EU INTERNATIONAL RELATIONS LAW

In the post-9/11 world, the European Union has been trying to define its international presence in a way which corresponds to its economic power and enlarged membership. In an effort to assert its identity on the international scene, it has developed a very wide range of economic relations with third countries and international organisations. It has also developed a Common Foreign and Security Policy in the context of which it is gradually shaping its Security and Defence Policy. These policies are carried out on the basis of distinct, albeit inter-related sets of legal rules. This book provides a comprehensive and systematic analysis of these economic, political and security aspects of the relations of the European Union with the rest of the world. It examines their genesis, development and interactions and places them in the specific context of the establishment of the internal market and the broader context of the increasingly interdependent international economic and geopolitical environment. Issues covered include the co-existence of Community and national competence in external relations, the approach of the Court of Justice to international law, the negotiation, conclusion and implementation of international agreements, the relationship between EC and WTO law and the development of the political and security policies of the Union. The book will be of interest to academics, practitioners and students of EU law.

Volume 9 in the Series Modern Studies in European Law

Modern Studies in European Law

EU International Relations Law

Panos Koutrakos

·HART·
PUBLISHING
OXFORD AND PORTLAND, OREGON
2006

Published in North America (US and Canada) by
Hart Publishing
c/o International Specialized Book Services
5804 NE Hassalo Street
Portland, Oregon
97213-3786
USA
Tel: +1 503 2873093 or toll-free (1) 800 944 6190
Fax: +1 503 280 8832
E-mail: orders@isbs.com
Web Site: www.isbs.com

© Panos Koutrakos 2006

First published 2006; reprinted 2007 and 2008

Panos Koutrakos has asserted his right under the Copyright, Designs and Patents Act 1988, to be
identified as the author of this work.

Hart Publishing, 16C Worcester Place, Oxford, OX1 2JW
Telephone: +44 (0) 1865 517 530 Fax: +44 (0) 1865 510 710
email: mail@hartpub.co.uk
WEBSITE: http//:www.hartpub.co.uk

British Library Cataloguing in Publication Data
Data Available

ISBN 10: 1-84113-311-6 (paperback)
ISBN 13: 978-1-84113-311-9 (paperback)

Typeset by Compuscript, Shannon
Printed and bound in Great Britain by
TJI Digital, Padstow, Cornwall

Στη Νατάσσα

Acknowledgments

Part of this book was written on research leave granted by the School of Law, University of Birmingham and the Department of Law, University of Durham. The latter was funded by the Arts and Humanities Research Council. The last parts of the book were written in Ann Arbor, Michigan, where I spent six months as a Jean Monnet Research Fellow at the University of Michigan Law School. To these institutions I am grateful.

Eileen Denza read parts of the book: for her comments, suggestions, corrections and kindness I am deeply grateful. Aurel Sari commented on other parts of the book and helped me enormously with his editorial assistance: I thank him very much.

In Ann Arbor, I benefited from conversations with Judge Koen Lenaerts, Daniel Halberstam and Eric Stein. Frank Hoffmeister has been very helpful with a number of queries over the past two years. Sebastian Harter-Bachmann helped me efficiently at the early stages of writing. All omissions and errors are, of course, my own.

Supported by

A · H · R · B
arts and humanities research board

Outline Table of Contents

Contents

Table of Cases

A. EUROPEAN COURT OF JUSTICE

B. COURT OF FIRST INSTANCE

C. INTERNATIONAL COURT OF JUSTICE

D. EUROPEAN COURT OF HUMAN RIGHTS

E. NATIONAL COURTS

F. WTO DECISIONS

Table of Legislation

Agreements

SECONDARY EUROPEAN LEGISLATION

EC Directives

EC Regulations

EC Decisions

EU Joint Actions

EU Common Positions

EU Common Strategies

Other CFSP Acts

EU Miscellanous

MISCELLANEOUS

Council

European Commission

European Council–Presidency Conclusions

European Parliament

National Instruments

Introduction

1. SCOPE

IN HIS STUDY on Treaty law, Anthony Aust notes that '[a]nything to do with the European Communities is complex, and this is particularly so for the law governing their external relations'.[1] When I was writing this book, not a day went by when this observation was not on my mind. And yet, this area of endless fascination for academic lawyers has become central to discussions about the future of the European Union at various levels. The long process leading to the signing of the Treaty establishing a Constitution for Europe made academic lawyers focus on the pillar structure of the Union and examine ways which would facilitate the conduct of the Union's international relations, whilst respecting the rights of Member States to act as fully sovereign subjects of international law. The uncertain fate of the Constitutional Treaty made politicians wonder about the future role of the Union on the international scene. The war in Iraq raised questions about the commitment of national governments to a truly common EU foreign policy. And Robert Kagan's discussion about Americans and Europeans and Mars and Venus[2] made lawyers, politicians and the public wonder about the distinctiveness of the EU international identity.

Indeed, the question whether Europeans are from Venus appears to be raised in every discussion about the Union's international actions. This is a question which this book will try to avoid. This is mainly because such thesis is as ubiquitous as it is impervious to the *rationale*, dynamics, development and interactions of legal mechanisms.[3] This book will focus on those mechanisms. It will analyse their manifestations in the areas of trade, foreign policy, security and defence and will examine their multifarious interactions.

This study does not aim to produce an encyclopaedia of all areas of EU international relations neither does it seek to provide an exhaustive analysis of specific EU external policies. Instead, it should be viewed as work in progress the aim of which is to focus on the trade, political and defence dimensions of the ways in which the Union relates to the outside world. It will analyse the legal rules which have shaped their genesis, development and interaction both in theory and in practice. By doing so, it will seek to define the threads which underpin these different areas of activity and ascertain how they seek to bring them together in a coherent whole.

---

[1] A Aust, *Modern Treaty Law and Practice* (2nd edn, Cambridge: Cambridge University Press, 2000) 55.

[2] R Kagan, *Paradise and Power: America and Europe in a New World Order* (New York: Knopf, 2003).

[3] For an analysis of the oversimplifications of this thesis from an international relations perspective, see T Garton Ash, *Free World* (London: Penguin, 2005).

2. STRUCTURE

The book is structured in five parts. The first part deals with the regulation of the Community's international relations. Its main focus is the constitutional foundations of the Community's external actions. Chapter one examines the areas where the Community is endowed with express competence to act on the international scene with particular emphasis on the Common Commercial Policy. The Court of Justice ruled, early on, that the competence of the Community to act in this area is exclusive. The chapter analyses the notion of exclusivity in a two-fold manner. On the one hand, it examines the legal context within which the Court articulated it and the ways in which it has applied it over the years. On the other hand, it sets out the approach of the Community institutions and the Member States to the regulation of the Common Commercial Policy and the ways in which it has evolved in parallel with the process of the establishment of the internal market and the international economic environment. The picture of the policy which emerges is characterised by a considerable degree of subtlety and variation. Chapter two analyses the scope of the Common Commercial Policy by focusing on its interpretation by the Court of Justice and its redefinition by the masters of the Treaty at Nice. By focusing on the gradual shift of emphasis characterising the Court's approach and the logic of the 'new' Common Commercial Policy, this chapter identifies the threads which bring together the express and implied sources of the Community's external competence. Chapter three analyses the implied competence of the Community to act on the international scene. Originating in the early 1970s, this principle has had major implications not only for the external dimension of the Community legal order but also the constitutional relationship between the Member States and the Community. Focusing on the evolution of this principle on the basis of the case law of the Court of Justice, this chapter examines the various ways in which its application determines the interaction between the Community and national actors.

The second part of this book is dedicated to the management of the EC international relations. The term 'management' is used in its broadest sense and refers to the various ways in which the Community and the Member States, on the one hand, and the Court of Justice, on the other, translate the constitutional principles of external competence into practice. Chapter four examines the processes under which the Community assumes, negotiates and concludes international agreements and participates in international organisations. The analysis focuses on the coexistence of the Community and the Member States in the negotiation, conclusion and implementation of international agreements. This phenomenon of mixity, much-maligned in the academic literature, is assessed in the light of the legal, political and practical mechanisms which have underpinned its application over the years. Chapter five analyses the approach of the Court of Justice to the existence and exercise of its jurisdiction over mixed agreements. Chapter six examines the approach of the Court of Justice to the interpretation of international rules in the Community legal order. Again, the emphasis is on the mixed agreements and the ways in which the Court has sought to ensure that their adoption and application complies with constitutional and substantive law of the Community. It identifies different categories of international rules and examines the rights of individuals as well as Member States to invoke them before national courts and the Community judiciary. Chapter seven focuses on the approach of the Community judiciary to the application of rules adopted within the framework of the World Trade Organisation. Tracing its origins back in the interpretation given to GATT rules, this chapter studies the various factors underpinning the Court's approach and identifies their interrelation with other strands of its caselaw.

Chapter eight examines the legal position of international agreements concluded by Member States prior to their membership of the European Union. Whilst apparent in the light of the recent enlargement, the significance of this topic is further highlighted by recent caselaw of the Court and initiatives undertaken by the Community institutions. This chapter will examine their implications for the development of the Community legal order in general and the role of national courts in particular.

The third part of the book provides an overview of the substantive content of the Community's international relations. Chapter nine deals with autonomous measures adopted in the context of the Common Commercial Policy. After a brief introduction to the main imports and exports rules, the 'Everything But Arms' initiative and the trade policy instruments, it focuses on one of the most popular of the latter, namely the rules on anti-dumping. The chapter summarises the ways in which the discretion of Community institutions to make substantive policy choices has been construed and juxtaposes it with the degree of intensity of judicial control in procedural and other aspects of that policy. Chapter ten examines international agreements concluded by the Community, either alone or with its Member States. Its particular focus is on the Partnership and Cooperation Agreements with members of the ex-Soviet Union, the Stabilisation and Association Agreements with countries in the West Balkans and the Euro-Mediterranean Agreements. Rather than providing an exhaustive analysis of their content, this chapter seeks to assess them within the context of the Union's gradually evolving approach as presented in the European Neighbourhood Policy. To that effect, these different sets of relationships are examined as parts of a potentially coherent system of international relations.

The fourth part of the book analyses the political aspects of the international relations of the European Union. Chapter eleven studies the Common Foreign and Security Policy. It examines the legal rules underpinning its development and the constitutional and political factors which affect the Union's effort to assert its identity on the international scene. In addition, this chapter addresses the strong criticism against the handling of the war in Iraq by the Member States and places it within the proper international and legal framework of that crisis. Chapter twelve analyses the European Security and Defence Policy. It examines the legal rules laid down in the Treaty on European Union and assesses them in the context of the economic and political parameters which determine their effectiveness. Furthermore, the chapter identifies the recent momentum which characterises this policy and examines its more prominent position in the Treaty establishing a Constitution for Europe. Chapter thirteen analyses the interactions between trade and foreign policy. It examines the legal rules governing sanctions against third countries and describes the development of the common rules on exports of dual-use goods. It also analyses the rules on exports of armaments and their position within the more general framework of the Common Foreign and Security Policy.

In the concluding part of the book, Chapter fourteen examines the extent to which the provisions of the Treaty establishing a Constitution for Europe set out a new framework for the conduct of EU international relations. Whilst focusing on the provisions on Common Foreign and Security Policy and Common Security and Defence Policy, this chapter seeks to address the proposed, and partly rejected, amendments and assess them in the light of both their intended effect and the existing structures and mechanisms of EU international relations law.

Part I

The Regulation of EC International Relations

1

Express Powers—Theory and Practice of Exclusivity in Common Commercial Policy

1. INTRODUCTION

IN THE BRIEFEST of its provisions, the EC Treaty addresses the issue of the legal personality of the European Community. According to Article 281 EC:

> The Community shall have legal personality.

Express legal personality is also provided for in the European Atomic Energy Community[1] and in the now expired European Coal and Steel Community.[2] The express provision for the Community's legal personality was one of the factors illustrating the unique nature of the Community legal order and its ensuing supremacy over national law. In its oft-quoted ruling in *Costa* in the mid-1960s, the Court stated that:[3]

> By creating a Community of unlimited duration, having its own institutions, its own personality, its own legal capacity, and capacity of representation on the international plane and, more particularly, real powers stemming from a limitation of sovereignty or a transfer of powers from the states to the Community, the Member States have limited their sovereign rights, albeit within limited fields and have thus created a body of law which binds both their nationals and themselves.

In terms of its relationship with the jurisdiction of its Member States, the existence of the Community's legal personality has the following implications:[4]

> In each of the Member States, the Community shall enjoy the most extensive legal capacity accorded to legal persons under their laws; it may, in particular, acquire or dispose of movable and immovable property and may be a party to legal proceedings. To this end, the Community shall be represented by the Commission.

---

[1] Art 184 EURATOM.
[2] Art 6 ECSC.
[3] Case 6/64 *Costa v ENEL* [1964] ECR 585 at 593.
[4] Art 282 EC.

According to the principles of public international law, the Community's legal personality entails a number of powers, such as the right to negotiate, conclude and implement international agreements, the right of legation, the right to present international claims by diplomatic procedures or in other available forms and the capacity to be the subject of such rights, the existence of liability for any breach of international law.[5] The precise scope of the powers and duties of the Community is determined pursuant to its primary law. As the International Court of Justice put it in the seminal case on the legal personality of international organisations:[6]

> Whereas a State possesses the totality of international rights and duties recognised by international law, the rights and duties of an entity such as the [United Nations] Organization must depend upon its purposes and functions as specified or implied in its constituted documents and developed in practice.

The definition of the precise scope of the Community's rights, as well as the legal implications of their exercise, both within the Community legal order and in the domestic legal order of its Member States, has proved to be far from easy: inter-institutional tensions, efforts by national authorities to preserve the autonomy of their action, the balance of powers on the international scene, the practical necessities of international negotiations and the pace of the establishment and management of the internal market, all have made the scope and implications of the Community's external powers the subject-matter of an institutional, legal and political debate which has yet to settle.

In the case of the European Union, the position has been the reverse: it has been the practice of the Union institutions which has been studied in order to ascertain the existence of the Union's legal personality. Indeed, neither the Treaty on European Union at Maastricht nor its amendments at Amsterdam and Nice provided for express legal personality. Instead, the latter endowed the Union with treaty-making capacity in the areas covered by both the Common Foreign and Security Policy and Police and Judicial Cooperation in Criminal Matters (Articles 24 and 38 TEU).[7] The issue of the legal personality of the Union has arisen again in the context of the Treaty Establishing a Constitution for Europe which provides for it expressly.[8]

In terms of their acts in the area of EC external relations, the Community institutions do not enjoy any autonomous competence. Instead, they are to comply with the provisions set out in the EC Treaty. As the Court put it:[9]

> it is the Community alone, having legal personality pursuant to Article [281] of the Treaty, which has the capacity to bind itself by concluding agreements with a non-member country or an international organization.

---

[5] See I Brownlie, 'International Law at the Fiftieth Anniversary of the United Nations—General Course on Public International Law' (1995) 25 *Recueil des Cours* 9 at 52 and 63–5.

[6] *Reparations for Injuries Suffered in the Service of the United Nations* [1949] ICJ Rep 174 at 179–180.

[7] For the legal personality of the EU, see Ch 11 below.

[8] Art I–7.

[9] Case C-327/91 *France v Council (re: Competition Agreement with USA)* [1994] ECR I–3641 at para 24.

2. EXPRESS COMPETENCE IN PRIMARY LAW

The areas in which the Community is endowed with express external competence have been limited. The original Treaty of Rome only referred to the Common Commercial Policy (Article 133 EC) and the negotiation and conclusion of association agreements (Article 310 EC), the latter establishing an association between the Community and one or more states or international organisations 'involving reciprocal rights and obligations, common action and special procedure'.

Apart from the conclusion of international agreements in the above areas, the Treaty of Rome also provided for other forms of international cooperation. There was, and still is, provision for the establishment and maintenance of 'all appropriate relations' with the organs of the United Nations and its specialised agencies as well as all international organisations under Article 302 EC, which confers the relevant responsibility upon the Commission. In a similar vein, Article 303 EC provides for the establishment of all appropriate forms of cooperation with the Council of Europe,[10] whereas Article 304 EC provides for close cooperation with the Organisation for Economic Cooperation and Development.

The subsequent amendments of the EC Treaty broadened the scope of the areas in which the Community is expressly competent to act externally. These are expressed in different ways. In the areas of education (Article 149(3) EC), vocational training (Article 150(3) EC), culture (Article 151(3) EC) and public health (Article 152(3) EC), the Community is expressly competent to foster cooperation with third countries and international organisations. In the area of trans-European networks (TENS) (Article 155(3) EC), the Community is competent to cooperate with third countries to promote projects of mutual interest and to ensure the interoperability of networks. In the area of research, Article 170 EC provides that, in the context of its multiannual framework programme, the Community may provide for cooperation with third countries and international organisations. The negotiation and conclusion of international agreements pursuant to Article 300 EC are defined as ways in which such cooperation may materialise, in areas such as environment (Article 174(4) EC), development policy (Article 181 EC) and economic, financial and technical cooperation with third countries (Article 181a(3) EC). Finally, the EC Treaty provides for the conclusion of international agreements on an exchange-rate system for the European currency in relation to non-Community currencies (Article 111 EC).

The absence of an express reference to negotiation and conclusion of international agreements notwithstanding, the power of the Community to foster cooperation with third countries and international organizations covers the negotiation

---

[10] See G de Vel, 'L'Union européenne et les activités du Conseil de l'Europe' in D Dormoy (ed), *L'Union européenne et les organisations internationales* (Brussels: Bryulant, 1997) 105 and T Ouchterlony, 'The European Communities and the Council of Europe' (1984) 1 *Legal Issues of European Integration* 59.

and conclusion of international agreements too.[11] However, the different wording in the EC Treaty provisions endowing the Community with express external competence is not irrelevant. This became clear in *Opinion 2/00*, where the Commission questioned the conclusion of the Cartagena Protocol on Biodiversity pursuant to Article 175(1) EC, rather than Articles 174(4) and 133 EC.[12] Having rejected the argument about the relevance of the CCP to the conclusion of the Protocol,[13] the Court went on to examine which EC provision on environment was the appropriate legal basis for its conclusion. It made a distinction between Articles 174 and 175 EC: the former sets out the objectives of the Community's environmental policy, whereas the latter constitutes the legal basis pursuant to which legislation is adopted. To that effect, the express power laid down in Article 174(4) EC is to be relied upon in relation to agreements setting out arrangements for international cooperation. However, in cases where an agreement goes further than that by introducing specific substantive rules, the general Community competence on environment should be relied upon. This was the case regarding the Cartagena Protocol on Biosafety which laid down precise rules and control procedures relating to living modified organisms covering their transboundary movements, risk assessment and management, handling, transport, packaging and identification.[14] In other words, the express competence to negotiate and conclude international agreements for the arrangement of international cooperation in the areas of environment and development, for instance, is to be construed rather restrictively. That is not to say that the Community may not conclude more wide-ranging agreements in those areas: the competence to do so is deemed to be implied from the general EC Treaty provision endowing the Community with internal decision-making competence in that area. This distinction, and in particular the application of the implied competence, has significant implications regarding the right of Member States to act externally along with the Community in a given area.[15]

Furthermore, the EC Treaty provisions on environment, development and economic, financial and technical cooperation with third countries share a significant legal characteristic: whilst endowing the Community with express external competence, they also acknowledge expressly the continuing role of the Member States. Not only is it stated that, along with the Community, the Member States are to cooperate with third countries and international organizations within their sphere of competence, but it is also pointed out that the exercise of the Community's competence would be without prejudice to the competence of the

---

[11] See I Macleod, ID Hendry and S Hyett, *The External Relations of the European Communities* (Oxford: 1996, OUP) 47 where the different wording is seen as merely reflecting the sensitivity of the relevant areas of activity which is also illustrated internally by the prohibition on the adoption of fully harmonising legislation.

[12] *Opinion 2/00* [2001] ECR I–9713.

[13] See the analysis in Ch 2 below.

[14] N12 above, at para 43.

[15] See the analysis of the principle of implied competence in Ch 3 below.

Member States to negotiate in international bodies and to conclude international agreements. The legal implications of this provision for the powers of the Member States are noteworthy. Be that as it may, it should be pointed out that, according to a Declaration attached to the Treaty on European Union, 'the provisions of Article [111(5)], Article [174(4)], second subparagraph, and Article [181] do not affect the principles resulting from the judgment handed down by the Court of Justice in the AETR case'.

In the light of the above, the amendments to the original EC Treaty which introduced the Community's express competence in those areas are significant: they broadened the areas of activities over which the Community is expressly competent to act whilst recognising the continuous role that the Member States would still have to play. Therefore, they facilitate the external action of the Community without compromising the right of the Member States to act as fully sovereign subjects of international law. This formula of coexistence between the Community and the Member States gives rise to certain legal and practical issues which will be examined later in this book.[16]

3. COMMON COMMERCIAL POLICY

The Common Commercial Policy (CCP) is provided for in Title IX of EC Treaty which covers Articles 131–133 EC. Its basis is the establishment of a customs union between the Member States. In that respect, Article 131 EC reads as follows:

> By establishing a customs union between themselves Member States aim to contribute, in the common interest, to the harmonious development of world trade, the progressive abolition of restrictions on international trade and the lowering of customs barriers.
>
> The common commercial policy shall take into account the favourable effect which the abolition of customs duties between Member States may have on the increase in the competitive strength of undertakings in those States.

The wording of Article 131 EC indicates that the establishment of the CCP merely follows from the establishment of a customs union, hence highlighting the link between the internal and external spheres of Community action. In addition, it suggests a commitment to the liberalisation of international trade which, whilst understandable in the light of the economic climate of the era, raises questions as to the precise ambit of the policy: would it also cover measures aimed at the regulation of international trade? This question, along with the more general issue of the definition of the outer limits of the CCP, has been addressed by the Court of Justice and will be examined in a later chapter.[17]

---

[16] See Chs 4–5 below.
[17] See Ch 2 below.

As to the effects of Article 131 EC, other than highlighting the function of the CCP as intrinsically linked to the Community legal order and setting out its main policy characteristics, no precise legal obligation upon the Community institutions may be discerned on the basis of its wording. This was indicated early on in an action against Community measures imposing import levies on agricultural products.[18] The applicant argued that such levies were very high and, hence, in violation of the principles laid down in Article 131 EC. The Court held that the relevant measures 'do not contravene Article [131], since it has not been established, nor has there been any offer to do so, that by adopting such measures the Council overstepped the wide power of assessment conferred on it by this provision'.[19] Therefore, the commitment of the Community institutions to trade liberalisation, as expressed in Article 131 EC and illustrated by the adoption of unilateral as well as conventional measures, constitutes a policy choice not amenable to judicial review.

The link between the internal market and trade with third countries is also illustrated by Article 132 EC which provides for the progressive harmonisation of aid for exports to third countries.[20]

It is Article 133 EC which provides for the core of the CCP. Its first paragraph reads as follows:

> The common commercial policy shall be based on uniform principles, particularly in regard to changes in tariff rates, the conclusion of tariff and trade agreements, the achievement of uniformity in measures of liberalization, export policy and measures to protect trade such as those to be taken in the event of dumping or subsidies.

This provision raises various questions about the scope of the activities to which it refers. These will be examined in detail in the next chapter. For the purposes of its analysis, suffice it to point out that the CCP covers both unilateral measures adopted by the Community institutions and conventional measures negotiated with third countries and international organisations. As the Court pointed out in Massey Fergusson, the proper functioning of the customs union 'justifies a wide interpretation of Articles [23, 26 and 133] of the Treaty and of the powers which these provisions confer on the institutions to allow them thoroughly to control external trade by measures taken both independently and by agreement'.[21]

---

[18] Case 5/73 *Balkan Import Export GmbH v Hauptzollamt Berlin Packhof* [1973] ECR 1091.

[19] *Ibid*, at para 27.

[20] Art 132(1) reads as follows: 'Without prejudice to obligations undertaken by them within the framework of other international organisations, Member States shall progressively harmonise the systems whereby they grant aid for exports to third countries, to the extent necessary to ensure that competition between undertakings of the Community is not distorted'. In a second subpara, the Council is given the power to adopt the necessary directives by qualified majority following a proposal by the Commission. Art 132(2) EC provides for an exception: 'The preceding provisions shall not apply to such a drawback of customs duties or charges having equivalent effect nor to such a repayment of indirect taxation including turnover taxes, excise duties and other indirect taxes as is allowed when goods are exported from a Member State to a third country, in so far as such a drawback or repayment does not exceed the amount imposed, directly or indirectly, on the products exported'. On the application of this provision, see M-L, Houbé-Masse, *La CEE et les crédits à l'exportation: l'intégration en question* (Rennes: Apogée, 1992).

[21] Case 8/73 *Hauptzollamt Bremerhaven v Massey Fergusson GmbH* [1973] ECR 897 at para 4.

The second significant feature of the CCP is related to decision-making: the Council is to adopt legislation implementing the policy by qualified majority (Article 133(4) EC) following a proposal by the Commission (Article 133(2) EC). This supranational feature marks the significance of the CCP for the establishment of the internal market. This became all the more important when the Court articulated the legal position of the Member States in the areas covered by Article 133. This will be the focus of the following analysis. In its examination of the nature of Community competence, this chapter will adopt a two-fold approach: on the one hand, it will examine its construction by the Court of Justice as it developed from the early 1970s to the present; on the other hand, it will set it against the evolution of the approach adopted by the Community institutions in that period. This is essential to the proper understanding of the competence assumed by the Community which proved to be neither static in nature nor one-dimensional in its implications.

4. INTRODUCING EXCLUSIVITY

In *Opinion 1/75,* the starting point for the assessment of the nature of the CCP was 'the manner in which [it] is conceived in the Treaty'.[22] Having concluded that financing local costs linked to export operations fell within the scope of Article 133 EC, the Court opined as follows:[23]

'[The Common Commercial Policy] is conceived in [Article 133 EC] in the context of the operation of the Common Market, for the defence of the common interests of the Community, within which the particular interests of the Member states must endeavour to adapt to each other.

Quite clearly, however, this conception is incompatible with the freedom to which the Member States could lay claim by invoking a concurrent power, so as to ensure that their interests were separately satisfied in external relations, at the risk of compromising the effective defence of the common interests of the Community.

In fact, any unilateral action on the part of the Member States would lead to disparities in the conditions for the grant of export credits, calculated to distort competition between undertakings of the various Member states in external markets. Such distortion can be eliminated only by means of a strict uniformity of credit conditions granted to undertakings in the Community, whatever their nationality.

It cannot therefore be accepted that, in a field such as that governed by the Understanding in question, which is covered by export policy and more generally by the common commercial policy, the Member States should exercise a power concurrent to that of the Community, in the Community sphere and in the international sphere. The

---

[22] *Opinion 1/75 (re: OECD Local Cost Standard)* [1975] ECR 1355 at 1363.
[23] *Ibid,* at 1364.

provisions of Article [133] show clearly that the exercise of concurrent powers by the Member States and the Community in this matter is impossible.

To accept that the contrary were true would amount to recognising that, in relations with third countries, Member States may adopt positions which differ from those which the Community intends to adopt, and would thereby distort the institutional framework, call into question the mutual trust within the Community and prevent the latter from fulfilling its task in the defence of the common interest.

The Court deems its own conception of the CCP central to the nature of the competence of the Community, whereas the complications caused by any concurrent national competence only follow: it is the position of the CCP in the wider context of the common market with which national competence is incompatible, rather than the other way round. In other words, the Court appears to have *une certain idée* of the CCP which, then, shapes the manner in which the Community and the Member States are to act. Whilst, initially, this may appear rather curious, this concept articulated by the Court makes more sense if viewed within its specific context, namely the operation of the Common Market. The various justifications for the exclusive nature of the competence of the Community are characterised by a clear emphasis on the link between the emerging policy and the operation of the common market: this link is expressed both in general terms, that is the requirement for the defence of the common interests of the Community, and in specific terms, that is the danger of distortion of competition between undertakings of the Member States in external markets. Article 133 EC is only one of the last reasons to be mentioned in the judgment—one assumes that this is because its wording does not appear to provide any indication regarding exclusivity. It is noteworthy that, in concluding that part of its ruling, the Court returned to the general line of reasoning underpinned by the focus on its position within the Community legal order and referred to the consequences that any solution other than exclusivity would have for the Community's institutional framework, the mutual trust within the Community and the defence of the common interest.

In practical terms, the link between the CCP and the common market is apparent in the light of the operation of the Community on the basis of a customs union which entails, amongst others, the application of a common customs tariff in the relations between Member States and third countries. It is within this context that the EC Treaty rules on the abolition of both fiscal and non-fiscal impediments to trade are to apply not only to products originating in Member States but also those coming from third countries which are in free circulation in the Community. In other words, the complete abolition of impediments to trade internally requires the adoption and application of common rules in relation to trade in those goods externally. It is this link between the CCP and the internal market which may explain the force with which the Court chose to articulate the foundation of exclusivity: the CCP properly understood is 'quite clearly' incompatible with any concurrent competence as the wording of Article 133 EC shows 'clearly that the exercise of such competence is 'impossible'. This force becomes all the more remarkable in the light of the earlier part of the ruling where the scope of CCP was construed very widely: in fact, the Court opined that commercial policy should have 'the same content whether it is applied in the context of the international action of a State or to that of the Community'.[24]

In expressing exclusivity in such uncompromising terms, the Court appears to suggest two points: on the one hand, the exclusive nature of the competence of the Community in the area of the CCP exists *a priori*, that is irrespective of the exercise of such competence; on the other hand, there appear to be no exceptions which might justify the concurrent competence of Member States. If correct, these positions would have been quite attractive in their absolutist reach: the endless debates about the circumstances under which the exercise of implied competence would render such competence exclusive[25] would be avoided and there would be no need to develop a typology of cases in which national powers were justified.

However, it is not only the benefit of hindsight which questions these assumptions. Whilst bolstering the foundation of exclusivity, the link between the CCP and the common market also serves to highlight the limits of the former by drawing upon practice under the latter. Indeed, the very development of the common market and the processes of establishing and managing the internal market attest to the paramount importance of observing the dividing line between Community and national competence: this line has not only been extremely fine but has also proved to be in need of constant redefinition.[26] In other words, to construe the CCP as the necessary adjunct to the establishment of the internal market was tantamount to implying the existence of inherent limitations to the exercise of the express competence granted to the Community.

This became apparent, albeit in a rather ackward manner, only three years later. In *Opinion 1/78*, another request by the Commission pursuant to Article 300(7) EC, the main question was whether the conclusion of a commodity agreement fell within the exclusive nature of the Community.[27] The construction of exclusivity three years earlier in *Opinion 1/75* and the uncompromising language used by the Court had rendered this issue central to the conduct of EC external relations in general and the concerns of the institutions to enhance their input in decision-making in particular. Having interpreted the scope of Article 133 EC in wide terms, the Court went on to examine the mechanism set up under the Agreement aimed at ensuring the financing of the buffer stock. The relevance of this had been

---

[24] At 1362: see the analysis in Ch 2 below.

[25] See the analysis in Ch 3.

[26] It is indicative, for instance, that, whilst the Member States had been deemed to have limited their sovereign powers 'within limited fields' in Case 26/62 *van Gend en Loos* [1963] ECR 1 at 12, they were held to have done so 'within ever wider fields' 30 years later (*Opinion 1/91* (*re: Draft EEA Agreement*) [1991] ECR I–60 6079 para 21*)*; on the other hand, in the *Tobacco Advertising* judgment, the Court had made it clear that the power of the Community to adopt legislation in order to facilitate the functioning of the internal market did not amount to an all-encompassing power to regulate that market (Case C–376/98 *Germany v European Parliament and Council* [2001] ECR I–2247).

[27] *Opinion 1/78* [1979] ECR 2871.

highlighted by the Member States. In particular, they had argued that, under the International Agreement on Natural Rubber, the buffer stock would be financed by public funds which, in their view, justified their participation in the conclusion of the Agreement. On the other hand, the Commission had argued that the financial arrangements regarding the implementation of an international agreement should be irrelevant to the more general issue of competence.

However, the Court deemed the financing arrangements central to the very application of the Agreement. Not only were they 'an essential feature of the scheme for regulating the market [to be set up by the Agreement]', but also their specific implications for the participation of the Member States would have had an impact on the actual application of the mechanism established thereunder. It noted that 'the financial structure which [the Agreement] is proposed to set up will make necessary . . . co-ordination between the use of the specific financial means put at the disposal of the future International Rubber Council and those which it might find in the Common Fund which is to be set up'. The Court then concluded as follows:[28]

> If the financing of the agreement is a matter for the Community the necessary decisions will be taken according to the appropriate Community procedures. If on the other hand the financing is to be by the Member States that will imply the participation of those States in the decision-making machinery or, at least, their agreement with regard to the arrangements for financing envisaged and consequently their participation in the agreement together with the Community. The exclusive competence of the Community could not be envisaged in such a case.

The thrust of the Court's ruling in *Opinion 1/78* highlighted the first crack in the principle of exclusivity which, according to *Opinion 1/75*, had been one of the pillars of the Common Commercial Policy. In essence, the Court indicated that, whilst in existence *a priori*, the exclusive competence of the Community in the area of the CCP did not necessarily entail the conclusion of an agreement exclusively by the Community. Put in another way, Member States are not necessarily precluded from concluding, along with the Community, an agreement falling within the scope of Article 133 EC despite the fact that their exclusion is inextricably linked to the nature of the Community's competence in that area.

In the context of the specific ruling, this illustration of pragmatism is remarkable in that it arose from the issue of the financing of the structure set up by the Agreement in question. It was curious that the Court should draw a link between the issue of financing and that of competence, all the more so in the light of the link made earlier between the CCP and the common market and the uncompromising language in which that had been articulated. If the exclusive nature of the competence bestowed upon the Community was as essential to the functioning of the common market as the Court had implied in *Opinion 1/75*, how could it be diluted simply because the Member States would choose to finance the application

---

[28] Para 60.

of the Agreement? After all, the financial aspects of an Agreement to be concluded under Article 133 EC had been expressly deemed irrelevant to the issue of competence three years before. Having pointed out that 'it is of little importance that the obligations and financial burdens inherent in the execution of the agreement envisaged are borne directly by the Member States', the Court had ruled in *Opinion 1/75* as follows:[29]

> The 'internal' and 'external' measures adopted by the Community within the framework of the common commercial policy do not necessarily involve, in order to ensure their compatibility with the Treaty, a transfer to the institutions of the Community of the obligations and financial burdens which they may involve: such measure [*sic*] are solely concerned to substitute for the unilateral action of the Member States, in the field under consideration, a common action based upon uniform principles on behalf of the whole of the Community.

What was it that justified the opposite view in *Opinion 1/78?* Given that finance was allowed to determine competence, would it not be open to the Member States to instrumentalise the financing of the mechanisms set up by commodity agreements in order to ensure their participation in their conclusion along with the Community? Would such an outcome not negate the essence of the exclusive nature of the Community over one of the very few areas in which it enjoyed express competence? The criticism levelled against this part of the ruling for 'putting the cart before the horse'[30] is correct in so far as the Court appears to strike at the very core of its construction of the CCP by undermining the principle of exclusivity in an unprincipled manner. Cut to its bare essentials, the ruling appears to suggest that the degree of national involvement in the practical components of what is deemed central to the implementation and application of an international agreement should be relevant to the exercise of the express competence over the CCP. This acknowledgment of the implications of the pronounced role enjoyed by the Member States in the management of areas of activity where their competence had been transferred to the Community echoes the pronounced role that the Member States actually played in the regulation of the CCP during that period. In order to appreciate this parallelism between judicial construction and political reality, an overview of the historical development of the CCP is useful.

5. DIVERSITY PREVAILING

The provision of Article 133 EC makes it clear that the CCP would be carried out on the basis of uniform principles. In articulating the exclusive nature of the

---

[29] *Opinion 1/75*, n22 above, at 1364.
[30] JHH. Weiler, 'The External Legal Relations of Non-Unitary Actors: Mixity and the Federal Principle' in HG Schermers and D O'Keeffe (eds), *Mixed Agreements* (Daventer: Kluwer, 1981) 35 at 72; reprinted in JHH. Weiler, *The Constitution of Europe* (Cambridge: Cambridge University Press 1999) 130 at 174.

competence of the Community in that area, the Court referred to the common interests of the Community which should be defended and the mutual trust within the Community which ought not to be called into question. The uniformity mentioned in the EC Treaty is not identical to the commonality referred to by the Court: the former served to highlight the nature of the CCP as a necessary component of the common market and to indicate the *modus operandi* of the emerging policy; the latter served to justify what the Court considered the necessary component of that policy, namely the exclusive nature of the Community. Yet, the structure and line of reasoning of the ruling in *Opinion 1/75*, as analysed above, appeared to suggest that it would be far from controversial to wonder whether, the exclusive nature of Community competence notwithstanding, there were circumstances in which Member States were allowed some leeway in the areas covered by Article 133 EC.

In terms of the regulation of the CCP by the Community institutions, the absence of uniformity was illustrated by various examples. For instance, in the area of imports, the relevant rules acknowledged the existence of national quotas in specific cases. This was the case regarding the common rules on imports in general[31] and the rules on imports from the former Communist countries of Eastern Europe in particular.[32] The management of this system required the annual review of the quotas opened to the Member States. Another popular practice consisted of division of quotas on imports of products from third countries to the Community into national subquotas. In terms of the relationship between the Community and third countries, this method often consisted of the negotiation, conclusion and application/of voluntary export restraints. These proved to be quite popular in relation to categories of products for which national industries were deemed to be too weak to face foreign competition and too sensitive for their Member States to subject them to it. One such area was the textiles sector, for which the Community concluded a voluntary restraint agreement with the major supplying countries within the framework of a GATT regime called the Multi-Fibre Arrangement. The main aim of that Arrangement was to enable the developed countries to react to falling production and employment by maintaining quotas in order to fence off competition from developing countries.[33] The protection of national textile and clothing sectors was so important that the Community negotiated agreements within the Multi-Fibre Arrangement with a number of

---

[31] Reg 288/82 on common rules on imports [1982] OJ L 31/1.
[32] See Reg 3420/83 on import arrangements for products originating in State-trading countries [1983] OJ L 346/6.
[33] Following the liberalisation of global trade in textiles from 1 Jan 2005, the volume of imports of textiles from China to the EU and United States arose sharply. This was met by intense lobbying from textiles manufacturers in certain Member States favouring the introduction of protective measures and considerable reactions from other Member States opposing such a solution. In fact, a temporary arrangement was reached on 12 June 2005 entitled Memorandum of Understanding Between the European Commission and the Ministry of Commerce of the People's Republic of China on the Export of Certain Chinese Textile and Clothing Products to the European Union. For its implementation see Commission Reg 1478/2005 [2005] OJ L 236/3.

Asian and South American countries.[34]Another area where such a differentiated approach prevailed consisted of the automobile industry, which the Member States deemed too weak to become subject to competition from Japan.[35] It is noteworthy that voluntary restraint agreements, negotiated by the industry and applied informally, had already been in existence in various Member States: one such agreement had been concluded between the British Society of Motor Manufacturers and the Japanese Automobile Manufacturers Association.[36]

In terms of the trade relations between the Community and the rest of the world, what emerges is a significantly differentiated approach operated on the basis of Community quotas divided into national subquotas and voluntary export restraint arrangements not only negotiated and concluded by the Community but also individually concluded by Member States. This is a picture of a highly fragmented policy. As far as the introduction of national subquotas was concerned, the practice was significant for both policy and legal reasons. On the one hand, it reflected the concern of the Member States to ensure that their industries would be protected from what they deemed to be unrestrained competition from imported products. Therefore, national interests did affect the determination of what the Court referred to in *Opinion 1/75* as 'the common interests of the Community'. On the other hand, these interests were protected by means of Community legislation, thus enabling the Community institutions to allow Member States to do legally within the CCP framework what they might choose to do illegally beyond it.

The existence of national quotas on imports proved to be a popular practice in the late 1970s and throughout the 1980s.[37] It would be too easy to dismiss this practice as overtly protectionist and indicative of the inertia which underpinned decision-making within the Community legal order. However, a number of other economic and international factors need to be taken into account. During the Tokyo Round, for instance, the international economic arena was met with a considerable expansion of protectionist practices throughout the world. This was largely due to the increasing oil prices, the structural changes in various industrial activities, floated exchange rates and rising unemployment.[38] Therefore, far from constructing a 'fortress Europe' by favouring wildly divergent national interests, the Community's practice was consistent with the patterns characterising the

---

[34] See P Eeckhout, *The European Internal Market and International Trade: A Legal Analysis* (Oxford: OUP, 1994) 186–97 and RJPM van Dartel, 'The EEC's Commercial Policy Concerning Textiles' in ELM Völker (ed.), *Protectionism and the European Community* (Deventer: Kluwer, 1983) 121.

[35] See Eeckhout, n34 above, at 197–225.

[36] See MCEJ Bronckers, 'A Legal Analysis of Protectionist Measures Affecting Japanese Imports into the European Community' in Völker, n34 above, 57 at 79.

[37] In the early 1990s, approximately 10000 quotas were estimated to be in existence in individual Member States: see R Madelin, 'Trade Policy-Opening World Markets for Business' in M Darmer and L Kuyper, *Industry and the European Union—Analysing Policies for Business* (Cheltenham: Elgar, 2000) 155 at 160.

[38] See M Elsig, *The EU's Common Commercial Policy—Institutions, Interests and Ideas* (Aldershot: Ashgate, 2002) 28.

policies of its major trading partners. Viewed from this angle, the measures adopted under Article 133 EC during that period appeared to define a process aiming at a two-fold objective: to develop a Community-defined external trade policy whilst ensuring that the common market would not become an oasis of trade liberalisation in a desert of increasing protectionism. This process was acknowledged by the Community legislature: the preamble to Council Regulation 3589/82 on common rules on imports on certain textile products originating in third countries, for instance, stated that:[39]

> the extent of the disparities existing in the conditions for importation of these products into the Member States and the particularly sensitive position of the Community textiles industry mean that the said conditions can be standardised only gradually.

This gradual process of standardisation[40] did not just render the application of the 'uniform principles' referred to in Article 133 EC an objective of the emerging policy rather than a requirement; it also necessitated the adoption of further measures the effect of which was to undermine the common market. This was because a Member State in whose territory the importation of certain products was subject to a quota would have to ensure that this quota would not be undermined by the import of the same products from another Member State where they had been imported from a third country either freely or subject to a higher quota. Therefore, divergence in import conditions entailed divergence in the operation of intra-Community trade.

This practice was also envisaged in primary law. The Treaty of Rome provided an exceptional clause in Article 115 EC. As amended at Maastricht, its first paragraph read as follows:[41]

> In order to ensure that the execution of measures of commercial policy taken in accordance with this Treaty by any Member State is not obstructed by deflection of trade, or where differences between such measures lead to economic difficulties in one or more of the Member States, the Commission shall recommend the methods for the requisite cooperation between Member States. Failing this, the Commission shall authorize Member States to take the necessary protective measures, the conditions and details of which it shall determine.

In referring to the possibility of deflection of trade or economic difficulties, the proviso of Article 115(1) EEC assumed both the absence of completely harmonised

---

[39] [1982] OJ L 374/106.

[40] See M Cremona, 'The Completion of the Internal Market and the Incomplete Commercial Policy of the European Community' (1990) 15 *ELRev* 283.

[41] According to Art 115(2) EC, 'in case of urgency during the transitional period, Member States may themselves take the necessary measures and shall notify them to the Member States and to the Commission, which may decide that the States concerned shall amend or abolish such measures'. According to Art 115(3), 'in the selection of such measures, priority shall be given to those which cause the least disturbance to the functioning of the common market and which take into account the need to expedite, as far as possible, the introduction of the common customs tariff'.

common rules under Article 133 EC and the ensuing application of divergent national commercial policies.[42] It was for this reason that, in its original version in the Treaty of Rome, it referred expressly to the transitional period. In a way, the provision for safeguard measures that the Member States were allowed to take, albeit pursuant to a specific procedure involving the Commission, recall the system of the application of the prohibition on quantitative restrictions and measures of equivalent effect under Articles 28 and 30 EC: the principle of free movement of goods, at the very core of the establishment of the common market, was laid down in the former provision and was accompanied by the exception under the latter provision enabling Member States to protect certain clearly identified social interests in certain circumstances. The measures approved by the Commission reaching their peak in the period between 1978 and 1987.[43]

Against this background, the forceful construction of exclusivity by the Court in the early 1970s takes a different dimension: instead of seeking to exclude Member States from the regulation and management of trade relations with the rest of the world, it serves to highlight the essential role of the emerging policy for the achievement of the main objectives of the EC Treaty. Such an approach was all the more necessary in the light of the stagnation which characterised the decision-making procedures of the Community following the Luxembourg Compromise. In theoretical terms, if examined against the antithesis between normative and decisional supranationalism articulated early on by Weiler,[44] the approach adopted in *Opinion 1/75* is easily explained. However, it also risks losing its iconic role as the foundation for an external policy developed to be supranational *par excellence*. The first indication that exclusive competence over the content of the CCP did not necessarily entail exclusivity in the conclusion of an international agreement became apparent in *Opinion 1/78*. Subsequent caselaw confirmed it by sanctioning the various arrangements which, as applied by the Community institutions and the Member States, were to render the notion of 'uniform principles' provided for in Article 133 EC very flexible indeed.

6. SANCTIONING DIVERSITY

In a judgment delivered only a year after *Opinion 1/75*, the Court articulated the practical implications of exclusivity in terms of the position of the Member States. In *Donckerwolcke*, the issue referred by a French court was the legality of national measures aiming at establishing the origin of products imported into France

---

[42] See the analysis in P Vogelenzang, 'Two Aspects of Article 115 E.E.C. Treaty: Its Use to Buttress Community-set Sub-quotas, and the Commission's Monitoring System' (1981) 18 *CMLRev* 169.

[43] The maximum number approved by the Commission was 260 in 1979: see the table in BT Hanson, 'What Happened to Fortress Europe? External Trade Policy Liberalization in the European Union' (1998) 52 *International Organization* 55 at 69.

[44] JHH Weiler, 'The Community System: the Dual Character of Supranationalism' (1981) 1 *Yearbook of European Law* 267.

from another Member State into which they had been imported from a third country.[45] The action before the referring court had been brought by traders established in Belgium who imported into France cloth and packing sacks originally imported from Lebanon and Syria. Those products, deemed to be in free circulation once they entered the Community under Article 23(2) EC, ought to have been declared under French customs law. In particular, the importer had to declare not only the exporting Member State but also the original source of the products. According to the French government, such measures were necessary for monitoring purposes in order to enable the authorities to decide whether to exercise the exceptional powers granted under the original Treaty of Rome and the then provision of Article 115.

In its judgment, the Court pointed out that, in terms of intra-Community trade, import licences or any other similar measures were contrary to the principle of free movement of goods. As the case was about products first entered into the exporting State by a third country, the Court noted that they enjoyed the status of products in free circulation provided that they were imported under the procedures laid down in Article 24 EC: according to those conditions, all import formalities should have been complied with, any customs duties or charges of equivalent effect should have been levied in the importing state and the products in question should not have benefited from a total or partial drawback of such duties or charges. Once these conditions had been met, the original source of a product in free circulation in the Community would have been irrelevant to the final state of importation and, consequently, any import requirements or similar measures would have been illegal.

However, the Court observed that, despite the expiry of the transitional period, the CCP had not in fact been complete, as it was possible for different rules to apply to products originating in a third country when they originally entered the Community. It was precisely this disparity which raised the possibility of deflections of trade and which underpinned the exceptional clause of Article 115 EEC. In this context, the right of Member States to deviate from the CCP was acknowledged, albeit not unconditionally:[46]

> As full responsibility in the matter of commercial policy was transferred to the Community by means of Article [133(1)] measures of commercial policy of a national character are only permissible after the end of the transitional period by virtue of specific authorization by the Community.

On the facts of the case, the Court concluded that national measures requiring that an importer declare the actual origin of products even when the latter were in free circulation would be consistent with Community law. However, the importer would be required to comply with them only 'in so far as he knows [the origin] or

---

[45] Case 41/76 *Suzanne Criel, née Donckerwolcke and Henri Pchou v Procureur de la République au Tribunal de Grande Instance, Lille and Director General of Customs* [1976] ECR 1921.

[46] *Ibid*, para 33.

may reasonably be expected to know it'.[47] Furthermore, non-compliance should not give rise to any administrative or penal measures which would be disproportionate to the offence.

The judgment in *Donckwerwolcke* was very significant in a number of ways. In terms of the position of the CCP within the Community legal order, it highlighted its construction as intrinsically linked to the establishment of the common market. In doing so, the Court did not take the principle of uniformity, laid down in Article 133 EC, as a given simply because the transitional period had expired. Instead, it adopted a pragmatic approach, observed what the reality had been and pointed out its repercussions for intra-Community trade. The Court noted the following:[48]

> The fact that at the expiry of the transitional period the Community commercial policy was not fully achieved is one of a number of circumstances calculated to maintain in being between the Member States differences in commercial policy capable of bringing about deflections of trade or of causing economic difficulties in certain Member States.

By pointing out the incomplete nature of the CCP, the Court did not hesitate to acknowledge the central role retained by the Member States in the area in question. In terms of the balance of powers between the Community and the Member States, it made it clear that, even following the expiry of the transitional period, the exclusive nature of the competence of the Community did not actually deprive Member States of their power to act by deviating from the CCP provided that certain conditions were met.

In terms of the manner in which it approached the relevant issues, the Court adopted a non-formalistic approach: it relied upon a factual consideration, that is the incomplete nature of the CCP, in order to determine the context in which a legal principle, that is the exclusivity competence of the Community, was to be applied. In doing so, it exhibited a considerable degree of pragmatism: it would have been highly problematic for the Court to seek to bolster the exclusive nature of the Community in an area where the Community institutions had either been very slow to act or very cautious in taking national policy concerns into account. Viewed from this angle, the judgment in *Donckewolcke* is based on a teleological approach which, actually, favours the Member States rather than the Community. However, that is not to say that national authorities were given *une carte blanche* in that area: on the one hand, the exercise of the national power to deviate from CCP had become an issue of Community law in so far as the Member State seeking to rely upon it should do so pursuant to a 'specific authorization by the Community';[49] on the other hand, the determination of how 'specific' the relevant Community authorisation should be became a matter ultimately to be determined by the Court.

---

[47] *Ibid*, para 35. See also Case 52/77 *Leonce Cayrol v Giovanni Rivoira & Figli* [1977] ECR 2261.
[48] *Ibid*, para 27.
[49] N45 above para 33.

In *Donckwerwolcke,* the Court applied to autonomous measures the approach it would adopt to conventional ones two years later. The issue of the 'specific' Community authorisation required for a unilateral deviation was raised in *Bulk Oil,* a reference from the English High Court.[50] The subject-matter of the reference was British policy confining the exportation of oil only to a number of countries other than Member States: these included Member States of the International Energy Agency and Finland, a country with which there had been an existing pattern of trade. This policy, never incorporated in a formal legislative instrument, aimed at controlling the direct and indirect export of crude oil. There had already been Community rules on exports adopted under Article 133 EC and incorporated in Regulation 2603/69.[51] Article 1 of that instrument established the principle of free exportation of products from the Community according to which no quantitative restrictions should be applied. However, there was an exceptional clause laid down in Article 10 of the Regulation according to which the principle of free exportation would not be applicable to a number of products specifically mentioned in a list annexed to the Regulation until the adoption of common rules by the Council. As crude oil and petroleum oils were included in this list, the question which arose was whether the exceptional clause of Article 10 was a 'specific authorization by the Community' in the meaning of *Donckerwolcke:* could the British authorities deviate from the principle of free exportation laid down in Article 1 of the Regulation?

The Court answered this question in the affirmative. In doing so, it expressly allowed not only the maintenance of national restrictions already in existence when Regulation 2603/69 entered into force but also the introduction of new ones. The other significant aspect of the judgment was the acknowledgment by the Court of the power of the Council to restrict the scope of CCP measures. The Court ruled as follows:[52]

> Having regard to the discretion which it enjoys in an economic matter of such complexity, in this case the Council could, without contravening Article [133 EC], provisionally exclude a product such as oil from the common rules on exports to non-member countries, in view in particular of the internationai commitments entered into by certain Member States and taking into account the particular characteristics of that product, which is of vital importance for the economy of a State and for the functioning of its institutions and public services.

In acknowledging the fact that the common rules on exports may not be all that common, albeit provisionally, the Court sanctions the central role still enjoyed by the Member States in the areas covered by the CCP. This approach entails a wide interpretation of the 'specific' Community law authorisation, one which was seen

---

[50] Case 174/84 *Bulk Oil (Zug) AG v Sun International Limited and Sun Oil Trading Company* [1986] ECR 559.

[51] [1969] OJ Spec Ed (II) 590.

[52] N50 above, para 36.

as rendering the requirement first mentioned in *Donckerwolcke* as 'extremely generous'.[53] Whilst the specific authorisation referred to in *Bulk Oil* does not, indeed, appear to be specific, it should be noted that the type of product to which it applied was quite sensitive. In that respect, it should be recalled that the nature of that product had already given rise to an equally pragmatic approach by the Court in the area of free movement of goods: in *Campus Oil*, it was held that a measure of equivalent effect to quantitative restriction was justified as necessary and proportionate to protect public security, even in the presence of Community legislation regulating that area, the reason being the inability of the latter to ensure sufficient supplies for Member States in all eventualities.[54] Therefore, the Court's approach to the commercial treatment of that specific product in the area of external trade was not all that different from that already adopted in the process of the establishment of the common market. In addition to further highlighting the link between the regulation of the CCP and that of the common market as related to the very core of Article 133 EC, the judgment in *Bulk Oil* also serves to illustrate a practical consideration: it was vital that the specific interests of the Member States should have been seen to be adequately protected at Community level. Had this not been the case, and in the light of the highly protectionist and unpredictable international economic climate of that period, the national administrations would have been very reluctant to cooperate in the establishment of even the incomplete CCP. Viewed from this angle, the gradual process of its completion to which reference was made in secondary legislation[55] became a politically feasible short-term objective rather than a mere aspiration.

The issue of the disuniform application of CCP rules and the right of Member States to deviate unilaterally was further raised in *Tezi Textiel*.[56] This was an action brought by importers of cotton trousers from Italy into the Netherlands. These products originated in Macao and were in free circulation in the Community. However, the Dutch authorities refused to authorise their importation on the basis of two measures: the first one was Regulation 3589/82 on textile products originating in third countries which had applied to imports into the Community of certain specifically defined textile products and imposed quotas which were, then, divided between the Member States;[57] on the other hand, the Benelux countries had been authorised pursuant to a Commission Decision adopted under Article 115 EC to exercise intra-Community surveillance of imports of certain products, including those sought to be imported by Tezi, making them subject to the grant of a licence. It was that Decision which was challenged by the applicant.

[53] CWA Timmermans, 'Community Commercial Policy on Textiles: A Legal Imbroglio' in Völker, n34 above, 159 at 161. See also the criticism in EML Völker, annotation on *Bulk Oil*, (1987) 24 *CMLRev* 99.

[54] Case 72/83 *Campus Oil Ltd v Minister for Industry and Energy* [1984] ECR 2727. In the context of indirect taxation, see Case 140/79 *chemical* [1981] ECR 1.

[55] See text accompanying n39 above.

[56] Case 5/84 *Tezi Textiel BV v Commission* [1986] ECR 887.

[57] See n39 above.

The judgment of the Court may be divided into two parts. In the first one, the Court examined whether the Commission had violated Article 133 EC in authorising national deviations from the CCP pursuant to Article 115 EEC in terms of the treatment of products in free circulation. The Court answered this question in the negative. It observed that, for products in free circulation to be wholly assimilated to Community products, common rules should have been applied at the point of their importation from the third country into the Community territory. However, no such rules had been applicable to textile products at the time. The Court viewed the rules contained in Regulation 3589/82 as merely one step in the process of gradually removing national disparities in the light of the various interests of the Community textile industry. In its judgment, the Court sanctioned the imposition of quantitative limits on the importation of specific products from third countries along with the division of these quotas into national and even regional ones.[58] In doing so, the Court nods approvingly to the policy objective expressed in the preamble to the Regulation according to which 'in order to ensure the best possible utilization of the Community quantitative limits, they should be allocated in accordance with the requirements of the Member States and with the quantitative objectives established by the Council'.[59]

In the second part of its judgment, the Court proceeded to examine whether the Commission had acted lawfully in authorising the Benelux countries to introduce an import surveillance system. Two points are relevant to this analysis: it was held that there was nothing to prevent the Commission from authorising the deviation from the CCP in terms of a wide category of products. However, the strict construction of the exception laid down in Article 115 EEC entailed that the Commission had to act with 'great prudence and moderation' and authorise the adoption of protective measures 'solely for serious reasons and for a limited period, after a full examination of the situation in the Member State seeking a decision under Article 115 and having regard to the general interests of the Community'.[60] All these conditions were held to have been met.

The judgment in *Tezi Textiel* consolidated the approach apparent in earlier case law: not only was the lack of uniformity in the application of CCP rules sanctioned, but also the right of Member States to tackle the ensuing practical repercussions by means of unilateral deviation from those rules was construed in wide terms. In terms of the latter, whilst *Donckwerwolcke* had highlighted the limits placed upon the Member States, that is the need to act pursuant to a specific Community authorisation, *Tezi Textiel* serves to underline the limits placed upon the Commission; in fact, both are so open-ended as to be adjustable to the needs of the specific stage of completion of the CCP. Whilst sensible with the benefit of hindsight and understandable when placed in its wider context, the Court's

---

[58] The Benelux countries were treated as a single unit in terms of the application of Reg 3589/82.
[59] Quoted in para 40 of the judgment.
[60] Paras 58 and 59 respectively.

approach did appear at that time to be too cautious and deferential to Community practice. In his Opinion, Advocate General VerLoren van Themaat argued as follows:[61]

> I do not regard the attainment of a genuinely uniform commercial policy pursuant to Article [133] and the Court's decisions . . . merely as an ultimate ideal and an objective for the future but as a legal duty which ought to have been fulfilled by the end of the transitional period.

For the purpose of this analysis, suffice it to point out that, whilst in legal terms the above statement is correct, the political climate in the Community and the international economic climate were bound to complicate the issue of the achievement of the CCP.[62] Another factor that should be considered was the level of development of the Community legal order: during the period in question, the national administrations were faced with the steady process of constitutionalisation of Community law. To ignore national concerns as well as the repercussions of a very difficult international economic cycle and frustrate the efforts of the Community executive to pursue a gradually evolving, yet balanced, policy would have been counterproductive. In any case, neither the Community nor the national administrations were given a free hand. In another case on the legality of national subquotas, the Court was at pains to point out what would have been self-evident had it not been for the broad construction of the specific Community authorisation: the division of a Community-set quota into national subquotas would be consistent with Community law under[63]

> the express condition that it does not hinder the free movement of the goods forming part of the quota after they have been admitted to free circulation in the territory of one of the Member States.

Whilst the above proviso might sound too weak and general a limit to be placed upon the Commission, it was articulated in a period when the tendency to approve national deviations pursuant to Article 115 EC had already reached its peak and was in the process of being gradually reduced. In 1989, for instance, the Commission approved 119 requests for an authorisation under then Article 115 EC as opposed to 260 in 1979.[64]

---

[61] N56 above at 904.

[62] As was pointed out in relation to the position of any given Member State in the 1970s and 1980s, 'if its only choice is between its own national measures that provide national protection, and accepting a Community regime denying national protection, the choice will inevitably be against the Community regime. Only a non-uniform Community regime that provides for national protection will induce that Member State to give up its own national regime. One may regret the failure of such a common commercial policy to reflect the uniform principles mandated by Article [133]; but unavailability of the intermediate option of a common policy along non-uniform lines will frustrate the development of any common policy': Vogelenzang, n42 above, at 175–6.

[63] Case 218/82 *Commission v Council* [1983] ECR 4063, para 13.

[64] See the Answer by the Commission to Written Question 2133/90 [1991] OJ C 85/29.

7. MANAGING DIVERSITY

The Court had been increasingly keen to set out a number of parameters, mainly of a procedural nature, within which the Community quotas ought to be administered. For instance, it was made clear that, once the overall Community quota had been exhausted, a mechanism had to ensure that goods would be imported into a Member State which had exhausted its share without having to bear customs duties at the full rate or to be rerouted via another Member State whose share had not been exhausted.[65] In setting out the requirements that ought to be met for the division of Community quotas into national subquotas, the Court made it clear that that practice was viewed as exceptional. The acknowledgement of exceptions, with the consequent definition of substantive and procedural requirements seeking to ensure that their application would be the least detrimental to compliance with the main principles, is hardly novel in the history of the development of the Community legal order. In relation to the fundamental area of free movement, for instance, not only have such exceptions been formalised in primary law, but even further exceptions have been developed by the Court of Justice in order to accommodate the evolution of its interpretation of that principle: these rules have taken the form of 'mandatory requirements'[66] or 'the general good'.[67] Furthermore, the judicial construction of those exceptions has been directly linked to the intensity and scope of secondary legislation adopted by the Community institutions: it is the latter which determines the scope for deviation left for Member States, the assumption being that national authorities need to protect an interest other than free movement only if that interest is not already protected at Community level pursuant to secondary legislation—and sometimes not even then.[68]

Viewed from this angle, the approach of the Court of Justice to the deviations from the CCP does not appear to be all that remarkable. Quite the contrary, it seems to further illustrate the strong links between the CCP and the single market which have always been at the very core of the elaboration of the former. However, the interpretation of the CCP by the Court is distinct in both its objective and implications. On the one hand, rather than dealing with an exception set out in the EC Treaty and adjusting it to the legal and political realities of the time, the Court itself acknowledged a practice whose application had no foundation in primary law. On the other hand, rather than enabling the Member States to deviate from fundamental Community principles, the approach of the Court enabled the

---

[65] See Case 35/79 *Grosoli v Ministry of Foreign Trade* [1980] ECR 177 and Case 199/84 *Procuratore della Repubblica v Migliorini* [1985] ECR 3325.

[66] Case 120/78 *Cassis de Dijon* [1979] ECR 649.

[67] Case 33/74 *Van Binsbergen* [1974] ECR 1299 at para 12 and Case 279/80 *Criminal proceedings against Webb* [1981] ECR 3305 at para 17. On the application of these requirements in the area of free movement of goods, see M Jarvis, *The Application of EC Law by National Courts: The Free Movement of Goods* (Oxford: OUP, 1998), MP Maduro, *We the Court: The European Court of Justice and the European Economic Constitution* (Oxford: Hart Publishing, 1998). As for the area of services, see S O'Leary and JM Fernandez-Martin, 'Judicial Exceptions to the Free Provision of Services (1995) 1 *European Law Journal (ELJ)* 303.

[68] See Case 72/83 *Campus Oil*, n54 above.

Community to achieve its objectives in the only manner which its institutions deemed realistic. What makes this approach noteworthy is its adoption in parallel to the forceful elaboration of the principle of exclusive Community competence.

As the approach of the Court reflected the policy choices made by the Community institutions, it was subject to change. In 1987, the Commission challenged the legality of Regulation 3294/86 applying generalised tariff preferences for that year on certain industrial products and Regulation 3295/86 for achieving the same objective in respect to textile products.[69] This system was based on suspension of customs duties granted within the framework of Community quotas, the latter divided between the Member States on the basis of a formula elaborated upon a number of economic criteria. There was a distinct shift of emphasis in the judgment from acknowledging the division of Community quotas into national subquotas as indicative of the development of the CCP to underlining the exceptional nature of that practice. Not only did the Court reiterate the conditions that had to be met for such practice to be justified, but it also noted that such practice should be justified by administrative, technical or economic constraints which preclude the administration of the quota on a Community basis.

In its judgment, it reached the conclusion that that requirement was not, in fact, met. The Council had deviated from the Commission proposal and provided for the suspension of duties pursuant to specific national subquotas, hence extending the application of a system of importation first introduced in 1971 under Regulation 1308/71.[70] The Court pointed out that the *raisond'être* of that system, as set out in the contested Regulation, was essentially the same as that set out in Regulation 1308/71. It then, concluded that 'the statement of reasons . . . does not set out the reasons justifying, 15 years later, the continuation of the system without alteration'.[71] In annulling Regulation 3294/86, the Court also reiterated the Commission's argument that it was, in fact, in a position, due to new means of telecommunication, to administer centrally the Community quota in an efficient manner, a claim which had not been seriously challenged.

The judgment in Case 51/87 *Commission v Council* is important for our understanding of the development of the CCP. First, it rendered the substantive and procedural requirements attached to the pragmatic construction of the CCP a flexible instrument of judicial review. Secondly, the Court made it clear that the exercise of discretion by the Community legislature could be a double-edged sword: whilst necessary in order to facilitate the adjustment of ultimate objectives set out in primary law to the political realities of the time, it was by no means impervious to judicial control. In fact, it was precisely the interpretation of that notion which, having made the Court subject to severe criticism for being overly deferential to the Community policy-makers, ultimately enabled it to curtail the perpetuation of old policies. Thirdly, in doing so, the Court appeared quite astute

---

[69] Case 51/87 *Commission v Council* [1988] ECR 5459.
[70] [1971] OJ L 142/1.
[71] N69 above, at para 14.

in its interaction with the Community legislature: the arguments put forward before the Court made it clear that the deviation from the CCP illustrated by the division of a Community quota into national subquotas had ceased to attract consensus amongst the Community actors as its function had ceased to be regarded as necessary and uncontroversial. Finally, the judgment in Case 51/87 *Commission v Council* serves as a reminder of the important contribution of the Court of Justice to the development and establishment of the CCP in a pragmatic and dynamic manner: whilst appearing to link its substantive content to the notion of exclusivity, it then proceeded to deconstruct it in order to interact with the Community legislature and respond to the practical and political realities of the time, only to revert to highlighting the importance of the CCP as a *common* policy.

In engaging in this imaginative course of action, the Court was not alone. The gradual development of the CCP highlights various instances where the Community institutions appeared willing to try new methods of establishing a CCP as a common policy. One such case was about the importation of cars from Japan. Whilst at the end of 1960s Japan's exports were rather insignificant, the 1970s saw a very considerable rise throughout the Community. This development alarmed the national industries in so far as it gradually threatened their labour forces, positively undermined their competitiveness and, ultimately, raised the prospect of significant market losses. It goes without saying that the extent to which national industries were affected varied: in 1980, for instance, Japanese firms had approximately 43 percent of the automobile market in Greece and only 0.14 percent in Italy. The reason for this disparity was that, depending on the strength of the individual domestic industries, each Member State sought to resist the penetration of its market by Japanese imports pursuant to arrangements negotiated individually. Those arrangements took the form of national quotas and voluntary export restraints the terms of which varied accordingly: in 1977, for instance, France imposed a limit on Japanese products of 3 per cent of its market, whereas Portugal only allowed the importation of 20,000 passenger cars.[72] This overtly protectionist policy was, at that time, justified in the light of the importance of domestic automobile industries for the economy of Member States: for instance, a study carried out by the European Commission in 1991 concluded that one in every 10 jobs in the Community as a whole was dependent upon the automobile industry either directly or indirectly.[73]

However, in 1991, after three years of negotiation, an agreement was concluded between the Commission and the Japanese Ministry of Trade and Industry. The agreement, entitled 'Elements of Consensus', aimed at establishing the progressive and complete liberalisation of the importation of Japanese cars, off-road vehicles and light commercial vehicles by the beginning of 2000. For the period until the end of 1999, it provided for a regulated regime for imports in the five most important

---

[72] See M Mason, 'Elements of Consensus: Europe's Response to the Japanese Automotive Challenge' [1994] *Journal of Common Market Studies (JCMS)* 433 at 436.
[73] See Hanson, n43 above, at 75.

European motor vehicle markets, namely France, Italy, Spain, Portugal and United Kingdom, albeit one whose quotas were substantially increased. This development should not be seen in isolation; instead, it was part of a broader relaxation of the attitude of the Community and its Member States towards their economic relations with Japan.[74]

As it is beyond the scope of this analysis to examine the content of this agreement in detail,[75]suffice it to point out the following. First, the process of the negotiation and conclusion of the Elements of Consensus was as important as its content. Whilst not introducing common rules applicable immediately throughout the Community market, the European Commission sought to merge a number of disparate individual national policies into a common, albeit provisionally diverse, policy negotiated and administered at Community level. Therefore, it represented a significant step forward, not only for reducing the scope of diversity within the Community market and rendering complete liberalisation a concrete objective, but also for subjecting diversity to a Community discipline in order to create a common policy.

Secondly, this initiative, and the momentum it created for the curtailment of the substantive deficiencies of the CCP apparent in the 1970s and 1980s, may be understood in the light of the momentum created by the Single European Act. The concrete goal of achieving by 1992 what should have been achieved years previously questioned the role of preexisting and individually negotiated national arrangements in the area of the CCP. This provides yet another illustration of the inescapable link between the common market and the CCP which had been at the core of the Court's case law. Therefore, the incomplete nature of the latter had been understood as necessitated by the existing state of the process establishing the former. Put another way, the impetus underpinning the completion of the internal market by 1992 rendered the case for an incomplete CCP untenable.

Thirdly, in terms of the content of the Elements of Consensus, the interests of the major national industries were taken into account and protected by the Commission, which negotiated individual arrangements with the Japanese authorities. In that respect, the substitution of individually negotiated national agreements for one negotiated and concluded by the Commission appears to be an imaginative exercise in policy-making; as such, it became all the more interesting in the light of the exclusive nature of the competence that the Community had been deemed to enjoy since the early 1970s. Viewed from this angle, the development of the EC policy regarding the importation of Japanese motor vehicles points in two directions: on the one hand, the existence of exclusive Community competence did not necessarily rule out all national policies; on the other hand, the exercise by the Community of that competence by no means entails the substitution of national concerns for an inflexible and centrally designed European policy model.

---

[74] See M Johnson, *European Community Trade Policy and the Article 113 Committee* (London: Royal Institute of International Affairs, 1998) 42.

[75] See Hanson, n43 above, at 74–80, Mason, n72 above and CRA Swaak, *European Community Law and the Automobile Industry* (The Hague: Kluwer, 1999) 187–204.

Finally, in political and practical terms, it could be argued that the negotiation and conclusion of the Elements of Consensus might not have been possible had it not been for the gradual evolution of the CCP: the acknowledgment of national concerns by the Community institutions and the sanctioning of the ensuing policies by the Community judiciary had created the political environment necessary both for the Commission to step in and seek to address national concerns within a common framework and for the Member States to entrust the defence of their interests to the Community executive. In other words, the implied acknowledgement by the Court in the 1970s and early 1980s that neither was the CCP a genuinely common policy nor was the Community's exclusive competence truly exclusive was central to the development of that policy. Viewed from this angle, the contribution of the Court of Justice to the development of EC intenrational relations was no less significant than that underpinning the establishment of the single market pursuant to its construction of the principle of free movement.

8. CONCLUSION

The analysis in this chapter sought to chart the development of one of the very few external policies of the Community expressly provided for in the original EC Treaty. By focusing on the historical development of the Common Commercial Policy, it identified its principal normative characteristic, namely the exclusive nature of the Community competence, and examined its implications for the legal position of the Member States. Placed in their specific legal and political context, the originally bold statements of the Court of Justice were applied in a flexible manner so that the parallel existence of the Member States was not necessarily excluded. To that effect, the policy laid down in Article 133 EC has been viewed as less common than originally envisaged.[76] Not only did the Community institutions, the Member States and the Community judicature appear to share this view of the CCP, but they also interacted in indirect ways in order to shape incrementally a regulatory space which was expressly provided for under primary law as complete by the end of the transitional period. This process becomes all the more noteworthy if viewed in the broader context of the longstanding debate about the precise scope of Article 133 EC and its much-debated reform. The following chapter will, therefore, reveal another dimension of the construction of the CCP as an adjunct to the establishment of the internal market and its relation to the other sources of external competence.

---

[76] See M Cremona, 'The External Dimension of the Signle Market: Building (on) the Foundations' in C Barnard and J Scott (eds), *The Law of the Single European Market—Unpacking the Premises* (Oxford: Hart Publishing, 2002) 352 for a detailed analysis of the limits of uniformity in external commercial policy as reflecting the limits of uniformity in the establishment and functioning of the internal market.

2

The Scope of the Common Commercial Policy: Interpretation and Constitutional Logic

1. INTRODUCTION

IN ANALYSING THE competence enjoyed by the Community in the areas covered by the Common Commercial Policy, the last chapter examined the introduction of exclusivity by the Court of Justice and assessed its development. The exclusive competence of the Community rendered the issue of the definition of the scope of the CCP of considerable practical significance: the wider the scope of the policies covered by the CCP, the less control the Member States would be able to exercise in the area of external trade and the more significant the powers of the Community institutions. This was all the more so in the light of the qualified-majority voting introduced by Article 133(4) EC.

These normative and procedural features of the CCP have given rise to a long-standing debate between the Community institutions and the Member States as to the delineation of the scope of activities which should be deemed to be covered by Article 133 EC. It is the various forms that this debate has taken over the years that this chapter will analyse.

2. LAYING DOWN THE LEGAL FOUNDATION

The central provision of the CCP merely refers to a number of activities which fall within the scope of the CCP:

> The common commercial policy shall be based on uniform principles, *particularly* in regard to changes in tariff rates, the conclusion of tariff and trade agreements, the achievement of uniformity in measures of liberalization, export policy and measures to protect trade such as those to be taken in the event of dumping or subsidies.[1]

The wording of Article 133(1) EC indicates that this list is non-exhaustive, a conclusion confirmed by the Court's case law.[2] As to the type of measures which may

---

[1] Emphasis added.
[2] *Opinion 1/78* [1979] ECR 2871, at para 45, Case 165/87 *Commission v Council* [1989] ECR 5545, para 15.

be adopted pursuant to that provision, both unilateral measures adopted by the Community alone and international agreements concluded with third countries and international organisations are covered. The Court has pointed out that:

> [a] commercial policy is in fact made up by the combination and interaction of internal and external measures, without priority being taken by one over the others. Sometimes agreements are concluded in execution of a policy fixed in advance, sometimes that policy is defined by the agreements themselves.[3]

It was against this background that the issue of the scope of the CCP arose. In *Opinion 1/75*, the Court was asked to rule on a draft Understanding on a Local Cost Standard, an agreement drawn up under the auspices of the Organisation of European Economic Cooperation and Development.[4] This agreement was about credits for the financing of local costs linked to export operations. Asked to rule on its consistency with the Community legal order, the Court referred to the CCP as follows:[5]

> [measures concerning credits for the financing of local costs linked to export operations] constitute an important element of commercial policy, that concept having the same content whether it is applied in the context of the international action of a State or to that of the Community.

This broad reading of the scope of Article 133 EC was accompanied by the construction of a dynamic policy:[6]

> The common commercial policy is above all the outcome of a progressive development based upon specific measures which may refer without distinction to "autonomous" and external aspects of that policy and which do not necessarily presuppose, by the fact that they are linked to the field of the common commercial policy, the existence of a large body of rules, but combine gradually to form that body.

The combined implications of these statements are very significant. The definition of the scope of the CCP with reference to that of the external commercial policy of a state may appear to render the former potentially unlimited; furthermore, its development independently of the adoption of internal harmonising legislation not only highlights the central powers of the Community institutions in that area but also brings the Court of Justice to the very centre of the conduct of international trade relations. Indeed, an ill-defined external policy which falls within the exclusive nature of the Community was likely to render the Community judicature the ultimate arbiter in an area challenging directly the autonomy of Member States to act on the international economic arena.

---

[3] *Opinion 1/75 (re: OECD Local Cost Standard)* [1975] ECR 1355 at 1363.
[4] *Ibid.*
[5] *Ibid*, 1362.
[6] *Ibid*, 1363.

The significance of this dynamic definition of the CCP in *Opinion 1/75* is further highlighted by the remaining part of the ruling. As analysed in a previous chapter, the Court went on to articulate the exclusive nature of the competence which the Community enjoys *a priori*. Its *raison d'être* was to ensure that the institutional framework of the Community would not be distorted, the mutual trust within the Community would not be called into question and the Community would not be prevented from fulfilling its task in the defence of the common interest. Viewed in this context, *Opinion 1/75* appeared to lay down the foundation of one of the most supranational policies of the Community. It has been argued, for instance, that the CCP 'represents the EC at the height of its legal powers, control, and supremacy over the member states'.[7]

A number of subsequent rulings appeared to support such views. In *Opinion 1/78*, the Court was asked to rule on whether the Community was exclusively competent pursuant to Article 133 EC to conclude an agreement aimed at the stabilisation of prices of natural rubber by means of setting up a buffer stock.[8] The Agreement aimed at achieving two objectives: on the one hand, to serve the interests of the exporting states by guaranteeing stable export earnings and, on the other hand, to serve the interests of the importing states by ensuring reliability of supplies at a fair price level. The Contracting States would meet those objectives by building up a buffer stock purchased when prices were in decline and then sold when prices were rising. The effect of this arrangement would be to contain the price of natural rubber within a predetermined fluctuating margin.

The very wide construction of the CCP put forward by the Court in *Opinion 1/75* was the canvas against which the Commission and the Council, the latter supported by a number of Member States, developed two contrasting lines of reasoning as to the proper definition of the scope of Article 133 EC. The agreement in question was a commodity agreement; therefore its aim was to regulate rather than liberalise international trade. The Commission viewed such agreements as necessary for the complete and consistent management of international trade and argued that the CCP should be construed widely enough to cover them. Therefore, the EC would be able to use trade instruments already at the disposal of states. Therefore, it viewed the instruments listed in Article 133(1) EC as classic mechanisms of international trade relations with which it sought to contrast a modern and dynamic policy, mainly on the basis of the earlier pronouncement of the Court in *Opinion 1/75*. This argument led to what has been known as the instrumentalist approach to Article 133 EC according to which the character of a given legal measure would determine whether it should be covered by the CCP and, hence, the exclusive competence of the Community: if that measure was an instrument regulating international trade, then it should be deemed to fall within the scope of Article 133 EC.

---

[7]   D McGoldrick, *International Relations Law of the European Union* (London: Longman, 1997) 70.
[8]   See n2 above.

The Council, on the other hand, articulated an objective approach according to which the question whether a given legal measure should be adopted pursuant to the CCP would be determined on the basis of its objective: any measure whose aim was to influence the volume or flow of trade should be considered as a commercial policy measure, hence falling within the scope of Article 133 EC. This approach was underpinned by the concern that, in the alternative, there would be no limit on what the Community institutions could do in the area of external trade relations. Furthermore, the Council pointed out that the negotiation and conclusion of the Agreement on Natural Rubber had been carried out within a distinctly political context. In particular, rubber was a strategic raw material whose regulation had been attempted as a matter of general economic policy and not trade policy, the former remaining within the sphere of national responsibility. Furthermore, the international regulation of natural rubber had been attempted within the context of the responsibilities which Member States had towards developing countries independently of the Community. This approach was also supported by the British and French governments.

In its ruling, the Court did not address the merits and drawbacks of these approaches in a comprehensive manner.[9] Instead, having identified the main features of the Agreement on Natural Rubber, it acknowledged both the distinct nature of commodity agreements in the context of international economic relations and their comprehensive scope. It stated the following:[10]

> As an increasing number of products which are particularly important from the economic point of view are concerned, it is clear that a coherent commercial policy would no longer be practicable if the Community were not in a position to exercise its powers also in connexion with a category of agreements which are becoming, alongside traditional commercial agreements, one of the major factors in the regulation of international trade.

Having construed the CCP in the light of this particular type of agreements, the Court went on to articulate its scope in the following terms:[11]

> it seems that it would no longer be possible to carry on any worthwhile common commercial policy if the Community were not in a position to avail itself also of more elaborate means devised with a view to furthering the development of international trade.

---

[9] See JHJ Bourgeois, 'The Common Commercial Policy: Scope and Nature of the Powers' in ELM Voelker (ed), *Protectionism and the European Community* (2nd edn, Deventer: Kluwer, 1986) 1 who points out that, if the approach adopted by the Council were to be taken to its logical conclusion, measures inherent in the conduct of commercial policy such as rules of origin would not be covered by Art 133 EC (at 5). See also P Gilsdorf, 'Portée et délimitation des compétences communautaires en matière de politique commerciale' [1989] *Revuedu Marché Commun* 195 and CWA Timmermans, 'Common Commercial Policy (Article 113 EEC) and International Trade in Services' in F Capotorti *et al* (eds), *Du droit international au droit de l'intégration - Liber Amicorum Pierre Pescatore* (Nomos: Bade-Baden, 1987) 675.

[10] N2 above at para 43.

[11] *Ibid*, para 44.

It is therefore not possible to lay down, for Article [133 EC], an interpretation the effect of which would be to restrict the common commercial policy to the use of instruments intended to have an effect only on the traditional aspects of external trade to the exclusion of more highly developed mechanisms such as appear in the agreement envisaged. A common commercial policy understood in that sense would be destined to become nugatory in the course of time. Although it may be thought that at the time when the Treaty was drafted liberalization of trade was the dominant idea, the Treaty nevertheless does not form a barrier to the possibility of the Community's developing a commercial policy aiming at a regulation of the world market for certain products rather than at a mere liberalization of trade.

And as if the point had not been brought home, the Court went on to rule that Article 133 EC made it clear that 'the question of external trade must be governed from a wide point of view and not only having regard to the administration of precise systems such as customs and quantitative restrictions'.[12]

The above approach of the Court of Justice might appear to bring the principles introduced in *Opinion 1/75* to their logical conclusion: being defined in parallel to the external commercial policy of a state, the CCP should be dynamic and construed in wide terms in order for it to be 'worthwhile' as well as 'coherent' and 'practicable'. However, when viewed in the light of the legal and political context in which the Court was called upon to rule, a more nuanced picture emerges. The type of agreement which formed the subject-matter of the request for an Opinion rendered any outcome other than that reached by the Court difficult to justify.

There was an increasing tendency in international economic relations in 1970s towards developing a regulatory approach to international trade. This aimed at taking into account, amongst others, the emerging concerns of developing countries. Both the establishment of systems of export credits and the conclusion of commodity agreements were part of this approach. To exclude them from the scope of the CCP would not only illustrate a shortsighted view of international trade but would also indicate a reading of Article 133(1) EC so restrictive as to run counter to the essence of the clearly non-exhaustive enumeration of activities laid down therein. Viewed from this angle, in *Opinions 1/75* and *1/78* the Court was asked to adjudicate on 'normal instrumentalities of commercial policy'.[13]

Furthermore, both rulings were delivered in the period of stagnation which characterised the Community legal system following the so-called Luxembourg compromise. Against this political background, the Court of Justice sought to define the normative foundation of the Community's external trade policy and ensure that its legal implications for the Member States would be accepted. In this respect, it is recalled that the twin principles of the CCP, namely its wide scope and the exclusive nature of Community competence, were introduced in what

---

[12] *Ibid*, para 45.
[13] E Stein, 'External Relations of the European Community: Structure and Process' (1990) 1 *Collected Courses of the Academy of European Law* 115, 137.

appeared to be quite uncompromising terms in *Opinion 1/75*. The Court's preoccupation with shaping as solid a foundation for the CCP as possible was illustrated
by the express linkages made in its rulings with the internal market. In *Opinion
1/78*, for instance, it was pointed out that 'a restrictive interpretation of the concept of common commercial policy would risk causing disturbances in intra-
Community trade by reason of the disparities which would then exist in certain
sectors of economic relations with non-member countries'.[14] As this link was
made in order further to justify the need for a dynamic interpretation of the scope
of the external trade policies of the Community, it is recalled that a similar link
had already been made three years earlier in order to justify the need for the competence of the Community to be exclusive. Indeed, Article 133 EC was seen as
'conceived ... in the context of the operation of the Common Market, for the
defence of the common interests of the Community, within which the particular
interests of the Member States must endeavour to adapt to each other'.[15] Therefore, the force with which the Court sought to define the scope of a 'worthwhile'
commercial policy may serve a very specific function in the gradual shaping of the
emerging CCP.

Finally, whilst the principles purporting to lay down the foundation of the CCP
were put forward in uncompromising terms, in fact the Court adopted a more
flexible approach to its application. In *Opinion 1/78*, for instance, it is recalled that
the assertion of the exclusive nature of the Community notwithstanding, the participation of the Member States in the conclusion of the International Agreement
in Natural Rubber was sanctioned.[16] This illustration of pragmatism on the facts
of the case[17] does not only suggest that the ramifications of exclusivity may not be
as severe as they appeared originally; it also questions whether the uncompromising terms in which the broad scope of the CCP was construed should be taken,
in fact, at face value.

Instead of abating the debate about the scope of Article 133 EC, the pronouncements of the Court of Justice were so general that they enabled the Council, the
Commission and the Member States to put forward their contrasting approaches
in a number of cases. In the *Generalised Tariff Preferences*, the Commission challenged the adoption of two Council regulations applying generalised tariff preferences to a number of industrial and textile products originating in developing
countries.[18] It argued that the contested measures should have been adopted by
the Council by qualified majority voting under Article 133 EC. The Council defended the absence of a reference to a precise legal basis in the contested measures as
well as their adoption by unanimity. It argued that they pursued commercial aims

---

[14] N2 above, at para 45.

[15] N3 above, at 1364.

[16] See the analysis in Ch 2 above.

[17] See T Tridimas and P Eeckhout, 'The External Competence of the Community and the Case-Law
of the Court of Justice: Principle versus Pragmatism' (1994) 14 *YEL* 143.

[18] Case 45/86 *Commission v Council (re: GSP)* [1987] ECR 1493.

as well as aims of development policy. It was for that reason that Article 133 EC had been considered irrelevant to the establishment of a system of generalised tariff preferences.

This line of reasoning was rejected by the Court of Justice. Having noted that a system of generalised tariff preferences was based on changes in tariff rates, it opined that it fell within the scope of the indicative list of activities laid down in Article 133(1) EC. Therefore, it was covered by the CCP without doubt. It then repeated that the CCP should have the same content as that of national commercial policy and proceeded as follows:[19]

> The link between trade and development has become progressively stronger in modern international relations. It has been recognized in the context of the United Nations, notably by the United Nations Conference on Trade and Development (UNCTAD), and in the context of GATT …

Against this legal and political background, the Community system of generalised preferences was seen as reflecting 'a new concept of international trade relations in which development aims play a major role'.[20] This construction of the CCP was also justified in the light of Article 131 EC which referred to the 'harmonious development of world trade' as one of the objectives of the CCP.[21]

In the *Generalised Tariff Preferences (GTP)* judgment, the Court was faced with the considerable difficulty of delineating a commercial policy broadly understood in the light of its interactions with other policies with which it shared legal instruments to considerable extent. It did so by relying upon one of the most expansive statements it had made in the previous decade, namely the parallelism between the content of the CCP and the external commercial policy of a state. It is also noteworthy that, in his Opinion, Advocate General Lenz had stressed the trade objectives pursued by the Community's generalised system of tariff preferences as well as the benefits it was expected to accrue for national economies.[22]

The judgment in the *GTP* case illustrated the difficulties that the Court would have to face in order to delineate a widely construed CCP in the light of its interactions with a number of other policies over which the competence enjoyed by the Community was not exclusive. The most prominent examples were provided in the context of the interaction between trade and foreign policy in 1990s. In the light of the specific legal and constitutional issues raised by the regulation of trade policy with foreign policy or security implications, the relevant body of case law will be analysed in a separate chapter.[23] For the purposes of this analysis, suffice it to point out that the Council and a number of national governments argued that

---

[19] *Ibid*, paras 17.
[20] *Ibid*, para 18.
[21] *Ibid*, para 19.
[22] See paras 67–69 of his Opinion.
[23] See Ch 12 below.

Community measures in that area should not be adopted under Article 133 EC because foreign policy and defence fell entirely beyond the scope of the Community legal system. This argument was rejected by the Court which, ruling on the consistency of national policies with trade sanctions imposed pursuant to an Article 133 EC Regulation and a non-EC measure, held as follows: '[t]he Member States have indeed retained their competence in the field of foreign and security policy. At the material time, their cooperation in this field was governed by *inter alia* Title III of the Single European Act [that is the precursor of the Common Foreign and Security Policy entitled European Political Cooperation]. ... None the less, the powers retained by the Member States must be exercised in a manner consistent with Community law'.[24] This principle was fully consistent with prior case law, where it had been held that 'a measure ... whose effect is to prevent or restrict the export of certain products, cannot be treated as falling outside the scope of the common commercial policy on the ground that it has foreign policy and security objectives. ... The specific subject-matter of commercial policy, which concerns trade with non-member countries and, according to Article [133 EC], is based on the concept of a common policy, requires that a Member State should not be able to restrict its scope by freely deciding, in the light of its own foreign policy or security requirements, whether a measure is covered by Article [133 EC]'[25].

Finally, individual Member States were also keen to advocate a commercial policy restrictively construed for the Community. The Greek government, for instance, sought the annulment of an Article 133 EC Regulation setting out the conditions of imports of agricultural products originating in third countries following the Chernobyl accident.[26] The Court rejected that action on the basis that, in the light of its objective and content, the contested measure was clearly intended to regulate trade between the EC and third countries. By doing so, it supported the argument put forward by Advocate General Darmon in his Opinion, according to which the definition of conditions of imports of products originating in a non-Member State was a CCP measure by its very nature.[27]

3. THE RULING IN OPINION 1/94: A POLICY NOT QUITE AS WIDE AS ORIGINALLY ENVISAGED?

The subject of *Opinion 1/94* was the competence of the Community to conclude a number of agreements annexed to the Agreement establishing the World Trade Organisation. In particular, the Commission, which requested the Opinion pursuant

---

[24] Case C–124/95 *The Queen v HM Treasury and Bank of England, ex parte Centro-Com* [1997] ECR I–81, paras 24–25.

[25] Case C–70/94 *Fritz Werner Industrie-Ausrustungen GmbH v Germany* [1995] ECR I–3189, paras 10–11.

[26] Case C–62/88 *Greece v Council* [1990] ECR 1527.

[27] *Ibid* para 32 of his Opinion.

to Article 300(6) EC, argued that the Community was exclusively competent to conclude the following: the General Agreement on Tariffs and Trade (GATT 1994) as far as products covered by the European Coal and Steel Community and the Euratom Community were concerned; the General Agreement on Trade in Services (GATS) and the Agreement on Trade-Related Aspects of Intellectual Property Rights (TRIPs).[28] The Community institutions and the Member States had chosen to set aside the issue of Community competence during the period of the negotiation of the WTO Agreements in order to enhance the effectiveness of the representation of the Community interests. Therefore, whilst they had authorised the Commission to act as the sole negotiator on behalf of the Community and the Member States, they had done so without prejudice to the determination of the Community and national competence on issues covered by those agreements.

3.1. The Ruling of the Court

It is in relation to GATS and TRIPS that the arguments put forward by the Commission and the line of reasoning underpinning the Court's ruling raise the most interesting issues. As far as the Multilateral Agreements on Trade in Goods were concerned, the exclusive nature of the Community was affirmed in rather uncompromising terms. First, the Court ruled, rather uncontroversially in the light of the absence of any argument to the contrary, that it covered Euratom products. Secondly, as to trade in ECSC products, a number of Member States and the Council argued that national competence was retained in the light of Article 71 ECSC, which provided that the powers of the Member States in matters of commercial policy would not be affected by the conclusion of that Treaty. However, the Court addressed this argument by interpreting the scope of that provision in very restrictive terms, namely as confined to international agreements relating specifically to ECSC products. Furthermore, it referred to *Opinion 1/75*, where it had been concluded that Article 71 ECSC should not be interpreted in a way which would render the CCP 'inoperative'.[29] In the light of this wide reading of Article 133 EC following the very strict reading of Article 71 ECSC, the Court concluded that the exclusive nature of the Community's competence to conclude the Multilateral Agreements on Trade in Goods 'cannot be impugned on the ground that they also apply to ECSC products'.[30]

Thirdly, in relation, specifically, to the Agreement on Agriculture, the Court opined that Article 133 EC was the appropriate legal basis for its adoption. This was the case despite the fact that the it had already ruled on the specific EC Treaty provision on agriculture, that is Article 37 EC: this was considered the appropriate legal basis for secondary legislation on the conditions under which products,

---

[28] *Opinion 1/94 (WTO Agreements)* [1994] ECR I–5267.
[29] N3 above, at 1365.
[30] N28 above, para 27.

including those originating in non-Member States, could be marketed.[31] This was because the Agreement on Agriculture did not aim at pursuing any of the CAP objectives; instead, its objective was 'to establish, on a worldwide basis, "a fair and market-oriented agricultural trading system"'.[32] The fact that the Community would have to comply with its obligations under that Agreement by adopting internal legislation pursuant to the CAP was deemed irrelevant.[33]

Fourthly, the Agreement on the Application of Sanitary and Phytosanitary Measures was also deemed to fall within the scope of Article 133 EC in the light of its objective, that is the establishment of a legal framework which would 'minimize [the] negative effects [of the development, adoption and enforcement of such measures] on trade'.[34]

Finally, in relation to the Agreement on Technical Barriers to Trade, the Court rejected the argument of the Netherlands government that, in the absence of either current or prospective complete harmonisation, it should be concluded by the Member States. Instead, it ruled that its conclusion was a CCP measure because its objective was 'merely to ensure that technical regulations and standards, along with the procedures underpinning their adoption, would not create unnecessary obstacles to international trade'.[35]

Having established the exclusive competence of the Community to conclude the Multilateral Agreements on Trade in Goods in their entirety, the Court turned its attention to the conclusion of GATS. The Commission had argued that Article 133 EC was applicable because trade in services was a CCP measure. To that effect, it advanced three main arguments. The first one was the broad construction of the CCP introduced by the Court of Justice in the 1970s and consolidated in the 1980s. The second was of a practical nature, namely the close link between trade and services: it was argued that, in a globalised economy, services had become the main focus of international economic activity. Therefore, it was increasingly difficult to distinguish between trade in goods and trade in services. The final argument was of a contextual nature: the purpose of GATS was to lay down rules aimed at the regulation and liberalisation of trade in services; in addition, the instruments that the Contracting Parties would be called upon to adopt would be of a commercial nature. As such, they would be covered by the instrumentalist approach which the Commission deemed to have been sanctioned by the Court in *Opinions 1/75* and *1/78* as well as the *GSP* judgment.

All these arguments were rejected by the Court of Justice. The starting point for its ruling was to accept the main premise of the Commission's analysis: the non-exhaustive nature of the activities set out in Article 133(1) EC and the principle that the scope of the CCP be interpreted widely, both articulated in past case law, were reaffirmed. The increasing economic significance of trade in services and its

---

[31] See Case C–131/87 *Commission v Council* [1989] ECR I–3764.
[32] Preamble to the Agreement, as referred to in *Opinion 1/94*, n28 above, para 29.
[33] *Ibid.*
[34] Preamble to the Agreement, as referred to in *Opinion 1/94* (n 28 above) para 31.
[35] *Ibid*, at para 33.

central position on the international economic arena was not only acknowledged but also viewed as borne out by the WTO Agreement and its annexes. However, its conclusion was significantly more nuanced: [36]

> it follows ... that trade in services cannot immediately, and as a matter of principle, be excluded from the scope of Article [133] ....

Whilst in accordance with the main contention of the Commission about trade in services in general, this statement was clearly of a negative character, not only in its wording but also its tone. What the Commission saw as sufficient to bring GATS within the scope of the CCP, the Court saw as insufficient to exclude it from it *a priori*. This rather cautious approach was illustrated by the convoluted statement which followed: [37]

> one must take into account the definition of trade in services given in GATS in order to see whether the overall scheme of the Treaty is not such as to limit the extent to which trade in services can be included within Article [133].

The Court identified the four modes of supply of services covered by GATS as follows: cross-frontier supply not involving the movement of a person; consumption abroad entailing the movement of a consumer in the territory of a WTO party where the supplier is established; commercial presence, that is the presence of a subsidiary or branch in the territory of the WTO party where the service is rendered; the presence of natural persons from a WTO member country, enabling a supplier from one member country to supply services within the territory of any other member country.

Of these four modes of supplies, only the first, involving no movement of a natural or legal person, was deemed to fall within the scope of Article 133 EC on the ground of its similarity to trade in goods. The supply of a service involving the physical movement of a natural person, either as a supplier or a consumer, was viewed as beyond the scope of the CCP in the light of the textual distinction laid down in different paragraphs of Article 3 EC between the CCP and measures concerning the entry and movement of persons. In the light of this, it was concluded that the treatment of third country nationals on crossing the external frontiers of Member States was beyond the scope of the CCP. The same conclusion was reached about the movement of legal persons, as the Court noted the existence of a specific EC Treaty chapter on the matter.

A specific point was made about transport services. The Court noted that not only was there a specific Title in the EC Treaty dedicated to transport, but also the implied competence of the Community to negotiate and conclude international agreements had been introduced in relation to a transport agreement.[38]

---

[36] Para 41.
[37] Para 42.
[38] See Case 22/70 *Commission v Council (European Road Transport Agrement)* [1971] ECR 263.

The conclusion of international transport agreements was therefore deemed to fall beyond the scope of Article 133 EC. It is noteworthy that the Court rejected the Commission's argument that economic sanctions regimes imposed on third countries under Article 133 EC had, in fact, covered transport services too: on the one hand, the Court opined that the suspension of transport services had been the necessary adjunct to the principal sanctions, as its absence would have undermined the effectiveness of any type of trade sanctions; on the other hand, it was pointed out that 'a mere practice of the Council cannot derogate from the rules laid down in the Treaty and cannot, therefore, create a precedent binding on Community institutions with regard to the correct legal basis'.[39]

The Commission's line of reasoning regarding TRIPs was also rejected. In particular, it had been argued that there is a very close link between intellectual property rights and trade in the products and services to which they apply; this link was deemed so strong as to bring them within the scope of the legal framework regulating the latter. In response to this argument, the Court's approach was developed in a manner similar to that already articulated in relation to GATS. First, it started off by making a distinction similar to that underpinning its analysis of GATS: it identified a specific area of trade-related intellectual property rights covered by TRIPs which was closely linked to trade in goods already regulated under Article 133 EC. This was about measures for the prohibition of the release for free circulation of counterfeit goods. Such measures, applied by customs officials at the external frontiers of the Community, had been laid down in Regulation 3842/86.[40] Then, the Court accepted the main premise upon which the Commission's contention was based, that is the link between trade in goods and the enforcement of intellectual property rights. However, this was deemed to be insufficient to bring them within the scope of Article 133 EC as 'intellectual property rights do not relate specifically to international trade; they affect internal trade just as much, if not more than, international trade'.[41]

The Court further substantiated its conclusion as to the inapplicability of Article 133 EC to the conclusion of TRIPs by relying upon the internal effects of that agreement within the Community legal order. Having identified the main objective of TRIPs as the world-wide strengthening and harmonisation of the protection of intellectual property, it pointed out that its conclusion would introduce harmonisation within the Community system too, hence affecting the establishment and functioning of the internal market. Whilst competent to adopt such harmonising legislation internally, the Community could only do so under either Article 100 EC or Article 100a EC or Article 235 EC. However, the procedural requirements laid down in these provisions were different from those under Article 133 EC, namely unanimity and consultation with the Parliament in the case of Articles 100 and 235 EC. The Court concluded as follows: [42]

---

[39] Para 52 with reference to Case 68/86 *UK v Council* [1988] ECR 855.
[40] [1986] OJ L 357/1.
[41] N28 above, para 57.
[42] Para 60.

If the Community were to be recognized as having exclusive competence to enter into agreements with non-member countries to harmonize the protection of intellectual property and, at the same time, to achieve harmonization at Community level, the Community institutions would be able to escape the internal constraints to which they are subject in relation to procedures and to rules as to voting.

Having ruled out the existence of exclusive Community competence on the basis of the insufficient link between intellectual property and trade in goods and the disparities between the international effects of TRIPs and the procedural constraints laid down in primary EC law, the Court went on to dismiss specific examples of secondary legislation affecting protection of IP rights as irrelevant. First, measures adopted in the context of the so-called new commercial policy instrument in order to protect the intellectual property interests of the Community were 'unrelated to the harmonization of intellectual property protection which is the primary objective of TRIPs'.[43] Secondly, the fact that the Community has suspended generalised tariff preferences in response to discrimination by a third state as regards protection of intellectual property rights was also irrelevant to the competence of the Community to conclude an agreement aiming at international harmonisation of intellectual property protection: 'since the grant of generalized preferences is a commercial policy measure ..., so too is their suspension'.[44] Thirdly, provisions on the protection of intellectual property rights in a number of agreements with third countries[45] were 'extremely limited in scope'[46] and, therefore, 'ancillary'.[47] They either provided merely for consultations or called on the Community's partners to raise the level of protection of intellectual property within their territory. Fourthly, the inclusion in agreements with third countries of provisions reserving the names of specific regions exclusively to producers of those countries[48] was 'directly linked' to CAP measures on wine and winegrowing and, in any case, too specific in scope to be relevant to the conclusion of an Agreement as wide in scope as the TRIPs.[49]

---

[43] Para 63. The Commission had referred to Commission Decision 87/251 on the initiation of an international consultation and disputes settlement procedure concerning a United States measure excluding imports of certain aramid fibres into USA [1987] OJ L 117/18, Notice of initiation of an illicit commercial practice procedure concerning the unauthorized reproduction of sound recordings in Indonesia [1987] OJ C 136/3 and a similar notice regarding piracy of Community sound recordings in Thailand [1991] OJ C 189/26.

[44] Para 65.

[45] The Commission referred to the Agreements with China and the then USSR on trade in textile products [1988] OJ L 380/2 and [1989] OJ L 397/2 respectively and three interim Agreements with Hungary [1992] OJ L 116/2, the Czech and Slovak Republic [1992] OJ L 115/2 and Bulgaria [1993] OJ L 323/2.

[46] N28 above, para 67.

[47] *Ibid*, para 68.

[48] The Commission mentioned the Agreement with Austria on the control and reciprocal protection of quality wines and 'retsina' wine [1989] OJ L 56/2 and the Agreement with Australia on trade in wine [1994] OJ L 86/3.

[49] N28 above, para 70.

3.2. Comment on *Opinion 1/94*

The ruling in *Opinion 1/94*, whose conclusions were subsequently affirmed in the *Public Procurement Agreement* judgment,[50] turned out to be quite controversial.[51] It was seen as 'fatal for the coherence of the Union'[52] and, famously, a 'programmed disaster'.[53] Pescatore's attack was quite violent: the Court's analysis was seen as 'lopsided', its logic 'disconcerting' and its arguments 'microscopic'.[54] The Court's conclusions were seen as a step back with respect to the definition of the CCP because, whilst repeating earlier statements about a wide interpretation, they rendered them redundant in practice.[55] In essence, the criticism levelled against the Court is focused on the following two charges: first, the Court adopted an inward approach in defining the scope of Article 133 EC which ignored both the context of the agreements concluded under the umbrella of WTO and the evolution of that framework; secondly, the construction of Article 133 EC was interpreted in such narrow terms as to undermine the effective pursuit of the Community interest on the international scene.

It cannot be denied that, set against earlier case law, the ruling in *Opinion 1/94* is characterised by a shift of emphasis: the former was focused on the establishment of the normative foundation of the CCP through the principle of exclusivity and the consolidation of its dynamic construction within an evolving international framework; the latter is focused on the internal constitutional ramifications, that is within the Community legal order, of that construction in a particular case. This shift of emphasis might be seen to confirm the assumption, widely shared in the late 1980s and 1990s, that the Court responded to the progress towards the establishment of the internal market by adopting a more cautious approach to the construction of the powers of the Community.[56]

However, the above shift could also be seen as an adjustment of the earlier principles to their proper constitutional setting. In essence, the main premise of *Opinion*

---

[50] Case C–360/93 *Parliament v Council* [1996] ECR I–1195 annotated by M Cremona in (1997) 34 *CMLRev* 389 and AJ Halford in (1996) 21 *ELRev* 478.

[51] See, for instance, A Appella, 'Constitutional Aspects of *Opinion 1/94* of the ECJ concerning the WTO Agreement' (1996) 45 *International and Comparative Law Quarterly (ICLQ)* 440, N Emiliou, 'The Death of Exclusive Competence?' (1996) 21 *ELRev* 294, D Chalmers, 'Legal Base and the External Relations of the European Community' in N Emiliou and D O'Keeffe (eds), *The European Union and World Trade Law after the GATT Uruguay Round* (Chichester: Willey, 1996) 46, 59–60, T Flory and F-P Martin, 'Remarques à propos des Avis 1/94 et 2/92 de la Cour de Justice des Communautés Européennes au regard de la Notion de Politique Commerciale Commune', [1996] *Cahiers de Droit European* 376, M Hilf, 'The ECJ's *Opinion 1/94* on the WTO—No Surprise, but Wise?-' (1995) 6 *European Journal of International Law (EJIL)* 245.

[52] A Maunu, 'The Implied External Competence of the European Community after the ECJ *Opinion 1/94* – Towards Coherence or Diversity?' [1995] *LIEI* 115 at 124.

[53] P Pescatore, '*Opinion 1/94* on Conclusion of the WTO Agreement: Is There an Escape from a Programmed Disaster?' (1999) 36 *CMLRev* 387.

[54] *Ibid* at 401, 398 and 400 respectively.

[55] JHJ Bourgeois, 'The EC in the WTO and Advisory *Opinion 1/94*: An Echternach Procession' (1995) 32 *CMLRev* 763 at 779.

[56] See the argument about 'legal minimalism' underpinning the Court's case law in T Koopmans, 'The Role of Law in the Next Stage of European Integration' (1986) 35 *ICLQ* 925.

1/94 is the Court's refusal to separate the exercise of the powers conferred by Article 133 EC from the internal system of the Community and the division of powers established therein. This should not have come as a surprise. After all, the introduction of the main principles of the CCP was based on the express link between that policy and the internal market: the exclusive nature of Community competence, for instance, had been read into Article 133 EC because the policy laid down in that provision 'is conceived ... in the context of the operation of the Common Market, for the defence of the common interests of the Community';[57] a restrictive interpretation of the CCP had been rejected because it 'would risk causing disturbances in intra-Community trade by reason of the disparities which would then exist in certain sectors of economic relations with non-member countries'.[58] Viewed from this angle, the constitutional approach underlying the reasoning in *Opinion 1/94* amounts to no more than bringing the main tenets of earlier case law, that is the main principles of the CCP, to their logical conclusion. An external commercial policy dissociated from the internal system of the Community would lead, inevitably, to a construct developed far beyond the system to which it owed its existence. This would entail a fundamental change in the logic underlying that system which would, then, become an independent policy aimed at accommodating the development of international trade rather than enabling the Community to respond to them in a manner consistent with its constitutional structure.

This is the main flaw in the sustained attack against *Opinion 1/94*. For instance, the argument that the Court ignores the context of WTO Agreements and the evolution of the framework they established[59] approaches the CCP as an independent, fully-fledged policy originating in a constitutional vacuum. More importantly, it requires that the Court act as an international tribunal entrusted with the task of furthering the development of international trade whereas, in fact, its function is only related to the application of Community law. Therefore, what is viewed as 'inward-looking vision' in the Court's reasoning[60] amounts to no more than the performance of the function laid down in Article 220 EC and the judicial acknowledgment of the constitutional parameters of the conduct of EC international relations.

There is another problem with the above criticism against the Court in that it treats the CCP as the only legal framework within which the Community may carry out its external relations. It is a truism that the decision-making procedure laid down in Article 133 EC and the exclusive competence of the Community facilitate such action considerably. However, account should be taken of the extent to which the legal alternative to CCP, that is the negotiation, conclusion and implementation of international agreements pursuant to the formula of mixity,

---

[57] *Opinion 1/75*, n3 above, at 1363–4.
[58] *Opinion 1/78*, n2 above, at para 45.
[59] See Bourgeois, n55 above, and Pescatore, n53 above.
[60] Pescatore, n53 above at 391.

may provide a viable framework for the conduct of external relations. Prior to the development of the main characteristics of the CCP, the Court had already introduced the existence of the Community's implied competence in the *AETR* case and had recognised the conditions under which it could be rendered exclusive.[61] The subsequent permutations of the principle of implied competence suggest that the effectiveness of the external action of the Community should not be seen as depending entirely upon the exercise of the competence conferred under Article 133 EC. In a way, the charge against *Opinion 1/94* for formalism is just as formalistic as it ignores the development of other mechanisms of conduct of external relations within the Community legal system. The Court's ruling appears to highlight precisely those mechanisms by concluding on the duty of cooperation between the Member States and the Community institutions. The construction of this duty and the parallel assessment of how mixed agreements are to be concluded and implemented in the wider context of EC external relations will shed further light on the approach to the CCP adopted in *Opinion 1/94*. At this juncture, suffice it to point out that the emphasis on the 'devastating' and 'catastrophic' consequences of the ruling[62] appears not only exaggerated, but also highly questionable in so far as it views the construction of Article 133 EC in isolation from the overall system of EC external relations.

4. BRINGING THE POINT HOME: THE RULING IN *OPINION 2/00*

Whilst avoiding the debate about the instrumental or objective approach advocated by the Commission and the Council, the Court had made it clear that the policy laid down in Article 133 EC was far from unlimited in scope. And yet, the controversy caused by the ruling in *Opinion 1/94* enabled the Commission to suggest that the issue of the definition of the scope of the CCP was far from settled. The same issue arose, albeit regarding the interaction between trade and environmental policy, when the Community was called upon to conclude the Cartagena Protocol on Biosafety. This Protocol was adopted in January 2000 within the framework of the Convention on Biological Diversity.[63] The Cartagena Protocol concerned the biosafety, in particular as regards to transboundary movement, of any living modified organisms (LMOs) resulting from modern biotechnology that might have adverse effect on the conservation and sustainable use of biological diversity.[64] The Protocol was adopted unanimously by the Council under

---

[61] Case 22/70 *Commission v Council*, n38 above.

[62] Pescatore, n53 above at 389.

[63] See B Chaytor, R Gerster and T Herzog, 'The Convention on Biological Diversity—Exploring the Creation of a Mediation Mechanism' (2002) 5 *Journal of World Intellectual Property* 157 and D Thieme, 'European Community External Relations in the Field of the Environment' (2001) 10 *European Environmental Law Review* 252, 260 *ff*.

[64] See PWB Phillips and WA Kerr, 'The WTO *versus* the Biosafety Protocol for Trade in Genetically Modified Organisms' (2000) 34 *Journal of World Trade (JWT)* 63 and O Rivera-Torres, 'The Biosafety Protocol and the WTO' (2003) 26 *Boston College International and Comparative Law Review* 263.

Article 175(1) in conjunction with Article 300(2) EC.[65] However, the proposal by the Commission had relied upon Articles 133 and 174(4) EC in conjunction with Article 300(2) EC.[66]

Following this deviation from its proposal, the Commission requested an Opinion pursuant to Article 300(6) EC.[67] This case attracted considerable interest amongst the Member States: in addition to the European Parliament and the Council, seven governments submitted observations.[68] The main objective of the Commission was to clarify a matter of principle, namely to 'ensure a framework of legal certainty for management of the Protocol, in particular when voting rights are exercised'. Indeed, the divergence of views with the Council was irrelevant in procedural terms in so far as the Council would have to act by qualified majority voting under either of the above options.

The line of reasoning put forward by the Commission was centred around the contention that the Protocol fell predominantly within the scope of the CCP because of its objective and content. Whilst it accepted that a number of issues fell within the powers retained by the Member States, it argued that those were limited in scope and were confined to measures not affecting trade in LMOs: they covered the application of safety conditions to the development, transport, use, transfer and release of any LMOs outside international trade and those covering unintentional transboundary movement of LMOs.

The line of reasoning followed by the Commission in *Opinion 2/00* typifies an expansive view of the CCP, one which appears to take the statements of the Court of Justice in the 1970s at face value. In addition to the above, it argued that the CCP had been held to be broadly construed and had, in fact, been construed widely enough to cover trade measures pursuing, amongst others, objectives related to public health protection,[69] development cooperation,[70] foreign and security policy[71] and agricultural policy.[72] Finally, the conclusion of the Cartagena Protocol as a CCP measure was seen as necessary for the effectiveness of Community action on the international scene.

---

[65] Art 175(1) EC reads as follows: 'The Council, acting in accordance with the procedure referred to in Article 251 and after consulting the Economic and Social Committee and the Committee of the Regions, shall decide what action is to be taken by the Commission in order to achieve the objectives referred to in Article 174'.

[66] Art 174(4) EC reads as follows: 'Within their respective spheres of competence, the Community and the Member States shall cooperate with third countries and with the competent international organisations. The arrangements for Community cooperation may be the subject of agreements between the Community and the third parties concerned, which shall be negotiated and concluded in accordance with Article 300 EC'. Its second sub-para reads as follows: 'The previous subparagraph shall be without prejudice to Member States' competence to negotiate in international bodies and to conclude international agreements'.

[67] *Opinion 2/00* [2001] ECR I–9713.

[68] Namely the Danish, Greek, Spanish, French, Italian, Austrian and British.

[69] Case C–62/88 *Greece v Council,* n 26 above.

[70] *Opinion 1/78* n 2 above, Case 45/86 *Commission v Council* n 18 above.

[71] Case C–70/94 *Werner,* n 25 above, Case C–83/94 *Leifer and Others* [1995] ECR I–3231, Case C–124/95 *Centro-Com,* n 24 above.

[72] *Opinion 1/94,* n 28 above, paras 28–30.

For the purpose of this analysis, the ruling of the Court in *Opinion 2/00* may be divided into three parts. The first one deals with the issue of legal basis in general. Having reaffirmed the principle that its choice should be determined on the basis of 'objective factors ... amenable to judicial review' which should include 'in particular the aim and the content of the measure',[73] the Court ruled that that also covered EC measures adopted in order to conclude an international agreement. The Court then referred to the rule of interpretation laid down in the Vienna Convention on the Law of Treaties: according to Article 31 thereof, 'a treaty shall be interpreted in good faith in accordance with the ordinary meaning to be given to the terms of the treaty in their context and in the light of its object and purpose'. In relation to the Cartagena Protocol in particular, the Court defined the essential question as:[74]

> whether the Protocol, in the light of its context, its aim and its content, constitutes an agreement principally concerning environmental protection which is liable to have incidental effects on trade in LMOs, whether, conversely, it is principally an agreement concerning international trade policy which incidentally takes account of certain environmental requirements, or whether it is inextricably concerned both with environmental protection and with international trade.

In the second part of its ruling, the Court analysed the context, the objectives and the content of the Protocol. It reached the conclusion that the former should be determined on the basis of the Convention on Biological Diversity, within the framework of which it had been drawn up in the first place. It was pointed out that the environmental nature of that instrument was apparent: it had been adopted under Article 130s EC and, in its first Article, it referred to its objectives as 'the conservation of biological diversity, the sustainable use of its components and the fair and equitable sharing of the benefits arising out of the utilisation of genetic resources'.[75] As to the Protocol's purpose, the Court noted that it was 'clear beyond doubt' that it pursued an environmental objective: its Article 1 refers to Principle 15 of the Rio Declaration on Environment and Development dealing expressly with environmental protection; it mentions the precautionary principle which is a fundamental principle of environmental protection laid down in Article 174(2) EC;[76] its title illustrates its objective of ensuring an adequate level of protection in the field of the safe transfer, handling and use of LMOs which is also underlined in its preamble.[77] Finally, in dealing with the substantive content

---

[73] Para 22 with reference to Case C–268/94 *Portugal v Council* [1996] ECR I–6177, para 22, Case C–269/97 *Commission v Council* [2000] ECR I–2257, para 43 and Case C–36/98 *Spain v Council* [2001] ECR I–779, para 58.

[74] N67 above, para 25.

[75] Para 27. Furthermore, the Protocol included various references to the Convention and the Conference of the Parties.

[76] Para 29.

[77] In particular, reference is made to risks to human health from biotechnology, the need for biotechnology to be used with adequate safety measures for the environment and human health and the crucial importance to humankind of centres of origin and centres of genetic diversity.

of the Cartagena Protocol, the Court ruled that its environmental aim was clearly reflected in the fundamental obligation it imposed on the parties: this was to prevent or reduce the risk to biological diversity in the development, handling, transport, use, transfer and release of any LMOs.[78] A number of provisions clearly illustrated the predominantly environmental character of the Protocol: control mechanisms, some of which were typically associated with environmental policy, were established in order to enable the parties to adhere to their obligations; the Protocol deals with the assessment and management of risks associated with the use, handling and transboundary movement of LMOs, unintentional transboundary movements and emergency measures, the handling, transport, packaging and identification of LMOs; the substantive duties imposed upon the contracting parties cover any kind of transboundary movement.

In the light of the above, the Court had no difficulty concluding that the Protocol's 'main purpose or component is the protection of biological diversity against the harmful effects which could result from activities that involve dealing with LMOs, in particular from their transboundary movement'.[79]

In the final part of its ruling in *Opinion 2/00*, the Court dealt with the specific arguments put forward by the Commission. Having held that 'the Protocol is, in the light of its context, its aim and its content, an instrument intended essentially to improve biosafety and not to promote, facilitate or govern trade',[80] it ruled that, in dealing with transboundary movement of LMOs, the Protocol covered not only trade in but also any form of movement of LMOs between states: these included illegal and unintentional movement and movement for charitable or scientific purposes or serving public interest.

As to the wide interpretation advocated by the Commission, the Court opined that 'if accepted, [the Commission's interpretation] would effectively render the specific provisions of the Treaty concerning environmental protection policy largely nugatory, since, as soon as it was established that Community action was liable to have repercussions on trade, the envisaged agreement would have to be placed in the category of agreements which fall within commercial policy'.[81] The 'effectiveness' argument had the same fate as it was pointed out that practical difficulties associated with the implementation of mixed agreements, 'whatever their scale, ... cannot be accepted as relevant when selecting the legal basis for a Community measure'.[82]

---

[78] See Art 2(2) of the Cartagena Protocol.

[79] Para 34.

[80] Para 37. As to the choice between Arts 174(4) and 175(1) EC, the Court concluded in para 43 that the latter was the correct legal basis. This was because the Cartagena Protocol did not merely provide for cooperation arrangements, as required under Art 174(4) EC, but it set out precise rules on control procedures regarding transboundary movements, risk assessment and management, handling, transport, packaging and identification of LMOs. Finally, the Community was held not be exclusively competence under Art 175 (1) EC, as 'the harmonisation achieved at Community level in the Protocol's field of application covers ... only a very small part of such a field' (para 46).

[81] Para 40.

[82] Para 41.

Following the ruling in *Opinion 2/00*, the Council Decision concerning the conclusion, on behalf of the Community, of the Cartagena Protocol was adopted on 25 June 2002 under Article 175(1) EC.[83] In its preamble, it pointed out that the Protocol 'contributes to the achievement of the objectives of the environmental policy of the Community'.

5. GRASPING THE NETTLE

On the international economic scene, it becomes increasingly difficult not only to dissociate the negotiation and conclusion of a trade agreement from the more general geopolitical context, but also to define the material scope of such agreement strictly in terms of trade policy. The interaction between trade and other interests, including development, foreign policy, health and environment, is at the very core of the functioning of a globalised market place. Viewed from this angle, the exercise in which the Court of Justice was called upon to engage in *Opinion 2/00* would appear to present problems similar to those facing any judicial body. However, it is the constitutional underpinnings of the regulation of different policies under the EC Treaty that render this task even more fraught with problems. This is all the more so in the light of the manner in which the Court had sought to foster the normative foundation of these policies, that is the *a priori* exclusivity of Community competence over a widely construed commercial policy. On the internal plane, the Court had been familiar with delineating the relationship between interacting policies: in *Titanium Dioxide*,[84] for instance, a central case in the legal basis debate, it was precisely the classification of secondary legislation as an internal marker measure or an environmental one which was at issue.[85] Whilst not uncontroversial in the context of the internal market, the choice of legal basis in the area of external relations is all the more complex in the light of the involvement of third states.

However, both the wording and the substantive content of the Cartagena Protocol were hardly unclear as to its predominantly environmental character.[86] Furthermore, the line of reasoning in *Opinion 2/00* was consistent both with the Court's approach to the overall system of EC external relations and the construction of Community competence as regards the establishment and functioning of

---

[83] Dec 2002/628 [2002] OJ L 201/48.

[84] Case C–300/89 *Commission v Council (re: Titanium Dioxide)* [1991] ECR I–1689.

[85] See the criticism in S Crosby, 'The Single Market and the Rule of Law' (1991) 16 *ELRev* 451. The Court, then, dealt with the issue of the interaction between trade and environmental policies in Case C–155/91 *Commission v Council* [1993] ECR I–939 and Case C–187/93 *Parliament v Council* [1994] ECR I–2857.

[86] This point was also borne out by the Protocol's negotiating history: see C Bail, J-P Decaestecker and M Joergensen, 'European Union' in C Bail, R Falkner and H Marquard (eds), *The Cartagena Protocol on Biosafety – Reconciling Trade in Biotechnology with Environment & Development* (London: The Royal Institute of International Affairs, 2002) 166, 168: all three authors were involved in the negotiations, the first leading the Commission delegation.

the internal market. In relation to the former, the Court rejected with considerable force the Commission's alarmist view that any alternative to Article 133 EC would impair the pursuit of the Community interest. It opined that the choice of legal basis could not be influenced by the practical difficulties associated with the implementation of mixed agreements, 'whatever their scale'.[87] In doing so, it followed its approach in *Opinion 1/94* where it had pointed out that, whilst 'quite legitimate', practical problems about shared competence could not render the Community's competence exclusive.[88] It is noteworthy that, in its ruling, the Court is as elaborate in articulating the alternatives to the CCP as it is forceful in rejecting the requirement for recourse to Article 133 EC as a matter of necessity. For instance, having pointed out that the delineation of powers shared by the Community and the Member States exceeded its jurisdiction under Article 300(6) EC, it held that:

> In any event, where it is apparent that the subject-matter of an international agreement falls in part within the competence of the Community and in part within that of the Member States, it is important to ensure close cooperation between the Member States and the Community institutions, both in the process of negotiation and conclusion and in the fulfillment of the commitments entered into. That obligation to cooperate flows from the requirement of unity in the international representation of the Community.[89]

It is recalled that an elaborate reference to that duty had concluded the Court's ruling in *Opinion 1/94*, where the Court had rejected the Commission's claim for exclusivity on almost all grounds. In other words, *Opinion 2/00* constitutes the natural continuation of the ruling in *Opinion 1/94* in a two-fold manner: on the one hand, it makes it clear that neither legal nor practical reasons may justify the transformation of the widely construed CCP into an all-encompassing external economic relations policy; on the other hand, instead of treating mixity as a legal abomination, it highlights the emergence of general principles which may address any ensuing complications.

Viewed within the context of its overall approach to the issue of Community competence, in rejecting too broad a reading of the CCP, *Opinion 2/00* was consistent with its case law on the competence of the Community to introducing harmonising legislation on the internal plane. In the now famous judgment in *Tobacco Advertising*,[90] when dealing with the issue whether a directive effectively banning tobacco advertising constituted a measure whose object was 'the establishment and functioning of the internal market', the Court opined that 'other articles of the Treaty may not ... be used as a legal basis in order to circumvent the express exclusion of harmonisation [on public health] laid down in Article

---

[87] N 67 above, para 41.
[88] See *Opinion 1/94,* n 28 above, para 107.
[89] Para 18.
[90] Case C–376/98 *Germany v European Parliament and Council* [2001] ECR I–2247.

[152(4)] of the Treaty'.[91] This was so despite the fact that such a prohibition 'does not mean that harmonizing measures adopted on the basis of other provisions of the Treaty cannot have any impact on the protection of human health'.[92] Therefore, the great difficulty in defining areas of activities and complying with their respective procedural and substantive requirements cannot entail the abolition of any such distinctions. The constitutional implications of this for the scope of the CCP had already been implied in *Opinion 1/94*: the principle of a dynamically understood external trade policy may not undermine the balance of competences as set out in primary law. In this respect, there is a parallelism underlying the Court's approach to the regulation of the internal market and that of the CCP. This parallelism, apparent in the continuous need to redefine the limits of these two spheres, is but an illustration of a thread which appears to underlie not only the Court's construction of EC external relations but also the emerging constitutional logic of the new CCP. This thread, also illustrated by the later amendments of Article 133 EC, will be analysed further below in this analysis.

At this juncture, suffice it to point out that the parallelism between the construction of the CCP and the internal spheres of the Community legal order may also be seen from another, substantive angle focusing on the position of other related policies under primary law. The Commission's arguments in *Opinion 2/00* about the relationship between trade and environment effectively undermined the EC provisions on environmental protection. It was for that reason that the language in which the Court stressed the position of environmental policy in the EC Treaty was identical to that used 25 years earlier in relation to the CCP itself.[93] Furthermore, the EC Treaty itself identifies limits to the scope of Article 133 EC. A case in point is the regulation of economic sanctions against third countries. Since the adoption of the Maastricht Treaty, Article 301 EC constitutes the legal basis for the imposition of sanctions against a third country by means of a Council Regulation adopted following a common position or joint action adopted within the Common Foreign and Security Policy. That provision applies to 'an action by the Community [whose aim is] to interrupt or to reduce, in part or completely, economic relations with one or more third counties'. The wording of this provision suggests that its scope is broader than that of the CCP pursuant to Article 133 EC,[94] a conclusion also confirmed by the sanctions regimes imposed thereafter. This conclusion indicates that Article 133 EC was clearly not meant to bestow a general external economic relations competence to be exercised exclusively by the Community.

---

[91] *Ibid*, para 79. For a comment, see C Hillion, 'Tobacco Advertising: if You Must, You May' (2001) 60 *Cambridge Law Journal* 486 and G Tridimas and T Tridimas, 'The European Court of Justice and the Annulment of the Tobacco Advertisement Directive: Friend of National Sovereignty or Foe of Public Health?' (2002) 14 *European Journal of Law and Economics* 171.

[92] Para 78.

[93] Para 40.

[94] See C Schmitter, 'Article 228a' in V Constantinesco, R Kovar and D Simon (eds), *Traité sur l'Union européenne (signé le 7 fevrier 1992): commentaire article par article* (Paris: Economica, 1996) 763.

Therefore, the line of reasoning put forward by the Commission and rejected by the Court appeared to read literally the Court's general pronouncements on the interpretation of the CCP.[95] In doing so, it failed to place them in their specific context: this covered not only the substantive content of the agreements in relation to which those pronouncements had been made, but also the emerging character of the CCP, its pronounced linkages with the internal market and the period of stagnation in decision-making in the Community at large. As has been pointed out, *Opinion 1/94* contains no reference to the substantive parallelism between the content of the CCP and that of the external trade policy of a state;[96] the same is true of *Opinion 2/00*. There is no such reference because there is no need for one: the principle of the dynamic interpretation of Article 133 EC and the exclusive nature of the Community competence are now well entrenched in our Community vocabulary. The development of the international economic arena should also be taken into account when assessing the approach of the Court: whilst the negotiation and conclusion of commodity agreements was part of mainstream international practice in the 1970s and early 1980s, the 1990s saw the collapse of commodity prices and the marginalisation of commodity agreements.[97] Viewed from this angle, to argue that a worthwhile, widely construed commercial policy is all-encompassing in scope is a logical misnomer: the dynamic development of a policy requires its construction in a manner which is sufficiently consistent to accommodate international developments and flexible to take into account the constitutional underpinnings of the legal system within which it is bound to be carried out. In the light of this, it is noteworthy that the scope of the CCP was articulated in *Opinion 2/00* in a manner which, whilst broad in nature, was distinguished from the early pronouncements of the 1970s: it aims at governing agreements which, in the light of their context, aim and content, are intended essentially to promote, facilitate or govern trade.

In February 2003, the Commission brought an action under Article 230 EC against the Council challenging the conclusion of the Rotterdam Convention on the Prior Informed Consent Procedure for certain hazardous chemicals and pesticides in international trade.[98] The Council Decision approving the conclusion of the Convention on behalf of the Community was adopted unanimously under Article 175(1) EC, whereas the Commission had proposed its adoption under Article 133 EC.[99] The Commission's line of reasoning that the Convention was, essentially,

---

[95] For a more detailed critique of the Commission's arguments, see P Koutrakos, ' "I Need to Hear You Say It": Revisiting the Scope of the EC Common Commercial Policy' (2003) 22 *YEL* 407 at 420 *ff*.

[96] See J Dutheil de la Rochère, 'L'ère des compétences partagées' [1995] *Revue du Marché Commun et de l'Union européenne* 461, 469

[97] See A Maizels, *Commodities in Crisis* (Oxford: Clarendon Press, 1992) 5–22 and C Michalopoulos, *Developing Countries in the WTO* (Basingstoke: Palgrave, 2001) 32–33.

[98] Case C–94/03 *Commission v Council* [2003] OJ C 101/27.

[99] Council Dec 2003/106 [2003] OJ L 63/27.

a trade measure was rejected by Advocate General Kokott, who found any conse-quences on international trade to be, at most, indirect.[100]

6. BEYOND MINIMALISM: THE ENERGY STAR AGREEMENT JUDGMENT

The above analysis suggested that the early pronouncements of the Court about the wide construction of the CCP and the parallelism between the external com-mercial policy of a state and that of the EC should be assessed in the light of the establishment of the legal foundations of the, then, emerging policy. Viewed from this angle, the rulings in *Opinions 1/94* and *2/00* merely placed the CCP within the broader context of the principles underpinning the conduct of EC external rela-tions: once the Community's exclusive competence and its scope beyond the indicative list laid down in Article 133 EC had been entrenched, it was only a mat-ter of time before the limits of the CCP and, in parallel, the proper role of the legal alternatives, that is mixed agreements, would be highlighted. However, that should not be taken to suggest either that the position of Article 133 EC is mar-ginalised or to signal a minimalistic approach to its interpretation. Such a position would oversimplify the role of the CCP as a part within the wider system of EC international relations.

This point was made clear by the Court in the *Energy Star Agreement* case.[101] For the second time within a year, the Commission asked the Court to determine the outer limit of Article 133 EC by questioning the conclusion of the US–EC Agreement on the coordination of energy-efficient labelling programmes for office equipment. This programme, called 'Energy Star Programme', originated in United States and aimed at encouraging manufacturers to introduce energy-saving features and raising consumer awareness of the energy losses of office equipment in stand-by motion. In doing so, it introduced a logo, the Energy Star logo, for the labeling of equipment which adhered to the relevant rules. This programme proved to be very popular with manufacturers around the world, including the Community. This prompted the Commission to adopt it. Following its signature, the relevant Agreement was approved on behalf of the Community by Decision 2001/469[102] based on Article 175(1) EC in conjunction with Article 300(2) and (4) EC. The Commission challenged that Decision on the

---

[100] Opinion delivered on 26 May 2005. However, in concluding that there was no reason for the Council Dec to be based on a dual legal basis, Kokkot AG relies upon the absence of any procedural advantages that such a formula would entail rather than the predominantly trade character of the Convention. The Commission also challenged Council Reg 304/2003 [2003] OJ L 63/1 which aimed at implementing the Convention in Case C–178/03 *Commission v Partiament and Council* [2003] OJ C 146/33: in her Opinion of 26 May 2005, Kokkot AG proposed the dismissal of that action, too.

[101] Case C–281/01 *Commission v Council* [2002] ECR I–12049.

[102] [2001] OJ L 172/1.

ground that it constituted a CCP measure which had to be adopted pursuant to Article 133 EC.

The Court repeated the need for the choice of legal basis to rest on objective factors amenable to judicial review and, then, noted that the Energy Star Agreement 'simultaneously pursues a commercial-policy objective and an environmental-protection objective':[103] the former on grounds of its aim to coordinate energy-efficient labelling programmes which 'necessarily facilitates trade inasmuch as manufacturers henceforth need to refer to just one standard as regards labeling and to comply with just one registration procedure with a single management entity in order to sell equipment bearing the Energy Star logo on the European and American markets';[104] the latter because, 'on reading the preamble to the Energy Star Agreement and Article I thereof, ... by stimulating the supply of and demand for energy-efficient products, the labeling programme in question is intended to promote energy savings'.[105]

As to its predominant aim, the Court concluded that the Agreement was '[a]n instrument having a direct impact on trade in office equipment'.[106] It did accept that 'in the long term ... the programme should have a positive environmental effect'. However, it went on to conclude that that 'is merely an indirect and distant effect, in contrast to the effect on trade in office equipment which is direct and immediate'.[107]

The Council had sought to underline the environmental character of the Energy Star Agreement by referring to various internal EC measures concerning the award of voluntary eco-labels adopted as environmental instruments under Article 175(1) EC. This argument was rejected by the Court, which suggested that the legal basis of those measures had been justified in the light of their intra-Community scope. Those measures were not 'sufficient to establish that the same basis must be used when approving an international agreement with similar subject-matter'.[108]

Whilst the judgment in the *Energy Star Agreement* case might appear to be at odds with the ruling in *Opinion 2/00*, it is suggested that this is not the case. On the facts of the case, the conclusion in the former is entirely justified: whereas the aim of the Energy Star Programme was to promote energy-efficient equipment, that of the Energy Star Agreement was, as far as the Community was concerned, to facilitate the

---

[103] Para 39 of the judgment.
[104] Para 37 of the judgment.
[105] Para 38 of the judgment.
[106] Para 40 of the judgment.
[107] Para 41 of the judgment. The optional character of the Energy Star Programme was deemed irrelevant to the commercial-policy objective of the Agreement, not only because the latter was 'none the less designed to have a direct impact on trade in office equipment' (para 44) but also because 'non-binding labelling provisions may constitute an obstacle to international trade' (para 45).
[108] Para 46 of the judgment. To that effect, the Court mentioned Dir 92/75 on the indication by labeling and standard product information of the consumption of energy and other resources by household appliances [1999] OJ L 297/16, adopted under Art. 95 EC due to its link to the establishment of the internal market.

commercial activities of traders originating in the Member States, hence enabling them to penetrate foreign markets more efficiently. This objective distinction, apparent in the judgment itself,[109] was central to the Court's reasoning. This was also implied by Advocate General Alber, who referred to the exploratory memorandum accompanying the Commission's proposal for the contested Decision: this viewed the Energy Star logo as the 'de facto required standard for office equipment sold on the United States market. In addition, the Energy Star requirements were becoming the applicable standard world-wide and therefore in the Community as well'.[110] Viewed from this angle, what was truly at the core of the matter was the extent to which market access could be guaranteed to Community traders of products falling within the scope of the Programme. Indeed, in his Opinion, Advocate General Alber implied a similarity between the Energy Star Agreement and technical standards agreements.[111] Therefore, the subject-matter of the *Energy Star Agreement* case is altogether different from that in *Opinion 2/00*.

The principles determining the choice of legal basis in EC international relations, as elaborated in the *Energy Star* judgment, have been applied by the Court in the context of protection and control of wine names. The Community relied upon Article 133 EC and concluded such an agreement with Hungary in 1993 which, protected, amongst others, the Hungarian geographical indication 'Tokaj'. In implementing its provisions, the Italian authorities prohibited the use in Italy of the grape variety names 'Tocai friulano' and its synonym 'Tocai italico' on wine labels with effect from 2007. The autonomous region where these varieties are produced, and an organisation called the Regional Agency for Rural Development challenged this prohibition before the Italian courts. One of their arguments was that the Agreement with Hungary should not have been adopted as the Community did not have exclusive competence to protect intellectual property rights. In its judgment, the Court dismissed this argument.[112] It applied the line of reasoning put forward in the *Energy Star* case, and noted that the specific objective of agreements on the protection and control of wine names is to guarantee reciprocal protection for certain geographical indications which are mentioned on the labelling. These are used to market the wines in the Community and in the third country concerned. Therefore, such agreements constitute an instrument directly affecting trade in wines.

---

[109] According to the Court, the American Energy Star Programme 'was devised in order to stimulate the supply of, and demand for, energy-efficient products and therefore to promote energy conservation', an objective which the extension of the Agreement to the EC would 'undoubtedly help' (para 42). The Energy Star Agreement 'does not contain new energy-efficiency requirements', hence 'merely render[ing] the specifications initially adopted by the [Programme] applicable on both the American market and the European market and mak[ing] their amendments subject to the agreement on both contracting parties' (*ibid*).

[110] Quoted in para 66 of this Opinion.

[111] See para 74 of his Opinion.

[112] Case C–347/03 *Regione autonom Friuli-Venezia Giulia and ERSA v Ministero delle Politiche Agricole e Forestali*, judgment of 12 May 2005, not yet reported.

7. THE 'NEW' COMMON COMMERCIAL POLICY

What emerges from the analysis of the principal normative aspects of the CCP so far is the picture of a policy which is far from static. In terms of its scope, it has turned out to be far from the open-ended policy which was read into the early rulings of the Court of Justice; as for the exclusivity of the Community competence, neither did it lead automatically to the exclusion of the Member States from the conclusion of an international agreement, nor did it necessarily entail a truly strict construction of the circumstances under which they might be allowed to deviate from rules adopted pursuant to Article 133 EC. This evolving construction might appear an illustration of judicial pragmatism: in effect, the Court readjusted principles introduced in the relatively early days of the Community to the reality subsequently shaped by factors as diverse as the establishment of the internal market, the furthering of the constitutionalisation process of the Community legal order and the increasingly assertive plans for an ambitious EU role on the international scene. Alternatively, it may be seen as an entrenchment of a deferential attitude to the most intergovernmental reflexes of the Member States which would lead, gradually but steadily, to the mutation of the very pillars of the external trade policies of the Community. In essence, both these views are underpinned by a particular conception of not only the development of the CCP through the years but also the proper function of the Court of Justice and its interactions with the Community institutions. For the purpose of this analysis, the amendments of Article 133 EC introduced by the Amsterdam and Nice Treaties tell a fascinating story about these issues, albeit one with various twists.

At Amsterdam, the scope of the CCP was expressly extended to cover services and intellectual property rights, albeit in a less than straightforward manner. Article 133(5) EC read, as follows:

> The Council, acting unanimously on a proposal from the Commission and after consulting the European Parliament, may extend the application of paragraphs 1 to 4 to international negotiations and agreements on services and intellectual property insofar as they are not covered by these paragraphs.

Rather than extending the scope of CCP, the Amsterdam amendment provided for the *possibility* of such an extension to services and intellectual property rights.[113] Whilst now merely of historical significance, this provision is noteworthy for paving the way for the more comprehensive articulation of the new CCP which would follow. In substantive terms, the extension of the scope of application of the CCP was limited in a number of ways: services and intellectual property rights could only be covered by international agreements and not autonomous measures adopted by the Community institutions; no reference to

---

[113] See O Blin, 'L'Article 113 CE après Amsterdam' (1998) 420 *Revue du Marché commun et de l'Union européenne* 447.

investment was made; most importantly, it was subject to a unanimous Council decision that this extension could actually take place. It is recalled that the decision-making procedure laid down in Article 133(4) EC, that is qualified majority voting, has been one of the distinct features of the CCP which has made it so popular with the Commission. The Amsterdam amendment merely enabled the Community institutions to agree unanimously to act by qualified majority voting.

In practical terms, to stress the limited effect of this provision is to point out the obvious. Furthermore, it is not dissimilar to a provision laid down in Title V TEU on the Common Foreign and Security Policy (CFSP) by the Maastricht Treaty: the Council could decide by unanimity whether to implement by qualified majority voting a decision already adopted under the second pillar. Laid down in Article J.3(2) TEU, that provision had been deemed necessary to indicate that decision-making in the CFSP area was not bound to be hostage to national concerns and preferences. Equally, it was the semantics of the Amsterdam amendment which rendered Article 133(5) EC significant: it indicated a degree of willingness of the Member States to respond to the challenges highlighted in *Opinion 1/94*. It is recalled that, in stating that the Community did not enjoy exclusive competence to conclude GATS and TRIPS, the Court had highlighted the role of the Community institutions and the intensity of the legislation they introduce internally in determining the competence of the Community to act externally. In making express reference to services and intellectual property rights, the Member States appeared to recognise the significance of services and intellectual property rights in international trade negotiations.

Whilst appearing willing to envisage their incorporation in the regime laid down in Articles 133(1)–(4) EC, the Member States also left no doubt as to the acutely political nature and underlying difficulties of such a move. It was for this reason that services and intellectual property rights appeared to be a *sui generis* sub-category within the scope of the CCP. This is also illustrated by the formalisation of the role of the European Parliament which, for the first time in the area of the CCP, is to be consulted on whether the rules of the 'old' CCP should apply to the negotiation of international agreements on services and intellectual property rights. Rather paradoxically, had the Council decided to act, the Parliament would have been consulted as to whether it would agree not to be formally consulted in the future.

The provision of the Amsterdam amendment was clearly the result of a compromise which did not satisfy the Commission. A member of the Santer Commission viewed the compromise illustrated by Article 133(5) EC at Amsterdam as 'tremendously disappointing', and added that 'the States sinned for lack of vision and showed an entirely deplorable mistrust towards the institutions'.[114] Quite how acute the difficulties underlying the Amsterdam amendment actually were became clear by both the drafting and substance of the new CCP in the Nice Treaty.

---

[114] Statement by then Commissioner Oreja before a parliamentary committee: *Agence Europe*, No 7012 of 9 July 1997 at 2.

8. THE NICE AMENDMENT

The Nice Treaty drastically rewrote Article 133 EC in terms of its application to services and intellectual property rights. In three paragraphs of dense content and with a number of cross-references, the Nice amendment seeks both to bring services and intellectual property rights within the scope of CCP and actively to avoid the application of the main tenets of that policy in a manner other than that envisaged by its drafters.

8.1 The Rule and its Limited Scope

The Nice amendment aims at bringing a wider range of services and intellectual property rights within the scope of the CCP: under Article 133(5)(1) EC, trade in services and commercial aspects of intellectual property are brought within the scope of Article 133(1)–(4) EC. This principle is limited in effect: it applies only to international agreements and does not cover autonomous measures adopted by the Community institutions. Therefore, not all services and intellectual property rights would be subject to the same treatment in terms of external relations: whilst those already covered by Article 133(1) EC could be covered by both international agreements and autonomous measures, others would be confined to international measures. The former category includes the cross-frontier supply of services, that is supply which would not involve the movement of physical persons and measures enforcing intellectual property rights which would be applicable at border crossing points in order to prevent the release into free circulation of counterfeit goods.[115] However, this enumeration is by no means exhaustive, as it was put forward by the Court in relation to specific agreements, namely GATS and TRIPs. More importantly, it was held that, in the light of the increasingly dominant position of services in international trade, 'it follows from the open nature of the common commercial policy, within the meaning of the Treaty, that trade in services cannot immediately, and as a matter of principle, be excluded from the scope of Article [133 EC]'.[116]

This restriction on the scope of the new CCP is in striking contrast to the CCP as construed by the Court consistently since its establishment. It is recalled that, in the light of the proper functioning of the customs union, external trade covered 'measures taken both independently and by agreement'.[117] The fact that this wide construction of the typology of implementation of the CCP is precluded by Article 133(5) EC is the first illustration of the legal features that distinguish the new CCP from Article 133 EC.

In practical terms, this distinction raises the question of the legal basis of Community measures intended to implement agreements that the Council concluded

---

[115] See *Opinion 1/94*, n28 above, paras 44 and 55 respectively.
[116] Para 41.
[117] Case 8/73 *Hauptzollamt Bremerhaven v Massey Gergusson GmbH* [1973] ECR 897, para 4.

pursuant to Article 133(5)(1) EC. It has been suggested that such measures should be adopted pursuant to the legal basis which would allow the Community to act internally.[118] In doing so, reference is made to the fact that reliance upon different legal bases for the negotiation and conclusion of an international agreement and the adoption of internal EC rules within the same area of activity has already been sanctioned by the Court. Indeed, the Court had pointed out in *Opinion 1/94* that 'the fact that the commitments entered into under [the Agreement on Agriculture] require internal measures to be adopted on the basis of Article 43 of the Treaty does not prevent international commitments themselves from being entered into pursuant to Article 133 alone'.[119] However, that reference was about the Agreement on Agriculture and Directives laying down uniform rules on the conditions under which products would be marketed; whilst both were in the area of agriculture, the Decision adopting the former on behalf of the Community relied upon Article 133 EC, whereas the latter relied upon Article 43 EC. This discrepancy arose for a reason: the adoption of internal measures on agriculture aimed at fulfilling the general objectives of agricultural policy laid down in the EC Treaty; the Agreement on Agriculture aimed at shaping the international agricultural trading system. In other words, the discrepancy in legal basis between external and internal measures was explained in the light of the different objectives of the relevant measures. The situation would be different where an internal measure was necessary in order to implement an external measure: they would both serve the same objective, their only difference being the former's adoption as a matter of necessity in order to enable the EC to comply with its contractual obligations under the latter. In the light of the above, Article 133(5)(1) EC could constitute the legal basis of the adoption of internal measures whose aim is to implement agreements concluded under that provision.[120]

8.2. The Material Scope

The material scope of the Nice amendments is far from clear. In relation to services, for instance, Community law approaches them not only as distinct from establishment but also as the subject matter of a residual freedom. This distinction between services and establishment does not appear in the GATS, whose wide definition of services covers establishment. Should the term 'services' in Article 133(5)(1) EC be interpreted strictly or widely? In the light of the link between the

---

[118] See M Cremona, 'A Policy of Bits and Pieces? The Common Commercial Policy after Nice' (2001) 4 *CYELS* 61 at 73 and C Herrmann, 'Common Commercial Polict After Nice: Sisyphus Would have Done a Better Job' (2002) 39 *CMLRev* 7 at 17.

[119] N28 above, at para 29.

[120] It follows that this would not be the case in the absence of an agreement adopted, on behalf of the Community, under Art 133(5)(1) EC in which case that provision could not be used as the legal basis for the adoption of internal measures. To that effect, see J Heliskoski, 'The Nice Reform of Article 133 EC on the Common Commercial Policy' (2002) 1 *Journal of International Commercial Law* 1 at 7.

new CCP and the GATS, it would be wrong to interpret 'services' under Article 133(5) EC consistently with the strict definition afforded within the Community legal order. The question is whether they should be interpreted as widely as the GATS suggests. Cremona answers this in the affirmative, hence concluding that the new CCP would, in fact, cover aspects of investment, too.[121]

Similar problems are raised in relation to the 'commercial aspects of intellectual property'. The first point of reference appears to be TRIPS which covered copyright and related rights, trade marks, geographical indications, industrial designs, patents, layout designs of integrated circuits, protection of undisclosed information and control of anti-competitive practices in contractual licences. Given the general position of *Opinion 1/94* as the context within which the re-drafting of Article 133 EC has taken place, it may be assumed that agreements in all the above rights fall within the new CCP 'insofar as [they] are not covered by [Article 133(1)EC]'.[122] The question which is then raised is whether that definition of the commercial aspects of intellectual property with reference to TRIPS should be static: if the scope of the TRIPS Agreement were to change, would the scope of Article 133(5)(1) EC change accordingly? Whilst both views have attracted support,[123] it is suggested that it is a strict reading of the scope of intellectual property rights as defined in Article 133(5)(1) EC which is faithful to the wording and spirit of the new CCP. Indeed, Article 133(7) provides as follows:

> Without prejudice to the first subparagraph of paragraph 6, the Council, acting unanimously on a proposal form the Commission and after consulting the European Parliament, may extend the application of paragraphs 1 to 4 to international negotiations and agreements on intellectual property insofar as they are not covered by paragraph 5.

This provision maintains the Amsterdam amendment, albeit by confining it to intellectual property rights not already covered by the Nice amendment. The possibility of rendering unanimously a broader category of intellectual property rights within the scope of the CCP suggests a strict reading of those already mentioned in Article 133(5)(1) EC.

---

[121] See Cremona, n118 above, at 72.

[122] There is a textual difference: TRIPS refer to 'trade-related intellectual property rights', whereas Art 133(5)(1) EC refers to 'the commercial aspects of intellectual property rights'. However, this appears by no means significant. Indeed, the term used in the French version of both texts is identical: Art 133(5)(1) EC refers to '*des aspects commerciaux de la la propriété intellectuelle*' and TRIPS refers to '*les aspects des droits de propriété intellectuelle qui touchent au commerce*'.

[123] See HG Krenzler and C Pischas, 'Progress or Stagnation? The Common Commercial After Nice' [2001] *EFA Review* 291 at 302 where it is argued that the scope of the commercial aspects of intellectual property in Art 133 EC should be flexible enough to accommodate future amendments of the scope of TRIPS. On the other hand, see Hermann, n118 above at 18–19 where an argument for a static definition of this term on grounds of the drafting history of Art 133(5) and the *raison d'être* of Art 133(7) EC.

8.3 Substantive Deviations: the Harmonisation Exception

Whilst extending Article 133(1)–(4) to services and commercial aspects of intellectual property rights, the Nice amendment expressly excludes a category of such rights. Article 133(6)(1) EC reads as follows:

> An agreement may not be concluded by the Council if it includes provisions which would go beyond the Community's internal powers, in particular by leading to harmonisation of the laws or regulations of the Member States in an area for which this Treaty rules out such harmonisation.

This subparagraph appears to draw upon the principle of limited powers enshrined in Article 5 EC. In doing so, it adds nothing to the legal framework of EC external relations. There has been no doubt as to the scope of the fundamental principle of limited powers: indeed, in *Opinion 2/94*, the Court had held that the principle of conferred powers 'must be respected in both the internal action and the international action of the Community'.[124] The significance that the drafters of the Treaty attached to this principle is highlighted by the second limb of Article 133(6)(1) EC, which refers to a specific case where an agreement in one of the areas covered by Article 133(5)(1) EC may not be concluded, namely where the content of that agreement would lead to harmonisation in an area where this is ruled out under the EC Treaty. Harmonisation is expressly excluded in the areas of education and vocational training,[125] culture[126] and public health.[127] As an illustration of an example of what the principle of conferred powers would entail in the area of the new CCP its usefulness is questionable. If the intention of the Member States was to eliminate any possibility of a liberal interpretation by the Court, its inclusion was unnecessary. As the construction of the CCP in *Opinion 1/94* had clearly illustrated, the Court had been unwilling to interpret Article 133 EC as a general external economic relations policy.

In relation to the internal sphere of EC activities, the express prohibition of harmonisation sets a clear limit beyond which the Court would not go. This was made painfully clear to the EC institutions with the *Tobacco Advertising* judgment, where the Court stressed that the express prohibition on harmonisation in the area of public health, enshrined in Article 152(4) EC, could not be circumvented by reliance upon the general decision-making clause of Article 95 EC.[128] It would be in exactly the same vein that the express prohibition on harmonisation could not be circumvented by reliance upon Article 133 EC. That this would be so, an express provision to that effect notwithstanding, had already been made apparent in *Opinion 1/94*. It is recalled that the Court had held that the conclusion of TRIPS

---

[124] *Opinion 2/94 (ECHR)* [1996] ECR I–1759, para 24.
[125] Arts 149(4) and 150(4) EC.
[126] Art 151(5) EC.
[127] Art 152(4) EC.
[128] Case C–376/98 *Germany v Parliament and Council (re: Tobacco Advertising)* [2001] ECR I–2247.

did not fall within the scope of the CCP in its entirety because the harmonising effect of that Agreement could not be achieved in the Community legal order in a manner which would render irrelevant the internal constraints laid down in primary law. Given that this approach to the CCP had been adopted by the Court in the absence of an express prohibition on full harmonisation internally, the second limb of Article 133(6)(1) EC sought to introduce an exception whose effect had never been in any doubt.

Whilst, in legal terms, Article 133(6)(1) EC adds nothing in our understanding of how the Community's external relations are to be carried out consistently with the EC Treaty, it is in more general terms that its main function may be ascertained. In defining the outer line of the scope of the new CCP, that provision highlights the parallelism between the internal and external policies of the Community as at the very core of the CCP. It is recalled that this parallelism was a distinctive feature of the Court's ruling in *Opinion 1/94* not only in relation to the construction of the CCP but also to that of implied competence: the Court's conclusion that the exclusive competence of the Community, pursuant to the *AETR* principle, did not cover the conclusion of either the GATS or TRIPS, was firmly based on the assumption that the nature of exclusive competence should be dependent on the exercise of the internal competence. It is that parallelism which appears to underpin the substantive exception laid down in Article 133(6)(1) EC too.

The importance attached to the principle by the drafters of the Nice amendment of the CCP was clearly illustrated by the addition of the following clause to Article 133(3): '[t]he Council and the Commission shall be responsible for ensuring that the agreements negotiated are compatible with internal Community policies and rules'. Viewed along with the provision of Article 133(6)(1) EC, this clause renders the expression of parallelism between the CCP and the internal aspects of the Community legal order at the very core of the Nice amendment, a fact also highlighted by its position as the starting point for the substantial restriction on the scope of Article 133(5) EC.

8.4. The Cultural Exception

The interpretation of the second subparagraph of Article 133(6) presents a host of legal problems. It introduces an express derogation from Article 133(5)(1) EC regarding agreements relating to trade in cultural and audiovisual services, educational services and social and human health services. It reads as follows:

> In this regard, by way of derogation from the first subparagraph of paragraph 5, agreements relating to trade in cultural and audiovisual services, educational services, and social and human health services, shall fall within the shared competence of the Community and its Member States. Consequently, in addition to a Community decision taken in accordance with the relevant provisions of Article 300, the negotiation of such agreements shall require the common accord of the Member States. Agreements thus negotiated shall be concluded jointly by the Community and the Member States

This subparagraph introduces the so-called 'cultural exception'. Of those areas mentioned therein, culture, education and health may not be regulated by fully harmonising rules internally pursuant to an express EC Treaty prohibition, namely Articles 151(5), 150(4) and 152(4)(c) EC respectively. Therefore, in so far as these services are concerned, the second subparagraph of Article 133(6) merely illustrates a particular field of application of the derogation laid down in the first subparagraph of Article 133(6). This is not the case as regards the remaining areas: as regards social policy, Article 136 EC states that 'the functioning of the common market ... will favour the harmonisation of social systems'; in relation to audio-visual services, there is no specific EC Treaty provision dealing with their internal regulation and the reference to its status as beyond the scope of the CCP was made at the insistence of the French government.

The relation between the 'cultural exception' and the 'harmonisation exception' is not immediately apparent. In the light of the range of policy areas mentioned in Article 133(6)(2) EC and the different objectives served by their inclusion therein, it is suggested that that provision does not serve to define the latter exception in exhaustive terms.[129] In fact, it appears to serve two other functions. First, it provides for the express external competence of the Community in the specific areas to which it refers. It is noteworthy that, in most of those areas, the EC Treaty had already provided for external action: Article 149(3) EC on education, Article 150(3) EC on vocational training, Article 151(3) EC on culture and Article 152(3) EC on public health provide that the Community and the Member States are to 'foster cooperation with third countries and international organizations'. To exclude the negotiation and conclusion of international agreements from this provision would be to deprive it of much of its significance. Viewed from this angle, rather than endowing the Community with express treaty-making competence for the first time, Article 133(6)(2) EC clarifies the competence which the Community has already had. In deviating from the scope of Article 133(5) EC, the cultural exception laid down in Article 133(6)(2) EC 'is here not just providing a specific procedural safeguard ... for the Member States; it excludes certain sectoral agreements from the express CCP-based Community competence of paragraph 5'.[130] Therefore, as the latter provision extends the scope of the CCP, albeit in a heavily circumscribed manner, Article 133(6)(2) EC introduces a derogation from the entire system of the CCP.

The second function carried out by the so-called cultural exception is expressly to render that competence shared. Again, that had already been the case pursuant to the EC Treaty provisions requiring fostering of cooperation. The clarification of the nature of the external competence in the EC Treaty provision on the CCP and the requirement that it be exercised by common accord illustrate the immense significance attached to decision-making at international level in those

---

[129] Cf Krenzler and Pitschas, n123 above, at 309.
[130] Cremona, n118 above, at 74.

areas. However, this procedural provision is problematic on various grounds. First, one limb of that provision undermines another: the requirement of common accord for the negotiation of agreements renders the voting procedures laid down in Article 300 EC redundant. This is because common accord is the most onerous voting procedure for decision-making, as an abstention prevents the adoption of a rule; this is not the case with unanimity, which merely connotes the absence of negative votes.[131] What does the provision that common accord be required in addition to a Community decision adopted under Article 300 EC actually entail? This may only refer to the position of the subject-matter of the agreements in question as within the shared competence of the Community and the Member States.[132] Indeed, this is what the introduction of that requirement with the word 'consequently' appears to entail.

Secondly, if the above reading is correct, what does the reference to 'the relevant provisions of Article 300' entail in practical terms? It has been argued that it actually refers to the involvement of the European Parliament and, in particular, its consultation pursuant to Article 300(3) EC.[133] Whilst it is difficult to reach any other conclusion which would make some sense of the reference to Article 300 EC, nonetheless the ensuing legal situation is puzzling: parliamentary control over areas where the Community is exclusively competent takes place only pursuant to informal arrangements, whereas in areas falling within shared competence and, hence, would be subject to national parliamentary control, the involvement of the European Parliament enjoys EC Treaty recognition.

8.5. The Transport Exception

The analysis of the substantive exceptions introduced in the new CCP at Nice indicated that, to a very considerable extent, their drafting did not change the state of the law as applied by the Court of Justice; instead, it aimed at establishing beyond doubt the status of a number of policy areas as beyond the scope of Article 133 EC. This rather declaratory function was also performed by Article 133(6)(3) EC which reads as follows:

> The negotiation and conclusion of international agreements in the field of transport shall continue to be governed by the provisions of Title V and Article 300 EC.

The only interesting point about this provision is its wording, which does not pretend to do anything more than attributing primary law status to what we already know to be the case.

---

[131] AM Arnull, AA Dashwood, MG Ross and DA Wyatt, *Wyatt and Dashwood's European Union Law* (London: Sweet and Maxwell, 2000) 49, as indicated in Art 205(3) EC.

[132] As Cremona puts it, 'strictly speaking, this is, a case of shared competence rather than unanimous voting within the Council': n118 above, at 82.

[133] See Cremona, n118 above, at 82–3 and Herrmann, n118 above, at 25.

8.6. Procedural Deviations: the Parallelism Exception

A central feature of the CCP has always been the simplicity of its decision-making procedures: the Council acts by qualified majority voting pursuant to a proposal by the Commission and having consulted with the European Parliament on a non-formalised basis. The various ways in which the extension of the application of Article 133(1)–(4) EC is circumscribed by the Nice Treaty include the requirement that, in a number of cases, agreements be concluded by the Community unanimously.

The first such exception is provided in Article 133(5)(2) EC which reads as follows:

> By way of derogation from paragraph 4, the Council shall act unanimously when negotiating and concluding an agreement in one of the fields referred to in the first subparagraph, where that agreement includes provisions for which unanimity is required for the adoption of internal rules or where it relates to a filed in which the Community has not yet exercised the powers conferred upon it by this Treaty by adopting internal rules.

As for the first case, the unanimous adoption of internal rules on services is still provided in areas for which the establishment of the internal market and development of European integration have yet to assuage national concerns: for instance, they include tax harmonisation pursuant to Article 93 EC and visas immigration and asylum matters pursuant to Article 67(1) EC. They also cover EC Treaty provisions the wording of which has been deemed by Member States to be too broad, such as Article 94 EC on the approximation of national laws and the residual clause of Article 308 EC. In the area of services, unanimity is required under Articles 47(2) EC on establishment and 57(2) EC on movement of capital to and from third countries when new restrictions are introduced.

As for the case of the absence of internal rules, the requirement that international agreements be concluded unanimously reflects the nature of international negotiations where, in order not to prevent the adoption of package deals, agreement is reached on specific points for which no such agreement would be reached internally were they to be discussed in the Council. That international practice should not impose upon the Community arrangements which its institutions had been unable or unwilling to introduce internally is a principle acknowledged by the Court itself in *Opinion 1/94*. Whilst the *rationale* underlying this exception is far from controversial, two points need to be made. First, it constitutes yet another illustration of the parallelism between the internal and external spheres of EC activity as the foundation of the new CCP—the first being the so-called harmonisation exception from the substantive scope of the CCP. It is interesting that the Member States should feel compelled to attribute Treaty status to the Court's interpretation. Secondly, the precise scope of the parallelism exception is far from clear. How should 'internal rules' be construed so that their presence would be deemed sufficient to enable the Community to act under Article 133(4) EC? Is it necessary for the internal rules to introduce full harmonisation? If so, would the scope of this exception not become so broad as to render it the rule within the new CCP? If not, what should the intensity of the internal rules be in order to trigger the applicability of the unanimity rule? Would it be sufficient if, whilst in force, internal rules covered only part of the area over which the Community might wish to act externally? Should this part be central or merely peripheral to the core of the agreement?[134]

It is not the function of primary law to provide exhaustive answers to every question that may arise from its application. However, the host of questions which the wording of Article 133(5)(2) EC opens is noteworthy. On the one hand, the range and type of questions are not dissimilar to those raised in the 1990s in relation to the internal rules whose adoption would render the implied external competence of the Community exclusive. In that respect, even the question left unanswered in that provision provides yet another illustration of the parallelism between the internal and external spheres of the EC activity and the construction of the system of EC international relations. That this parallelism is spelled out in a primary rule articulating the effects of express competence associated with exclusivity is very significant for the development of this policy within the broader system of EC external relations. However, the fact that such questions are left unanswered following the Nice amendment is telling: whilst it may be easy to attack the judiciary for not laying down the precise parameters of their rulings when adjudicating upon specific disputes, it by no means follows that the express provision of legal principles in primary law would introduce more clarity.

8.7. The 'Horizontal Agreement' Exception

Article 133(5)(3) EC also provides for unanimity in relation to the negotiation and conclusion of a horizontal agreement 'insofar as it also concerns the preceding subparagraphs or the second subparagraph of paragraph 6'.

The EC Treaty itself does not provide a definition of horizontal agreements. For the purpose of this analysis, such agreements may be understood as covering other areas in addition to services and commercial aspects of intellectual property rights, in the area of which internal rules would be adopted unanimously or where there are no internal rules on cultural and audiovisual services, educational services, social and human health services. Again, the wording of Article 133(5)(3) EC is far from clear as to the extent to which such services or intellectual property rights should form a central or significant or just ancillary part in the agreement in question.

8.8. Procedural Deviations: the Cultural Exception

Agreements on trade in cultural and audiovisual services, educational services and social and human health services are to be negotiated pursuant to the common

---

[134] See Herrmann, n118 above, at 22–3 for a broad reading of the exception; also Krenzler, n123 above, at 305.

accord of the Member States under Article 133(6)(2) EC. This exception follows from the express position of such agreements as within the competence shared by the Community and the Member States. As common accord rules out decision-making with abstention, its provision leaves no doubt as to political significance attached to its subject-matter.

9. COMMENT ON THE NICE PROVISIONS OF ARTICLE 133 EC AND BEYOND

The provisions on the CCP introduced by the Nice Treaty render Article 133 EC very difficult to read: extending the scope of the CCP in a heavily circumscribed manner, introducing qualifications and exceptions, both substantive and procedural, relying upon continuous cross-references and raising as many questions as they sought to address, the rules laid down in Article 133(5)–(7) EC are difficult to navigate and introduce a degree of complexity which is disconcerting.

Be that as it may, in an attempt to define the logic of the Nice amendments to the CCP, a number of threads may be identified. The first is that of parallelism between internal and external powers. According to the European Commission, this is the key to understanding the new provisions.[135] The so-called logic of parallelism and the ensuing principle that the internal rules and policies define the outer limit of the Community's external action clearly draws upon the case law of the Court of Justice on the construction of implied external competence, as illustrated not only in *Opinion 1/94* but also in the more recent *Open Skies* judgments.[136] What makes this principle of parallelism significant is its gradual effect which permeates the entire system of the CCP. It is in the light of this that one should approach the duty of the Commission and the Council under Article 133(3) EC to ensure that agreements negotiated in the exercise of the CCP competence be compatible with the internal Community rules and policies. Indeed, this provision, added at Nice, applies to all agreements concluded under Article 133 EC. It is not so much in legal terms that this addition is significant: contrary to international agreements which are inconsistent with primary law,[137] agreements inconsistent with secondary legislation may be adopted, the question then being how to amend the latter so as to give effect to the former.[138] It is rather in

---

[135] European Commission, 'The Reform of Article 133 by the Nice Treaty. The Logic of Parallelism': this was a document drawn up in Dec 2000 and which had been placed on the Commission's External Trade website for some time.

[136] See Case C–466/98 *Commission v UK* [2002] ECR I–9427, Case C–467/98 *Commission v Denmark* [2002] ECR I–9519, Case C–468/98 *Commission v Sweden* [2002] ECR I–9575, Case C–469/98 *Commission v Finland* [2002] ECR I–9627, Case C–471/98 *Commission v Belgium* [2002] ECR I–9681, Case C–472/98 *Commission v Luxembourg* [2002] ECR I–9741, Case C–475/98 *Commission v Austria* [2002] ECR I–9797, Case C–476/98 *Commission v Germany* [2002] ECR I–9855 as analysed in Ch 3 below.

[137] See Art 300(6) EC which renders their entry into force conditional upon an amendment of the EC Treaty.

[138] See Cremona, n118 above, at 75–6 and Herrmann, n118 above, at 26–7.

symbolic terms that this addition should be understood: it appears to draw upon the more nuanced construction of implied competence which has emerged from the case law on external relations since the early 1990s.[139]

Secondly, the amendments introduced at Nice strike at the principal normative feature of that policy, namely its exclusive nature as defined by the Court in its early case law.[140] It is recalled that Member States are excluded *a priori* from acting in an areas falling within the scope of the CCP, save pursuant to express authorisation granted under Community law.[141] The Nice amendments deviate from this principle in two ways: on the one hand, by enabling the Member States to negotiate and conclude agreements whose scope falls within Article 133(5)(1) EC with third countries and international organisations (Article 133(5)(4) EC); on the other hand, by rendering agreements relating to the so-called cultural exception expressly within shared competence (Article 133(6)(2) EC). In introducing these provisions, not only does the Nice Treaty dilute the exclusive nature of the CCP, but it also does so in a manner whose legal implications vary. In terms of agreements in services and commercial aspects of intellectual property rights covered by Article 133(5)(1) EC, the external competence of the Community is expressly affirmed and may be exercised independently, albeit without undermining the parallel competence of the Member States. As far as agreements falling within the cultural exception are concerned, the Community may not act alone.[142]

The formalisation of shared competence as above raises a number of questions. In terms of Article 133(6)(2) EC, is the type of mixity introduced compulsory? In other words, are Member States stripped of their competence to act alone? Whilst such strict reading has been suggested,[143] it appears to be contrary to the spirit of the Nice amendments. The latter are clearly focused on endowing the Community with express competence, albeit in a heavily circumscribed manner. Indeed, this follows from the formalisation of shared competence in the area traditionally based on Community exclusive competence. As for the type of shared competence envisaged under Article 133(5)(4) EC, the question which arises is whether its scope, and ultimately its very existence, is subject to redefinition. It is recalled that the external competence of the Community is deemed to become exclusive following the adoption of completely harmonising rules in the internal sphere. Whilst articulated in the *AETR* judgment in the context of implied competence, this principle is not irrelevant to the exercise of express competence: after all, the introduction of express external competence regarding monetary matters,

---

[139] In another reading of the application of the 'logic of parallelism', the Nice amendments were seen as introspective and indicative of the focus of the IGC on internal matters: see JHJ Bourgeois, 'The EC's Trade Policy Powers after Nice: Painting Oneself in a Corner?' in G Vandersanden (edn), *Mélanges en hommage à Jean-Victor Louis* (Brussels: Editions de l'Université de Bruxelles, 2003) ii, 29 at 34–5.

[140] See *Opinion 1/75* in n3 above and the subsequent case law as analysed in Ch 2 above.

[141] Case 41/76 *Criel, née Donckerwolke et al v Procureur de la République au Tribunal de Grande Instance, Lille et al* [1976] ECR 1921 at para 32.

[142] See Cremona, n118 above, at 84.

[143] See Herrmann, n118 above, at 21–2.

environmental policy and development cooperation at Maastricht was accompanied by the following Declaration:[144]

> The Conference considers that the provisions of Article [111(5), 174 and 181] do not affect the principles resulting from the judgment handed down by the Court of Justice in the *AETR* case.

Such a declaration is conspicuously absent from the Nice amendments of Article 133 EC. Does this suggest that the shared competence established under Article 133(5)(4) EC formalises the parallel exercise of Community and national competence in the literal sense of the word, that is by ensuring that they would never 'meet'? Whilst open-ended, the wording of the provision suggests so. There is another indication to that effect, namely the accompanying requirement that the exercise of national competence comply with Community law and other international agreements. This emphasis on the obvious, as emanating from Article 10 EC, appears to counteract the formalisation of the permanently parallel coexistence of the Member States with the Community within the scope of application of Article 133(5)(1) EC.[145]

The formalisation of shared competence within the context of Article 133 EC by the Nice reform appears to introduce a considerable deviation from the principal normative qualities of the CCP. However, its practical effects should not be overstated. The construction of exclusivity by the Court of Justice, as analysed in chapter 1, indicated a much more nuanced approach to its application than the early judicial pronouncements might have suggested. That notion was applied in a flexible manner, with due regard to the degree of the actual completion of the common commercial policy as well as the specific circumstances under which a given agreement was negotiated. Similar flexibility was also illustrated by the interpretation of trade measures with foreign policy implications, a topic examined in a later chapter. In other words, *a priori* exclusivity did not necessarily exclude the parallel participation of Member States in the negotiation and conclusion of international agreements. Viewed from this angle, exclusivity had ceased to appear the sacrosanct foundation upon the existence of which the CCP was dependent and had become one of the principles which shaped the evolving implementation of that policy.

Therefore, as the principle of exclusivity had not been sufficient in itself to guarantee either the completion of the CCP in time or its effective conduct on the international scene, neither is the formalisation of shared competence in the Nice provisions sufficient in itself to justify the doomed predictions about the implementation of that policy. The problem lies elsewhere: as Cremona puts it, a more substantial threat to the development of the CCP is 'the threat of "deconstruction", of a lack of coherence arising out [of] the formidable complexity of the

---

[144] Declaration 10 attached to TEU.
[145] Cf Krenzler and Pischas, n123 above, at 307.

revised Treaty provisions, the number of different permutations and procedures applicable to different aspects of commercial policy'.[146] It is this practical risk which renders the Nice version of Article 133 EC a sum of problematic provisions.

Compared to the current provisions on the CCP, the text agreed upon in the Treaty Establishing a Constitution for Europe is considerably easier to read. Its provisions are laid down in Article III–315 and read as follows:

1. The common commercial policy shall be based on uniform principles, particularly with regard to changes in tariff rates, the conclusion of tariff and trade agreements relating to trade in goods and services, and the commercial aspects of intellectual property, foreign direct investment, the achievement of uniformity in measures of liberalisation, export policy and measures to protect trade such as those to be taken in the event of dumping or subsidies. The common commercial policy shall be conducted in the context of the principles and objectives of the Union's external action.

2. European laws shall establish the measures defining the framework for implementing the common commercial policy.

3. Where agreements with one or more third countries or international organisations need to be negotiated and concluded, Article III-325 shall apply, subject to the special provisions of this Article.

The Commission shall make recommendations to the Council, which shall authorise it to o1pen the necessary negotiations. The Council and the Commission shall be responsible for ensuring that the agreements negotiated are compatible with internal Union policies and rules.

The Commission shall conduct these negotiations in consultation with a special committee appointed by the Council to assist the Commission in this task and within the framework of such directives as the Council may issue to it. The Commission shall report regularly to the special committee and to the European Parliament on the progress of negotiations.

4. For the negotiation and conclusion of the agreements referred to in paragraph 3, the Council shall act by a qualified majority.

For the negotiation and conclusion of agreements in the fields of trade in services and the commercial aspects of intellectual property, as well as foreign direct investment, the Council shall act unanimously where such agreements include provisions for which unanimity is required for the adoption of internal rules.

The Council shall also act unanimously for the negotiation and conclusion of agreements:

(a) in the field of trade in cultural and audiovisual services, where these agreements risk prejudicing the Union's cultural and linguistic diversity;
(b) in the field of trade in social, education and health services, where these agreements risk seriously disturbing the national organisation of such services and prejudicing the responsibility of Member States to deliver them.

---

[146] N118 above, at 89.

5. The negotiation and conclusion of international agreements in the field of transport shall be subject to Section 7 of Chapter III of Title III and to Article III-325.6. The exercise of the competences conferred by this Article in the field of the common commercial policy shall not affect the delimitation of competences between the Union and the Member States, and shall not lead to harmonisation of legislative or regulatory provisions of the Member States insofar as the Constitution excludes such harmonisation.

At the time of writing, the fate of the Constitutional Treaty is uncertain at best. Nonetheless, two brief points need to be made. First, the above provisions rationalise the extension of the Community's competence whilst retaining the link between external policy and internal decision-making.[147] Secondly, Article III–315 is part of a set of provisions grouped together in Part III under Title V 'External Action'. This Title includes provisions on the CCP, cooperation with third countries and humanitarian aid, economic, financial and technical cooperation with third countries, economic sanctions, the negotiation and conclusion of international agreements and the EU relations with international organisations and third countries. In addition, it covers the rules on Common Foreign and Security Policy and Common Security and Defence Policy. By grouping all these provisions together, the Constitutional Treaty makes the conduct of the entirety of the Union's international relations subject to a unified set of principles and objectives which are set out in Article III–292. The principles are defined as those which 'have inspired [the Union's] own creation, development and enlargement' and include democracy, the rule of law, the universality and indivisibility of human rights and fundamental freedoms, respect for human dignity, the principles of equality and solidarity, and respect for the principles of the United Nations Charter and international law. The objectives include references to, amongst others, sustainable economic, social and environmental development of developing countries, with the primary aim of eradicating poverty, the encouragement of the integration of all countries into the world economy, the development of international measures to preserve and improve the quality of the environment and the sustainable management of global natural resources, in order to ensure sustainable development, assistance to populations, countries and regions confronting natural or man-made disasters and the promotion of an international system based on stronger multilateral cooperation and good global governance. These objectives will be examined further in this book. At this juncture, suffice it to point out that the definition of a set of unified principles and objectives is a positive step towards ensuring the coherence of the Union's international action.[148]

---

[147] See the analysis in M Krajewski, 'External Trade Law and the Constitution Treaty: Towards a Federal and More Democratic Common Commercial Policy?' (2005) 42 *CMLRev* 91.

[148] See M Cremona, 'The Draft Constitutional Treaty : External Relations and External Action' (2003) 40 *CMLRev* 1347 at 1363.

10. CONCLUSION

The requirement that the scope of the Common Commercial Policy be interpreted in broad terms was one of the main parameters of this policy as emerging from the case law of the Court of Justice in the early 1970s. In analysing its various adjustments up to the reform of Article 133 EC at Nice, this chapter examined the various legal, practical and political factors which have shaped the evolving interpretation of the open-ended provision of Article 133(1) EC. In making it clear in no uncertain terms that, broadly though it might be construed, Article 133 EC could not be an all-encompassing external economic relations policy, the Court sought to define the outer-limit of the CCP. This was not the only adjustment to the fundamental principles of the CCP brought about over time by the case-law: as the broad scope of the CCP did not necessarily cover commercial activities whose materialisation was deemed to fall within the scope of other specific EC Treaty provisions, so did the exclusive nature of the Community competence not necessarily exclude the parallel presence of Member States in the process of negotiation and conclusion of international agreements.

This approach to the CCP has often been characterised as pragmatic. This definition is correct in so far as it reflects the responsiveness of the Community judicature to the regulatory climate of the era and the consolidation of the emerging policy. However, pragmatism does not necessarily entail timidity. In approaching the CCP as but one of the external policies of the Community, the Court of Justice shifts the emphasis on the various ways in which the Community carries out its external relations in accordance with its constitutional idiosyncrasies. This contextual approach to the CCP is apparent by the increasing emphasis in the CCP case law on the legal techniques aimed at ensuring the effective coexistence between the Community and the Member States on the international scene. The implications of this approach may only be appreciated in the light of the interpretation of the Community's implied powers and the circumstances under which these may become exclusive. This will be the subject of the next chapter.

3

Implied Competence

1. INTRODUCTION

T HE ANALYSIS SO far has focused on the express external competence of the Community, in particular in the area of the Common Commercial Policy. Its genesis and development have been shown to be characterised by considerable diversity. This was the case not only in terms of its regulation by the Community institutions but also of the application of its principal normative features by the Court of Justice. This has also been one of the main characteristics of the amendment of Article 133 EC at Nice.

However, to appreciate fully both the development of the express competence and the logic of the Nice amendment, one needs to analyse the concept of implied competence. The existence of the implied competence of the Community to act externally, along with the legal implications of its exercise, has formed the subject-matter of a line of rulings by the European Court of Justice stretching back to the early 1970s. Whilst not quite voluminous, the relevant case law has given rise to controversy as to its repercussions and even more considerable academic debate as to its precise meaning. This Chapter will analyse the genesis, development and application of this type of competence.

2. THE FOUNDATION PERIOD: THE *AETR* PRINCIPLE

The first time the implied competence of the Community to act in international relations was raised was in Case 22/70 *Commission v Council (re: European Road Transport Agreement).*[1] Its subject-matter was transport policy. The Member States had participated in the conclusion of the European Transport Road Agreement. This agreement regulated the work of crews engaged in international transport and was signed in 1970 under the auspices of the UN Economic Commission for Europe. The Member States passed a resolution within the Council stating that they would conclude the Agreement. The Commission challenged that measure under Article 230 EC, claiming that it was the Community which should conclude the agreement rather than the Member States; this argument was based on the assumption that competence in the field of transport had passed on to the Community following

---

[1] [1971] ECR 263.

the adoption of Regulation 543/69 concerning the harmonisation of certain social provisions in the field of road transport.[2]

The *AETR* judgment introduced the principle of implied powers in the external action of the Community according to which the conferment of internal competence in a specific area of activities upon the Community by the EC Treaty implies the conferment of external competence in that area. The relevant extract of the judgment is worth citing in full:

12. In the absence of specific provisions of the Treaty relating to the negotiation and conclusion of international agreements in the sphere of transport policy—a category into which, essentially the AETR falls—one must turn to the general system of Community law in the sphere of relations with third countries.

13. Article 210 provides that "The Community shall have legal personality".

14. This provision, placed at the head of Part Six of the Treaty, devoted to 'General and Final Provisions', means that in its external relations the Community enjoys the capacity to establish contractual links with third countries over the whole field of objectives defined in Part One of the Treaty, which Part Six supplements.

15. To determine in a particular case the Community's authority to enter into international agreements, regard must be had to the whole scheme of the Treaty no less than to its substantive provisions.

16. Such authority arises not only from an express conferment by the Treaty—as is the case with Articles 113 [now 133] and 114 [now deleted] for tariff and trade agreements and with Article 238 [now 310] for association agreements—but may equally flow from other provisions of the Treaty and from measures adopted, within the framework of those provisions, by the Community institutions.

17. In particular, each time the Community, with a view to implementing a common policy envisaged by the Treaty, adopts provisions laying down common rules, whatever form these may take, the Member States no longer have the right, acting individually or even collectively, to undertake obligations with third countries which affect those rules.

18. As and when such common rules come into being, the Community alone is in a position to assume and carry out contractual obligations towards third countries affecting the whole sphere of application of the Community legal system.

19. With regard to the implementation of the provisions of the Treaty the system of internal Community measures may not therefore be separated from that of external relations.

20. Under Article 3(e) [now 3(f)], the adoption of a common policy in the sphere of transport is specially mentioned amongst the objectives of the Community.

21. Under Article 5 [now 10], the Member States are required on the one hand to take all appropriate measures to ensure fulfilment of the obligations arising out of the Treaty or resulting from action taken by the institutions and, on the other hand, to abstain from any measure which might jeopardize the attainment of the objectives of the Treaty.

---

[2] [1969] OJ L 77/49.

22. If these two provisions are read in conjunction, it follows that to the extent to which Community rules are promulgated for the attainment of the objectives of the Treaty, the Member States cannot, outside the framework of the Community institutions, assume obligations which might affect those rules or alter their scope.

23. According to Article 74 [now Article 70], the objectives of the Treaty in matters of transport are to be pursued within the framework of a common policy.

24. With this in view, Article 75 (1) [now Article 70(1)] directs the Council to lay down common rules and, in addition, 'any other appropriate provisions'.

25. By the terms of subparagraph (a) of the same provision, those common rules are applicable ' to international transport to or from the territory of a Member State or passing across the territory of one or more Member States'.

26. This provision is equally concerned with transport from or to third countries, as regards that part of the journey which takes place on Community territory.

27. It thus assumes that the powers of the Community extend to relationships arising from international law, and hence involve the need in the sphere in question for agreements with the third countries concerned.

28. Although it is true that Articles 74 [now 70] and 75 [now 71] do not expressly confer on the Community authority to enter into international agreements, nevertheless the bringing into force, on 25 March 1969, of Regulation no 543/69 of the Council on the harmonization of certain social legislation relating to road transport (OJ l 77, p. 49) necessarily vested in the Community power to enter into any agreements with third countries relating to the subject-matter governed by that Regulation.

29. This grant of power is moreover expressly recognized by Article 3 of the said Regulation which prescribes that: 'the Community shall enter into any negotiations with third countries which may prove necessary for the purpose of implementing this Regulation'.

30. Since the subject-matter of the AETR falls within the scope of Regulation no 543/69, the Community has been empowered to negotiate and conclude the agreement in question since the entry into force of the said Regulation.

31. These Community powers exclude the possibility of concurrent powers on the part of Member States, since any steps taken outside the framework of the Community institutions would be incompatible with the unity of the common market and the uniform application of Community law.

The Court makes a distinction between the 'capacity' of the Community to negotiate and conclude international agreements and its 'authority' to do so: the former stems from the Community's legal personality; the latter refers to whether it is legally possible for the Community to exercise this authority in relation to a specific subject-matter and is determined on the basis of specific provisions of primary and secondary EC law. From a theoretical perspective, this distinction, elaborated upon in the judgment as the starting point for the introduction of the principle of implied powers, is significant: it aims at reconciling that principle with that of limited powers laid down in Article 5 EC. Whilst the Community 'shall act within the limits of the powers conferred upon it by th[e EC] Treaty and of the objectives assigned to it therein', the Court seeks to assuage fears that the principle of implied powers would lead to the extension of the Community's competence.[3]

Central to the operation of the principle of implied competence is the distinction between the issue of the existence and nature of that competence. The former will indicate whether, consistently with the principle of limited powers, the Community has the authority, that is the competence, to conclude an international agreement: the latter would determine whether that competence is exclusive or merely coexistent with a parallel competence enjoyed by the Member States. This is a distinction to which the *AETR* judgment does not appear to adhere very strictly. Indeed, the judgment is surprising short on its analysis of the existence of implied competence and the circumstances in which this may arise. A close analysis of the judgment will reveal that this is not its only shortcoming.

2.1. The General Formulation: Existence and Nature of the Competence (paragraphs 15–19)

Having stated that the Community's competence to act externally 'may flow' from primary or secondary Community law, the Court seeks, in just one paragraph, to define the fundamental parameters of the principle of exclusivity. On the one hand, it addresses the question when is the Community's implied competence exclusive, the answer to which is 'each time the Community, with a view to implementing a common policy envisaged by the Treaty, adopts provisions laying down common rules, whatever form these may take'; on the other hand, in explaining what exclusivity means, it held that 'the Member States no longer have the right, acting individually or even collectively, to undertake obligations with third countries which affect those rules'. The corollary of this is spelled out in the following paragraph, hence bringing the point home: 'the Community alone is in a position to assume and carry out contractual obligations towards third countries affecting the whole sphere of application of the Community legal system'.

These two paragraphs leave open as many questions as they seek to answer. First, is the term 'common policy envisaged by the Treaty' in relation to which the Community's authority may become exclusive to be interpreted literally? If the answer is affirmative, the implications of exclusivity would be very limited indeed, as it would be confined to the common agricultural and transport policies. However, it is not only for the *effet utile* of this new doctrine that this question should be answered in the negative: according to the judgment, it is only 'in particular' with regard to a common policy that the Community's authority may become exclusive. This implies that other instances are envisaged.

Secondly, the opening words of paragraph 17 as to when exclusivity may arise raise another question: exactly how wide is the scope for the implied competence

---

[3] A Dashwood and J Heliskoski, 'The Classic Authorities Revisited' in A Dashwood and C Hillion (eds), *The General Law of EC External Relations* (London: Sweet and Maxwell, 2000) 3 at 7.

to become exclusive? In other words, is exclusivity dependent upon the adoption of 'provisions laying down common rules' or may it arise independently of the adoption of secondary legislation? Are there EC Treaty provisions which may constitute the inherent source of external competence which is both implied and exclusive? Are there circumstances under which the implied competence conferred by an EC Treaty provision or secondary legislation, whilst initially shared, should be exercised exclusively by the Community?

Thirdly, what is the scope of 'common rules' that may give rise to exclusivity? Should they completely harmonise the subject-matter they intend to cover? The determination of this issue was directly relevant to the assessment of the impact of exclusive implied competence, all the more so in the light of the regulatory model prevailing at that time. Indeed, when the Court delivered the judgment in *AETR*, the establishment of the internal market was based on the notion of complete harmonisation which underpinned the introduction of secondary legislation. Is this what the term 'common rules' entailed? And if so, is its definition static or should it vary according to the regulatory mode prevailing at the time? If the latter were the case, then to define that term so as to encompass the model of minimum harmonisation followed in the mid-1980s would be tantamount to construing exclusivity in rather wide terms. Would such an interpretation be appropriate merely on the basis of a judgment delivered in quite opaque terms in the early 1970s?

Fourthly, what exactly are the implications of exclusivity on Member States in practical terms? Whilst the judgment views its effect arising 'as and when . . . common rules come into being', it does not define quite how national action should affect common rules. It is clear that Member States are prevented from assuming international obligations which would undermine the existing obligations of the Community or its negotiating position. But what about obligations which, when assumed by the Member States, do not raise any threat whatever for the Community's interests? Is the possibility of a future conflict sufficient to deprive Member States of their freedom to engage in contractual relations with third countries in areas where the Community has adopted 'common rules'? If so, would that mean that there would be no scope whatever for Member States to act in a field occupied by common rules? In other words, how severe are the legal implications of exclusivity actually in terms of their effect on the positions of the Member States?

Fifthly, what exactly is the source of the existence of the Community's implied competence? Is it the EC Treaty provision itself enabling the Community to act internally from which the external competence 'flows'? In its judgment, the Court refers to EC Treaty provisions not expressly providing for external competence 'and . . . measures adopted, within the framework of those provisions, by the Community institutions'.[4] If the existence of external competence were implied from EC Treaty provisions, why was the reference to secondary law adopted

---

[4] N1 above, para 16.

pursuant to those provisions necessary? Would it not be more accurate to argue that the external competence may flow from either primary or secondary Community law? The reference to 'common rules' in the subsequent paragraph seems to suggest that 'measures adopted within the framework of' 'other provisions of the Treaty' would be relevant to the nature of the Community's competence rather than its existence, hence determining whether it would be exclusive or not.

The above questions notwithstanding, the *raison d'être* of exclusivity lies in the link between secondary law adopted internally and external relations: the former may not be separated from the latter. This abstract formulation of the principle of implied powers is followed by three paragraphs in which a reformulation, adjusted to EC Treaty provisions, is being presented. However, this reformulation is even less revealing than the original one. On the basis of the insertion of transport policy amongst the EC Treaty objectives and the duty of solidarity laid down in Article 10 EC, the Court infers that 'Member States cannot, outside the framework of the Community institutions, assume obligations which might affect [those Community rules promulgated for the attainment of Treaty objectives] which might affect those rules or alter their scope'.[5]

The above extract is puzzling in so far as it puts forward a construction of exclusivity which differs from that already laid down in paragraph 17: according to the former, Member States would be prevented from 'assum[ing] obligations which might affect [EC rules] or alter their scope'; according to the latter, Member States would be prevented from undertaking obligation which 'affect [common] rules'. Two definitions of the same duty in six brief consecutive paragraphs are rather puzzling. Furthermore, it is not immediately apparent why the above construction of exclusivity 'follows' from a combined reading of Articles 3 and 10 EC; this is all the more so in the light of the construction of exclusivity in relation to 'Community rules promulgated for the attainment of the objectives of the Treaty' rather than 'common rules'.

Apart from further obscuring the requirements for and implications of exclusivity, the above extract from the *AETR* judgment does add to the theoretical foundation of the principle of implied powers by referring to Article 10 EC. The reference to the duty of solidarity serves two purposes: on the one hand, it justifies the apparently severe implications of exclusivity by rendering it an extension of the core of national duties under primary Community law; on the other hand, it adds yet another layer to the constitutional foundation of the exclusive nature of the Community's implied competence.

2.2. The Application of the Principle (paragraphs 23–31)

What follows in paragraphs 23–31 of the judgment is the application of the principle on the basis of the specific EC provisions on transport. Perhaps not

---

[5] N1 above, para 22.

unsurprisingly, this part of the judgment is as fraught with problems as the ones preceding it. The Court refers to two types of EC rules, namely the provisions of EC Treaty on transport and Regulation 543/69. Whilst it acknowledges that the relevant EC Treaty provisions assume the extension of the Community's power to cover the negotiation of international agreements, the Court goes on to argue that the adoption of Regulation 543/69 'necessarily vested in the Community power' to negotiate agreements within the scope of that Regulation. In this part of the judgment, the Court appears to be referring to the issue of the existence of the implied competence of the Community. If that is the case, the question which is raised is why it deemed the reference to secondary legislation necessary. It had already been established that external competence need not be expressly conferred; does it not follow that such competence 'flows' from Articles 70 and 71, all the more so in the light of the reference in that provision to international transport? The adoption of Regulation 543/69 is relevant only to the assessment of the nature of Community's competence and, yet, this is not what paragraphs 23–28 are about. Therefore, it is arguable that the reference to the adoption of Regulation 543/69 serves to reinforce the point about the existence of the Community's competence. This appears to be supported by the wording of the following paragraph which refers to 'this *grant* of power' which 'is *moreover* recognised by Article 3' of the Regulation.[6] If the power, that is to say the authority of the Community, followed from Article 71 EC, let alone Article 3 EC, was the reference to the specific provisions of the secondary measure necessary? It is suggested that the answer is negative: not only is reference to that provision the very last reference of the Court, but it was also viewed as 'recognis[ing]', that is not granting or conferring or even implying, the Community's power. What makes that paragraph of the judgment all the more interesting is the specific content of Article 3 of that Regulation which enables the Community to negotiate with third countries, if that were to prove necessary, in order to implement Regulation 543/69. In other words, the specific legal context is presented in such a way as to leave no doubt as to the existence of the Community's external competence: it 'flows' from primary law and is 'expressly recognised' by secondary law.

And yet, the Court goes on to state that the Community had been 'empowered' to negotiate the AETR agreement since the entry into force of Regulation 543/69. This is as redundant in the context of the establishment of the Community's implied competence as it is unhelpful for the determination of the latter's nature. Instead, the explanation given for the exclusivity enjoyed by the Community in the area covered by Regulation 543/69 is devoid of any analysis: it follows from the existence of Community powers 'since any steps taken outside the framework of the Community institutions would be incompatible with the unity of the Common Market and the uniform application of Community law'.[7] The Court

---

[6] Emphasis added.
[7] N1 above, para 31.

made no reference whatever to how collective action by the Member States would undermine the Community's policies in the area covered by the Agreement.

2.3. An Overall Comment

The introduction of the principle of implied powers has been characterised as 'a purely judicial construction'.[8] The teleological undertones of the concept, along with its implications for the right of the Member States to negotiate and conclude international agreements, are similar to the tone which had already defined the introduction of the major constitutional principles of the Community legal order. Indeed, the judgment in *AETR* should be examined in the broader context of the introduction of the principle of supremacy of Community law in *Costa*[9] and direct effect in *van Gen en Loos*.[10] Delivered in the very early 1970s, it followed from the constitutional milestones produced by the Court in order to consolidate the foundations of the new legal order which was in search of a normative identity.[11] In fact, by articulating the exclusive nature of the Community's implied external competence, the Court essentially applies the principle of supremacy broadly understood in so far as the exercise of the internal competence pre-empts Member States from acting either internally or externally.[12] In the area of EC external relations, it is this feature which distinguishes the exclusive nature of express competence from that of implied competence: the former is deemed as an *a priori* concept which produces its legal effects irrespective of any Community action.[13]

Viewed from this angle, the introduction of the *AETR* principle and the provision for the exclusivity of the Community's implied competence appear to be yet another illustration of the elaborate 'response' of the Court of Justice to the policy paralysis originating in the Luxembourg Accord. That infamous compromise, a deviation from primary law which lacked Treaty status, had occurred only six years earlier.[14] In his earlier work, Weiler juxtaposed decisional supranationalism, that is transfer of powers from the Member States to the Community pursuant to secondary legislation, and normative supranationalism, that is empowerment of the Community structures pursuant to legal principles introduced by the Court;

---

[8] A Dashwood, 'Implied External Competence of the EC' in M Koskenniemi. (ed), *International Law Aspects of the European Union* (The Hague: Kluwer Law International, 1998) 113.

[9] Case 6/64 *Costa v ENEL* [1964] ECR 585.

[10] Case 26/62 *van Gend en Loos v Nedherlandse Administratie der Belastingen* [1963] ECR 1.

[11] For criticism of the principle and its foundations, see T Hartley, *Constitutional Problems of the European Union* (Oxford: Hart Publishing, 1999) 35 ff.

[12] For an analysis of this judgment, along with the subsequent line of case law, as an illustration of the principle of pre-emption, see R Schütze, 'Parallel External Powers in the European Community: From "Cubist" Perspectives Towards "Naturalist" Constitutional Principles?' (2004) 23 *YEL* 225.

[13] This would be made clearer in the subsequent ruling in *Opinion 2/91* (re: *Convention No 170 ILO on safety in the use of chemicals at work*) [1993] ECR I–1061.

[14] See Bull EC 3–1966, 9.

he showed how, in the period of legislative stagnation following the Luxembourg compromise, when decisional supranationalism was malfunctioning, the Court was quite active and innovative.[15] Indeed, the case law of that era was of major constitutional significance: the wide scope of the principle of supremacy of Community law had been clearly affirmed[16] and its considerable implications for national courts spelled out;[17] the principle of direct effect had already been introduced[18] and would be extended to directives[19] not too long after the *AETR* judgment. Therefore, the *AETR* judgment appeared to be linked organically with the constitutional case law of the Court of that time.

And yet, there is something deeply troubling about the lack of clarity and consistency of the line of reasoning followed in *AETR*: as has been pointed out, the part of the judgment dealing with the specific issue of competence to conclude the AETR agreement 'reads as if separate versions had been written and then patched together rather untidily'.[20] Indeed, in setting out the definition, scope and implications of the principle of implied powers, the *AETR* judgment follows three degrees of abstraction: first, it does not refer to any EC Treaty provision at all (paragraphs 15–18); secondly, it refers to the general provision of Article 3 which mentions transport amongst the Community's objectives (paragraphs 20–22); finally, it refers to the specific primary and secondary rules on transport (paragraphs 23–31). This structure of the judgment, the underlying confusion between the issues of the existence and the nature of the Community's implied competence and the lack of clarity as to the implications of the positions laid down in each of the above parts of the judgment, all make the whole very difficult to read.

This is illustrated not only by the number of questions outlined above but also by the reception the new doctrine received. Pescatore even turned the confusion between existence and exercise which seemed to permeate the judgment into a principle. Writing in an extra-judicial capacity, he argued that 'it appears, on balance, that though the Court does by no means disregard the fact that a given agreement may in some of its parts pertain to the province of the Community and in part to the jurisdiction of the Member States, there is no place in the system for the construction of "concurrent" or "parallel" powers. In other words, whenever and so far as the matter belongs to the Community's sphere, jurisdiction over it is exclusive of any concurrent power of Member States'.[21] This was an extraordinary

---

[15] See JHH Weiler, 'The Community System: the Dual-Character of Supranationalism' (1981) 1 *YEL* 267.

[16] Case 11/70 *Internationale Handelsgesellschaft v. Einfuhr- und Vorratstelle für Getreide und Futtermittel* [1970] ECR 1125.

[17] Case 106/77 *Administrazione delle Finanze dello Stato v. Simmenthal SpA (Simmenthal II)* [1978] ECR 629.

[18] Case 26/62 *van Gend en Loos v Nederlandse Administratie der Belastingen* [1963] ECR 1, Case 9/70 *Grad v. Finanzamt Traunstein* [1970] ECR 825.

[19] Case 41/74 *Van Duyn v. Home Office* [1974] ECR 1337.

[20] Dashwood and Heliskoski, n3 above, at 7.

[21] P Pescatore, 'External Relations in the Case-Law of the Court of Justice of the European Communities' (1975) 12 *CMLRev* 615 at 624.

position to take as it was based on a homogenised conception of competence with no place for more subtle understanding of external relations.

Admittedly, a fully articulated analysis of all the implications of a legal doctrine rarely accompanies its very introduction, desirable though this might be. After all, the function of a judgment is to apply the law to the specific set of circumstances surrounding a specific legal question; the full details of the implications of that doctrine may be irrelevant to the questions sought to be addressed by the Court and unknown to the judges at the time of the judgment. However, even with this qualification in mind, the inconsistencies in which the judgment in *AETR* is shrouded and the lack of coherence of its structure are striking. This is all the more so when assessed against the judgments introducing the main constitution-al principles of Community law which the *AETR* principle purports to follow. The overtly teleological approach, articulated in the early parts of *Costa* and *van Gend en Loos*, was clear in providing the foundation for the constitutionalisation of the Community legal order.[22] Controversial though it may be, what Pescatore famously defined as '*une certaine idée de l'Europe*'[23] provided those judgments with a degree of internal coherence which one is longing to find in *AETR*.

The deficiencies of the judgment in *AETR* illustrate the highly controversial nature of the principles it sought to articulate. This had already become apparent before the Court. In his Opinion, Advocate General Dutheillet de Lamothe had asked the Court to declare the action inadmissible and concluded that 'it appears clear from the general scheme of the Treaty of Rome that its authors intended strictly to limit the Community's authority in external matters to the cases which they expressly laid down'.[24] He objected to the construction of Article 71 EC as the basis for implied external competence,[25] arguing that the reference to 'any other appropriate measures' was too vague a term to be capable of bestowing such important and specific power to the Community. Having pointed out that there were various EC Treaty provisions on commercial policy with general stipulations which were similar to that in Article 71 EC, he stated that 'it is certain that the authors of the Treaty did not consider that such provisions were sufficient to pro-vide a basis for a Community authority in external affairs'.[26] He also argued, 'albeit with some regret',[27] that not even the adoption of secondary legislation should be deemed as implying a corresponding external competence for the Community.[28]

This position was not unique. In the early days of European integration, one of its most prominent advocates and a subsequent member of the Court which

---

[22] For the elements of this process, see C Timmermans, 'The Constitutionalization of the European Union' (2002) 21 *YEL* 1.

[23] P Pescatore, 'The Doctrine of "Direct Effect": An Infant Disease of Community Law?' (1983) 8 *ELRev* 155, 157.

[24] At 293.

[25] At 290.

[26] *Ibid.*

[27] At 291.

[28] At 291–2.

delivered the judgment in *AETR*, had argued for a restrictive reading of the external competence of the Community.[29] The significance of the new principle was not lost on the wider public either: for instance, it was met with an editorial in *Le Monde* which expressed grave reservations about what was viewed as a supranational step *par excellence*.[30]

The specific challenges that the introduction of the principle of implied powers posed may also be understood in the light of another factor which placed the Court firmly within the territory of political controversy, namely the third states and international organisations with which the Community may enter into contractual relations. Whilst the application of constitutional principles and decision-making procedures in the internal sphere may be underpinned by legal disputes regarding the equilibrium of power between Members States and the Community, the involvement of third parties places these disputes in an entirely different context. It adds an international dimension which renders internal disputes about competence and procedure of a rather secondary nature. The legal obligations assumed by the Community and its Member States have specific legal consequences for the third countries and international organisations with which the Community negotiates; these consequences are not altered simply because of a dispute between the Community institutions or the Member States. The addition of this international dimension in the constitutionalisation of Community law introduces an element of irreversibility which renders the construction of the principles underlying the Community's external relations all the more significant.

Finally, when the Court of Justice delivered the *AETR* judgment, the first signs of the reactions that the principle of supremacy of Community law would provoke amongst national courts had appeared. The German Administrative Court had already referred the question of the relationship between Community law and the protection of human rights under national constitutional law and the Court had responded with the seminal *Internationale Handelsgesellschaft* judgment.[31] That judgment was to place the symbiosis of the Court of Justice with the German Constitutional Court upon a basis of doctrinal ambivalence for a long period of time.[32]

The above considerations may explain the deficiencies of the reasoning and structure of the judgment in *AETR*. They may even suggest that the distinct

---

[29] P Pescatore, 'Les relations exterieures des communautés européennés' (1961) 103/II *RdC* 1 at 97 which he later reconsidered expressly in n21 above, at n5.

[30] Reference to that editorial in JA Frowein, 'The Competences of the European Community in the Field of External Relations' in J Schwarze (ed), *The External Relations of the European Community, in particular EC-US Relations* (Baden-Baden: Nomos, 1989) 29.

[31] Case 11/70 [1970] ECR 1125.

[32] See the judgment of the Federal Constitutional Court (*Bundesverfassungsgericht*) in *Internationale Handelsgesellschaft v EVFG* [1974] 2 CMLR 540. That period appeared to have come to an end with the judgment of the *Bundesverfassungsgericht* in *Wüensche Handelsgesellschaft* [1987] 3 CMLR 225, only to get into a new phase with the landmark judgment in *Brunner v European Union Treaty* [1994] 1 CMLR 57. On the relationship between the Court of Justice and national courts more generally, see A-M Slaughter, A Stone Sweet and JHH Weiler (eds), *The European Court of Justice and National Courts: Doctrine and Jurisprudence* (Oxford: Hart Publishing, 1998).

emphasis of the judgment on the exclusive nature of the implied competence and its lingering confusion with the issue of existence might have been seen as necessary in order to buttress the introduction of this new principle in the Community legal order. The combined effect of these factors shed some light on the principal messages that the ruling in *AETR* conveys. First, the 'system of external relations'[33] of the Community is not immune to the constitutionalising process of the Community legal order. Instead, it is intertwined with the establishment of the internal market and stems from its regulation. Secondly, the reality of international relations may affect the application of legal principle. On the substance of the dispute, the Commission's action was dismissed. The negotiations for the conclusion of the AETR Agreement were viewed by the Court as merely another part of the negotiating process which had already produced an agreement as early as in 1962, albeit one which had not been ratified. As Regulation 543/69 had not been adopted then, the competence of the Member States in the area covered by the Agreement had not been given up. Therefore, whilst the Agreement originated in and had been negotiated at a period when the Member States were competent in the area covered therein, at the time of its conclusion that competence had been transferred to the Community. However, this legal development had to be assessed in its factual context in relation to which the Court ruled as follows:[34]

> At that stage of the negotiations, to have suggested to the third countries concerned that there was now a new distribution of powers within the Community might well have jeopardized the successful outcome of the negotiations, as was indeed recognized by the Commission's representative in the course of the Council's deliberations.

It was for that reason that the solution articulated in the Resolution challenged by the Commission was sanctioned and the action dismissed. The application of strict and broadly-worded principles in a restrictive manner is not a novelty in the Court's constitutional case law. It is recalled, for instance, that the introduction of the controversial principle of direct effect of directives in *Van Duyn* was of no help to Mrs van Duyn.[35] In their influential critique, Tridimas and Eeckhout show that the balance between legal principle and pragmatism illustrated in *AETR* constitutes a common theme underlying the Court's case law on EC international relations.[36] In terms of this analysis, suffice it to point out the following: its deficient reasoning and problematic structure notwithstanding, the judgment in *AETR* made it clear that, in its international relations, the exclusive nature of the Community's implied competence would not necessarily exclude the Member States from negotiating and concluding international agreements. This is a point which will re-emerge in subsequent case law.

---

[33] N1 above, at para 19.
[34] N1 above, para 86.
[35] Case 41/74 *Van Duyn v Home Office* [1974] ECR 1337.
[36] T Tridimas and P Eeckhout, 'The External Competence of the Community and the Case-Law of the Court of Justice: Principle versus Pragmatism' (1995) 14 *YEL* 143.

3. BUILDING UPON THE FOUNDATION

The messages conveyed by the judgment in *AETR* were also present in the judgment delivered in Joined Cases 3, 4 and 6/76 *Cornelis Kramer and others*.[37] These were references from Dutch district courts about the application of the 1959 North East Atlantic Fisheries Convention. All but two of the then Member States were parties to the Convention whose aim was 'to ensure the conservation of the fish stocks and the rational exploitation of the fisheries of the North-East Atlantic Ocean and adjacent waters'. The Convention set out a specific institutional framework: a Fisheries Commission was established in order to make recommendations to the Contracting States on measures falling within the scope of the Convention. Pursuant to a measure adopted in 1970, the Commission became responsible for recommending measures aimed at the regulation of the amount of total catch and fishing effort and the allocation of those amounts to Contracting States. Each Contracting State was under a legal duty to give effect to those recommendations adopted under certain procedural requirements unless an objection was raised within a set period. The references from the Dutch courts were about criminal proceedings initiated against fishermen on grounds of violation of Netherlands rules implementing a recommendation about fishing for sole and plaice.

One of the questions referred to the Court of Justice was about competence: did the Community alone have the competence to enter into commitments such as those undertaken by most of its Member States under the system established by the North-East Atlantic Fisheries Convention? In addressing this question, the Court followed the path already set in *AETR* five years previously. In the absence of an EC Treaty provision endowing the Community with express external competence, regard should be had of the 'general system of Community law'. Its express legal personality entails the Community's capacity to enter into contractual relationships with third countries and international organisations over the whole field of objectives set out in Part One of the EC Treaty; it is 'the whole scheme of Community law' and 'its substantive provisions' which establish the competence of the Community in a particular case; that competence 'may equally flow implicitly' from other provisions of the Treaty and from measures adopted by the Community institutions within the framework of those provisions. It is in this last limb of its line of reasoning that the Court deviates slightly from its *AETR* judgment by adding the Act of Accession to the measures which may establish the external competence.[38]

The Court then stated that the Community did have the competence 'on the internal level . . . to take any measures for the conservation of the biological resources of the sea, measures which include the fixing of catch quotas and their allocation between the different Member States'.[39] This 'follows' from a number of

---

[37] [1976] ECR 1279.
[38] *Ibid*, paras 19–20.
[39] *Ibid*, paras 30–33.

primary and secondary EC rules, along with the Act of Accession, 'taken as a whole'.[40] Primary rules cover Article 3(e) EC including the adoption of a common agricultural and fisheries policy in the Community's objectives; Article 32(3) and Annex II to the EC Treaty on fishery products; Article 33 EC specifying the rationalisation of production and the guarantee of availability of supplies as objectives of CAP; Article 34(1)–(3) EC requiring the establishment of a common organisation of agricultural markets and Article 37(2) EC authorising the Council to adopt secondary rules to that effect. Finally, secondary rules include Regulations 2141/70[41] and 2142/70[42] which authorise the Council 'to adopt the necessary conservation measures' in cases where 'there is a risk of over-fishing of certain stocks in the maritime waters' under the sovereignty of a Member State. Finally, the Act of Accession expressly enables the Council to 'determine conditions for fishing with a view to ensuring protection of the fishing grounds and conservation of the biological resources of the sea'.[43]

The Court held that the authority of the Community was not confined to the sea under the sovereignty of its Member States; instead, it extended to fishing on the high seas, a conclusion deemed to 'follow' from the objectives of Regulation 2141/70 and Article 102 of the Act of Accession and 'moreover from the very nature of things'.[44] This assertion led to the following conclusion: [45]

> The only way to ensure the conservation of the biological resources of the sea both effectively and equitably is through a system of rules binding on all the states concerned, including non-member countries. In these circumstances it follows from the very duties and powers of the Community on the internal level that the Community has authority to enter into commitments for the conservation of the resources of the sea.

Having established the existence of the Community's competence, the Court went on to assess whether the Member States retained the power to assume international obligations in the area of fisheries conservation. The starting point for its analysis was the fact that, when the Netherlands gave effect to international duties adopted within the framework of the 1959 Convention, the authority of the Community to adopt similar measures, whilst in existence, had not been exercised, at least 'not . . . fully'.[46] Indeed, the secondary measures adopted within the fisheries framework had merely enabled the Community to adopt legislation in order to regulate the areas subsequently regulated by the Member States under the framework of the 1959 Convention.

It was in the absence of Community action that the Member States retained their power to act externally, hence under the 1959 Convention too, and subsequently

---

[40] *Ibid.*
[41] [1970] OJ Spec Ed (III) 703.
[42] *Ibid*, at 707.
[43] Art 102 of the Act of Accession.
[44] Paras 30–33 of the judgment.
[45] *Ibid.*
[46] Para 39.

ensure compliance with their international obligations by adopting internal legislation. However, the national competence, whilst retained, was qualified in two ways: on the one hand, it was of a transitional nature because it would come to an end at the date on which, according to Article 102 of the Act of Accession, the Council would have adopted internal legislation for the conservation of the resources of the sea; on the other hand, it was held that 'the Member States are now bound by Community obligations in their negotiations within the framework of the Convention and of other comparable agreements'.[47] Those obligations were based on the duty of loyal cooperation laid down in Article 10 EC and the, now repealed, duty of common action in international organisations of an economic character.[48]

The first remarkable feature of the judgment in *Kramer* is the wide construction of the scope of Community's competence. The reference to the aim of 'encouraging rational use of' and the 'conservation of the biological resources of the sea' in secondary legislation and the Act of Accession respectively is viewed as extending the material scope of EC competence to fishing on the high seas, too. That conclusion was reached not only on the basis of the wording of the above provisions but also 'from the very nature of things'. It might appear curious that the judgment in *Kramer* should be as much about internal competence as about external one—and yet, it was the emphasis on the teleological interpretation of the former that led to the equally teleological interpretation of the latter. This is what has been called 'the principle of complementarity'.[49]

In terms of the construction of the Community's competence to conclude the Agreement, the tone of the judgment is similar to that in *AETR*: whilst widely defined and forcefully articulated, the external competence had not as yet excluded Member States from negotiating international agreeements. In a clear illustration of the dynamic nature of the Community's international relations, that effect was to come about three years later: in an action by the Commission against the United Kingdom, the Court opined that the expiry of the transitional period of the provision of the Act of Accession of Denmark, Ireland and the United Kingdom on fisheries conservation had affected the position of the Member States: these had become 'no longer entitled to exercise any power of their own in the matter of conservation measures in the waters under their jurisdiction' as 'the adoption of such measures, with the restrictions which they imply as regards fishing activities, is a matter . . . of Community law'.[50]

4. REINFORCING THE PRINCIPLE OF IMPLIED COMPETENCE

In introducing the principle of implied competence in *AETR*, the Court drew upon the link between the internal and external powers of the Community in

---

[47] *Ibid.*
[48] This duty had been laid down in Art 116 EC.
[49] Dashwood and Heliskoski, n3 above, 10.
[50] Case 804/79 *Commission v United Kingdom* [1981] ECR 1054, para 18. See also Case 21/81 *Criminal proceedings against Daniël Bout and BV I. Bout en Zonen* [1982] ECR 381, at para 6.

order to establish exclusivity. Combined with the confusion between the issues of the existence and nature of external competence, this raised questions about the Community's competence in areas where there had been no internal legislation. Such questions were addressed in *Opinion 1/76*.[51] The Commission asked the Court to rule on the compatibility of a draft Agreement establishing a European laying-up fund for inland waterway vessels with the EC Treaty. The Agreement aimed at setting out a system which would eliminate the disturbances arising from the surplus carrying capacity for goods by inland waterway in the Rhine and Moselle basins and by the Dutch waterways and the German inland waterways linked to the Rhine basin. It was negotiated by the Commission, on behalf of the Community pursuant to a Council Decision, and Switzerland. In addition, six Member States, namely Belgium, Germany, France, Luxembourg, the Netherlands and Great Britain, participated, as they had already been parties either to the revised Convention for the Navigation of the Rhine, signed in 1868, or to the Convention for the Canalization of the Moselle signed in 1956. What was at the core of the Commission's request was the provision in the draft Agreement for a decision-making and adjudicating system which involved for the Community a certain delegation of powers to bodies independent from the Community institutions. The Commission argued that that delegation was compatible with the EC Treaty and its request for an Opinion was merely based on its concern for legal certainty.

The issue which first arose was whether the Community had the competence to conclude that Agreement in the absence of internal legislation on the matter. The Court opined as follows:

1.   The object of the system laid down by the draft agreement and expressed in the statute Annexed thereto is to rationalize the economic situation of the inland waterway transport industry in a geographical region in which transport by inland waterway is of special importance within the whole network of international transport. Such a system is doubtless an important factor in the common transport policy, the establishment of which is included in the activities of the Community laid down in Article 3 of the EEC Treaty. In order to implement this policy, Article 75 of the Treaty [now Article 71] instructs the Council to lay down according to the prescribed procedure common rules applicable to international transport to or from the territory of one or more Member States. This Article also supplies, as regards the Community, the necessary legal basis to establish the system concerned.

2.   In this case, however, it is impossible fully to attain the objective pursued by means of the establishment of common rules pursuant to Article 75 of the Treaty [now Article 71], because of the traditional participation of vessels from a third state, Switzerland, in navigation by the principal waterways in question, which are subject to the system of freedom of navigation established by international agreements of long standing. It has thus

---

[51] *Opinion 1/76 (re: Draft Agreement establishing a European laying-up fund for inland waterway vessels)* [1977] ECR 741.

been necessary to bring Switzerland into the scheme in question by means of an international agreement with this third state.

3.   The power of the Community to conclude such an agreement is not expressly laid down in the Treaty. However, the court has already had occasion to state, most recently in its judgment of 14 July 1976 in Joined Cases 3, 4 and 6/76, *Cornelis Kramer and Others*, (1976) ECR 1279, that authority to enter into international commitments may not only arise from an express attribution by the Treaty, but equally may flow implicitly from its provisions. The court has concluded *inter alia* that whenever Community law has created for the institutions of the Community powers within its internal system for the purpose of attaining a specific objective, the Community has authority to enter into the international commitments necessary for the attainment of that objective even in the absence of an express provision in that connexion.

4.   This is particularly so in all cases in which internal power has already been used in order to adopt measures which come within the attainment of common policies. It is, however, not limited to that eventuality. Although the internal Community measures are only adopted when the international agreement is concluded and made enforceable, as is envisaged in the present case by the proposal for a Regulation to be submitted to the Council by the Commission, the power to bind the Community *vis-à-vis* third countries nevertheless flows by implication from the provisions of the Treaty creating the internal power and in so far as the participation of the Community in the international agreement is, as here, necessary for the attainment of one of the objectives of the Community.

The Court went on to apply these principles to the specific EC Treaty provisions on transport. It interpreted Article 75(1)(d) EC, according to which the Council has the power to lay down 'any other appropriate provisions' in order to attain the common transport policy, as entailing that 'the Community is . . . not only entitled to enter into contractual relations with a third country in this connexion but also has the power, while observing the provisions of the Treaty, to cooperate with that country in setting up an appropriate organism such as the public international institution which it is proposed to establish under the name of the "European Laying-up Fund for Inland Waterway Vessels"'.[52]

The main contribution of the ruling in *Opinion 1/76* in our understanding of the principle of implied competence is the dissociation of its existence from the exercise of the internal competence. This was a welcome clarification of the application of the doctrine of implied competence. Viewed from this angle, the principles articulated by the Court may be summarised as follows: a system of rationalisation of the inland waterway transport industry such as the one laid down in the Draft Agreement was an important factor in the Common Transport Policy covered by Article 71 EC which also provides the legal basis for its establishment. However, the adoption of common rules under that provision would not 'fully attain the objective pursued' for practical reasons. That turns out not to be a problem because the Community has the power to conclude international agreements

---

[52] Para 5.

'whenever Community law has created for the institutions of the Community powers within its internal system for the purpose of attaining a specific objective' provided that the conclusion of such agreement is 'necessary for the attainment of that objective'.[53]

A first reading of the ruling reveals the absence of any reference to the nature of the Community's competence: the part of the Court's ruling dealing with the general principle of external competence (paragraphs 1–5) appears to refer only to the existence of implied competence. This is all the more striking in the light of the confusion between the issues of existence and nature of the implied competence which had underpinned the *AETR* judgment. In *Opinion 1/76*, the participation of the six Member States was sanctioned. The reason for this was the substantive context of the Agreement: the mechanism which it aimed at establishing entailed the amendment of provisions of two pre-existing Agreements, namely the Convention of Manheim for the Navigation of the Rhine and the Convention of Luxembourg on the Canalization of the Moselle. As these agreements had been concluded in 1868 and 1956 respectively, their amendment could only be achieved by the Member States which had concluded them. After all, Article 307(2) EC requires that Member States take all appropriate measures to eliminate incompatibilities between agreements they had concluded prior to their accession to the Community and EC law. The amendment of those pre-existing duties was laid down in Article 3 of the Agreement and undertaken by the six Member States. It was for this reason that the participation of Member States along with the Community was sanctioned by the Court. In order to bring this point home, the Court went on to stress that 'the participation of these States in the Agreement must be considered as being solely for this purpose and not as necessary for the attainment of other features of the system'.[54]

To summarise, the participation of a number of Member States in the conclusion of the Agreement in question was sanctioned only because the conclusion of the latter would bring about the amendment of obligations already assumed by those States prior to the establishment of the Community. Whilst avoiding the reference to the term 'exclusivity', the line of reasoning followed by the Court may appear to be couched in such terms. Followed up to its logical conclusion, it appears to suggest that, had there been no prior legal regime binding on Member States and affected by the Draft Agreement, the participation of those Member States would not have been considered necessary for the establishment of the new navigation system and, hence, their participation in the conclusion of the Agreement would not have been sanctioned.

Is the above not an acknowledgment of exclusivity? Whilst the line of reasoning put forward in *Opinion 1/76* appears to provide an affirmative answer,[55] it is

---

[53] Para 3.
[54] *Ibid.*
[55] See, for instance, T Tridimas, 'The WTO and OECD Opinions' in Dashwood and Hillion, n3 above, 48 at 55.

difficult to see how such conclusion may be sustained. As the common transport policy does not fall within the exclusive competence of the Community, it is difficult to see how, in the absence of common rules, the Member States would have violated their Community law obligations had they concluded an agreement with Switzerland in the area covered by the Rhine Convention.[56] What complicates matters even further is the Court's apparent effort to present the participation of Member States as legally necessary when, in fact, this is questionable. Indeed, the duty of Member States to comply with Article 307(2) EC does not necessarily entail their participation in an Agreement: instead, the Member States could have amended the pre-existing Manheim and Luxembourg Conventions unilaterally on the basis of public international law. Furthermore, were it accurate, the above reading of the ruling in *Opinion 1/76* would be tantamount to suggesting a potential expansion of the scope of exclusivity. Could that have been the intention of the Court in delivering only its third ruling on what appeared to be a highly controversial principle?

This question would arise again in subsequent case law. At this juncture, suffice it to point out that what emerges from the above is a picture of fragmentation: the first part of the judgment appears to refer to the existence of the Community's implied external competence, whereas the second part appears to make a leap to a rather convoluted articulation of the nature of that competence. The confusion as to the precise implications of the principles laid down in *Opinion 1/76* is compounded by yet another piece of the 'implied competence puzzle', that of necessity. It is recalled that the Court ruled that, in the absence of internal legislation, the Community's external competence is implied 'in so far as the participation of the Community in the international agreement is . . . necessary for the attainment of one of the objectives of the Community'.[57] Whilst ruling that it was applicable on the conclusion of the Agreement in question, the Court did not elaborate on the definition of this term: would it be subject to an inherently indeterminate policy assessment?[58] To what extent would considerations related to the political expedience or efficiency be relevant?

The lack of clarity underlying the Court's line of reasoning is striking.[59] And in a perverse way, it also provides the link between *Opinion 1/76* and the judgment in *AETR*: in both, the Court seeks to set out the principles pursuant to which the external competence of the Community may be exercised within the framework of a legal order functionally understood; in neither is there a consistent normative foundation for the newly introduced principles articulated or a coherent account

---

[56] Tridimas and Eeckhout, n36 above, at 167; Dashwood and Heliskoski, n3 above, at 13.

[57] N51 above, para 4.

[58] See, for instance, M Hardy, '*Opinion 1/76* of the Court of Justice: The Rhine Case and the Treaty-Making Powers of the Community' (1977) 14 *CMLRev* 561.

[59] However, it has been pointed out that it reflects the substance of the request before the Court:, that is whether the participation of Member States in the Agreement on navigation on the Rhine which had already been decided to be concluded by the Community would produce undermining effects: see Dashwood and Heliskoski, n3, above, at 14.

of their legal implications provided. These deficiencies notwithstanding, the principal message conveyed in both rulings is clear: widely though the competence of the Community to act externally may be construed, it does not necessarily prevent the Member States from participating in the conclusion of international agreements along with the Community as a matter of fact.

5. THE PERIOD OF ADJUSTMENT: IN SEARCH OF LIMITS

The construction of the principle of implied competence, as introduced in *AETR* and further developed in *Opinion 1/76*, was outlined above as based upon two assumptions: the forceful articulation of the presence of the Community's external competence coexisted with the parallel presence of the Member States in the context of the negotiation and conclusion of international agreements. However, that presence was attributed to the specific practical and legal contexts raised before the Court, whilst their normative foundation, precise preconditions and general legal implications were left unclear.

In the early 1990s, the case-law of the Court of Justice appeared to be more focused on the clarification of the application of the principle of implied competence. This became apparent in *Opinion 2/91*.[60] The subject matter of this request was the conclusion of a Convention signed in 1990 under the auspices of the International Labour Organisation (ILO) on safety in the use of chemicals at work. The Commission argued that the Community alone was competent to conclude the agreement on the basis of its internal competence on health and safety under Article 137(2) (ex 118a) EC. Whilst not a party to the ILO Convention, the Community has observer status. However, its participation in the implementation of the Convention had already been an issue of contention. Any controversies had been addressed on the basis of *ad hoc* procedural arrangements which appeared to come to an end when the Council, with the agreement of the Commission, adopted a decision in December 1986. That measure set out a procedural mechanism whose objective was the general management of the participation of the Community and the Member States in the ILO framework.

The material scope of this arrangement is strictly confined to areas falling within the exclusive competence of the Community. In terms of decision-making, it provided that the Community would reply to the ILO questionnaires by means of a Council decision following a proposal from the Commission. In terms of representation, it provided that the Commission would speak on behalf of the Community in the Conference and act in close consultation with the Member States whilst the latter could retain their right to speak at the plenary sessions of the Conference. It was on the basis of that Decision that the Commission submitted a proposal to the Council in relation to an ILO questionnaire on Convention

---

[60] *Opinion 2/91 (re: Convention No 170 ILO on safety in the use of chemicals at work)* [1993] ECR I–1061.

No 170. Various Member States chose to reply to the ILO directly, hence deviating from the system set out in the above Decision. The reason for this was the Member States' contention that the subject matter of the Convention was not covered by the Community's exclusive competence. The Commission then requested that it be authorised to negotiate the Convention on behalf of the Community. The Council gave its agreement. The decision adopted to that effect also required that the Commission be in close consultation with the Member States and provided that the latter would retain their right to express views on aspects of the Convention which fell within their competence. Following the adoption of Convention No 170, the Commission informed the Council that it was under a legal duty to inform the International Labour Office that, in terms of the ILO Constitution, the competent authorities were the Community institutions. It was following that request that the dispute about the nature of the Community competence resurfaced, as a number of Member States did not accept that Convention No 170 fell within the scope of the Community's exclusive competence.

The objective of Convention No 170 was to protect workers against the harmful effects of using chemicals in the workplace. Its content sought to achieve this in various ways: it set out consultation procedures between Contracting States and representative organisations of employers and workers, it authorised national authorities to prohibit, restrict or regulate the use of hazardous chemicals, it laid down rules on the classification of chemical products and their transport, labelling and marketing, it defined the relevant responsibilities of employers and the duties and rights of workers.

5.1. Restating the General Principles

The core of the substantive issues raised by the Commission in its request for an Opinion was whether the conclusion of Convention No 170 fell within the competence of the Community and, if so, whether that competence was exclusive. In approaching this issue, the Court deemed it necessary to articulate the general premises on which the Community's implied competence may arise and the circumstances in which that competence may become exclusive. It did so in a distinct part of its ruling which reads like a summary of the general principles of EC external relations in the light of the pre-existing case law.

The Court's analysis may be divided into three parts. First, it deals with the issue of the existence of implied competence using its ruling in *Opinion 1/76* as the starting point of its analysis: [61]

> authority to enter into international commitments may not only arise from an express attribution by the Treaty, but may also flow implicitly from its provisions. The Court concluded, in particular, that whenever Community law created for the institutions of the Community powers within its internal system for the purpose of attaining a specific

---

[61] Para 7 of the ruling.

objective, the Community had authority to enter into the international commitments necessary for the attainment of that objective even in the absence of an express provision in that connection. At paragraph 20 in its judgment in . . . *Kramer and Others* . . . , the Court had already pointed out that such authority could flow by implication from other measures adopted by the Community institutions within the framework of the Treaty provisions or the acts of accession.

Secondly, the Court examines the issue of the nature of the Community's external competence and makes a distinction: when expressly provided for in the EC Treaty, that competence is exclusive; as regards its implied competence, its exclusive nature 'may . . . depend on the scope of the measures which have been adopted by the Community institutions for the application of [EC Treaty] provisions and which are of such kind as to deprive the Member States of an area of competence which they were able to exercise previously on a transitional basis'.[62] The foundation for that proposition is the *AETR* statement: 'where Community rules have been promulgated for the attainment of the objectives of the Treaty, the Member States cannot, outside the framework of the Community institutions, assume obligations which might affect those rules or alter their scope'.[63]

In addition, the Court for the first time expressly clarifies the material scope of exclusivity in relation to the Community's implied powers: it is not only in relation to common policies that the Member States are precluded from acting when the Community's competence has become exclusive. This conclusion was based on two premises: on the one hand, the broad material scope of the requirement of loyalty laid down in Article 10 EC covers 'all the areas corresponding to the objectives of the Treaty';[64] on the other hand, there was the need to ensure that the Community's 'tasks and the objectives of the Treaty would [not] be compromised if Member States were able to enter into international commitments containing rules capable of affecting rules already adopted in areas falling outside common policies or altering their scope'.[65]

Thirdly, the Court deals with the cases where the Community's implied competence is not exclusive. As that competence 'is shared between the Community and the Member States', 'negotiation and implementation of the agreement require joint action by the Community and the Member States'.[66]

5.2. Applying the Principles to Convention No 170 ILO

In approaching the specific question of competence raised by the Commission, the Court started off by identifying the objective of Convention No 170, namely

---

[62] Para 9.
[63] *Ibid,* referring to para 22 of the judgment in *AETR.*
[64] Para 10.
[65] Para 11.
[66] Para 12 with reference to *Kramer,* n37 above, paras 39–45 and *Opinion 1/78* [1979] ECR 2871, para 60.

to prevent or reduce the incidence of chemically induced illnesses and injuries at work. It, then, noted that that also fell within the social provisions of the EC Treaty. Indeed, the improvement of the working environment to protect workers' health and safety is defined in Article 137(1)(a) EC as an area where the Community supports and complements national actions by means of directives setting out minimum standards. Having established the existence of internal competence over the areas covered by Convention No 170, the Court had no difficulty in asserting the existence of an external implied competence, albeit not without pointing out that the subject-matter of that Convention coincided with that of several directives adopted under the above EC Treaty provision.[67]

The analysis, then, turned to whether the implied external competence was exclusive. The Court focused on the effects of the rules laid down in Convention No 170. In the light of the fact that the adoption of internal legislation pursuant to Article 137(2) EC would 'not prevent any Member State from maintaining or introducing more stringent protective measures compatible with this Treaty',[68] the Court ruled as follows:

> the provisions of Convention No 170 are not of such a kind as to affect rules adopted pursuant to Article [137 EC]. If, on the one hand, the Community decides to adopt rules which are less stringent than those set out in an ILO convention, Member States may, in accordance with Article [137(4) EC], adopt more stringent measures for the protection of working conditions or apply for that purpose the provisions of the relevant ILO convention. If, on the other hand, the Community decides to adopt more stringent measures than those provided for under an ILO convention, there is nothing to prevent the full application of Community law by the Member States under Article 19(8) of the ILO Constitution, which allows Members to adopt more stringent measures than those provided for in conventions or recommendations adopted by that organization.[69]

In other words, ILO Convention No 170 did not fall within the exclusive competence of the Community because its conclusion by the Member States could not affect the content of secondary legislation to be adopted pursuant to Article 137(2) EC. This was a conclusion which the Commission had sought to challenge on the basis of two further arguments. The first one was of a practical nature: it would be difficult to assess whether a specific provision would be more favourable for the protection of working conditions or not; therefore, in order to avoid a violation of the ILO Convention, Member States might become reluctant to adopt measures necessary for the working environment under Article 137(2) EC, hence impairing the development of Community law. The legal argument put forward

---

[67] Para 17.
[68] Art 137(4) EC.
[69] Para 18.

by the Commission consisted of an alternative foundation for exclusivity, namely secondary legislation adopted under Article 100 EC.

Both arguments were rejected by the Court. The practical one was dismissed in a rather summary manner: 'difficulties, such as those referred to by the Commission, which might arise for the legislative function of the Community cannot constitute the basis for exclusive Community competence'.[70] As for the legal argument, the Court pointed out that the secondary provisions adopted under Article 100 EC laid down minimum requirements, with specific reference to legislation on the protection of workers from the risks related to exposure to chemical, physical and biological agents at work[71] and other detailed directives adopted pursuant to this.

5.3. A Foundation for Exclusivity

However, the Court identified a specific area which fell within the exclusive competence of the Community. The basis for this conclusion was a number of directives whose subject-matter fell within that covered by Part III of ILO Convention No 170. The main characteristic was the introduction of more than minimum requirements. Reference was made to Community rules on the classification, packaging and labelling of dangerous substances[72] and dangerous preparations,[73] adopted under Articles 100 EC and 100a EC respectively. The Court observed that these rules were, in certain respects, more favourable for workers, and their content was quite detailed. Having pointed out that the scope of ILO Convention No 170 was wider than that of the abovementioned Directives, the Court went on to opine as follows:[74]

> While there is no contradiction between these provisions of the Convention and those of the directives mentioned, it must nevertheless be accepted that Part III of Convention No 170 is concerned with an area which is already covered to a large extent by Community rules progressively adopted since 1967 with a view to achieving an ever greater degree of harmonization and designed, on the one hand, to remove barriers to trade resulting from differences in legislation from one Member State to another and, on the other hand, to provide, at the same time, protection for human health and the environment.
>
> In those circumstances, it must be considered that the commitments arising from Part III of Convention No 170, falling within the area covered by the directives cited above in paragraph 22, are of such a kind as to affect the Community rules laid in those directives and that consequently Member States cannot undertake such commitments outside the framework of the Community institutions.

---

[70] Para 20.
[71] Dir 80/1107/EEC [1980] OJ L 327/8.
[72] Dir 67/548/EEC [1967] OJ Spec Ed. 234, amended by Dir 79/831/EEC [1979] OJ L 259/10.
[73] Dir 88/379/EEC [1988] OJ L/187/14.
[74] Paras 25–26.

5.4. Other Areas of Shared Competence

Finally, in examining the content of ILO Convention No 170, the Court identified other areas which fell within the joint competence of the Community and the Member States. These are included in the general principles relating to the implementation of the Convention laid down in its Part II. Whilst general in nature, it was held that they fell within the Community's competence 'in so far as it has been established that the substantive provisions of Convention No 170 come within the Community's sphere of competence'.[75] These provisions are about the development of cooperation between organisations of employers and workers as regards the adoption and periodical review of safety measures on the use of chemicals at work. The Court then pointed out the following:[76]

> Admittedly, as Community law stands at present, social policy and in particular cooperation between both sides of industry are matters which fall predominantly within the competence of the Member States.

> This matter, has not, however, been withdrawn entirely from the competence of the Community. It should be noted, in particular, that, according to Article 118b of the Treaty, the Commission is required to endeavour to develop the dialogue between management and labour at European level.

> Consequently, the question whether international commitments, whose purpose is consultation with representative organizations of employers and workers, fall within the competence of the Member State or of the Community cannot be separated from the objective pursued by such consultation.

Similarly, the Community was competent over the assumption of supervisory powers aimed at ensuring compliance with the substantive content of the Convention even if those powers were to be exercised by national authorities. After all, even on the internal plane, Member States could be authorised to exercise supervisory powers in areas covered by Community law.[77] The logic of this provision is clear: once competence over the substantive content of an international agreement has been established, that competence is presumed to extend to the supervisory framework designed to ensure compliance with that agreement. However, this should not be viewed as an unqualified statement. The wording of the ruling infers that the extent of those powers could be central to the issue of competence; it might be the case that, if the supervision of the agreement were to be exercised entirely by the Member States, the Community's competence would not extend over the relevant provisions.

---

[75] Para 28.
[76] Paras 30–32.
[77] The Court referred to Dir 80/1107, n71 above, and the provision of Art 4.

5.5. The Duty of Cooperation

Having established that the conclusion of ILO Convention No 170 fell within the joint competence of the Community and its Member States, the Court went on to point out the following:

> [I]t is important to ensure that there is close association between the institutions of the Community and the Member States both in the process of negotiation and conclusion and in the fulfilment of the obligations entered into. This duty of cooperation, to which attention was drawn in the context of the EAEC Treaty, must also apply in the context of the EEC Treaty since it results from the requirement of unity in the international representation of the Community.

> In this case, cooperation between the Community and the Member states is all the more necessary in view of the fact that the former cannot, as international law stands at present, itself conclude an ILO convention and must do so through the medium of the Member States.

5.6. Comment on the Ruling in *Opinion 2/91*

In its ruling, the Court sought for the first time to articulate the principles underpinning the Community's external competence with a certain degree of clarity. In so doing, it clarified a number of issues pertaining to the implied competence: its exclusive nature may follow from the adoption of internal legislation in areas not falling within the common policies; whilst the scope of Community legislation adopted pursuant to the exercise of the internal competence would determine whether the external competence became exclusive, when the former consists of minimum rules the latter would be shared with the Member States. This function of *Opinion 2/91* was highlighted by the clear division between the issues of existence and exercise of the Community's external competence which underlies the Court's analysis.

The clarification of certain issues notwithstanding, the Court's line of reasoning did not provide complete clarity. One feature of the ruling is the Court's attempt to avoid a detailed analysis of the internal rules whose scope was deemed to give rise to exclusivity externally. Indeed, whilst reference was made in general 'to a number of directives adopted in the areas covered by the ILO Convention No 170' which 'contain rules which are *more than minimum requirements*', specific analysis was provided only 'for instance' to two such measures.[78] What light does this shed to the correlation between the scope of internal legislation and the nature of external competence? Is the existence of merely a handful of secondary measures sufficient to give rise to exclusivity? Indeed, the Court further pointed out that the external competence becomes exclusive when the subject-matter of

---

[78] Para 22 (emphasis added).

the agreement to be concluded falls within an area which is 'already covered *to a large extent* by Community rules *progressively* adopted . . . *with a view to achieving an ever greater degree of harmonization*'.[79]

This formula may appear problematic in so far as it does not provide for a clear test which would allow the Community institutions and the Member States to ascertain the nature of their competence. How advanced should harmonisation be in order to give rise to exclusivity, and on which criteria should this assessment be based? Whilst this process may be fraught with uncertainty and subject to a qualitative judgment, the Court's ruling appears to suggest a rather automatic deduction. It is noteworthy that this line of reasoning corresponds with the regulatory climate of the era: in the light of the status of minimum harmonisation legislation as the cornerstone of the single market project, to have concluded otherwise would have been tantamount to rendering exclusivity the norm in the Community's external relations; on the other hand, in those specific areas which appear to be subject to detailed regulation, the external competence should be presumed to be exclusive.

Be that as it may, compared to the judgment in *AETR,* the Court's approach in *Opinion 2/91* suggests a stricter definition of the conditions under which the Community's implied competence may become exclusive. It also suggests that, once it has arisen, exclusivity produces its effects in a rather automatic manner. What is noteworthy in the ruling is the absence of any assessment as to whether unilateral action by the Member States might, in fact, undermine the exercise by the Community of its implied competence. In *Opinion 2/91*, the Court accepted that such an assessment was not necessary, hence construing the effect of national action in very broad terms.[80] If this analysis is correct, then a point of convergence between express and implied competence of the Community emerges. It is recalled that, in its ruling, the Court suggested that the exclusive nature of the express competence follows precisely from its express provision—this is what has been described as 'pre-emptive exclusivity'.[81] In the case of implied competence, once the internal competence has been exercised in a detailed manner, the exclusive nature of the external competence follows from the harmonising effect of internal legislation, the absence of a specific contradiction notwithstanding. In both cases, the assessment of the nature of the external competence is independent of a substantive determination of whether exclusivity is in fact essential for the protection of the *acquis communautaire* pursuant to the characteristics of the specific case under review.

Another interesting feature of *Opinion 2/91* is the light it appears to shed on the doctrine of necessity already elaborated in *Opinion 1/76*. It is noteworthy that, in the first part of the ruling, the starting point for the Court's analysis of the

---

[79] Para 25 (emphasis added).

[80] See D O'Keeffe, 'Exclusive, Concurrent and Shared Competence' in Dashwood and Hillion, n3 above, 179 at 187.

[81] Dashwood and Heliskoski, n3 above, at 16.

general principles of external competence was *Opinion 1/76* rather than the *AETR* judgment.[82] This might appear to provide a link with the *rationale* underpinning the argument that the conclusion of ILO Convention No 170 falls within the scope of Community competence. It is recalled that the Court referred to the internal competence of the Community to adopt legislation in the area of health and safety requirements for workers under Article 138 EC.

In that regard, Dashwood and Heliskoski have suggested that the principle of necessity may explain this conclusion: 'possession of treaty-making power by the Community facilitates the adoption of such measures: for instance, the raising of minimum standards for Community workers may prove more easily acceptable if the possibility exists of negotiating a similar improvement in third countries, thereby countering so-called "social dumping". The test applied in practice by the Court may, we suggest, be formulated thus: does the Community need treaty-making power to ensure the optimal use, over time, of its expressly conferred internal competence?'.[83] Whilst the first part of the above extract is undoubtedly true, the second is less so in so far as it appears to view 'necessity' in the light of what is desirable in policy terms. Such an interpretation is not supported by the relevant part of the Court's ruling which contains no suggestion as to whether policy-oriented consideration should apply. Indeed, the wording of the ruling suggests a rather automatic process: once the subject-matter of the Convention has been identified as within Chapter 1 of Title III EC Treaty which confers on the Community an internal legislative competence in the area of social policy, it is immediately concluded that 'consequently, Convention No 170 falls within the Community's area of competence'.[84] Would this be taken to imply that the Community enjoys external competence in all areas over which it is endowed with internal legislative competence? The Court is careful not to make such a statement. Indeed, the affirmation of the existence of the external competence in *Opinion 2/91* is accompanied by reference to the fact that the subject-matter of Convention No 170 coincides with that of several directives adopted pursuant to the exercise of the internal legislative competence. This illustrates a tendency which characterises all rulings of the Court affirming the existence of external competence, including the *AETR* judgment.

The above analysis highlights the specific implications of the Court's ruling for the construction of the Community's implied competence: the introduction of a stricter definition of the *AETR* test coupled with a broader reading of the effects of exclusivity points towards the most important function of *Opinion 2/91*, that is

---

[82] Dashwood and Heliskoski point out that 'the principle is cited in a context which shows the intention of the Clourt to disconnect it from the unusual circumstances of both *Opinion 1/76* and, previously, *Kramer*. Paragraph 3 is evidently to be taken as an expression of the normal (though not necessarily the only) way in which external competence may arise for the Community in the absence of explicit attribution' (n3 above, at 15).

[83] Dashwood and Heliskoski, n3 above, 16.

[84] Para 17 (emphasis added).

the implicit sanctioning of mixity. More importantly, the message conveyed by the ruling is that, in EC bilateral and multilateral relations, mixity is the rule. Indeed, the starting point for the Court's analysis appears to be the presumption that the Member States could participate in the conclusion of the agreement, albeit one that may be rebutted.

In this respect, two points need to be made. First, whilst in *AETR* and *Opinion 1/76* the participation of Member States along with the Community in the negotiation and conclusion of the Agreements in question had been sanctioned for reasons related to the practical realities of international negotiations, Convention No 170 ought to be concluded by both because the competence over its content was shared. This indicates a shift in emphasis from the application of mixity as a matter of practice to its articulation as a matter of principle and legal logic.

Secondly, the principle of shared competence is accepted by the Court without taking account of the practical problems to which it may give rise. The ruling in *Opinion 2/91* constituted the first time where arguments to that effect submitted by the Commission were rejected; this will become quite prominent in subsequent disputes where arguments about the practical problems regarding the international representation of the Community and the Member States in the case of mixed agreements will have the same fate. This suggests the emergence of a practice which confines the determination of the nature of the Community's external competence to legal issues pertaining to the implementation of the EC Treaty rather than practical considerations. That is not to say that the Court appears oblivious to the reality of the conduct of international relations. In its ruling in *Opinion 2/91*, it makes reference to the duty of cooperation which is deemed binding both on the Community institutions and the Member States in the process of the negotiation, conclusion and implementation of international agreements over which they share competence.

The significance of this principle cannot be overstated: it is being set out in a distinct manner in the concluding part of the Court's ruling and it is sanctioned by the Court in the context of both the Community's express and implied competence.[85] Most importantly, its construction suggests a duty which is distinct from the general duty of loyalty laid down in Article 10 EC. Indeed, the duty of cooperation to which the Court refers in *Opinion 2/91* is viewed as stemming from the requirement of unity in the international representation of the Community. As such, it is not merely a procedural instrument aimed at mitigating any undermining effects that may follow from mixity; it is also a legal principle which makes the executive authorities of the Community and the Member States assume responsibility for the conduct of EC external relations. In that regard, it is true that the duty of cooperation appears to be quite vague and the Court offered no indications of the specific ways in which it could be construed. However, whilst its supervision is entrusted to the Court of Justice, its prominent position in the

---

[85] Reference is made to *Kramer*, n37 above, paras 39–45 and *Opinion 1/78*, n66 above, para 60.

ruling also indicated that the *locus* of power in the conduct of EC external relations lies with the legislative and executive institutions of the Community and the Member States and the way in which they would manage their coexistence.

All in all, by clarifying the conditions giving rise to exclusivity, ruling on the effects of internal legislation introducing minimum standards and focusing on the function of the duty of cooperation, *Opinion 2/91* offered the first illustration of the Court's approach to the principle of mixity. In its subsequent case law, the Court elaborated upon the duty of cooperation and transformed it into one of the cornerstones of the Community's external economic policies. In other words, *Opinion 2/91* contains the seeds of what is to become the constitutional core of EC external relations.

6. THE CONTROVERSIAL *OPINION 1/94*

In *Opinion 1/94*, the Court was asked to rule on the competence of the Community to conclude the General Agreement on Trade in Services (GATS) and the Agreement on Trade-Related Aspects of Intellectual Property Rights (TRIPS).[86] In Chapter 2, it was examined how the Court, in rejecting the principal contention by the Commission, ruled that the content of those agreements fell beyond the scope of the Common Commercial Policy and, therefore, was not covered by the Community's exclusive competence.[87]

The Court, then, dealt with the alternative submission, namely that the conclusion of the GATS and TRIPS fell within the Community's exclusive competence impliedly. This submission was based on three main arguments, namely the effect of the *AETR* principle, the effect of the necessity principle laid down in *Opinion 1/76* and, finally, the effect of the general clauses laid down in Articles 95 and 308 EC.

6.1. The Application of the *AETR* Principle

As far as the *AETR* principle was concerned, the Commission argued that it was applicable to both the GATS and TRIPS. In relation to the former, the Commission focused on a number of areas covered by the Agreement over which the Community enjoyed competence to adopt rules internally, namely the right of establishment, the freedom to provide services and transport. It claimed that internal competence had given rise to exclusive external competence. In relation to TRIPS, it was argued that a number of secondary provisions adopted by the Community institutions internally would be affected were the Member States to participate in its conclusion.

---

[86] *Opinion 1/94 (WTO Agreements)* [1994] ECR I–5267.
[87] See Ch 2 above at section 3.

This line of reasoning was rejected by the Court. As far as transport was considered:

> the Community's exclusive external competence does not automatically flow from its power to lay down rules at internal level. As the Court pointed out in the *AETR* judgment . . .., the Member States, whether acting individually or collectively, only lose their right to assume obligations with non-member countries as and when common rules which could be affected by those obligations come into being. Only in so far as common rules have been established at internal level does the external competence of the Community become exclusive. However, not all transport matters are already covered by common rules.[88]

The absence of common rules on all transport matters was the first point the Court made in order to reject exclusivity. The second point had to do with the practical reasons for which the Commission had argued for exclusivity. In particular, it had been argued that, in the absence of exclusive Community competence, the authority of Member States to conclude individually international agreements with third countries would 'inevitably lead to distortions in the flow of services and will progressively undermine the internal market'.[89] The Court rejected that practical argument on the basis of a legal principle:

> there is nothing in the Treaty which prevents the institutions from arranging, in the common rules laid down by them, concerted action in relation to non-member countries or from prescribing the approach to be taken by the Member States in their external dealings.[90]

That conclusion was supported by reference to specific secondary rules on transport which provided for such arrangements: Regulation 4058/86, for instance, deals with the possibility of third states restricting free access by shipping companies of Member States to the transport of linear cargoes by enabling the Council to decide on coordinated action.[91]

Having rejected the exclusive nature of the Community's external competence on transport, despite the reference in Article 75(1)(a) EC to 'relationships arising from international law', the Court had no difficulty reaching the same conclusion in relation to the right of establishment and the freedom to provide services. The Court pointed out that 'the sole objective of [the chapters on the above freedoms] is to secure the right of establishment and freedom to provide services for nationals of Member States'.[92] It then, went on to point out that:

---

[88] N86 above para 77.

[89] *Ibid*, para 78.

[90] *Ibid*, para 79.

[91] [1986] OJ L 378/21, Art 3. The Court also referred to Reg. 4055/86 [1986] OJ L 378/1 on the freedom to provide services to maritime transport between Member States and third countries which requires that Member States phase out or adjust existing cargo-sharing arrangements, as their conclusion became subject to a Community authorisation procedure.

[92] Para 81.

They contain no provision on the problem of the first establishment of nationals of non-member countries and the rules governing their access to self-employed activities. One cannot infer from those chapters that the Community has exclusive competence to conclude an agreement with non-member countries to liberalize first establishment and access to service markets, other than those which are the subject of cross-border supplies within the meaning of GATS which are covered by Article [133].[93]

However, the fact that the Community did not enjoy exclusive competence externally to conclude an agreement on the rights of third-country nationals in the above areas should not be taken to mean that the Community is prevented from relying upon the powers conferred by the relevant provisions in order to specify the treatment which is to be accorded to such nationals. In a later part of its judgment, the Court returns to this issue to point out that that power has actually been exercised by the inclusion of external relations provisions in secondary rules adopted by the Council pursuant to Articles 44 and 47(2) EC. Such provisions may serve different objectives: disclosure requirements imposed on branches established by companies governed by the laws of third countries were included in secondary legislation in order to avoid disparities with similar requirements imposed on companies governed by the laws of a Member State;[94] the Second Banking Directive included a specific Title III for credit institutions in third countries setting out various measures which rendered reliance by them upon the system introduced therein conditional upon obtaining comparable competitive opportunities for Community credit institutions in those countries;[95] the same applied to secondary rules in the area of insurance.[96]

However, that was not sufficient to endow the Community with exclusive competence. The relevant part of the Court's ruling is worth citing in full:

95. Whenever the Community has included in its internal legislative acts provisions relating to the treatment of nationals of non-member countries or expressly conferred on its institutions powers to negotiate with non-member countries, it acquires exclusive external competence in the spheres covered by those acts.

96. The same applies in any event, even in the absence of any express provision authorising its institutions to negotiate with non-member countries, where the Communtiy has achieved complete harmonization of the rules governing access to a self-employed activity, because the common rules thus adopted could be affected within the meaning of the *AETR* judgment if the Member States retained freedom to negotiate with non-member countries.

97. That is not the case in all service sectors, however, as the Commission has itself acknowledged.

---

[93] *Ibid.*
[94] Art 54 of Council Dir 89/666 [1989] OJ L 395/36 mentioned in para 92.
[95] Council Dir 89/646 [1989] OJ L 386/1.
[96] See, for instance, Council Dir 90/618 [1990] OJ L 330/44, amongst other measures mentioned in para 93.

It was on similar grounds that the Court rejected the Commission's claim to exclusivity for the conclusion of TRIPS. It pointed out that 'the harmonization achieved within the Community in certain areas covered by TRIPS is only partial and . . ., in other areas, no harmonization has been envisaged'.[97]

6.2. The Application of the Necessity Principle Pursuant to *Opinion 1/76*

The alternative claim for exclusivity put forward by the Commission was based on the principle of necessity elaborated upon in *Opinion 1/76*. In particular, it was argued that exclusivity was necessary at both internal and external levels for different reasons: in terms of the former, it would maintain the coherence of the internal market, whereas, in terms of the latter, it would enable the Community to remain active, as the need for the conclusion of the WTO Agreements was not in itself disputed.

The Court rejected both arguments on the basis that they did not reflect the issues raised in *Opinion 1/76*. The latter was viewed as a case where the objective of the Draft Agreement was impossible to be achieved in any way other than by concluding an international agreement; similarly, in *Kramer*, the objective of conservation of biological resources of the high seas 'would hardly be effective' if not applicable to non-Community vessels. It was in that context that 'external powers may be exercised, and thus become exclusive, without any internal legislation having first been adopted'.[98] The Court, then, made a distinction:[99]

> That is not the situation in the sphere of services: attainment of freedom of establishment and freedom to provide services for nationals of the Member States is not inextricably linked to the treatment to be afforded in the Community to nationals of non-member countries or in non-member countries to nationals of Member States of the Community.

The same conclusion applied to TRIPS in relation to which the Court was quite direct: 'unification or harmonization of intellectual property rights in the Community context does not necessarily have to be accompanied by agreements with non-member countries in order to be effective'.[100]

6.3. The Application of the General Clauses of Articles 95 and 308 EC

The Commission's last resort in order to claim exclusivity was to rely upon the general clauses laid down in Articles 95 and 308 EC. The wording of their provisions

---

[97] Para 103. As examples of partial harmonisation, the Court mentioned trade-mark law, whereas the areas of undisclosed technical information, industrial designs and patents are cited as examples of absence of harmonising legislation.

[98] Para 85.

[99] Para 86.

[100] Para 100.

was deemed sufficiently broad to be construed as giving rise to exclusivity under the circumstances: the former enables the Council to adopt by qualified majority harmonising measures 'which have as their object the establishment and functioning of the internal market', whereas the latter enabled the Council to adopt unanimously the measures 'necessary to attain, in the course of the operation of the common market, one of the objectives of the Community' in cases where the EC Treaty 'has not provided the necessary powers'.

However, both provisions were held to be insufficient in themselves to render the Community's external competence exclusive. The Court ruled that only the exercise of the internal competence conferred therein could give rise to exclusive external competence.

6.4. Comment on the Construction of the *AETR* Principle

The ruling of the Court in *Opinion 1/94* appeared to be a remarkable defeat for the Commission: the core of its line of reasoning, in all its forms, was rejected in a manner which was as comprehensive as it was forceful. It was pointed out in Chapter 2 that, in dissociating the conclusion of the GATS and TRIPS from the CCP, the Court attracted heavy criticism. The parts of the Court's judgment rejecting the Commission's claim for exclusivity pursuant to the principles laid down in *AETR* and *Opinion 1/76* were no less controversial. Its line of reasoning was seen as couched in open-ended terms with a propensity to vagueness.[101] Its forceful sanctioning of shared competence was seen as undermining the coherence of the external representation of the Community, and its emphasis on the duty of cooperation was seen as an inadequate remedy for potential inter-institutional conflicts.[102] The interpretation of the necessity principle was seen as unduly restrictive and the construction of exclusivity pursuant to the *AETR* principle as undermining the very *raison d'être* of the latter's introduction.[103]

In the context of the implied competence of the Community pursuant to the *AETR* principle, exclusivity was construed in strict terms: rather than arising from the existence of 'common rules' (*AETR*) or even 'Community rules covering an area to a large extent' (*Opinion 1/76*), it required the existence of complete harmonisation following the exercise of the Community's internal competence. This formulation appeared to mark the apogee of a progressive tightening of the criteria laid down by the Court over the years. Does this mean the logic underpinning the ruling in *Opinion 1/94* is markedly different to that of previous case law?

A close examination of the ruling suggests a negative answer. After all, *Opinion 2/91* had already made it clear that internal rules introducing minimum standards

---

[101] See N Emiliou, 'The Death of Exclusive Competence?' (1996) 21 *ELRev* 294 at 310.

[102] See A Maunu, 'The Implied External Competence of the European Community after the ECJ *Opinion 1/94*—Towards Coherence or Diversity?' (1995) 2 *LEI* 115 at 123 ff.

[103] JHJ Bourgeois 'The EC in the WTO and Advisory *Opinion 1/94*: An Echternach Procession' (1995) 32 *CMLRev* 763 at 780 ff.

would not give rise to exclusive competence externally. In any case, to view the reference to complete harmonisation as a departure from the broader conditions of exclusivity laid down in earlier case law presumes that the latter actually sanctioned such a liberal reading of the competence of the Community to negotiate and conclude international agreements to the exclusion of the Member States. However, the analysis of the rulings in *AETR*, as well as those in *Kramer* and *Opinion 1/76*, earlier in this chapter, showed that that had not been the case. In fact, in both legal and practical terms the definitions given by the Court in those cases suggested a positively compromised reading of exclusivity: on the one hand, the examination of the nature of implied competence was intertwined with that of its existence to such an extent that no safe assumption could be made about its legal requirements; on the other hand, the participation of Member States along with the Community had been sanctioned, the 'broad' construction of the latter's exclusive competence notwithstanding. In other words, the requirement in *Opinion 1/94* that complete harmonisation be present internally in order for exclusivity to arise externally provides a clarification of, rather than a departure from, the previous statements of the law.

Admittedly, such an interpretation of *Opinion 1/94* is possible, at least partly, with the benefit of hindsight. However, to argue that the approach adopted in *Opinion 1/94* would render it very difficult for exclusivity to arise is to ignore that, under the previous case law, exclusivity had not, in fact, excluded Member States from participating in the negotiation and conclusion of the Agreements examined by the Court. In other words, far from construing implied competence in too restrictive terms, the ruling in *Opinion 1/94* interpreted exclusivity in the light of the context within which it had been intended to function. Viewed from this angle, the criticism levelled against the Court appears to be based on assumptions about exclusivity which had no actual foundation in the Court's case law. This argument highlights a link between the Court's approach in *Opinion 1/94* to the nature of implied competence and the construction of the scope of the Common Commercial Policy. It is recalled that, in its ruling, the Court held that TRIPS was excluded from the scope of Article 133 EC because, otherwise, the harmonising effect of the TRIPS provisions would be binding upon the Community in deviation from its internal rules. This concern that the external competence of the Community should not produce effects which the Member States had been unable or unwilling to sanction internally is also present in the construction of implied competence. Indeed, the requirement that exclusivity arise following complete harmonisation internally is aimed at addressing precisely that concern. Viewed from this angle, the ruling in *Opinion 1/94* is characterised by a degree of internal coherence which, in the light of prior case law, is both surprising and welcome.

To argue that harmonisation of national laws has always been a politically charged issue is to state the obvious: the evolving institutional balance addressed in the EC Treaty legal bases and the long process of transformation from complete to minimum harmonisation indicate that the adoption of harmonising rules

constitutes a political choice left to the Community institutions and implemented on the basis of legal rules laid down in primary law. It is difficult to see how the
Court could sanction a practice whereby such a choice is made by bypassing the
internal legislative system. This point is brought home by the express reference in
the ruling to one example, namely the protection of undisclosed technical information as regards industrial designs. Whilst the Commission had put forward
proposals in this area, the legislative process provided internally had been far from
complete. In fact, had the assessment of exclusivity been dissociated from the existence of internal harmonising legislation, the effectiveness of the Community's
implied competence would have been undermined. Indeed, faced with the possibility of engaging in international negotiations which might lead to a choice of
legal regulation deemed unsatisfactory internally, the Council would become
increasingly reluctant to give the Commission a negotiating mandate.

Furthermore, the construction of exclusivity in *Opinion 1/94* is consistent with
the logic of the doctrine as introduced in the early 1970s. As the Community's
implied competence was deemed to flow from the existence of the internal competence in order to pursue the Community's objectives, a different definition of
exclusivity in *Opinion 1/94* would have rendered that principle an alternative
instrument of internal regulation rather than the inevitable consequence of
supremacy. In this respect, it is hardly surprising that what underpins the parts of
the ruling dealing with external competence pursuant to the *AETR* doctrine is the
linkage between the internal and external competences. In treating it as critical to
the definition of the nature of the latter, the Court follows closely the approach it
had adopted since the genesis of its relevant case law. Indeed, so central was that
link in *AETR* that, as mentioned above, the whole judgment was characterised by
a distinct confusion between the issue of the existence of the Community's
implied competence and that of its nature.

6.5. Comment on the Construction of the *Opinion 1/76* Principle

In terms of the interpretation of the principle first introduced in *Opinion 1/76*, the
Court's approach raises certain questions. In its effort to clarify the vague concept
of 'necessity', the Court introduced an equally vague one: the conclusion of the
GATS was not 'necessary' for the attainment of freedom of establishment and
freedom to provide services for nationals of the Member States because the latter
was not 'inextricably linked' to the scope of that Agreement which covered the
treatment to be afforded to nationals of third countries. In so far as it required to
be further clarified, the purported clarification of the 'necessity' doctrine is regrettable. And yet, the ruling in *Opinion 1/94* does shed some light on how 'necessity'
is to be understood in so far as the link it suggests between the fulfilment of the
Community's objectives and the exercise of the external competence is considerably closer than originally assumed. It is in order to highlight this point that the
Court juxtaposes the GATS with the issues of the navigation of the Rhine and

fisheries conservation which had arisen in *Opinion 1/76* and *Kramer* respectively: the relevant objectives, as laid down in the EC Treaty, could not possibly have been achieved unless an international agreement had been concluded.

However, the question is not completely answered: how close should this link be and on what basis should it be assessed? Would the conclusion of an international agreement be inextricably linked to the optimal use of the exercise of the internal competence? In relation to TRIPs, the relevance of the 'necessity' principle was ruled out in a very short paragraph where it was held that 'unification or harmonization of intellectually property rights in the Community context does not necessarily have to be accompanied by agreements with non-member countries in order to be effective'.[104] Can this be taken to suggest that, after all, there might be scope for a teleological assessment of whether the exercise of the Community's implied competence would be effective?[105] This question might appear all the more justifiable in the light of the French wording of the Opinion which refers to the '*effet utile*' of internal legislation.

A second question regarding the construction of the principle of 'necessity' in *Opinion 1/94* is related to the subject-matter of that notion. What the clarifications in the relevant parts of the ruling do not clarify is whether they refer to the existence of the Community's implied competence or its nature. In that respect, the ruling compounds the confusion originating in *Opinion 1/76*. The paragraph rejecting the Commission's claim in relation to TRIPs appears to refer to the need for the Agreement to be concluded, whereas the relevant section of the ruling concludes on the shared competence of the Community and the Member States. However, if the clarification of the principle of 'necessity' refers to the nature of the Community's competence, it provides no explanation of why this should be assumed to be exclusive.[106] Indeed, the questions about this issue raised in relation to *Opinion 1/76* are still pertinent.

There is one formulation of the doctrine of necessity in *Opinion 1/94* which is noteworthy. When applying it to the GATS, the Court concludes that 'external powers may be exercised, and thus become exclusive, without any internal legislation having first been adopted'.[107] Applying the objective definition of necessity, this appears to suggest the following: as the internal competence cannot possibly be exercised except through the conclusion of an international agreement, that is through the exercise of the external competence, the legal implications for the position of the Member States would be determined by approaching the provisions of that agreement as if it provided for internal rules. Therefore, as the exercise of the internal competence would have given rise to exclusivity externally and,

---

[104] N86 above, para 100.
[105] For a different view, see Dashwood 'The Attribution of External Relations Competence' in Dashwood and Hillion, n3 above, 115 at 133–4.
[106] See P Eeckhout, *External Relations of the European Union* (Oxford: OUP, 2004) at 78.
[107] Para 85.

therefore, prevented the Member States from acting, so would the exercise of the external competence. However, to identify the effects of the exercise of external competence in an *Opinion 1/76* senario with those of the exercise of the internal competence is problematic: it does not follow that the latter would give rise to exclusivity externally because it does not follow that it would produce complete harmonisation. After all, this is one of the main tenets of the ruling in *Opinion 1/94*.

The answer to the above two questions, namely the precise definition of the 'necessity' requirement along with its material scope, may be interrelated. In other words, the interpretation of the principle originating in *Opinion 1/76* should be taken to refer to the exclusivity of the Community's competence, albeit in circumstances very strictly construed. In other words, rather than being dependent upon a subjective value judgement as to what is desirable in policy terms, the notion of 'necessity' is to be applied as an objective one, hence referring to what is factually a *sine qua non* for the exercise of the internal competence. All in all, the ruling in *Opinion 1/94* appears to suggest that arguments as to the desirability, in policy terms, of the conclusion of an international agreement as a facilitator of the attainment of internal objectives are irrelevant to the application of the 'necessity' principle. Instead, what really matters is whether the conclusion of that agreement is the only way for the internal competence to be exercised.

6.6. An Overall Comment on *Opinion 1/94*

It is noteworthy that the Court is distinctly reluctant to say anything not strictly necessary on the existence of the Community's implied competence. As a result, there is a lingering uncertainty about the precise preconditions for and implications of the principles governing that type of competence. At the very core of this lies the apparent confusion between the existence and the nature of that competence, an unfortunate characteristic that the ruling in *Opinion 1/94* shares with past case law. This is partly due to the maximalistic claims of the Commission that the Community's competence was exclusive on all possible grounds. However, it is noteworthy that, more than 30 years following the introduction of implied external competence in our legal vocabulary, the relevant rulings should still generate conflicting readings of such fundamental a question as that related to its existence.[108]

This uncertainty notwithstanding, the ruling is not only clearer in its emphasis but also characterised by a degree of internal coherence. This is illustrated, for instance, in rendering the notion of 'necessity' an instrument aimed at the factual assessment of whether the internal competence may be exercised only through the exercise of the external competence. At the core of both the application of the

---

[108] See, for instance, Dashwood, n105 above, 115 at 130 and Tridimas in *ibid*, 48 at 54.

AETR principle and the interpretation of the 'necessity' doctrine is the exercise of the internal competence or, in the case of the latter doctrine, the impossibility thereof. By focusing on this link between the internal and external rules, the ruling highlights the normative characteristics of the Community's external competence within the broader context of the Community legal order: in the absence of an expressly provided competence, any other external competence is implied because of its position as a necessary adjunct to the establishment of the single market and the attainment of the EC Treaty objectives. Indeed, it had been pointed out in *Kramer* that the competence of the Community to enter into international commitments for the conservation of the resources of the sea 'follows from the very duties and powers which Community law has established and assigned to the institutions of the Community on the internal level'.[109] Put in another way, the conduct of the EC external relations by the Community itself, rather than being an aim in itself, is developed because it has been conceived as instrumental to the exercise of the internal competences. Viewed from this angle, the general statement included in the *AETR* judgment according to which 'with regard to the implementation of the provisions of the Treaty the system of internal Community measures may not . . . be separated from that of external relations' is less maximalistic than it might have originally appeared: far from being construed in isolation and developed into a free-standing system, the latter cannot possibly be conceived and carried out but in the light of the former.

Therefore, to view the thrust of *Opinion 1/94* as a curtailment of the scope of the *AETR* principle and the 'necessity' doctrine is tantamount to dissociating the Court's earlier, albeit admittedly vague and often confusing, pronouncements from their specific legal context and attributing to them a meaning which they were not intended to carry. This approach to the Court's judgments is hardly novel. It is recalled that the general statements about the scope of the Common Commercial Policy contained in the rulings delivered in the 1970s and 1980s were often misconstrued and interpreted in a maximalistic manner, so much so that, even after the ruling in *Opinion 1/94*, the Commission insisted on invoking them in its quest for an all-encompassing CCP.[110] In its more recent case law, the Court clarified the scope of those early pronouncements and, therefore, that of the Community's express external competence. It was in the same vein that implied competence was construed by the Court in *Opinion 1/94*, hence enabling that ruling to unify different strands of the EC external relations case law.

Another point which is noteworthy in *Opinion 1/94* is the distinct reluctance of the Court to delineate which areas of the GATS and TRIPS fall within whose competence. It is quite forceful in its articulation of which areas do *not* fall within the *exclusive* competence of either the Community or the Member States: in the case

---

[109] Para 33, n37 above.
[110] See Ch 2 above, in particular in relation to *Opinion 2/00 (re: Cartagena Protocol)*.

of the latter, for instance, the ruling leaves no doubt as to the fact that no *domaine réservé* for the Member States exists in relation to a number of issues covered by TRIPS, such as procedural rules for violations of intellectual property rights or interim measures and the award of damages. There is also no doubt as to the existence of the Community's internal competence to introduce harmonising legislation in those areas. However, having ruled out the exclusive competence of either the Community or the Member States, the Court moves on to make two points. The first is that any problems which may arise in the process of the negotiation of a mixed agreement in terms of coordination between the Member States and the Commission and their effect on the Community's unity of action may not possibly justify exclusivity. The second related point is that both the Member States and the Community institutions are bound by a duty of cooperation. The Court dedicates a separate section, the final one of its Opinion, to that duty compliance with which is deemed 'essential' and which is viewed 'all the more imperative'[111] in the WTO context, where the possibility of cross-retaliation should make it possible for either the Community or the Member States to be able to retaliate in an area of GATS or TRIPS falling beyond their competence.

In this phase of maturity of the main tenets of the EC external relations principles, the more the exclusive implied competence appears to be the exception rather than the rule, the more the duty of cooperation becomes a focal point in the Court's rulings. This duty might appear to be a procedural tool too vague to be of any practical significance in the conduct of international relations. However, to dismiss it in those terms would be a mistake. Close cooperation between the Community institutions and the Member States is an obligation imposed upon them pursuant to Community law, and compliance with it is a matter falling within the jurisdiction of the Court of Justice. To argue that the establishment of the internal market and the development of the Community legal order owe a great debt to the development of legal principles based upon broadly worded Community law duties is to state the obvious. In the context of international agreements, the gradual realisation that mixity is the rule will not only reinforce the central position of the duty of cooperation but will also render its construction by the Court essential to the development of the law of EC international relations. This point will be further analysed later in this book.

In emphasising the central position of the duty of cooperation in *Opinion 1/94*, the Court seeks to convey its second message to the Member States and the Community institutions: having already made it clear that, in essence, it is for them to render the external competence of the Community exclusive by exercising its internal competence in order to adopt harmonising rules, it makes it equally clear that, in the absence of such development, it is for them to ensure the Community's unity of action. In essence, the ruling in *Opinion 1/94* may be seen as an important part of the dialogue in which the Court of Justice engages with

---

[111] Para 109.

the Community's institutions and the Member States. To define the approach of the Court as a mere illustration of judicial restraint is to ignore the subtle terms in which the above dialogue is carried out. Whilst ruling out maximalistic conceptions of exclusivity and underlining the decisive role of the Member States and the Community legislature, by providing, in return, a general duty as a remedy for any ensuing practical difficulties, the Court reserves for itself a position at the very centre of the conduct of EC international relations. Indeed, it will be the elaboration of the implications of that duty in specific cases which will define the legality of the external action of the Member States.

In other words, far from being a *conditio sine qua non* for the curtailment of any unilateralist and divisive initiatives that Member States might wish to undertake, exclusivity is not the only way for the unity of the Community's external representation to be ensured. Instead, it will be the construction of the alternative substantive and procedural instruments developed by the Court that will contribute to the achievement of that objective. If this analysis of *Opinion 1/94* is correct, the ruling is very significant not only for what it rejected, that is broad readings of exclusivity, but also for what it suggested with considerable clarity by bringing the conduct of both Community institutions and Member States in areas of shared competence within a Community law framework at the centre of which stands the Court itself. This was an unequivocal sanctioning of the parallel existence of the Community and the Member States and, accordingly, a call for attention to the phenomenon of mixity.

7. CONSOLIDATING THE PRINCIPLES: THE *OPEN SKIES* JUDGMENTS

The Court's ruling in *Opinion 1/94* appeared to render any paean to the indispensable nature of exclusivity broadly construed redundant. Drawing upon prior case law, it also consolidated the position of implied competence in the EC international relations framework. This consolidating function is reflected by its acceptance by the Community institutions. In its Decision concluding the WTO Agreements, for instance, the Council expressly referred to it:[112]

> Whereas the competence of the Community to conclude international agreements does not derive only from explicit conferral by the Treaty but may also derive from other provisions of the Treaty and from acts adopted pursuant to those provisions by Community institutions[.]

The position articulated in *Opinion 1/94* was also confirmed in *Opinion 2/92*, where the Court ruled that the conclusion of the Third Revised Decision of the Organisation for Economic Cooperation and Development fell within

---

[112] Council Dec 94/800 concerning the conclusion on behalf of the European Community, as regards matters within its competence, of the agreements reached in the Uruguay Round multilateral negotiations (1986–1994) [1994] OJ L 336/1.

the competence of both the Community and its Member States.[113] However, the questions it left unanswered regarding the preconditions for and implications of exclusivity were raised by the Commission in a series of enforcement proceedings it initiated against Member States pursuant to Article 226 EC. The subject-matter of those actions was a number of bilateral agreements concluded by eight Member States with the United States in the 1990s.[114] The judgments of the Court of Justice attracted considerable attention, not only for the further clarification of the state of the law in the area of EC international relations but also for their implications for policy-making in the area of international aviation.[115]

7.1. The Legal Background

Whilst the EC Treaty provisions on transport apply to transport by rail, road and inland waterway, Article 84(2) EC provides that '[t]he Council may, acting by a qualified majority, decide whether, to what extent and by what procedure appropriate provisions may be laid down for sea and air transport'. In the area of air transport, Community rules were adopted in the form of three separate legislative initiatives.[116]

The so-called 'third package' was adopted by the Council in 1992. Regulation 2407/92 set out a regime under which carrying passengers, mail and cargo by air for remuneration or hire within the Community territory was subject to the appropriate operating licence.[117] Such licence is to be granted by national authorities only to undertakings which are majority owned and effectively controlled by Member States or their nationals and whose principal place of business and registered office are in the territory of the authorising Member State. Once granted an operating licence, such undertakings are deemed to be Community air carriers within the meaning of Regulation 2408/92[118] and may exercise traffic rights on

---

[113] *Opinion 2/92 (re: OECD)* [1995] ECR I–521, Part V, paras 31 ff.

[114] Case C–466/98 *Commission v UK* [2002] ECR I–9427, Case C–467/98 *Commission v Denmark* [2002] ECR I–9519, Case C–468/98 *Commission v Sweden* [2002] ECR I–9575, Case C–469/98 *Commission v Finland* [2002] ECR I–9627, Case C–471/98 *Commission v Belgium* [2002] ECR I–9681, Case C–472/98 *Commission v Luxembourg* [2002] ECR I–9741, Case C–475/98 *Commission v Austria* [2002] ECR I–9797, Case C–476/98 *Commission v Germany* [2002] ECR I–9855.

[115] See L Heffernan and C McAuliffe, 'External Relations in the Air Transport Sector: the Court of Justice and the Open Skies Agreements' (2003) 28 *ELRev* 601, PJ Slot and J Dutheil de la Rochère, annotation on *Open skies agreements* judgments (2003) 40 *CMLRev* 697, R Greaves, 'The Community's External Competence: Air Transport Services' (2003) 52 *ICLQ* 499, R Holdgaard, 'The European Community's Implied External Competence after the *Open Skies* Cases' (2003) 8 *European Foreign Affairs Rev* 365, R Abeyratne, 'The Decision of the European Court of Justice on Open Skies and Competition Cases' (2003) 26 *World Competition* 335, H Wassenbergh, 'A Mandate to the European Commission to Negotiate Air Agreements with Non-EU States: International Law versus EU Law' (2003) 28 *Air & Space Law* 139, N Lavranos, annotation on *Open Skies* judgments (2003) 30 *LIEI* 81.

[116] See PS Dempsey, *European Aviation Law* (The Hague: Kluwer, 2004) Ch VI.

[117] [1992] OJ L 240/1.

[118] [1992] OJ L 240/8.

routes within the Community. Member States may regulate the distribution of traffic between their airports without discrimination on grounds of nationality or identity of the air carriers. The establishment of fares and rates charged by Community air carriers for carriage wholly within the Community is subject to Regulation 2409/92,[119] the latter expressly being inapplicable to fares and rates charged by non-Community air carriers. Furthermore, the right to introduce new products or lower fares than the ones existing for identical products was expressly reserved for Community air carriers. In addition, common rules had already been set out regarding computerised reservation systems (CRSs)[120] as well as the allocation of slots at Community airports.[121]

Against that background, a number of bilateral aviation agreements had been concluded between individual Member States and United States. All but one, that concluded with United Kingdom, were Open Skies Agreements which provided for the exchange of certain rights to be exercised by airlines designated by one contracting party and authorised by the other. These Open Skies Agreements shared a number of features including the following:

—free access to all routes between all points situated within the territory of the parties, without limitation of capacity or frequency and with all desired combinations of aircraft;

—opportunities for the designated airlines to conclude code-sharing agreements;

—provisions for furthering competition or non-discrimination in relation to, amongst others, computerised reservation systems;

—exchange of third freedom, that is the right for an airline to carry passengers from its home country to another country;

—exchange of fourth freedom, that is the right to carry passengers from another country to the home country;

—exchange of fifth freedom, that is the right for an airline to carry passengers to a third country provided that the flight had originated in one of the contracting parties;

—a clause on airline ownership and control according to which the authorisation required for the airlines designated by one of the parties to exercise the rights laid down in the agreement would be subject to the condition that a substantial part of the ownership and effective control of that airline be vested in the contracting party designating the airline or/and nationals of it;

—a minority shareholders provision according to which United States had the right to withhold or revoke the necessary authorisation to airlines designated by the other contracting party in which citizens of or legal persons based in that party hold less than 50 per cent of its capital.

---

[119] [1992] OJ L 240/15.
[120] See Reg 2299/89 [1989] OJ L 220/1, amended by Reg 3089/93 [1993] OJ L 278/1.
[121] [1993] OJ L 14/1.

Against this background of extensive secondary legislation on air transport and the conclusion of individual bilateral aviation agreements, the Commission had consistently sought to obtain a mandate by the Council to negotiate an air transport agreement with the United States. Its first two efforts in 1990 and 1992 were rebuffed. A third request in 1995 was met with granting a limited mandate in 1996 confined to specific matters,[122] albeit one which did not result in the conclusion of an agreement.

The Commission decided to attack all Open Skies agreements with the United States concluded by Member States, along with the more limited aviation agreement between the United Kingdom and the United States. As far as the law of EU international relations is concerned, the main charge levelled by the Commission was that, in negotiating and concluding Open Skies Agreements, the Member States had exercised a competence which they did not have. Instead, the subject matter of the Agreements fell within the scope of the competence of the Community which was exclusive on two grounds: on the one hand, it was necessary, in the meaning of *Opinion 1/76*, for the Community to undertake the commitments laid down in the Open Skies Agreements; on the other hand, those commitments affect, within the meaning of the *AETR* principle, the existing Community rules governing that area.

7.2 The Judgments

The Court's rulings on the Open Skies Agreements were identical in substance. The following analysis will be referring to that delivered in the case against Germany. The Court first qualified the existence of the Community's competence in the area of international aviation. It was pointed out that the relevant Treaty provision, namely Article 84(2) EC, made the power of the Community to act in the area of external aviation dependent on a prior Council decision. This makes it clear that 'although that provision may be used by the Council as a legal basis for conferring on the Community the power to conclude an international agreement in the field of air transport in a given case, it cannot be regarded as in itself establishing an external Community competence in that field'.[123]

The interpretation of the 'necessity' doctrine put forward by the Commission was rejected. The conclusion of an aviation agreement with the USA was not 'necessary' in order to achieve the aims of the Treaty in the area of air transport because these aims could be achieved by the establishment of autonomous rules:[124]

---

[122] These covered competition law, airline ownership and control, computerised reservation systems, code-sharing, dispute resolution, leasing, environmental clauses and traditional measures. Pursuant to a later request, these matters were extended to cover state aids, slot allocation at airports, economic and technical fitness of airlines, security and safety clauses, safeguard clauses and any other matter relating to the regulation of the sector.

[123] Para 81.

[124] Para 85.

there is nothing in the Treaty to prevent the institutions arranging, in the common rules laid down by them, concerted action in relation to the United States of America, or to prevent them prescribing the approach to be taken by the Member states in their external dealings, so as to mitigate any discrimination or distortions of competition which might result from the implementation of the commitments entered into by certain member states with the United States of America under 'open skies' agreements.

This point was brought home by reference to the establishment of the internal market in air transport pursuant to the 'third package': it was the principle of free movement of services which made this possible rather than any negotiation of an agreement with the United States. In fact, it was following the exercise of the internal competence that the question of the exercise of the external one arose when the Commission was granted a limited negotiating mandate.

The second argument put forward by the Commission was that the conclusion of Open Skies Agreements by the Member States was contrary to the competence of the Community, which had been rendered exclusive pursuant to the adoption of internal legislation establishing an internal market in air transport. The starting point for the Court was to assess whether the principle emerging from its *post-AETR* case law, namely that the adoption of internal measures entailed recognition of exclusive external competence for the Community, was also applicable to the specific provision of Article 84(2) EC; this was necessary because the competence to act, both internally and externally, was subject to a Council decision providing 'whether, to what extent and by what procedure' Community rules would be adopted. This question was answered in the affirmative on the basis of the, by now familiar, *effet utile* rationale.[125]

The Court, then, went on to summarise the state of the law in a concise manner which makes the relevant extract worth citing in full:

> 107 It must next be determined under what circumstances the scope of the common rules may be affected or distorted by the international commitments at issue and, therefore, under what circumstances the Community acquires an external competence by reason of the exercise of its internal competence.
>
> 108 According to the Court's case-law, that is the case where the international commitments fall within the scope of the common rules (*AETR* judgment, paragraph 30), or in any event within an area which is already largely covered by such rules (*Opinion 2/91*, paragraph 25). In the latter case, the Court has held that Member States may not enter into international commitments outside the framework of the Community institutions, even if there is no contradiction between those commitments and the common rules (*Opinion 2/91*, paragraphs 25 and 26).
>
> 109 Thus it is that, whenever the Community has included in its internal legislative acts provisions relating to the treatment of nationals of non-member countries or expressly

---

[125] The Court pointed out that 'if the Member States were free to enter into international commitments affecting the common rules adopted on the basis of Article 84(2) of the Treaty, that would jeopardise the attainment of the objective pursued by those rules and would thus prevent the Community from fulfilling its task in the defence of the common interest' (para 105).

conferred on its institutions powers to negotiate with non-member countries, it acquires an exclusive external competence in the spheres covered by those acts (*Opinion 1/94*, paragraph 95; *Opinion 2/92*, paragraph 33).

110   The same applies, even in the absence of any express provision authorising its institutions to negotiate with non-member countries, where the Community has achieved complete harmonisation in a given area, because the common rules thus adopted could be affected within the meaning of the *AETR* judgment if the Member States retained freedom to negotiate with non-member countries (*Opinion 1/94*, paragraph 96; *Opinion 2/92*, paragraph 33).

111   On the other hand, it follows from the reasoning in paragraphs 78 and 79 of *Opinion 1/94* that any distortions in the flow of services in the internal market which might arise from bilateral `open skies' agreements concluded by Member States with non-member countries do not in themselves affect the common rules adopted in that area and are thus not capable of establishing an external competence of the Community.

112   There is nothing in the Treaty to prevent the institutions arranging, in the common rules laid down by them, concerted action in relation to non-member countries or to prevent them prescribing the approach to be taken by the Member States in their external dealings (*Opinion 1/94*, paragraph 79).

The Court went on to repeat its *dictum* in *Opinion 1/94*: 'any distortions in the flow of services in the internal market which might arise from bilateral "open skies" agreements concluded by Member States with non-member countries do not *in themselves* affect the common rules adopted in that area and are thus not capable of establishing an external competence of the Community'.[126]   Instead, what needs to be established is whether the common rules adopted internally are capable of being affected by the international commitments undertaken by the Member States in the context of their Open Skies Agreements.

The Court, then, dealt with the general argument put forward by the Commission that the cumulative effect of the Open Skies Agreements would give rise to discrimination and distortions of competition which would, then, affect the normal functioning of the internal market in air transport. That was dismissed: the Court repeated that distortions alone were not capable of affecting the common rules. According to the Court, this clearly indicated that the Third Package did not, in fact, establish complete harmonisation in the area of air transport.

Instead, what was required was a detailed assessment of the specific issues covered by the Open Skies Agreements and their effect, or lack thereof, on the common rules laid down in the Third Package. The fifth-freedom rights conferred upon American airlines were deemed not to affect the Community's competence because they fell beyond the scope of the common rules. Indeed, the latter did not apply to non-Community air carriers operating within the EC.[127]

---

[126]   Para 111 (emphasis added).
[127]   Para 118 where it was pointed out that 'the international commitments in issue do not fall within an area already covered by [those regulations and, therefore,] cannot be regarded as affecting [them]'.

On the other hand, the common rules did lay down a number of provisions applicable to third countries and their carriers. These included the introduction of new products or fares lower than the ones existing for identical products and the provision for access to computerised reservation systems. The former was confined to Community air carriers, whereas the latter was also applied to third country air carriers subject to reciprocity. Therefore, by extending those rights to US air carriers, the Member States had acted in an area which had fallen within the Community's exclusive competence. The latter was also deemed to cover the allocation of slots at Community airports.[128] Finally, the Court went on to conclude that the ownership control clause of the Open Skies Agreements was contrary to the principle of free movement of services.

7.3 Comment on the *Open Skies* Judgments

A noteworthy, albeit not surprising, feature of the Court's rulings is the confusion between the issues of the existence and nature of the Community's external competence.[129] The parts of the judgment examining the applicability of the 'necessity' doctrine and the *AETR* principle are preceded by a heading referring to the 'alleged existence of an external Community competence'.[130] On the one hand, the Court started off its analysis of whether the Community's external competence exists at all in the light of the specific wording of Article 84(2) EC and in the absence of internal rules;[131] on the other hand, it concluded that part of the judgment by ruling out the Community's 'exclusive external competence within the meaning of *Opinion 1/76*'.[132] More than 30 years since the recognition of the implied external competence of the Community, such confusion is striking. However, in order to appreciate the implications of this apparent confusion, the main thrust of the judgments in the *Open Skies* cases need to be examined first.

In terms of the principle of necessity as first elaborated in *Opinion 1/76*, the judgments in *Open Skies* leave no doubt as to the strictly defined circumstances under which it would apply: it is only in so far as the objectives of the Community may not possibly be achieved pursuant to the exercise of the internal competence that the external one applies. In its judgment, the Court's determination to confirm the objective definition of 'necessity' was at the expense of a clearer definition of exclusivity. In his Opinion, Advocate General Tizzano had argued against the assumption that the competence of the Community would become exclusive

---

[128] However, the Commission's claim that the Member States had violated that competence was dismissed as unfounded because no commitments undertaken under the Agreements were identified by the Commission as capable of affecting the relevant rule of Reg 95/93.

[129] See R Holdgaard, 'The European Community's Implied External Competence after the *Open Skies* Cases' (2003) 8 *EFA Rev* 365 at 388–9.

[130] Paras 71 *ff.* and 91 *ff.*

[131] Paras 81 and 82.

[132] Para 89.

automatically when necessary. Relying upon a clear parallelism between the internal and external spheres, he had argued for the 'proceduralisation' of necessity, that is its assessment by the EC institutions pursuant to the procedures laid down in the EC Treaty for the exercise of the internal competence or, in the absence thereof, under Article 235 EC.[133] This analysis was ignored. Instead, the line of reasoning followed by the Court was characterised by a distinct determination to construe necessity in objective terms, with no scope for policy-oriented and inevitably subjective considerations to be taken into account.

This approach has been viewed as not only unduly restrictive of the scope of the *Opinion 1/76* principle[134] but also as making it virtually impossible for the implied competence to arise under such circumstances.[135] However, whilst the principle of necessity played an important role in buttressing the introduction of the Community's implied competence in the 1970s, its adjustment to its current formulation does not necessarily render it irrelevant. In the increasingly interdependent international environment the conditions under which the Community will be called upon to exercise its constitutionally limited internal competence are not easy to predict.[136]

Be that as it may, it is worth pointing out that the ruling in the *Open Skies* litigation is consistent with the logic underpinning the ruling in *Opinion 1/94* in so far as both are centred around the link between the internal and the external spheres of Community action. This takes various forms. At the constitutional level, this is manifested by approaching implied external competence as an adjunct to the ultimate exercise of internal competence, hence rendering it an instrument for pursuing the EC objectives. The primary objective of the establishment of the internal market in air transport, for instance, is the freedom of the nationals of Member States to provide services: an international agreement regulating the legal treatment of Community nationals in a non-Member State or that of third country nationals in the Community would be necessary within the meaning of *Opinion 1/76* only if the freedoms of the nationals of Member States could not be achieved except through the conclusion of such agreement. After all, had the exercise of the internal competence been possible separately from the external, the latter would have become exclusive pursuant to the *AETR* principle.

The above construction of the relationship between internal and external competence is also evident in the Court's application of the *AETR* principle. It is recalled that potential distortions in the internal market which might arise following the

---

[133] See paras 47–57 of his Opinion.

[134] See L Grard, 'La Cour de justice des Communautés européennes et la dimension externe du marché unique des transports aériens – A propos des huit arrêts du 5 novembre 2002 dans l'affaire dite "open skies" [2002] *CDE* 695.

[135] See Eeckhout, n106 above, at 91.

[136] See, for instance, PJ Kuijper, 'The Evolution of the Third Pillar from Maastricht to the European Constitution: Institutional Aspects' (2004) 41 *CML Rev* 609 at 618 who refers to the possibility of agreements on readmission within the context of the Area of Liberty, Security and Justice.

conclusion of bilateral agreements by Member States were considered insufficient to establish exclusive competence in the absence of internal harmonisation. This strict approach has been criticised as too deferential to the Member States and dismissive of the realities of the regulation of international aviation.[137] However, the approach adopted in the *Open Skies* judgments should be viewed in the light of two principal considerations. The first has to do with the line of reasoning upon which the Commission had sought to base its claim to exclusivity, that is arguments of a practical nature and clearly policy-oriented: domestic and international aviation was presented as incapable of being separated either economically or legally and purely internal measures were deemed ineffective in the light of the international character of the activities carried out. It is not the first time the Commission put forward this type of reasoning in order to suggest that exclusivity was essential to the conduct of the Community's external relations: similar arguments had supported its claims in relation to the GATS and TRIPS in *Opinion 1/94* as well as a very broadly defined CCP both in that case and in *Opinion 2/00*. Indeed, its construction of the Common Commercial Policy, and the exclusive competence underlying its exercise, has been based on precisely such assumptions about the effectiveness of internal rules and the dynamic nature of international trade.[138] In adopting this approach so consistently, the Commission appears to view exclusivity as an instrument for effective Community policy-making on the international scene. This is diametrically opposed to the Court's *rationale* of exclusivity which has been the attainment of the Community's objectives and the supremacy of Community law. As Dashwood has pointed out, the *AETR* principle 'is derived, not from the elusive notion of *l'effet utile*, but from the fundamental constitutional principle that Community rules prevail over national ones'.[139] It is noteworthy that the point of departure in the Court's judgment appears entirely different from that of the Commission: whereas the latter relies upon the problems raised by the external actions of the Member States as evidence of the need for exclusive Community competence, the Court approaches these problems as merely practical issues which need to be tackled.

This approach is explained by the strict construction of the implications of exclusivity. It is recalled that in *Opinion 2/91* it had already been made clear that, once the Community competence has been rendered exclusive, any action undertaken by the Member States individually or collectively beyond the Community framework would be contrary to Community law, irrespective of whether its content would be compatible or not with that of the relevant internal rules. In the *Open Skies* litigation, the Court confirmed this strict construction of exclusivity:

---

[137] See Slot and de la Rochère, n115 above at 709–10, L Grard, 'L'Union européenne et le droit international de l'aviation civile' (2004) 49 *Annuaire Français de Droit International* 492 at 498.

[138] See Ch 2 above.

[139] A Daswhood, 'The Attribution of External Relations Competence' in Dashwood and Hillion (eds), n3 above, 115 at 135.

a Member State may not argue, in its defence, that the substance of the international commitments it undertook individually was not in conflict with internal common rules; or that there is a provision in the bilateral international agreement requiring that Community measures in existence at that time be complied with. As a matter of principle, Community law is deemed to have been violated and the Member State concerned to have failed to fulfil its obligations by undertaking international commitments without authorisation even if the substance of that commitment does not necessarily conflict with Community law.[140]

This rather automatic conclusion as to the illegality of national action is not dissimilar to the approach adopted by the Court in other enforcement procedures initiated by the Commission against Member States: the Court has been particularly sceptical to the various defences put forward by the defendant states in general, all the more so in particular cases where national law maintains 'an ambiguous state of affairs' in relation to compliance with Community law.[141] However, it should be stressed that the implications of exclusivity would not be of a sweeping scope; the judgments in *Open Skies* make it clear that the international obligations undertaken by Member States would be examined against existing Community legislation not as a whole but in relation to particular, individually assessed matters.

As for the concerns regarding the so-called 'timid' approach to national competence, it should be stressed that the Court's line of reasoning on the issue of competence should not be dissociated from the overall legal context within which the judgments were delivered. It is recalled that the Member States were found to have violated Article 56 EC on the free movement of services by agreeing upon an 'ownership and control' clause with the United States. The Court did reject the Commission's claim to exclusivity over the totality of the Open Skies Agreements as well as the determination of routes, that is their most central aspect. However, by carving out what were considered a number of peripheral issues[142] and asserting the exclusive nature of the Community's competence over the negotiation of their content, the Court created the momentum for which the Commission had been looking for years. Without the right to negotiate on computerised reservation systems, slot allocation and pricing, the negotiation of international aviation agreements unilaterally by individual Member States became a distinctly unattractive option.[143]

The developments following the judgments illustrate the point made above. Within less than two weeks after the judgments had been delivered, the Commission issued a Communication in which it laid down its policy objectives in the

---

[140] In relation to the right to charge lower fares or introduce new products, see para 127; in relation to computerised reservation systems, see para 131.

[141] See, for instance, Case 167/73 *Commission v France* [1974] ECR 359 at para 41.

[142] See L Grard, 'La Court de Justice des Communautés européennes et la dimension externe du marché unique des transports aériens' (2002) 38 *CdE* 695 at 722.

[143] As Slot and de la Rochère put it, 'without the possibility to discuss slots, CRS's and prices and with the duty to allow other Community carriers to share traffic rights, negotiating and concluding agreements with third countries is no longer an attractive option': n115 above at 711.

area of international aviation.[144] It argued for a unified approach which would enable the Community to negotiate air transport agreements of a broad scope, covering not only the areas which the Court had held to be covered by the Community's exclusive competence but also areas falling within shared competence such as safety, competition and the environment. It also made it clear that it expected the Member States to denounce their Open Skies Agreements.[145] The following year the Commission, again, urged the Council to grant it a general mandate for Community negotiations with third countries which was viewed necessary in policy terms and desirable for rendering the bilateral agreements compatible with Community law.[146] In particular, the Commission envisaged the conclusion of an agreement which would establish a Transatlantic Aviation Area the aim of which would be 'to go beyond the current "open skies" agreements and to eliminate fragmentation of the European market that results from existing bilateral agreements and create more operational and financial flexibility for Community airlines'.[147]

It is beyond the scope of this chapter to analyse how the process of the redefinition of the international aviation policy has developed and to examine the outcome of the negotiation with the United States.[148] What is noteworthy in terms of this analysis is that, in approaching the implied competence of the Community from the angle of its intrinsic link with the internal market and construing it in a pragmatic manner, the Court continues to set the tone and pace of the development of the EC international relations. It is difficult to imagine how the implications of its rulings would have been more profound in practical terms had they defined exclusivity in bolder terms. All in all, the construction of the exclusive nature of implied competence is by no means the most decisive factor in the framework within which the Community is called upon carry out its international relations. It is also the legal effects of the fundamental principles of the internal market and the evolving and interdependent international environment which shape the ways in which the Community acts.

In a coda to the *Open Skies* rulings, the following might be worth mentioning. In relation to the right to charge lower fares or introduce new products, the

[144] COM(2002)649 final *on the consequences of the Court judgments of 5 November 2002 for European air transport policy*.

[145] See also Answer by Commissioner de Palacio in Written Question E-3511/02, [2003] OJ C 161E/98.

[146] *Declaration on relations between the Community, its Member States and third countries in the field of air transport* [2003] OJ C 69/03 and COM(2003)94 final *Communication on relations between the Community and third countries in the field of air transport*. On the practical problems of EC–US negotiations of an aviation agreement of a broad scope, see Wassenbergh, n115 above.

[147] Answer to Written Question E-3510/02 [2003] OJ C 222E/78.

[148] See the interesting account provided in C Woll, *Transatlantic Relations as a Catalyst to European Integration—The Activism of the European Commission in the Case of International Aviation* (Washington, DC, American Institute for Contemporary German Studies, The Johns Hopkins University, 2003). On the negotiating mandates given to the Commission, see CNK Franklin, 'Flexibility vs. Legal Certainty: Article 307 EC and Other Issues in the Aftermath of the Open Skies Cases' (2005) 10 *EFA Rev* 79 at 103–14.

defending Member States were found to have acted contrary to the Community's exclusive competence because they included a clause in the Open Skies Agreements with the United States to that effect without having been authorised to do so.[149] Might this suggest that it would not be inconceivable for a Member State to be authorised to act unilaterally in an area where the Community's implied competence has been rendered exclusive? It had already been recognised that, in cases where the Community's external competence may not be exercised for objective reasons, the Member States may act jointly on its behalf.[150] What is noteworthy about this point in the *Open Skies* judgments is that the possibility of unilateral action subject to authorisation appears to be envisaged in relation to individual Member States in the process of enforcement actions against them. This is significant because, as regards that aspect of exclusivity, it brings the case law on implied competence closer to that on express competence. It is recalled that, in relation to areas covered by the CCP, it has long been the case that Member States could not deviate from Community rules unless specifically authorised to do so by Community law.[151] Whist this proviso is only mentioned in relation to the right to charge lower fares or introduce new products, and even then in passing, its relevance should not be ruled out. It highlights a significant dimension of the principle of exclusivity in relation to the Community's implied competence: not only is it clearly the exception rather than the rule, but also the possibility of derogation may not be ruled out. As this derogation would be a matter of Community law and, as such, its application a matter upon which the Court of Justice would adjudicate, what might appear to be the possibility of a concession to the Member States is also the implied assertion of the central position of the Community judicature.

8. FURTHER LIMITS ON IMPLIED COMPETENCE

The above analysis on the construction of the implied competence of the Community has focused on the construction of exclusivity as this has been the aspect upon which the Court has placed considerable emphasis. However, there are also limits to the very existence of implied competence. This became clear in *Opinion 2/94* where the Court dealt with the question of the Community's accession to the European Convention on Human Rights.[152] The request for this Opinion under Article 300(6) EC had been made by the Council and was focused on the compatibility of accession with the EC Treaty. The significance of the issue discussed was

---

[149] See n114 above, at para 127.

[150] See *Opinion 2/91*, n60 above, at para 5: the ILO Constitution reserves membership to states only.

[151] See Case 41/76 *Suzanne Criel, née Donckerwolcke and Henri Schou v Procureur de la République au Tribunal de Grande Instance, Lille and Director General of Customs* [1976] ECR 1921 and Case 174/84 *Bulk Oil (Zug) AG v Sun International Limited and Sun Oil Trading Company* [1986] ECR 559.

[152] *Opinion 2/94 (re: Accession of the European Communities to the European Human Rights Convention)* [1996] ECR I–1759.

illustrated by the fact that, in addition to the Commission and the European Parliament, 11 governments submitted observations.

The ruling of the Court on the substance of the request was quite brief. First, it referred to the principle of conferred powers enshrined in Article 5 (1) EC and pointed out that it should be respected in both the internal and the international action of the Community. It, then, restated the main principles of implied powers with reference to *Opinion 2/91* and pointed out that:[153]

> [N]o Treaty provision confers on the Community institutions any general power to enact rules on human rights or to conclude international conventions in this field.

The Court went on to examine whether such competence might be based on the general clause of Article 308 EC. That provision reads as follows:

> If action by the Community should prove necessary to attain, in the course of the operation of the common market, one of the objectives of the Community and this Treaty has not provided the necessary powers, the Council shall, acting unanimously on a proposal from the Commission and after consulting the European Parliament, take the appropriate measures.

The Court was keen not to render Article 308 EC an instrument which would extend the Community's competence unduly:[154]

> That provision, being an integral part of an institutional system based on the principle of conferred powers, cannot serve as a basis for widening the scope of Community powers beyond the general framework created by the provisions of the Treaty as a whole and, in particular, by those that define the tasks and the activities of the Community. On any view, Article [308] cannot be used as a basis for the adoption of provisions whose effect would, in substance, be to amend the Treaty without following the procedure which it provides for that purpose.

In its ruling, the Court emphasised the special significance of respect for human rights in Community law: not only was this expressly mentioned in the preamble to the Single European Act, as well as the Treaty on European Union and the EC Treaty, but it had also been well-established in the case law of the Court. Indeed, fundamental human rights formed an integral part of the general principles of law the observance of which the Court ensures 'by drawing inspiration from the constitutional traditions common to the member States and from the guidelines supplied by the international treaties for the protection of human rights on which the Member States have collaborated or of which they are signatories'.[155]

---

[153] *Ibid*, at para 27.
[154] *Ibid*, at para 30.
[155] *Ibid*, at para 33.

However, the fact that respect for human rights constituted a condition of the legality of Community law did not entail the Community's competence to accede to ECHR:[156]

> Accession to the Convention would . . . entail a substantial change in the present Community system for the protection of human rights in that it would entail the entry of the Community into a distinct international institutional system as well as integration of all the provisions of the Convention into the Community legal order.
>
> Such modification of the system for the protection of human rights in the Community, with equally fundamental institutional implications for the Community and the Member States, would be of constitutional significance and would therefore be such as to go beyond the scope of Article [308]. It could be brought about only by way of Treaty amendment.

The significance of this ruling in terms of the human rights policy of the European Community is self-evident and has given rise to a healthy academic debate.[157] In terms of the construction of implied competence, there are a number of issues which emerge. First, the overall tone as well as the substance of the line of reasoning followed by the Court highlights its emphasis on the principle of limited powers. Whilst this might appear a statement of a self-evident fact, at the time it was a timely reminder of the inherently confined function of the principle of implied powers. It is recalled that, when Dutheillet de Lamothe, the then Advocate General, delivered his Opinion in *AETR*, it was precisely on the basis of the principle of conferred powers that he objected to the introduction of the notion of implied competence.[158] The Court had sought to address this in that judgment by distinguishing between the Community's power to conclude international agreements and its authority to do so. That the principle of conferred powers acquired such a central position in its ruling in *Opinion 2/94* is consistent with the overall tenor of the external relations case law in the 1990s which was also more explicit in articulating the limits to the function and implications of external competence. In addition, the question of the limits of Community's competence had recently acquired considerable weight following the ruling of the German Federal Constitutional Court in *Brunner* and its emphasis on the significance of the principle of conferred powers.[159]

---

[156] *Ibid*, paras 34–35.

[157] See AM Arnull, 'Left to its Own Devices? Opinion 2/94 and the Protection of Fundamental Rights in the European Union' in Dashwood and Hillion, n3 above, 61, M Cremona, 'The EU and the External Dimension of Human Rights Policy' in S Konstadinidis (ed), *A Peoples' Europe—Tuning a Concept into Content* (Aldershot: Ashgate, 1999) 155 and JHH Weiler and SC Fries, 'A Human Rights Policy for the European Community and Union: The Question of Competences' in P Alston (ed), *The EU and Human Rights* (Oxford: OUP, 1999) 147.

[158] See above under 2.3.

[159] See n32 above.

Whilst ruling out the existence of implied competence in the area of human rights as primary law stood then, the Court is careful not to make a general pronouncement on the external competence of the Community to act in that area pursuant to Article 308 EC: having identified the limits imposed by the principle of limited powers upon the function of that provision, it proceeds to reject the Community's competence to accede to the ECHR on the basis of its implications upon the constitutional and institutional system of the Union. This leaves open the question of reliance upon Article 308 EC for other external activities on human rights.[160]

It is not only constitutional limits which define the Community's competence. The latter is also subject to the institutional provisions as set out in the EC Treaty. This was raised in an action brought by the French government under Article 230 EC against the Commission seeking the annulment of an international agreement with the United States.[161] That Agreement was about the application of competition rules and had entered into force in September 1991. Its controversial aspect was its signature by the European Commission. The French government objected to that on the basis of Article 300(2) EC which expressly reserves such power to the Council and confines the role of the Commission to the negotiation of international agreements. One of the arguments put forward by the Commission[162] was that it had the power to conclude international agreements on competition law in the light of its extensive internal powers pursuant to Articles 81 and 82 EC. This was rejected by the Court which ruled as follows:[163]

> Even though the Commission has the power, internally, to take individual decisions applying the rules of competition, a field covered by the Agreement, that internal power is not such as to alter the allocation of powers between the Community institutions with regard to the conclusion of international agreements, which is determined by Article 228 of the Treaty.

This conclusion points out that the Community's implied external competence, however broadly construed, may not alter the institutional balance as established in the internal sphere under primary law. This care not to upset the organisation of power on the internal sphere illustrates a thread which underlies the case law on external relations: only three months after the judgment under discussions the Court of Justice went on to deliver another one following a similar approach.[164]

---

[160] See L Bartels, *Human Rights Conditionality in the EU's International Agreements* (Oxford: OUP, 2005) Ch 7, E Cannizzaro, 'The Scope of the EU Foreign Policy Power—Is the EC Competent to Conclude Agreements with Third States Including Human Rights Clauses?' in E Canniozzaro (ed), *The European Union as an Actor in International Relations* (The Hague: Kluwer, 2002) 296, Eeckhout, n106 above, 86.

[161] Case C–327/91 *France v Commission* [1994] ECR I–3641.

[162] For a detailed discussion of the institutional implications of the judgment, see Ch 5 below.

[163] N161 above, para 41.

[164] *Opinion 1/94*, n86 above, at para 60.

This clearly highlights the limits of the link between the internal and external spheres of the Community legal order and, accordingly, that between internal and external competences.[165]

9. CONCLUSION

The legal rules governing the existence and exercise of the Community's implied external competence are complex; so much so that any attempt to reformulate them succinctly without reference to their specific legal and factual context runs the risk of missing the subtleties of their construction. This is illustrated by the relevant provision of the Treaty establishing a Constitution for Europe. In its objective to provide a clear delimitation of competences between the Union and its Member States, it sets out and classifies the Union's competences in Part I, Title III. In its Article I-13, it deals with the areas in which the Union would enjoy exclusive competence. In its second paragraph, it refers to the Union's treaty-making competence as follows:

> The Union shall also have exclusive competence for the conclusion of an international agreement when its conclusion is provided for in a legislative act of the Union or is necessary to enable the Union to exercise its internal competence, or insofar as its conclusion may affect common rules or alter their scope.

This provision refers to concepts which, whilst originating in the 1970s, have since been subject to considerable adjustment as to the conditions of their application. However, it appears to ignore it. The bare reference to the principle of 'necessity'; for instance, ignores the strict construction of the link between the exercise of the external and internal competences which requires that the latter only be exercised simultaneously with the former.[166] Admittedly, primary law may not capture the subtleties of the application of legal principles developed incrementally by the judiciary. However, it is a measure of the complexity of their articulation that, whilst deeply entrenched in our Community law vocabulary, their fundamental aspects still remain somewhat mysterious.

It is due to this complexity and the controversy it still generates that this chapter sought to engage in a detailed analysis of the relevant judgments. The approach of the Court to EC international relations emerges as pragmatic: its emphasis is on the intrinsic link between the nature of the implied competence of the Community and the content of the internal policies, the emphasis on the objectives of the Community at the core of the construction of the issue of competence, the strict

---

[165] See M Cremona, 'External Relations and External Competence: The Emergence of an Integrated Policy' in P Craig and G de Búrca (eds), *The Evolution of EU Law* (Oxford: OUP, 1999) 137 at 150.

[166] See M Cremona, 'The Draft Constitutional Treaty: External Relations and External Action' (2003) 40 *CMLRev* 1347 at 1362 and A Dashwood, 'The Relationship Between the Member States and the European Union/European Community' (2004) 41 *CMLRev* 355 at 372–73.

construction of the doctrine of necessity, the merging of the issue of the exclusive nature of implied competence with that of its existence. As Tridimas and Eeckhout point out, 'in effect, it is as difficult to establish that the Community has no competence on a given area as it is to establish that the Community's competence is truly exclusive'.[167]

And yet, pragmatism, accurate though it is in this context, does not quite capture the subtleties of the overall approach to the conduct of EC international relations. It is not only what is sensitive in political terms or desirable in practical terms that appears to be addressed in the case law. For instance, in terms of the fundamental principles of implied competence, the approach of the Court is as noteworthy as it is consistent: on the one hand, its distinct reluctance to engage in a strict separation between the issues of existence and nature of the Community's competence is matched by the positive focus of its rulings on the affirmation or rejection of exclusivity; on the other hand, having opined on the issue of exclusivity, the Court stops short of delineating areas of competence within the scope of a given agreement. As the scope of internal legislation constitutes the criterion for exclusivity externally, it follows that the construction of the nature of implied competence will require continuous redefinition. This in itself renders the exercise of external competence a matter of a constantly evolving legal context. However, it is not only the construction of competence which renders the conduct of EC international relations dynamic in nature: it is also the rapidly evolving international climate where regulation becomes steadily globalised and the areas it seeks to cover not only diverse but also increasingly interdependent.

In the light of the above, the case-law on the manner in which the Community is to carry out its international relations in accordance with its constitutionally limited function suggests a shift of emphasis: as exclusivity becomes a concept requiring constant redefinition, the Community institutions and the Member States should draw their attention to the management of their parallel presence on the international scene. It is recalled that, in the context of the case law examined in this chapter, even the confirmation of the Community's exclusive competence did not actually exclude the Member States. This approach is consistent with the construction of the scope of the Common Commercial Policy by the Court of Justice: in rejecting the maximalistic claims of the Commission for exclusivity, for instance in *Opinion 1/94* and, more recently, in *Opinion 2/00*,[168] not only did it safeguard the substantive and institutional rules underpinning the internal sphere of the Community, but it also underlined the legal mechanisms within which the coexistence between Community institutions and Member States should be managed in the process of the negotiation, conclusion and application of international agreements.

---

[167] Tridimas and Eeckhout, n36 above, 143 at 172.
[168] See n110 above.

In effect, this shift of emphasis is illustrated by the Court's effort to strip exclusivity of its apparent appeal and concentrate the minds of the Community institutions and the Member States on the effective management of their parallel existence, the latter translated in legal terms by the phenomenon of mixity. This approach has at least three interrelated implications. First, it highlights the specific function of implied powers in serving the Community objectives as defined in primary law. Secondly, it stresses the principal role of the Community legislature: should it find the quest for effectiveness within the context of shared competence impossible or counterproductive, it has the choice to render the external competence exclusive by means of internal legislation. Thirdly, it confirms the position of the Court at the very centre of the conduct of EC international relations as it is the ultimate arbiter for any dispute which may arise from its pragmatic approach to the regulation of those relations.

Part II

The Management of EC International Relations

4

International Commitments and the Management of Mixity

1. INTRODUCTION

THE ANALYSIS OF the caselaw on the constitutional foundations of EC external action has shown that the Court has been distinctly reluctant to engage in a detailed delineation of competence within the context of a specific agreement. First, it assesses the nature of the Community's competence. Once exclusivity over the entirety of the agreement has been dismissed, the Court may point out that its scope falls within the competence of both the Community and the Member States. In this case, it then shifts its attention to how best the negotiation, conclusion and implementation of such an agreement may be managed.

The coexistence of Community and national competence in the context of an international agreement gives rise to the concept of mixity. Mixed agreements have proved a source of endless fascination for European and international lawyers alike.[1] Their position within the system of EC international relations raises the question whether the *modus operandi* of this formula has proved sufficiently flexible to accommodate both the legal requirements set by individual agreements and the political realities prevailing in the Community landscape. This question touches upon two aspects of the application of mixity: the first consists of the reliance upon it by the Community institutions in the process of the negotiation, conclusion and implementation of international agreements; the second consists of the interpretation of such agreements by the Court of Justice. Neither may fully reveal the role of mixity in EC international relations on its own. This chapter will seek to focus on the first aspect of the application of mixity.

2. ACCEPTING INTERNATIONAL OBLIGATIONS

In order to appreciate the issues raised by the management of shared competence, a brief overview of the general procedural rules pursuant to which the Community carries out its international relations is necessary. The procedural aspects of

---

[1] For earlier analyses, see MJFM Dolmans, *Problems of Mixed Agreements—Division of Powers within the EEC and the Rights of Third States* (The Hague: TMC Asser Instituut, 1985) and D O'Keeffe and HG Schermers (eds), *Mixed Agreements* (Deventer: Kluwer, 1983).

treaty-making are laid down in Article 300 EC. This provision defines the role of the Community institutions and their interaction in the process of negotiating, signing and concluding international agreements.[2] However, apart from the internal substantive and procedural limitations on the exercise of its treaty-making power, there are objective limits regarding participation in international organisations as the overwhelming majority of them confine membership to states. In relation to the United Nations Organisation, neither the Union nor the Community can be a member and it is through the Member States that their interests are presented pursuant to the specific provisions set out in Title V TEU.[3] Whilst a member of the Food and Agriculture Organisation and the World Trade Organisation, the Community holds only the status of an observer in the other Specialised Agencies of the United Nations including the International Monetary Fund and World Bank.[4]

In those cases where the subject-matter of an international organisation falls, even partly, within the competence of the Community but that competence may not be exercised because of the limitations set out in that organisation's constitutional document, the Community's 'external competence may, if necessary, be exercised through the medium of the Member States acting jointly in the Community's interest'.[5] The Council, relying upon the legal basis under which it would have concluded the agreement in question on behalf of the Community, adopts a Decision authorising the Member States, in the interest of the Community, to sign and ratify that agreement. Examples of such agreements include the International Convention on Civil Liability for Bunker Oil Pollution Damage 2001[6] and the International Convention on Liability and Compensation for Damage in Connection with the Carriage of Hazardous and Noxious Substances by Sea, 1996.[7] Such authorisations may be accompanied by the express requirement that Member States 'shall, at the earliest opportunity, use their best endeavours to ensure that the [agreement in question] is amended in order to allow the Community to become a Contracting Party'.[8]

---

[2] For a detailed analysis, see D Verwey, *The European Community, the European Union and the International Law of Treaties* (The Hague: TMC Asser Press, 2004) Ch 3.

[3] See Ch 11 below. See K Lenaerts and E de Smijter, 'The United Nations and the European Union: Living Apart Together' in K Wellens (ed), *International Law: Theory and Practice—Essays in Honour of Eric Suy* (The Hague: Kluwer, 1998) 439.

[4] See E Denza, 'The Community as a Member of International Organizations' in E Emiliou and D O'Keeffe (eds), *The European Union and World Trade Law After the GATT Uruguay* Round (Chichester: Wiley, 1996) 3 and J Sack, 'The European Community's Membership of International Organizations' (1995) 32 *CMLRev* 1227.

[5] *Opinion 2/91 (re: Convention No 170 ILO on safety in the use of chemicals at work)* [1993] ECR I–1061, para 5.

[6] See Council Dec 2002/726/EC [2002] OJ L 256/7.

[7] See Council Dec 2992/971/EC [2002] OJ L 337/55. See also Council Dec 2005/367 authorising Member States to ratify, in the interests of the European Community, the Seafarers' Identity Documents Convention of the International Labour Organisation (Convention 185) [2005] OJ L 136/1.

[8] Art 4 of Council Dec 2004/246/EC authorising the Member States to sign, ratify or accede to, in the interest of the European Community, the Protocol of 2003 to the International Convention on the Establishment of an International Fund for Compensation for Oil Pollution Damage 1992 and authorising Austria and Luxembourg, in the interest of the European Community, to accede to the underlying instruments [2004] OJ L 78/22.

2.1. Negotiation

In accordance with its role in the decision-making internally, it is for the Commission to recommend to the Council that negotiations with a third country or countries or within the framework of an international organisation be carried out pursuant to Article 300(1) EC. Once the Council has authorised such negotiations, the Commission conducts them under Council supervision. The Council authorisation is given in the form of a directive, known informally as a 'negotiating mandate' under which the Commission is to negotiate. In some cases, the Commission is required to carry out its negotiating mandate in consultation with special committees appointed by the Council. In relation to agreements in the area of the Common Commercial Policy, the existence of such a committee is expressly provided for under Article 133(3) EC.[9] Whilst purely advisory,[10] the role of the Committee is important. It is for this reason that it has raised concerns by the European Parliament in terms of the transparency of its work. The Commission agreed in January 2000 to transmit to the Parliament 'significant documents' it sends to the Committee as well as 'other important reports established by the Commission'.[11]

In authorising the negotiation of international agreements, the Council acts by qualified majority. However, two exceptions are provided for in the EC Treaty: on the one hand, the negotiation of agreements which cover an area for which unanimity is required for the adoption of internal rules (Article 300(1) and (2) EC); on the other hand, the negotiation of agreements establishing an association involving reciprocal rights and obligations, common action and special procedures (Articles 300(1), (2) and 310 EC). In those cases, the Council authorises the negotiation of international agreements by unanimity.

The notion of an agreement has been interpreted broadly by the Court. In relation to the Understanding on a Local Cost Standard, negotiated under the auspices of the Organisation for Economic Cooperation and Development, it ruled that 'the formal designation of the agreement envisaged under international law is not of decisive importance'. The Court pointed out that Article 300 EC 'uses the expression in a general sense to indicate any undertaking entered into by entities subject to international law which has binding force, whatever its formal designation'.[12] In essence, the intention of the parties is the decisive criterion for determining whether or not a document is binding. In annulment proceedings brought in the case of *France v Commission*, the Court examined the nature of a document entitled 'Guidelines on Regulatory Cooperation and

---

[9] For an account of its functioning, see M Johnson, *European Community Trade Policy and the Article 113 Committee* (London: Royal Institute of International Affairs, 1998).

[10] See Case C–61/94 *Commission v Germany (International Dairy Agreement)* [1996] ECR I–3989 at para 14.

[11] Answers to Written Questions P-3674/00 [2001] OJ C 163E/221 and E-4035/00 [2001] OJ C 187E/122.

[12] *Opinion 1/75 (re: OECD Local Cost Standard)* [1975] ECR 1355 at 1359–60 reaffirmed in Case C–327/91 *France v Commission* [1994] ECR I–3641 at para 27.

Transparency'.[13] This was drawn up between the Commission and the United States authorities in the context of the Transatlantic Economic Partnership Action Plan. The French government argued that the Commission was not competent to conclude the contested measure because, under Article 300 EC, the conclusion of international agreements is a matter falling within the competence of the Council. In its judgment, the Full Court rejected that argument. It noted that the intention of the parties left no doubt as to the non-binding nature of the Guidelines. Therefore, their conclusion fell beyond the scope of Article 300 EC.

In focusing on the nature of the measure as the criterion for the applicability of Article 300 EC, the Court adopts a functional approach to the scope of that provision. This is not unique in the caselaw on international relations. It is recalled, for instance, that in the caselaw on direct effect, the possibility of relying on directives as against the state or the emanation of the state is dependent upon the specific functions and status of the body in question rather than its designation under national law.[14]

Finally, it is worthpointing out that the role of the Commission as the sole negotiator of international agreements on behalf of the Community is not absolute: agreements concerning monetary or foreign exchange regime matters are negotiated pursuant to a procedure which deviates from that laid down in Article 300(1) EC. In accordance with Article 111(3) EC, the negotiation and conclusion of such agreements are decided by the Council acting by a qualified majority on a recommendation from the Commission and after consulting the European Central Bank. The Commission is merely to be 'fully associated with the negotiations'.[15]

2.2. Conclusion

Following the successful negotiation of an agreement, the Commission submits a proposal to the Council regarding its signing and conclusion. According to Article 300(2) EC, it is the Council which is responsible for those two acts. In Community practice, the term 'conclusion' is equivalent to national ratification or accession. In concluding an international agreement, the Council carries out two functions: on the one hand, it signifies the assumption of the international obligations laid down in the agreement in question, hence binding the Community under international law; on the other hand, it acts under the constitutional powers given in the EC Treaty and under the procedure laid down therein. These internal and external functions are carried out usually by means of a Council decision and occasionally a regulation.

[13] Case C–233/02 *France v Commission* [2004] ECR I–2759.

[14] See Case C–188/89 *Foster and others v British Gas plc* [1990] ECR I–3313 at para 18. See P Craig and G de Búrca, *EU Law* 3rd ed. (Oxford: OUP, 2003) 208–11.

[15] On the external relations of EMU, see CW Herrmann, 'Monetary Sovereignty over the Euro and External Relations of the Euro Area: Competences, Procedures and Practice' (2002) 7 *EFA Rev* 1 and M Selmayr and C Zilioli, 'The External Relations of the Euro Area: Legal Aspects' (1999) 36 *CMRev* 273.

The period of time between the signing and conclusion of an agreement may be long, especially in the case of mixed agreements which must be ratified by all Member States. For this reason, the Council decision to sign an agreement on behalf of the Community is sometimes accompanied by another decision on provisional application before the entry into force. This provision was added in Article 300(2) EC at Amsterdam. In the case of the Europe–Mediterranean Agreement between the Community and its Member States and Lebanon, for instance, its provisions on trade and trade-related matters were singled out in an Interim Agreement between the Community and Lebanon.[16] However, this practice is not confined to mixed agreements.[17] Again, the voting rule for the conclusion of international agreements is qualified majority with two exceptions where unanimity prevails, namely agreements covering areas for which unanimity is required for the adoption of internal rules (Article 300(2)) and agreements establishing an association involving reciprocal rights and obligations, common action and special procedures (Article 310 EC).

In concluding international agreements pursuant to Article 300(2) EC, the role of the Council is to be carried out 'subject to the powers vested in the Commission in this field'. This qualification refers to the privileges and immunities of members and servants of the Community institutions: the Commission has the authority to conclude agreements with third countries on the recognition of Community documentation as valid travel documents in their territory.[18]

The definition of this qualification was examined in an action brought by the French Government under Article 230 EC against the Commission seeking the annulment of an international agreement with the United States.[19] That Agreement was about the application of competition rules and had entered into force in September 1991. Its controversial aspect was the fact that it was actually signed by the European Commission represented by its then Vice President, Sir Leon Brittan. Aiming at promoting cooperation and coordination between the US competition authorities and the Commission, the Agreement set out certain mechanisms which would minimise the possibility of differences between them in the application of their competition laws. These included the following: the notification of measures taken in the enforcement of competition law which might affect important interests of the other party; the exchange of information related to matters of mutual interest pertaining to the application of competition laws; coordination of enforcement activities; reciprocal consultation procedures; cooperation regarding anti–competitive activities in the territory of one party that adversely affect important interests of the other party.

---

[16] See Council Dec 2002/761/EC [2002] OJ L 262/1.

[17] See, for instance, Council Dec 2002/54/EC concerning the provisional application of the Agreement between the European Community and South Africa on trade in spirits [2002] OJ L 28/131.

[18] See Art 7(1)(2) of the Protocol on Privileges and Immunities of the European Communities.

[19] Case C–327/91 *France v Commission* [1994] ECR I–3641.

The main objection put forward by the French Government was that the conclusion of the Agreement by the Commission was contrary to Article 300(2) EC which expressly reserves such power to the Council and confines the role of the Commission to the negotiation of international agreements. The Commission counter–argued that the Agreement was in fact one of an administrative nature which it had the right to conclude under Community law. To that effect, it argued that non-compliance with the Agreement would not render the Community liable; instead, it would merely result in its termination. According to the Commission, this 'secondary' nature of the Agreement was further illustrated by a clause which precluded the parties from interpreting its provisions in a manner inconsistent with their own laws.

This Commission defence was summarily rejected by the Court, which relied upon its well-established functional test in order to determine whether the contested act produced legal effects.[20] The Agreement with the USA was without doubt an international agreement in that sense: it was binding upon the Community and the fact that the Commission was not the proper signatory would not prevent the Community from being internationally liable.

The second line of defence pursued by the Commission was related to its own competence to conclude international administrative agreements. It suggested that this was acknowledged by Article 300(2) EC itself, whose wording should be interpreted broadly, in accordance with practice and by analogy with the Euratom Treaty. In fact, the Commission had concluded a number of agreements regarding the status of Commission delegations in third countries.[21] The Commission argued on this basis that it was competent to conclude any international agreements whose implementation would not require action by the Council and which could be effected within the limits of the relevant budget without giving rise to any new financial obligations on the part of the Community, provided that the Council was kept informed.

That argument was also rejected by the Court. On the one hand, it pointed out that the wording of Article 300(2) EC, examined in its various versions in different official languages, by no means suggested the existence of powers other than those conferred expressly by its provision. Therefore, the broad interpretation suggested by the Commission could not be sustained, both because Commission practice in other instances could not override the EC Treaty provisions and because the procedure for the negotiation and conclusion of international agreements by the Community was distinct from that laid down in Euratom Treaty. Finally, the Court ruled that the specific role of the Commission in the area of competition law, namely to ensure the application of the principles laid down in primary and secondary law, by no means implied the conferment of the power to conclude international agreements in that area. As the Court put it:[22]

---

[20] This test was elaborated upon in Case 22/70 *Commission v Council (ERTA)* [1971] ECR 263.

[21] See I MacLeod, ID Hendry and S Hyett, *The External Relations of the European Communities* (Oxford: Clarendon Press, 1996) 95.

[22] See n19 above, at para 41.

the internal power [in a field covered by the Agreement] is not such as to alter the allocation of powers between the Community institutions with regard to the conclusion of
international agreements, which is determined by Article [300] of the Treaty.

In rejecting the broad interpretation of the Commission powers under Article
300(2) EC, the Court defined the procedural rules laid down in the EC Treaty as
a system whose functioning relies upon the specific allocation of powers to the
Community institutions. As it links this allocation to the balance between the
institutions, the Court transposes into the EC external relations system the main
logic of the internal decision-making process, as underpinned by compliance with
the institutional balance. In the context of the internal market, compliance with
the logic of institutional balance was mainly aiming at ensuring that the powers
conferred upon Community institutions in general and the Parliament in particular would not be undermined. In addition to illustrating a coherent approach to
the procedural foundations of Community law in its internal and external aspects,
compliance with the logic of institutional balance in the area of EC external relations has an additional fundamental objective: it aims at preventing the
Community from becoming legally bound under international law in contraven-
tion of its internal rules. The Court's approach in *France v Commission* appears
firmly based on the constitutional propriety of the Commission's measure.[23] That
is not to say that international rules are ignored. In fact, the legally binding character of the Agreement under international law was in no doubt, that being distinct, for the purposes of the action brought by the French government, from the
question of compliance with the constitutional requirements internal to the
Community legal order. According to the 1986 Vienna Convention on the Law of
Treaties between States and International Organisations, 'an international organisation may not invoke the fact that its consent to be bound by a treaty has been
expressed in violation of the rules of the organization regarding competence to
conclude treaties as invalidating its consent unless that violation was manifest and
concerned a rule of fundamental importance'.[24] Indeed, not only had the validity
of the Agreement not been disputed, but the latter was also later renewed by the
Council.[25]

The judgment in *France v Commission* adopted a restrictive approach to the
scope of the power of the Commission to conclude international agreements, confined to those cases expressly provided for under primary law. In addition to the
agreements mentioned in the Protocol on Privileges and Immunities, these
include the approval of modifications on behalf of the Community where the
agreement provides for them to be adopted by a simplified procedure or by a body
set up by the agreement, albeit pursuant to an authorisation by the Council which

---

[23] See C Kaddous, 'L'arrêt *France c. Commission* de 1994 et le contrôle de la "légalité" des accords
externes en vertu de l'art. 173 CE: la difficile réconciliation de l'orthodoxie communautaire avec
l'orthodoxie internationale' (1996) 32 *CDE* 613.
[24] Art 46(2): [1986] ILM 543.
[25] See Council Dec 95/145 [1995] OJ L 95/45.

may be accompanied by specific conditions (Article 300(4) EC). Finally, Article 302 EC enables the Commission to agree upon administrative arrangements for ensuring the maintenance of all appropriate relations with the organs of the United Nations and of its specialised agencies.[26]

As amended by the Treaty of Amsterdam, the EC Treaty provides for the suspension of the application of an agreement. In accordance with Article 300(2) subparagraph 2 EC, the rule of qualified majority, albeit subject to the express exceptions provided for in Article 300(2) subparagraph 1 EC, also applies to the adoption of the relevant provision by the Council. This is also the case regarding Council decisions establishing the position to be adopted on behalf of the Community in a body set up by an agreement, when that body is called upon to adopt decisions having legal effects.[27] In all these cases, as well as that of Council decisions on the provisional application of an agreement, the European Parliament is to be 'immediately and fully informed'.[28]

2.3. The Role of the European Parliament and Inter-institutional Conflicts

As to the participation of the European Parliament in the process of the conclusion of international agreements, Article 300(3) EC provides only for consultation. This is noteworthy as it applies even to agreements covering areas for which, were internal rules to be adopted, the Parliament would be involved pursuant to the codecision or cooperation procedures. This restrictive position may be understood in the light of the practical considerations related to the length of the process of negotiation and conclusion of international agreements by the Community, all the more so in the case of mixed agreements. However, this restrictive provision of the Parliament's power might appear less striking if examined in the context of trade agreements concluded under Article 133 EC for which there was no formal role for the Parliament at all.[29]

The evolution of the EC Treaty showed a gradual increase in the powers of the Parliament. The Single European Act provided that the conclusion of association agreements, as well as agreements providing for the accession of new states to the Community, were dependent upon the assent of the Parliament, to be granted by the absolute majority of its members. Under the Maastricht Treaty, the scope of this powerful provision was further broadened to cover three additional types of agreements:[30] first, agreements establishing a specific institutional framework

---

[26] See Macleod, Hendry and Hyett, n21 above, at 167.

[27] This is not the case regarding decisions supplementing or amending the institutional framework of the agreement (Art 300(2)(2) EC).

[28] Art 300(2)(3) EC.

[29] On the role of the Parliament in the conclusion of international agreements, see R Bieber, 'Democratic Control of International Relations of the European Union' in E. Cannizzaro, *The European Union as an Actor in International Relations* (Dordrecht: Kluwer, 2002) 105 and R Gosalbo Bono, 'The International Powers of the European Parliament, the Democratic Deficit, and the Treaty of Maastricht' (1992) 12 *YEL* 85.

[30] See Art 300(3)(2) (old 228(3)(2))

by organising cooperation procedures;[31] secondly, agreements having important budgetary implications for the Community and, thirdly, agreements whose adoption entails the amendment of an act already adopted under the codecision procedure.

As Article 300(3)(2) does not elaborate on the definition of agreements with important budgetary implications, it becomes immediately apparent that that issue would become the subject of inter–institutional conflicts. Indeed, the Parliament sought to protect its right of assent by raising it in Case C–189/97 *Parliament v Council* in relation to the conclusion of a fisheries agreement between the Community and Mauritania.[32] This Agreement enabled Community fishermen to fish in waters under the jurisdiction of Mauritania, in return for which the Community would grant financial compensation and support at its own expense. It was the Council Regulation on the conclusion of the Agreement, which also laid down provisions for its implementation, that was challenged by the Parliament pursuant to Article 230 EC. In particular, it was argued that, rather than having been consulted under Article 300(3)(1) EC, the Parliament ought to have been asked to give its assent under Article 300(3)(2) EC.

The line of reasoning put forward by the Parliament was based on both principle and practice. In relation to the former, it was argued that its involvement in the conclusion of international agreements should be interpreted broadly, as the Maastricht Treaty increased its powers substantially. According to the Parliament, this indicated that its position was closer to that of national parliaments and it was the latter which ought to be the main point of reference in relation to the Parliament's own powers in the field. As for the practical argument, the Parliament stressed its role as a constituent part of the budgetary authority regarding the law of the internal market and suggested a number of specific criteria which would determine whether the conclusion of an agreement would have important budgetary implications. On the other hand, rather predictably, the Council put forward a strict interpretation of this procedural deviation from the consultation principle and suggested that the implications of an agreement be assessed against the overall budget of the Community.

Having repeated the well-established principle that the choice of legal basis is determined by objective factors amenable to judicial review,[33] the Court went on to rule out the Council's suggestion: a comparison between the annual financial cost of an agreement and the overall Community budget 'scarcely appears significant' and 'might render the relevant wording of the second subparagraph of

---

[31] As the establishment of institutional frameworks becomes a popular practice, a number of agreements fall within the scope of this provision: see C Flaesch-Mougin, 'Le Traité de Maastricht et les compétences externes de la Communauté européenne: à la recherche d'une politique externe de l'Union' (1993) 29 *Cahiers de Droit Européen* 351 at 385–6.

[32] Case C–189/97 *Parliament v Council* [1999] ECR I–4741.

[33] Reference was made to Case 45/86 *Commission v Council* [1987] ECR 1493, para 11, Case C–22/96 *Parliament v Council* [1998] ECR I–3231, para 23 and Joined Cases C–164/97 and C–165/97 *Parliament v Council* [1999] ECR I–1139, para 12.

Article [300(3)] of the Treaty wholly ineffective'.[34] Instead, the financial implications of an agreement should be examined in the context of EC external relations in particular. Therefore, expenditure under the agreement should be set against the amount of the appropriations designed to finance the Community's external operations.

This test is intended to apply in a flexible manner, account being taken of the specific nature of the agreement and the circumstances surrounding its implementation. To that effect, whether expenditure under the agreement is spread over several years is an issue which should be taken into account as the total amount may end up representing a significant budgetary outlay. Equally, in relation to sectoral agreements, an additional comparison may be carried out between the expenditure entailed by the agreement and the whole of the budgetary appropriations for the sector in question, the latter including both its internal and external aspects. However, this comparison may only be secondary in nature in so far as its findings may not render the financial implications of an agreement significant if they do not represent a significant share of the appropriations designed to finance the Community's external operations.[35]

On the basis of those considerations, the Court concluded that the Fisheries Agreement with Mauritania did not have significant financial implications: it was concluded for five years, that is a not particularly lengthy period of time, and it provided for financial compensation which represented barely more than 1 per cent of the whole of the payment appropriations allocated for the Community's external operations. This proportion was seen as 'far from negligible', yet one which 'can scarcely be described as important'.[36] This was deemed to be the case despite the fact that it exceeded 5 percent of expenditure on fisheries in general.

The judgment of the Court is sensible in its assessment of the circumstances under which an agreement is to be deemed to be of significant financial implications. In particular, it is entirely consistent with the degree of significance suggested by Article 300(3)(2) EC which is more clearly borne out in its French version referring to financial implications as *notables*.[37] However, whilst providing a more solid basis on which the character of an international agreement should be assessed, the Court's approach did not articulate a set of strict rules which would form part of the relevant test. This flexibility is inevitable as the application of the test set out in the EC Treaty may only be determined by practice. What is noteworthy, however, is a point made by the Court about the general role of the Parliament regarding the conclusion of international agreements by the Community. It reads as follows:[38]

---

[34] N32 above, para 26.
[35] *Ibid*, at paras 29 and 32.
[36] *Ibid*, para 33.
[37] See also Flaesch-Mougin, n31 above, at 386.
[38] N32 above, para 34.

the scope [of Article 300(3) second subparagraph] . . . , as set out in the Treaty, cannot, despite what the Parliament suggests, be affected by the extent of the powers available to national parliaments when approving international agreements with financial implications.

In the above statement, made in the concluding paragraph of the judgment, the Court dismissed the maximalistic position of the Parliament about its role in EC external relations. That was an extraordinary position for the Parliament to have taken. In terms of the wording of the EC Treaty, it ran counter to the differentiated distribution of powers underpinning the process of the conclusion of international agreements and the exceptional character of the assent procedure. By relying upon its increasing powers in that area, and suggesting a parallelism with the position of national parliaments, the Parliament made a logical leap: it appeared to ignore not only the specific character of the Community legal order but also the logic of the system of EC external relations. In particular, the provision of Article 300(3) EC on the principal role of consultation expressly dissociates decision-making externally from that underpinning the adoption of internal rules. In any case, it is recalled that the Court itself has not been immune to such suggestions of parallelism between national and Community policies in the area of EC external relations: in 1975, for instance, it had ruled that the concept of commercial policy has 'the same content whether it is applied in the context of the international action of a State or to that of the Community'.[39] However, the legal context was entirely different as, in the latter case, the Court sought to foster the normative foundation of the then emerging Common Commercial Policy. In any case, the subsequent caselaw left no doubt as to the specific position of the CCP within the broader system of EC external relations and, hence, the limitations in the above parallelism with the external commercial policy of a state.[40]

A proper assessment of the role of the European Parliament should also take into account a number of informal mechanisms. Developed incrementally through time and in line with the more general enhancement of the powers of the Parliament, these established channels of communication between the Council and Commission, on the one hand, and the Parliament, on the other, have been relied upon throughout the process of the negotiation and conclusion of international agreements. They include the so-called Luns Procedure which was introduced in the early 1960s for association agreements, the so-called Westerterp (or Luns II) procedure on trade agreements developed in 1973, the commitment to consult the Parliament for all significant international agreements undertaken in the Solemn Declaration on European Union of 1981.[41] Whilst adding significantly

---

[39] *Opinion 1/75 (re: OECD Local Cost Standard)* [1975] ECR 1355, 1362 also repeated in Case 45/86 *Commission v Council* [1987] ECR 1493 at para 16.
[40] See the analysis in Ch 2 above.
[41] See the analysis in *Commentaire Mégret, Vol. 12 Relations Extérieures* (Brussels: Editions de l'Université de Bruxelles, 2005) 98–100.

to the formal powers available to the European Parliament, these mechanisms are by no means equivalent to the latter in terms of their legal effectiveness.[42]

The European Parliament and the Commission have established a relationship of cooperation formalised by the adoption of a Framework Agreement. First adopted in July 2000,[43] it was revised in May 2005.[44] Its section entitled 'External relations, enlargement and international agreements' is worth quoting in full:

> 19.   In connection with international agreements, including trade agreements, the Commission shall provide early and clear information to Parliament both during the phase of preparation of the agreements and during the conduct and conclusion of international negotiations. This information covers the draft negotiating directives, the adopted negotiating directives, the subsequent conduct of negotiations and the conclusion of the negotiations.
>
> The information referred to in the first subparagraph shall be provided to Parliament in sufficient time for it to be able to express its point of view if appropriate, and for the Commission to be able to take Parliament's views as far as possible into account. This information shall be provided through the relevant parliamentary committees and, where appropriate, at a plenary sitting.
>
> Parliament undertakes, for its part, to establish appropriate procedures and safeguards as regards confidentiality, in accordance with the provisions of Annex 1.
>
> 20.   The Commission shall take the necessary steps to ensure that Parliament is immediately and fully informed of:
>
> (i)   decisions concerning the provisional application or the suspension of agreements; and
> (ii)   a Community position in a body set up by an agreement.
>
> 21.   Where the Commission represents the European Community, it shall, at Parliament's request, facilitate the inclusion of Members of Parliament as observers in Community delegations negotiating multilateral agreements. Members of Parliament may not take part directly in the negotiating sessions.
>
> The Commission undertakes to keep Members of Parliament who participate as observers in Community delegations negotiating multilateral agreements systematically informed.
>
> ...
>
> 24.   The Commission shall keep Parliament fully informed of the progress of accession negotiations and in particular on major aspects and developments, so as to enable it to express its views in good time through the appropriate parliamentary procedures.

In setting out the context within which the revision of the Framework Agreement was deemed necessary, its preamble states that the EU, EC and EAEC Treaties strengthen the democratic legitimacy of the European Union's decision-making

---

[42] See also MacLeod, Hendry and Hyett, n21 above, at 98–100.
[43] Framework Agreement on relations between the European Parliament and the Commission, CS–0349/2000 [2000] OJ C 121/122.
[44] See Annex to EP Decision 2005/2076 (ACI).

procedures. It also suggests that it does not affect the powers and prerogatives of any EU institution or organ but, instead, seeks to ensure that those powers and prerogatives are exercised as effectively as possible. Compared to the previous Framework Agreement, the 2005 one is more streamlined; as for the provisions on international agreements, they are now part of the main body of the Agreement rather than an Annex, as was the case before.

The above arrangement was met with opposition by the Council. Following a recommendation by COREPER, it issued a statement which was published in the *Official Journal*. This expressed its concern 'at the fact that several provisions of the new framework agreement seek to bring about, even more markedly than the framework agreement of 2000, a shift in the institutional balance resulting from the Treaties in force'.[45] In relation to the Parliament's involvement in the negotiation of international agreements, the Council pointed out that it is Article 300 EC which sets out the relevant procedures and that practical arrangements concerning the presence of Members of the European Parliament in Community delegations or representing the EU at international conferences were, in fact, adopted in 1998. Having pointed out that 'it regrets not being informed earlier, in a spirit of sincere cooperation, of the negotiations on this new framework agreement' and that its concerns, whilst expressed in advance, were ignored, it concluded as follows:[46]

> The Council stresses that the undertakings entered into by these institutions cannot be enforced against it in any circumstances. In reserves its rights and in particular the right to take any measure appropriate should the application of the provisions of the framework agreement impinge upon the Treaties' allocation of powers to the institution or upon the institutional equilibrium that they create.

It is not immediately apparent why the arrangements between the Commission and the Parliament have provoked such a strong reaction from the Council. A significant, and justifiable, concern would be about the confidentiality of information: for instance, in the case of the negotiating mandates issued by the Council, it would be undesirable and counter-productive for their details to become known to other parties to the negotiation. However, the Framework Agreement does refer to the adoption of the necessary protective mechanisms by the Parliament.

On a final note on the role of the European Parliament: following amendment in the Treaty of Nice, it became entitled to submit a request to the European Council under Article 300(6) EC for an Opinion on the legality of an envisaged agreement under the EC Treaty. It exercised this right in June 2004 in relation to the EC–USA Agreement on the processing and transfer of passenger name record data by air carriers to the United States Department of Homeland Security, Bureau of Customs and Border Protection. However, the Council, considering the

---

[45] Council statement concerning the framework agreement on relations between the European Parliament and the Commission [2005] OJ C 161/1.
[46] *Ibid.*

deadline for consultation with the Parliament had expired, concluded the Agreement citing 'the urgent need to remedy the situation of uncertainty in which airlines and passengers found themselves, as well as to protect the financial interests of those concerned'.[47] Following this development, the Court has initiated annulment proceedings against the Council.[48]

2.4. The Proposals in the Constitutional Treaty

The Treaty Establishing a Constitution for Europe abolishes the pillar structure of the European Union. Therefore, it brings all agreements currently negotiated and concluded under EC law, as well as the rules on Common Foreign and Security Policy and Judicial Cooperation in Criminal Matters, into one set of provisions. These are set out in Chapter VI of Part III, entitled 'International Agreements'. The significance of the abolition of the pillar structure and the procedure and practice of treaty-making as currently carried out by the European Union will be examined in a subsequent Chapter. At this juncture, suffice it to focus on the agreements currently concluded under Community law. Under Article III–325(3) of the proposed Treaty, the Council would nominate the Union negotiator on the basis of the subject-matter of the envisaged agreement: if that referred exclusively or principally to the Common Foreign and Security Policy, it would be negotiated by the Union Minister for Foreign Affairs; if not, it would be negotiated by the Commission. Equally, it would be for either the Minister or the Commission to submit a recommendation to the Council suggesting the conduct of negotiations.

The European Parliament would be asked to give its 'consent' under Article III–325(6)(a) to all the cases currently requiring its assent, along with two more: the accession of the Union to the European Convention on Human Rights and agreements covering fields to which 'the ordinary legislative procedure applies', including the area of the Common Commercial Policy. Its power in that area is further strengthened under Article III–315(3), as the Commission should report to the Parliament regularly on the process of negotiation international agreements.

3. THE VARIOUS DISGUISES OF MIXITY

Mixity may be defined as the legal formula enabling the Community and the Member States to negotiate, conclude and implement an international agreement whose subject-matter falls within the competence of both. In its conception and implications, the phenomenon of mixity is multi-dimensional: aiming at facilitating the coexistence of the Community and the Member States in international contractual relations, it manifests itself in various ways and contexts.

---

[47] Council Dec 2004/496 [2004] OJ L 183/83, second preambular para.
[48] Case C–317/04 *Parliament v Council*, notice in [2004] OJ C 228/31. The Parliament's request for an accelerated procedure has been rejected: Order of the President of 21 Sept 2004.

The definition of mixity may be as complex as its application. Rosas articulates a detailed typology of mixity,[49] distinguishing first between parallel and shared competence: the former denotes cases where the Community is competent to conclude an agreement in its entirety, whilst the Member States have the competence to do so too;[50] the latter denotes cases where an agreement falls partly within the competence of the Community and partly within that of the Member States. He then focuses on shared competence which gives rise to mixity *stricto sensu* and distinguishes between coexistent or concurrent competence: the former denotes cases where distinct parts of an agreement fall within the competence of either the Community or the Member States in a way which 'could, in fact, be seen as two different treaties presented in one and the same document';[51] the latter denotes cases where both the Community and the Member States have competence to conclude an agreement in its entirety without, however, either being, in principle, exclusive. The competences conferred upon the Community by the Single European Act and the Maastricht Treaty in the areas of environment[52] and development co-operation[53] expressly provide for the concurrent existence of national competence. The same applies to the area of the economic and monetary union.[54]

Eeckhout correctly points out that the various ways in which the coexistence of the Community and the Member States is organised in international practice are difficult to be captured in detailed, yet easily accessible, categorisations.[55] For the purpose of this analysis, suffice it to point out that, in practical terms, mixity may take various forms. It may involve the negotiation and conclusion of an international agreement by the Community and only a number of Member States. This was the case of the Convention on the protection of the Alps (Alpine Convention) which was concluded by the Community pursuant to Article 130s(1) EC because its subject-matter was deemed 'a major challenge to all Member States owing to the cross-frontier nature of the economic, social and ecological problems of the Alpine area';[56] the Member States which concluded the Convention were Germany, Italy, France and Austria. Another such example was the Agreement on cooperation on management of water resources in the Danube Basin concluded in 1990 between Germany and the then EEC, on the one hand, and Austria, on the

---

[49] A Rosas, 'The European Union and Mixed Agreements' in A Dashwood and C Hillion (eds), *The General Law of E.C. External Relations* (London: Sweet and Maxwell: 2000) 201 at 203–207.

[50] The example given by Rosas is that of the Agreement establishing the European Bank for Reconstruction and Development: *ibid*, at 203. In that case, the coexistence of the Community and the Member States is not legally necessary as a matter of Community law and entails no division of duties between them.

[51] *Ibid* at 204.

[52] Art 174(4) EC.

[53] Art 181(2) EC.

[54] Art 11(5) EC. However, Declaration No 10 annexed to the TEU at Maastricht makes it clear that those three provisions 'do not affect the principles resulting from the judgment handed down by the Court of Justice in the *AETR* case'.

[55] P Eeckhout, *External Relations of the European Union* (Oxford: OUP, 2004) 191–2.

[56] Council Dec 96/191/EC [1996] OJ L 61/31 third recital.

other hand.[57] This possibility is also provided under the law of the European Atomic Energy Community.[58] Furthermore, it is also possible for the Community to conclude an agreement along with a number of Member States and the European Atomic Energy Community.[59]

Mixity enables the Community institutions and the Member States to avoid debates about the legal bases of envisaged agreements and arguments about precise delineation of competences. Rosas refers to 'mixity at all costs' in cases where clauses about political dialogue are inserted in international agreements so as to render the participation of Member States uncontroversial.[60] In certain cases, the participation of Member States in addition to that of the Community is deemed necessary for practical reasons. This was the case of the International Coffee Agreement 2001 which was concluded by the Community under Article 133 EC: the relevant Decision provided that 'notwithstanding the exclusive Community competence in this matter, and in order to avoid certain temporary operational difficulties, it is appropriate to authorise the Member States to conclude the Agreement at the same time as the Community and to participate on a temporary basis in the new arrangement'.[61]

4. MIXITY WITHIN THE CONTEXT OF THE CASELAW OF THE COURT OF JUSTICE

The analysis of the caselaw on the external competence of the Community has illustrated the distinct reluctance of the Court of Justice to engage in a detailed delineation of areas of competence within the context of mixed agreements: once the issue of the exclusive competence of the Community has been addressed and the nature of the agreement as mixed ascertained, the definition of precise demarcation lines appears to the Court a far less attractive prospect than academic lawyers might wish. The tone had been set quite early on in the *AETR* judgment, where the line of reasoning for the recognition of implied competence was underpinned by confusion between the questions of its existence and nature.[62] The ruling in *Opinion 1/94* illustrates that approach. It appears to carry out three

---

[57] See Council Dec 90/160/EEC [1990] OJ L 90/18.

[58] See, for instance, the Agreement between the French Republic, the European Atomic Energy Community and the International Atomic Energy Agency for the application of safeguards in connection with the Treaty for the Prohibition of Nuclear Weapons in Latin America and Caribbean [2000] OJ C 298/1.

[59] See, for instance, the Framework Agreement on a Multilateral Nuclear Environmental Programme in the Russian Federation and its Protocol on Claims, Legal Proceedings and Indemnification concluded by Council Dec 2003/462/EC [2003] OJ L 155/35.

[60] A Rosas, 'Mixed Union—Mixed Agreements' in M Koskenniemi, (ed), *International Law Aspects of the European Union* (The Hague: Kluwer Law International, 1998) 125 at 145.

[61] Fifth preamble to Council Dec 2001/877/EC [2001] OJ L 326/22. Issues relating to voting procedures and membership of the Executive Board had not been finalised between the Commission and Member States in time for signing the Agreement. It was for this reason that the membership of the Member States was provided for for a period of up to one year.

[62] Case 22/70 *Commission v Council* [1971] ECR 263: see the analysis in Ch 3 above.

main functions: first, to define the limited areas of the WTO framework which fell within the Community's exclusive competence; then, to put forward a detailed examination of the reasons for which the GATS and TRIPS as a whole fell beyond that competence as well as clarifying that they did not fall within a *domaine reservée* for the Member States; and finally, to articulate the duty of cooperation which ought to define the management of shared competence in practice.[63]

This emphasis on the existence of shared competence and the hesitancy in addressing the precise allocation of competences may be explained in the light of the nature of the specific context within which the Court is asked to adjudicate: it is the claim for exclusivity which is usually at the centre of the request of the Commission either in direct actions or requests under Article 300(6) EC. It may also be explained by the constant development of Community law and its link to the determination of the nature of Community competence which, hence, renders the allocation of competences subject to continuous redefinition. In fact, the definition of competences is clearly a constitutional question related to the nature and development of the Community legal order and, as such, is viewed as internal to the Community. This was made clear by the Court when asked, in 1978, to rule on the compatibility of the Draft Convention of the International Atomic Energy on the Physical Protection of Nuclear Materials, Facilities and Transports. It ruled as follows:[64]

> It is not necessary to set out and determine, as regards other parties to the Convention, the division of powers ... between the Community and the Member States, particularly as it may change in the course of time. It is sufficient to state to the other contracting parties that the matter gives rise to a division of powers within the Community, it being understood that the exact nature of that division is a domestic question in which third parties have no need to intervene.

It is in accordance with this 'internal logic' that the Court has consistently dismissed arguments by the Commission as to the potentially undermining effects of shared competence on the protection of the Community interests internationally. In doing so, the relevant caselaw has been characterised by an increasing emphasis on the ways in which shared competence should be managed: this was apparent in its rulings on the conclusion of both the WTO Agreements and the Cartagena Protocol.[65]

5. THE EXERCISE OF SHARED COMPETENCE BY THE COMMUNITY

In its judgment in *Portugal v Commission*, the Court shed some light on the exercise of concurrent competence by the Community.[66] Portugal challenged Council Decision 94/578 concluding the Cooperation Agreement with India on Partnership

---

[63] See the analysis in Ch 3 above.

[64] *Ruling 1/78* [1978] ECR 2151, para 35. The ruling was delivered under the procedure laid down in Art 103 of the EAEC Treaty.

[65] See *Opinion 2/00* [2001] ECR I–9713.

[66] Case C–268/94 *Portugal v Council* [1996] ECR I–6177 annotated by S Peers, (1998) 35 *CMLRev* 539.

and Development.[67] That Decision had been adopted by qualified majority voting pursuant to Articles 133 EC and 181 EC. Portugal objected to a number of clauses contained in the Agreement for which, it argued, the EC Treaty provisions on the CCP and development cooperation did not endow the Community with competence. These clauses provided for respect for human rights and democratic principles, cooperation in the areas of energy, tourism and culture, drug abuse control and intellectual property.

In relation to the human rights clause, Portugal argued that it should have been adopted by the Community only unanimously pursuant to Article 308 EC. Whilst accepting the significance of respect for human rights and acknowledging the reference to it in the EC Treaty, Portugal argued that the latter specified no powers of action. The human rights clause constituted an essential element of the Cooperation Agreement with India. Portugal argued that such a provision was contrary to the programmatic nature of the statements included in the EC Treaty in general and Article 130u(2) EC in particular.

This argument was rejected by the Court, which pointed out that Article 177(2) EC requires the Community to take account of the objective of respect for human rights when it adopts measures in the field of development cooperation. According to the Court, this wording entailed that the Community should adapt its development policy to that requirement. The fact that respect for human rights had been rendered an essential element of an international agreement did not go beyond that requirement. In addition, two points were made: on the one hand, respect for human rights was subordinate to development policy as it was merely one of the factors which ought to be taken into account before the Community exercised its right to suspend or terminate the Agreement with India; on the other hand, both the context and wording of the human rights clause made it clear that it did not constitute a specific field of cooperation provided for by the Agreement.

In relation to the other specific forms of cooperation, Portugal argued that Member States retained competence in the areas of intellectual property, drug abuse control, tourism and culture; therefore, their inclusion in an international agreement by the Community required their participation. As to cooperation in the area of energy, in the absence of any specific provision, action could only be taken under Article 308 EC. The Court started off its analysis by pointing out that Title XVII EC Treaty endowed the Community with express competence in the area of development of cooperation which was complementary to that of the Member States. It, then, set the tone of its judgment by pointing out that the objectives of development cooperation as defined in Article 130u EC were 'broad', hence entailing action covering 'a variety of specific matters', in particular in the case of an agreement establishing the framework of such cooperation.[68] In practical terms, this meant that:[69]

---

[67] [1994] OJ L 223/23.
[68] N66 above, para 37.
[69] *Ibid*, para 38.

to require a development cooperation agreement concluded between the Community and a non-member country to be based on another provision as well as on Article [177] and, possibly, also to be concluded by the Member States whenever it touches on a specific matter would in practice amount to rendering devoid of substance the competence and procedure prescribed in Article [177].

It was for that reason that the Court ruled as follows:[70]

the fact that a development cooperation agreement contains clauses concerning various specific matters cannot alter the characterization of the agreement, which must be determined having regard to its essential object and not in terms of individual clauses, provided that those clauses do not impose such extensive obligations concerning the specific matters referred to that those obligations in fact constitute objectives distinct from those of development cooperation

The Court identified the needs of a developing country, in that case India, as the main thread of the Agreement, the latter providing the framework of cooperation rather than defining specific courses of action: 'those provisions establishing the framework of cooperation between the contracting parties . . . contain nothing that prescribes in concrete terms the manner in which cooperation in each specific area envisaged is to be implemented'.[71] In relation to other provisions of the Agreement which suggest the possibility of further cooperation in specific areas, the Court noted the following:[72]

The mere inclusion of provisions for cooperation in a specific field does not . . . necessarily imply a general power such as to lay down the basis of competence to undertake any kind of cooperation action in that field. It does not, therefore, predetermine the allocation of spheres of competence between the Community and the Member States or the legal basis of Community acts for implementing cooperation in such field.

This approach underlay examination of the specific clauses to which Portugal had objected. In relation to those on energy, tourism and culture, the Court pointed out that the relevant provisions of the Agreement did pursue the objectives referred to in Article 130u EC and, in fact, laid down the framework of cooperation applicable to those areas. In relation to the clauses on drug abuse control, again the Court stressed their link to the objectives of development cooperation by pointing out that production of narcotics, drug abuse and related activities can constitute serious impediments to economic and social development. As to the content of that specific provisions of the Agreement, they were properly concluded under Article 177 EC because they merely provided for a declaration of intent. As for the provisions referring to specific actions such as training, education, treatment and rehabilitation of addicts, they were clearly linked to development

---

[70] *Ibid*, para 39.
[71] *Ibid*, para 45.
[72] *Ibid*, para 47.

policy in so far as they defined the Community's contribution to the efforts of India to combat drug trafficking.

The link with development policy was also made in relation to the clause of the Agreement providing for the improvement in protection of intellectual property rights: the Court deemed it relevant to the EC Treaty objective of smoothly and gradually integrating the developing countries into the world economy. As to the content of that clause, it merely laid down an obligation 'of a very limited scope and is ancillary in nature, even in relation to the substance of intellectual property protection'.[73]

The judgment is important for the light it shed, first, on the relationship between development policy as laid down in Article 177 EC and human rights and, secondly, on the practice of the exercise by the Community of its non-exclusive competence in the area of development. In relation to the former, the judgment suggests clearly a broad construction of development by the Court. However, this is by no means unqualified. Whilst the objective of respect for human rights ought to be taken into account in the implementation of development cooperation and the latter ought to adapt to human rights principles, the language used was rather general and non-prescriptive as to quite how this requirement of compliance should be observed. Furthermore, the judgment ignores the enthusiastic statements earlier advanced by Advocate General La Pergola: not only had he argued that 'the democrary clause must . . . be deemed *necessary* if development cooperation policy is to be lawfully pursued' but he had also suggested that 'it would be the *failure to adopt* a clause of that type that would compromise the legality of Community action, because compliance with the specific wording of Article [170(2) EC] would no longer be guaranteed'.[74] In this respect, it is interesting that the starting point for the relevant part of the ruling is expressed in negative terms: the 'mere fact' that the human rights clause constituted an 'essential element' of the Agreement did 'not justify the conclusion that that provision [went] beyond the objective stated in Article [172 EC]'. Equally, the final point made by the Court in paragraph 28 of its judgment suggests a further qualification: it indicates that the insertion in a development agreement of a human rights clause setting out a mechanism of cooperation between the Community and its contracting party would be questionable under Article 177(1) EC.[75] In essence, this suggests that the legality of the clause in the Agreement with India

---

[73] *Ibid*, para 75. Art 10 of the Agreement with India provided as follows: 'The Contracting Parties undertake to ensure as far as their laws, regulations and policies allow that suitable and effective protection is provided for intellectual property rights, including patents, trade or service marks, copyright and similar rights, geographical designations(including marks of origin), industrial designs and integrated circuit topographics, reinforcing this protection where desirable. They also undertake, wherever possible, to facilitate access to the data bases of intellectual property organizations': [1994] OJ L 223/24.

[74] Emphasis in the original: n66 above, at para 29 of his Opinion.

[75] Cf S Peers, 'Fragmentation or Evasion in the Community's Development Policy? The Impact of *Portugal v Council*' in Dashwood and Hillion, n49 above, 100 at 103–6.

was affirmed because that clause was confined to exercising pressure upon India by acting as a threat rather than by entailing any specific sanction.

This broad, albeit qualified, reading of the Community's non-exclusive competence on development cooperation was also apparent in the Court's approach to the other contested clauses, namely those on energy, tourism, culture, drug abuse control and intellectual property.[76] Their inclusion in the Agreement was sanctioned because their content entailed no specific legal duty or course of action. The emphasis on their limited effect underpinned the entire judgment. After all, as the Court underlined, the Agreement with India was a framework agreement which merely set out the context within which specific cooperation was to be carried out. This approach reflects the Court's reluctance to construe external competence so broadly as to affect the constitutional balance of powers in internal decision-making: the Court noted that the contested clauses did not constitute 'general enabling powers for their implementation'.[77] This highlights a thread which links this judgment with other strands of EC international relations law: another express competence, that provided under Article 133 EC, had also been construed in *Opinion 1/94* and the Nice Treaty in such a manner as to address the concern about the parallelism between the exercise of external competence and the internal rules and procedures.

Therefore, in terms of the substantive scope of the autonomous exercise of Community competence under Title XX EC, the judgment in *Portugal v Council* lacks clarity in much the same way as the caselaw on the construction of implied competence does: is there a substantive core of development policy over which the Community would be competent to conclude alone an international agreement containing substantial legal undertakings? Is the autonomous exercise of the Community's shared competence under Article 177 EC sanctioned only because it may appear to be innocuous? In practical terms, the judgment is important because it facilitates the exercise of the Community's external competence on a pragmatic basis, hence illustrating a second thread linking the *Portugal v Council* case to the EC external relations caselaw: it is recalled that the exercise of the exclusive external competence over Article 133 EC was sanctioned even when it included ancillary provisions for the organisation of purely consultative procedures.[78]

6. THE EXERCISE OF SHARED COMPETENCE BY THE MEMBER STATES

In Joined Cases C–181/91 and C–248/91 *Parliament v Council and Commission*, the Parliament relied upon Article 230 EC to challenge the legality of a decision to

---

[76] In his Opinion, La Pergola AG argued that 'it is clear that the objectives laid down in Article [177 EC] reflect a complex vision of development, the product of interaction between its economic, social and political aspects': n66 above, para 13.

[77] *Ibid*, para 67.

[78] See *Opinion 1/94* [1994] ECR I–5267 at para 68 to which the ruling in *Portugal v Council* referred in para 77.

grant special aid to Bangladesh.[79] This decision required that such aid be granted as part of the Community's policy towards that country. As such, it would be provided by the Member States either directly or by means of an account administered by the Commission. The contested act had been adopted by the Member States meeting in the Council following a Commission proposal and had been incorporated in the conclusions of the relevant Council meeting. The Court ruled that 'acts by representatives of the Member States acting, not in their capacity as members of the Council, but as representatives of their governments, and thus collectively exercising the powers of the Member States, are not subject to judicial review'.[80] However, it also noted that that would be case only if, 'having regard to its content and all the circumstances in which it was adopted', the contested act was not actually a Council decision intending to produce legal effects within the Community legal order.[81]

First, the Court ascertained the nature and implications of the competence of the Community in the subject-matter of the contested act:[82]

> the Community does not have exclusive competence in the field of humanitarian aid, and . . . consequently the Member States are not precluded from exercising their competence in that regard collectively in the Council or outside it.

The significance of this statement for the exercise of the competence shared by the Member States with the Community may hardly be overstated: Community institutions, procedures and forms of action are available to the Member States in addition to the intergovernmental forms of cooperation to which they may decide to have recourse. This conclusion was confirmed in the remaining part of the judgment. In terms of the involvement of Community institutions in the implementation of such policies, Community law 'does not prevent the Member States from entrusting the Commission with the task of coordinating a collective action undertaken by them on the basis of an act of their representatives meeting in the Council'.[83] In terms of the mode of implementation of such policies, 'nothing in the Treaty precludes the Member States from making use outside the Community context of criteria taken from the budgetary provisions for allocating the financial obligations resulting from decisions taken by their representatives'.[84] In terms of relying upon the Community budget in order to give effect to such policies, 'since the contested act does not require the use of the Community budget for the part of the aid to be administered by the Commission, the budget entry made by the latter cannot have any bearing on how the act is categorized'.[85]

---

[79] Joined Cases C–181/91 and C–248/91 *Parliament v Council and Commission (re: Bangladesh aid)* [1993] ECR I–3685.

[80] *Ibid*, para 12.

[81] Para 14.

[82] Para 16.

[83] Para 20.

[84] Para 22.

[85] Para 24.

The exercise of national competence in the context of development coopera-tion was also the subject-matter of the *European Development Fund (EDF)* case.[86] This was an action brought by the Parliament under Article 230 EC challenging the financial aspects of the Fourth Lomé Convention as laid down in a Financial Protocol attached to it. That Protocol provided for the financing and administra-tion of Community aid to the African, Caribbean and Pacific countries. In order to carry out the obligations undertaken thereunder, the representatives of the gov-ernments of the Member States, meeting within the Council, adopted an Internal Agreement. This document provides that the Member States set up the European Development Fund and specifies the contribution of each state; Community institutions became involved in various ways: the Commission was responsible for the administration of the Fund and the Court of Auditors was to control its oper-ations, whereas the discharge for its financial management was to be given to the Commission by the Parliament on the recommendation of the Council. The implementation of the Agreement would be further defined by a Financial Regulation adopted by the Council. It was the latter measure which was chal-lenged by the Parliament: it argued that it dealt with Community expenditure and, as such, it ought to have been adopted pursuant to the budgetary provisions of the EC Treaty which required that the Parliament be consulted.

In its action, the Parliament focused on the provision of financial aid by the Community under the Fourth Lomé Convention. It argued that that entailed an international law obligation for the Community which was distinct from that undertaken by the Member States. Again, the Court first identifies the nature and implications of Community competence:[87]

> The Community's competence in that field is not exclusive. The Member states are accordingly entitled to enter into commitments themselves vis-à-vis non-member States, either collectively or individually, or even jointly with the Community.

This conclusion was substantiated by the wording of the EC Treaty provision on development cooperation which had just been incorporated at Maastricht accord-ing to which the Member States and the Community were to coordinate their policies and to consult each other on their aid programmes and for the possibili-ty of joint action.

In the second part of the judgment, the Court points out that the Fourth Lomé Convention had been concluded by the Community and its Member States on the one part and the ACP states on the other part: following an examination of a number of its provisions, it pointed out the 'essentially bilateral character of the cooperation'. It, then, concluded that, 'in the absence of derogations expressly laid down in the Convention, the Community and its Member States as partners of the

---

[86] Case C–316/91 *Parliament v Council* [1994] ECR I–625.
[87] Para 26.

ACP States are jointly liable to those latter States for the fulfilment of every obligation arising from the commitments undertaken, including those relating to financial assistance'.[88]

In the third part of the judgment, the Court examines how precisely these obligations were to be performed. It points out that it was for the Community and the Member States to choose how to perform their obligation, and in that case to choose the source and method of financing their cooperation with the ACP countries. The contested action merely expresses the choice made by the Member States: as to the mode of its implementation and its reliance upon Community institutions and procedures, their legality has already been sanctioned in the *Bangladesh* judgment.

7. NEGOTIATION OF MIXED AGREEMENTS

If it were possible to identify certain threads in Community practice related to the negotiation of international agreements,[89] the following two would become easily apparent: on the one hand, the determination of the dividing line between Community and national competence is dissociated from the process of the actual negotiation of a given agreement; on the other hand, no firm commitment is undertaken by either the Community or the Member States as to the allocation of their competence. In practical terms, the application of those principles entails the assumption of the main negotiating role by the Commission, albeit without prejudice to the allocation of competence between the Community and the Member States. Therefore, the Commission acts as the sole negotiator on the basis of the mandate provided by the Council, regarding the issues falling within the Community competence, and the representatives of the governments of the Member States, regarding issues falling within national competence.[90]

It was on the basis of that formula that the WTO Agreement was actually negotiated. It was stated by the Council that 'in order to ensure the maximum consistency in the conduct of the negotiations, it was decided that the Commission would act as the sole negotiator on behalf of the Community and the Member States', albeit without 'prejudg[ing] the question of the competence of the Community or the Member States on particular issues'.[91]

This arrangement, which has been applied so extensively as to cover association and cooperation agreements,[92] has various advantages. In legal terms, it is consistent with the logic of implied competence. By linking the scope of legislation

---

[88] Para 29.

[89] See J Groux, 'Mixed Negotiations' in O'Keeffe and Schermers (eds), n1 above, 87.

[90] To that effect, see the Opinion by Jacobs AG in Case C–316/91 *Parliament v Council*, n86 above, at para 82.

[91] Opinion 1/94 , n78 above, at I–5282.

[92] Heliskoski refers to the exceptional cases of the first and second Yaoundé Conventions signed in July 1963 and July 1969 respectively which were negotiated by representatives of the Member States as well as the Commission: *Mixed Agreements as a Technique for Organizing the International Relations of the European Community and its Member States* (The Hague: Kluwer, 2001) at 80.

adopted pursuant to the exercise of the internal competence to the nature of the external competence, this clearly suggests that the dividing line between Community and national competence may require redefinition even during the process of negotiating a given international agreement. In practical terms, it provides continuity in the representation of the position of the Community and national positions. In symbolic terms, it ensures that the determination of competence, that is an issue owing its existence to the constitutional idiosyncrasies of the Community legal order, remains internal to that order.

However, the representation of the Community and national positions by the Commission in the context of the negotiation of mixed agreements raises specific questions relating to the coordination between the Commission and the Member States. As the latter enjoy competence over parts of the agreement and, hence, are entitled to express and protect their interests in the negotiations of those parts, the Commission is constrained as to the substance of the position it may present to its negotiating partners. There is no single formula applying to all mixed agreements as to quite how a joint position is to be determined and presented by the Commission. It is recalled that, in its caselaw on the external competence of the Community, the Court of Justice has increasingly relied upon the duty of cooperation: binding upon both the Community institutions and the Member States, this duty applies to the process of negotiation, conclusion and implementation of international agreements.[93] The coordination between the Commission and representatives of the Member States aiming at enabling the former to present a joint position is a case in which this duty is entirely relevant.

A most interesting example of quasi-formal arrangement as to the coordination between the Community and the Member States was illustrated by PROBA 20. This was an arrangement applied to commodity agreements negotiated within the context of the 1970s Integrated Commodity Programme of UNCTAD. As this particular type of international agreement was popular in the 1970s, the Community institutions sought to agree upon how to represent the interests of the Community. It is noteworthy that PROBA 20, which was agreed upon by the COREPER on 27 March 1981, had been suggested by the Commission.

In terms of the negotiation of agreements, PROBA 20 provides as follows:[94]

The Community and the Member States will participate a joint delegation:

(i) within which the Member States will be individually identifiable (accreditation, and nameplate).

In the conference rooms the Member States will gather around the nameplate 'EEC'. In the list of delegations the names of the national and Community delegates will be arranged in a single list. . .

[93] See, for instance, *Opinion 1/94*, n78 above, at paras 107–109.
[94] Translation from by the author.

(ii) which will operate on the basis of a common position previously established pursuant to the usual procedures (positions arrived at within the bodies of the Council—coordination on the spot—the possibility of recourse to the Council in case of difficulties on the spot); amongst the matters to be specifically discussed by the management bodies, will be certain matters, notably of a technical nature or which concern only certain Member States which will not require a common position. As far as possible, these matters shall be established previously by common agreement.

(iii) which will express the common position with a single voice. The spokesman will normally be the representative of the Commission. However, depending on tactical or technical circumstances, the common position may also be presented by the representative of the Member State holding the Presidency or by a representative of another Member State. In certain cases, interventions may be made by Member States provided that they are strictly within the framework of the common position, they aim at supporting and developing that common position and are made in cooperation with the spokesman and the representative of the Member State holding the Council Presidency.

In particular, such flexibility will occur in cases where the personality and experience of representatives of Member States could facilitate the defence of the common interests or in cases where a specific issue does not require a common position (cf. ii);

(iv) which will be represented pursuant to informal means or restraints by the representative of the Commission, normally accompanied by the representative of the Member state holding the Presidency whilst the Member States are being kept constantly informed.

The flexibility provided for under (iii) will also apply to this case.

Two interrelated features of this arrangement are worth-exploring. The first is the subject-matter of the agreements to which PROBA 20 is applicable: commodity agreements, it is recalled, had been held by the Court to fall, in principle, within the scope of the Common Commercial Policy and, therefore, to be covered by the Community's exclusive competence.[95] And yet, it was precisely for such agreements that arrangements for coordination between the Commission and representatives of the Member States were deemed necessary. What makes this all the more interesting is the fact that the above formula had been suggested by the Commission itself, that is the institution which would normally be the sole negotiator in any case. In addition, it is also recalled that the ruling in *Opinion 1/78* sanctioned the actual participation of the Member States in the negotiation and conclusion of the Agreement on Natural Rubber, depending on the determination of the issue of financing. As the conclusion reached by the Court suggested a degree of flexibility, so does the content of the arrangements laid down in PROBA 20. Rather than defined in terms of merely the procedural ways in which national interests could be expressed, flexibility was also given a substantive content.

---

[95] *Opinion 1/78* [1979] ECR 2871.

At the Council meeting approving of RPOBA 20, the German, Danish, French and British delegations insisted on attaching the following general statement to the minutes:[96]

> These delegations start from the principle that the Arrangement between the Council and the Commission provides for the effective participation of the Community and its Member States in the negotiations, the preparatory work and the institutions of international commodity agreements and, equally, takes into account their national interests regarding commodity policy. If, in the light of essential interests in wholly exceptional cases, the above objective is not met, it should be possible to make national declarations. This should be the case provided that every effort has been made in a persistent manner in order to find a common position and that the interests of the Community are respected.

The arrangements laid down in PROBA 20, whilst formalising the parallel participation of the Member States, did not provide for the circumstances under which no common position could be reached. It was in the light of this incomplete character that the above declaration was made. The legality of this formula was questioned in the light of the exclusive competence of the Community over commodity agreements pursuant to Article 133 EC.[97] In responding to a written question in the European Parliament, the Commission sought to justify it as follows:[98]

> This arrangement is intended to achieve the basic objective of enabling the Community to participate and speak externally as a single entity. It would thus succeed, pragmatically and without prejudice to the various legal arguments advanced, in ending the difficulties which for many years have resulted from the division of powers between the Community and the Member States in respect of their participation in international activities and agreements in connection with commodities.

Whilst apparently deviating from the principle asserted (rather than the practice sanctioned) in *Opinion 1/78*, the above approach suggested by the Commission and agreed upon by the Council is an improvement from past practice where the Community delegation had consisted of representatives of the Commission, the Presidency and the Member States.[99] At this juncture, it is appropriate to return to one of the themes of the previous chapters, that is pragmatism: it is not only the Court of Justice which construes the management of EC external relations on the basis of various legal and practical considerations. At times, the Community institutions appear equally willing to resort to legal arrangements which would

---

[96] See n94 above. Extracts from the PROBA Agreement are also included in E.L.M. Voelker and J. Steenbergen, *Leading Cases and Materials on the External Relations Law of the E.C.* (Deventer: Kluwer, 1985) 59 *ff*.

[97] See JHH Weiler, 'The External Legal Relations of Non-Unitary Actors: Mixity and the Federal Principle' in O'Keefe and Schermers (eds), n1 above, 35 at 75. For a different view, see R Barents, 'The European Communities and the Commodity Organisations' (1984) 10 *LIEI* 77 at 85–8.

[98] Answer to Written Question 343/81 [1981] OJ C 274/3.

[99] See E Wellenstein, 'Participation of the Community in International Commodity Agreements' in St John Bates *et al* (eds), *In Memorial J.D.B. Mitchell* (London: Sweet and Maxwell, 1983) 65.

ensure a degree of unity whilst reserving their position as a matter of principle. Indeed, in the above extract describing the Commission's position, the phrase 'pragmatically and without prejudice to the various legal arguments advanced' is central to its approach which, therefore, appears responsive to that emerging from the caselaw of that era: the question of the precise delimitation of competences did not detract from the need to set out pragmatic arrangements for the negotiation of international agreements. And, its open-ended character notwithstanding, PROBA 20 is important for formalising an understanding shared with the Council that the Community should speak, and appear to speak, with a single voice.

The efforts by the Commission and the Member States to reconcile their interests in the process of the negotiation of international agreements do not always lead to the adoption of a unitary formula. In the case of the United Nations Convention on the Law of the Sea, for instance, Member States were particularly insistent in making their presence clear and distinct.[100] Furthermore, the determination of a common position to be presented by the Commission is not always easy. In this respect, the Treaty of Rome had provided for a mechanism for coordination between the Member States in areas of particular interest to the common market relevant within the context of international organisations. This provision, laid down in Article 116 EC which was deleted at Maastricht, imposed a duty on Member States to proceed by common action. It even endowed the Council with the power to define the scope and implementation of such action by qualified majority pursuant to a proposal by the Commission.

In practical terms, the adoption of a common position to be presented in the international negotiations of mixed agreements is determined on a case-by-case basis. In the event of failure to reach a common position, and independently of the issue of the application of the duty of cooperation, the involvement of the Member States in the negotiations is not ruled out.[101] This has been criticised as contrary to the principle of unity in the international representation of the Community and potentially undermining Community competence.[102] This issue will be further explored below in relation to the participation of the Community and the Member States in the process of the application of mixed agreements. Be that as it may, it has been the rule rather than the exception that, in such contexts, the Community does speak with one voice. If not due to the overarching shadow of the duty of cooperation, this has been due to practical considerations. After all, both the Community institutions and the Member States agree that, in this context, they do not need to agree on the division of treaty-making competence. In addition, they do realise that third parties should not be enabled to benefit from internal difficulties in the Community camp.

---

[100] See KR Simmonds, 'The European Community and the New Law of the Sea' (1989) 218 *RdC* 9 at 112–15. See also T Treves, 'The European Community and the Law of the Sea Convention: New Developments' in Cannizzaro (ed), n29 above, 279 at 281–90.

[101] See *Commentaire Megret*, n41 above, 183.

[102] See C Timmermans, 'Organising Joint Participation of EC and Member States' in Dashwood and Hillion (eds), n49 above, 239 at 242.

8. CONCLUSION, RATIFICATION AND PARTICIPATION

In terms of the conclusion of mixed agreements, there is a degree of coordination between the Community and the Member States in the process of accession to international conventions and ratification of agreements. In relation to Vienna Convention for the Protection of the Ozone Layer and the Montreal Protocol on Substances that Deplete the Ozone Layer, for instance, the relevant Council Decision sets out a deadline by which the Member States are to 'take the necessary steps to permit the deposit, as far as possible simultaneously, of the instruments of ratification, acceptance, approval or accession . . . by the Community and the Member States';[103] to that effect, there is express provision for cooperation between the Commission and the Member States. At other instances, the simultaneous ratification of an agreement is expressly recognised as necessary for the latter's uniform and complete application within the Community legal order.[104] In any case, the limits of this practice are apparent, as ratification of an international agreement falls within the sovereign discretion of states.

As to the issue of the entry into force of mixed agreements, in contrast to the EC Treaty, the European Atomic Energy Community provided for a specific rule. Article 102 EAEC read as follows:

> Agreements or contracts concluded with a third State, an international organization or a national of a third State to which, in addition to the Community, one or more Member States are parties, shall not enter into force until the Commission has been notified by all the Member States concerned that those agreements or contracts have become applicable in accordance with the provisions of their respective national laws.

This arrangement[105] is also followed in the Community legal order as a matter of practice. Whilst often applied smoothly, there have been instances where the period between the conclusion of an agreement and its entry into force is unnecessarily long because of delays in the process of ratification in national legal orders. The Cooperation and Customs Union Agreement with San Marino is an infamous example of such delay often mentioned in academic literature:[106] the Agreement actually entered into force on 28 March 2002, that is more than 10 years after its approval by the Parties.[107] Delays in the implementation of legal rules due to inadequate coordination are not novel in the area of EU external relations. In the area of economic sanctions on third countries, for instance, there are sometimes delays due to the imposition of the sanctions regime on the basis of

---

[103] Art 3(1) Council Dec 88/540/EEC [1988] OJ L 297/8.

[104] See Council Dec 2001/539/EC on the conclusion by the European Community of the Convention for the Unification of Certain Rules for International Carriage by Air (the Montreal Convention) [2001] OJ L 194/38.

[105] This was recently illustrated in the case of the Additional Protocols to the Treaty on the Non-Proliferation of Nuclear Weapons: see E Denza, 'Non-proliferation of Nuclear Weapons: The European Union and Iran', (2005) 10 *EFA Rev* 289.

[106] See Rosas, n49 above, at 208, Eeckhout in n55 above, at 218 and *Commentaire Megret*, n41 above, at 186.

[107] [2002] OJ L 84/43.

two instruments, namely a common position adopted under Title V TEU and a Council Regulation adopted under Article 301 EC.[108] In the context of mixed agreements concluded by the Community and the Member States, this problem is generally dealt with by separating, where possible, the component of the agreement falling with the exclusive competence of the Community and incorporating it in an Interim Agreement concluded by the Community under Article 133 EC and its contracting partner. Indeed, this was the case in the abovementioned Agreement with San Marino.[109] The practice of concluding interim agreements was formalised in Article 300(2)(1) EC at Amsterdam.

It is often the case that, when concluded pursuant to the mixed formula, international agreements providing for accession by international organisations require that international organisations specify the areas of the agreements in question falling within their competence. The first in which the Community agreed to provide such a declaration was the Law of the Sea Convention in which, despite the fact that the Community did not participate in its negotiation, participation by international organisations was permitted.[110] The Declaration submitted by the Community reads in part as follows:

1. Matters for which the Community has exclusive competence:
The Community points out that its Member States have transferred competence to it with regard to the conservation and management of sea fishing resources. Hence in this field it is for the Community to adopt the relevant rules and regulations (which are enforced by the Member States) and, within its competence, to enter into external undertakings with third States or competence international organisations. This competence applies to waters under national fisheries jurisdiction and to the high seas. Nevertheless, in respect of measures relating to the exercise of jurisdiction over vessels, flagging and registration of vessels and the enforcement of penal and administrative sanctions, competence rests with the member States whilst respecting Community law. Community law also provides for administrative sanctions.
2. Matters for which the Community shares competence with its Member States
With regard to fisheries, for a certain number of matters that are not directly related to the conservation and management of sea fishing resources, for example research and technological development and development cooperation, there is shared competence.

Declarations of competence are also required in agreements concluded by the European Atomic Energy Community.[111]

---

[108] See P Koutrakos, *Trade, Foreign Policy and Defence in EU Constitutional Law* (Oxford: Hart Publishing, 2001) at 86–90.

[109] [1992] OJ L 359/14.

[110] Annex IX to the Convention. For the participation of the Community, see KR Simmonds, 'The Community's Participation in the U.N. Law of the Sea Convention' in D. O'Keeffe and H.G. Schermers (eds), *Essays in European Law and Integration* (Deventer: Kluwer, 1982) 179. For a more favourable assessment in the light of its specific context, see R Barents, 'The European Communities and the Commodity Organisations' (1984) 10 *LIEI* 77 at 85 ff.

[111] See for instance the Convention on Nuclear Safety (1996) concluded under the auspices of the International Atomic Energy Agency. The content of the required declaration of competence was the subject-matter of Case C–29/99 *Commission v Council* [2002] ECR I–11221 annotated by P Koutrakos in [2004] 41 *CMLRev* 191.

A declaration of competence reflects the division between the Community and national competence in the context of a specific agreement to which both (intend to) become parties. Its main function is to inform other parties to the Agreement as to whether the Community or the Member States are responsible for the perform-ance of particular obligations. As the provisions of international agreements and the balance between EC and national competence are subject to change, so is the con-tent of a declaration. This was the case with the General Fisheries Commission for the Mediterranean (1998):[112] its amendment establishing an autonomous budget and the ensuing financial contribution by the Community necessitated the submis-sion of an amended declaration of competence and voting rights.[113]

In the case of the Cartagena Protocol on Biosafety and in accordance with Article 34(3) of the Convention on Biological Diversity, the Community submit-ted a declaration of competence following the ruling of the Court of Justice in *Opinion 2/00*.[114] The declaration submitted is interesting not only for the degree of generality which it shares with other declarations but mainly for its concluding phrase which reads as follows: '[t]he exercise of Community competence is, by its nature, subject to continuous development'.[115]

In terms of the practice of the participation of the Community and its Member States in international organisations, the voting rights of the Community are exer-cised on the basis of the underlying principles of competence. As the International Agreement on Jute and Jute Products specifies, 'in the case of voting on matters within their competence, such intergovernmental organisations shall vote with a number of votes equal to the total number of votes attributable to their member States in accordance with [the specific provisions of the Agreement]. In such cases, the member States of such intergovernmental organisations shall not be entitled to exercise their individual rights'.[116]

There is no single formula applying to all mixed agreements for how the Community position is determined and presented. In some cases, provision to that effect is made in the Council Decision concluding the agreement on behalf of the Community. In relation to the Joint Committee set up under the Interbus Agreement on the international occasional carriage of passengers by coach and bus, for instance, the relevant measure provides that the position to be taken by the Community within the Committee shall be adopted by the Council acting by a qualified majority on a Commission proposal, except in relation to issues about the Committee's Rules of Procedure in which case decision-making is by simple majority.[117] Furthermore, the Member States may formalise the way in which they are to participate in an agreement concluded along with the Community; a case

[112] It was concluded on behalf of the Community by Council Dec 98/416/EC [1998] OJ L 190/34.
[113] See Annex to Council Dec 2004/815EC [2004] OJ L 357/30.
[114] [2001] ECR I–9713.
[115] Annex B to Council Dec 2002/628/EC [2002] OJ L 201/48.
[116] Art 5(2) [1991] OJ L 29/4 adopted by the Community by Council Dec 91/5/EEC [1991] OJ L 29/1.
[117] Council Dec 2002/917/EC [2002] OJ L 321/11.

in point is the Cotonou Agreement for which the Commission submitted a draft.[118]

Questions about representation are not unique in the context of the Community legal order. Under the second pillar, for instance, the Union has participated in the efforts of the international community to find a solution to the issue of nuclear proliferation in the Korean peninsula. To that effect, it participates in the Korean Peninsular Energy Development Organisation (KEDO). The Common Position adopted by the Council under Article 15 TEU on the participation of the Union includes provisions about the determination of the EU position within KEDO's Executive Board: the Council and the Commission have agreed that if KEDO's Executive Board were to address any matter falling outside Euratom's competence, it would be the Presidency of the Council of the European Union which took the floor to express the position taken by the Council.[119]

The case of the participation of the Community and its Member States in the Food and Agriculture Organisation (FAO) is interesting.[120] The Community is a member along with the Member States. This was achieved following an amendment of the FAO's constitution which, *inter alia,* permitted international organisations to accede to it. As a result, the Community was required to submit a declaration of competence specifying the areas in which it was endowed with exclusive competence, the latter including all matters concerning fisheries aimed at protecting fishing grounds and conserving the biological resources of the sea.[121] In terms of decision-making and voting rights, the General Rules of FAO provided as follows:

> Rule XLI(2). Before any meeting of the organization the Member Organization or its Member States shall indicate which, as between the Member Organization and its Member States, has competence . . . and which, as between the Member Organization and its Member States, shall exercise the right to vote in respect of each particular agenda item.

> Rule XLI(3). In cases where an agenda item covers both matters in respect of which competence has been transferred to the Member Organization and matters which lie within the competence of its Member states, both the Member Organization and its Member States may participate in the discussions. In such cases the meeting, in arriving at its decisions, shall take into account only the intervention of the party which has the right to vote.

In relation to the coordination of the positions between the Community and the Member States, the Council and the Commission concluded an Arrangement on the preparation for FAO meetings, statements and voting. The following section of that Arrangement is worth-quoting in full:

---

[118] Internal Agreement between the representatives of the governments of the Member States, meeting with the Council, on measures to be taken and procedures to be followed for the implementation of the ACP–EC Partnership Agreement [2000] OJ L 317/376.

[119] Art 1 of Council Common Position 2001/869/CFSP [2001] OJ L 325/1.

[120] See Denza, n4 above, at 7–9 and Sack, n4 above, at 1243–7.

[121] See R Frid, *The Relations Between the EC and International Organizations—Legal Theory and Practice* (The Hague: Kluwer, 1995) Ch 5.

1.12.   In the absence of an agreement between the Commission and the Member States
. . ., the matter will be decided according to the procedure provided for in the Treaty and
the agreed practice. In the absence of agreement on this basis, the matter will be referred
to the Permanent Representatives Committee.

1.13.   Decisions referred to in 1.12 are without prejudice to the respective competences
of the Community and its Member States

2.1.   Where an agenda item deals with matters of exclusive Community competence, the
Commission shall speak and vote for the Community.

2.2.   Where an agenda item deals with matters of national competence, Member States
shall speak and cote.

2.3.   Where an agenda item deals with matters containing elements both of national and
of Community competence, the aim will be to achieve a common position by consensus. If a common position can be achieved:

　　—the Presidency shall express the common position when the thrust of the issue lies
　　in an area outside the exclusive competence of the Community. Member States and
　　the Commission may speak to support and/or to add to the Presidency statement.
　　Member States will vote in accordance with the common position.

　　—the Commission shall express the common position when the thrust of the issue
　　lies in an area within the exclusive competence of the Community. Member States
　　may speak to support and/or add to the Commission's statement. The Commission
　　will vote in accordance with the common position.

2.4.   Should it prove impossible to reach a common position, Member States shall speak
and vote. In accordance with the FAO rules of procedure, the Commission would be able
to participate in the discussion.

The precise interpretation of the provisions of FAO voting arrangements
agreed upon by the Council and the Commission is not without ambiguities.[122]
An interesting case of its application was raised before the Court in an action for
annulment. In Case C–25/94 *Commission v Council (FAO)*,[123] the Commission
challenged a decision adopted by the Council in November 1993 giving the
Member States the right to vote in the FAO for the adoption of the Agreement to
Promote Compliance with International Conservation and Management
Measures by Fishing Vessels on the High Seas. The clauses on the attribution and
changing of flags which were included in a first draft caused controversy between
the Commission and the Member States: registration of vessels lies within national competence, whereas the conservation and management of fishery resources
falls within the exclusive competence of the Community. Whilst both the
Commission and the Member States agreed that the negotiation and conclusion
of the agreement was a matter of shared competence, they disagreed as to the
exercise of the right to vote, each arguing that the thrust of the draft Agreement
fell within their respective sphere of competence. The disagreement persisted
despite the removal of the clauses on registration and flagging in a second draft,

---

[122] See J Heliskoski, 'Internal Struggle for International Presence: The Exercise of Voting Rights
Within the FAO' in Dashwood and Hillion (eds), n49 above, 79 at 84.
[123] Case C–25/94 *Commission v Council (FAO)* [1996] ECR I–1469.

following which it was indicated to the FAO that it would be the Member States which would vote. This they duly did. Following the adoption of the Agreement, the Commission requested that the Council, meeting in its Fisheries formation, approve a declaration not only stating that the Agreement ought to have been approved by the Commission alone but also that, in the future, it would be the Commission which would vote on matters of that nature. It was the refusal of the Council to do so and its confirmation of the approach already adopted that constituted the subject-matter of the action brought before the Court of Justice.

Having applied its well-known functional approach to the material scope of the action for annulment under Article 230 EC, the Court accepted the admissibility of the action by concluding that the Council's decision as to voting rights in the FAO had legal effects. These applied to 'relations between the Community and the Member States, between the institutions of the Community and, finally, between the Community and its Member States on the one hand and other subjects of international law, especially the FAO and its Member States, on the other'.[124]

As to the substance of the dispute, the Court affirmed that the competence of the Community on the conservation of the biological resources of the sea was exclusive, a fact recognised by its caselaw but also illustrated by the Community's declaration of competence sent to the FAO.[125] It was also pointed out that, as regards the high seas and in areas falling within its authority, the Community had regulatory powers identical to those enjoyed under international law by the state whose flag the vessel flew or in which it was registered.[126] It then went on to identify the essential object of the draft Agreement as confined to compliance with international conservation and management measures by fishing vessels on the high sea.

The Council's contention that the main thrust of the draft Agreement fell within national competence was based on two arguments: on the one hand, it set out a system of fishing licences which was comparable to the system of authorisation to fly a particular flag given by national authorities; on the other hand, it included provisions referring to the possibility of imposing penal sanctions and to the provision of assistance to developing countries. Both were rejected by the Court. As regards the former, fishing licences had constituted traditional instruments of managing fishing resources and, as such, were fundamentally different from the international law rights of every state to regulate which ship would fly its flag. In relation to the latter argument, the relevant provisions were deemed not to occupy a prominent position in the draft Agreement.

Having defined the thrust of the draft Agreement as within the scope of Community competence, the Court went on to recapitulate the significance of the duty of cooperation between the Community institutions and the Member

---

[124] Para 37. The fact that, in its Conclusions, the Council had noted that 'the substantive questions of competence and exercise of voting rights in matters coming under the future Agreement had not been settled' and that it had asked COREPER to reconsider the question of voting in due course was considered irrelevant: para 38.

[125] See Joined Cases 3/76, 4/76 and 6/76 *Kramer and Others* [1976] ECR 1279 at para 33.

[126] Para 44 with reference to Case C–405/92 *Mondiet v Islais* [1993] ECR I–6133 para 12.

States in the process of the negotiation, conclusion and implementation of mixed agreements. In doing so, it reaffirmed the role of the requirement of unity in the international representation of the Community as the basis of the duty of cooperation,[127] the latter requiring that the Community institutions and the Member States take all necessary steps to ensure the best possible cooperation.[128] It was precisely the voting rules contained in the Arrangement between the Commission and the Council which represented fulfilment of that duty within the FAO. As those rules were clearly intended to bind both institutions to each other, the Council decision to allow the Member States to vote for the adoption of the draft Agreement despite the fact that its main thrust fell within Community competence constituted a violation of the voting rules laid down in the Arrangement. Therefore, it ran counter to Community law.

In terms of its approach to the definition of external competence, the judgment in *FAO* is entirely consistent with the caselaw setting out the constitutional foundations of competence as examined in previous Chapters. Indeed, rather than deconstructing all the elements of the subject-matter of the Agreement, the Court ascertained whether that covered areas over which the competence of the Community was exclusive. Once those have been found to constitute the core of the Agreement, the Court moves on to the issue of the management of shared competence. In this respect, it should be pointed out that the Court did not conclude that the Community's exclusive competence covered the entire scope of the Agreement;[129] neither did it identify which parts of the latter fell within national competence or over which, if any, the competence of the Community was shared. However, the Court had no difficulty in finding that the 'thrust' of the Agreement or its 'essential object' fell within the Community's exclusive competence by relying upon the absence of provisions on registration and flagging in its final draft. In this respect, it deviated from the advice of Advocate General Jacobs, who had argued that 'at the time of deciding on the indication of competence it was . . . legitimate to take account of the flagging dimension of the negotiation'.[130] This argument had led him conclude that it was difficult to define competence in terms of the 'thrust of the issue'.

In his analysis, Advocate General Jacobs appears to adopt a pragmatic approach to the conduct of negotiations: as issues perceived to fall within national competence could re-emerge at a later stage of the negotiations, competence could not be determined on the basis of the Commission's arguments. It is recalled that, in the past, such practical considerations had influenced the Court in applying the principles of competence to the facts of cases brought before it. In *AETR*, for instance, the negotiation of the Agreement in question by the Member States had

---

[127] *Ruling 1/78* [1978] ECR 2151 at paras 34–36, *Opinion 2/91 (re: ILO)* [1993] ECR I–1061 at para 36 and *Opinion 1/94*, n78 above, at para 108.

[128] *Opinion 2/91*, n127 above, at para 38.

[129] See N Neuwahl, 'Shared Powers or Combined Incompetence? More on Mixity' (1996) 33 *CMLRev* 667 at 682.

[130] Para 69 of his Opinion in n123 above.

been sanctioned in order to avoid undermining the successful outcome of the negotiations by suggesting to the negotiating parties a new distribution of powers within the Community.[131] It is interesting that the Court should have chosen not to take this practical aspect of negotiations into account in *FAO*. And yet, its judgment had distinct pragmatic overtones in its approach to the Arrangement between the Commission and the Council. It is remarkable that the content of the Arrangement was not assessed in the light of Community law, nor were its effects questioned in any way. This might be explained by the fact that, rather than being an inter-institutional agreement *stricto sensu*, the document in question was broader in its scope, as it expressed the commitment of the Member States as to how to manage their competence.

In giving effect to the FAO Arrangement, the Court applied the duty of cooperation in a rigorous manner. One factor which might have rendered this less controversial than might have been assumed originally was the substantive content of the position of the Commission and the Member States: there was no dispute as to the desired outcome of the negotiations and a common position had been formed throughout that process.[132] In other words, the rigorous application of the procedural rules laid down in the FAO Arrangement had no effect on the substance of the negotiating position of the Community and the Member States. At a more general level, the judgment in *FAO* appears to convey two messages to both the Community institutions and the Member States: on the one hand, the *ad hoc* arrangements about the management of their shared competence upon which they both agree would be accepted by the Community judicature as the valid expression of their will to comply with their duty of cooperation. On the other hand, the effects of such arrangements would be enforced by the Court. This may be a double-edged sword in so far as the encouragement to adopt formalised methods of cooperation is accompanied by the clear threat of judicial intervention.[133] However, the Court's approach in *FAO* is linked to a theme illustrated more clearly in the rulings in *Opinions 1/94* and *2/00*, namely the emerging emphasis on the duty of cooperation. Conceived to be binding upon the Community institutions and the Member States in the process of negotiation, conclusion and implementation of international agreements, this duty is central to the management of EC external relations. In enforcing it rigorously by relying upon the very arrangements reached voluntarily by the Community institutions and the Member States, the Court indicates the binding character of that duty.

It is not only the question of the modalities of the participation of the Community and the Member States which raises questions. It is also that of

---

[131] Case 22/70 *Commission v Council (AETR)* [1971] ECR 263 at para 86.

[132] See Jacobs AG n123 above, at para 59 and Heliskoski, n122 above, at 99.

[133] See I Govaere, J Capiau and A Vermeersch, 'In-Between Seats: The Participation of the European Union in International Organizations' (2004) 9 *EFA Rev* 155 at 167 who point out that no code of conduct similar to the FAO Arrangement has been concluded following the *FAO* judgment.

responsibility. It is recalled that the European Community, which is endowed with express legal personality, incurs international responsibility: as the International Court of Justice put it:[134]

> international organisations are subjects of international law and, as such, are bound by any obligations incumbent upon them under general rules of international law, under their constitutions or under international agreements to which they are parties.

In certain cases of mixed agreements where there is express allocation of competence over specific provisions, the declarations submitted by the Community may clarify the issue of responsibility. This was the case regarding the Convention on the Transboundary Effects of Industrial Accidents: the declaration of competence submitted by the Community included the following clause: '[a]s regards the application of the Convention, the Community and its Member States are responsible, within their respective spheres of competence'.[135] In other cases, the question is raised whether the Community and the Member States are jointly and severally liable. In his Opinion in the *EDF* case, Advocate General Jacobs argued that 'under a mixed agreement the Community and the Member States are jointly liable unless the provisions of the agreement point to the opposite conclusion'.[136] In relation to a procedural provision of TRIPS, Advocate General Tesauro argued in his Opinion in *Hermès* that '[i]n these circumstances, it should be recognised that the Member States and the Community constitute, vis-à-vis contracting non-member States, a single contracting party or at least contracting parties bearing equal responsibility in the event of failure to implement the agreement'.[137] In its judgment in *EDF* case, the Court held as follows:[138]

> The Convention was concluded, according to its preamble and Article 1, by the Community and its Member States of the one part and the ACP States of the other part. It established an essentially bilateral ACP-EEC cooperation. In those circumstances, in the absence of derogations expressly laid down in the Convention, the Community and its Member States as partners of the ACP States are jointly liable to those latter States for the fulfilment of every obligation arising from the commitments undertaken, including those relating to financial assistance.

However, Advocate General Mischo reached a different conclusion in his Opinion in the *Berne Convention* case where he argued in the following terms:[139]

---

[134] ICJ Advisory Opinion *Interpretation of the Agreement of 25 March 1951 between the WHO and Egypt* [1980] ICJ Rep 73 at 89.

[135] Annex II to Council Dec 98/685 [1998] OJ L 326/1.

[136] N86 above, at para 69 of his Opinion.

[137] Case C–53/96 *Hermès International v FHT Marketing Choice BV* [1998] ECR I–3603, para 14.

[138] Case C–316/91, n86 above, para 29. On joint responsibility, see Eeckhout n55 above, at 222–3, MacLeod, Hendry and Hyett, n21 above, at 158–60, C Tomuschat, 'The International Responsibility of the European Union' in Cannizzaro, n29 above, 177 at 185. However, see the analysis in J Heliskoski, *Mixed Agreements as a Technique for Organizing the International Relations of the European Community and its Member States* (The Hague: Kluwer, 2001) 147–53.

[139] Case C–13/00 *Commission v Ireland* [2001] ECR I–2943, para 30.

It does not appear certain to me, however, that the simple fact that the respective obligations of the Community and the Member States to the other Contracting Parties have not been defined enables the latter to infer that the Community assumes responsibility for fulfilment of the whole of the agreement in question, including those provisions which do not fall within its competence. On the contrary, the very fact that the Community and its Member States had recourse to the formula of a mixed agreement announces to non-member countries that that agreement does not fall wholly within the competence of the Community and that, consequently, the Community is, *a priori*, only assuming responsibility for those parts falling within its competence.

In relation to the Fourth Lomé Convention in particular, the Court ruled in the *EDF* judgment as follows:[140]

The Convention was concluded, according to its preamble and Article 1, by the Community and its Member States of the one part and the ACP States of the other part. It established an essentially bilateral ACP-EEC cooperation. In those circumstances, in the absence of derogations expressly laid down in the Convention, the Community and its Member States as partners of the ACP States are jointly liable to those latter States for the fulfilment of every obligation arising from the commitments undertaken, including those relating to financial assistance.

In practical terms, the issue of responsibility may be addressed on the basis of specific provisions included in the international treaties concluded by the Community and the Member States. The UN Convention on the Law of the Sea, for instance, provides for such a clause in Article 6(2) of Annex IX which reads as follows:

Any State Party may request an international organization or its member States which are States Parties for information as to who has responsibility in respect of any specific matter. The organization and the member States concerned shall provide this information. Failure to provide this information within a reasonable time or the provision of contradictory information shall result in joint and several liability.

The significance of *ad hoc* solutions and practical arrangements should not be underestimated in relation to the issue of the definition of international responsibility: in the absence of a clear demarcation of competence, practice may clarify which party has been involved in the (mis)implementation of which rule.[141] This is a point which will be further elaborated in this Chapter. At this juncture, suffice it to note that, in the context of the work of the International Law Commission on Responsibility of States for Internationally Wrongful Acts, there is a provision according to which 'where several States are responsible for the same internationally wrongful act, the responsibility of each State may be

---

[140] Case C–316/91, n86 above, para 29.
[141] See M Bjoerklund, 'Responsibility in the EC for Mixed Agreements—Should Non-Member Parties Care?' (2001) 70 *Nordic Journal of International Law* 373.

invoked in relation to that Act'.[142] However, the accompanying commentary qualifies that rule and points out that it:[143]

> neither recognizes a general rule of joint and several responsibility, nor does it exclude the possibility that two or more States will be responsible for the same internationally wrongful act. Whether this is so will depend on the circumstances and on the international obligations of each of the States concerned.

9. MANAGING MIXITY WITHIN THE WORLD TRADE ORGANISATION

The above section highlighted the *ad hoc* nature of arrangements aiming at the management of the coexistence of the Community and its Member States in international organisations. It also examined their acceptance and enforcement by the Court of Justice, as illustrated by the judgment in the *FAO* case regarding voting. However, the structure of international organisations may raise further challenges to the manner in which the Community and the Member States agree to manage their competences. The WTO framework is a case in point, due to the variety of the agreements it comprises, the various forms of coexistence of Community and national competence it encompasses and the structure of its enforcement. Under the Dispute Settlement Understanding, the principle of cross-retaliation makes it entirely possible for a third country to be found by WTO bodies to have suffered injury in an area covered by the EC competence and, yet, be enabled to impose countermeasures in an area perceived to fall within national competence. It is recalled that, in the concluding part of its ruling in *Opinion 1/94*, the Court had referred specifically to the rule of cross-retaliation the application of which made the duty of cooperation between the Community and the Member States all the more necessary. The relevant extract is worthciting in full:[144]

> The duty to cooperate is all the more imperative in the case of agreements such as those annexed to the WTO Agreement, which are inextricably interlinked, and in view of the cross-retaliation measures established by the Dispute Settlement Understanding. Thus, in the absence of close cooperation, where a Member State, duly authorized within its sphere of competence to take cross-retaliation measures, considered that they would be ineffective if taken in the fields covered by GATS or TRIPS, it would not, under Community law, be empowered to retaliate in the area of trade in goods, since that is an area which on any view falls within the exclusive competence of the Community under Article 113 of the Treaty. Conversely, if the Community were given the right to retaliate in the sector of goods but found itself incapable of exercising that right, it would, in the absence of close cooperation, find itself unable, in law, to retaliate in the areas covered by GATS or TRIPs, those being within the competence of the Member States.

---

[142] Art 47(1) in Resolution of the General Assembly A/56/83.
[143] ILC Report A/56/10, 317. See the analysis in PJ Kuijper and E Paasivirta, 'Further Exploring International Responsibility: the European Community and the ILC's Project on Responsibility of International Organisations' (2004) 1 *International Organizations Law Review* 111.
[144] N78 above, para 109.

In the light of the above, it is interesting that the experience so far should have illustrated a remarkable ability of all the parties involved to tackle substantive issues whilst avoiding addressing matters of principle. A couple of examples are worth mentioning. A dispute arose in 1996 about the classification of local area network (LAN) equipment and multimedia personal computers for tariff purposes. The United States authorities argued that the classification carried out by the customs authorities of the Community and those of Great Britain and Ireland resulted in the imposition of higher tariffs and was in violation of Article II GATT 1994. The US authorities initiated separate proceedings against the Community, the UK and Ireland, the latter two covering the alleged violations by the respective national authorities despite the fact that those violations had also formed part of the proceedings initiated against the Community. The Community claimed that the initiation of separate proceedings against its Member States was unacceptable in the light of its exclusive competence over the application of tariff policy. This position was also supported by Ireland and the United Kingdom. The problem was addressed by means of a procedural device: following the suggestion by the Commission, the US authorities agreed that the panel established for the complaint against the EC examine the complaints against its two Member States too.

The uncontroversial existence of the Community's exclusive competence over the GATT did not render the *LAN* dispute as challenging as it might have been. In relation to the issue of responsibility, for instance, both the Commission's argument that, due to the transfer of competence, no violation could possibly have been committed by its Member States and the US counter-argument that the latter were independent WTO members were not addressed directly: in the light of the factual and procedural context of the complaints, neither the Panel[145] nor the Appellate Body addressed the issue of responsibility.[146] However, things could be more difficult in the case of disputes which arose in the context of TRIPS, that is the agreement about which the Court rejected the Commission's claims for exclusivity in a comprehensive manner in *Opinion 1/94*. In 1998, the United States initiated identical, albeit separate, proceedings against Ireland[147] and the Community,[148] alleging the violation of a number of TRIPS provisions by Irish legislation on copyright and neighbouring rights. Again, these proceedings were joined, as indeed was the case in another set of complaints by United States against Greece and the Community regarding the enforcement of intellectual property rights in the area of motion picture and television rights.[149]

---

[145] See WTO doc WT/DS62/R, WT/DS67/R, WT/DS68/R of 5 Feb 1998.
[146] See WTO doc WT/DS62/AB/R, WT/DS67/AB/R, WT/DS68/AB/R of 5 June 1998.
[147] See WTO doc WT/DS82/2 of 12 Jan 1998.
[148] See WTO doc WT/DS115/2 of 12 Jan 1998.
[149] See WTO doc WT/DS124/1 and WTO doc WT/DS125/1 respectively, both of 7 May 1998.

These and other examples[150] indicate that the ambiguities and complexities of determining competence have not seriously challenged the ability of the Community to act within the WTO structures. Both the Community and the Member States have succeeded in fencing off attempts by third parties to divide them and exploit the general distinct reluctance to allocate competences. This in itself is an example of fulfilment of the duty of cooperation. However, viewed from this angle, compliance with that duty is dependent not only upon the determination of the Commission and the Member States to present a common front, but also the willingness of the other WTO members to accept the arrangements suggested to them. As neither is guaranteed, the limits of procedural ingenuity and tactical cooperation may be challenged.[151]

It is for this reason that, in recent years, the issue of the formalisation of a permanent mechanism regulating the participation of the Community and the Member States in the WTO has been under discussion. It is recalled that, following the conclusion of the Uruguay Round, a Code of Conduct had been drawn up between the Council, the Commission and the Member States authorising the Commission to carry out the negotiations on transport and investment services.[152] A number of proposals were made subsequently by countries holding the Presidency and the Commission suggested the drafting of a Code of Conduct which would govern participation in the WTO.[153] All failed to win consensus. At the Nice Intergovernmental Conference, a number of proposals were also tabled. The one submitted by the Portuguese Presidency to the Feira European Council in June 2000 was entitled 'Protocol on arrangements for participation by the European Union (European Community and Member States) in WTO proceedings'.[154] It provided for a single procedure applicable to all cases, whether involving the exercise of Community powers, national powers or powers shared between the Community and the Member States. The Commission would become the sole spokesman and negotiator, presenting the common position as determined by the Council by qualified majority. Not only would Member States have the right to participate in all WTO meetings directly or indirectly, that is through the Council Presidency, but there would also be channels of continuous communication and interaction between them and the Commission and the Presidency. The Protocol also suggested a procedural simplification: rather than determined by the Council, the common position would be determined by the Article 133 Committee in cases

---

[150] See the detailed analysis in J Heliskoski, 'Joint Competence of the European Community and its Member States and the Dispute Settlement Practice of the World Trade Organization' (1999) 2 *CYELS* 61. Also, C Ni Cathain, 'The European Community and the Member States in the Dispute Settlement Understanding of the WTO: United or Divided?' (1999) 5 *ELJ* 461.

[151] See Heliskoski, n150 above, at 76 and 80 ff.

[152] The text of this Code of Conduct is reproduced in *Opinion 1/94*, n78 above, at 5365–6.

[153] See J Heliskoski, 'The "Duty of Cooperation" between the European Community and its Member States within the World Trade Organization' (1996) 7 *The Finnish Yearbook of International Law* 59 at 116 ff.

[154] CONFER 4750/00 Presidency report to the Feira European Council (Brussels, 14 June 2000).

where its purpose would be to comment on WTO texts of no legal effect for the Community or for the Member States and no delegation had asked for the matter to be referred to the Council.

In terms of its position under the DSU, the Draft Protocol required that the unity of the Union's representation be upheld. To that effect, the Commission would be responsible for the representation of the Member States and the preparation of their defence, albeit in close cooperation with the states in question. The potential conflict of interests between the Community and the relevant Member States would be avoided by requiring that every effort be made to ensure that WTO procedures do not result in the calling into question of advantages enjoyed by the Community or other Member States. As to the Union's position as a claimant, the Draft Protocol provided for the Commission's involvement in the relevant consultations, whereas the decision to request the establishment of a panel or submit an appeal would be taken by the Article 133 Committee by qualified majority. In cases where it would not be possible to establish a common position by qualified majority in order to request the establishment of a panel, it would be for the Member State concerned to make such a request. However, this exception was qualified in so far as it would not be applicable where the Council had decided by a qualified majority against such an individual request. The Draft Protocol submitted by the Portuguese Presidency, along with the others drafts circulated at the IGC, was not deemed acceptable by all delegations.

The above overview suggests that, rather than functioning on the basis of clearly pre-determined principles, the Community and the Member States manage their participation in WTO on the basis of *ad hoc* procedural arrangements, leaving, amongst others, the question of responsibility in an ambiguous state. Clarity in the conduct of international relations is both necessary and desirable. In the case of a Code of Conduct, the clarity that such an arrangement would bring in the participation of the Community and the Member States in the WTO should be welcome.[155] However, the advantages of such formalisation notwithstanding, one should neither overestimate the seriousness of the complications to which the existing dynamic state of affairs has given rise, nor underestimate the advantages that flexibility may provide in practical terms. Whilst the possibilities of challenging the ability of the Community and the Member States to manage their participation in WTO as a matter of practice are endless, no crisis has actually occurred. Equally, one should be aware of the inherent limits of legal rules which cannot possibly provide for every eventuality, all the more so in the light of the constantly evolving state of Community law and, hence, the ensuing re-definition of the

---

[155] On the desired content of such an arrangement, see A Antoniadis, 'The Participation of the European Community in the World Trade Organisation: An External Look at European Union Constitution-Building' in T Tridimas and P Nebia (eds), *European Union Law for the Twenty-First Century* Vol. 1 (Oxford: Hart Publishing, 2004), 321 at 338–40, PJ Kuiper, 'The Conclusion and Implementation of the Uruguay Round Results by the European Community' (1995) 6 *EJIL* 222 at 243–44, Timmermans, n102 above, at 246–7.

dividing line between Community and national competence. After all, it is recalled that the genesis and development of EC international relations has been defined by the flexible application of apparently strict principles. As it is the problematic cases which are brought before the Court of Justice and attract the attention of academic literature and, occasionally, give rise to alarmist comments and predictions of doom, it might be easy to underestimate the significance of the constant channels of cooperation between the Community institutions and the Member States. Developed incrementally and relied upon as a matter of practice, these arrangements indicate a culture of cooperation which, the absence of a formal foundation notwithstanding, underlie not only areas of potential controversy but also areas of certainty: in the negotiations leading to the adoption of the Cartagena Protocol on Biodiversity, for instance, the informal arrangements provided by the Commission and the Council were of such wide scope as to allow for meetings aiming at achieving a common position even on issues of exclusive competence.[156]

In other words, there is a tendency to underestimate the culture of cooperation which has developed over the years amongst the negotiators of and advisors on the Community's external policies and which manifests itself even in areas where the definition of competence is not an issue.[157] Similarly, the specific circumstances under which problematic cases reach the Court of Justice put any alarmist views into perspective: it is recalled, for instance, that in *FAO*, the dispute about voting notwithstanding, the Community and the Member States had had no difficulty during the negotiations in reaching a common position.

The above is not to suggest that, in the context of EC international relations, complacency is a virtue. Every effort aiming at facilitating the exercise of the Community's external competence and its coexistence with national competence should be encouraged. To that effect, in addition to the discussions about the formalisation of the procedural arrangements between the Community and the Member States, attention should also be drawn to the role of the duty of cooperation. Whilst an emerging theme in the Court's caselaw, its construction is developed incrementally as well as sparingly. Its incorporation in primary law,[158] as well as the determination of its legal basis on the EC provision endowing the Community with implied competence to act jointly with the Member States,[159] has been suggested. Both are useful and interesting.[160] However, similarly to the

---

[156] See l M Kritikos, 'Mixity and Ad Hoc Arrangements in EU Negotiating Strategies for the Biosafety Protocol' in F Snyder (ed), *International Food Security and Global Legal Pluralism* (Brussels: Bruylant, 2004) 153 at 166.

[157] See the empirical analysis in A Niemann, 'Between Communicative Action and Strategic Action: the Article 113 Committee and the Negotiations on the WTO Basic Telecommunications Services Agreement' (2004) 11 *Journal of European Public Policy* 379.

[158] See J Heliskoski, 'Should There Be a New Article on External Relations?' in M Koskenniemi (ed), *International Law Aspects of the European Union* (The Hague: Kluwer Law International, 1998) 273.

[159] See Editorial, 'The Aftermath of Opinion 1/94 or How to Ensure Unity of Representation for Joint Competence' (1995) 32 *CMLRev* 385.

[160] See the analysis in J Heliskoski, n92 above.

duty of loyal cooperation laid down in Article 10 EC, the duty binding the Community institutions and the Member States in the process of the negotiation, conclusion and application of international agreements cannot but reveal its precise implications through practice and, ultimately, its interpretation by the Court of Justice. After all, no mechanism aiming at precisely delineating competences and, accordingly, regulating their exercise can be capable of capturing all the aspects and ramifications of the relationship between the Community and Member States within the context of a mixed agreement. For instance, even in areas where the Member States are entirely competent to act, the exercise of their rights ought to be consistent with the requirements laid down in Community law.[161] In the light of this somewhat elusive quest for certainty, the interpretation of mixed agreements is central to the proper assessment of their role.

10. CONCLUSION

In a succinct analysis in 1997, Dashwood cogently described the function of mixed agreements in the context of the Community legal order and approached them as 'a necessary complication, rather than a necessary evil'.[162] The outline provided in this chapter endorses this view. The constitutional limitations inherent in the Community legal order, the rapidly developing interdependence of international regulation of different spheres of activities, the constantly evolving state of Community law and, hence, the need for redefinition of the dividing line between Community and national competence, all place mixed agreements at the very centre of EC international relations. Indeed, in addition to its accession to the FAO and the WTO and a number of other agreements, the Agreements with the countries of Central and Eastern Europe paving their way to EU membership, the Partnership and Cooperation Agreements with the countries of the former Soviet Union, the Agreement establishing the European Economic Area, the Agreements with its Mediterranean neighbours, all have been negotiated and concluded as mixed agreements. Once the principal role of this method has been accepted, the emphasis of the interested parties should focus on effective methods of managing the exercise of shared competence. These would include the use of mixed agreements only when truly necessary and the elaboration of appropriate procedural

---

[161] This principle has been articulated in areas considered to be of acute sensitivity to the Member States, both in the external and internal spheres: see, for instance, Case C–124/95 *The Queen, ex parte Centro-Com Srl v HM Treasury and Bank of England* [1997] ECR I–81 at para 27 and Case C–158/96 *Raymond Kohll v Union des caisses de maladie* [1998] ECR I–1931 at para 19 respectively.

[162] A Dashwood, 'Why Continue to Have Mixed Agreements at All?' in JHJ Bourgeois, J-L. Dewost, M-A Gaiffe (eds), *La Communauté européenne et les accords mixtes. Quelles perspectives?* (Brussels: Presses Interuniversitaires Européennes, 1997) 93. For an earlier analysis of the distinct role of mixed agreements as indicative of the Community's *sui generis* nature, see JHH Weiler, 'The External Legal Relations of Non-Unitary Actors: Mixity and the Federal Principle' in O'Keefe and Schermers, n1 above, 35.

mechanisms. In any case, the limits of legal rules in dealing with the various manifestations of mixity in the evolving international framework should not be underestimated; neither should the capacity of the informal Community and national structures to respond to legal challenges as a matter of practice be ignored. It is in the light of those structural limitations of any system managing shared competence that the role of the Court of Justice becomes all the more significant. After all, any assessment of the function of mixed agreements and the mechanisms of managing shared competence is dependent upon the system of enforcement of international obligations within the Community legal order. This is all the more so in the light of the caselaw of the Court of Justice which has clearly sanctioned the central position of mixed agreements. The approach of the Court of Justice to their interpretation will be examined in the next Chapter.

5

International Agreements, Member States and the Jurisdiction of the Court of Justice

1. INTRODUCTION

THE EXERCISE OF judicial authority over the conduct of any international actor presents special challenges for the balance between the judiciary and the executive and legislative branches. To a certain extent, this is due to the wide margin of discretion that the latter are presumed to enjoy in the area of international affairs. However, international law is applied as a matter of course by domestic courts, a phenomenon which has become all the more significant in this era of increasing and intense interdependence underpinning the current geopolitical environment. This phenomenon has enabled international law to penetrate all aspects of domestic legal orders, hence increasing the significance of the judiciary.

When applied to the European Community, this rather obvious observation raises even more challenging questions due to the unique constitutional arrangements which underpin this 'new legal order of international law'.[1] The previous chapter assessed one manifestation of this uniqueness in the central position of mixed agreements in the system of EC external relations. In examining its *raison d'être* and typology, it showed how it reflects the constitutional idiosyncrasies of the Community legal order. It also underlined its position as deeply entrenched in the ways in which the Community is bound to assert its identity on the international scene. Whilst the phenomenon of mixity has become the rule rather than the exception in the conduct of EC external relations, a number of questions about the jurisdiction of the Court of Justice to supervise their application and interpretation have been raised: does it extend to the entirety of the provisions of a mixed agreement? Does its scope vary depending on the provision of the agreement upon which the Court has been called to adjudicate? Is there any role left for the national courts, in addition, that is, to the one they enjoy in the context of the preliminary reference procedure?

---

[1] Case 26/62 *Van Gend en Loos* [1963] ECR 1 at 12.

Whilst the answer to these have been far from apparent for a considerable peri-od of time, its significance is self-evident: the existence, scope and exercise of the jurisdiction of the Court of Justice over the interpretation and application of mixed agreements have profound implications for the constitutional structure of the Union at various levels, namely in terms of the interaction between the legis-lature and the judiciary, that between the Community judicature and national courts, the latter and national legislature and, last but not least, courts and Com-munity citizens. In addition, the role of the Court of Justice in the interpretation of international agreements concluded by the Community may have serious repercussions for the way in which the legislature and executive would chose to represent the Community interests on the international scene.

2. OBLIGATIONS UNDER INTERNATIONAL AGREEMENTS

When the Community concludes an international agreement, it becomes bound under international law to fulfill the commitments undertaken pursuant to its provisions. This *pacta sunt servanda* principle constitutes a principle of custom-ary international law which is expressly laid down in Article 26 of the Vienna Convention of the Law on Treaties:

> Every treaty in force is binding upon the parties to it and must be performed by them in good faith.

However, the question which this raises is what other dimension the conclusion of such agreements adds to the legal position of the Community institutions and the Member States. Article 300(7) EC provides as follows:

> Agreements concluded under the conditions set out in this Article shall be binding on the institutions of the Community and on Member States.

The implications of this provision in the context of agreements falling within the exclusive competence of the Community and actually concluded by the Com-munity alone were highlighted by the Court quite early on. In a reference from the German Federal Finance Court on the interpretation of the Free Trade Agreement (FTA) between the Community and Portugal, the Court was asked to deal with the legality of the imposition of charges under German law upon quantities of port imported from Portugal.[2] In its judgment in *Kupferberg*, the Court relied upon Article 300(7) EC and opined that 'it is incumbent upon the Community institutions, as well as upon the Member States, to ensure compliance with the obligations arising from such agreements'.[3] As a corollary of this responsibility, the Court articulated the following duty imposed upon the Member States:[4]

---

[2] Case 104/81 *Hauptzollamt Mainz v C.A. Kupferberg & Cie KG a.A.* [1982] ECR 3641.
[3] *Ibid*, para 11.
[4] *Ibid*, para 13.

In ensuring respect for commitments arising from an international agreement conclud-ed by the Community institutions the Member States fulfill an obligation not only in relation to the non-member country concerned but also and above all in relation to the Community.

Therefore, the assumption of international obligations by the Community on its own carries with it the assumption of a Community law obligation by the Member States. This is related to the duty of loyal cooperation, that is the duty of Member States under Article 10 EC 'to take all appropriate measures, whether general or particular, to ensure fulfilment of the obligations arising out of this Treaty or resulting from action taken by the institutions of the Community'. After all, the conclusion of an agreement pursuant to Article 300 EC is an action taken by the Community the effects of which are formalised within the Community legal order by means of the Council measure actually concluding the Agreement. By referring to it expressly, the provision of Article 300(7) EC serves to articulate the effects of agreements concluded under Article 300 EC in a more comprehen-sive manner, hence completing the scope of the *ratio* of Article 300 EC.

Viewed from this angle, the construction of the obligations imposed upon the Member States in *Kupferberg* is strict in so far as it refers to the internal effects of the agreement on the legal position of the Member States, that is the effects pro-duced within the Community legal order. Arguments to the contrary have been advanced seeking to establish independent legal duties binding the Member States against third parties. [5] However, this position is not convincing: when based on an agreement concluded by the Community alone, the obligation of the Member States to non-member countries is only indirect: their actions or inactions may be the medium through which the Community would have to comply with its rele-vant international obligations. Indeed, in *Kupferberg* the Court referred to the possibility of an agreement being implemented by means of Community and national law, despite its conclusion by the Community alone.[6] To that effect, it is worth recalling the Agreement on competition law between the Community alone and the United States concluded contrary to the procedure laid down in Article 300 EC. In its judgment in *France v Commission*, the Court pointed out that the agreement was nonetheless binding on the Community and that, in the event of non-compliance, it would be the Community which would incur liability.[7] Therefore, it should be concluded that, whilst confirming the duty of Member States, Article 300(7) EC may not transform it into an international law one. It is for this reason that compliance by the Member States and Community institu-tions may only be ensured pursuant to the system of judicial review set out in the EC Treaty.

---

[5] For a summary and convincing counter arguments see I Macleod, ID Hendry and S Hyett, *The External Relations of the European Communities* (Oxford: OUP, 1996) 127 in n30.

[6] *Ibid*, para 12.

[7] Case C–327/91 *France v Commission* [1994] ECR I–3641 at paras 23–25.

The interpretation of Article 300(7) EC in the case of agreements concluded by the Community and the above analysis of its implications do not answer the question of the Community dimension of the obligations assumed by Member States in the context of mixed agreements. This question was addressed expressly by the Court in an action brought by the Commission against Ireland regarding the latter's accession to the Berne Convention for the Protection of Literary and Artistic Works.[8] Accession to the Berne Convention was an obligation laid down in Protocol 28 to the European Economic Area Agreement which had been concluded both by the Community and the Member States. In its judgment, the Court affirmed the right of the Commission to initiate enforcement proceedings for an obligation imposed under a mixed agreement because that obligation 'relates to an area covered in large measure by the Treaty'.[9]

Both the above formulation of the legal obligation of Member States and its foundation upon past case law are worthy of further analysis. However, their articulation and implications may not be properly appreciated unless placed within the evolving construction by the Court of the scope of its jurisdiction over international agreements. The reason for this is that the position of mixed agreements within the Community legal order and the interpretation of the procedures pursuant to which the Court determines that position appear to be intertwined. It is this link which informs the structure of this chapter.

3. BROAD CONSTRUCTION OF PRE-EMPTIVE JURISDICTION UNDER ARTICLE 300(6) EC

The EC Treaty provides for a mechanism of preventive control of the legality of international agreements. Article 300(6) reads as follows:

> The European Parliament, the Council, the Commission or a Member State may obtain the opinion of the Court of Justice as to whether an agreement envisaged is compatible with the provisions of this Treaty. Where the opinion of the Court of Justice is adverse, the agreement may enter into force only in accordance with Article 48 of the Treaty on European Union.

It is not only in the EC Treaty, that special procedures are set out regarding the examination of international agreements. Similar provisions are included in the European Atomic Energy Community Treaty[10] as well as the European Coal and Steel Community.[11] In relation to Article 300(6) EC, the right of the Parliament to request an Opinion was added at Nice. Whilst there is no provision for it in the

---

[8] Case C–13/00 *Commission v Ireland* [2001] ECR I–2943.
[9] *Ibid*, para 20.
[10] See Arts 103–105.
[11] See Art 75 (2) where this role is to be carried out by the Commission.

EC Treaty, the views of the Advocates General are heard by the Court which, sitting in closed session, then delivers the Opinion.[12]

There can be no doubt about the legally binding effects of the Court's rulings under Article 300(6) EC. Therefore, the term 'Opinion' may be explained in the light of the non-contentious nature of the procedure. As to the function of this exceptional procedure, it was described by the Court early on as follows:[13]

> It is the purpose of [the procedure laid down in Article 300(6) EC] to forestall complications which would result from legal disputes concerning the compatibility with the Treaty of international agreements binding upon the Community. In fact, a possible decision of the Court to the effect that such an agreement is, either by reason of its content or of the procedure adopted for its conclusion, incompatible with the provisions of the Treaty could not fail to provoke, not only in a Community context but also in that of international relations, serious difficulties and might give rise to adverse consequences for all interested parties, including third countries

In terms of the material scope of the procedure laid down in Article 300(6) EC and, in particular, the definition of the term 'agreement', the Court ruled that the designation of the document in question was irrelevant to the exercise of its jurisdiction. Instead, it was its nature which would determine its binding effects and, hence, the applicability of the procedure set out in Article 300(6) EC.[14] Furthermore, the preventative purpose of the procedure justified a broad approach to the subject-matter of requests:[15]

> This procedure must . . . be open for all questions capable of submission for judicial consideration, either by the Court of Justice or possible by national courts, in so far as such questions give rise to doubt either as to the substantive or formal validity of the agreement with regard to the Treaty.

When general issues of division of competence between the Community and the Member States were raised in *Opinion 1/75* about the conclusion of the Local Cost Understanding under the auspices of the OECD, the Council argued that Article 300(6) EC was inappropriate for the assessment of such issues.[16] This argument was rejected, as the broad interpretation of the subject-matter of Article 300(6) EC was seen as necessary in the light of its purpose. This conclusion is now incorporated in the Court's Rules of Procedures.[17]

---

[12] Art. 108(2) of the Court's Rules of Procedures.

[13] *Opinion 1/75 (re: OECD Local Cost Standard)* [1975] ECR 1355 at 1360–1.

[14] *Ibid*, at 1359–60.

[15] *Ibid*, at 1361.

[16] *Opinion 1/78* [1979] ECR 2871.

[17] According to Art 107(2) of the Rules of Procedure, '[t]he Opinion may deal not only with the question whether the envisaged agreement is compatible with the provisions of the EC Treaty but also with the question whether the Community or any Community institution has the power to enter into that agreement'.

The Court's jurisdiction under Article 300(6) EC also covers agreements which the Community may not actually conclude. This was made clear in relation to the compatibility of Convention No 170 of the International Labour Organisation, that is an organisation whose membership is confined to states.[18] The Court justified the admissibility of the request on the basis of two arguments. The first one was rather formalistic: the obstacles that the Community may actually encounter in the exercise of is competence are not for the Court to assess, as a request under Article 300(6) EC is related only to the competence of the Community and the Member States in the areas covered by the Convention. The second argument is convincing: despite the objective obstacle to the exercise of the Community's competence, in fact the latter may be exercised, albeit through the medium of the Member States acting jointly in the Community's interests.

The temporary scope of Article 300(6) EC has been interpreted in similarly broad terms. The procedure may be invoked about an agreement whose negotiation is at an end[19] or has yet to reach an advanced state. Indeed, in cases where the request for an Opinion is about the definition of competence, the Court opined that 'it is clearly in the interests of all States concerned, including non-Member countries, for such a question to be clarified as soon as any particular negotiations are commenced'.[20] However, such questions are bound to be assessed on an *ad hoc* basis: in *Opinion 1/78*, for instance, the Court had first pointed out that the subject-matter of the Agreement was already known and it was 'possible to form a sufficiently certain judgment on the question raised' on the basis of the documents submitted to the Court and the information provided at the hearing of the parties.[21] Indeed, to assess the timeliness of a request for an Opinion on the basis merely of the interests of third countries, even prior to the undertaking of any legal obligation, might appear slightly disingenuous. After all, only a month following the ruling in *Opinion 1/78*, the Court opined that the delimitation of competence is a matter internal to the Community and of no concern to third parties.[22]

An international agreement may constitute the subject-matter of a request for an Opinion even prior to the commencement of negotiations, provided that sufficient information exists at the time of the request. This issue was raised in *Opinion 2/94* regarding the accession of the Community to the European Convention on Human Rights.[23] The Court was asked to rule on two main issues, namely the competence of the Community to accede to the Convention and the compatibility of the latter with the EC Treaty. As regards the former, the Court pointed out that the general purpose and subject-matter of the Convention was

---

[18] *Opinion 2/91* [1993] ECR I–1061. paras 4–5.
[19] See *Opinion 1/94* [1994] ECR I–5267, para 12.
[20] *Opinion 1/78*, n16 above, para 35.
[21] *Ibid*, at para 34.
[22] *Ruling 1/78* [1978] ECR 2151 at para 35.
[23] *Opinion 2/94* [1996] ECR I–1759.

clear and would not be affected by whichever mechanism the Community might choose to accede to it. It also pointed out that an Opinion at that early stage would address the legitimate concerns of the Council to know the extent of the Community's powers prior to any decision on the opening of negotiations. As to the question of the compatibility of the Convention with the Community's judicial system, the Court held that it could not possibly address it: there was no sufficient information on the mechanisms pursuant to which the Community would submit to the jurisdiction of the European Court of Human Rights.

Furthermore, the Community institutions and the Member States may rely upon Article 300(6) EC even in relation to an agreement which has already been signed. To the argument to the contrary by the Spanish Government in relation to the WTO Agreements, the Court, in one short paragraph, ruled that a request for an Opinion may be made 'at any time before the Community's consent to be bound by the agreement is finally expressed. Unless and until that consent is given, the agreement remains an envisaged agreement'.[24] This line of reasoning was brought to its natural conclusion in *Opinion 3/94* where the Court held that to deliver an Opinion once the Agreement in question has been concluded is devoid of purpose.[25] In that case, the request had been submitted by the German government on the legality of the framework agreement on the Community import regime for bananas concluded between the Community and Colombia, Costa Rica, Nicaragua and Venezuela. That agreement was subsequently incorporated in the list of the Community's commitments contained in the GATT. The request for an Opinion was lodged following the signature of the WTO Agreements but prior to their conclusion. The Court opined that the critical issue was whether, at the time when its Opinion would be rendered, it would be possible to address any adverse effects in accordance with Article 300(6) EC, that is by relying upon Article 48 TEU and amending the EC Treaties. This would not be the case if the Agreements had already been concluded. Therefore, 'it would . . . be contrary to the internal logic of Article [300(6)] to accept that it is appropriate for the Court to rule on the compatibility with the Treaty of an agreement which has already been concluded, since a negative Opinion would not have the legal effect prescribed in that article'.[26]

This conclusion is entirely sensible. And yet, in essence, it allows practical considerations entirely unrelated to the institution or the state submitting the request to determine its admissibility. Such considerations include the case-load of the Court and are bound to affect the assessment of matters of considerable legal and political significance. In its ruling, the Court opined that the procedure laid down in Article 300(6) EC is not to protect the interests and rights of the parties requesting an opinion. These may be protected pursuant to an action for annulment and

---

[24] *Opinion 1/94* [1994] ECR I–5267, para 12.
[25] *Opinion 3/94* [1995] ECR I–4577, paras 11–23.
[26] *Ibid*, para 13.

the ensuing possibility of an application for interim relief.[27] As this is hardly satisfactory, one way of avoiding this, admittedly exceptional, chain of events might
be the establishment of a mechanism enabling the Court to deal with a request for
an Opinion as a matter of urgency. As such requests are the exception rather than
the rule, this would not put too much of a strain on the Court.[28] These issues
became relevant in June 2004 in relation to the EC–USA Agreement on the processing and transfer of passenger name record data by air carriers to the United
States Department of Homeland Security, Bureau of Customs and Border
Protection. When submitted for consultation to the Parliament, the latter requested an Opinion under Article 300(6) EC. However, the Council went on to conclude the Agreement. The Parliament, then, withdrew its request and initiated
annulment proceedings against the Council.[29]

The wide interpretation of the circumstances under which the request for an
Opinion may be submitted raises the question of the relationship between the
procedure under Article 300(6) EC and the other means of recourse to the Court
of Justice. This was examined by the Court in the context of the request submitted by the Belgian government about the competence of the Community to participate in the Third Revised OECD Decision on national treatment.[30] Two of the
questions submitted were about the correct legal basis of the Council Decision on
the Community's participation in the OECD Decision. The Council and the
Spanish and British governments argued that this was beyond the scope of Article
300(6) EC and, instead, should be dealt with within the context of an action under
Article 230 EC challenging the annulment of the relevant Council Decision. This
view was rejected: the Court ruled that the existence of alternative procedures
capable of bringing certain questions before the Community judicature cannot
preclude recourse to Article 300(6) EC, provided that such questions are related
to the substantive or formal validity of the agreement in question.[31]

The significance of the procedure laid down in Article 300(6) EC may not be
overstated.[32] Some of the most significant principles of EC international relations
law have been articulated in Opinions rendered in the exercise of this exceptional jurisdiction. That the Court has construed it in broad terms should not come

---

[27] See R Plender, 'The European Court's Pre-emptive Jurisdiction: Opinions under Article 300(6)
EC' in D O'Keeffe and A Bavasso (eds), *Liber Amicorum in Honour of Lord Slynn of Hadley—Judicial
Review in European Union Law* Vol. 1 (The Hague: Kluwer, 2000) 203 at 213–14 where he explores the
application of the duty of cooperation in order to prevent the conclusion of an agreement following a
request for an Opinion. However, this might give rise to the manipulation of the procedure for the
pursuit of short-term political or practical interests.

[28] However, in seeking to explain what they perceive as the shortcomings of *Opinion 1/94*, its critics
pointed out the extremely short period of time within which the Court delivered its ruling.

[29] Case C–317/04 *Parliament v Council*, notice in [2004] OJ C 228/31. Its request for an accelerated
procedure was rejected by Order of the President delivered on 21 Sept 2004.

[30] *Opinion 2/92* [1995] ECR I–521.

[31] *Ibid*, para 7.

[32] See V Christianos, 'La compétence consultative de la Cour de justice à la lumière de Traité sur
l'Union européenne' (1994) 374 *Revue du Marché Commun et de l'Union européenne* 37 who places
emphasis on its constitutional ramifications of the procedure. See also P Eeckhout, *The External
Relations of the European Union* (Oxford: OUP, 2004) at 232.

as a surprise in the light of its functional approach to the interpretation of its jurisdiction in the other, non-exceptional procedures laid down in the EC Treaty. This has been the case both in the sphere of the law of the internal market and that of EC international relations. In *Opinion 1/00*, for instance, the Court reformulated the question put forward by the Commission because of the lack of clarity resulting from the various language versions;[33] it is recalled that, in the context of preliminary references pursuant to Article 234 EC, it is by no means unusual for the Court to reformulate the question referred by national courts.[34] As for the EC international relations context, one hardly needs reminding of the broad construction of the notion of a legally binding act pursuant to Article 230 EC in the *AETR*[35] and *FAO*[36] cases.

What is most interesting in the interpretation of the procedure set out in Article 300(6) EC is the existence of a thread which links its broad construction to the substantive strands of EC international relations case law. In relation to the Cartagena Protocol on Biodiversity, for instance, the Court reaffirmed the broad scope of its jurisdiction by ruling that a request for an Opinion does not need to refer to a dispute about the existence of the competence of the Community or to the compatibility of the envisaged provisions with the substantive provisions of the EC Treaty: its jurisdiction under Article 300(6) EC arises in relation to any dispute about the legal basis of the Community's competence, its nature and the definition of its scope in relation to the competence of the Member States.[37] However, it made it clear that once the legal basis pursuant to which the Community competence may be exercised has been ascertained, it is beyond its jurisdiction under Article 300(6) EC to engage in a precise delineation of competences. The relevant extract is worth quoting in full:[38]

[The] procedure [laid down in Article 300(6) EC] is not intended to solve difficulties associated with implementation of an envisaged agreement which falls within shared Community and Member State competence.

In any event, where it is apparent that the subject-matter of an international agreement falls in part within the competence of the Community and in part within that of the Member States, it is important to ensure close cooperation between the Member States and the Community institutions, both in the process of negotiation and conclusion and in the fulfilment of the commitments entered

---

[33] *Opinion 1/00 (re: European Common Aviation Area)* [2002] ECR I–3493 at para 1.
[34] See, for instance, Case 28/85 *Deghillage v Caisse Primaire d'Assurance Maladie* [1986] ECR 991 at para 13.
[35] Case 22/70 *Commission v Council* [1971] ECR 263 at para 42.
[36] Case C–25/94 *Commission v Council* [1996] ECR I–1469 at paras 32 *ff*.
[37] *Opinion 2/00* [2001] ECR I–9713 at paras 4 *ff*.
[38] *Ibid*, paras 17–18. See the annotation on the ruling by A Dashwood, (2002) 39 *CMLRev* 353. For a call for a broader reading of Art 300(6) EC, see G Gattinara, 'La compétence consultative de la Cour de justice après les avis 1/00 et 2/00' [2003] *Revue du Droit de l'Union Européenne* 688.

into. In confining the scope of its exceptional jurisdiction in the above terms, the Court links this procedural issue with one trend underpinning its case law and one principle articulated therein: the former is its distinct reluctance to allocate competences once the exclusive nature of the Community's competence to negotiate and conclude an agreement has been ruled out and the existence of shared competence affirmed; the latter is the duty of cooperation which is intended to address any practical problems raised by the management of shared competence.

4. WHAT TYPE OF JURISDICTION UNDER THE PRELIMINARY REFERENCE PROCEDURE?

The significance of the role of international law in the exercise of the Court's jurisdiction under Article 234 EC became apparent quite early on. In *International Fruit Company*, the Court dealt with a reference from a Dutch court about a set of Community measures restricting the importation of apples from third countries and their validity in the light of the General Agreement on Tariffs and Trade (GATT).[39] This Agreement, to which all Member States were parties, had been concluded in 1947. The very first question referred to the Court was whether its jurisdiction pursuant to the preliminary reference procedure to rule on the validity of Community measures also covered their validity under international law. In two very short paragraphs, the Court interpreted the wording of Article 234(1) EC broadly: as that provision did not limit it by the grounds on which the validity of Community measures might be contested, its jurisdiction extended to all grounds capable of invalidating those measures. These include international law.[40]

The precise conditions under which the legality of Community law would be assessed in the light of international law were further elaborated in the judgment and will be analysed below. At this juncture, suffice it to point out that a different construction of the position of international law it the Community legal order would be impossible to envisage, all the more so in the light of the subject-matter of the agreement in question. After all, trade in goods and tariffs constituted one of the very few areas in which the Community enjoyed express treaty-making capacity. In any case, the function of the Court is described in Article 220 EC as 'ensur[ing] that in the interpretation and application of this Treaty the law is observed'. In interpreting 'the law' broadly, albeit conditionally, as the subsequent analysis will show, the Court made it clear that it is the Community judiciary

---

[39] Joined Cases 21 to 24/72 *International Fruit Company NV and Others v Produktschap voor Groenten en Fruit* [1972] ECR 1219.

[40] That conclusion also includes customarty international law: Case C–162/96 *Racke v Hauptzollampt Mainz* [1998] ECR I–3655 at para 27.

which is the ultimate authority on the legality of Community law. This conclusion was to be spelled out more clearly 15 years later in the judgment in *Foto-Frost*, according to which national courts were precluded from declaring a Community measure invalid.[41]

In more general terms, the judgment in *International Fruit Company* ought to be viewed within the broader context of the Court's constitutional case law: having shaped the unique normative qualities of the Community legal order in the 1960s by asserting the supremacy and direct effect of its rules, the process of constitutionalisation of the EC Treaty had already built sufficient momentum to enable the Court to address its external implications, that is its position within the international legal order. Viewed from this angle, the ruling in *International Fruit Company* further highlighted the constitutional function of the Court of Justice: in asserting its authority as the ultimate arbiter of the legality of Community law, it clearly impinged directly upon the role of national courts in the process of the enforcement of international law. However, most importantly, it assumed a function more akin to that of a domestic court: having followed an imaginative combination of legal techniques in order to enable Community law to penetrate national law, it then assumed the function of controlling the ways in which international law would penetrate Community law.

Similar issues arose two years later in the context of the interpretation of a mixed agreement. In *Haegeman*, a Belgian court referred a number of questions about the Association Agreement concluded between the Community and its Member States and Greece in 1961 (Athens Agreement).[42] The applicant in the main proceedings had challenged a national decision imposing countervailing duties on imports of wine from Greece, arguing that it was a violation of a Protocol annexed to the Athens Agreement. The issue of the existence of its jurisdiction was the very first point made by the Court. Having pointed out that the Agreement in question had been concluded by the Council pursuant to the procedures laid down in Articles 300 and 310 EC, it ruled that the Agreement 'is therefore, in so far as concerns the Community, an act of one of the institutions of the Community within the meaning of [Article 234 EC]'.[43] The Court then ruled that the provisions of the Athens Agreement 'form an integral part of Community law' from their entry into force[44] before affirming its jurisdiction 'within the framework of this law'.[45]

This line of reasoning, put forward in four one-phrase paragraphs and prior to any reference even to the first question referred by the Belgian court, purported to address the issue of the Court's jurisdiction in a comprehensive manner.

---

[41] Case 314/85 *Firma Foto-Frost v Hauptzollamt Lübeck-Ost* [1987] ECR 4199.
[42] Case 181/73 *R & V Haegeman v Belgian State* [1974] ECR 449.
[43] *Ibid*, para 4.
[44] *Ibid*, para 5.
[45] *Ibid*, para 6.

In doing so, it has been criticised as 'dubious, to say the least'[46] and 'extremely sweeping'.[47]

A particular objection has been raised regarding the alleged failure of the Court to distinguish between the Agreement concluded by the Community and the secondary measure adopted by the Council actually concluding the Agreement. However, it should be pointed out that the Council measure carries out a more important function than merely to express the Community's assent to the agreement.[48] It expressly concludes the Agreement on behalf of the Community and includes its text in an annex, hence defining the subject matter of the obligation to which Article 300(7) EC refers. Furthermore, the scope of the Court's conclusion is not as all-encompassing as the terseness of its reasoning might appear to suggest: the agreement constitutes an act of the Community's institutions 'in so far as concerns the Community' and the Court is to exercise its jurisdiction 'within the framework of [Community] law'.[49] However, these qualifications do not address the questions raised by the pythic manner in which the Court chose to articulate its line of reasoning.

This lack of clarity as to the implications of the ruling in *Haegeman* was illustrated by a direct challenge to the Court's jurisdiction to interpret mixed agreement. This occurred in the context of a preliminary reference on the interpretation of the Association Agreement with Turkey (Ankara Agreement). It is interesting that this case should have been referred to the Court in 1984, that is 12 years after the judgment in *Haegeman*. This is indicative of the capacity of the system of Community law to adjust to periods of normative uncertainty and organise its legal affairs on the international scene on a pragmatic basis. In *Demirel*, the dispute was about the provisions of the Ankara Agreement on free movement of workers and its Additional Protocol.[50]

Having started off its analysis by referring to the judgment in *Haegeman*, the Court went on to address the specific objections to its jurisdiction raised by the British and German governments. These centred on the mixed character of the Ankara Agreement and its Protocol. In particular, it was argued that the subject-matter of the provisions invoked before the referring court, that is free movement of workers, fell within national competence. As such, the commitments they entailed had been entered into by the Member States in their capacity as fully sovereign subjects of international law and were excluded from the jurisdiction of the Court of Justice.

This objection was rejected on the basis of two separate, albeit interrelated, arguments regarding the nature of the Ankara Agreement and its Protocol and the

---

[46] T Hartley, *Constitutional Problems of the European Union* (Oxford: Hart Publishing, 1999) 31–3.

[47] I Cheyne, '*Haegeman, Demirel* and their Progeny' in A Dashwood and C Hillion (eds), *The General Law of E.C. External Relations* (London: Sweet & Maxwell, 2000) 20 at 23.

[48] This is the phrase used by Hartley in n46 above, at 32.

[49] N42 above, paras 4 and 6 respectively.

[50] Case 12/86 *Demirel v Stadt Schwäbisch Gmünd* [1987] ECR 3719. See the annotations by N Neuwhahl, (1988) 13 *ELRev* 360 and G Nolte, (1988) 25 *CMLRev* 403.

duties imposed by them in relation to the implementation of their provisions on free movement of workers. As far as the former was concerned, the Court ruled that the Agreement provisions on free movement were not adopted in the exercise of national powers: as the free movement of workers was covered by the EC Treaty, commitments in that area "fall within the powers conferred on the Community by Article [310 EC]".[51] The reason for this was that the Ankara Agreement 'is an association agreement creating special, privileged links with a non-member country which must, at least to a certain extent, take part in the Community system'.[52] The Court then ruled that Article 310 EC 'must necessarily empower the Community to guarantee commitments towards non-member countries in all the fields covered by the Treaty',[53] including that of free movement of workers. In order to bring this point home, it then concluded that, in interpreting the free movement of workers provisions of the Ankara Agreement, the Court would not interpret 'a provision in a mixed agreement containing a commitment which only the Member States could enter into in the sphere of their own powers'.[54]

On the other hand, the judgment focused on the obligations imposed by the Agreement in the area of free movement of workers. Whilst the above provisions or the relevant decisions of the Association Council needed to be implemented in the territory of the Member States by means of national measures, the Court did not accept any encroachment on its jurisdiction: it opined that, 'in ensuring respect for commitments arising from an agreement concluded by the Community institutions the Member States fulfil, within the Community system, an obligation in relation to the Community, which has assumed responsibility for the due performance of the agreement'.[55]

Once more, whilst addressing the questions referred to it, the Court did not offer a comprehensive answer regarding the scope of its jurisdiction over the provisions of mixed agreements. In his Opinion, Advocate General Darmon had sought to articulate such an answer by adopting a broad approach. He argued that 'in the absence of any reservations of powers in the Agreement, and subject to the various prerogatives as to its implementation, both the nature and the scope of its provisions suggest that, having regard to the principles defined in the case-law, the interpretation of those provisions is within the jurisdiction of this Court, particularly with a view to ensuring their uniform application'.[56] This approach was endorsed by Advocate Ganeral Tesauro who provided a broad reading of the Court's position in the subsequent *Hermès* case. He argued as follows:[57]

---

[51] *Ibid*, para 9.
[52] *Ibid*.
[53] *Ibid*.
[54] *Ibid*.
[55] *Ibid*, para 11.
[56] *Ibid*, at para 15 of his Opinion.
[57] Case C–53/96 *Hermès International v FHT Marketing* [1998] ECR I–3603, 3617–18. See also N Neuwahl, annotation on *Demirel*, (1988) 13 *ELRev* 360, A Rosas, 'Mixed Union—Mixed Agreements' in M Koskenniemi (ed), *International Law Aspects of the European Union* (The Hague, Kluwer, 1998)

It appears to follow from [the] statements [in *Demirel*], first, that the Court itself considers that the only matters on which it has no interpretative jurisdiction pursuant to Article [234] are matters within the exclusive competence of the Member States . . . and, second, that in the case of an agreement (even a mixed agreement) concluded by the Community institutions the Community is competent with respect to the agreement in its entirety . . . I should add that I do not think these considerations can be confined solely to association agreements, where the Community's exclusive competent to conclude the agreements is based on the Treaty itself, in this case Article [310]. While it must be recognized that mixed agreements vary considerably in nature and type, depending on the degree of participation by States, . . . the fact remains that the problem with which we are concerned in the present case inevitably arises in the same terms in the case of an association agreement, when it is concluded in the form of a mixed agreement, and in the case of agreements (also mixed) which have no *ad hoc* legal basis in the Treaty.

It is difficult to see what justification there could be for the exercise of the Court's jurisdiction over provisions of mixed agreements whose subject matter would fall within the exclusive competence of the Member States. For instance, in the unlikely event that the Community negotiated and concluded an agreement whose provisions contained commitments in the area of trade in goods as well as defence, those covering the latter would be excluded from its jurisdiction.[58] An argument to the contrary would be difficult to sustain not only on practical but also on legal grounds, not least in the light of Article 46 TEU which excludes from its jurisdiction Title V TEU covering the foreign and security policy of the EU.[59]

Whilst the objections raised in *Demirel* were about the existence of the Court's jurisdiction, the judgment itself was underpinned by a distinct effort to reject any national claim to exclusivity. It was for this reason that it appears to assume that, in relying upon the authority provided under Article 310 EC, the Community actually exercised its competence in the entire sphere covered by the Agreement.[60] Indeed, in relation to the area of free movement of workers in particular, the Court held that the Ankara Agreement did not provide for commitments 'which *only* the Member States could enter into in the sphere of their own

---

at 140–1, J Rideau, 'Les accords internationaux dans la jurisprudence de la cour de justice des communautés européennes: reflexions sur les relations entre les ordres juridiques internationaux, communautaire et nationaux' [1990] RGDIP 289 at 347, albeit with criticism. For a restrictive view, see A Dashwood, 'Preliminary Rulings on the Interpretation of Mixed Agreements' in O'Keeffe and Bavasso (eds), n27 above, 167 at 170–1 and J Heliskoski, 'The Jurisdiction of the European Court of Justice to Give Preliminary Rulings on the Interpretation of Mixed Agreements' (2000) 69 *Nordic Journal of International Law* 395 at 400–1.

[58] It is interesting that, in its intervention in *Demirel*, the Commission argued that it would be 'illogical' to refer to the Court of Justice provisions over which the Member States have exclusive jurisdiction: see Opinion of Darmon AG, n50 above, at para 5.

[59] See Macleod, Hendry and Hyett, n5 above, at 157; D Anderson and M Demetriou, *References to the European Court* (2nd edn, London: Sweet and Maxwell, 2002) 67.

[60] See JHH Weiler, 'Thou Shalt Not Oppress a Stranger: On the Judicial Protection of the Human Rights of Non-EC Nationals—A Critique' (1992) 3 *EJIL* 65, 72 *ff*.

powers'.[61] Therefore, exclusivity was rejected, not only in terms of national but also Community competence.

This 'competence-based' line of reasoning is noteworthy for two reasons. First, it indicates the wide implications of reliance upon Article 310 EC: it is assumed to amount to the exercise of EC competence. The agreement concluded thereunder becomes part of Community law and gives rise to the exercise of the Court's jurisdiction. It is for these reasons that the Ankara Agreement could have been concluded by the Community alone.[62] Secondly, the tenor of the judgment in *Demirel* is entirely consistent with that of the case law on EC international relations which has laid down the foundations of the Community's external competence. Its distinct reluctance to define the scope of its jurisdiction over provisions falling within the scope of exclusive national power is reminiscent of the distinct reluctance to delineate competences between the Community and the Member States in the rulings delivered over the years under Article 300(6) EC. In both cases, the main focus was exclusivity or, rather, its absence. Therefore, the judgment in *Demirel* is an interesting link in a line of cases whose underlying premises are as consistent as they are ambiguous. This is a line which was not broken by subsequent judgments.

5. BROAD CONSTRUCTION OF JURISDICTION UNDER ARTICLE 234 EC

In *Hermès*,[63] a judgment delivered ten years after *Demirel*, the Court elaborated further on its jurisdiction over provisions of mixed agreements. The case was referred by a Dutch court and was about the interpretation of Article 50(6) of the TRIPS Agreement. In accordance with Article 50 TRIPS, the judicial authorities of the Members are under a duty to protect the intellectual property rights which fall within the scope of the Agreement by means of provisional measures. The provision of Article 50(6) requires that a decision imposing such measures and adopted *inaudita altera parte* be revoked or otherwise cease to have effect if proceedings on the merits are not initiated within a reasonable time. Having been granted interim relief for the infringement of their trade mark, the applicant in the main proceedings asked the referring court to set a period after the expiry of which the defendant would not have the right to ask that the order against him or her be

---

[61] N50 above, para 9 (emphasis added).

[62] See JHJ Bourgeois, 'The European Court of Justice and the WTO: Problems and Challenges' in JHH Weiler, (ed), *The EU, the WTO and the NAFTA. Towards a Common Law of International Trade* (Oxford: OUP, 2000) 71 at 83.

[63] Case C–53/96 *Hermès*, n57 above. See the annotation by A von Bogdandy, (1999) 36 *CMLRev* 663; see also Dashwood, n57 above, AF Gagliardi, 'The Right of Individuals to Invoke the Provisions of Mixed Agreements before the National Courts: a New Message from Luxembourg?' (1999) 24 *ELRev* 276, Heliskoski, n57 above.

lifted. The referring court, then, asked the Court of Justice to rule, under the pre-liminary reference procedure, whether that request was consistent with Article 50(6) TRIPS.

Once again, the Court's jurisdiction was directly challenged, this time in the submissions made by the Dutch, French and British governments. They argued that the interpretation of Article 50 of the TRIPs Agreement fell beyond the Court's jurisdiction. Their objection was based on *Opinion 1/94*[64] where it had been held that the TRIPs Agreement did not fall within the exclusive competence of the Community, either pursuant to Article 133 EC or the doctrine of implied competence articulated in *ERTA*[65] or the general clauses of Articles 95 and 308 EC. They recalled that the Court had referred specifically to the issue of enforcement of intellectual property rights and had ruled that the Community had not exer-cised its powers to introduce harmonising legislation, except on the release for free circulation of counterfeit goods.[66] As this had remained the case until the refer-ence in *Hermès*, they claimed that the Court should not exercise its jurisdiction.

This line of reasoning did not convince the Court. It observed that the conclu-sion of the TRIPS Agreement by the Community and its ratification by the Member States contained no allocation of obligations between them What fol-lowed in the judgment was an elaborate line of reasoning which may be sum-marised as follows. First, at the time of the signature of the Final Act and the WTO Agreement, the Council had already adopted a Regulation on the Community trade mark.[67] As the Community is a party to the WTO, the adoption of this Regulation entailed that, when national courts were to protect rights stemming from a Community trade mark, they should apply national remedies in the light of Article 50 TRIPs. This was the case on two grounds: first, Article 50 TRIPs applies in order to protect the proprietor of trade marks conferred under the laws of the Members; secondly, Regulation 40/94 provided that rights from a Community trade mark are to be safeguarded by means of provisional measures.

The Court, then, ruled that 'it follows that [it] has, in any event, jurisdiction to interpret Article 50 of the TRIPs Agreement'.[68]

However, the reference by the Netherlands was about a dispute which arose from the application of national trade mark law. Did that not add another dimension to the exercise of the Court's jurisdiction? This point was addressed by two argu-ments: the first one was formalistic and familiar from the Court's overall approach to questions referred by national courts under Article 234 EC: it was pointed out that it was the responsibility of the referring court to assess the need for the

[64] *Opinion 1/94*, n24 above.
[65] Case 22/70 *ERTA*, n35 above.
[66] See n24 above, at para 104.
[67] Council Reg 40/94 [1994] OJ L 11/1.
[68] N57 above, para 29.

reference.[69] The second argument sought to articulate the issue of jurisdiction in more general terms:[70]

> where a provision can apply both to situations falling within the scope of national law and to situations falling within the scope of Community law, it is clearly in the Community interest that, in order to forestall future differences of interpretation, that provision should be interpreted uniformly, whatever the circumstances in which it is to apply.

Whilst further clarifying the terse line of reasoning originating in *Haegeman* and developed in *Demirel*, the conclusion of the Court in *Hermès* does not appear to provide a definitive answer to the scope of its jurisdiction under Article 234 EC. Would it cover only provisions of mixed agreements which may apply to situations both within a national and a Community legal context?[71] Would it extend to all provisions of a mixed agreement which cover areas under Community competence when the latter is non-exclusive? Would the issue of the actual exercise of that competence be relevant?[72]

These questions were subsequently raised in *Dior and Others*, two further cases referred by Dutch courts, one of them the Dutch Supreme Court.[73] Their subject-matter was the interpretation of Article 50 of the TRIPS Agreement and, in particular, whether the ruling in *Hermès* was confined to situations covered by trade mark law.

In his Opinion, Advocate General Cosmas suggested a strict reading of the ruling in *Hermès*. He argued that the jurisdiction of the Court of Justice should be confined to provisions of mixed agreements which would be applicable to both national and Community areas of competence only when there was actually legislation in both which would be affected by those provisions. Therefore, the absence of Community legislation would render the jurisdiction of the Court redundant. He argues that 'in the context of Article [234] of the Treaty, to extend the Court's interpretative jurisdiction to TRIPs provisions relating to areas in which the (potential) Community competence has not yet been exercised would constitute pursuit of a policy of judge-made law in conflict with the

---

[69] Reference was made to Joined Cases C–297/88 and C–197/89 *Dzodzi* [1990] ECR I–3763 and Case C–231/89 *Gmurzynska-Bscher* [1990] ECR I–4003.

[70] Reference was made to Case C–130/95 *Giloy v Hauptzollamt Frankfurt am Main-Ost* [1997] ECR I–4291, para 28, and Case C–28/95 *Leur-Bloem v Inspecteur der Belastingdienst/Ondernemingen* [1997] ECR I–4161.

[71] See Heliskoski, n57 above at 404 *ff*.

[72] See Dashwood, n57 above, at 173–4 Rosas, n57 above, at 215. See the criticism in S Weatherill and P Beaumont, *EU Law* (London: Penguin Books, 1999 and 3rd ed) 319–20. See also P Koutrakos, 'The Interpretation of Mixed Agreements under the Preliminary Reference Procedure' (2002) 7 *EFA Rev* 25 at 36.

[73] Joined Cases 300/98 and 392/98 *Parfums Christian Dior SA and Tuk Consultancy BV and Assco Gerüste GmbH, Rob van Dijk, and Wilhelm Layher GmbH & Co. KG* [2000] ECR I–11307.

constitutional logic of the Treaty and would be difficult to justify on grounds of expediency'.[74]

In its judgment, the Court started off by asserting its jurisdiction as follows:[75]

> [As the TRIPs Agreement] was concluded by the Community and the Member States under joint competence . . . [i]t follows that where a case is brought before the Court in accordance with the provisions of the Treaty, in particular, Article 177 [now 234] thereof, the Court has jurisdiction to define the obligations which the Community has thereby assumed and, for that purpose, to interpret TRIPs.

This statement is as forceful in its tone as it is broad in its scope. On the one hand, the Court appears to assert its jurisdiction in relation to all types of procedures whereby a provision of a mixed agreement is brought before it. In this respect, why is this the case regarding 'in particular' the preliminary reference procedure? Why is not 'including' the preliminary reference procedure? One way of reading this is in the light of the requirement of uniform interpretation, already mentioned in *Hermès*, and its central role in the function of Article 234 EC. On the other hand, the Court asserts its jurisdiction in order to define the obligations assumed by the *Community*: that would imply that the definition of the obligations assumed by the *Member States* would be excluded from its jurisdiction. However, if this qualification is intended to confine the scope of the Court's jurisdiction, how is it to apply in the light of the distinct reluctance of the Court to delineate areas of competence within the context of mixed agreements? And why is there no reference to the judgment in *Hermès*?

This latter question may be explained by the following paragraphs of the judgment in *Dior*:[76]

> *In particular*, the Court has jurisdiction to interpret Article 50 TRIPs in order to meet the needs of the courts of the Member States when they are called upon to apply national rules with a view to ordering provisional measures for the protection of rights arising under Community legislation falling within the scope of TRIPs (see *Hermès*, paragraphs 28 and 29).

> Likewise, where a provision such as Article 50 of TRIPs can apply both to situations falling within the scope of national law and to situations falling within that of Community law, as is the case in the field of trade marks, the Court has jurisdiction to interpret it in order to forestall future differences of interpretation (see *Hermès*, paragraphs 32 and 33).

---

[74] Para 51 of his Opinion.
[75] *Ibid*, para 33.
[76] *Ibid*, paras 34–36, emphasis added.

In that regard, the Member States and the Community institutions have an obligation of close cooperation in fulfilling the commitments undertaken by them under joint competence when they concluded the WTO Agreement, including TRIPs (see, to that effect, *Opinion 1/94*, . . . paragraph 108)

The above extracts appear to define the ruling in *Hermès* as merely one example of a provision of mixed agreements whose interpretation falls within the Court's jurisdiction. It is recalled that Article 50 of the TRIPs Agreement is a provision of procedural content. However, again, the above extracts are unclear in terms of their underlying *rationale* as well as their implications: the reference to the duty of close cooperation appears to be rather out of place. Does it suggest that it should be interpreted broadly enough to cover national courts in the application of mixed agreements? Would it require that they give a uniform meaning to provisions of mixed agreements which might, conceivably, be applied in another, Community law, context? The paragraphs immediately following the above extracts appear to support this view: [77]

Since Article 50 of TRIPs constitutes a procedural provision which should be applied in the same way in every situation falling within its scope and is capable of applying both to situations covered by national law and to situations covered by Community law, that obligation requires the judicial bodies of the Member States and the Community, for practical and legal reasons, to give it a uniform interpretation.

Only the Court of Justice acting in cooperation with the courts and tribunals of the Member States pursuant to Article [234] of the Treaty is in a position to ensure such uniform interpretation.

The jurisdiction of the Court of Justice to interpret Article 50 of TRIPs is thus not restricted solely to situations covered by trade-mark law.

If the above analysis is correct, the judgment in *Dior*, as a whole, constitutes a significant advancement in the construction of the role of the Court of Justice in EC international relations. On the one hand, it appears to define the twin principles governing the status of mixed agreements within the Community legal order, namely the jurisdiction of the Court of Justice over their interpretation and the duty of close cooperation imposed upon Community institutions and Member States over their application. On the other hand, both these principles are construed in very broad terms. Whilst not atypical in the case law on EC international relations, the absence of a clearer line of reasoning is regrettable. This is all the more so as the limits of the Court's jurisdiction are so ill-defined. Its general formulation in *Dior* is a case in point. In principle, the role of the Court appears to be confined to the definition of the obligations assumed by the Community. In practice, in the light of the Court's reluctance to allocate competences within the

---

[77] Paras 37–39.

context of mixed agreements, it appears that only in areas clearly falling within the exclusive competence of the Member States would it be precluded from exercising its jurisdiction.

6. THE EXISTENCE OF BROAD JURISDICTION
CONFIRMED—THE CASE OF ARTICLE 226 EC

The line of reasoning underpinning the *Dior* judgment leaves no room for doubt as to the broad scope of the Court's jurisdiction to interpret mixed agreements. This is all the more so if viewed as yet another link to the line of cases originating in *Haegeman* and *Demirel* and leading to *Dior* via *Hermès*: these judgments appear to articulate, albeit in an incremental and often cryptic manner, a broad jurisdiction for the Court of Justice. Interestingly enough, a judgment delivered in the context of an enforcement action pursuant to Article 226 EC may appear to shed some light on the foundation of the principles examined in this chapter. The enforcement proceedings brought against Ireland for its failure to adhere to the Berne Convention for the Protection of Literary and Artistic Works were mentioned above. It is recalled that this failure was challenged as contrary to Article 300(7) EC and Article 5 of Protocol 28 to the European Economic Area Agreement.[78] The Full Court first examined whether the subject-matter of the dispute fell within the scope of Community law. It ruled as follows:

> 14. The Court has ruled that mixed agreements concluded by the Community, its Member States and non-member countries have the same status in the Community legal order as purely Community agreements, as these are provisions coming within the scope of Community competence (see, to that effect, Case 12/86 *Demirel* [1987] ECR 3719, paragraph 9).

> 15. From this the Court has concluded that, in ensuring respect for commitments arising from an agreement concluded by the Community institutions, the Member States fulfil, within the Community system, an obligation in relation to the Community, which has assumed responsibility for the due performance of the agreement (*Demirel*, cited above, paragraph 11).

The above extracts do not merely clarify the position of mixed agreements in the Community legal order: they read previous statements by the Court in a new light. It is recalled that the judgment in *Demirel* was delivered under the preliminary reference procedure about the interpretation of an association agreement. It is also recalled that, when delivered, it raised various questions about whether it should be interpreted broadly or restrictively, which were then addressed in other judgments delivered under Article 234 EC in quite specific contexts. And yet, in *Commission v Ireland* the statements in *Demirel* become the foundation for the

---

[78] Case C–13/00 *Commission v Ireland* [2001] ECR I–2943.

complete assimilation of all mixed agreements, that is not only those establishing an association, to purely Community law agreements. Once this sweeping reading of *Demirel* has been adopted, the broad reading of the duties of Member States only follows. Indeed, paragraph 15 of the above extract refers to a passage of *Demirel* which had been articulated expressly in the context of the exercise of a Community competence and with a further reference to *International Fruit Company*, that is a judgment concerning the status of a 'purely Community agreement'.

To sum up, the following development appears to have occurred: having affirmed the Community law duties of Member States in the context of an agreement whose scope falls within Community competence (*International Fruit Company*),[79] the Court went on to read the conclusion of an association agreement as the exercise of the competence of the Community over the entire scope of the EC Treaty (*Demirel*) and, then, to assimilate all mixed agreements to Community agreements in a judgment delivered under Article 226 EC. This gradual generalisation of the position of mixed agreements within the Community legal order is relevant to the construction of the Court's jurisdiction. This becomes apparent in the remaining part of the judgment where, prior to any assessment of the substance of the dispute, the Court examines whether the contested obligations fell within the scope of Community law. In so doing, it pointed out that 'there can be no doubt' that the Berne Convention covers an area which falls 'in large measure' within the scope of Community competence.[80] In order to substantiate this assessment, it referred to the objective of the Berne Convention, that is the protection of literary and artistic works, and stated that it is 'to a very great extent governed by Community legislation'.[81] To that effect, it cited as examples the protection of computer programs, rental and lending intellectual property rights, copyright protection in the area of satellite broadcasting and cable retransmission, the protection of databases and the terms of protection of copyright and certain related rights. Following this assessment, the Court concluded as follows:[82]

> The Berne Convention thus creates rights and obligations in areas covered by Community law. That being so, there is a Community interest in ensuring that all Contracting Parties to the EEA Agreement adhere to the Convention.

> It follows that the requirement of adherence to the Berne Convention which Article 5 of Protocol 28 to the EEA Agreement imposes on the Contracting Parties comes within the Community framework, given that it features in a mixed agreement concluded by the Community and its Member States and relates to an area covered in large measure by the Treaty. The Commission is thus competent to assess compliance with that requirement, subject to review by the Court.

---

[79] See n39 above: this was the case even though GATT had not, actually, been concluded by the Community.
[80] N78 above, para 16.
[81] *Ibid*, at para 17.
[82] *Ibid*, at paras 19–20.

Having assimilated the position of mixed agreements to that of purely Community agreements and deemed them as wholly within the Community legal order, the Court established the Community law nature of the obligations laid down therein on the basis of a very brief examination. It was only in a short paragraph in which the subject-matter of the Agreement was deemed within the scope of Community law by reference to a handful of related areas in which the Community has legislated. No reference was made to specific secondary measures, neither was there any attempt to define the extent to which the mixed nature of the agreement might affect the nature of the Community duty imposed upon the Member States. The judgment in *Commission v Ireland* is viewed as affirming the position that, in effect, mixed agreements do not expand the scope of Community's competence.[83] Whilst this is correct, it is also noteworthy that the assessment made by the Court should have been very general and confined to identifying the scope of the Agreement with that of secondary Community law 'in large measure' and 'to a very great extent'. This approach suggests a reluctance to engage in detailed analysis of the provisions of the Berne Convention against Community law. In that respect, it is not dissimilar to the reluctance of the Court to delineate precise areas of competence when asked to do so in the context of its pre-emptive jurisdiction under Article 300(6) EC.

This approach may be understood within the proper context of the case: the existence of a Community law obligation was not in dispute. Indeed, the Irish government had informed the Commission that the draft legislation required was at an advanced stage of its scrutiny by the Irish Parliament. That was not the case in a subsequent enforcement action against France.[84] This was about the application of the Convention for the Protection of the Mediterranean Sea against Pollution.[85] The Commission argued that it had been violated because the French authorities had failed to take all appropriate measures to prevent, abate and combat heavy and prolonged pollution of a saltwater marsh called Etang de Berre. The French government argued that the action was inadmissible because the obligations alleged to have been infringed fell beyond the scope of Community law. In its judgment, delivered without an Opinion, the Court rejected this objection and referred *verbatim* to the line of reasoning of the judgment in *Commission v Ireland*.[86] Again, the subject matter of the Convention is deemed to fall within that of Community law 'without doubt' and 'in large measure'.[87] It is noteworthy that the Court referred to a number of specific Community measures on the protection of waters against pollution, which indicated that the subject-matter of the

---

[83] See Eeckhout, n32 above, at 220.

[84] Case C–239/03 *Commission v France*, [2004] ECR I–9325

[85] Concluded by Council Dec 77/585/EEC [1977] OJ L 240/1.

[86] In its English version, the judgment in *Commission v France* states that the position of the mixed agreements has been 'inferred' (para 26) rather than 'concluded' (*Commission v Ireland*, n78 above, para 15). However, in French, both judgments use the term 'la Court en a tiré la conséquence'.

[87] N84 above, para 27.

Convention 'is in very large measure regulated by Community legislation'.[88] However, the French government had argued against the existence of Community competence because there was no Community directive regulating the specific type of the alleged pollution, that is discharges of fresh water and alluvia into a saltwater marsh. The Court appears to have found this degree of specificity unnecessary for the establishment of the Community competence and, hence, its jurisdiction.

All in all, there appears to be a thread between the interpretation of the Court's jurisdiction under Article 234 EC and Article 226 EC in so far as in both cases it is a broadly construed criterion which gives rise to judicial review pursuant to the EC Treaty. In the case of preliminary references, it is the possibility of the provision of the mixed agreement being applied in a Community law context in a future dispute which gives rise to the requirement for uniform interpretation, hence necessitating the exercise of the Court's jurisdiction. In the case of Article 226 EC it is the assessment that the provision of the mixed agreement falls within the scope of Community law 'in large measure' and 'to a very great extent'. If the above analysis is correct, then the thread which brings together different aspects of the Court's jurisdiction under primary law appears to suggest that only in cases where an area clearly falling within the exclusive competence of the Member States in a mixed agreement would not be covered by the broad, albeit ill-defined, jurisdiction of the Court.

7. THE COOPERATION OF NATIONAL COURTS

In the judgments examined in this chapter, the central questions raised by either the referring court or intervening governments or both were about the existence and scope of the jurisdiction of the Court of Justice over mixed agreements. A common feature of these questions is the underlying concern that, if broadly construed, this jurisdiction would give rise to judicial review whose intensity would undermine the competence of Member States as exercised in the context of mixed agreements. The above analysis indicated that, over the years, the Court developed an evolving definition of its jurisdiction, one which is broad in scope and ill-defined as to its limits. However, this does not necessarily entail the assumption of an intrusive judicial role, neither does it imply *ipso facto* undue interference with the national legal order. The assessment of the implications of the Court's jurisdiction requires the examination of the role of national courts.

It is a truism to argue that the relationship between the Community and national judicature is far from the outcome of a zero-sum power game. In fact, the main principles of Community law have become a deeply entrenched part of the domestic legal order precisely because the Court of Justice has entrusted their application to the active involvement of national courts. The preliminary reference procedure set out in Article 234 EC provided the obvious mechanism

---

[88] *Ibid*, at para 28.

for the interaction between national and Community courts, one which has been gradually adjusted by the Court of Justice to the evolving requirements of the Community legal order and the increasing familiarity of national courts with Community law. A case in point is the construction of the duty of certain national courts to refer when a decision on a question raised before them is necessary to enable them to give judgment. By developing the *acte claire* formula in *CILFIT*,[89] for instance, the Court has acknowledged the function that national courts are expected to carry out in the process of the application of Community law.[90]

However, the significance of this function is revealed if assessed in the light of less apparent and more indirect mechanisms. These consist of the Court's construction of the general cooperation clause set out in Article 10 EC, according to which Member States 'shall take all appropriate measures, whether general or particular, to ensure fulfillment of the obligations arising out of this Treaty'. This provision has been consistently interpreted widely enough to impose specific Community law duties on national courts in the area of enforcement of Community law.[91] Another mechanism is provided through the specific construction of the various constitutionalising principles developed by the Court of Justice. For instance, a number of specific conditions relating to the application of the principle of state liability in damages for breach of Community law are to be defined under national law.[92] Another example is the area of free movement where national courts are to determine whether a national measure which, in principle, violates the EC Treaty principle, is actually justified as necessary and proportionate for the protection of other public interests.[93]

In the context of the application of mixed agreements, a significant role emerges from the Court's case law. This may take various forms, including the determination of the effects of the relevant provisions or the application of specific concepts in accordance with national law.

7.1. Assessing the Effect of Provisions of Mixed Agreements

Apart from the scope of the Court's jurisdiction, another question referred in *Dior* was about the rights of individuals to invoke Article 50(6) of the TRIPs Agreement before the referring courts.

---

[89] Case 283/81 *Srl CILFIT and Lanificio di Gavardo SpA v Ministry of Health* [1982] ECR 3415.

[90] On different readings of this formula, see A Arnull, 'The Use and Abuse of Article 177' (1989) 52 *MLR* 622 and H Rasmussen, 'The European Court's *Acte Claire* Strategy in *CILFIT*' (1984) 9 *ELRev* 242.

[91] See, for instance, Case C–213/89 *R v Secretary of State for Transport, ex parte Factortame Ltd & Others* [1990] ECR I–2433.

[92] See Cases C–46/93 and C–48/93 *Brasserie du Pêcheur SA v Germany* and *R v Secretary of State for Transport, ex parte Factortame Ltd and others* [1996]ECR I–1029.

[93] See, for instance, Case C–405/98 *Konsumentombudsmannen (KO) v Gourmet International Products AB (GIP)* [2001] ECR I–1795. For a study of the role of national courts in the area of free movement of goods, see M Jarvis, *The Application of EC Law by National Courts: The Free Movement of Goods* (Oxford: OUP, 1998).

A detailed examination of the state of the law on the effects of WTO agreements within the Community legal order and the contribution of the ruling in *Dior* is beyond the scope of this chapter. For the purposes of this analysis, suffice it to point out the following. Prior to the conclusion of the WTO Agreements, the Court had ruled out the direct effect of the GATT 1947 on the ground that it provided for a system of rules the application of which was characterised by considerable flexibility.[94] However, the tighter legal regime set out in the WTO Agreements raised that question once more. It had been only a year prior to the *Dior* judgment had the Court had ruled on the effect of the WTO Agreements in determining the legality of Community legislation pursuant to Article 230 EC. In the *Portuguese Textiles* case, it had ruled that the WTO Agreements did not constitute rules in the light of which the legality of Community measures could be reviewed.[95] This conclusion was substantiated by reference to the considerable scope of negotiation enjoyed by the WTO parties, not least in the area of dispute settlement. The Court also mentioned that the most important trading partners of the Community had also excluded them from the rules applied by their courts in reviewing the legality of domestic legislation. It was in the light of this considerations that the Court had pointed out that '[to] accept that the role of ensuring that Community law complies with those rules devolves directly on the Community judicature would deprive the legislative or executive organs of the Community of the scope for manoeuvre enjoyed by their counterparts in the Community's trading partners'.[96]

In its judgment in *Dior*, the Court referred to the above line of reasoning in order to reject the direct effect of WTO rules and, hence, Article 50(6) TRIPs. However, the Court proceeded to point out that 'the finding that the provisions of TRIPs do not have direct effect in that sense does not fully resolve the problem raised by the national courts'.[97] Having, then, underlined once more the procedural nature of Article 50 of the TRIPs Agreement and the fact that it is intended to be applied by both Community and national courts in relation to commitments undertaken both by the Community and the Member States, the Court made the following distinction:

> In a field to which TRIPs applies and in respect of which the Community has already legislated, as is the case with the field of trade marks, it follows from the judgment in *Hermès*, in particular paragraph 28 thereof, that the judicial authorities of the Member States are required by virtue of Community law, when called upon to apply national rules with a view to ordering provisional measures for the protection of rights falling within such a field, to do so as far as possible in the light of the wording and purpose of Article 50 of TRIPs.

<hr>

[94] Cases 21–4/72 *International Fruit Company*, n39 above, Case 9/73 *Schlüeter* [1973] ECR 1135, Case 38/75 *Nederlandse Spoorwegen* [1975] ECR 1439, Case 266/81 *SIOT* [1983] ECR 731, Case 267–9/81 *Amministrazione delle Finanze dello Stato v SPI SpA* [1983] ECR 801.
[95] Case C–149/96 *Portugal v Council* [1999] ECR I–8395, para 47.
[96] N73 above, at para 46.
[97] *Ibid*, para 45 of the judgment.

On the other hand, in a field in respect of which the Community has not yet legislated and which consequently falls within the competence of the Member States, the protection of intellectual property rights, and measures adopted for that purpose by the judicial authorities, do not fall within the scope of Community law. Accordingly, Community law neither requires nor forbids that the legal order of a Member State should accord to individuals the right to rely directly on the rule laid down by Article 50(6) of TRIPS or that it should oblige the courts to apply that rule of their own motion'.[98]

By distinguishing between areas covered by the TRIPS Agreement in which the Community has legislated and areas in which there is no EC legislation, the Court enhances the position of national courts in the area of the application of mixed agreements. This is further highlighted in the final part of the judgment in *Dior*, where the Court dealt with the substantive questions referred by the Dutch Supreme Court. One of them was whether industrial designs fall within the scope of TRIPS. The Court responded in the affirmative and left it to the national courts to decide whether the requirements for their protection, laid down in Article 25 TRIPS, were met. Therefore, national courts are entrusted not only with the application of procedural rules contained in TRIPs but also the determination of their legal effects in a case where there is no Community legislation.

The emergence of a significant role for national courts in the above context is understandable. It is consistent with the role of national courts at the various stages of the preliminary reference procedure, from the choice and definition of the questions referred to the application of the interpretation given by the Court to the facts of the case.[99] Within the context of EC international relations, it also operates as a considerable counterweight to the assertion of the Court's jurisdiction. However, the criterion on the basis of which this role of national courts is introduced, namely the existence of Community legislation in the area covered by the specific provision of TRIPs, is puzzling. This is the case not only because of its lack of clarity: indeed, it remains to be seen how the existence of harmonising Community rules or rules laying down minimum standards might affect its application. First, it sits uncomfortably with the logic underpinning the broad jurisdiction of the Court of Justice, namely the need for uniform interpretation of the TRIPs Agreement: is this not paramount in terms of the effects of WTO provisions, all the more so in the light of the reluctance of the Community's trading partners, to grant WTO rules direct effect? And is it significant that the right of Member States to determine this was laid down in a case referred by a Dutch court which is traditionally sympathetic to the direct effect of international treaties? Secondly, it ignores the link between the direct effect of WTO rules and the discretion enjoyed by the Community legislature and executive when acting within

---

[98] *Ibid*, paras 47–48.

[99] To that effect, see Anderson and Demetriou, n59 above, Ch 5. For the evolution of the preliminary reference procedure and the involvement of national courts, see T Tridimas, 'Knocking on Heaven's Door: Fragmentation, Efficiency and Defiance in the Preliminary Reference Procedure' (2003) 40 *CMLRev* 9.

the WTO framework.[100] The importance of this link was highlighted in *Hermès* at the hearing of which the French government had asked the Court to give the national court some indication as to whether or not the provisions of the WTO Agreement, including those of the TRIPS, have direct effect. That request had been made precisely in order to forestall differences of interpretation on such an important matter.[101] Thirdly, the acknowledgment of the right of national courts to determine the effect of Article 50 of the TRIPs Agreement in areas where the Community has not legislated sits uncomfortably with the logic of denying direct effect. Indeed, if uniformity in the application of TRIPs justified the lack of direct effect, this would apply to the agreement as a whole.[102]

7.2. Applying the Provisions of Mixed Agreements

Having defined its jurisdiction in broad terms and confirmed the right of national courts to determine the direct effect of a provision of the TRIPs Agreement in areas where there is no Community legislation, the Court went on in *Dior* to address the substantive issues about the interpretation of Article 50(6). One such question was about the right to sue in accordance with general provisions of national law in order to protect an industrial design against copying: does it constitute an intellectual property right within the meaning of Article 50 of the Agreement? As there was no express definition of the term 'intellectual property right' in the Agreement, the Court proceeded to interpret it 'in its context and in the light of its objective and purpose'.[103] Having referred in detail both to the preamble to and a number of substantive provisions of the TRIPs Agreement,[104] it pointed out that:[105]

> TRIPs leaves to the Contracting Parties, within the framework of their own legal systems and in particular their rules of private law, the task of specifying in detail the interests which will be protected under TRIPs as 'intellectual property rights and the method of protection, provided always, first, that the protection is effective, particularly in preventing trade in counterfeit goods and, second, that it does not lead to distortions of or impediments to international trade.

The answer given to the referring court was affirmative. Whilst acknowledging the autonomy of national law in the application of procedural aspects of TRIPs, this

---

[100] See M Cremona, 'EC External Commercial Policy after Amsterdam: Authority and Interpretation within Interconnected Legal Orders' in Weiler, n62 above, 27 *ff*.

[101] Tesauro AG in his Opinion in *Hermès*, n57 above, at n28 where he refers to this request as 'somewhat unorthodox and contentious'.

[102] See the criticism in Koutrakos, n72 above, at 43–47.

[103] N73 above, para 55.

[104] Reference is made to Arts 1(1) and 62 TRIPs.

[105] N73 above, para 60.

part of the judgment also affirms the broad construction of the scope of the Court's jurisdiction: it actually interprets the TRIPs Agreement in a dispute about an industrial design governed by national law and with no reference whatever to Community rules in the judgment.

The role of national courts in the application of mixed agreements was further acknowledged in the subsequent judgment in *Schieving-Nijstad*.[106] This was a preliminary reference from the Dutch Supreme Court to interpret Article 50(6) of the TRIPs Agreement. The dispute before the referring court was about the protection of a trade mark registered in the Netherlands. The applicant, the owner of a club in the Netherlands, operated a café called 'Route 66', a name which was displayed in various ways throughout the club. This name of an old expressway in the United States had been registered as a trade mark in the Netherlands by the respondent in the main proceedings in respect of various classes of goods and services. He, then, granted licences to manufacturers for the marketing of products sold under the mark 'Route 66'. As the applicant was not one of the respondent's licensees, the latter obtained an order from the District Court under which Schieving-Nijstad was required to refrain from using the name 'Route 66' for the café and the services provided therein, along with the mark 'Route 66'. On appeal, that order was upheld and it was the latter judgment which, on appeal before the Supreme Court, raised the issue of the application of TRIPs before the Court of Justice.

The Supreme Court referred a number of questions, all but one of which dealt with specific aspects of the content of Article 50(6) TRIPs and its application in the Netherlands. Whilst there was no objection to its jurisdiction to give a ruling, the Court reaffirmed the existence of its jurisdiction in just one paragraph by stating that 'in the field of trade marks to which TRIPs is applicable and in respect of which the Community has already legislated, the Court has jurisdiction to interpret Article 50 of TRIPs—as, indeed, it has previously had the occasion to do'.[107] This part of the judgment was accompanied by a reference to both *Hermès* and *Dior*. Rather than clarifying the position, this statement raises a new host of questions, in particular regarding the reference to the existence of Community legislation. In that context, the reference to *Dior and Others* was also puzzling, as that dispute was about industrial designs and no reference was made to Community rules.

Be that as it may, the Court went on to interpret Article 50 of the TRIPs Agreement by identifying two principles underpinning the system of interim protection established thereunder, namely procedural autonomy and the balance of interests between the right holder and the defendant. The former was for the national legal system to construe, as there were no Community rules in the area. The latter was for the judicial authorities to apply, albeit with due regard for certain conditions. The relevant paragraph of the judgment reads as follows: [108]

---

[106] Case C–89/99 *Schieving-Nijstad vof and Others and Robert Groeneveld*, [2001] ECR I–5851.
[107] *Ibid*, para 30.
[108] *Ibid*, para 38.

It is . . . for the judicial authorities, when called upon to apply national rules with a view to ordering provisional measures, to take into account all the circumstances of the case before them, so as to ensure that a balance is maintained between the competing rights and obligations of the right holder and of the defendant.

The Court provided guidance to national courts by placing the balance between the above competing rights within the objectives of Article 50 TRIPs.[109] It identified the objectives of the procedural provision of Article 50 TRIPs and the logic which should underpin its application. By doing so, it defined the parameters within which national courts are expected to adjudicate as Community courts. Indeed, the balance between the rights enjoyed by the trade mark holders and other traders and the need to be struck in the light of the overall context of the dispute before the referring court is linked to the duty of interpretation imposed upon the national judiciary in the absence of direct effect of TRIPs. In *Schieving-Nijstad*, the Court repeated in a very short paragraph the fact that the rules of that Agreement may not be invoked by individuals before the national courts. However, in a longer paragraph which followed, it stressed what national courts should actually do in the light of the general principles put forward in prior case law and the specific ones articulated in *Schieving-Nijstad*:

> It should . . . be made clear that . . ., where the judicial authorities are called upon to apply national rules with a view to ordering provisional measures for the protection of intellectual property rights falling within a field to which TRIPs applies and in respect of which the Community has already legislated, they are required to do so as far as possible in the light of the wording and purpose of Article 50(6) of TRIPs, taking account, more particularly, of all the circumstances of the case before them, so as to ensure that a balance is struck between the competing rights and obligations of the right holder and of the defendant.[110]

The role that national courts are expected to play in the application of non-directly effective international agreements concluded by the Community is tied in with the role of national law in determining various aspects of their interpretation. In *Schieving-Nijstad*, for instance, it was for each Member State to determine the point in time at which the period prescribed by Article 50(6) of TRIPs is to start, provided always that the period thus fixed is 'reasonable having regard to the circumstances of each case and taking into account the balance to be struck between the competing rights and obligations of the intellectual property right holder and of the defendant'.[111] In the same vein, as regards the limits of the powers of the judicial authorities in ordering provisional measures, it was for each Member State to determine them in the light of the absence of any Community

---

[109] *Ibid*, paras 39–40.
[110] *Ibid*, para 54 of the judgment.
[111] Para 65.

rule.[112] Another procedural aspect of the application of Article 50(6) TRIPs dealt with was whether it was necessary for the defendant against whom a provisional decision has been adopted to make a request for that measure to be revoked or to cease to have effect. Whilst answering this question in the affirmative, the Court stated that there was no reason to consider whether national law may expressly provide for the provisional measure to lapse automatically. This may be interpreted as an implied endorsement of the position put forward by Advocate General Jacobs, who had argued for the right of Member States to provide for more extensive protection than that granted under Article 50(6) TRIPS.[113]

The above overview of the Court's approach to the interpretation of various procedural aspects of Article 50(6) TRIPs highlights not only the role of national law in the application of international agreements concluded by the Community but also the function that national courts are expected to carry out in that respect. The latter becomes all the more significant in the light of the following three interlinked considerations. First, the broad jurisdiction of the Court of Justice over mixed agreements renders various aspects of their application a matter of Community law whose uniform interpretation is deemed of paramount significance. Secondly, it is within these Community law parameters that national law may determine specific aspects of the interpretation of such agreements. Thirdly, in assessing such determinations, national courts carry out a function of a Community character in the exercise of which they are to be aided by the Court of Justice, as illustrated by its conclusions in *Schieving-Nijstad*. This approach sheds more light on the statement made in *Dior* according to which 'only the Court of Justice acting in cooperation with the courts and tribunals of the Member States pursuant to Article [234] of the treaty is in a position to ensure such uniform interpretation [of Article 50 TRIPs]'.[114] Viewed from this angle, whilst the judgment in *Hermès* appeared to highlight the first part of that statement, that is the role of the Court of Justice, the subsequent case law shed light on its second part, that is the role of the national courts.

8. PROCEDURAL INTEGRATION AND COOPERATION

In examining the case law on the interpretation of mixed agreements within the Community legal order, the analysis in this chapter has identified two threads. The first is related to the broad construction of the jurisdiction of the Court of Justice

---

[112] Para 68. In practical terms, this approach reads Art 50(6) TRIPs as neither requiring nor forbidding national rules to allow the judicial authorities to determine a reasonable time limit within which substantive proceedings are to be instituted (paras 69–70). That provision was also read as neither requiring nor forbidding national rules to confer that power both on appellate courts and on courts of first instance (paras 71–73).

[113] See para 49 of his Opinion where he suggested that the exercise of this right could not undermine the balance between the interests of the right holder and the defendant.

[114] *Dior*, n73 above, para 38.

not only to rule on the application of mixed agreements pursuant to Article 234 EC but also to determine their legality prior to their adoption pursuant to Article 300(6) EC. The second is concerned with the ensuing role of national courts in the application of mixed agreements and the emphasis on their cooperation with the Court of Justice. In relation to the jurisdiction of the latter, the interpretation of Article 300(6) is clearly not related to the interpretation of mixed agreements as such. However, it was included in this analysis not only because of the parallel development of its scope, but also because the principles to which it has given rise have been relied upon consistently by the Court in order to articulate the foundation for the role of national courts in the application of mixed agreements.

This evolving process of procedural integration and cooperation adds another dimension to the position of mixed agreements within the Community legal order. The analysis in the previous Chapter highlighted the principal role of mixity as sanctioned by the Court of Justice and managed by the Community institutions and the Member States. It also examined the various pragmatic mechanisms which have been developed as a matter of practice in order to deal with the practical issues raised by the absence of a clear delimitation of competences. It was against that background that the principle of close cooperation, articulated by the Court in the 1970s and emphasised in the 1990s, has been assessed and its role underlined. The analysis of the jurisdiction of the Court of Justice to interpret mixed agreements and its cooperation with national courts shapes the other pillar of the management of mixed agreements under Community law. In other words, originating in the constitutional idiosyncrasies of the Community, necessitated by the comprehensive and multifarious scope of international negotiations and favoured by the distinct reluctance of the Court to allocate non-exclusive competences, mixity has now become the focus of a two-fold mechanism aimed at curtailing its problems: first, the negotiation, conclusion and application of mixed agreements are subject to compliance with the duty of close cooperation which is binding on the Community institutions and the Member States; secondly, the interpretation of such agreements becomes the subject-matter of the jurisdiction of the Court of Justice which is acting in close cooperation with national courts.

Viewed from this angle, there is a clear thread which brings together various strands of the case law on mixed agreements and is centred on the role of the Court of Justice: by introducing binding principles in an area developed by practice, extending its scope of application and interacting with a variety of institutional and judicial actors, it shapes a flexible mechanism aiming at the effective supervision of all aspects of mixed agreements. The incremental development of this mechanism carries out a variety of functions. In practical terms, it succeeds in fencing off maximalistic claims for exclusivity. In legal terms, it illustrates the various elements whose interaction forms the foundation of the system of EC international relations law. In this respect, the following statement by Advocate General Tesauro in his Opinion in *Hermès* is noteworthy: [115]

---

[115] N57 above, 3621.

The Community legal system is characterized by the simultaneous application of provisions of various origins, international Community and national; but it nevertheless seeks to function and to represent itself to the outside world as a unified system. That is, one might say, the inherent nature of the system which, while guaranteeing the maintenance of the realities of States and of individual interests of all kinds, also seeks to achieve a unified *modus operandi*. Its steadfast adherence to that aim, which the Court itself has described as an obligation of solidarity, is certainly lent considerable weight by the judicial review mechanism which is defined in the Treaty and relies on the simultaneous support of the Community courts and the national courts.

In fleshing out the 'unified *modus operandi*' mentioned above, the Court of Justice has assumed a constitutional function. In the light of the analysis in this chapter, that is not to say that the system emerging from its case law is either complete or flawless. The specific legal and factual context within which the Court has delivered its judgments should not be dismissed. For instance, the provision whose interpretation gave rise to this case law, that is Article 50 of the TRIPs Agreement, is one of a strictly procedural nature, as the Court underlined time and again in its judgments.[116] In the absence of Community law, diversity in the application of procedural rules has been accepted by the Court of Justice as the foundation for the application of Community law by national courts provided that the latter comply with certain conditions defined and supervised by the Court itself.[117] In addition, the host of questions raised by the line of reasoning followed in these judgments suggests that the mechanism emerging from the case law on EC international relations is still evolving. On the other hand, the implications of those questions should not be overestimated: for instance, the right of national courts to ascertain the direct effect of international provision should be viewed in the context of the rapid development of Community law.[118]

9. CONCLUSION

The analysis in this chapter focused on the various mechanisms pursuant to which the Court of Justice has assumed the role of interpreting mixed agreements. The assessment of the exercise of its jurisdiction and its implications for national courts aimed at complementing the analysis in the previous chapter on the various mechanisms pursuant to which the formula of mixity is regulated in the process of the negotiation, conclusion and application of international agreements. It has taken the Community legal order more than 30 years to develop

---

[116] In addition, the TRIPS Agreement has been criticised for the considerable discretion it grants its contracting parties: see JH Reichman, 'Securing Compliance with the TRIPs Agreement After *US v India*' (1998) 1 *JIEL* 585.

[117] See the principle of procedural autonomy articulated in Case 33/76 *Rewe-Zentralfinanz eG and Rewe-Zentral AG v Landwirtschaftskammer für das Saarland* [1976] ECR 1989. For its development and adjustments, see P Craig and G de Búrca, *EU Law* (3rd edn, Oxford: OUP, 2003) ch 6.

[118] See Koutrakos, n72 above, at 50–51.

incrementally the system of principles emerging from this analysis. Whilst under-lining the multi-faceted implications of the phenomenon of mixity within the context of Community law, its articulation in ways which raise as many questions as they answer indicates a rather inward-looking posture. In other words, the approach to the interpretation of mixed agreements was clearly focused on the constitutional idiosyncrasies of the Community and aimed at striking the balance between the various actors these involved, namely the Community legislature and executive, the national institutions as well as the Community and national courts. This approach is apparent in the early statement in *Ruling 1/78* regarding the allo-cation of competences between the Community and Member States and its char-acter as internal to the Community.[119] Whilst this is undoubtedly correct, the increasing interdependence of international activities and the ensuing prolifera-tion of international legal mechanisms will raise other types of challenges for Community law. The relationship between those mechanisms and the Community legal order and their direct impact on the role of the Court of Justice is a case in point.[120] It is hoped that the response to those challenges will further clarify the function and implications of the principles governing the position of mixity within the Community legal order.

[119] *Ruling 1/78*, n22 above, para 35.
[120] See the action in Case C–459/03 *Commission v Ireland* [2004] OJ C 7/39: Ireland instituted dis-pute settlement proceedings against UK under the UN Convention for the Law of the Sea concerning the MOX Plant located at Sellafield. The Commission argued that this should be dealt with as a mat-ter of Community law and, therefore, the action by the Irish government constituted a violation of the duty of loyal cooperation under Art 10 EC and the exclusive jurisdiction of the Court under Art 292 EC. On the dispute between the two countries, see R Churchill and J Scott, 'The Mox Plant Litigation: The First Half-Life' (2005) 53 *ICLQ* 643, V Shany, 'The First *MOX Plant* Award: The Need to Harmonize Competing Environmental Regimes and Dispute Settlement Procedures' (2004) 17 *Leiden Journal of International Law* 815. On the issue of the jurisdiction of the Court of Justice, see J Cazala, 'La contestation de la compétence exclusive de la Cour de justice des communautés européennes' (2004) 40 *Revue Trimestrielle de Droit Européen* 505.

6

Effects of International Rules in the Community Legal Order

1. INTRODUCTION

THE LAST CHAPTER examined the ways in which the Court of Justice has gradually elaborated its jurisdiction to interpret international agreements concluded by the Community. It also identified the role entrusted to national courts in the process of application and interpretation of such agreements and the ways in these courts are expected to interact with the Court of Justice. Whilst significant in principle, the construction of the Court's jurisdiction is not a sufficient criterion for the assessment of the Court's approach to the international rules. That may only be determined in the light of the specific ways in which international rules penetrate the Community legal order. It is this approach that will be examined in this chapter. A substantial part of the case law to be examined deals with provisions laid down in the GATT and WTO agreements: because of the special questions their effects in the Community legal order raise, the relevant judgments will be examined in detail in a subsequent chapter; the present one will only refer to their role within the more general scheme of the case law on the effects of international agreements.

2. THE INTRODUCTION OF THE PRINCIPLE OF DIRECT EFFECT: LAYING DOWN THE FOUNDATION

In developing the principle of supremacy, that is the fundamental constitutional quality of the Community legal order, the Court made it clear that national law was entirely irrelevant to the assessment of the validity of Community law. In declaring the applicability of this principle to national constitutional law, the Court enabled its jurisprudence to develop in areas such as the protection of fundamental human rights.[1] The relationship of Community law with international

---

[1] See the case law initiated by the reference of the Federal Constitutional Court in Case 11/70 *Internationale Handelsgesellschaft mbH v Einfuhr- und Vorratsstelle für Getreide und Futtermittel* [1970] ECR 1125.

law, however, raised an entirely different host of questions which the principle of supremacy alone could not address. These questions were centred around the extent to which the Community was bound by international law, and the rights of individuals to rely upon it in order to challenge the validity of Community measures either directly before the Community judicature or indirectly before national courts.

It is ironic that the Court should have dealt explicitly with these issues, including that of the binding effect upon the Community, for the first time in a case about an agreement to which the Community, as opposed to all its Member States, was not a party. This was the General Agreement on Tariffs and Trade (GATT) concluded in 1947. In *International Fruit Company*,[2] a Dutch court referred to the Court questions about a set of Community measures restricting the importation of apples from third countries and their validity in the light of the GATT. The first issue which was dealt with was the existence of its own jurisdiction under the preliminary reference procedure when the consistency of Community law with international law was at stake. As examined in chapter 5, the Court interpreted the wording of Article 234(1) EC broadly: its jurisdiction covers all grounds of review of the validity of Community law, including international law.

The next question, then, was whether its consistency with international law was one such ground for a Community measure to be invalidated. The Court ruled that the answer would be affirmative provided that two conditions were met: on the one hand, the international rule in question should be binding upon the Community; on the other hand, that rule should be capable of conferring rights upon Community citizens upon which the latter could rely before national courts. The first condition was deemed by the Court to have been met, a conclusion reached on the basis of two main arguments. First, it was pointed out that not only were all Member States bound by GATT at the time of the establishment of the then European Economic Community but they also intended to observe their obligations in formulating and implementing Community law. This was illustrated by the rule of Article 307 EC which recognised the application of the principle of *pacta sunt servanda* within the Community legal order; it also underpinned Article 110 of the original Treaty of Rome, now deleted, which stated that the Community was to adhere to the same aims as those of GATT. Secondly, the Court held that the Community 'has assumed the functions inherent in the tariff and trade policy' within the context of its Common Commercial Policy, progressively during the transitional period and in their entirety on the expiry of that period.[3] It was in the light of this development that the Court opined that 'by conferring those powers on the Community, the Member States showed their wish to

---

[2] Joined Cases 21 to 24/72 *International Fruit Company NV and Others v Produktschap voor Groenten en Fruit* [1972] ECR 1219.

[3] *Ibid*, para 14.

bind it by the obligations entered into under [GATT]'.[4] In order to substantiate this position, the Court drew upon the autonomous involvement of the Community, through its own institutions, as a party to the various agreements concluded within the GATT framework pursuant to the now repealed provision of Article 114 of the Treaty of Rome.[5] It was on that basis that the Court concluded that 'in so far as under the EEC Treaty the Community has assumed the powers previously exercised by Member States in the area governed by [GATT], the provisions of that agreement have the effect of binding the Community'.[6]

Having established the binding effect of GATT upon the Community, the Court went on to examine whether that Agreement was capable of conferring rights which individuals could invoke before national courts. The answer to this question relied upon 'the spirit, the general scheme and the terms' of GATT.[7] As a detailed examination of the line of reasoning followed by the Court will be provided in a subsequent section, suffice it to point out that the Court deemed the GATT an agreement which could not affect the validity of Community measures: this was so because the great flexibility of its provisions rendered it incapable of conferring rights enforceable by Community citizens before national courts.

In terms of its contribution in the law of EC international relations, the judgment in *International Fruit Company* carried out three main functions: it laid down the foundation of the Court's jurisdiction within the framework of the preliminary reference procedure, it defined the basis for the reception of international law within the Community legal order and signalled its cautious approach to the effect of the most important multilateral trade agreement of the time. As the first and the last of those functions are examined elsewhere, this analysis will focus on the second one.

The legal context within which the Court was asked to clarify the position of international agreements in *International Fruit Company* was not as controversial as it might have been as it did not raise questions of competence. The subject matter of the GATT, that is the conclusion of tariff and trade arrangements, fell within the scope of the Common Commercial Policy as defined expressly in Article 133 EC. As such, it was covered by the exclusive competence of the Community: had it been negotiated and concluded following the expiry of the transitional period, and had the GATT provided for membership of international organisations, it would have been the Commission and the Council respectively which would have been responsible, the latter acting by qualified majority voting. The issue of the prior conclusion of the GATT was addressed by the Court by what has

---

[4] *Ibid*, para 15.
[5] That provision read as follows: 'The agreements referred to in Article 111(2) [that is tariff agreements] and in Article 113 [now 133] shall be concluded by the Council on behalf of the Community, acting unanimously during the first two stages and by a qualified majority thereafter'.
[6] N2 above, para 18 of the judgment.
[7] N2 above, para 20 of the judgment.

been described as 'its succession theory'.[8] The principle of state succession in respect of treaties is a recognised principle of international law.[9] However, the introduction of the concept of succession by an international organisation to state obligations by the Court was noteworthy for a number of reasons. First, the exclusive nature, which is not stated in express terms in the EC Treaty, had not yet been spelled out by the Court at the time of the reference in *International Fruit Company*: it would take three more years for the exclusive nature of Community competence over the Common Commercial Policy to be articulated.[10] With the benefit of hindsight, the ruling of the Court appears to signal what was to become one of the pillars of its external trade relations.

Secondly, in practical terms, as far as the fulfilment of their obligations under the GATT was concerned, the Member States had been replaced by the Community; this necessary corollary of the judgment in *International Fruit Company*, was spelled out three years later in *Nederlandse Spoorwegen*.[11] This case was about the effect of the Convention on Nomenclature for the Classification of Goods in Customs Tariffs and the Convention establishing a Customs Cooperation Council in relation to which the Court repeated its formula of substitution.[12] Thirdly, the determination of the effect of GATT provisions in both domestic and the Community legal order became a matter for the Court of Justice: as the Community had replaced the Member States in the fulfilment of their obligations, the interpretation and application of the GATT within the context of a domestic dispute under domestic law was *ipso facto* a dispute governed by Community law. The significance of the implications of this type of judicial exclusivity became apparent in the judgment in *International Fruit Company* itself with reference to the legal effect of the GATT: in ruling out even the possibility of a national court being receptive to a more direct enforcement of the GATT, the Court's judgment determined the effectiveness of that agreement in the territory of one of the most important international trade actors.

In addition to the wide construction of the Court's jurisdiction and the statement on succession to the obligations undertaken within the framework of the GATT, the third main thrust of the judgment in *International Fruit Company* was the acknowledgment of the possibility of international agreements concluded by the Community being directly effective. In this, the Court transposed one of the foundations of the process of constitutionalisation of the internal market law into the area of EC external relations. It is recalled that the premise under which individuals were deemed to enjoy rights under Community law which they could

[8] J Klabbers, 'The *Bustani* Case before the ILOAT: Constitutionalism in Disguise?' (2004) 53 *ICLQ* 455 at 456.

[9] See the analysis in I Brownlie, *Principles of Public International Law* (6th edn, Oxford: OUP, 2003) at 633–8.

[10] See *Opinion 1/75 (re: OECD Understanding on a Local Cost Standard)* [1975] ECR 355.

[11] Case 38/75 [1975] ECR 1439 at para 21.

[12] *Ibid*. Both Conventions had been concluded in 1950.

enforce before national courts was the very first proposition of the Court on the effect of Community law within the domestic legal orders.[13] Applicable originally to EC Treaty provisions, its scope was broadened to cover regulations,[14] decisions[15] and, most controversially, directives.[16] The introduction of the principle of direct effect provided considerable momentum for the development of Community law, being at the very centre of the process of constitutionalisation of the EC Treaty. In the light of the multi-faceted role of the principle of direct effect on the internal plane, its endorsement in the area of external relations raised a number of questions as to the approach the Court would adopt to the interpretation of international law: would it adopt an internationalist approach, aiming at enforcing international rules as actively as it possibly could? In doing so, would it show the creative ingenuity which had underpinned its approach to the development of the principles of supremacy and direct effect? How receptive would it be to the approach adopted by other international courts?

The long and still evolving process of the construction of direct effect of directives[17] indicates that the introduction of the principle itself does not necessarily determine the effectiveness of the instrument to which it applies: it is the application of the principle in specific instances which really matters. Indeed, the judgment in *International Fruit Company* appears to illustrate the very specific context within which the principle of direct effect is to be applied to international agreements: the Court did not engage in a detailed examination of the proviso of Article XI GATT; instead, it held that the agreement of which it was part was incapable of conferring rights enforceable before national courts because of its very nature, scheme and wording. This approach suggests that the application of direct effect in the area of international agreements requires a general assessment of the overall legal nature of the agreement prior to the specific assessment of the provision put forward before a court. This two-tier test which would determine the application of the principle of direct effect may be seen as an acknowledgment, by the Court, of the special challenges that the enforcement of international agreements within the Community legal order raises for the latter's constitutional balance. After all, the principle of direct effect of international agreements as a matter of Community law was introduced in a case where the agreement in question had not even been concluded by the Community. Viewed from this angle, the judgment in *International Fruit Company* struck the balance between the introduction of bold principles (broad jurisdiction of the Court, succession to the obligations of Member States by the Community and direct effect of international agreements)

---

[13] Case 26/62 *NV Algemene Transporten Expeditie Onderneming van Gend en Loos v Nederlandse Administratie der Belastingen* [1962] ECR 1.

[14] Case 50/76 *Amsterdam Bulb BV v Produktschap voor Siergewassen* [1977] ECR 137.

[15] Case 9/70 *Franz Grad v Finanzamt Traunstein* [1970] ECR 825.

[16] Case 41/74 *Van Duyn v Home Office* [1974] ECR 1337.

[17] For an updated analysis, see S Prechal, *Directives in EC Law* (2nd edn, Oxford: OUP, 2005) Ch 9 and T Tridimas, 'Black, White and Shades of Grey: Horizontality of Directives Revisited' (2002) 21 *YEL* 327

and their cautious application. This was an approach which, as examined in earlier chapters, would become increasingly prominent in EC international relations case law.

In the case of GATT, it was its 'great flexibility' which ruled out direct effect: the Court referred in particular to GATT's provisions conferring the possibility of derogation, the measures to be taken when the parties were confronted with exceptional difficulties and the settlement of conflicts between the contracting parties. Would the absence of flexibility in the substantive content of an international agreement be a necessary prerequisite for its ability to be invoked by individuals? If so, would it not be extremely difficult for any agreement to qualify as directly effective? If not, which criteria would determine what degree of flexibility was acceptable for an international rule to qualify as directly effective? These were not the only questions raised by the judgment in *International Fruit Company*. As it sought to confine its conclusion to the parameters set by the questions referred to it, the Court avoided other questions related to the scope of the principles laid down therein. One question referred to the type of procedure in which invalidity of a Community measure in the light of international law could be invoked: did it cover direct actions before the Community judicature? If so, would the direct effect of that rule be essential for an individual to be able to invoke it? Were there any further conditions for Member States to be able to challenge Community measures before the Court of Justice on the ground of their inconsistency with international law?

3. THE DEVELOPMENT OF THE PRINCIPLE OF DIRECT EFFECT: THE PERIOD OF CONSOLIDATION

Some of the questions raised above were addressed in subsequent case law within a short time. Four years after the judgment in *International Fruit Company* was delivered, the relevance of the Yaoundé Convention to the legality of national law in the area of charges of an equivalent effect to customs duties was raised. The Yaoundé Convention was an association agreement concluded between the Community and its Member States, on the one hand, and the African states and Madagascar, former dependent territories of France, Belgium and the Netherlands, on the other. This precursor of the Lomé and Cotonou Conventions, signed in 1963, was invoked in *Bresciani* by an importer of raw cowhides from France and Senegal into Italy.[18] He objected to being charged a fee for a compulsory veterinary and public health inspection of his imports, and argued that that fee constituted a charge of an equivalent effect to a customs duty and, as such, was contrary not only to Article 25 EC but also to Article 2(1) of the Yaoundé Convention which provided for the progressive prohibition of such charges on goods originating in any of the associated states.

---

[18] Case 87/75 *Conceria Daniele Bresciani v Amministrazione Italiana delle Finanze* [1975] ECR 129.

Having interpreted the notion of a charge of an equivalent effect to a customs duty in Article 25 EC broadly enough to cover the contested charge, the Court went on to ascertain whether the latter was also illegal under Article 2(1) of the Yaoundé Convention. In order to address this question, the Court turned to the issue of the direct effect of the Convention for the examination of which 'regard must be simultaneously paid to the spirit, the general scheme and the wording of the Convention and that of the provision concerned'.[19] First, the Court identified the specific context within which the Convention had been adopted. Its aim was to replace an arrangement concluded pursuant to Part IV of the EEC Treaty, which had established an association between the Community and dependent territories of some of its Member States. Following the expiry of that arrangement and the process of independence of many of the associated states, the Community and its Member States concluded the Yaounde Convention in order to maintain the special preferential economic and political connections between them.

Secondly, the Court examined the spirit of the Convention and concluded that it was characterised by an 'imbalance' between the obligations assumed by the Community and those assumed by the associated states: whilst Article 2(1) of the Convention provided for the progressive abolition of customs duties and charges of an equivalent effect to a customs duty, Article 3(2) enabled the associated states to retain or introduce such charges if they were deemed to correspond to their needs or their industrialisation requirements or were intended to contribute to their budget; this exceptional clause did not alter the obligation of the Community and its Member States to adhere to their duty under Article 3(2). It was in the light of these provisions that the Court concluded that:[20]

> it is apparent . . . that the Convention was not concluded in order to ensure equality in the obligations which the Community assumes with regard to the associated states, but in order to promote their development in accordance with the aim of the first convention annexed to the Treaty.

However, 'this imbalance' was deemed 'inherent in the special nature of the Convention' and did 'not prevent recognition by the Community that some of its provisions have a direct effect'.[21]

The Court then proceeded to examine the specific provision of the Yaoundé Convention invoked by the applicant before the referring court. It reached the conclusion that it was capable of conferring rights directly upon individuals. In doing so, it construed the obligation contained in Article 2(1) of the Convention in very strict terms: on the one hand, whilst the application of the prohibition laid down therein could be subject to consultations within the Association Council at the request of an associated state, that was deemed to be irrelevant to the nature

---

[19] *Ibid*, para 16.
[20] *Ibid*, para 22.
[21] *Ibid*, para 23.

of the obligation imposed upon the Community, the latter having to comply with it automatically; on the other hand, Article 2(1) of the Convention referred expressly to the similar prohibition laid down in Article 25 EC. This was read by the Court to imply that the nature of the obligation the Community had assumed towards the associated states was precisely the same as that which its Member States had assumed towards one another: since the latter was 'specific and not subject to any implied or express reservation', so was the former.[22]

The judgment in *Bresciani* is underpinned by a more liberal interpretation of direct effect in EC external relations: it was neither dependent upon reciprocity of obligations undertaken under the agreement in question nor restricted by the existence of consultation mechanisms in relation to the application of the specific provision invoked before the national court. This approach may be juxtaposed to that in *International Fruit Company*: whilst the latter was keen to stress the parameters within which the principle of direct effect would be applied, the former illustrated the flexibility with which it could be employed. This makes the absence of reasoning in the judgment all the more remarkable: why did the imbalance of obligations not prevent the possibility of direct effect? Was it only because the Convention was of a special nature, that is to maintain and develop the relations between the Community and a number of countries traditionally linked with some of its Members? Is this both a sufficient and necessary condition for the imbalance of obligations to be irrelevant to the direct effect of the Agreement?

The conditions under which the principle of direct effect would be applied were clarified in *Kupferberg*, a reference from the German Federal Finance Court on the interpretation of the Free Trade Agreement (FTA) between the Community and Portugal.[23] A German importer of port from Portugal into Germany was asked to pay a charge imposed upon all imported spirits under national law. He brought an action before German courts arguing that the imposition of that charge was contrary to Article 21(1) of the FTA with Portugal.

The governments of four Member States, Denmark, Germany, France and Great Britain, had argued against the direct effect of FTA provisions. In its judgment, the Court defined the principles under which the principle of direct effect may be applied to international agreements concluded by the Community. These may be summarised as follows. First, the Court referred to the international origin of the rules in question. It noted that, in accordance with public international law, it is for the parties to an agreement to determine its effect within their domestic legal order: the Court of Justice would determine whether the provision of an international agreement concluded by the Community would be directly effective before national courts only if the Community institutions had not addressed this issue in the agreement itself.

---

[22] *Ibid*, para 25.
[23] Case 104/81 *Hauptzollamt Mainz v C.A. Kupferberg & Cie KG a.A.* [1982] ECR 3641.

Secondly, the Court referred to what may be called judicial reciprocity. It pointed out that 'the fact that the courts of one of the parties consider that certain of the stipulations in the agreement are of direct application whereas the courts of the other party do not recognize such direct application is not itself such as to constitute a lack of reciprocity in the implementation of the agreement'.[24] What is significant is that the obligations contained in the agreement are fulfilled, in accordance with the general rules of international law, *bona fide*: whilst under a duty to comply fully with their contractual obligations, the parties are free, in the absence of an express provision in the agreement, to determine how to do so.

Thirdly, the Court referred to the establishment of a special institutional framework by an agreement concluded by the Community. The FTA with Portugal, for instance, had entrusted its administration to joint committees which enjoyed the power to make recommendations about the proper implementation of the Agreement and take decisions in the areas specified therein. However, 'the mere fact' that such structures had been established was deemed 'not in itself sufficient to exclude all judicial application of that Agreement'.[25] The Court justified this conclusion by pointing out that a provision viewed as directly applicable by the judiciary of one of the parties would not adversely affect the powers of the committee set up by the FTA given that that provision would be presumed to be unconditional.

Fourthly, the Court referred to the provision of safeguard clauses which was also viewed as 'not sufficient in itself to affect the direct applicability' of certain provisions of the agreement.[26] This was because of their limited scope: the contracting parties were allowed to deviate from the Agreement only in specific circumstances and following consultations in the Joint Committee.

In the light of the above considerations, the Court deemed the FTA with Portugal capable of conferring rights upon individuals enforceable before national courts. The construction of the first part of the two-tier test for determining the direct effect of international rules in *Kupferberg* is so liberal that its actual function in the process of enforcing these rules becomes questionable: neither judicial reciprocity nor the establishment of autonomous bodies with decision-making power nor the provision for safeguard clauses is alone sufficient to make provisions of an agreement incapable of conferring rights upon individuals, provided, that is, that they meet the specific conditions for direct effect.

In dealing with this issue in *Kupferberg*, the Court examined Article 21(1) of the Agreement in the light of the object and purpose of the Agreement and of its context. The purpose of the FTA was the establishment of 'a system of free trade in which rules restricting commerce are eliminated in respect of virtually all trade in products originating in the territory of the parties'.[27] As the main pillars of this system referred to the abolition of customs duties and charges of an equivalent

---

[24] *Ibid*, para 18.
[25] *Ibid*, para 20.
[26] *Ibid*, para 21.
[27] *Ibid*, para 24.

effect as well as quantitative restrictions and measures of an equivalent effect, the Court had no difficulty in viewing the prohibition on fiscal measures laid down in Article 21(1) of the Agreement as a necessary part of that system. Therefore, that provision:[28]

> imposes on the contracting parties an unconditional rule against discrimination in matters of taxation, which is dependent only on a finding that the products affected by a particular system of taxation are of like nature, and the limits of which are the direct consequence of the purpose of the Agreement. As such this provision may be applied by a court and thus produce direct effects throughout the Community.

In the line of reasoning in *Kupferberg*, the structure of the judgment is noteworthy: what precedes the detailed assessment of the number of characteristics which may not deprive the provisions of an agreement of direct effect is the assertion of the right of the parties to the agreement to determine its effect. In other words, the jurisdiction of the Court on that matter is only residual: it is for the Community institutions either on their own or along with the Member States as regards mixed agreements to render any willingness of the Court to adopt an internationalist position redundant. In making this point, the Court not only acknowledges their primary role on that matter but it also points out an alternative, should the Member States find its interpretation of direct effect detrimental to the international interests of the Community.

Following the clarifications of the conditions under which the principle of direct effect would be applied, a number of provisions of international agreements were found to meet the relevant criteria. In *Legros*, the Court held that the dock dues imposed upon all products imported into the French region of Réunion were contrary to the prohibition on charges of an equivalent effect to customs duties under Article 25 EC as well as Article 6 of the FTA with Sweden, concluded in 1972.[29] In *Texaco*, the prohibition on internal fiscal measures discriminating, directly or indirectly, against imported products laid down in the Free Trade Agreement with Sweden was held to be directly effective.[30] This was also the case with a similar prohibition in the Free Trade Agreement with Austria concluded in 1972.[31]

4. THE INTERPRETATION OF DIRECTLY EFFECTIVE PROVISIONS OF INTERNATIONAL AGREEMENTS

The construction of direct effect of provisions contained in an agreement concluded by the Community has been shown to be directly linked to a preliminary

---

[28] *Ibid*, para 26.
[29] Case C–163/90 *Administration des Douanes et Droits Indirects v Leopold Legros and others* [1992] ECR I–4625.
[30] Joined Cases C–114/95 and C–115/95 *Texaco A/S v Middelfaert Havn and others* [1997] ECR I–4263.
[31] Case C–312/91 *Metalsa* [1993] ECR I–3751.

assessment of the nature and spirit of the agreement which, in turn, determines whether that agreement may provide grounds for challenging the legality of Community law. Once this assessment has been made, questions about its interpretation by the Court of Justice arise: how broadly would the Court be prepared to interpret the wording and context of such provisions? To what extent would it be prepared to infuse the product of the international contractual actions of the Community with the constitutionalising qualities it had attributed to Community law? To what extent would it be prepared to draw upon provisions of primary and secondary Community law for inspiration in interpreting similarly worded provisions of international agreements?

4.1. A Conflict?

These questions arose in *Polydor,* a preliminary reference from the Court of Appeal about the application and interpretation of the FTA with Portugal.[32] The dispute before the referring court arose because the proprietor of the copyright of recordings by the group Bee Gees had relied upon national law in order to exercise their rights to exclusive commercial exploitation and to prevent the parallel import of recordings from Portugal. As regards intra-Community trade, the Court had held that whilst the existence of intellectual property rights could justify a deviation from the rules on free movement of goods, their exercise by their proprietor would constitute a measure of equivalent effect to a quantitative restriction if it targeted imports of products from another Member State where they had been put on the market by the proprietor himself or with his consent.[33] As the imported recordings had originated in Portugal, the question was whether the exercise of the exclusive rights granted under national law to the copyright proprietor was consistent with the FTA governing trade relations between the Community and Portugal. The Agreement provided for the abolition of quantitative restrictions and measures of equivalent effect on imports; it also introduced an exception enabling the parties to protect a number of public interests, including industrial and commercial property, albeit not in a way which would amount to arbitrary discrimination or a disguised restriction on trade.[34]

In order to decide whether the transposition of the Court's case law on Article 28 EC would be appropriate regarding the Agreement in question, the Court set out to assess its object, purpose and wording. The former was 'to consolidate and to extend the economic relations existing between the Community and Portugal and to ensure, with due regard for fair conditions of competition, the harmonious

---

[32] Case 270/80 *Polydor Ltd and RSO Records Inc v Harlequin Records Shops Ltd and Simons Records Lmd* [1982] ECR 329.

[33] See, for instance, Case 16/74 *Centrafarm BV et Adriaan de Peijper v Winthrop BV* [1974] ECR 1183.

[34] See Arts 14(2) and 23 of the FTA respectively.

development of their commerce for the purpose of contributing to the work of constructing Europe'.[35] In pursuance of this objective, a set of provisions was introduced in order to liberalise trade in goods: customs duties and charges of equivalent effect were to be abolished along with quantitative restrictions and measures of equivalent effect; fiscal measures amounting to discrimination and all restrictions on payments relating to trade in goods were prohibited; provisions on competition law, state aids and anti-dumping were included and a joint committee responsible for the administration and proper implementation of the Agreement was established.

The Court, then, proceeded to examine the wording of the relevant FTA provisions which was similar to that of the prohibition laid down in Article 28 EC and the exceptional clause of Article 30 EC. However, such similarity was deemed 'not a sufficient reason for transposing to the provisions of the Agreement' the Court's case law on the relationship between intellectual property rights and free movement of goods as their scope had to be assessed in different contexts: the relevant case law on Articles 28 and 30 EC had developed 'in the light of the Community's objectives and activities as defined in the . . . EC Treaty [which] . . . by establishing a common market and progressively approximating the economic policies of the Member States, seeks to unite national markets into a single market having the characteristics of a domestic market';[36] on the other hand, the FTA with Portugal, 'although it makes provision for the unconditional abolition of certain restrictions on trade between the Community and Portugal, such as quantitative restrictions and measures having equivalent effect, it does not have the same purpose as the EEC Treaty'.[37] The Court went on to argue that that conclusion was supported by the absence, within the framework set up by the FTA, of the significant legal tools the EC has at its disposal in order to ensure the uniform application of EC law and its progressive harmonisation.

The starting point for the Court's interpretation of the prohibition on measures having equivalent effect to quantitative restrictions laid down in an FTA is sensible: as legal rules are interpreted in the light of their context, similarly worded rules cannot possibly be dissociated from the set of provisions of which they form part. However, the judgment in *Polydor* provides no firm guidance on the conditions which need to be met for such similarly worded provisions to be interpreted in a similar manner. The Court underlines the distinct objectives of the EC Treaty and the unique legal machinery available to Community institutions to pursue them: is this intended to be a precondition for the interpretation given to EC provisions to apply to other treaties? In other words, is this a normative standard which ought to be met before similarly worded provisions are interpreted in the light of the EC Treaty?

---

[35] N32 above, para 10 of the judgment referring to the preamble to FTA.
[36] *Ibid*, para 16.

The relevance of the difference between the objectives pursued by an FTA and the EC Treaty was also mentioned in *Kupferberg*. In that judgment, the Court pointed out that the interpretation given to the prohibition on discriminatory taxation in Article 90 EC could not be applied by way of simple analogy to the equivalent provision of the FTA with Portugal.[38] The same conclusion was later reached in *Metalsa* in respect of the analogous prohibition contained in the FTA with Austria: whilst Article 90 EC had been interpreted as prohibiting the penalisation of offences concerning the payment of VAT on imports more severely than those concerning the payment of VAT on domestic products, no such prohibition could be inferred on imports from Austria.[39]

So far in this analysis a number of FTAs have been identified the provisions of which on measures of equivalent effect to quantitative restrictions, charges of equivalent effect to customs duties and discriminatory taxation were given a different interpretation from that of the similar provisions laid down in the EC Treaty. However, in other cases on the interpretation of FTAs, the Court reached a different conclusion. In the context of the FTA with Sweden, the French government relied upon the judgment in *Polydor* and argued in *Legros* that dock dues imposed upon all products imported into the French region of Réunion, whilst contrary to Article 25 EC, were not contrary to the analogous prohibition of the FTA.[40] This argument was rejected by the Court, which stressed the central role of the prohibition on charges of equivalent effect to customs duties in the context of the objective of eliminating obstacles to trade. It was in the light of this consideration that it concluded that 'the agreement would . . . be deprived of much of its effectiveness if the term "charge having equivalent effect" contained in Article 6 of the agreement were to be interpreted as having a more limited scope than the same term appearing in the [EC] Treaty'.[41]

In *Eurim-Pharm*, questions about the interpretation of the Free Trade Agreement with Austria were referred by a German court.[42] The applicant had bought consignments of a medicine in Austria and had sought to import it into Germany. However, the Federal Health Authority did not authorise the placing of the product in circulation on the German market on the ground that significant information such as the method of its manufacture, its length of storage and the quality control methods used had not been established. The applicant challenged that decision, arguing that it was contrary to the FTA with Austria, in particular Article 13 which prohibited quantitative restrictions and measures of equivalent effect and Article 20 which allowed the parties to deviate from Article 13 in order

[37] *Ibid*, para 18.
[38] See n23 above, at para 30.
[39] See n31 above.
[40] See n29 above.
[41] *Ibid*, para 26.
[42] Case C–207/91 *Eurim-Pharm GmbH v Bundesgesundheitsaut* [1993] ECR I–372.

to protect certain public interests which included intellectual property rights. What was interesting about this case was the fact that the Federal Authority had already authorised the placing of the medicine in question on the market by the trade mark owner; it was the placing of the parallel imported medicine in the market that was not authorised.

The substantive point in question had already been addressed in the judgment in *De Peijper,* where it was held that a national rule rendering the grant of an authorisation to a parallel importer of medicines subject to the production of documents which had already been supplied to the competent health authority by the manufacturer of that medicine constituted a measure of an equivalent effect to a quantitative restriction on imports which was not necessary in order to protect the life and health of humans.[43] The question was whether that interpretation could be applied in the context of an FTA. The British and Italian governments, along with the Commission, argued before the Court for a negative response in the light of the absence of any provision in the Agreement for legislative harmonisation or administrative cooperation in the pharmaceutical sector. That argument was rejected:[44]

> Even on the assumption that the Court's case-law on Articles [28] and [30] of the Treaty cannot be applied to the interpretation of Articles 13 and 20 of the Agreement, it is sufficient to note that, since the German health authority already possessed all the necessary information about the medicine and there was no dispute that the imported medicine and the authorized medicine were identical, the authority had no need to secure cooperation of any kind from the Austrian authorities.

It was then concluded that the interpretation already given to Articles 28 and 30 EC in *De Peijper* should also apply to Articles 13 and 20 of the FTA with Austria for, otherwise, the latter would be deprived 'of much of their effectiveness'.[45]

What emerges is an apparent conflict: on the one hand, in cases such as *Polydor, Kupferberg* and *Metalsa,* the Court denies any automatic extension of the interpretation of EC Treaty prohibitions in the area of free movement of goods to similarly or identically worded provisions of FTAs; on the other hand, in cases such as *Eurim-Pharm* and *Legros,* the Court suggests that the effectiveness of prohibitions set out in the latter would be undermined if the liberal interpretation of the analogous EC prohibitions were not transposed. Are these cases inconsistent? The answer should be negative. These judgments, all delivered under the preliminary reference procedure, should be viewed within their specific factual and legal context. In *Polydor,* for instance, it would be very difficult to envisage any other answer to the question of the transposition to the FTA of the case law on exhaustion of

---

[43] Case 104/75 *De Peijper* [1976] ECR 613.
[44] Para 24 of the judgment in *Eurim-Pharm,* n42 above.
[45] N43 above, para 25.

intellectual property rights. It is recalled that the definition of the territorial scope of that principle has given rise to considerable controversy at various levels: in the negotiations leading to the adoption of the Trade Marks Directive,[46] for instance, the idea of introducing the principle of international exhaustion was rejected; the provision for EEA-wide exhaustion has been interpreted by the Court as introducing complete harmonisation in the area, hence enabling trade mark owners in a Member State to rely upon their right to object to parallel imports of a trade-marked product from a non-EEA state.[47] For the Court to have ruled otherwise in *Polydor* would have been tantamount to extending, as early as in 1982, the scope of the principle of exhaustion beyond the reach of what would be considered necessary by the Community legislature 20 years later. Not to have done so has two advantages: first, it acknowledges the distinct origin and, hence, meaning of the provisions laid down in international agreements; secondly, it illustrates a certain degree of deferment to the discretion enjoyed by the executive and the legislature in the area of external relations. It is one thing for the Court to enhance the penetration of national legal orders by a dynamic reading of the rules contained in primary law and quite another to extend this reading to the international obligations assumed by the Community. With hindsight, *Polydor* contains an element of what would become the cornerstone of the Court's approach to the WTO rules after more than two decades. The caution of the Court is all the more understandable in the light of the number of agreements concluded by the Community with third countries. In fact, the caution underpinning the Court's approach to the application of the FTA prohibition on measures of equivalent effect to quantitative restrictions goes even further than limiting the material scope of that prohibition: the judgment appears to suggest a presumption of legality of the national deviation from the prohibition on measures of equivalent effect to quantitative restrictions. This is not merely dissimilar to the construction of the exception laid down in Article 30 EC; it is quite the opposite of the construction of any exceptional clause contained in primary and secondary Community legislation. Normally, the Court is keen to point out that the exceptions to the principle of free movement should be interpreted restrictively: in relation to Article 30 EC, for instance, the Court has made it clear quite early on that the social interests set out therein do not reserve the relevant areas of activity to the exclusive competence of the Member States; instead, the latter may deviate from the principle of free movement in order to protect those interests only if, in doing so, certain standards of necessity and proportionality are met.[48]

---

[46] First Council Dir 89/104/EEC to approximate the laws of the Member States relating to trade marks [1989] OJ L 40/1.

[47] See Case C–355/96 *Silhouette International Schmied GmbH & Co. KG v Hartlauer Handelsgesellschaft mbH* [1998] ECR I–4799 as confirmed and refined in Joined Cases C–414–416/99 *Davidoff and Levi Straus* [2001] ECR I–8691.

[48] See, for instance, Case 35/76 *Simmenthal v Minister for Finance* [1976] [1976] ECR 1871.

As to the conclusion in *Legros*, it is clearly explained within its specific context: had the notion of charges of equivalent effect to customs duties been interpreted as restrictively as the French government had suggested, there would have been nothing to prevent the Member States from establishing internal customs borders so as to levy similar charges upon imports from third states with which the Community had concluded an FTA. In a similar vein, the ruling in *Eurim-Pharm* is not inconsistent with the conclusion in *Polydor*: as the judgment was delivered in response to a reference from a German court, the Court of Justice had established that the marketing of the medicine in question had been authorised in Germany and that the relevant authorities had been in possession of all the necessary information about its production, manufacture and storage; 'in those circumstances',[49] to have sanctioned the prohibition on the authorised marketing of the same product simply because it had been imported from Austria would indeed have been unduly formalistic.

4.2. The Significance of the Context

It was argued above that the specific factual and legal context of the cases brought before the Court of Justice explain the potential divergence of interpretation of provisions of international agreements whose wording is similar to or even identical with provisions of the EC Treaty. Such divergence may also be explained as a matter of principle. To point out the conception of Community law as a 'new legal order of international law' as the fundamental factor underpinning all aspects of interpretation of EC law is to state the obvious; so is to identify its links to the interconnecting nature of the various supranational and intergovernmental features of this system and the interaction between national and Community actors.[50] In rendering the specific context within which a provision of an international agreement is set central to its interpretation, the Court acknowledges the specific challenges that the enforcement of international rules in the Community legal order must meet. This is apparent in the Court's overall approach: on the one hand, not all international agreements concluded by the Community are presumed to be capable of being directly justiciable before the EC courts; on the other hand, even those which are may not necessarily be interpreted in a manner analogous to that of EC primary and secondary law irrespective of whether their wording is similar or identical.

Viewed from this angle, the overall interpretation of the Court is as consistent as it is sensible. An interesting case in point is its approach to agreements providing for a more integrated relationship between the Community and third countries or

---

[49]   Para 25 of the judgment in Case C–207/91, n42 above.
[50]   See the analysis in JHH Weiler, 'The Community System: the Dual Character of Supranationalism' (1981) 1 *YEL* 267.

group of countries. The Community is endowed with competence to conclude them pursuant to Article 310 EC which provides as follows: '[t]he Community may conclude with one or more States or international organisations agreements establishing an association involving reciprocal rights and obligations, common action and special procedure'. The issue of the interpretation of such an agreement with Greece concluded in 1961 was raised before the Court in *Pabst* the year of the accession of Greece to the then EEC.[51] Imports of spirits from Greece had been subject to a consumption tax which was deemed by the importer to be contrary to, amongst other provisions, Article 53(1) of the Agreement. Having concluded that the charge in question constituted a tax measure favouring German producers, hence being contrary to the directly effective rule of Article 90 EC, the Court went on to examine whether the similarly worded provision of Article 53(1) of the Association Agreement with Greece had been violated. The Court answered this in the affirmative, pointing out that:

> that provision, the wording of which is similar to that of Article [90] of the Treaty, fulfils, within the framework of the association between the Community and Greece, the same function as that of Article [90]. It forms part of a group of provisions the purpose of which was to prepare for the entry of Greece into the Community by the establishment of a customs union, by the harmonization of agricultural policies, by the introduction of freedom of movement for workers and by other measures for the gradual adjustment to the requirements of Community law.[52]

Following this assessment, the Court had no difficulty in transposing its interpretation of Article 90 EC to that of Article 53(1) of the Agreement with Greece, the latter provision also declared directly effective from the expiry of the period within which all conflicting measures ought to have been abolished. It is noteworthy that the judgment in *Pabst* was delivered only three months after that in *Polydor*. What seemed to differentiate the two agreements was the ultimate objective of membership which was served by a number of policies referred to by the Court. It should be pointed out that establishment of an association between the Community and its Member States and a third country or group of countries by no means entails membership as a matter of course. The association with the ACP countries, for instance, denotes the special nature of the relationship between the parties without preparing the Community's partners for membership. In *Razanatsiba*, where issues regarding the interpretation of the Lomé Convention were referred to the Court of Justice, the latter's case law on establishment and services was deemed non-applicable to Article 62 of the Convention which prohibited discriminatory treatment.[53] That provision also absolved a party to the

---

[51] Case 17/81 *Pabst & Richarz KG v Hauptzollamt Oldenburg* [1982] ECR 1331.
[52] *Ibid*, para 26 of the judgment.
[53] Case 65/77 *Jean Razanatsiba* [1977] ECR 2229.

Convention from the obligation imposed thereunder towards the nationals or firms of another party unable to provide non-discriminatory treatment in a given area. The question referred under the preliminary reference procedure was whether Article 62 of the Convention conferred upon an individual of Madagascan nationality the right to establish himself in the territory of a Member State without any condition as to nationality. This would entail the transposition to the Lomé Convention of the judgment in *Reyners* on the right of residence accorded to Community citizens wishing to establish themselves in another Member State.[54] The answer provided by the Court was negative: the wording of Article 62 of the Convention did not oblige the parties to the Convention to give the nationals of the other parties treatment identical to that given to their own nationals. Furthermore, it also allowed a Member State party to enter into arrangements which would reserve more favourable treatment to the nationals of one ACP country in relation to specific activities provided that such treatment resulted from an international agreement comprising reciprocal rights and advantages.

Yet, there can be no test which would determine the interpretation of international rules linked to similarly worded Community provisions simply in the light of the intensity of the relationship established under the agreement in question. A case in point is the Court's approach to Article 7 of Decision 1/70 adopted by the Association Council pursuant to the Association Agreement with Turkey. That provision defines the rights of the family members of Turkish workers. The Court ruled that a Member State is free to require that, save in exceptional circumstances justified by objective reasons, such family members actually live with the worker for the period of three years laid down in that provision.[55] This interpretation is in contrast to that given in the context of nationals of Member States exercising their right to free movement pursuant to Regulation 1612/68 where, provided that the marriage is genuine, cohabitation was not a prerequisite for the rights of family members to be enjoyed.[56] To argue for a different interpretation would be tantamount to ignoring the entirely different objectives of the provision of family rights in each case: the provision for family rights in Regulation 1612/68 was aimed at facilitating the exercise of the right of free movement whereas the one in the Association Agreement with Turkey and the subsequent Association Council Decision was intrinsically linked to the status of the worker as lawfully employed in the host Member State.

The acknowledgment of the central role that the context of an international rule binding on the Community governs its interpretation has one drawback, that is uncertainty. It is not always easy to determine how this context is to be approached by the Court. And yet this, in fact, may be positive: as the context within which international agreements operate evolves, so should the judiciary be

---

[54] Case 2/74 *Reyners v Belgian State* [1974] ECR 631.
[55] Case C–351/95 *Kadiman* [1997] ECR I–2133, para 45.

free to take any developments into account when interpreting international rules. In other words, the approach of the Court appears inherently flexible enough to adjust to the evolving legal and political circumstances surrounding the application of international agreements. This need for flexibility has two dimensions. The first one is internal and is related to the manner in which the Community implements its international commitments. As the state of Community law is in flux, with the effect of redefining the nature of competence enjoyed by the Community and that retained by the Member States, so should the assessment of the effects of international commitments be left inherently flexible. In *Kupferberg,* the Court had pointed out that 'the measures needed to implement the provisions of an agreement concluded by the Community are to be adopted, according to the state of Community law for the time being in the areas affected by the provisions of the agreement, either by the Community institutions or by the Member States. That is particularly true of agreements such as those concerning free trade where the obligations entered into extend to many areas of a very diverse nature'.[57]

The second dimension is external and is related to the evolving international context within which the Community may be called upon to comply with international obligations. This may be illustrated by the relationships between the Community and the Maghreb countries, namely Algeria, Tunisia and Morocco. This was defined by a number of cooperation agreements signed in the late-1970s.[58] Concluded on behalf of the Community under Articles 133 EC and 308 EC, these mixed agreements covered trade and economic as well as technical and financial cooperation, along with freedom of movement of workers. In particular, the Community and its Member States exchanged letters with the other parties which were annexed to the Agreements, and in which they expressed their readiness to examine possibilities of making progress towards achieving equal treatment for Community and non-Community workers and members of their families regarding respect of living and working conditions. More than 15 years later, the Community launched the Europe–Mediterranean Partnership, a process which sought to bring the Community and its Member States closer together with not only the Maghreb countries but also the other Mediterranean and Middle Eastern countries. At the first Euro–Mediterranean Conference in 1995 in Barcelona, the Community, the Member States, the Maghreb countries, the Mashrek countries, namely Egypt, Jordan, Lebanon and Syria, along with Israel and the Palestinian Authority signed the Barcelona Declaration. Setting the objective of establishing a Euro–Mediterranean free trade zone by 2010, the Declaration set out the framework for the negotiation and conclusion of a new wave of association agreements. For the purpose of this analysis, suffice it to point out that the Barcelona

---

[56] Case 267/83 *Diatta* [1985] ECR 567, paras 11–12.

[57] N23 above, para 12.

[58] These agreements were concluded with Algeria [1978] OJ L 263/2, Morocco [1978] OJ L 264/2 and Tunisia [1978] OJ L 265/2.

Declaration contains references to existing commitments undertaken by the parties and provides them with added momentum: in relation to the welfare of third-country nationals resident in a Member State, for instance, the parties 'undertake to guarantee protection of all rights recognized under existing legislation of migrants legally resident in their respective territories'.[59] What this overview indicates is that the international rules concluded by the Community which the Court is asked to interpret often operate in a constantly evolving legal and political context. Whilst mindful of the discretion enjoyed by the executive and legislature in international negotiations, the Court needs to be prepared to take this context into account. This is not a question of non-legally binding developments determining the interpretation of legally binding rules;[60] it is rather one of flexibility that the system of interpreting international rules may be prepared to exhibit under certain circumstances.

5. THE COURT'S APPROACH TO THE INSTITUTIONAL STRUCTURES ESTABLISHED UNDER ASSOCIATION AGREEMENTS

The diversity of the contractual relations between the Community and the rest of the world and the sophistication of their development are illustrated by the various mechanisms established under some agreements the aim of which is the management of their application and development of the relationship between the contracting parties.[61] When these mechanisms involve the establishment of bilateral bodies with decision-making powers, a number of important questions are raised about the effects of their acts within the Community legal order: can the Court's case law treating international agreements concluded by the Community as an integral part of Community law apply to them? Can they grant rights which individuals may enforce before national courts?

These questions were addressed in *Demirel,* where the Court was asked to deal with the interpretation of the Association Agreement with Turkey concluded in 1963.[62] The applicant before the referring court, the Turkish wife of a Turkish citizen who had been working in Germany for five years since the date he arrived there in order to join his family, had returned to Germany in order to rejoin her family. However, her visa was valid only for the purposes of a visit and not for

---

[59] Barcelona Declaration, 'Partnership in Social, Cultural and Human Affairs: developing human resources, promoting understanding between the cultures and exchanges between civil societies', 10th indent.

[60] See M Hedemann-Robinson, 'An Overview of Recent Legal Developments at Community Level in Relation to Third Country Nationals Resident within the European Union, with Particular Reference to the Case Law of the European Court of Justice' (2001) 38 *CMLRev* 525, 560–1.

[61] See B Martenczuk, 'Decisions of Bodies Established by International Agreements and the Community Legal Order' in V Kronenberger, *The European Union and the International Legal Order: Discord or Harmony?* (The Hague: TMC Asser Press, 2001) 141.

[62] Case 12/86 *Meryem Demirel v Stadt Schwäbisch Gmünd* [1987] ECR 3719.

family reunification. Following its expiry, she was asked to leave the country or otherwise be expelled. The reason was that national law required a period of eight years of continuous and lawful residence for the right of reunification to arise. Ms Demirel attacked this order, arguing that it violated a number of provisions of the Association Agreement: Article 12 provided that the Contracting Parties would be guided by the EC Treaty provisions on free movement of persons for the purpose of progressively securing free movement of workers between them; Article 36 of the Additional Protocol attached to the Agreement provided that freedom of movement would be secured in progressive stages on the basis of the principle set out in Article 12 of the Agreement and pursuant to Decisions adopted by the Association Council; Decision 1/80 of the Association Council prohibited the imposition of further restrictions on the conditions of access to employment on Turkish workers already integrated in the labour force of a Member State.

The Court started off its analysis by recalling the standard definition of direct effect in EC international relations:[63]

> A provision in an agreement concluded by the Community with non-member countries must be regarded as being directly applicable when, regard being had to its wording and the purpose and nature of the agreement itself, the provision contains a clear and precise obligation which is not subject, in its implementation or effects, to the adoption of any subsequent measure.

In applying this two-tier test, the Court first identified the objective of the Agreement, that is the provision of a preparatory stage to enable Turkey to strengthen its economy with aid from the Community, then the progressive establishment of a customs union and the alignment of economic policies on the basis of a transitional stage and, finally, the functioning of the customs union and close coordination of economic policies. Then, its structure was pointed out with particular emphasis on the establishment of the Association Council, its function and decision-making powers.

Finally, the Court focused on the specific provisions which formed the subject-matter of the reference, and concluded that they could not be invoked by individuals before national courts because, far from being precise and unconditional, they were of a programmatic nature; to that effect, it pointed out that, in the sphere of family reunification, no implementing provision had been adopted by the Association Council. This conclusion was not altered by the provision of Article 7 of the Agreement which is equivalent in content and wording to the cooperation clause laid down in Article 10 EC: the Court pointed out that that provision 'does no more than impose on the contracting parties a general obligation to cooperate in order to achieve the aims of the Agreement and it cannot directly confer on individuals rights which are not already vested in them by other

---

[63] *Ibid*, para 14.

provisions of the Agreement'.[64] This point was brought home by the Court's refusal to rule on whether the German measure contested before the referring court was in violation of the European Convention on Human Rights: in the absence of rules adopted by the Association Council on family reunification, national measures regulating this issue were beyond the reach of Community law, hence rendering the applicability of ECHR in this context a matter beyond the jurisdiction of the Court of Justice.

It is noteworthy that the Court did not examine in great detail whether the first condition of its two-tier test was met, namely whether the Association Agreement with Turkey was capable of conferring rights upon individuals directly enforceable before national courts: there was a leap from outlining the objective and structure of the Agreement to the wording and context of the specific provisions invoked before the referring court. The Court seems to presume that the Agreement was potentially directly effective, a presumption all the more noteworthy in the light of the programmatic nature of all the provisions mentioned in the judgment. This technique is quite astute in practical terms: the institutional structures established by the Agreement ensure its dynamic development; in other words, the Agreement itself provides for the legal means to ensure that its programmatic content would be transformed into concrete rules. To rule out the possibility of producing direct effect would be tantamount to ignoring its *raison d'être* as the foundation for gradual integration between the Contracting Parties. Indeed, the incremental development of the relationship provided for in the Agreement was inherent in its structure: Article 36 of the Protocol granting the Association Council exclusive powers to adopt detailed rules on the movement of workers, for instance, makes it clear that such powers are to be exercised 'in accordance with political and economic considerations arising in particular out of the progressive establishment of the customs union and the alignment of economic policies'.

The point made in *Demirel* appeared to reach its logical conclusion in *Sevince* where a number of decisions of the Association Council had been adopted and their relevance to the interpretation and application of the Association Agreement with Turkey were raised before the Court.[65] The applicant was a Turkish citizen whose application for an extension of his residence permit had been turned down by the Dutch authorities on the ground that the family circumstances which had justified the grant of the permit no longer existed. He challenged that decision as contrary to two Decisions of the Association Council: Decision 2/76 provided in its Article 2(1)(b) that a Turkish worker employed legally in a Member State for five years would enjoy free access to any paid employment of his choice; Decision 1/80 provided in Article 6(1) third indent that a Turkish worker duly registered as belonging to the labour force of a Member State would enjoy free access to any paid employment in that state after four years' legal employment. Having ruled

---

[64] *Ibid*, para 24.
[65] Case C–192/89 *S.Z. Sevince v Staatssecretaris van Justitie* [1990] ECR I–3461.

that the interpretation of these provisions fell within its jurisdiction under the preliminary reference procedure, the Court referred to the formula for direct effect of a provision contained in an international agreement concluded by the Community, and ruled that it was also applicable to provisions contained in a decision of an Association Council.

The Court, then, proceeded to find the provisions invoked before the referring court directly effective. This was illustrated not only by their wording, as they provided in clear, precise and unconditional terms for the right of a Turkish worker, after a number of years' legal employment, to enjoy free access to any paid employment, but also their nature and purpose: they formed part of Decisions 2/76 and 1/80 which had been adopted precisely in order to give flesh to the programmatic aims of Article 12 of the Agreement and Article 36 of the Additional Protocol. The Court, then, went on to provide for a typology of rules whose presence in an Association Council Decision would not affect its direct effect. First, the requirement under Decision 1/80 that the procedures for applying the rights conferred on Turkish workers be established under national law was deemed irrelevant: such provisions 'merely clarify the obligation of the Member States to take such administrative measures as may be necessary for the implementation of those provisions, without empowering the Member States to make conditional or restrict the application of the precise and unconditional right which the decisions of the Council of Association grant to Turkish workers'.[66] Secondly, the provisions of Decisions 12/76 and 1/80 requiring the parties, each for its own part, to take any measures necessary for the purpose of implementing the decisions were also irrelevant to the direct effect of the Decisions: they were seen as 'merely lay[ing] emphasis on the obligation to implement in good faith an international agreement, an obligation which, moreover, is referred to in Article 7 of the Agreement itself'.[67] Thirdly, the fact the Decisions had not been published, whilst possibly preventing their direct effect horizontally, did not affect the right of private individuals relying upon them before state authorities. Fourthly, the existence of safeguard clauses enabling the parties to derogate from the provisions of the Decisions did not affect the latter's direct effect as they were of limited scope, hence applying only to very specific situations.

Interestingly enough, whilst the applicant before the referring court was allowed to rely upon Decisions 2/76 and 1/80 of the Association Council, the substance of those Decisions turned out to be of no help: he could not be considered to be legally employed during the period within which his appeal was examined, as that would have enabled him to contrive to fulfil the conditions laid down in the Decisions relied on.

There is a degree of internal logic in the approach of the Court to the Association Agreement with Turkey: whilst its provisions on free movement of

---

[66] *Ibid*, para 22.
[67] *Ibid*, para 23.

workers were viewed as of a programmatic nature and, hence, in themselves incapable of producing direct effect (*Demirel*), the Decisions adopted by the Association Council implementing them did have such effects (*Sevince*). As the Court pointed out in the latter judgment, 'the fact that the . . . provisions of the Agreement and the Additional Protocol essentially set out a programme does not prevent the decisions of the Council of Association which give effect in specific respects to the programmes envisaged in the Agreement from having direct effect'.[68] It is also interesting that in *Sevince* the Court appeared to presume that the Association Agreement with Turkey was capable of conferring rights upon individuals, as it had done in *Demirel*: having reiterated the two-tier test of direct effect of international agreements, it proceeded to examine the content and wording of the specific provisions invoked before the referring court. Furthermore, the liberal construction of direct effect of provisions contained in Association Council Decisions is similar to that underpinning the judgment in *Kupferberg*: both cases provided a list of legal features of the Agreements referred under Article 234 EC which were considered as not undermining their capability of conferring rights upon individuals.

The interpretation of the decisions adopted by the EC–Turkey Association Council provide an interesting insight into the differentiated approach to the principle of direct effect adopted by the Court.[69] In relation to the rights of third-country nationals resident in a Member State, the Association Council adopted Decision 1/76 which was applicable for the first stage of association provided by the Agreement. Following that, Decisions 1/80 and 3/80 were adopted, the former on the development of the Association and the latter on the application of the social security schemes of the Member States to Turkish workers and their families. As the effects of Decision 1/80 were outlined above, the interpretation of Decision 3/80 on social security is indicative of the Court's approach. First, it was pointed out that the principle of aggregation for workers employed in more than one Member State could not be applied in so far as supplementary implementing measures had not been adopted by the Association Council.[70] This was the case despite the fact that 'the binding effect of decisions of the Association Council cannot depend on whether implementing measures have in fact been adopted by the Contracting Parties'.[71] Secondly, the denial of direct effect to a number of provisions of Decision 3/80 by no means ruled out the direct effect of the non-discrimination clause of its Article 3.[72] Thirdly, however, the practical implications of these rulings for the regulation of the very sensitive sector of social security are

---

[68] *Ibid*, para 21.
[69] For an examination of the reception that such decisions have found within both the Community and national legal orders, see N Lavranos, *Decisions of International Organizations in the European and Domestic Legal Orders of Selected EU Member States* (Groningen: Europa Law Publishing, 2004) 61–76.
[70] Case C–277/94 *Taflan-Met* [1996] ECR I–4085, para 37.
[71] *Ibid*, para 20.
[72] Case C–262/96 *Sürül* [1999] ECR I–2685.

taken into account by the Court: its ruling on the direct effect of the above clause was expressly confined to future applications and proceedings initiated prior to the date of the delivery of the judgment.[73]

6. THE FORMULA OF DIRECT EFFECT WITHIN THE BROADER CONTEXT OF ENFORCEMENT OF INTERNATIONAL RULES

The application of the principle of direct effect, as introduced in *International Fruit Company* and articulated in *Kupferberg*, depends upon whether two distinct conditions are satisfied: on the one hand, the agreement in question should be capable, in the light of its objectives and spirit, of conferring rights upon individuals; on the other hand, the specific provision of such an agreement invoked by individuals should be clear, unconditional and not dependent on further implementing measures. This two-tier test might appear to suggest that construction of direct effect in the area of EC external relations has been very cautious with significantly detrimental effects for the legal position of individuals.[74] However, it is the construction of the conditions of direct effect rather than their existence which determines the impact of the formula. The frequent use of the principle, as illustrated by the above overview, suggest that the criticism levelled against the Court is exaggerated. This conclusion is also supported by a brief examination of the construction of direct effect of internal market law as well as the application of customary international rules by the Community judicature.

6.1. The Function of Direct Effect

As regards the general assessment of the nature of an international agreement prior to the assessment of its direct effect, suffice it to make three points. First, whilst appearing to render the application of direct effect in the area of EC external relations more difficult, in fact, it has no such effect. Even on the internal plane the assessment of whether individuals may rely upon specific rules of Community measures before national courts was dependent upon a more general assessment of the nature of those measures. This assessment has remained largely implied as it appeared to be addressed by the all-encompassing notion of 'the new legal order of international law' introduced in *Van Gend en Loos*. However, the painfully long and protracted story of the direct effect of directives makes it clear that such an assessment is also carried out well into the phase of maturity of the Community legal order. It is recalled that the limited direct effect of directives, namely against

---

[73] *Ibid*, at para 109 ff.
[74] See, for instance, G Gaza, 'Trends in Judicial Activism and Judicial Self-restraint Relating to Community Agreements' in E Cannizzaro (ed.), *The European Union as an Actor in International Relations* (The Hague: Kluwer, 2002) 118, 128–30.

the state or the emanation of the state and not to other individuals,[75] was justified because of their very nature as instruments addressed to the Member States. This indicates that the acknowledgment of direct effect by the Court has always followed a preliminary assessment of the type of effects that a specific instrument may be deemed to carry in the light of its nature. Viewed from this angle, the two-tier test which is associated with the direct effect of international agreements is not unique to EC external relations—it is just that its presence is more pronounced in that area. Indeed, following the introduction of the principle in the context of international agreements, the Court often goes straight to whether the specific provision invoked before the national court confers rights upon individuals without mentioning the first part of the test, that is whether the agreement as a whole is capable of conferring such rights.[76]

Secondly, the two-tier test attached to the application of the principle of direct effect to international agreements is more pronounced because the stakes may appear to be higher: the extent to which domestic courts are prepared to enforce international commitments undertaken by the Community and the Member States may determine the extent to which the latter are prepared to undertake such commitments, hence affecting international negotiations. This point may be illustrated by a case on the interpretation of the Cooperation Agreement between the EC and Morrocco. In *Kziber*, the Court had ruled that its provision on social security was directly effective and should be viewed as analogous with the identical one in Regulation 1408/71, hence covering disability allowances.[77] When this issue, amongst others, was referred again in *Yousfi*, the German government submitted written observations urging the Court to review its case law.[78] In particular, it was argued that not only had the parties to the Agreement not intended to confer direct effect on its provision on social security, but also the Court's decision to grant such effect would have a negative effect on the negotiating position of the Member States in the conclusion of similar agreements, not least a new one negotiated with Morocco at that time. Whilst summarily dismissed by the Court in that specific context,[79] it is precisely this concern that appears to be addressed by the attachment to the direct effect test of the express requirement that the relevant agreement be capable, in principle, of conferring such effect. However, this function of the test signifies more than merely the Court's willingness to interact with the executive and the legislature in the area of international law; it also acknowledges the constitutional implications of any assessment of direct effect in the area of provisions contained in agreements concluded by the Community. It

---

[75] Case 152/84 *Marshall v Southampton and South-West Hampshire Area Health Authority (Teaching)* [1986] ECR 723.

[76] See, for instance, Case C–58/93 *Zoubir Yousfi v Belgian State* [1994] ECR I–1353.

[77] Case C–18/90 *Office national de l'emploi v Bahia Kziber* [1991] ECR I–199.

[78] See n76 above.

[79] This argument had also been dismissed by Tesauro AG who pointed out that 'the Court's interpretation cannot and may not be made to depend on the "approval" of the Member States' (para 7 of his Opinion).

should be recalled that the Court has been acutely aware of such implications even on the internal plane. When asked to extend the direct effect of directives to relations between individuals, for instance, it declined on the basis of, amongst others, the following argument:

> The effect of extending that case-law to the sphere of relations between individuals would be to recognize a power in the Community to enact obligations for individuals with immediate effect, whereas it has competence to do so only where it is empowered to adopt regulations.[80]

This was a constitutional argument[81] which determined the extent to which legally binding Community measures were allowed to penetrate the domestic legal orders. Similarly, the recognition that certain international rules, whilst legally binding, should not be granted unlimited ways of being enforced within the Community legal order is based on a constitutional premise related to the proper function of the judiciary and the scope for manoeuvre enjoyed by the executive and the legislature in international negotiations. This point becomes more apparent in the context of the discussion of WTO rules.

Thirdly, the recognition of the constitutional underpinnings of the application of direct effect renders the enforcement of international agreements a more nuanced exercise. Again, this is not unique in the area of external relations. The Court's insistence that directives may not be horizontally directly effective has given rise to a considerable body of case law seeking to consolidate and adjust the existing principles whilst introducing new ones: the vertical direct effect of directives has been broadly construed,[82] even though they may be relied upon in disputes between private parties in very limited circumstances[83] in order to prevent the enforcement of a national measure which they render void;[84] in any case, even if non-directly effective, they are relevant to the interpretation of national law which must be carried out by national courts in the light of their provisions,[85] albeit as far as possible.[86] The incremental development of these principles and the subtlety of their interaction illustrate that the application of the principle of direct effect, far from being a straightforward exercise, is a long process requiring various adjustments in the light of factors subject to constant evolution. Whilst

---

[80] Case C–91/92 *Faccini Dori v Recreb* [1994] ECR I–3325, para 24.

[81] S Weatherill and P Beaumont, *EU Law* (3rd edn, London: Penguin, 1999) 403.

[82] Case C–188/89 *A. Foster and others v British Gas plc* [1990] ECR I–3313.

[83] See Cases C–441/93 *Panagis Pafitis v Trapeza Kentrikis Ellados AE* [1996] ECR I–1347 and C–192/94 *El Corte ingles v Cristina Blazquez Rivero* [1996] ECR I–1281.

[84] See Case C–194/94 *CIA Security International SA v Signalson SA and Securitel SPRL* [1996] ECR I–2201, Case C–443/98 *Unilever Italia SpA v Central Food SpA* [2000] ECR I–7535 and Case C–159/00 *Sapod Audic v Eco Emballages SA* [2002] ECR I–5031.

[85] Case 14/83 *Von Colson and Kamann v Land Nordrhein-Westfalen* [1984] ECR 1891 and Case C–106/89 *Marleasing SA v La Comercial Internacionale de Alimentacion SA* [1990] ECR I–4135.

[86] Case 80/86 *Criminal proceedings against Kolpinghuis Nijmegen BV* [1987] ECR 3969.

controversial,[87] this process shows that, in order to assess the enforcement of international rules in the Community legal order, the focus should perhaps shift: whether there are alternative, indirect mechanisms of enforcement and how they are applied by the judiciary are as important questions as that of direct effect. This is all the more so in the light of the less than draconian effect of the two-tier test developed by the Court: only the rules contained first in GATT and then in the WTO system have been deemed to be in principle not enforceable before the Court. As the analysis in this chapter has highlighted, the principle of direct effect is regularly applied by the Court of Justice in a wide variety of contexts, including the Europe Agreements concluded with the Central and Eastern European countries,[88] Free Trade Agreements,[89] the Agreement with the Caribbean, African and Pacific countries and Cooperation Agreements,[90] including the Partnership and Cooperation Agreements with countries of the ex-Soviet Union.[91]

6.2. The Enforcement of Customary International Law

Another indication that the application of the principle of direct effect has not necessarily hampered the enforcement of international rules within the Community is provided by the approach of the Community judicature to international customary law. In general, whilst this source of law is accepted as part of the domestic legal order, there are problems in the approach adopted by domestic courts to its interpretation and application.[92]

The Court of Justice first ruled indirectly on the issue of compliance with customary international law: in the famous judgment in *Van Duyn*, it pointed out that the EC Treaty 'cannot be assumed to disregard in the relations between Member States' the principle of international law that a state is precluded from refusing its

---

[87] In the context of the so-called incidental horizontal direct effect, see, for instance, the criticism in M Dougan, 'The "Disguised" Direct Effect of Directives' (2000) 59 *CLJ* 586 and S Weatherill, 'Breach of Directives and Breach of Contract' (2001) 26 *ELRev* 177.

[88] See, for instance, the Agreement with Poland: Case C–162/00 *Pokrzeptowicz-Meyer* [2002] ECR I–1049.

[89] See, for instance, the one with Spain: Case 225/78 *Procureur de la République de Besançon v Bouhelier* [1979] ECR 3151, para 10.

[90] See, for instance, the one with Algeria: Case C–103/94 *Krid v CNAVTS* [1995] ECR I–719 (paras 21–23).

[91] See Case C–265/03 *Igor Simutenkov v Ministerio de Educación y Cultura, Real Federación Española de Fútbol*, judgment of Grand Chamber delivered on 12 Apr 2005, not yet reported.

[92] See P Daillier and A Pellet, *Droit International Public* (7th edn, Paris: LGDJ, 2002) 346 and E Denza, 'The Relationship Between International and National Law' in MD Evans (ed), *International Law* (Oxford: OUP, 2003) 415 at 428–9. See also the analysis of Jacobs AG in Case C–162/96 *Racke v Hauptzollampt Mainz* [1998] ECR I–3655 at paras 79–81 which refers to the general wording of customary rules of treaty law and the difficulty of interpreting them (paras 84–86). For a critical view, see J Wouters and D van Eeckhotte, 'Giving Effect to Customary International Law Through European Community Law' in JM Prinssen and A Schrauwen (eds), *Direct Effect—Rethinking a Classic of EC Legal Doctrine* (Groningen: Europa Law Publishing, 2002)183 at 230 ff.

own nationals the right of entry or residency;[93] in relation to the Community's jurisdiction to apply its competition rules it was pointed out in *Ahlström* that it 'is covered by the territoriality principle as universally recognized in public international law'.[94] However, in subsequent rulings, the focus of the Community judicature on the position of customary international law has been sharper.

In *Poulsen*,[95] a fishing vessel under a Panamanian flag whose owner and crew were Danish encountered motor trouble in heavy weather whilst sailing in Danish waters. When it called at a Danish port, its cargo, consisting of salmon caught in international waters, was seized by the authorities acting under EC Regulation 3094/86.[96] The thrust of the provision relied upon by the Danish authorities was the prohibition on the holding on board of salmon, even in cases where it had been caught in international waters. In essence, the questions referred by the Danish court were about the application of the Community measure in cases where there is potential conflict with international law.

The first paragraph of the judgment states the position of the Community in relation to international law: 'the European Community must respect international law in the exercise of its powers and . . ., consequently, [the relevant Community rule] must be interpreted, and its scope limited, in the light of the relevant rules of the international law of the sea'.[97] The rules in question were of customary international law as codified in a number of provisions in certain fisheries conventions, namely the Geneva Conventions on the Territorial Sea and the Contiguous Zone, on the High Seas and on Fishing and Conservation of the Living Resources of the High Seas; and finally the United Nations Convention on the Law of the Sea. These rules were to be taken into account 'in so far as they codify general rules recognized by international custom'.[98]

On the interpretation of the relevant regulation, the Court held that, in the light of the right of innocent passage and that of free navigation, the prohibition should not apply to third-country vessels when either in the exclusive economic zone or the territorial waters of a Member States. However, it would be applicable to them once in port. As to whether third-country vessels in distress should escape the prohibition laid down in the regulation, it was left to the referring court to decide 'in accordance with international law'.[99] There was in fact no Community provision dealing with this matter.

This approach was seen as a 'generous and far reaching recognition of the relevance' of rules of customary international law within the Community legal

---

[93] Case 41/74 *Van Duyn v Home Office* [1974] ECR 1337, para 22.
[94] Joined Cases 89, 104, 114, 116, 117 and 125 to 129/85 *A. Ahlström Osakeyhtiö and others v Commission* [1993] ECR I–1307.
[95] Case C–286/90 *Anklagemindigheden v Poulsen and Diva Navigation* [1992] ECR I–6019.
[96] Reg 3094/86 laying down certain technical measures for the conservation of fisheries resources [1986] OJ L 288/1.
[97] N95 above, para 9.
[98] *Ibid*, para 10.
[99] *Ibid*, para 38.

order.[100] In two subsequent rulings, this recognition was confirmed, albeit with an interesting twist.

In *Opel Austria*,[101] the rule of customary international law at issue was the obligation not to defeat the object and purpose of a treaty prior to its entry into force. In that case, the Council adopted Regulation 3697/93[102] withdrawing tariff concessions originally granted under the Free Trade Agreement between the Community and Austria. The additional duties were imposed one week after the conclusion of the European Economic Area Agreement, which prohibited charges of equivalent effect to customs duties. However, that prohibition had not yet entered into force: in fact, the Council measure imposing additional charges was adopted two weeks prior to the specific date on which the Agreement was to enter into force. The applicant sought the annulment of the Regulation by the Court of First Instance under Article 230 EC, arguing that its adoption at that time was contrary to the above principle of customary international law as codified in Article 18 of the Vienna Convention.[103]

The Court of First Instance annulled the Regulation. However, rather than directly applying the principle enshrined in Article 18 of the Vienna Convention, it read it into a Community law principle: it opined that 'the principle of good faith is the corollary in public international law of the principle of protection of legitimate expectations which, according to the case-law, forms part of the Community legal order' and added that '[a]ny economic operator to whom an institution has given justified hopes may rely on the principle of protection of legitimate expectations'.[104]

This method of asserting the position of customary international law in relation to Community law by applying it in a rather indirect way was not dissimilar to the approach adopted by the Court of Justice in *Racke*.[105] The subject-matter of this reference from Germany was about the effects of the suspension of the Co-operation Agreement between the Community and Yugoslavia following the war in that country. The suspension of the Agreement by the Community entailed the suspension of trade concessions which it provided. Racke was an importer of wine from Kosovo who had been asked by the Customs Office to pay the difference between the preferential rates of customs duty originally paid pursuant to the

---

[100] C Timmermans, 'The EU and Public International Law' (1999) 4 *EFA Rev* 181 at 187.

[101] Case T–115/94 *Opel Austria GmbH v Council* [1997] ECR II–39.

[102] [1993] OJ L 343/1.

[103] This provision reads as follows: 'A State is obliged to refrain from acts which would defeat the object and purpose of a treaty when: (a) it has signed the treaty or has exchanged instruments constituting the treaty subject to ratification, acceptance or approval, until it shall have made its intention clear not to become a party to the treaty; or (b) it has expressed its consent to be bound by the treaty, pending the entry into force of the treaty and provided that such entry into force is not unduly delayed.'

[104] N101 above, para 93 with reference to Case 112/77 *Töpfer v Commission* [1978] ECR 1019, para 19, and Joined Cases T–466/93, T–469/93, T–473/93, T–474/93 and T–477/93 *O'Dwyer and Others v Council* [1995] ECR II–2071, para 48.

[105] Case C–162/96 *Racke v Hauptzollampt Mainz* [1998] ECR I–3655.

Agreement and the full third-country rate. On appeal before the Federal Finance Court, he argued that Council Regulation 3300/91 suspending the trade concessions provide for by the Cooperation Agreement was contrary to international law.

The legal principle at the core of this dispute was the suspension of a treaty following a change of circumstances. In its judgment, the very first point made by the Court was to refer to the statement by the International Court of Justice that the articulation of this principle in Article 62 of the Vienna Convention on the Law of the Treaties constitutes a codification of existing customary international law.[106] Then, it was pointed out that the legality of the disputed regulation in the light of that rule was relied upon by the applicant in the proceedings only incidentally: in essence, it was Article 22(4) of the Cooperation Agreement and the preferential rates granted thereunder upon which the applicant sought to rely. Therefore, the question which had to be addressed first was whether that provision was capable of being invoked by individuals before national courts. The Court answered this question in the affirmative: in the light of the aim of the Agreement to promote trade relations with Yugoslavia, the provision granting trade concessions contained a clear and precise obligation which was not subject to the adoption of subsequent measures.

The Court, then, focused on the specific ground of invalidity relied upon before the referring court, namely the one providing that *pacta sunt servanda*, as well as the exception relied upon by the Community institutions, that is the fundamental change of circumstances. Two points were made: first, the Court noted that 'the rules of customary international law concerning the termination and the suspension of treaty relations by reason of a fundamental change of circumstances are binding upon the Community institutions and form part of the Community legal order';[107] secondly, it was held that, whilst relevant to the action before the referring court, the application of customary law in that context was not a case of giving it direct effect: 'the plaintiff is incidentally challenging the validity of a Community regulation under those rules in order to rely upon rights which it derives directly from an agreement of the Community with a non-member country'.[108]

That did not mean that Racke would be denied the possibility of invoking its directly effective rights by challenging Community law on the basis of customary international law. However,[109]

---

[106] *Ibid*, at para 24. Art 62, entitled 'Fundamental change of circumstance', reads as follows: '1. A fundamental change of circumstances which has occurred with regard to those existing at the time of the conclusion of a treaty, and which was not foreseen by the parties, may not be invoked as a ground for terminating or withdrawing from the treaty unless: (a) the existence of those circumstances constituted an essential basis of the consent of the parties to be bound by the treaty; and (b) the effect of the change is radically to transform the extent of obligations still to be performed under the treaty'. According to Art 62(3), '[i]f, under the foregoing paragraphs, a party may invoke a fundamental change of circumstances as a ground for terminating or withdrawing from a treaty it may also invoke the change as a ground for suspending the operation of the treaty'.

[107] *Ibid*, para 46.

[108] *Ibid*, para 47.

[109] *Ibid*, para 52.

> because of the complexity of the rules in question and the imprecision of some of
> the concepts to which they refer, judicial review must necessarily, and in particular
> in the context of a preliminary reference for an assessment of validity, be limited to
> the question whether, by adopting the suspending regulation, the Council made
> manifest errors of assessment concerning the conditions for applying those rules

The Court applied the conditions laid down in Article 62(1) of the Vienna
Convention and concluded that no manifest error of assessment had occurred.[110]
In the light of the wide-ranging objectives of the Cooperation Agreement, the
maintenance of peace in Yugoslavia and the existence of institutions capable of
ensuring implementation of the cooperation envisaged by the Agreement constituted an essential condition for initiating and pursuing that cooperation; the
statements made in the preamble to the contested regulation regarding the implications of the pursuit of hostilities on economic and trade relations were deemed
not to constitute a manifest error of assessment.

There appears to be a thread which brings together the ruling of the Court of
First Instance in *Opel Austria* and that of the Court of Justice in *Racke*: both
appear to be pulling in two directions. The first one is towards the facilitation of
the application of customary international law: in both judgments there are references to rulings of the International Court of Justice, the one in *Opel Austria* in
order to define the duties required by an international treaty which had not yet
entered into force.

The second aspect that these judgments have in common is the clear determination of the Courts to avoid the issue of direct effect: in *Opel Austria* that was
achieved by channelling the application of international law through that of
Community law; in its judgment in *Racke*, the Court of First Instance expressly
separated the application of customary international law from the issue of direct
effect. In doing so, it departed from the Opinion of Advocate General Jacobs.
Whilst he, too, had applied the test of manifest error of assessment, he had simply
suggested that that was justified by the limited entitlement of individuals because
of the nature and purpose of the law of treaties.[111] Therefore, the choice of the
more convoluted approach followed by the Court[112] is noteworthy. Viewed within
the broader context of its case law, the implications of the approach adopted in
Racke are not entirely dissimilar to those adopted in relation to the legal effects of
directives. In *Unilever*, for instance, the inconsistency of the adoption of a national measure with the procedure laid down in a directive on technical standards was
allowed to be invoked in proceedings between individuals whilst expressly defined
as not a case of direct effect.[113] In both cases, the effectiveness of the rule in question was enhanced, while the elaboration of controversial doctrines was avoided.

---

[110] *Ibid*, paras 54–56.
[111] See n105 above, paras 78–90.
[112] See P Eeckhout, *External Relations of the European Union* (Oxford: OUP, 2004) 331.
[113] See Case C–443/98 *Unilever*, n84 above, paras 48–51.

The imaginative, albeit somewhat convoluted, application of customary international law by the Court indicates that the two-tier test attached to the principle of direct effect does not necessarily undermine the enforcement of international rules within the Community legal order. On the other hand, the very specific factual and legal context of the cases examined above advises caution in any attempt to articulate a general theory of the application of customary international rules: rather than applying to all types of customary international law, the rulings in *Opel Austria* and *Racke* were delivered in the context of treaties. This appears to make the legal position of the individuals quite precarious: in his Opinion, Advocate General Jacobs argued that the overall nature and purpose of that set of rules are to apply to relations between states and are not intended to create rights for individuals, and he refers to the considerable difficulty of defining the content of the principle in question.[114] Furthermore, the exclusion of customary international rules would have been tantamount to offering *une carte blanche* to Community institutions: in both cases, provisions of international agreements concluded by the Community and granting specific rights which individuals could invoke before courts were undermined by actions by Community institutions.[115]

7. CONCLUSION

This chapter analysed the effects of international rules in the Community legal order and their construction by the Court of Justice. It indicated that, despite the apparently stricter definition of the principle of direct effect, both provisions of international agreements and rules of customary international law are applied on the basis of a highly sophisticated approach by the Court of Justice. However, in this analysis, the position of rules first laid down in the General Agreement on Tariffs and Trade and, subsequently, in the agreements concluded in the framework of the World Trade Organisation is central. The acknowledgment of the specific features of those rules by the Court has given rise to the development of an evolving system of principles whose interrelated application aims at completing the system of enforcement of international rules within the Community legal order. It is these principles which the next chapter will analyse.

---

[114] Paras 84–85 of his Opinion.

[115] See P-J Kuijper, 'From Dyestuffs to Kosovo Wine: From Avoidance to Acceptance by the European Community Courts of Customary International Law as Limit to Community Action' in IF Dekker and HHG Post (eds), *On the Foundations and Sources of International Law* (The Hague: TMC Asser Press, 2003) 151 at 162–63.

7

Effects of GATT and WTO Rules in The Community Legal Order

1. INTRODUCTION

THE APPROACH OF the Court of Justice to the principle of direct effect in the context of international agreements concluded by the Community has been shown to have as its main point of reference the context and spirit of the agreement in question. Not only is their examination a necessary requirement which needs to be met prior to the assessment of any specific provision, but it is also relevant to the interpretation of the substantive content of that provision. This approach may appear to impose a rather strict test for the application of direct effect and, therefore, the legal position of individuals. However, it has been shown to be justified: in legal terms, it takes into consideration the specific legal context of the questions referred to the Court; in constitutional terms, it does not lose sight of the internal developments of Community law and the possible repercussions of any internationalist interpretation of the effect of international rules binding upon the Community; in practical terms, the cases where the nature of an agreement has been deemed incapable of constituting a basis for challenging Community law and conferring rights upon individuals have been confined to the rules set out in the WTO system and its precursor, GATT 1947. It is the approach of the Court of Justice to those rules which will be examined in this chapter. Such a separate examination is necessary, not only in the light of the fundamental role of those rules in the process of liberalisation of international economic law but also because of the distinct features of the system of which those rules form part. It will be those features which this chapter will seek to assess by placing them in the context of the constitutional role of the Court of Justice.

2. THE LEGAL EFFECTS OF GATT 1947 UNDER EC LAW

It was in the early 1970s when the Court dealt with the issue of the effect of GATT in the Community legal order. It will be recalled that, in *International Fruit Company*, importers of apples into the Netherlands challenged a number of regulations adopted by the Council and the Commission subjecting the importation of eating apples to a system of import licences.[1] The referring court raised the issue of the compatibility of that system with GATT 1947. Having established that the Community was bound by GATT because it had assumed the rights previously exercised by the Member States, the Court proceeded to determine whether that Agreement was capable of conferring rights enforceable before national courts. By examining the spirit, the general scheme and the wording of GATT, it reached a negative conclusion. The main reason for this was the 'great flexibility' of the agreement which, according to the Court, was illustrated by a number of its provisions: these included the duty of contracting parties to engage in consultations on any issue pertaining to the operation of GATT and their right to engage in further consultation if a satisfactory solution was not reached; the settlement of a conflict provided for written recommendations or proposals to be given sympathetic considerations, consultations between the parties, authorisation to suspend the application of parts of GATT and, in that case, the right to withdraw from the Agreement; the possibility of derogation by means of unilateral suspension of GATT obligations in the event or the threat of serious damage. Therefore, compliance with the duties imposed by GATT upon the contracting parties provided for such flexibility as to render its rules incapable of conferring Community rights enforceable before national courts.

The above rationale, referred to GATT 1947 as a whole, was applied by the Court in a wide range of circumstances. First, it was applied in actions brought by individuals before national courts seeking to challenge indirectly the legality of Community measures, the dispute in *International Fruit Company* being such a case. Another example of this is provided in *Schlüter* where the applicant before the referring court argued that Community measures were inconsistent not only with Article XXVIII GATT but also with a bilateral agreement which the Community had concluded with Switzerland in accordance with that GATT provision.[2]

Secondly, the Court's approach in *International Fruit Company* precluded reliance on GATT in challenges brought by individuals against national legislation. This was the case in *SIOT* where an Italian company challenged Italian legislation levying charges on unloading and loading of goods in specified ports as contrary to Article V GATT.[3] In a similar vein, a claim in *Chiquita* that Italian legislation charging high taxes upon the importation of bananas from third countries was contrary to GATT was rejected.[4]

Thirdly, the line of reasoning underpinning the case law post-*International Fruit Company* was also applied by the Court to actions by Member States against

[1] Joined Cases 21 to 24/72 *International Fruit Company NV and Others v Produktschap voor Groenten en Fruit* [1972] ECR 1219.

[2] See Case 9/73 *Carl Schlüter v Hauptzollamt Lörrach* [1973] ECR 1135.

[3] See Case 266/81 *SIOT v Ministero delle Finanze* [1973] ECR 731. See also Joined Cases 267/81, 268/81 and 269/81 *Amministrazione delle Finanze dello Stato v Società Petrolifera Italiana SpA (SPI) and SpA Michelin Italiana (SAMI)* [1983] ECR 801.

[4] Case C–469/93 *Amministrazione delle Finanze dello Stato v Chiquita Italia* [1995] ECR I–4533.

Community acts. This most controversial development occurred when Germany sought to challenge the Community regime on imports of bananas.[5] This set of rules was introduced by Regulation 404/93 which set up a common market organisation.[6] The main objective of this system was not only to protect the limited production of bananas within the Community territory but, mainly, to ensure the protection afforded to imports of bananas by African, Caribbean and Pacific countries pursuant to the Lomé Convention. In order to achieve this objective, a complex system of annual tariff quotas was introduced which became accessible to importers pursuant to annual licences. This system was very controversial: on the one hand, imports from Latin American countries in excess of the quota allocated were subject to very high tariffs, whereas imports from ACP countries deemed to be in accordance with the volume of trade prior to the adoption of this system were to be imported duty free; on the other hand, the allocation of quotas favoured importers of ACP bananas to a very great extent.

Germany, which had been outvoted in the Council, was particularly hit by this system as the consumption of bananas in its territory relied exclusively on imports. In fact, prior to the adoption of the contested regime, Germany had been entitled to import an annual quota of bananas from third countries free of customs duties pursuant to a special arrangement.[7] Furthermore, the majority of its importers were trading in bananas from non-ACP countries.

It was in that context that Germany brought an action against the Council pursuant to Article 230(1) EC.[8] In particular, it attacked Title IV of Regulation 404/93 which referred to traditional imports of bananas from ACP countries into the Community, the quantity of which was set in an annex where it was also further divided up between those countries, and where it was provided that such imports could continue free of customs duty. Germany also attacked Article 21(2) of the Regulation which abolished the above Protocol on imports of bananas. In its action, supported by Belgium and the Netherlands, it put forward a number of arguments. It argued that Regulation 404/93 was adopted in violation of essential procedural requirements: it was alleged to have diverged from the Commission's original proposal without a new one being adopted formally by the Commission; in addition, the statement of reasons was defective and the Parliament was not consulted again. Germany, then, argued that the contested regime was adopted in violation of substantive Community rules, namely the common agricultural policy, the competition rules, a number of fundamental rights and general principles

---

[5] For an account of the bananas saga, see P Eeckhout, *External Relations of the European Union— Legal and Constitutional Foundations* (Oxford: OUP, 2004) 381–94 and E Vranes, 'From Bananas I to the 2001 Bananas Settlement: A Factual and Procedural Analysis of the WTO Proceedings' in F Breuss, S Griller and E Vranes (eds), *The Banana Dispute—An Economic and Legal Analysis* (Vienna/New York: Springer-Verlag, 2003) 1.

[6] [1993] OJ L 47/1.

[7] This arrangement was provided under Art 136 of the original Treaty of Rome and was annexed to the Implementing Convention on the Association of the Overseas Countries and Territories with the Community.

[8] Case C–280/93 *Germany v Council* [1994] ECR I–4973.

including the principle of non-discrimination, the right to property and the freedom to pursue a trade or business and the principle of proportionality; it was then alleged that the distinction between traditional and non-traditional importers as applied to ACP importers was in violation of the exemption of ACP products from all customs duties pursuant to Article 168 of the Lomé Convention; it was, then, argued that Regulation 404/93 was adopted in breach of GATT and, finally, in breach of the Banana Protocol. It is the Court's approach to the latter plea of law which is relevant to the present analysis.

The argument put forward by the German government was interesting in so far as it sought to distinguish between compliance with GATT as a condition for the legality of Community law and the direct effect of the Agreement. This position was rejected by the Court which expressed a distinction of its own: whilst the binding effect of GATT on the Community was reaffirmed, what was important was to consider the spirit, the general scheme and the terms of GATT in order to 'assess ... the scope of GATT in the Community legal system'.[9] Having, then, referred briefly to the main characteristics of GATT, already pointed out in its rulings pursuant to the preliminary reference procedure, the Court concluded as follows:[10]

> Those features of GATT, from which the Court concluded that an individual within the Community cannot invoke it in a court to challenge the lawfulness of a Community act, also preclude the Court from taking provisions of GATT into consideration to assess the lawfulness of a regulation in an action brought by a Member State under the first paragraph of Article 230] of the Treaty.

Prior to any analysis of this part of the judgment, it should be pointed out that the Court rejected all the arguments put forward by the German government. In procedural terms, the proposal of the Commission had been properly amended and submitted to the Council and its examination did not require that the Parliament be consulted again, as the amendments by the Commission did not affect the very essence of the Regulation taken as a whole. In terms of substantive Community law, the principle underpinning the common agricultural policy had not been violated: the discretion enjoyed by the Community institutions was exercised in accordance with the objectives of CAP, whereas the detrimental effects felt specifically by German importers were inevitable and should be assessed in the context of the benefits felt generally by traders throughout the common market; neither had the competition rules been violated, as it was for the Council to decide on the effects of competition law on CAP measures. In the same vein, the fundamental rights and general principles invoked by the German government were held not to have been violated by the Bananas Regulation: there was no discrimination against traders in third-country bananas not only because the prior existence of significantly compartmentalised national markets had rendered the

---

[9] *Ibid*, para 105.
[10] *Ibid*, para 109.

position of Community traders non-comparable but also because the difference in treatment resulting from the adoption of the Regulation was inherent in the objective of integrating these very markets; the right to property and the freedom to pursue a trade or business were not absolute and should be viewed as subject to changes which the Community institutions enjoy discretion to introduce; finally, in implementing the CAP objectives, the Community institutions enjoy wide discretion in the exercise of which the adoption of the Bananas Regulation did not appear to be in manifest breach of the principle of proportionality.

Despite the express reference to the legal position of individuals, it is not accurate to say that the ruling in *Germany v Council* made the direct effect of GATT, or rather the absence thereof, a condition for reliance upon it by a Member State in annulment proceedings: what it did hold was that the reasons which prevented GATT provisions from being directly effective in actions by individuals against Community measures also prevented Member States from attempting similar actions. This parallelism, based on the broad construction of the principle of direct applicability proper, had been envisaged long ago: in his Opinion in *International Fruit Company*, Advocate General Mayras had concluded his analysis of why individuals could not possibly derive any directly enforceable rights under GATT in the following terms: 'is it not right to think that if Article XI of GATT was directly applicable in the Community legal system, the Netherlands Government could have requested this Court, in pursuance of Article [230] of the Treat of Rome, to annul the regulations at issue, on the ground that it considered those Community regulations to be contrary to the General Agreement and, consequently, to the treaty obligations of the Community and of the Netherlands?[11]

Viewed from this angle, in rejecting the action brought by the German government, the Court identified a thread which brings together different aspects of the effects of GATT within the Community legal order, namely the legal position of individuals and Member States. This mitigates the implications of the two-tier test for the application of direct effect of international agreements in so far as both individuals and Member States are precluded from relying upon them in order to challenge Community measures. It also brings consistency in the system of the enforcement of international obligations undertaken by the Community. In the context of the WTO, Eeckhout views it as 'eminently defensible' as the identity of the claimant should not be relevant to the Court's conclusion on the effect of WTO rules.[12] It could be argued that, in this instance, consistency is brought by the Court because of the specific features of the GATT and, subsequently, the WTO rather than as a matter of principle. After all, the identity of the claimant is generally relevant to the effectiveness of their claims: the variation in the *locus standi* rules under Article 230 EC, for instance, does acknowledge variations in the effect of legal claims brought before the Court. This is not merely a procedural point in so far as the divergence illustrated by the different classes of applicants

---

[11] Joined Cases 21 to 24/72, n1 above, at 1240.
[12] Eeckhout, n5 above, 249.

under the annulment procedure reflects a divergence of substantive interests: the interest of privileged applicants in the legality of any Community measure is presumed by their very status.

The judgment in *Germany v Council* also highlights the limited scope of the GATT 1947 within the Community legal order: in principle, its provisions may not be relied upon by either individuals or Member States in order to challenge the validity of Community measures in either national courts or the European Court. This approach has been subject to criticism on various grounds. Even prior to the adoption of the WTO agreements, the emphasis on the incomplete legal nature of the GATT was seen as legally indefensible.[13] It was argued, for instance, that many provisions laid down in the GATT were more precise and unconditional than certain vague and conditional rules of the EC Treaty, Article 28 EC being such an example.[14] In dismissing every single basis of what was seen as 'an extremely compelling attempt' to use the GATT as 'a kind of economic constitution',[15] the Court was viewed as engaging in a process of judicial protectionism which undermined the ability of international law to penetrate the Community legal order. In addition, the identification of the legal position of Member States with that of individuals was criticised as legally indefensible.[16]

The force with which the line of reasoning put forward by the German government was rejected by the Court was considerable. It may be explained by three interlinked considerations. The first one is of a practical and political nature. The determination of the effect of an international agreement within the Community legal order is directly related to the manner in which the Community institutions may choose to defend the Community interests on the international economic scene. It is noteworthy that the Community interest as defined by the Community institutions is at the very core of the line of reasoning advanced by the Court. In dealing with the argument that the adoption of the Bananas Regulation had led to an increase in prices on the German market, the Court pointed out that 'the creation of a common organization of the market, taking the place of national arrangements characterized by considerable price differences, inevitably results in an adjustment of prices throughout the Community' and that 'the objective of ensuring reasonable prices for consumers must be considered not on each national market but in the common market as whole'.[17]

---

[13] See E-U Petersmann, 'The EEC as a GATT Member—Legal Conflicts Between GATT Law and European Community Law' in M Hilf, FG Jacobs and E-U Petersmann (eds), *The European Community and GATT* (The Hague: Kluwer, 1989) 23, 58–9.

[14] E-U Petersmann, 'The GATT Dispute Settlement System as an Instrument of the Foreign Trade Policy of the EC' in N Emiliou and D O'Keeffe (eds), *The European Union and World Trade Law* (Chichester: Wiley, 1996) 253 at 275.

[15] S Dillon, *International Trade and Economic Law and the European Union* (Oxford: Hart Publishing, 2002) 378.

[16] See C Kaddous, *Le droit des relations extérieures dans la jurisprudence de la Cour de justice des Communautés européennes* (Basel/Brussels: Helbing & Lichtenhahn/Bruylant, 1998) 374.

[17] N8 above, para 51.

In dealing with the argument that the subdivision of the tariff quota in favour of importers of Community and traditional ACP bananas was contrary to the principle of non-discrimination, the Court pointed out that:[18]

> such a difference in treatment appears to be inherent in the objective of integrating pre-viously compartmentalized markets, bearing in mind the different situations of the various categories of economic operators before the establishment of the common organization of the market. The Regulation is intended to ensure the disposal of Community production and traditional ACP production, which entails the striking of a balance between the two categories of economic operators in question.

Similarly, on the effect of this arrangement on the competitive position of economic operators on the German market, it was pointed out that it[19]

> is inherent in the establishment of a common organization of the market designed to ensure that the objectives of [CAP] are safeguarded and that the Community's interna-tional obligations under the Lomé Convention are complied with. The abolition of the differing national systems, in particular the exceptional arrangements still enjoyed by operators on the German market and the protective regimes enjoyed by those trading in Community and traditional ACP bananas on other markets, made it necessary to limit the volume of imports of third-country bananas into the Community. A common organization of the market had to be implemented while Community and ACP bananas were not displaced from the entire common market following the disappearance of the protective barriers enabling them to be disposed of with protection from competition from third-country bananas.

As if the need to strike the balance between defining the Community interest within the international legal commitments undertaken by the Community insti-tutions and seeking compliance with other conflicting international undertakings had not been brought home, the Court went on to stress the following:[20]

> The differing situations of banana traders in the various Member States made it neces-sary, in view of the objective of integrating the various national markets, to establish machinery for dividing the tariff quota among the different categories of traders con-cerned. That machinery is intended both to encourage operators dealing in Community and traditional ACP bananas to obtain supplies of third-country bananas and to encourage importers of third-country bananas to distribute Community and ACP bananas. It should also in the long term allow economic operators who have tradition-ally marketed third-country bananas to participate, at the level of the overall Community quota, in the two sub-quotas introduced.

In other words, it is the overall approach of the contested measure to striking the balance between competing interests with due regard to what the Community

---

[18] *Ibid*, para 74.
[19] *Ibid*, para 82.
[20] *Ibid*, para 83.

interest entails that underlies the judgment of the Court on the substance of the case. For instance, to the German attack on the phenomenon of transfers of import licences, the Court responded that:[21]

> the financial advantage which such a transfer may in some cases give traders in Community and traditional ACP bananas is a necessary consequence of the principle of transferability of licences and must be assessed in the more general framework of all the measures adopted by the Council to ensure the disposal of Community and traditional ACP products. In that context it must be regarded as a means intended to contribute to the competitiveness of operators marketing Community and ACP bananas and to facilitate the integration of the Member States' markets.

In the light of the above, it is suggested that the assessment of the right of a Member State to invoke the GATT in order to challenge a Community measure was directly linked to the assessment of what the Community institutions defined as 'Community interest'. It is for this reason that the discretion enjoyed by the Community legislature and executive was mentioned by the Court time and again. For the Court to accept the action against the Bananas Regulation would have been tantamount to enabling the German government to win by judicial means the political battle it had lost in the Council where its objections to the adoption of the Regulation had been overruled.

This point leads to the second consideration underpinning the Court's ruling, namely the distinction between the binding force of GATT and its scope in the Community legal order. In essence, the assessment of the nature and spirit of the Agreement prior to reliance on it by a Member State, as well as an individual, amounts to ascertaining its justiciability.[22] In fact, it does not determine whether the legally binding nature of the Agreement could be enforced by the Court; it merely provides the criterion for deciding how the legally binding nature of the Agreement could be enforced within the Community legal order. To that effect, an extract from the ruling in *SIOT* is noteworthy: having determined that Article V GATT was not capable of conferring rights enforceable by individuals before national courts, the Court of Justice concluded as follows: 'that [conclusion] in no way affects the Community's obligations to ensure that the provisions of GATT are observed in its relations with non-Member States which are parties to GATT'.[23]

This raises the final point, which is quite how the international obligations undertaken by the Community under GATT may be enforced by national courts and the European Court in the light of the coherent, albeit strict, construction of its direct effect. The other mechanisms of enforcing those obligations will be considered in the following section.

---

[21] *Ibid*, para 86.
[22] See I Cheyne, 'International Instruments as a Source of Community Law' in A Dashwood and C Hillion (eds), *The General Law of E.C. External Relations* (London: Sweet and Maxwell, 2000) 254 at 255 ff.
[23] N3 above, para 28.

3. OTHER MECHANISMS OF ENFORCING THE GATT

The force with which the line of reasoning advanced by the German government was dismissed must be viewed within the legal and constitutional context of the enforcement of international agreements in general and the provisions of the GATT in particular. In fact, there had already been two cases where a GATT provision was deemed a valid basis for challenging the legality of Community law.

3.1. The Genesis of the 'Reference' Case

The first case had arisen in a direct action against the Commission brought by the Seed Crushers' and Oil Processors' Federation in 1987.[24] The applicant challenged a decision addressed to them and adopted pursuant to Regulation 2641/84[25] in which the Commission declined to initiate a procedure in order to examine certain commercial practices of Argentina regarding the export of soya cake to the Community. Regulation 2641/84 had established a procedure aimed at enabling the Community to deal with illicit commercial practices other than dumping and subsidies; both the Member States and Community producers were given the right to submit a complaint to the Commission which, having examined the legality of the targeted practice and the alleged injury, would then decide whether it was necessary in the light of the Community interest to pursue the complaint. The argument of *Fediol* that a scheme of differential charges on exports of soya products and the imposition of quantitative restrictions on the exportation of soya beans were contrary to a number of GATT provisions was rejected by the Commission as unfounded and unsubstantiated.

The thrust of the Commission's defence before the Court was confined to the consistent case law so far: individuals may not rely upon GATT rules in order to challenge Community measures as those rules, because of their nature, are incapable of conferring rights upon them. This argument was rejected by the Court in the light of the legal context set out by Regulation 2641/84 which should be viewed as allowing individuals to rely upon GATT rules. The subject of the request made by individuals pursuant to that Regulation was the illicit nature of a commercial practice which, according to Article 2(1) of the Regulation, was defined as 'incompatible with international law or with the generally accepted rules'. The Court relied upon the preamble to Regulation 2641/84 and concluded that the GATT provisions form part of the international rules to which Article 2(1) refers.

Having established the interest of individuals to invoke GATT rules in the context of Regulation 2641/84, the Court went on to leave no doubt about the scope of its own jurisdiction. On the one hand, it made it clear that the reason which rendered GATT incapable of conferring rights upon individuals, that is its broad flexibility, did not prevent the Court from interpreting the Agreement in order to

---

[24] Case 70/87 *Fediol v Commission* [1989] ECR 1781.
[25] [1984] OJ L 252/1.

assess the consistency of a specific commercial practice with its provisions: 'the GATT provisions have an independent meaning which, for the purposes of their application in specific cases, is to be determined by way of interpretation'.[26] On the other hand, the existence of a special procedure under GATT rules for the settlement of disputes arising from the application of the Agreement did not preclude the interpretation of that Agreement: in drawing upon its case law on the institutional framework set up by agreements concluded by the Community, the Court concluded that 'the mere fact that the contracting parties have established a special institutional framework for consultations and negotiations *inter se* in relation to the implementation of the agreement is not in itself sufficient to exclude all judicial application of that agreement'.[27]

On the substance of the case, every single argument of the applicant was rejected on the basis of the interpretation of a number of GATT provisions by the Court. Two aspects of this ruling are particularly interesting. First, it took the Court only one paragraph to articulate the right of the applicant to challenge a Commission decision pursuant to the GATT; in this articulation, very specific terms were used, all in reference to the detailed procedure set up under Regulation 2641/84. Therefore, the Court appeared reluctant to articulate a general exception to the rule followed consistently after the ruling in *International Fruit Company*. While it is difficult to view the above Regulation as the only Community measure in the context of which GATT rules were relevant to actions brought by private applicants, the formulation used by the Court begs the following question: how clearly should a Community measure refer to the GATT in order to enable the latter's rules to be invoked in actions against Community decisions? Should the reference be expressed in either the operative part of the measure or its preamble? Would it be sufficient if the legislative history of the measure indicated that its adoption had aimed at ensuring compliance with GATT? Be that as it may, the tenor of the judgment was clear as to the exceptional nature of the effect of GATT rules in that case. Indeed, the Court was keen to stress that its conclusion was consistent with the thrust of its line of reasoning originating in *International Fruit Company* and reaffirmed in *Schlüter* and *SPI and SAMI*.

Secondly, in its judgment, the Court appeared willing to justify its conclusion in terms of its own jurisdiction too. In acknowledging the judicial application of an Agreement whose broad flexibility had been affirmed time and again, the Court assumed a considerable interpretative function: not only was it called upon to identify the 'independent meaning' of the GATT provisions,[28] but it also indicated that the discretion enjoyed by Community institutions in the area covered by GATT would become subject to judicial scrutiny.

---

[26] N24 above, para 20.
[27] *Ibid*, para 21.
[28] *Ibid*, para 20.

3.2. The Genesis of the 'Implementation' Case

This was reaffirmed in the ruling in *Nakajima*, an action brought by a producer of typewriters and printers against the Council.[29] Following a complaint by the European Printer Manufacturers, the Commission found dumping in imports of serial-impact dot-matrix printers and imposed provisional anti-dumping duties on the applicant and other importers pursuant to the general rules laid down in Regulation 2176/84.[30] Following the adoption of the new Basic Regulation,[31] the Council extended the provisional anti-dumping duties on Nakajima and, then, imposed definitive duties. Amongst other arguments, the applicant argued that the Regulation imposing definitive anti-dumping duties was void because it was adopted pursuant to an illegal measure, namely the Basic Regulation. In particular, it was argued that the latter's provisions on constructing the normal value of the imported product were in violation of essential procedural requirements, certain general principles of law and, most importantly for this analysis, the Anti-Dumping Code annexed to the GATT 1947. The Council counter-argued that the legality of the Basic Regulation could not be challenged in the light of the Anti-Dumping Code because, along with the GATT, it did not confer any rights upon individuals which could be enforced by the Court.

The Court rejected this line of reasoning. First, it pointed out that, in that context, reliance upon the provisions of the Anti-Dumping Code did not amount to direct effect: instead, the applicability of the Basic Regulation was being questioned 'in an incidental manner' under Article 231 EC, by relying upon the infringement of the Treaty or any rule of law relating to its application as laid down as grounds for review of legality pursuant to Article 230 EC.[32] The binding effect of the GATT and, hence, of the Anti-Dumping Code being in issue, the Court referred to the preamble to the Basic Regulation, according to which its provisions were adopted in accordance with international obligations, in particular those arising from the Anti-Dumping Code before concluding:[33]

> It follows that the new basic regulation, which the applicant has called in question, was adopted in order to comply with the international obligations of the Community, which, as the Court has consistently held, is therefore under an obligation to ensure compliance with the General Agreement and its implementing measures.

Having acknowledged the right of the applicant to challenge the Basic Regulation in the light of a set of rules annexed to the GATT, the Court proceeded to dismiss all the arguments put forward by the applicant and, therefore, to affirm the legality of that measure.

---

[29] Case C–69/89 *Nakajima v Council* [1991] ECR I–2069.
[30] [1984] OJ L 201/1.
[31] Reg 2423/88 [1988] OJ L 209/1.
[32] N29 above, para 27.
[33] *Ibid*, para 31.

The principle set out in *Nakajima* was of paramount significance in so far as it indicated a way of ensuring compliance with WTO rules within the Community legal order without compromising the logic of the *International Fruit* line of cases: indeed, the *Nakajima* principle was repeated on every occasion on which the Court felt compelled to reaffirm the special structure and nature of the GATT.[34] The rulings in both the *Fediol* and *Nakajima* enabled individuals to benefit from the binding effect of the GATT in challenging secondary Community measures without, strictly speaking, suggesting that specific rights enforceable before the Community courts were conferred upon them. The principles introduced in those judgments have been referred to as the 'reference' exception and the 'implementation' exception respectively.[35] However, strictly speaking, rather than introducing exceptions to the principle enunciated in *International Fruit Company*, they dissociate the enforcement of legally binding international rules from the principle of direct effect; or rather, more accurately, they view the duties undertaken by the GATT as 'internalised' in the Community legal order. It is this act of internalisation which renders the analysis of the nature and purpose of GATT irrelevant to its enforcement.

It is noteworthy that the Court was at pains to draw the distinction between the direct effect of GATT rules, whose rejection it presents as good law, and the incidental effect of such rules in strictly defined cases and in a manner which would enable the Court to review the legality of a Community measure. In seeking to maintain this distinction, the Court appears keen to strike the balance between, on the one hard, enabling the Community institutions to exercise considerable discretion in determining their trade policies within the WTO framework and, on the other hand, giving effect to the principle that GATT rules form an integral part of the Community legal order. Indeed, the latter proposition would be difficult to maintain convincingly if its effects within the Community legal order were to become apparent mainly in order to reduce the scope of powers exercised by the Member States as opposed to those granted by the Community, one such example being the substitution of the former by the latter in respect of the GATT. It is not only in international relations law that the Court seeks to observe this fine line between the above interests: in the area of the enforcement of the law of the single market, when the construction of direct effect of directives had reached its limits, the Court sought to introduce alternative ways in which they would affect the legal position of individuals whilst stressing that those would not amount to direct effect, the so-called 'incidental' or 'triangular' effect being a case in point.[36]

---

[34] See, for instance, Case C–280/93 *Germany v Council*, N8 above, at para 111.

[35] See, for instance, Case T–3/99 *Banatrading GmbH v Council* [2002] ECR II–47, para 49.

[36] See the controversial judgment in Case C–443/98 *Unilever Italia SA v Central Food SpA* [2000] ECR I–7535 and the criticism in M Dougan, 'The "Disguised" Vertical Direct Effect of Directives' (2000) 59 *CLJ* 586 and S Weatherill, 'Breach of Directives and Breach of Contract' (2001) 26 *ELRev* 177; for another view, see P Koutrakos, 'On Groceries, Alcohol and Olive Oil: More on Free Movement of Goods after Keck' (2001) 26 *ELRev* 391. The implications of the judgment appear to have been addressed in Case C–159/00 *Sapod Audic v Eco-Emballages SA* [2002] ECR I–5031 annotated by M Dougan in (2003) 40 *CMLRev* 206.

In effect, this approach is consistent with the logic underpinning the rulings in *International Fruit Company* and *Germany v Council*: as the main point of emphasis in the latter case law was the discretion of Community institutions within the flexible system set out by the GATT, it is the exercise of that discretion which determines the enforcement of specific GATT provisions within the Community legal order. Inevitably, this shifts the emphasis to the construction of the conditions under which the duties undertaken by the Community would be deemed to have been internalised to such an extent as to enable the Community courts to enforce them.

3.3. The Duty of Interpretation

Irrespective of the construction of the *Fediol* and *Nakajima* cases, another method of enforcing the duties undertaken under the GATT was articulated by the Court two years after the judgment in *Germany v Council*, albeit in the context of an enforcement action under Article 226 EC. In the *International Dairy Arrangement* case, the Commission challenged the authorisation granted by German authorities whereby imports of certain dairy products were made under inward processing relief arrangements.[37] The Commission argued that this practice was applied to products the customs value of which was lower than set out in the International Dairy Arrangement (IDA). That Agreement, to which the Community was a party, had been concluded under the GATT umbrella. It aimed at the liberalisation of world trade in dairy products under stable market conditions and the economic and social development of developing countries. The parties had undertaken to desist from importing certain categories of products, specified in three protocols annexed to the Agreement, at prices lower than the minimum prices defined therein. The provision on which the arguments of the parties focused was Article 6 of each of the above protocols which provided, in identical terms, that the parties to the IDA would cooperate in implementing the minimum prices objective of the protocols and ensure 'as far as possible' that those products were not imported at prices lower than the appropriate customs valuation equivalent to the minimum prices set.

One of the interesting features of this case is that the German government did not seek to rely upon and reverse the thrust of the Court's approach to the GATT as articulated in *Germany v Council* a short time prior to the action in question. In other words, it did not argue that the GATT was incapable of being invoked by Community institutions against Member States, given that the latter could not invoke it in actions against the former. That issue was not raised before the Court. Instead, the line of reasoning put forward by the German government was focused on the interpretation of IDA in general and the cooperation clause laid down in Article 6 of its Protocols in particular. Its argument that there was no legal duty

---

[37] Case C–61/94 *Commission v Germany* [1996] ECR I–3989.

imposed under the latter provision was rejected by the Court, which interpreted it in the light of the purpose of the Agreement, the context of Article 6 and the general rule of international law requiring the parties to any agreement to show good faith in its performance.

Having identified the purpose of IDA as seeking to achieve stability on the world market in dairy products in the mutual interests of exporters and importers, the Court held that 'the Community must interpret its terms in such a way as to encourage the attainment of the objective pursued'.[38] Examining the wording of the cooperation clause laid down in the IDA Protocols and placing it in its context, it pointed out that 'the phrase "as far as possible" ... is not intended to release participating States from the obligation laid down by those provisions but rather to relieve a participant of liability where, notwithstanding the means at its disposal, it is unable to prevent dairy products from being imported into its territory at prices below the minimum set by the IDA'.[39] The Court had no difficulty in concluding that the German authorities did possess all the means necessary to ensure compliance with the IDA because all processing operations were conditional upon authorisation granted by national authorities.

Therefore, the Court's approach to the application of IDA was underpinned by what appears to be a duty of interpretation accepted by the Community: that entails that the provisions of an international agreement binding upon the Community should be interpreted in a manner which enhances the attainment of its objectives. This was brought home in the remaining part of the *IDA* judgment where the Court dealt with the attempt by the German government to defend its position by relying upon secondary Community law. In particular, it argued that, under Commission Regulation 2228/91[40] implementing the Basic Regulation 3677/86,[41] specific commercial policy measures to which imports are subject do not apply where non-Community goods are entered for inward processing relief arrangements using the suspension system: therefore, Community law setting out specific arrangements was seen as precluding the application of the measures provided under IDA. This argument was rejected by the Court. It had been a well-established principle that, in cases where a Community provision was open to more than one interpretation, every effort should be made to interpret it consistently with the EC Treaty or, in the case of an implementing Community measure, with the basic regulation. The Court concluded as follows:[42]

> Similarly, the primacy of international agreements concluded by the Community over provisions of secondary Community legislation means that such provisions must, so far as is possible, be interpreted in a manner that is consistent with those agreements.

---

[38] *Ibid*, para 31.
[39] *Ibid*, para 37.
[40] [1991] OJ L 210/1.
[41] [1986] OJ L 351/1.
[42] N37, para 52.

The Court, then, applied this principle to the Community measures in question: the construction of their scope in a way which would exempt the goods covered by it from IDA was deemed incompatible with the Agreement.

In essence, the Court of Justice articulated two related duties regarding the effects of international agreements concluded by the Community. The first one is a duty applicable to 'the Community': this should be construed as relating to the process of the application of the agreement and imposed upon both the Community and the Member States. This conclusion is not affected by the reference to the Community only in the relevant part of the judgment: it has already been established that, within the context of international agreements concluded by the Community, the Member States are under a duty 'above all' towards the Community for the due performance of the commitments undertaken therein.[43] The second duty articulated in *IDA* was that of consistent interpretation which, whilst relevant to the actions of the Community institutions and the Member States, is mainly addressed to the judiciary. In effect, this is similar to the principle of indirect effect of directives, according to which national courts are under a duty to interpret national legislation in the light of non-directly effective directives.[44] In addition, the two principles are also similar in so far as they do not impose duties of unlimited scope: instead, they both are to apply 'as far as possible'. Following from the principle of primacy of international agreements, the duty of consistent interpretation applies to all agreements concluded by the Community and to any type of action bringing their interpretation before the Court of Justice.[45] However, its function is particularly useful in cases where it may mitigate the constraints imposed by the strict reading of direct effect of the GATT. To that effect, it is noteworthy that the principle of indirect effect of directives had been introduced precisely in order to counterbalance the limits of the construction of direct effect of directives.

4. THE APPROACH OF THE COURT OF JUSTICE TO WTO RULES

The analysis so far has stressed two main points. First, in principle, the considerable flexibility of the GATT was deemed by the Court sufficient to exclude assessment of the validity of Community law in the light of its provisions; this approach was applied consistently to any challenge, irrespective of whether or not it reached

---

[43] See Case 104/81 *Hauptzollamt Mainz v C.A. Kupferberg & Cie KG a.A.* [1982] ECR 3641, at para 13.

[44] See Case 14/83 *Von Colson* [1984] ECR 1891 and Case C–106/89 *Marleasing* [1990] ECR I–4135. See G Betlem, 'The Doctrine of Consistent Interpretation—Managing Legal Uncertainty' (2002) 22 *OJLS* 397.

[45] To that effect, see Case C–286/02 *Bellio F.lli Srl v Prefettura di Treviso* [2004] ECR I–3465 at para 33 in relation to the EEA Agreement, Case C–284/95 *Safety-Tech Srl v S.& T. Srl* [1998] ECR I–4301 at para 22 and Case C–341/95 *Giannio Bettati v Sagety Hi-Tech Srl* [1998] ECR I–4355 at para 20 in relation to the 1985 Vienna Convention for the Protection of the Ozone Layer and the 1987 Montreal Protocol on Substances that Deplete the Ozone Layer, and Case C–53/96 *Hermès International v FHT Marketing* [1998] ECR I–3603 at para 28 in relation to TRIPs.

the Court under the preliminary reference procedure or an action for annulment and irrespective of whether it was initiated by a private applicant or a Member State. Secondly, that did not render the provisions of the GATT irrelevant: on the one hand, the legality of Community law would be assessed in the light of the obligations undertaken under that Agreement if internalised along the lines indicated in *Fediol* and *Nakajima*; on the other hand, the provisions of international agreements should be read into Community legislation as far as possible.

The establishment of the World Trade Organisation, its distinctly developed character in relation to the GATT and the conclusion of a number of agreements within its framework appeared to change the context within which some of the above principles were developed. The adoption of the WTO Agreements in 1994 following the Marrakesh Round brought the issue of direct effect back to the centre of EC international relations law. The reason for this was the considerable juridification of this new framework for multilateral trade negotiations.[46]

4.1. The Tighter Legal Framework Laid Down in WTO Agremeents

The process of legalisation of the WTO system was illustrated by various instances, most notably in the dispute settlement rules which became applicable on 1 January 1995. Laid down in the Understanding on Rules and Procedures Governing the Settlement of Disputes (DSU), a system which drew upon and further developed the pre-existing GATT mechanism was established. As the nature and modalities of this system are central to the Court's approach to the effect of WTO rules under Community law, they are worth considering in brief.[47] Prior to reliance upon the detailed procedures set out in DSU, a WTO Member must enter into 'good faith' consultations with the Members with which it is in dispute.[48] If the dispute is not settled within 60 days, or 20 days in cases of urgency, the complaining WTO Member may request that the Dispute Settlement Body (DSB) establish a panel to examine the dispute. It is the General Council of the WTO which serves as the DSB, albeit operating under its own chairman and pursuant to distinct procedures. The panel, consisting of individuals appointed from a list maintained by the General Council Secretariat, submits first a draft and then an interim report on which the parties in dispute may comment. Its final report must be adopted by the DSB, unless the latter decides by consensus not to do so.[49] The

---

[46] See JHH Weiler, 'The Rule of Lawyers and the Ethos of Diplomats: Reflections on WTO Dispute Settlement' in RB Porter, P Sauve, A Subramanian and AB Zampetti (eds), *Efficiency, Equity, Legitimacy: The Multilateral Trading System at the Millennium* (Washington, DC: Brookings Institution Press, 2001) 334.

[47] For a more detailed overview, see AF Lowenfeld, *International Economic Law* (Oxford: OUP, 2003) 135 ff and M Matsushita, TJ Schoenbaum and PC Mavroidids, *The World Trade Organization—Law, Practice, and Policy* (Oxford: OUP, 2003) ch 2.

[48] Art 4(3) DSU.

[49] Art 16(4) DSU

report may be challenged on appeal by any party to the dispute before the Appellate Body which, within a period not exceeding 90 days, has the power to uphold, modify or reverse the legal reasoning and conclusions of the Panel report.[50] The Appellate Body's report must be adopted by the DSB, unless the latter decides by consensus not to do so.

Under Article 19(1) DSU, 'where a panel or the Appellate Body concludes that a measure is inconsistent with a covered agreement, it shall recommend that the Member concerned bring the measure into conformity with the agreement' whereas Article 21(1) DSU stresses that prompt compliance with recommendations or rulings of the DSB is essential in order to ensure effective resolution of disputes to the benefit of all Members. The losing party must inform the DSB of how it intends to proceed regarding the implementation of the recommendations and rulings of the DSB. In case of failure to comply within the reasonable period of time determined under the DSU procedures,[51] a number of options are available to the wining party. The first option consists of retaliation by means of suspension of trade concessions. In order to do so, it should submit the relevant request to the DSB within 20 days of the expiry of the abovementioned reasonable period; the DSB may either grant such authorisation or refer the matter to arbitration. The second option is compensation which is the subject of negotiation between the parties to the dispute and which ought to be mutually acceptable. In case of failure to reach such agreement, any party having invoked the DSU procedures may proceed to request authorisation in order to suspend trade concessions.[52] The level of retaliation should be equivalent to the level of violation and could apply to either the same economic sector in which the violation of WTO rules has been determined (parallel retaliation) or a different sector in the same agreement annexed to the WTO (cross-sector retaliation) or a different WTO agreement altogether (cross-agreement retaliation).[53] The retaliation is authorised and monitored by the DSB, whereas disputes over its level and procedures may be referred to arbitration.

The procedure outlined above is to be carried out within strict time-limits laid down in the DSU which also seeks to clarify the nature of sanctions it sets out: 'the suspension of concessions or other obligations shall be temporary and shall only be applied until such time as the measure found to be inconsistent with a covered agreement has been removed, or the Member that must implement recommendations or rulings provides a solution to the nullification or impairment of benefits, or a mutually satisfactory solution is reached'.[54]

---

[50] Art 17(13) DSU.

[51] What is a reasonable period of time within which the losing party must comply with WTO law is deterriiined either by the DSB following a proposal by the party concerned or by the parties to the dispute themselves or through binding arbitration, in which case it should not exceed 15 months from the date of the adoption of the report (Art 21(3) DSU).

[52] Art 22(2) DSU.

[53] Art 22(3) DSU.

[54] Art 22(8) DSU.

The introduction of this elaborate set of procedures has been viewed as the culmination of a considerable process of judicialisation of international economic law. Drawing upon increasing reliance upon and the concomitant maturity of the mechanisms provided under the GATT 1947, the DSU was seen as 'in many respects strengthening the "rule-orientation" and "legal methods" in the WTO dispute settlement system' and illustrating 'progressive "judicialization" of GATT dispute settlement procedures'.[55]

4.2. The Approach of the Court of Justice

The Court of Justice was initially quite reluctant to pronounce on the legal effects of the new rules laid down in WTO Agreements. In *Affish*,[56] importers of frozen fisheries products from Japan into the Netherlands challenged the prohibition or the importation of such products laid down in a Commission Decision.[57] That Decision aimed at protecting public health from the risks resulting from what the Commission deemed to be seriously defective hygienic conditions of production and storage. One of the arguments of the applicants was that the contested measure was incompatible with the Agreement on the application of sanitary and phytosanitary measures annexed to the WTO Agreement.[58] The Court declined to examine that argument because an examination of the contested Decision in the light of that Agreement had not been requested by the referring court, whilst such an examination by the Court of its own motion was considered 'unnecessary'.[59]

Within a short period of time, the issue of the effect of WTO rules was raised in the context of the bananas litigation in *T.Port III*[60] where German importers challenged the import regime on bananas laid down by the Council in Regulations 404/93 and 478/95. The referring court raised the question of the compatibility of that regime with the GATT and the right of the applicants to rely upon it before the national judiciary. Having pointed out that the exporting country, namely Ecuador, had not been a party to either the GATT 1947 or the GATT 1994, the Court of Justice deemed it unnecessary to answer either question. In both cases, the Advocates General had not hesitated to offer their views on the relationship between the WTO rules and Community law.

In *Affish*, Advocate General Cosmas argued that the rules laid down in the WTO Agreement and GATT 1994 were still characterised by 'great flexibility',

---

[55] E-U Petersmann, 'The Dispute Settlement System of the World Trade Organization and the Evolution of the GATT Dispute Settlement System since 1948' (1994) 31 *CMLRev* 1157 at 1189.

[56] Case C–183/95 *Affish* [1997] ECR I–4315.

[57] Dec 95/119 [1995] OJ L 80/56 adopted pursuant to Council Dir 90/675 [1990] OJ L 373/1 laying down the principles governing the organisation of veterinary checks on products entering the Community from third countries.

[58] [1994] OJ L 336/40.

[59] N56 above, para 28 of the judgment.

[60] Joined Cases C–364/95 and 365/95 *T. Port GmbH & Co v Hauptzollampt Hamburg-Joans (T. Port III)* [1998] ECR I–1023.

hence precluding individuals from relying upon them before national courts.[61] Similarly, Advocate General Elmer in *T.Port III* merely argued for the transposition of the Court's case law on the GATT 1947 to the WTO rules in the light of the preamble to Council Decision 94/800.[62] Another occasion where the Court chose to avoid the issue of the direct effect of the WTO rules was in *Hermès*, a preliminary reference from a Dutch court on the application of provisional measures laid down by national law in order to protect trade mark rights and their interpretation in the light of the TRIPS Agreement.[63] This was despite the call of Advocate General Tesauro to reconsider its case law in the light of the significantly different characteristics of the WTO regime.[64]

It was only in late 1999, that is nearly five years after the WTO Agreement had entered into force, that the Court of Justice dealt with the issue of the effect of the rules within the Community legal order. This was in the *Portuguese Textiles* case, where Portugal challenged a Council Decision concerning the conclusion of Memoranda of Understanding between the EC and Pakistan and India on arrangements in the area of market access for textile products.[65] These arrangements provided for the removal of restrictions on the importation of certain textile products into the Community and the latter's commitment to give favourable consideration to the flexible management of existing tariff and quotas. Having been outvoted in the Council, Portugal brought annulment proceedings under Article 230 EC on the basis of alleged incompatibility of the Decision with both WTO rules and fundamental principles of Community law. In relation to the former, it was argued that, in adopting the contested decision, the Council had violated GATT 1994, the Agreement on Textiles and Clothing and the Agreement on Import Licensing Procedures. In order to address the pre-existing approach of the Court to the GATT, Portugal put forward a two-fold argument: on the one hand, the WTO agreements were presented as significantly different from the GATT 1947, especially in relation to the rules governing dispute settlement; on the other hand, the issue of direct effect was irrelevant in so far as the dispute was about the right of a Member State to challenge the legality of a Community measure before the European Court of Justice.

The Court started off its analysis by reaffirming two general points: on the one hand, it was for the contracting parties to every agreement to determine whether that agreement should have direct effect—it was only in the absence of such a statement that it was left to the courts to determine the effect of the agreement; on the other hand, whilst there should be *bona fide* performance of every agreement under international law, each contracting party is free to determine the legal means through which the commitments entered into should be fully executed in its legal system provided that such means are not specified in the agreement itself.

---

[61] Paras 119–128 of his Opinion where he refers to specific provisions of the Agreement in question.
[62] Paras 27–30 of his Opinion.
[63] [1998] ECR I–3603.
[64] See paras 22–37 of his Opinion.
[65] Case C–149/96 *Portugal v Council* [1999] ECR I–8395.

As for the WTO Agreements themselves, the Court accepted that they differed 'significantly' from the rules laid down in the GATT 1947 with particular emphasis on the tighter regime provided in the system of safeguards and the dispute settlement procedure. However, after this briefest of statements, the Court proceeded to put forward a number of reasons which justified its conclusion that 'the WTO agreements are not in principle among the rules in the light of which the Court is to review the legality of measures adopted by the Community institutions'.[66] The arguments put forward by the Court may be summarised as follows. First, the subject-matter and purpose of the WTO Agreements indicated that 'the system resulting from [them] accords considerable importance to negotiation between the parties'.[67]This was illustrated by the DSU, whose Article 22(1) enables a contracting party whose actions have been found to be in violation of WTO law to grant compensation on an interim basis where the immediate withdrawal of the measure is impracticable. This is so despite the fact that such compensation is temporary in nature and that a preference is shown for full implementation of a DSB recommendation in order to ensure conformity with WTO law. Having mentioned the fact that compensation should be mutually acceptable and subject to negotiation between the parties involved in the dispute settlement procedures, the Court held that 'to require the judicial organs to refrain from applying the rules of domestic law, which are inconsistent with the WTO agreements would have the consequence of depriving the legislative or executive organs of the contracting parties of the possibility afforded by Article 22[DSU] of entering into negotiated arrangements even on a temporary basis.'[68]

The second argument put forward by the Court was based on the nature of the system set out by the WTO Agreements. The general purpose of the WTO agreements, namely to be implemented on the basis of the principle of negotiations with a view to entering into reciprocal and mutually advantageous arrangements, was similar to that of the GATT 1947. According to the Court, this feature distinguished the WTO framework from the typology of agreements concluded by the Community in order to provide either for an asymmetry of obligations or to create a special legal framework of integration with the Community.

Thie third argument may be called a balance-of-power one, and is based on the approach to the issue of direct effect taken by some of the most important commercial partners of the Community. Whilst in the case of many other international agreements a divergent approach to direct effect would not be problematic, the distinct nature of the WTO Agreements meant that the lack of reciprocity in their effect may lead to disuniform application of the WTO rules. The Court then concluded that '[t]o accept that the role of ensuring that those rules comply with

---

[66] *Ibid*, para 47.

[67] *Ibid*, para 36.

[68] *Ibid*, para 40. The Court then concluded that 'the WTO agreements, interpreted in the light of their subject-mater and purpose, do not determine the appropriate legal means of ensuring that they are applied in good faith in the legal order of the contracting parties' (para 41).

Community law devolves directly on the Community judicature would deprive the legislative or executive organs of the Community of the scope for manoeuvre enjoyed by their counterparts in the Community's trading partners'.[69]

This conclusion has since been repeated in relation to a number of agreements concluded under the WTO umbrella, such as the GATT 1994,[70] the Agreement on Technical Barriers to Trade,[71] the Agreement on Trade-Related Aspects of Intellectual Property Rights.[72] The judgment in *Omega* is interesting for the direct attack on the line of reasoning underpinning the ruling in *Portuguese Textiles* by the applicant. It was argued that the distinction between international agreements based on reciprocal and mutually advantageous arrangements such as those under the WTO umbrella and agreements not based on such arrangements was unhelpful: the conclusion of all international agreements aims at conferring advantages upon the contracting parties. Following the response already put forward by Advocate General Alber, the Court dismissed Omega's argument as misunderstanding 'the basis of [its] case-law', namely that:[73]

> the decisive factor … is that the resolution of disputes concerning WTO law is based, in part, on negotiations between the contracting parties. Withdrawal of unlawful measures is indeed the solution recommended by WTO law, but other solutions are also authorised, for example settlement, payment of compensation or suspension of concessions.

Following this 'clarification' of the thrust of its reasoning, the Court proceeded to repeat the arguments in the *Portuguese Textiles* judgment *verbatim*. Finally, the line of reasoning of that ruling was also relied upon in order to rule out the direct effect of TRIPs provisions within the scope of Community law in actions before national courts.[74]

5. ASSESSMENT OF THE COURT'S APPROACH

The approach of the Court of Justice to the legal effects of WTO rules within the Community legal order has been criticised heavily on a number of grounds. The following section will outline the various arguments and seek to assess them in the light of the legal, political and constitutional context.

---

[69] *Ibid*, para 46.

[70] Case C–307/99 *OGT v Hauptzollamt Hamburg-St Annen* [2001] ECR I–3159.

[71] Case C–27/00 and 122/00 *Omega and Others* [2002] ECR I–2569.

[72] Joined Cases 300/98 and 392/98 *Parfums Christian Dior SA v TUK Consultancy BV,and Assco Gerüste GmbH and Rob van Dyk v Wilhelm Layher GmbH and Co KG and Layher BV* [2000] ECR I–11307 and Case C–89/99 *Schieving-Nystad vof and Others and Robert Groeneveld* [2001] ECR I–5851.

[73] N71 above, para 89.

[74] Case C–300/98, n72 above, and Case C–491/01 *British American Tobacco (Investments) and Imperial Tobacco* [2002] ECR I–11453.

5.1. The View from the WTO Framework

The various strands of the criticism levelled against the Court's approach may be summarised as legal, constitutional and political arguments, all of which are intrinsically interrelated. In legal terms, the line of reasoning underpinning the *Portuguese Textiles* ruling has been seen as misconstruing the nature of the obligations laid down in WTO rules. In relation to the dispute settlement procedures set out in the DSU, the emphasis on the provision of compensation and the engagement of the relevant parties in negotiation in order to reach a mutually acceptable solution has been argued to be an attempt to cast doubt on the binding nature of the WTO rules.[75] According to this criticism, the provision for compensation or suspension of concessions or other obligations under Article 22(1) DSU does not constitute an alternative to full compliance with WTO rules: that provision makes it clear that both are to be temporary in nature as 'full implementation of a recommendation to bring a measure into conformity with the covered agreements' is 'preferred'. Furthermore, Article 21(1) DSU makes it clear that 'prompt compliance with recommendations or rulings of the DSB is essential in order to ensure effective resolution of disputes to the benefit of all Members' whereas 'the implementation of adopted recommendations or rulings' is to be kept 'under surveillance' by the DSB.[76] It is on the basis of those provisions that the final outcome of the dispute settlement procedures as ascertained in a DSB report is deemed to impose an international law duty to comply with its findings.

In a recent comment, Jackson has argued cogently for that conclusion on the basis not only of the DSU provisions but also the text, object and purpose, context and practice of the GATT and WTO.[77] He notes, for instance, Article XVI(4) WTO according to which 'each Member shall ensure the conformity of its laws, regulations and administrative procedures with its obligations as provided in the annexed Agreements'. Whilst popular amongst international economic lawyers, this view is not entirely uncontroversial. The wording of the relevant provisions of the DSU is not without ambiguities. For instance, full implementation of a DSB report is merely 'preferred'; furthermore, whilst the suspension of concessions should be temporary under Article 22(8) DSU, that same provision allows its application 'until such time as [amongst other options] a mutually satisfactory solution is reached'. Such provisions appear to enable the Members to choose a remedy which, in the light of the specific context of a dispute, they may consider appropriate.[78]

[75] See S Griller, 'Judicial Enforceabilty of WTO Law in the European Union—Annotation to Case C–149/96 *Portugal v Council*' [2000] *JIEL* 441 at 451 ff.

[76] Art 21(2) DSU.

[77] J Jackson, 'International Law Status of WTO Dispute Settlement Reports: Obligation to Comply or Option to "Buy Out"?' (2004) 98 *AJIL* 109.

[78] JO Berkey, 'The European Court of Justice and Direct Effect for the GATT: A Question Worth Revisiting' (1998) 9 *EJIL* 626 at 644 where he notes that 'the GATT 1994 may actually be a unique international agreement in that it attempts to utilize the "realpolitik" of the environment in which it operates to its benefit by providing methods of remedying violations which are flexible enough to maintain the functioning of the agreement: that is, the GATT 94 may provide a choice of remedy precisely because allowing such a choice helps preserve momentum for the trade liberalization process which is the ultimate purpose of the agreement' (at 645).

In constitutional terms, the approach of the Court of Justice may appear to run counter to the construction of international economic law as a legal process with distinct constitutional features in which the European Union ought to assume a leading role: it ought to promote a global democratic framework where individuals were active participants with specific legal rights conferred upon them which were enforceable before both national and transnational judicial bodies.[79] Capable of being interpreted in a more nuanced manner,[80] the perceived constitutionalisation of international economic law has been relied upon in order to attack the Court's construction of the legal effects of the WTO in the Community legal order. On the one hand, its direct effect may be deemed necessary in order to enhance the substantive and procedural rights of individuals. In that respect, the link has been made with the development of the law of the single market and the very considerable extent to which its success has been underpinned by the enhancement of the legal position of the individual though the conferment of legally enforceable rights. To that effect, it has been argued that 'this enlargement of "individual sovereignty" and the empowerment of EU citizens vis-a-vis EU member states has ... not been applied to the EU's external relations'.[81] On the other hand, by granting WTO rules direct effect, the European Courts would strengthen the enforcement mechanisms provided under the WTO umbrella and, hence, support the constitutionalising process.[82]

Finally, in political terms, another criticism levelled against the Court's approach in *Portuguese Textiles* is centred around the general scheme of the WTO framework. In setting out a rules-oriented system for the regulation of international trade, it took a considerable step towards trade liberalisation. As such, not only did it provide for the evolution of the system which originated in the Bretton Woods initiatives but it also ensured the maintenance and reinforcement of an incremental process towards economic interdependence and trade liberalisation on the international arena. The conclusion reached by the Court of Justice in *Portuguese Textiles* might be viewed as undermining the effective application of the WTO, hence raising potential obstacles to the process of trade liberalisation instigated by those rules.

Whilst not entirely without merit, the above arguments are not convincing. In legal terms, the process of juridification illustrated by the reform of the WTO rules is in no doubt and is acknowledged by the Court of Justice, both expressly and impliedly, in *Portuguese Textiles*. However, the emphasis on the binding

---

[79] See E-U Petersmann, 'European and International Constitutional Law: Time for Promoting "Cosmopolitan Democracy" in the WTO' in G de Búrca and J Scott (eds), *The EU and the WTO—Legal and Constitutional Issues* (Oxford: Hart Publishing, 2001) 81.

[80] See N Walker, 'The EU and the WTO: Constitutionalism in a New Key' in de Búca and Scott, n79 above, 31.

[81] E-U Petersmann, 'From State Sovereignty to the "Sovereignty of Citizens" in the International Relations Law of the EU?' in N Walker (ed), *Sovereignty in Transition* (Oxford: Hart Publishing, 2003) 145, 154.

[82] See KJ Kuilwijk, *The European Court of Justice and the GATT Dilemma* (Beuningen: Centre for Critical Legal Studies, 1996).

nature of the duties laid down in the WTO rules as ascertained by the DSB appears to misunderstand the reasoning of the Court. It is not the binding character of the WTO obligations which lies at the core of the Court's approach but the extent to which the contracting parties may be allowed to choose the method of enforcement of those obligations. In other words, it is the discretion enjoyed by the executive and legislative bodies of the Community and its Member States to negotiate mutually acceptable arrangements pursuant to the DSU that the Court seeks to ensure. It is expressly stated that that discretion should be preserved even if, in accordance with Article 22 DSU, it were to be exercised for negotiating arrangements on a temporary basis.[83] In other words, to stress the binding nature of the obligations imposed upon the Community under WTO rules does not refute the line of reasoning underpinning the judgment in *Portuguese Textiles*, for the latter did not question that nature, a point stressed by the Court even in the GATT 1947 context: in adjudicating upon the action brought by Germany against the bananas regime, the Court had opined as follows: 'the provisions of GATT have the effect of binding the Community. However, in assessing the scope of GATT in the Community legal system, the spirit, the general scheme and the terms of GATT must be considered'.[84]

Furthermore, to infer from the conclusion in *Portuguese Textiles* that the binding effect of WTO rules is negated within the Community legal order is to read a particular strand of the Court's approach out of its context: it is how the jurisprudence of the Court of Justice has enabled the binding effect of WTO rules to penetrate the Community legal order in practice at the various instances where they are relevant to the application of EC law that is truly important. As Jackson has pointed out, 'international law commands a variety of ways of dealing with breaches of [a "binding" international law] obligation, and some of the practical implications of "bindingness" will assist the general membership of an organization in encouraging the country to comply. Sometimes the implications of the legal effect within domestic systems will be involved; and sometimes subtler diplomatic and other pressures ... will gain additional help through the concept of "binding obligations".[85]

In constitutional terms, there is a choice underpinning the dispute settlement system under the WTO and that is to strive for negotiation; merely one illustration of this is provided by the absence of any remedy regarding financial compensation of past losses or interest. This indicates that the juridification of the WTO system, far from amounting to the establishment of a rules-oriented structure, constitutes a process which evolves around, rather than beyond, the political will of the contracting parties.[86] As has been pointed out, 'remedies ... in an integration system

---

[83] See para 40 of the *Portuguese Textiles* judgment, n 65 above.

[84] Case C–280/93 *Germany v Council*, n8 above, para 105.

[85] N77 above at 117.

[86] See RE Hudec, 'The New WTO Dispute Settlement Procedure: An Overview of the First Three Years' (1999) 8 *Minnesota Journal of Global Trade* 1, 10–15. See the overview by P-T Stoll and A Steinmann, 'WTO Dispute Settlement: The Implementation Stage' (1999) 3 *Max Planck UNYB* 407.

between unequal players like the WTO are there to "equalize" inequalities'.[87] The defining limits of the WTO system, as pointed out by the Court of Justice in *Portuguese Textiles*, are also borne out in the light of current practice. In relation to the foreign sales corporation tax imposed by the United States administration, for instance, the Commission was notably keen to avoid the imposition of trade sanctions in order to ensure compliance with the WTO rules.[88] Even after years of judicial proceedings involving the Community bananas import regime, the US administration never abandoned the policy of seeking to strike a deal with the Commission.[89] In the light of these considerations, to apply the logic that underpinned the constitutionalisation of the Community legal order to the rules laid down in the WTO framework is tantamount to ignoring the specific features of the latter and suggesting a parallelism which is supported neither in legal nor in practical terms.[90]

In political terms, it is not self-evident that the enhancement of the legal status of WTO law within the domestic legal order of its Members would speed up the process of trade liberalisation on the international economic arena. The substantive rules and procedures laid down in the WTO amount to a system of policies which is based as much on legal agreement as on political choice amongst the WTO Members. It is the interaction between these factors, in itself subject to a number of parameters such as the general economic climate, political stability and development of regional economic cooperation, that renders the WTO rules the dynamic framework within which trade liberalisation is to be achieved. In other words, trade liberalisation in general and the effectiveness of the WTO system in particular constitute an economic and political imperative to which the WTO Members ought to strive by relying upon multifarious legal, economic and political tools—they do not constitute a normative proposition compliance with which ought to be devolved to the judiciary of the WTO members. Quite the contrary, were the courts to intervene in order to impose a specific type of legal effectiveness contested amongst the WTO Members, the incomplete process of evolution generated by the functioning of the WTO system might be at risk: the more active the domestic courts were in enforcing WTO rules, the more intransigent the executive and legislature might prove to be in negotiating the further development of the WTO policies.

---

[87] PC Mavroidis, 'Remedies in the WTO Legal System: Between a Rock and a Hard Place' (2000) 11 *EJIL* 763, 811.

[88] See the statements of Commissioner Lamy in *Financial Times*, 26 Feb 2004, 10.

[89] See H Hauser and A Roitinger, 'Renegotiation in Transatlantic Trade Disputes' in E-U Petersmann and MA Pollack (eds), *Transatlantic Economic Disputes—The EU, the US, and the WTO* (Oxford: OUP, 2004) 487.

[90] As Howse and Nicolaidis point out, 'constitutionalization was made acceptable in Europe by characteristics whose functional equivalent cannot be obtained at the WTO level, including the complex relationship between constitutional politics and legislative politics in the European Union': R Howse and K Nicolaidis, 'Legitimacy and Global Governance: Why Constitutionalizing the WTO Is a Step Too Far' in Porter, Sauve, Subramanian and Zampeti (eds), n46 above, 227, 238.

In other words, the system set out under the WTO Agreements is multi-faceted in nature and evolving in its application: it provides the institutional machinery, the legal commitment and the political momentum for testing the commitment of its Members to trade liberalisation on the basis of successive rounds of negotiations on the adjustment of the existing agreements annexed to the WTO. Furthermore, the balance of powers between the various legislative, executive and judicial organs within the WTO system is far from settled.[91] Its enforcement system, whilst undoubtedly developed when compared to that laid down in the GATT 1947, is as flexible and open-ended in setting out ways to ensure compliance as it is clear in seeking to point out the binding nature of 'judicial' organs determinations.[92] In other words, in light of the deficiencies of the available remedies,[93] compliance is not only a matter of formal enforcement; it also depends on the various political interests whose interaction the multi-level structure and dynamic nature of the WTO system appears to envisage.[94]

In the light of the above, there may be a direct correlation between the activism that courts might be prepared to demonstrate domestically and the unilateralism that the executive might feel compelled to adopt internationally: should this underpin the approach of only a major economic actor or a handful of minor ones, it would be bound to influence the stance of other WTO members, hence stalling the evolution of the international economic order. Viewed from this angle, the endowment of WTO rules with direct effect would entail a shift in the balance of powers, not only within the Community legal order, but also the WTO framework itself, a development hardly envisaged by its contracting parties.[95]

Therefore, the internationalist position according to which domestic courts are responsible for the enforcement of conventional international law irrespective of the existence of a specific national political authorisation[96] may, in fact, endanger rather than enhance the achievement of the WTO aims and the successful development of the process of trade liberalisation. In the case of the Community judiciary, in particular, the internationalist position appears to ignore the specific constitutional character of the Community legal order. This is an issue which will be examined in the following section.

---

[91] See F Roessler, 'The Institutional Balance between the Judicial and the Political Organs of the WTO' in M Bronckers and R Quick (eds), *New Directions in International Economic Law. Essays in Honour of John H. Jackson* (The Hague: Kluwer Law International, 2000) 325 for criticism of the rulings of the Appellate Body on the balance-of-payments settlement procedures and regional trade agreements.

[92] The structure of this system has been characterised as 'peculiar': P-T Stoll and A Steinmann, 'WTO Dispute Settlement: The Implementation Stage' (1999) *3 Max Planck UNYB* 407 at 437.

[93] For a thoughtful analysis of the remedies provided under WTO rules, see Mavroidis, n87 above.

[94] See S Princen, 'EC Compliance with WTO Law: The Interplay of Law and Politics' (2004) 15 *EJIL* 555.

[95] See the arguments put forward in C-D, Ehlermann, 'Six Years on the Bench of the "World Trade Court". Some Personal Experiences as Member of the Appellate Body of the World Trade Organization' (2002) *JWT* 637.

[96] For a critical assessment of that position, see M Kumm, 'The International Rule of Law and the Limits of the International Model' (2003) 44 *Va J Int'l L* 19.

5.2. The View from the EC Framework

An interesting argument levelled against the approach of the Court of Justice to WTO rules is centred around the internal consistency of its case law on the effects of international agreements in the Community legal order. In its judgment in the *Portuguese Textiles* case, the Court of Justice sought to address it by distinguishing the WTO framework from other agreements which had been held in the past to be capable of conferring rights upon individuals: the latter were defined by 'a certain asymmetry of obligations' or the establishment of 'special relationships with the Community' as opposed to the objective of 'entering into reciprocal and mutually advantageous arrangements' served by the former.[97] This distinction is emphasised twice within four paragraphs in the judgment, the second time expressed in even stronger terms: the WTO Agreements 'must ipso facto be distinguished from agreements concluded by the Community'.[98] The Court further emphasises this special position of WTO rules by focusing on the lack of reciprocity regarding their effect by important trade partners of the Community. In other words, reciprocity is viewed by the Court as a two-fold concept: on the one hand, it refers to the rights and duties provided for under WTO rules (substantive reciprocity); on the other hand, it refers to the approach of the judiciary of the Community's partners (judicial reciprocity).

Both have been attacked on various grounds. In legal terms, the Court's reliance upon substantive reciprocity has been viewed as anachronistic, as the WTO framework contains principles the application of which is not subject to reciprocity.[99] In his Opinion in *Portuguese Textiles*, Advocate General Saggio had rejected the reciprocity argument as irrelevant to the effect of the WTO Agreements in the Community legal order; to that effect, he had pointed out that there are sufficient international law instruments to deal with this issue, namely the right of a contracting party, as a matter of customary international law, to suspend or extinguish an agreement in relation to which another contracting party has committed a material breach.[100] Furthermore, the notion of substantive reciprocity has been viewed as unhelpful: Griller wonders 'what is the borderline between agreements that are "reciprocal and mutually advantageous" and therefore depend on reciprocity at the level of implementation techniques, and "asymmetric" agreements or agreements creating special relations of integration, which do not rely on such an implicit recognition?'.[101]

Whilst the Court of Justice has not been as forthcoming as one might wish in distinguishing them from the other Agreements it was asked to deal with in the

---

[97] N65 above, para 42.

[98] *Ibid*, para 45.

[99] G Zonnekeyn, 'The Status of WTO Law in the Community Legal Order: Some Comments in the Light of the Portuguese Textiles case' (2000) 25 *ELRev* 293 at 300.

[100] Para 21 of his Opinion where he refers to Art 60 of the Vienna Convention on the Law of treaties and the principle *inadimplementi noen est adimplemendum.*

[101] Griller, n75 above, at 459.

past, there can be little doubt about the distinctive features of the WTO rules. It is not the multilateral nature itself of the WTO which, strictly speaking, underlines its unique character;[102] instead, it is the fact that it constitutes the most significant legal framework regulating the international economic order the scope of which is as comprehensive and its membership as wide as is realistically possible under present circumstances. It is not only the international front on which the Community deals with the other central world economic players on an equal footing but also the evolving legal, political and economic context within which it is called upon to shape its relationships with third countries and groups of countries as determined pursuant to its own Treaty objectives. Viewed from this angle, there is indeed a distinction to be drawn between the WTO Agreements and that agreement with Portugal to which the Court referred in *Portuguese Textiles*.[103] The criterion of this distinction is not the extent to which derogations from the substantive content of an agreement are available and the right to adopt safeguard measures unilaterally recognised: after all, it is difficult to find any agreement where the possibility of derogation is ruled out altogether. Instead, the distinction pointed out by the Court may be understood as referring to the overall character of the WTO system and the incremental development its dispute settlement procedures generate by enabling the fine balance between different interests to be subject to continuous redefinition, that is what the Court referred to as the nature and structure of the WTO Agreements. Another point needs to be clarified: the above analysis should not be taken to suggest that, under Community law, the legal effectiveness of an international agreement is in reverse correlation to its substantive significance. What it does suggest is that the complexity and distinct features of the system set out in the WTO Agreements demands an equally sophisticated and, inevitably, incrementally developed system of enforcement.

Furthermore, the line of reasoning developed by Advocate General Saggio in *Portuguese Textiles* is itself subject to criticism on two grounds. First, in dealing with the issue of reciprocity, his analysis focuses on reciprocity of implementation of the substantive content of the WTO Agreements. However, this fails to address the concern about the effects of judicial reciprocity. This issue is most important not only in the light of its effects on the balance of powers under the WTO umbrella but also in the light of the unique position of the Court of Justice within the Community legal order. Secondly, in his effort to highlight the various alternatives, short of denying the direct enforcement of WTO law, open to the Court of Justice, Advocate General Saggio points out that 'there is ... a strong case for holding that the rules of the agreement are not applicable or a fortiori binding even if the agreement was not suspended or extinguished, whenever the

---

[102] See JHJ Bourgeois, 'Effects of International Agreements in European Community Law: Are the Dice Cast?' (1984)82 *Mich L R* where he makes this argument in relation to GATT 1947 (at 1265); also N Neuwahl, 'Individuals and the GATT: Direct Effect and Indirect Effects of the General Agreement on Tariffs and Trade in Community Law' in Emiliou and O'Keeffe, n14 above, 313 at 320.

[103] See P Lee and B Kennedy, 'The Potential Direct Effect of GATT 1994 in European Community Law' (1996) 30 *JWT* 67 at 80 ff.

fulfilment of an obligation under the WTO entails a risk for the Community of jeopardising the balanced operation of the Community legal order and the pursuit of its objectives'.[104] He then goes on to argue that 'even if this may cause the Community to be held to be in breach of international law, the Court, which has the duty to ensure respect of the independence of the Community legal order, may not apply provisions that require the institutions to act in a manner that is inconsistent with the proper functioning and the objectives of the Treaty'.[105] Its vagueness aside, this position is rather curious as it is in itself contrary to the content of the DSU Article 23 of which prohibits unilateral retaliatory measures adopted beyond the framework of the procedures laid down therein.[106] Therefore, he appears to argue for the irrelevance of reciprocity to the full enforcement of the binding rules set out in WTO Agreements whilst suggesting that the Community judiciary violates those rules in the absence of such reciprocity.

As for the other aspect of reciprocity mentioned by the Court in *Portuguese Textiles*, namely judicial reciprocity, it is worth pointing out that the concern of domestic courts for the effect granted to international agreements by the courts of other contracting parties is not as uncommon as it might appear to be. It has been argued, for instance, that domestic courts seek to assess that effect as a matter of course when asked to adjudicate upon the application of an international agreement within their own legal order.[107] If this consideration is significant for the approach of domestic courts to international agreements as a matter of judicial policy, it is essential for the approach of the Court of Justice as a matter of constitutional balance. In this respect, it is worth recalling the considerations in the light of which the exclusive competence of the Community to conclude GATS and TRIPs was rejected in *Opinion 1/94*:[108] ensuring that harmonisation in the internal market would not be introduced through the exercise of external competence was central to the logic of mixity underpinning that ruling. Similarly, compliance with procedural rules laid down in the EC Treaty was relevant not only to that ruling but also to the rejection of the Commission's claim for a very broadly construed CCP.[109] This concern for parallelism between what the Community is equipped to do internally and what it decides to do externally is indicative of the constitutional function of the Court in the regulation of EC international relations; and the acknowledgment of the discretion enjoyed by the executive and the legislature in the evolving context of the WTO is another aspect of the exercise of this function.

In this respect, the intention of the executive and the legislature could not have been clearer. In the preamble to Decision 94/800 on the conclusion of the WTO

---

[104] N65 above, para 22 of his Opinion.

[105] *Ibid.*

[106] See A Rosas, Annotation of *PortugueseTextiles* (2000) 37 *CMLRev* 797 at 812.

[107] E Benvenisti, 'Judicial Misgivings Regarding the Application of International Law: An Analysis of Attitudes of National Courts' (1993) 4 *EJIL* 159.

[108] *Opinion 1/94* [1994] ECR I–5267: see the analysis in Ch 3 above.

[109] *Opinion 2/00* [2001] ECR I–9713: see the analysis in Ch 2 above.

Agreements on behalf of the Community, the Council had stated that 'by its nature, the Agreement establishing the World Trade Organisation, including the Annexes thereto, is not susceptible to being directly invoked in Community or Member State courts'.[110] Equally, the proposal by the Commission had pointed out that 'it is already known that the United States and many other of our trading partners will explicitly rule out ... direct effect. Without an express stipulation of such exclusion in the Community instrument of adoption, a major imbalance would arise in the actual management of obligations of the Community and other countries'.[111] It is noteworthy that, whilst referring to the express will of the Member States as to the effects of the WTO, the formula used by the Court in *Portuguese Textiles* was such as to make it impossible to assess the weight that it had attached to it. Having elaborated on the reasons why the WTO Agreements should not determine the legality of EC measures, the Court merely pointed out that that interpretation corresponded to the content of Decision 94/800.

In any case, the management of obligations within the framework set out pursuant to the dispute settlement procedures is by no means static. Indeed, these have cogently been described as assuming 'the role of shaping a new bargaining environment by attributing costs to the continuing violation of contract'.[112] Within such a legal environment, the judicial acknowledgment of the discretion that the Community executive should be allowed ought not to be seen as an illustration of judicial restraint; instead, it shows that the Court of Justice is receptive to the specific dynamics that underlie the international economic arena and the way they vary depending on the nature of the specific framework of cooperation under review.[113]

6. ALTERNATIVE WAYS OF ENFORCING WTO RULES

The analysis so far has suggested that WTO rules are enforced in the Community legal order within the parameters already set by the Court in the pre-WTO era: it is only in cases where the Community has intended to implement a particular obligation assumed in the WTO framework or where the Community measure refers expressly to the precise provisions of the WTO Agreement in question that the Court may review the legality of the Community measure in question in the light of the WTO rules. To that effect, the thrust of the ruling in *Nakajima* has

---

[110] Council Dec 94/800 concerning the conclusion on behalf of the European Community, as regards matters within its competence, of the agreements reached in the Uruguay Round multilateral negotiations (1986–1994) [1994] OJ L 336/1.

[111] COM(94) 414 final Uruguay Round of Multilateral Negotiations.

[112] Hauser and Roitinger, n89 above, at 506.

[113] It is interesting that a WTO Panel Report has noted that 'neither the GATT nor the WTO has so far been interpreted by GATT/WTO institutions as a legal order producing direct effect. Following this approach, the GATT/WTO did not create a new legal order the subjects of which comprise both contracting parties or Members and their nationals': US Sections 301–310 of the Trade Act of 1974, Panel Report of 8 Nov 1999, WT/DS 152, para 7.78.

been repeated every time the Court reaffirms the special features of the WTO.[114] Furthermore, as the special features of the WTO have affected the legal position both of individuals and Member States, so have the above specific ways of enforcement been applied to both.[115]

In the light of the line of reasoning in *Portuguese Textiles*, the actual significance of the principle articulated in *Nakajima* ought to be determined by the extent to which the Community judicature has been prepared to apply it liberally. It has been argued that, originally, both the Court of Justice and the Court of First Instance adopted a rather strict approach.[116] It is certainly true that, until recently, the case law has revealed a degree of ambivalence. On the one hand, the Court of First Instance deemed that principle irrelevant to the legality of the amendment of Regulation 404/93, which was the origin of the Bananas litigation, despite the fact that that amendment had been adopted following the adoption by the Dispute Settlement Body of a report declaring Regulation 44/93 incompatible with the GATT 1994. It was argued that 'neither the reports of the WTO Panel ... nor the report of the WTO Sanding Appellate Body ... which was adopted by the Dispute Settlement Body ... included any special obligations which the Commission intended to implement, within the meaning of the case-law, in Regulation No 2362/98 [ie the regulation amending Regulation 404/93] ... The regulation does not make express reference either to any specific obligations arising out of the reports of WTO Bodies, or to specific provisions of the agreements contained in the annexes to the WTO Agreement.[117]

This approach was subsequently confirmed by the Court of Justice, which regarded the matter so clear as to enable it to address it in an Order under Article 104(3) of its Rules of Procedure and declared simply that 'contrary to [the] assertions [by the applicant before the referring court], ... [t]he common organisation of the market in bananas, as introduced by Regulation No 404/93 and subsequently amended, is not designed to ensure the implementation in the Community legal order of a particular obligation assumed in the context of GATT, nor does it refer expressly to specific provisions of GATT'.[118] The paucity of reasoning notwithstanding, the Court appears to confine the application of the *Nakajima* principle to cases where the contested Community measure provides textual evidence as to the intention of the Community institutions to comply with

---

[114] See, for instance, the judgment in *Portuguese Textiles*, n65 above, para 49.

[115] For actions by Member States against Community measures, see Case C–352/96 *Italy v Council* (*re: tariff quotas on imports of rice*) [1998] ECR I–6937 at para 20 with regard to GATT 1994; Case C–150/95 *Portugal v Council* (*re: oilseeds*) [1997] ECR I–5863 in which area figures contained in an annex to the Blair House Agreement were mentioned in the challenged Regulation and the Court and its A G proceeded to examine the contested regulation in the light of, amongst others, the Blair House Agreement.

[116] See G Zonnekeyn, 'The ECJ's Petrotub Judgment: towards a Revival of the "Nakajima Doctrine"?', (2003) 30 *LIEI* 249.

[117] Case T–30/99 *Bocchi Food Trade International GmbH v Commission* [2001] ECR II–943, para 64, Case T–18/99 *Cordis, Obst and Gemüse Grosshandel GmbH v Commission* [2001] ECR II–913 at para 59, Case T–52/99 *T. Port GmbH & Co. KG v Commission* [2001] ECR II–981 at para 59.

[118] Case C–307/99, n70 above, 28.

an obligation imposed under WTO law. This is a formalistic criterion which may allow the Commission and the Council to be tempted to engage in textual manipulation. Furthermore, it appears to question the significance of the *Nakajima* principle as a way of mitigating the effects of the judgment in *Portuguese Textiles* in practical terms.

That is not to say that the approach adopted by the Court of Justice has been wholly objectionable. In *Portuguese Textiles,* for instance, the Portuguese government had invoked this principle in order to substantiate the alleged illegality of the contested Decision which concluded the Memoranda of Understanding with Pakistan and India. Whilst this argument was dismissed rather too swiftly by the Court,[119] it is very difficult to see how the contested Decision could possibly be viewed as intending to implement the GATT 1994 and the Agreement on Textiles and Clothing.

6.1. The Judgment in *Petrotub*

The issue of the construction of the *Nakajima* principle arose more recently in *Petrotub*.[120] This reached the Court on appeal from the Court of First Instance,[121] before which the applicants had challenged a Council regulation imposing definitive anti-dumping duties on their imports of seamless pipes and tubes of steel originating in Russia, the Czech Republic, Romania and the Slovak Republic. They challenged the contested judgment because they claimed that two of their pleas had not been adequately addressed by the CFI. The first referred to the choice of the assymetrical method in order to determine the degree of dumping which took place: in other words, the Council had chosen to compare the weighted average normal value with the individual export prices. Whilst this was allowed by Article 2(11) of the Basic Regulation, that provision made it clear that two conditions had to be met: there ought to be a pattern of export prices which differs significantly amongst different purchases, regions or time periods and the symmetrical methods should be deemed inadequate to reflect the full degree of dumping. The second plea referred to the determination of normal value and the fact that the Council had used prices between the two appellants despite the fact that they had been claimed to be in a compensatory arrangement with each other. Article 2(1)(3) of the Basic Regulation provides that such prices may not be used to establish normal value because they may not be considered to be in the ordinary course of trade unless it is determined that they are unaffected by the relationship.

The appellants claimed that their original pleas about the legal defects of the contested Regulation due to the lack of adequate reasoning had not been properly addressed by the Court of First Instance. One of the issues raised was whether the latter had been correct in refusing to take into account Article 2(4)(2) of the

---

[119] See n65 above, at para 51.
[120] Case C–76/00 P *Petrotub SA and Republica SA v Council and Commission* [2003] ECR I–79.
[121] Case T–34/98 *Petrotub and Republica v Council* [1999] ECR II–3837.

1994 Anti-dumping Code according to which the competent authorities of GATT parties should provide an explanation of why the use of symmetrical methods would be inadequate in order to take into account significant differences in the pattern of export prices amongst different purchases, regions or time periods. The Court of Justice answered this question in the negative. Whilst reiterating the special nature and structure of the WTO Agreements, it went on to state once more that the rules laid down therein would be taken into account by the Community's judiciary in reviewing the legality of EC law, where the Community intended to implement a particular obligation assumed in the context of the WTO or where the contested EC rule referred expressly to precise WTO provisions. It was the former which applied to the Basic Regulation whose preamble made it clear that its purpose was '*inter alia*, to transpose into Community law as far as possible the new and detailed rules contained in the 1994 Anti-dumping Code, which include, in particular, those relating to the calculation of dumping, so as to ensure a proper and transparent application of those rules'.[122]

Having established the relevance of the provisions laid down in the Anti-dumping Code, the Court went on to reiterate the principle that Community law be interpreted 'so far as possible' consistently with international law.[123] And then, it did exactly that: the absence of a reference in the Basic Regulation to the duty to state reasons in relation to the determination of dumping is viewed in the light of the general duty to state reasons laid down in Article 253 EC. Therefore, the specific duty provided for in the Anti-dumping Code is presumed to have been subsumed by the general duty imposed upon all Community institutions. The Court further substantiates this conclusion with reference to a Commission communication addressed to the WTO Committee on Anti-dumping Practices, according to which the reasoning required under Article 2(4)(2) of the 1994 Anti-dumping Code would be given directly to the parties and in regulations imposing anti-dumping duties. Having established the existence of a legal duty imposed on the Community institutions to give reasons in the choice of methods in the area of anti-dumping, the Court concluded that the CFI had erred in law because the contested regulation 'does not contain even the merest reference to the second symmetrical method or, a fortiori, the slightest explanation as to why that method would not enable [the elements mentioned in the Basic Regulation] to be taken appropriately into account'.[124] The same conclusion was reached in relation to the determination of normal value, too.

The judgment in *Petrotub* is important on various grounds. First, it illustrates that the *Nakajima* principle need not be interpreted in strict terms. The Court was not confined to a textual interpretation of the relevant provision of the Basic Regulation: it did not let the absence of any reference to the duty to state reasons to prevent it from giving effect to a WTO rule. Instead, it adopted a contextual

---

[122] N120 above, para 55 of the judgment
[123] *Ibid*, para 57 with reference to Case C–341/95 *Bettati* [1998] ECR I–4355, para 20.
[124] *Ibid*, para 61 of the judgment.

approach and read that specific objective of the Anti-Dumping Code into the Basic Regulation. Secondly, in interpreting the *Nakajima* formula widely, the Court ended up interpreting Community law widely, too. Indeed, in drawing upon the duty laid down in Article 253 EC, the Court not only enhanced the effect of an EC Treaty provision but also indicated that the Community legal order may, in fact, accommodate a variety of obligations imposed upon the Community institutions. It is recalled that it was on the basis of a similar approach, albeit in an entirely different legal and political context, that the Court started developing a Community law system of protection of human rights in the 1970s: an objective which was not expressly provided for in the EC Treaty was viewed as intrinsically linked the pursuance of the objectives actually provided for in that Treaty. In *Nakajima*, the issue of applicability of WTO law and the multifarious legal problems to which it had given rise over the years was not allowed to obstruct the application of what Advocate General Alber would have called, in the light of his Opinion in *Biret*, the principle of legality.

Thirdly, the line of reasoning in *Nakajima* illustrates with stark clarity how the duty of consistent interpretation may be applied in practice in a manner which would ensure compliance with the international legal obligations assumed by the Community without undermining the latter's overall approach to the application of WTO law. Viewed from this angle, the significance of the judgment is two-fold: on the one hand, it conveys a message to national courts as to how they are expected to discharge their Community law duty to interpret legislation in the light of international legal obligations; on the other hand, it conveys a message to the Court of First Instance that the acknowledgment of the discretion enjoyed by the Community institutions in their conduct of commercial policy within the WTO framework may be reconciled with compliance with and enforcement of the rules of that framework.

Following the above positive assessment of the judgment in *Petrotub*, a note of caution is necessary. For all its promising signals, that judgment was delivered in the context of anti-dumping law in which the *Nakajima* principle was introduced and for which there has never been any doubt as to its relevance. Furthermore, the dispute before the Court was about the right to state reasons, that is a right which, linked to the principle of transparency, has enabled the Community judiciary over the years to exercise quite an intensive level of review of secondary legislation.[125] It is noteworthy that, in the area of anti-dumping, the Court recently construed the duty laid down in Article 253 EC in quite wide terms.[126] Bearing all this in mind, the next question is whether the *Nakajima* principle may be relied upon in a way which would be more responsive to the various concerns raised about the intensity of judicial supervision pursuant to international trade rules over the

---

[125] See, for instance, Case C–76/01P *Comité des industries du coton et des fibres connexes de l'Union européenne (Eurocoton) and Others v Council* [2003] ECR I–10091 at para 91 and Case T–192/98 *Eurocoton v Council*, judgment of 17 Mar 2005, not yet reported.

[126] Case C–76/01 P *Eurocoton and Others v Council* [2003] ECR I–10091.

ways in which the Community institutions, often along with national authorities, choose to carry out their commercial policy.

6.2. The Relevance of DSB Acts

At the very core of the interpretation of the *Nakajima* principle is the question of the relevance of DSB decisions asserting the illegality of Community legislation. As far as the dispute settlement system in the WTO framework is concerned, a report adopted by the Appellate Body is the final stage of the legal process provided therein: once a violation of WTO law is being affirmed, the only question which arises is that of compliance. Put in another way, an Appellate Body report is as judicial and final a pronouncement on compatibility with WTO rules as a state can possibly get under the DSU system, hence consisting of the clearest illustration of the legalisation process of the international economic order. Once the Court of Justice, after a considerable period of procrastination, ruled out the direct effect of WTO law, it was only a matter of time before it would be confronted with the question of the effects of Appellate Bodies' reports.

It did so recently in *Van Parys*.[127] Referred by the Highest Administrative Court in Belgium, this was, again, an action which arose out of the Bananas litigation. Van Parys had been importing bananas into the Community from Ecuador and applied for import licences to the Belgian Intervention and Refund Bureau. Although granted, the import licences were not for the full amounts applied for: applying a Commission Regulation which provided for reduction coefficients for applications to import bananas from, amongst others, Ecuador, the Bureau deducted certain amounts corresponding to those coefficients. Van Parys challenged the legality of two such decisions by the Bureau: it argued that they implemented Community measures on imports of bananas which were illegal under WTO law.

The overall tone of the judgment indicates a willingness to reaffirm the state of the law. The question referred by the Belgian court about the validity of Community regulations in the light of the GATT 1994 is preceded by one formulated by the Court: do the WTO agreements give Community nationals a right to rely upon them in legal proceedings challenging the validity of Community legislation where the DSB has held that both that legislation and subsequent legislation adopted by the Community in order, amongst others, to comply with the relevant WTO rules are incompatible with those rules? Having summarized its position on the review of Community law in the light of WTO rules, the Court went on to rule that 'by undertaking after the adoption of the decision of the DSB ... to comply with the WTO rules ..., the Community did not intend to assume a particular obligation in the context of the WTO, capable of justifying an exception to the

---

[127] Case C–377/02 *Léon van Parys NV v Belgisch Interventie- en Restitutiebureau (BIRB)*, judgment of 1 Mar 2005 delivered by the Grand Chamber, (not yet reported).

impossibility of relying on WTO rules before the Community Courts and enabling the Community Courts to exercise judicial review of the relevant Community provisions in the light of those rules'.[128]

This conclusion is substantiated on the basis of two interrelated reasons. The first is the considerable importance that the WTO dispute settlement system accords to negotiation between the parties. The Court repeats the, by now well-rehearsed, line of reasoning put forward in *Portuguese Textiles*. However, the judgment places more emphasis on the DSU procedures and the legal implications of their fruitless conclusion in that case. For instance, it refers specifically to the provision of Article 22(8) DSU, according to which the dispute remains on the agenda of the DSB until it is resolved, that is until the inconsistent measure has been removed or the parties reach a mutually satisfactory solution. The Court also refers to Article 21(5) DSU, according to which, in the event of a failure to agree on the compatibility of the measures taken to comply with the DSB's recommendations and decisions, the dispute should be decided through recourse to DSB procedures, which include an attempt by the parties to reach a negotiated solution.[129]

It was in the light of the above that the Court referred to the discretion enjoyed by the legislative or executive organs of the contracting parties to reach a negotiated settlement, even on a temporary basis. Then, the Court summarised how, following the amendment of the bananas regime, the Community negotiated agreements with the United States and Ecuador in order to bring Community law into conformity with WTO law and pointed out the following:[130]

> Such an outcome, by which the Community sought to reconcile its obligations under the WTO agreements with those in respect of the ACP States, and with the requirements inherent in the implementation of the common agricultural policy, could be compromised if the Community Courts were entitled to judicially review the lawfulness of the Community measures in question in light of the WTO rules upon the expiry of the time-limit ... granted by the DSB within which to implement its decision....

In its first pronouncement on a point upon which considerable academic literature has focused in order to strengthen the effects of the WTO, the Court ruled as follows:[131]

> The expiry of that time-limit does not imply that the Community had exhausted the possibilities under the understanding of finding a solution to the dispute between it and the other parties. In those circumstances, to require the Community courts, merely on the basis that that time-limit has expired, to review the lawfulness of the Community measures concerned in the light of the WTO rules, could have the effect of undermining the Community's position in its attempt to reach a mutually acceptable solution to the dispute in conformity with those rules.

---

[128] *Ibid*, para 41.
[129] *Ibid*, paras 46–47.
[130] *Ibid*, para 50.
[131] *Ibid*, para 51.

The second reason for preventing the review of legality of Community law in actions brought by individuals is the lack of reciprocity. In the paragraph concluding that part of its judgment, the Court refers, again, to the position of some of the most important commercial partners of the Community and the need to enable the Community's legislative and executive bodies to enjoy discretion in dealing with them: 'such lack of reciprocity, if admitted, would risk introducing an anomaly in the application of the WTO rules'.[132]

It is interesting that, contrary to *Portuguese Textiles*, the line of reasoning in *Van Parys* should contain no reference to Council Decision 94/800 and the intention of the Council to determine the status of WTO rules within the Community legal order. And yet, the judgment is couched in such terms as to leave no doubt: the reformulation of the question referred by the Belgian court and the emphasis on the possibilities for negotiation between WTO members even following the adoption of a DSB report clearly suggest that the logic underpinning the ruling in *Portuguese Textiles* and the subsequent line of cases is here to stay.

6.3. The Principle of Interpretation

The principle of interpretation becomes of increasing significance in EC international relations law. It was articulated by the Court in an action where the Netherlands sought the annulment of Directive 98/44 on the legal protection of biotechnological inventions.[133] Adopted under Article 95 EC, the objective of this measure was to require the Member States to protect their biotechnological inventions through their patent laws whilst complying with their international obligations. In Article 2, the Directive provided that it 'shall be without prejudice to the obligations of the Member States pursuant to international agreements and in particular the TRIPs Agreement and the Convention on Biological Diversity'. In addition to a number of other pleas, the Dutch government argued that the content of the Directive was incompatible with international obligations laid down in a number of agreements, namely TRIPs, the Agreement on Technical Barriers to Trade (TBT), the Convention on the Grant of European Patents and the Convention on Biological Diversity (CBD).

Having repeated the thrust of the judgment in *Portuguese Textiles*, the Court pointed out that 'such an exclusion cannot be applied to the CBD, which, unlike the WTO agreements, is not strictly based on reciprocal and mutually advantageous arrangements'.[134] It then went on to rule as follows:[135]

Even if, as the Council maintains, the CBD contains no provisions which do not have direct effect, in the sense that they do not create rights which individuals can rely on

---

[132] *Ibid*, para 53.
[133] Case C–377/98 *Netherlands v Parliament and Council* [2001] ECR I–7079.
[134] *Ibid*, para 53.
[135] *Ibid*, paras 54–55.

directly before the courts, that fact does not preclude review by the courts of compliance with the obligation incumbent on the Community as a party to that agreement.

Moreover, and in any event, this plea should be understood as being directed, not so much at a direct breach by the Community of its international obligations, as at an obligation imposed on the Member States by the Directive to breach their own obligations under international law, while the Directive itself claims not to affect those obligations.

All the arguments put forward by the applicant in relation to this plea were rejected. The line of reasoning followed by the Court may raise a number of questions, not least because the Court examined the pleas of the applicant in relation to the European Patent Convention, which had not been concluded by the Community.[136] However, this judgment is significant because it appears to dissociate the issue of the enforcement of international obligations from that of their direct effect. In his Opinion, Advocate General Jacobs suggested as much, albeit in a way which would limit enforcement of non-directly effective agreements to the cases covered by the *Nakajima* and *Fediol* principles.[137] A broader approach might be warranted: in addition to those principles, it is also the duty of interpretation, articulated in the *IDA* judgment, which is relevant to the enforcement of international agreements within the Community legal order and to the application of which the direct effect of those agreements is irrelevant. To that effect, it is noteworthy that the Court's statement is accompanied by a reference to *Racke,* and in particular those paragraphs which seek to justify the enforcement of customary international rules as an issue distinct from that of their direct effect.[138] Viewed from this angle, the principle of consistent interpretation may provide a technique sufficiently broad to mitigate against the confining implications of the special nature of WTO rules.

7. THE ISSUE OF THE COMMUNITY'S LIABILITY

In accordance with Article 288 (2) EC, '[i]n the case of non-contractual liability, the Community shall, in accordance with the general principles common to the laws of the Member States, make good any damage caused by its institutions or by its servants in the performance of their duties'. This provision has been consistently interpreted to apply when three conditions are met, namely the existence of an unlawful measure adopted by the Community institutions, actual damage and a causal link between them.[139]

---

[136] See Eeckhout, n5 above, at 251–2.

[137] See n133 above, para 146; however, he also added that 'more generally, it might be thought that it is in any event desirable as a matter of policy for the Court to be able to review the legality of Community legislation in the light of treaties binding the Community. There is no other court which is in a position to review Community legislation; thus if this Court is denied competence, Member States may be subject to conflicting obligations with no means of resolving them' (para 147).

[138] Case C–162/96 *Racke* [1998] ECR I–3655, paras 45, 47, 51.

[139] See, for instance, Joined Cases 256/80, 257/80, 265/80, 267/80 and 5/81 *Birra Wührer SpA and others v Council and Commission* [1982] ECR 85 at para 9, Case C–87/89 *Sonito and Others v Commission*

These conditions were then refined in relation to the exercise of legislative function by the Community: the rule of law infringed must be intended to confer rights on individuals; the breach must be sufficiently serious; and there must be a direct causal link between the breach of the obligation resting on the author of the act and the damage sustained by the injured parties.[140] In order to ascertain whether the breach in question is sufficiently serious, the decisive test is whether the Community institution concerned has manifestly and gravely disregarded the limits on its discretion; where the institution in question has only a considerably reduced or even no discretion, the mere infringement of Community law may be sufficient to establish the existence of a sufficiently serious breach.[141]

The question whether the Community could be liable for breach of GATT/WTO rules first arose at the aftermath of the Bananas litigation.[142] Atlanta, a company established in Germany, was an importer of bananas which had challenged the legality of Regulation 404/93 before the Court of First Instance and had also sought damages under Article 288 EC.[143] Of the various pleas put before the CFI, the one relevant to this analysis was that relating to the GATT rules. The CFI relied upon the judgment of the Court of Justice in *Germany v Council*[144] and concluded that no illegality sufficient to establish non-contractual liability on the Community could be found. In challenging that conclusion before the Court of Justice, Atlanta relied first and foremost upon a decision adopted by the DSB after the CFI had delivered the contested judgment. It argued that that decision left no doubt about the inconsistency of Regulation 404/93 with WTO law and, hence, its illegality. This argument was rejected by the Court, albeit on procedural grounds. In particular, it had not been raised by the appellant because the DSB decision had been published six months after it had lodged its appeal. The Court viewed this decision as in 'an inescapable and direct link'[145] with the plea of breach of the GATT, one which, whilst rejected by the CFI, had not been repeated by Atlanta on appeal. Therefore, the argument based on the DSB decision was dismissed as inadmissible because 'to admit the plea based on the WTO decision would be tantamount to allowing the appellant to challenge for the first time at the stage of the reply the dismissal by the Court of First Instance of a plea it had raised before that court, whereas nothing prevented it from submitting such a plea at the time of its application to the Court of Justice'.[146]

[1990] ECR I–1981 at para 16, Joined Cases C–258/90 and C–259/90 *Pesquerias de Bermeo and Naviera Laida v Commission* [1992] ECR I–2901 at para 42 and Case C–295/03 P *Allesandrini Srl and Others v Commission*, judgment of 30 June 2005, not yet reported, at para 61.

[140] See Case C–352/98 P *Bergaderm and Goupil v Commission* [2000] ECR I–5291 at paras 41 and 42.

[141] *Ibid*, at para 44 and Case C–312/00 P *Commission v Camar and Others* [2002] ECR I–11355 at para 54.

[142] C–104/97 P *Atlanta AG v EC* [1999] ECR I–6983.

[143] Case T–521/93 [1996] ECR II–1707.

[144] See n8 above.

[145] N142 above, para 19 of the judgment.

[146] *Ibid*, para 22 of the judgment.

It is noteworthy that the Court did not refer to any link between the lack of direct effect of the GATT rules and the status of the DSB decision. Even the statement about the 'inescapable and direct link' was referred to only in procedural terms and confined to the conclusion that reliance upon the DSB decision could only be examined as part of a plea of illegality in the light of the GATT. In doing so, it did not follow the Opinion of Advocate General Mischo who, having argued for the inadmissibility of the appellant's argument, went on to conclude that 'the rights which a decision of the Appellate Body would intend to confer on individuals have nowhere near the scope which the appellant seeks to give them';[147] in other words, it does not constitute a rule intending to confer rights on individuals and, therefore, is unable to establish non-contractual liability of the Community.[148]

In a number of subsequent judgments, the Court of First Instance relied upon the Court of Justice's settled case law on the lack of direct effect of WTO rules in order to conclude that the Community cannot incur non-contractual liability as a result of infringement of those rules.[149] In these cases, the alleged unlawful conduct by the Commission had occurred following the adoption of the Appellate Body's report by the Dispute Settlement Body declaring the inconsistency between the Bananas legislation and the WTO rules; the applicants alleged that the legislation subsequently adopted by the Community was contrary to the WTO rules in general and the commitment undertaken by the Community to remedy the illegality concluded by the DSB. Their arguments were rejected rather swiftly by the Court of First Instance which did not see fit to engage in a discussion of whether a decision by the DSB might be relevant to the effects of the relevant WTO rules but in relation to the *Nakajima* doctrine.

This issue again reached the Court of Justice on appeal in *Biret*.[150] The question was whether the Community was liable in damages for a violation of the Agreement on the Application of Sanitary and Phytosanitary Measures following the expiry of the deadline for compliance set by the Dispute Appellate Body.[151] The Community had expressed its intention to comply with the DSB decision, albeit within a reasonable period of time. That was determined by the DSB to be 15 months. The Court of First Instance had pointed out that there was an 'inescapable and direct link between the decision and the plea alleging infringement of the SPS Agreement' and concluded that the former could only be taken

---

[147] *Ibid*, para 30 of his Opinion.

[148] Mischo AG went on to argue that 'unlike . . . a judgment in infringement proceedings, such a decision entails only an obligation to remedy the unlawful conduct in the future, accompanied by a number of conditions' (*ibid*, para 31).

[149] See Case T–18/99, n117 above at paras 44–60, Case T–30/99, n117 above, at paras 49–65, Case T–52/99, n117 above, at paras 44–60 and Case T–3/99, n35 above, at paras 43–45.

[150] Case C–93/02 P *Biret International SA v Council* and C–94/02 P *Etablissements Biret et Cie SA v Council* [2003] ECR I–10497; the CFI judgments were Cases T–174/00 *Biret International SA v Council* [2002] ECR II–17 and T–210/00 [2002] ECR II–47.

[151] For the application of Art 288 EC in such circumstances, see G Zonnekeyn, 'EC Liability for Non-implementation of Adopted WTO Panels and Appellate Body Reports—The Example of the 'Innocent

into account if the latter were directly effective. In doing so, the CFI relied upon the judgment in *Atlanta* from which it quoted the above phrase directly. On appeal, the Court of Justice concluded that, on the facts of the case, the Community could not possibly have been liable for the period alleged by *Biret*: when the period of time granted by the DSB as to enable the Community to comply with its decision expired, the appellant had been declared bankrupt by the national judicial authorities and payments had ceased.

However, the *Biret* judgment is most interesting for the comments the Court made about the CFI judgment. In particular, it also pointed out that the contested judgment contained two errors of law. The first one consisted of the failure of the Court of First Instance to comply with its duty to state reasons, for its line of reasoning was not sufficient to address Biret's argument regarding the violation of the SPS Agreement. In particular, the question which ought to have been addressed was whether the DSB decision was relevant to the conclusion already reached by the Court of Justice regarding the lack of direct effect of WTO rules. The second error consisted of misinterpreting the scope of the ruling of the Court of Justice in *Atlanta*.[152] According to the Court, the latter judgment was irrelevant to the case before it because it was confined to the facts of the case: whilst the decision of the Dispute Settlement Body was inescapably and directly linked to the issue of inconsistency with WTO rules, that plea had not been repeated on appeal. It was for this reason that the argument had been rejected as inadmissible.

The judgment in *Biret* has revived the academic debate about the effects of WTO rules within the Community legal order.[153] This is so not only because of the various ways in which it may be interpreted but also because of the rather severe criticism of the contested ruling. The CFI is criticised for not addressing a legal question which the Court itself chose not to address, albeit by reference to the facts of the case. This approach is similar to that adopted some years ago towards the general issue of the effect of WTO rules within the Community legal order; it is recalled that the Court addressed this issue in the *Portuguese Textiles* case, having avoided tackling it in a number of previous cases and contrary to the elaborate analyses of its Advocates General. Does the judgment in *Biret* constitute yet another step to a similar conclusion in relation to the effects of decisions adopted by the Dispute Settlement Body? In criticising the Court of First Instance, the Court of Justice makes it clear that its only prior statement on this issue, that is the one in *Atlanta* ruling out direct effect for such decisions too, was confined to the facts of that case. There is no doubt that, in referring to *Atlanta* and in repeating the wording of that judgment, the Court of First Instance had substituted a substantive argument for a procedural one. Furthermore, in both cases where

---

Exporters' in the Banana Case' in V Kronenberger (ed), *The European Union and the International Legal Order: Discord or Harmony?* (The Hague: TMC Asser Press, 2001) 251.

[152] Case C–104/97 P *Atlanta v European Community* [1999] ECR 1–6983.

[153] See for instance G Zonnekeyn, 'EC Liability for Non-implementation of WTO Dispute Settlement Decisions—Are the Dice Cast?' (2004) 7 *JIEL* 483 and J Wiers, 'One Day, You're Gonna Pay: The European Court of Justice in Biret' (2004) 31 *LIEI* 143.

the Court of Justice had declined to assess the effect of DSB decisions, it did so on either procedural or factual grounds. Would the force with which the judgment in *Biret* is expressed suggest that it is only a matter of time before the denial of direct effect of WTO rules was confined to cases where there was no decision adopted by the Dispute Settlement Body and where, whilst there was such a decision, the period of time granted to the Community to remedy the violation of WTO rules had not expired?

Advocate General Alber suggests an affirmative answer. In his detailed Opinion in *Biret* in which he concluded that the contested decision should be set aside and the case be sent back to the Court of First Instance, his line of reasoning is worth examining in some detail. First, he made it clear that the declaration of the Community, made by the Commission, that it intended to remedy the inconsistency of its legislation with WTO rules in accordance with the DSB decision was of no legal consequence within the Community legal order, and hence devoid of any substance which could be enforceable before the Community's judicature. Secondly, having examined the dispute settlement procedure set out in the DSU, Advocate General Alber concluded that, following the adoption of a decision by the DSB, WTO members were not given the option of not complying with its findings; in particular, neither the possibility of compensation nor that of retaliation was a permanent legal alternative, the former being temporary and the latter being subject to authorisation by the DSB. Thirdly, the absence of legal means of ensuring compliance with the DSB decisions does not negate their legal nature, all the more so as even in the Community legal order legal sanctions for non-compliance were only introduced under the Maastricht Treaty. Fourthly, the discretion granted upon the Community institutions in their conduct of trade policy under the WTO framework is not undermined by the right of individuals to rely upon WTO rules in an action arguing Community liability: this is so because the right to reparation under Article 288 EC would not interfere with the right of the Community institutions to determine the substance of their policy choice in their response to the DSB decision. Fifthly, the principle of reciprocity may not conceivably affect the recognition of the right of individuals to seek damages in a case of non-compliance with a DSB decision: on the one hand, the preamble to Decision 90/800 concluding the WTO Agreements may not bind the Court of Justice as a matter of Community law and, on the other hand, the negotiating position of the Community could only be affected in a case where it would be in agreement with another WTO member to retain legislation contrary to WTO law, a scenario not relevant to the case under dispute. Sixthly, the right of individuals to seek damages for a violation of WTO rules was similar to their equivalent right, already recognised by the Court of Justice, to seek damages for breach of an EC Treaty provision or a directive by a Member State before a national court. Seventhly, the right of individuals to carry out economic activities also supports their right to seek damages: otherwise, the statements by the Commission and the Council that they would remedy the illegality with WTO law would be inconsistent with their actual conduct. Finally, as the DSU aims at prompt compliance with the recommendations or rulings of DSB, it is sufficiently clear and unconditional within the meaning of the case law of the Court of Justice on direct effect.

At the very core of the analysis of Advocate General Alber in *Biret*, which was fully supported by Advocate General Tizzano in *Van Parys*, is what he calls 'the principle of legality': he relies upon the international law nature of the WTO rules whilst seeking to demonstrate how the arguments underlying the Court's conclusion in *Portuguese Textiles* would not be relevant once the deadline for compliance with a DSB decision had expired. However, whilst being put forward with conviction, his analysis is not without problems, of which the following are worth mentioning. First, there is reference, more than once, to the right of individuals to carry out commercial activities as a general principle of Community law which should inform the application of WTO rules within the Community legal order. In dealing with this point, the analysis of the learned Advocate General is regrettably short in detailed substantiation. Whilst such a right, and its multifarious implications, has been heralded enthusiastically by Petersmann,[154] it is supported by neither Community law nor its interpretation by the Court of Justice;[155] to rely upon it in order to introduce the direct effect of the WTO following a DSB decision would be tantamount to asking the Court to engage in a significant constitutional leap. The problematic nature of this point becomes all the more apparent in the light of the inconsistency between the approach of Advocate General Alber to the right to carry out commercial activities, however vaguely expressed in his Opinion, and the line of reasoning underpinning the Court's case law following the *Portuguese Textiles* case. Irrespective of whether the latter may be criticised on legal, political or practical grounds, it is characterised by its internal logic: it is the discretion allowed to the Community institutions in the light of the specific features of the WTO framework that has guided the Court's approach, and it is that element that has underlain the alternative routes to which the Court has had recourse in order to ensure alternative effects, albeit in clearly specified circumstances, of WTO rules within the Community legal order.

Secondly, in his Opinion, Advocate General Alber also seeks to justify the principle of Community liability for a breach of WTO rules by relying upon the rationale underpinning the introduction of the principle of state liability for a breach of Community law.[156] This is a curious parallel to draw, for the differences between the Community legal order and the WTO system are too numerous and obvious to analyse. Suffice it to point out that there is no legal basis which would assimilate the issue in *Biret* to a specific aspect of the constitutional approach adopted by the Court in order to ensure compliance by Member States with the new legal order of international law they established.

---

[154] See, for instance, his essay, 'National Constitutions and International Economic Law' in M Hilf and E-U Petersmann (eds), *National Constitutions and International Economic Law* (Deventer: Kluwer, 1993) 3.

[155] See the critique in S Peers, 'Fundamental Right or Political Whim? WTO Law and The European Court of Justice' in de Búrca and Scott (eds), n79 above, 111.

[156] See Part VII.B.1(iv) of his Opinion.

Thirdly, Advocate General Alber appears to view the direct effect of WTO rules as a precondition for recognising the non-contractual liability of the Community. It is not apparent why this should be the case.[157] Finally, in concluding on the direct effect of WTO rules following the expiry of a deadline within which the Community had stated it would comply with a DSB decision, Advocate General Alber argues that the WTO rules are directly effective.[158] This statement is staggering in its generality: it appears to refer to no WTO provision in particular and, consequently, it is supported by no textual and contextual analysis. Even on the assumption that the completion of the dispute settlement procedure might render a WTO rule directly effective, it remained to be seen whether the specific provisions at the centre of the dispute fulfilled the direct effect conditions.

And yet, for all the above criticism, there is something attractive about the analysis of Advocate General Alber in *Biret*: is it not proper for the Community to adhere to the application of an international set of rules which forms an integral part of its legal order? And is the expiry of the deadline within which the Community institutions had stated their intention to comply with a DSB decision not the right moment for that principle to be applied? After all, a decision by the DSB body may be seen as illustrating the legal dimension *par excellence* of the tighter regime set out by the WTO Agreements.

There are a number of problems with this view. First, if a decision adopted by the DSB were to be endowed with direct effect, or if such a decision, once the period for compliance had expired, were to endow a WTO rule with direct effect, the line of reasoning underpinning the judgment in the *Portuguese Textiles* case and the subsequent case law would be deprived of its internal coherence. It is recalled that, whilst recognising the tighter legal character of the WTO framework, the Court had relied upon the nature and structure of that Agreement and its implications for the discretion enjoyed by the Community institutions in order to deny its rules direct effect. This inherent feature of the WTO set of rules also applies to the decisions adopted by the DSB pursuant to the DSU; equally, the adoption of the latter acts may not alter the fundamental nature of the WTO rules. For the Court to adopt such a position simply because an act at the more legal end of the spectrum covering the WTO framework has been adopted would be tantamount to undermining the logic of its overall approach to the effects of WTO rules. Viewed from this angle, the analysis of that approach set out in this chapter is still valid: whilst potentially open to criticism in the light of legal, political and constitutional arguments, the presence of a DSB decision is not one of them.

Secondly, it is true that, if the Court were to qualify its approach to the effect of the WTO rules in the light of a DSB decision, it would contribute to the strengthening of the legal character of the WTO framework and the effective enforcement of its rules. However, commendable though it may appear to some quarters, this is

---

[157] See G Zonnekeyn, 'EC Liability for the Non-Implementation of WTO Dispute Settlement Decisions' (2003) 6 JIEL 761, 764–5.
[158] See Part VII.B.1(vi).

a task beyond those assumed by the Court within the context of the Community legal order. The hardening of that framework—or its constitutionalisation, as its more ambitious advocates would prefer it—is a process which involves its members. For the Court to contribute actively would be tantamount to assuming the role of an international court, which would have serious repercussions on two fronts. On the one hand, it would challenge the Court's relationship with the national legislative and executive authorities. This is al the more so in the light of the mixed character of the WTO Agreements except for the GATT: as the Court has been distinctly reluctant to distinguish clearly between the areas of agreements falling within national competence and those falling within Community competence, to become actively engaged in strengthening the legal nature of the WTO rules would be tantamount to assuming an executive function in international areas of activity which it has treated as within a twilight zone between Community and national competence. On the other hand, to grant direct effect to DSB decisions would have serious implications for the balance of power within the WTO framework itself. The robust approach of the Community's judiciary would influence the approach of other WTO members in future negotiating rounds.

8. CONCLUSION

The picture of the application of WTO law within the Community legal order emerging from the above analysis so far is rather fragmented: because of the particular nature and structure of the WTO Agreements, neither individuals (*Parfums Dior*) nor Member States (*Portuguese Textiles*) may invoke them in order to challenge the legality of EC secondary legislation; this is not the case where the legality of an EC measure is challenged in the light of a WTO rule which that measure was intended to implement (*Nakajima*) or to which that measure makes express reference (*Fediol*); this remains the case even where the DSB has held that Community law and subsequent measures adopted by the Community in order, amongst others, to comply with the relevant rules are incompatible with those rules (*Van Parys*). An issue which appears outstanding is whether the Community may incur non-contractual liability in cases where an inconsistency between an EC measure and a WTO rule has been declared by a DSB decision and the period of time set for compliance has expired despite the express assurance by the Commission that the inconsistency would be remedied: this appears to be unclear because the right question has yet to be presented before the Court of Justice under the right circumstances (*Atlanta, Biret*). This fragmented picture has been heavily criticised for failing individuals[159] and for rendering the exercise of commercial policy by the Community institutions beyond the reach of effective judicial supervision.[160]

[159] See the critiques by Petersmann in n13 above.
[160] See N van den Broek, 'Legal Persuasion, Political Realism and Legitimacy: The European Court's Recent Treatment of the Effects of WTO Agreements in the EC Legal Order' (2001) 4 *JIEL* 411.

However, this analysis has shown that the acknowledgment of the central role of the political institutions has not brought the enforcement of WTO rules to a halt. The multi-layered system articulated gradually by the Community judicature has been developed incrementally in various directions and has not reached its limits yet. This section will focus on three such aspects.

First, in relation to the implementation principle, there is some scope for further development. Indeed, the judgment in *Petrotub* does indicate that the Court is not oblivious to the circumstances in which EC secondary legislation is adopted. An advantage of this construction of the *Nakajima* principle is its consistency with the line of reasoning underpinning the Court's approach to the effects of the WTO rules following the judgment in *Portuguese Textiles*. It is recalled that the scope of manoeuvre deemed to have been granted to the Community institutions in the WTO framework was central to the Court's reasoning. It is also recalled that at the very core of the *Nakajima* principle was the position that it constituted a means of assessing the legality of EC legislation in the light of WTO rules in an incidental manner and in clearly defined circumstances—it did not amount to recognising those rules as directly effective. The same *rationale* would apply to a broader construction of the *Nakajima* principle: relevant to the issue of legality of EC law rather than that of applicability of WTO law, it would only apply when the Community's expressed and clear policy choice defines the adoption of secondary legislation.

However, if the ruling in *Petrotub* indicates the potential of the implementation principle, that in *Van Parys* highlights its outer limits: it may not be construed broadly enough to undermine the logic of the approach first articulated in *Portuguese Textiles*; too broad a reading of the *Nakajima* principle would undermine the scope of manoeuvre deemed by the Court to have been granted to Community institutions pursuant to WTO rules. In this respect, the facts of the *Biret* case are noteworthy: the Commission expressed its intention to remedy the incompatibility of Directive 96/22 with the Agreement on the Application of Sanitary and Phytosanitary Measures, hence complying with the DSB decision; during the period granted by the DSB and in the process of decision-making, the Community institutions decided that, whilst introducing legislation amending Directive 96/22, the prohibition on the use of a particular substance should be maintained as a permanent measure. In the light of these circumstances, it would be unreasonable to construe the amending legislation as intending to implement the DSB decision in so far as the maintenance of the above prohibition is concerned. It is precisely this type of discretion the Court deemed worthy of protection in *Portuguese Textiles*; to subsume it within a broadly construed 'implementation exception' would be tantamount to undermining the main tenet of the Court's approach to the effects of WTO rules.

The second aspect of the Court's approach is the principle of consistent interpretation. It is recalled that it was that principle that enabled the Court to construe the implementation principle in *Petrotub*. The significance of this principle is considerable not only because it provides alternative ways of monitoring compliance with international obligations undertaken under WTO law, but also because it would enable national courts to participate in this process. Indeed, in proceedings before national courts, it is for them to apply the duty of consistent interpretation under the supervision of the Court of Justice through the preliminary reference procedure. It is recalled that, in relation to TRIPs, national courts were deemed free to decide whether its provision on temporary measures granted rights to individuals in areas where the Community institutions had not legislated.[161] All in all, in decentralising the management of compliance with WTO rules, the Court gradually constitutionalises the system of EC international relations even in an area where the one of the core tenets of the constitutiolisation process of EC law, that is direct effect, is deemed not applicable.

Thirdly, another potential technique for mitigating the effects of the *Portuguese Textiles* line of reasoning may be centred around the issue of non-contractual liability of the Community. As illustrated in the above analysis, the Community judiciary has rejected the existence of such liability on the basis that the WTO rules were not intended to confer rights upon individuals and, therefore, their violation could not imply liability, an approach criticised,[162] not least for rendering direct effect a precondition for the existence of Community liability.[163] However, the Court has been clear on this point, as it viewed its 'finding that the WTO rules did not have direct effect' as 'central to the arguments relating to the scope of Article 228(7) of the Treaty'.[164]

However, what is worth examining is whether the Community may possibly incur liability for a valid act in a case of non-compliance with WTO law. This question was recently raised before the Court of First Instance by a number of importers of bananas.[165] Whilst by no means a remedy frequently relied upon, it was not the first time that the Community judicature had to address the issues of the existence, scope and conditions of non-contractual liability for a lawful act.[166] In *Dorsch Consult*, the Court of Justice held that 'in the event of the principle of Community liability for a lawful act being recognised in Community law, a precondition for such liability would in any event be the existence of "unusual" and "special" damage'.[167] In addition to these conditions, the damage should be real and a causal link should be established between the act on the part of the Community and the damage. Whilst expressed in rather qualified terms, this

---

[161] See *Dior*, n72 above, at para 48

[162] See I Schoisswohl, 'The ECJ's Atlanta Judgment: Establishing a Principle of Non-Liability?' in F Breuss, S Griller and E Vranes (eds), *The Banana Dispute—An Economic and Legal Analysis* (Vienna/New York: Springer, 2003) 309.

[163] See Zonnekeyn, n157 above at 764–65.

[164] N150 above, paras 57–8.

[165] Joined Cases T–64/01 and T–65/01 *Afrikanische Frucht-Compagnie GmbH and Internationale Fruchtimport Gesellschaft Weichert & Co v Council and Commission*, [2004] ECR II–521 paras 150–155.

[166] See Joined Cases 9/71 and 11/71 *Compagnie d'Approvisionnement v Commission* [1972] ECR 391, paras 45–6.

[167] Case C–237/98 P *Dorsch Consult Ingenieurgesellschaft mbH v Council and Commission* [2000] ECR I–4549, para 18.

statement appears to accept the possibility of non-contractual liability for a valid act.[168]

However, the conditions attached to it are very restrictive: damage is deemed 'unusual' if it exceeds the limits of the economic risks inherent in the activities of the traders sustaining it;[169] furthermore, in order to be considered 'special', it must affect a category of economic operators in a manner which distinguishes them from all other economic operators.[170] In the sparse case law in which this cause of action has been raised, the requirement that the damage be unusual and special has never been deemed to have been met.[171] This is hardly surprising: the requirement of the 'special' nature of the damage, for instance, is not dissimilar to that of individual concern which needs to be met for a private applicant to be able to challenge a Community decision addressed to a third party, that is one of the most notoriously difficult requirements to be met pursuant to the Court's case law.[172] Indeed, the language of the Court of First Instance in the recent *Afrikanische Frucht-Compagnie* judgment is reminiscent of that of the construction of the locus standi requirements: 'the reference quantity of each of the applicants for 1999 was determined on the basis of objective criteria contained in Regulation No 2362/98 and applicable without distinction to all economic operators in the same situation as the applicants. In particular, the applicants are concerned by the provisions of that regulation which they criticise in the same manner as any other traditional operator who supplied bananas to the new Member States in [the period under discussion]. There can thus be no question of a particular sacrifice made by them alone'.[173]

This extract illustrates the slim chances of success of any action for damages against the Community of a lawful act. The clarity of this is highlighted in a judgment of the Court of First Instance which arose within the context of the Convention on Future Multilateral Cooperation in the North-West Atlantic Fisheries.[174] As a result of a dispute between the Community and Canada and its management within the institutional structure of the Convention, the Community quota for fishing Greenland halibut for 1995, divided pursuant to Council regulations, was significantly reduced. These measures were attacked by a group of owners of refrigerating trawlers who sought damages. In examining the nature of the damage alleged by them, the Court of First Instance pointed out

---

[168] See HJ Bronkhorst, 'The Valid Legislative Act as a Cause of Liability of the Communities' in T Heukels and A McDonnell (eds), *The Action for Damages in' Community Law* (The Hague: Kluwer, 1997) 153.

[169] Case 59/83 *Biovilac v EEC* [1984] ECR 4057, para 29.

[170] See Case 81/86 *De Boer Buizen v Council and Commission* [1987] ECR 3677 as reiterated in Case T–184/95 *Dorsch Consult Ingenieurgesellschaft mbH v Council and Commission* [1998] ECR II–667 at para 80.

[171] See the strict construction of 'special' and 'unusual' damage in Case T–196/99 *Area Cova and Others v Council and Commission* [2001] ECR II–3597 at paras 174 ff.

[172] See generally AM Arnull, 'Private Applicants and the Action for Annulment since *Codorniu*' (2001) 38 *CMLRev* 7.

[173] Joined Cases T–64/01 and T–65/01, n165 above, para 153.

[174] Case T–196/99 *Area Cava*, n 171 above.

that 'it rested on the premise that they enjoyed a right to exploit the shoal of Greenland halibut' and stated: 'the applicants cannot claim such a right, whether it is alleged as a traditional fishing right, as a right deriving from the principle of relative stability, or as an acquired right. It should be noted in that respect that economic operators cannot rely on an acquired right to the maintenance of an advantage arising from Community legislation, *especially legislation worked out in the context of an international organisation in which the Community partici-pates*'.[175] Be that as it may, the possibility of non-contractual liability for lawful conduct remains open.[176]

Drawing upon the analysis so far, this conclusion has sought to further illustrate the various ways in which WTO rules may penetrate the Community legal order and affect legal disputes. In the light of the various limitations underpinning their conception and the conditions attached to their application, each one of them is far from unproblematic. However, their effectiveness in specific cases notwithstanding, it is their cumulative effects within the overall system of the Community legal order which is of paramount significance. It is recalled that, in articulating the principle of implied competence in *AETR* in the early 1970s, the Court referred to the *system* of the Community's external relations. The effectiveness of such a system should take into account the various ways in which its rules, principles, procedures, actors and practice interact. The sanctioning of the coexistence of Member States with the Community, the wide construction of the jurisdiction of the Court of Justice, the emerging role of national courts, the differentiated construction of direct effect, the development of indirect methods of applying international rules, all are central to the application of WTO law. Their interaction should not be forgotten when assessing its effectiveness within the Community legal order. Furthermore, as the system of EC external relations is still emerging in its multifaceted dimensions, the construction of the effects of WTO rules under Community law is also in flux.

---

[175] *Ibid*, para 177 (emphasis added).
[176] See A von Bogdandy, 'Legal Effects of World Trade Organization Decisions Within European Union Law: A Contribution to the Theory of the Legal Acts of International Organizations and the Action for Damages Under Article 288(2) EC' (2005) 39 *JWT* 45 at 64–66 where he refers to this possibility as a '"soft" solution' (at 65)

8

International Agreements Concluded by Member States Prior to their Membership of The European Union

1. INTRODUCTION

THE ANALYSIS SO far has focused on the various ways in which the progressive development of the Community as an international actor has interacted with the rights and duties of the Member States as sovereign subjects of international law. The specific case of international agreements concluded by states prior to their membership of the Union raises different, albeit no less interesting, questions.

The starting point is Article 307 EC, the first paragraph of which reads as follows:

> The rights and obligations arising from agreements concluded before 1 January 1958 or, for acceding States, before the date of their accession, between one or more Member States on the one hand, and one or more third countries on the other, shall not be affected by the provisions of this Treaty.

The above provision acknowledges that the establishment of the Community legal order should not be taken to undermine international law, a main tenet of which is the *pacta sunt servanda* principle as enshrined in Article 26 of the 1969 Vienna Convention on the Law of Treaties.[1] Article 30(4)(b) of the Vienna Convention further makes it clear that, in a case of successive treaties where the parties to the later one do not include all the parties to the earlier one, 'as between a State party to both Treaties and a State party to only one of the treaties, the treaty to which both States are parties governs their mutual rights and obligations'. Therefore, Article 307 EC appears to state the obvious:[2] instead of introducing an exception to the principle of supremacy of Community law, Article 307 EC acknowledges that the establishment of the Community legal order cannot possibly run counter to one of the foundation of public international law. As Advocate General Mischo pointed out, 'no-one has yet seriously defended the idea that, by creating

---

[1] UKTS No. 58 (1980), Cmnd 7964.
[2] A Aust, *Modern Treaty Law and Practice* (Cambridge: Cambridge University Press, 2000) 177.

a regional international organisation—and that is what the European Union certainly is under international law—States could, without recourse to any other procedure, release themselves from the obligation to fulfil earlier commitments to non-member countries'.[3] Be that as it may, the proviso of Article 307 EC is of paramount significance in the light of the normative qualities underlying the Community framework in its conception as 'a new legal order of international law'[4] whose foundation is viewed as 'an independent source of law'.[5]

2. THE INTERPRETATION OF ARTICLE 307 EC

International agreements concluded between Member States prior to their accession to the Community are clearly not within the scope of Article 307 EC in so far the EC Treaty applies automatically to all matters falling within the competence of the Community and supersedes earlier agreements between Member States to the extent of any incompatibility.[6] The material scope of Article 307 EC is unlimited in principle as it covers all types of international agreements, irrespective of their subject-matter, which may be capable of affecting the application of EC Treaty.[7] However, the existence of such an agreement is not sufficient in itself to justify a deviation from Community law. The ratio of Article 307(1) EC aims at ensuring that pre-existing international obligations of Member States are complied with and the corresponding rights of the third contracting parties are respected. In *Henn and Darby*, the House of Lords referred a number of questions relating to the prohibition on imports of pornographic material on grounds of public morality.[8] One of the questions referred was about the Geneva Convention of 1923 for the Suppression of Traffic in Obscene Publications and the Universal Postal Convention which had been renewed in 1974: could they justify the national deviation from the principle of free movement of goods? Whilst a violation of that principle, the Court found the national restriction justified on the basis of Article 30 EC. Therefore, it concluded that Article 307 EC did not preclude the national authorities from fulfilling their obligations under pre-existing treaties.

The sole focus of Article 307 EC is the obligation imposed upon a Member State by a pre-existing agreement. Therefore, it does not enable Member States to exercise rights conferred upon them by such agreements in violation of EC law.[9]

---

[3] Joined Cases C–62/98 and C–84/98 *Commission v Portugal* [2000] ECR I–5171, para 57.

[4] Case 26/62 *van Gend en Loos* [1963] ECR 1 at 12.

[5] Case 6/64 *Flaminio Costa v ENEL* [1964] ECR 585 at 593.

[6] Case 10/61 *Commission v Italy* [1962] ECR 1. For subsequent agreements between Member States, see B de Wittte, 'Old-fashioned Flexibility: International Agreements between Member States of the European Union' in G de Búrca and J Scott (eds), *Constitutional Change in the EU—From Uniformity to Flexibility?* (Oxford: Hart Publishing, 2000) 31.

[7] Case 812/79 *Attorney General v Juan C Burgoa* [1980] ECR 2787, para 6.

[8] Case 34/79 *R v Maurice Donald Henn and John Frederick Ernest Darby* [1979] ECR 3795.

[9] Case C–158/91 *Ministère public and Direction du travail et de l'emploi v Levy* [1993] ECR I-4287 at para 12, Case C–124/95 *The Queen, ex parte Centro-Com v HM Treasury and Bank of England* [1997] ECR I-81 at para 60, Case C–473/93 *Commission v Luxembourg* [1996] ECR I-3207, para 40 and Case C–147/03 *Commission v Austria*, judgment of 7 July 2005, not yet reported, at para 73.

Equally, Article 307 EC may not be invoked in relation to obligations based on pre-existing agreements if these obligations may not be invoked by a third party in a particular case. Therefore, the rules in the GATT, whilst binding on the Member States since 1947, could not be invoked by them in order to justify imports of bananas from Ecuador in 1995: this was because the latter became a member of the WTO, and hence a party to the GATT, only in 1996.[10]

Having acknowledged the binding nature of pre-existing contractual arrangements of Member States, Article 307 EC seeks to address ways in which any ensuing incompatibilities between such arrangements and EC law may be resolved. Its second paragraph reads as follows:

> To the extent that such agreements are not compatible with this Treaty, the Member State or States concerned shall take all appropriate steps to eliminate the incompatibilities established. Member States shall, where necessary, assist each other to this end and shall, where appropriate, adopt a common attitude.

There is no reference in the EC Treaty to the period of time within which the incompatibilities between pre-existing international duties of Member States and EC law may be addressed. However, such provision may be made in secondary legislation. This is illustrated by Regulation 4055/86 on maritime transport.[11] This measure gives shipping lines rights relating to the provision of maritime services between Member States and between Member States and third countries. Explicit reference is made to cargo arrangements contained in pre-existing bilateral agreements concluded by Member States with third countries: under Article 3, they should be phased out or adjusted, the latter option being carried out in accordance with Community law. Regulation 4055/86 makes a distinction on the basis of the United Nations Code of Conduct for Liner Conferences: trades not governed by it should be adjusted as soon as possible and in any event before 1 January 1993. As for trades governed by the Code, no deadline is set and Member States are required to comply with their obligations under EC rules implementing that Code.

In a case regarding compliance with Regulation 4055/86, the Court held that, in the absence of a specific period within which adjustment of a pre-existing bilateral treaty may be made in order to ensure compliance with EC law, such adjustment should be carried out immediately after the entry into force of the relevant EC rule.[12] However, this should not be taken to imply that, in general, the absence of a reference to a period for adjustment should impose an absolute legal obligation on Member States to adjust their pre-existing international duties with

---

[10] Joined Cases C–364/95 and C–365/95 *T. Port GmbH & Co. v Hauptzollamt Hamburg-Jonas* [1998] ECR I–1023 paras 60–64.

[11] [1986] OJ L 378/1.

[12] Case C–170/98 *Commission v Belgium (re: maritime transport agreement with Zaire)* [1999] ECR I–5493 at para 40. See also the judgment delivered on the same day in Joined Cases C–171/98, C–201/98 and C–202/98 *Commission v Belgium and Luxembourg (re: maritime transport agreements between the Belgo-Luxembourg Economic Union with Togo, Mali, Senegal and Cote d'Ivoire)* [1999] ECR I–5517.

immediate effect. That would not only be too harsh an obligation but would also ignore the practical realities of international relations; most importantly, it would run counter to the ratio of the first paragraph of Article 307 EC by providing for a disproportionately inflexible way of striking the balance between the international law duties of Member States and those based on Community law. Instead, the conclusion of the Court in Case C–170/98 *Commission v Belgium* is confined to the specific legal framework and justified in the light of the express distinction made in Regulation 4055/86.

2.1. 'All Appropriate Steps': Renegotiation, Adjustment, Denunciation

Article 307(2) EC refers to 'all appropriate measures' that Member States bound by a pre-existing agreement with a third country 'shall' take in order to eliminate incompatibilities with Community law. This is a Community law duty imposed on Member States, and it requires Member States to find a way of accommodating their international law obligations within the Community legal order.

The wording of this provision is reminiscent of the general duty of cooperation enshrined in Article 10 EC. Indeed, Article 307(2) EC may be viewed as a specific illustration of that duty. It is recalled that Article 10 EC has enabled the Court to articulate the practical implications of the principles of supremacy and direct effect by means of specific duties imposed on all national authorities, including the judiciary, hence becoming one of the cornerstones of the constitutionalisation of the Community legal order.[13] This special character of the duty of cooperation illustrates the significance of the ancillary duty applicable in the area of external relations as laid down in Article 307(2) EC. This is all the more so in the light of the foreign policy dimension of treaty-making: in negotiating and concluding an international treaty, Member States make foreign policy choices in their capacity as fully sovereign subjects of international law. The principle of Article 307(2) EC makes it clear that, in so far as such past choices may run counter to EC law, they must be reviewed. This constitutes a stark illustration of the interaction between foreign policy carried out by national authorities and Community law.

The way in which the above interaction should be regulated is often not apparent. In the light of the absence of a specific indication as to what the appropriate measures to be taken by Member States might be or when they should be taken, it follows that a case-by-case approach must be adopted. This makes perfect sense as the specific circumstances under which a Member State may be called to fulfil its international law obligations towards a third country may vary considerably. After all, it may take a considerable period of time for an incompatibility with EC law to become apparent either because the EC competence has not been fully exercised or because the implications of an EC measure are unclear and require interpretation by the Community judiciary. Furthermore, even in cases where the

---

[13] See, for instance, Case C–213/89 *The Queen v Secretary of State for Transport, ex parte Factortame* [1990] ECR I–2433.

incompatibility between a pre-existing agreement and EC law is not in doubt, there may be considerable scope for manoeuvre as to how this could be remedied. A number of factors may be relevant to this assessment, including the content of the agreement and the wishes of the contracting third party. Indeed, in most cases where the interpretation of Article 307 EC was relevant to a dispute before the Court of Justice, the main issue of contention has been the appropriateness of the response of the national authorities to the incompatibility rather than the determination of the latter.

Of the possible ways in which a Member State may remedy the incompatibility between a pre-existing agreement with a third country and EC law, adjustment of the agreement following renegotiation with the contracting third party is usually the least onerous. As most provisions of such an agreement are likely not to contravene EC law, its adjustment allows the Member State to retain rights that it may enjoy pursuant to those clauses which are either compatible with EC law or to the application of which EC law is irrelevant. The termination of a pre-existing treaty by a Member State, on the other hand, is a more drastic measure whose exercise is constrained by international law. Whilst most international agreements provide for their termination, the 1969 Vienna Convention on the Law of Treaties sets the general conditions for unilateral termination to be legal under international law.[14]

The place of denunciation within the options envisaged under Article 307(2) EC was at the centre of Case C–170/98 *Commission v Belgium*. The Commission attacked the failure of the Belgian government to adjust or denounce its preexisting Agreement with Zaire which, in the light of the cargo-sharing clauses it contained, was contrary to Regulation 4055/86. This measure set out the application of the principle of freedom to provide services to maritime transport between Member States and between Member States and third countries. A 'cargosharing' clause provided that the carriage of goods by sea between Belgian ports and ports of Zaire would be carried out on the basis of equal shares by vessels flying the flag of either of the parties or operated by persons or undertakings having the nationality of either of the parties. The effect of this clause was to exclude vessels operated by nationals of the remaining Member States from trade between the ports of Belgium and Zaire. There are two points worthy of comment in the Court's judgment. First, the Court dismissed the arguments put forward by the Belgian government regarding the practical difficulties in adjusting the Agreement due to the political developments in Zaire which made negotiations impossible: it was held that a difficult political situation in a third country may not justify the failure of a Member State to fulfil its EC obligations. Secondly, if such a situation makes the adjustment of the agreement impossible, the Member State concerned is under a duty to denounce it.

The brevity of analysis in the Court's judgment is as significant as its conclusions. In two short paragraphs, the Court leaves no doubt as to the Community law duty on the Belgian government to denounce its Agreement with Zaire. In

---

[14] See Art 42–45 and 54–65.

doing so, the Court went further than both the Commission, which had stated that it had not in fact requested the denunciation of the Agreement, and Advocate General La Pergola, who had argued that denunciation would have been necessary 'only if the other Contracting Party had not accepted the amendments needed'.[15] The Court's conclusion may be understood in the light of two considerations. On the one hand, the absence of an express reference to it in the operative part of the judgment notwithstanding, the Agreement with Zaire did contain a denunciation clause providing for only six months' notice. On the other hand, the disregard for the practical difficulties that a Member State must face in seeking to comply with EC law is entirely consistent with its approach to similar claims in enforcement actions under Article 226 EC when the relations with a third country are not an issue. In the well-known judgment about the blockades organised by French farmers, for instance, the Court had been equally dismissive of the argument that the French authorities had not prevented the free movement of goods from being disrupted because their intervention was likely to have resulted in civil unrest.[16] In other words, the objective nature of the Article 226 procedure and the automatic rejection of practical arguments put forward by the defending Member States constitute a thread which links the Court's approach to violations of EC law irrespective of whether these difficulties are due to the internal political scene in the Member State concerned or to a third country whose rights would be affected by that state's compliance.

The question whether a specific duty to denounce a pre-existing agreement was imposed upon a Member State under Article 307(2) EC arose again in two infraction cases brought by the Commission under Article 226 EC. Their subject matter was an agreement on merchant shipping with Angola[17] and the then Federal Republic of Yugoslavia.[18] Both agreements had entered into force prior to the accession of Portugal to the Community on 1 January 1986, the former in July 1979 and the latter in May 1981. As those Agreements included cargo-sharing clauses, the Commission argued that, having failed to adjust or denounce them, Portugal had violated Regulation 4055/86 on maritime transport.

The central finding of these actions was not in doubt as Portugal accepted that the application of cargo-sharing clauses was contrary to Regulation 4055/86. The dispute, however, centred on whether the failure to adjust or denounce the Agreements amounted to a violation of EC law. The Portuguese government argued in the negative on the basis of Article 307 EC and put forward three main arguments: first, no specific legal requirement is set out that Member States eliminate the incompatibility of their prior agreements irrespective of the legal and political implications of doing so; secondly, negotiations with Angola and Yugoslavia had been slow because of the political situations prevailing in those

---

[15] *Ibid*, 5499.
[16] Case C–265/95 *Commission v France* [1997] ECR I–6959.
[17] Case C–62/98 *Commission v Portugal* [2000] ECR I–5171.
[18] Case C–84/98 *Commission v Portugal* [2000] ECR I–5215.

countries, namely war and constant tension in the former and war and disintegration in the latter; finally, a combined reading of the first and second paragraphs of Article 307 EC indicates that such incompatibility should be eliminated in a manner which affects to the least extent possible the contracting third country, thus, rendering the denunciation of the agreement necessary only when that party clearly does not wish to adjust it.

The Court rejected this line of reasoning and concluded that Portugal had indeed violated Regulation 4055/86. It opined that a continuing failure of a Member States to comply with Community law may not be justified by the existence of a difficult political situation in the country with which the Agreement in question had been concluded. As to the denunciation of the agreements, the Court essentially made three points. First, it acknowledged that the rights that the contracting third country derives from the agreement should be respected in all cases. Secondly, it pointed out that the express provision for a denunciation clause in the contested Agreements made it clear that denunciation would not encroach upon the rights of the contracting third countries whilst ensuring compliance with Regulation 4055/86. Thirdly, whilst Article 307 EC enables Member States to make a choice as to how to eliminate incompatibilities between their pre-existing agreements and EC law, it also imposes a duty to ensure that such incompatibilities are actually eliminated. Therefore, 'if a Member State encounters difficulties which make adjustment of an agreement impossible, an obligation to denounce that agreement cannot . . . be excluded'.[19] This does not amount to disregarding the foreign policy interest that the Member State may wish to serve by approaching its pre-existing agreements in a particular manner. In an interesting description of Article 307 EC, the Court pointed out that:[20]

> the balance between the foreign-policy interests of a Member State and the Community interest is already incorporated in Article [307] of the Treaty, in that it allows a Member State not to apply a Community provision in order to respect the rights of third countries deriving from a prior agreement and to perform its obligations thereunder. That article also allows them to choose the appropriate means of rendering the agreement concerned compatible with Community law.

It is noteworthy that, in approaching the denunciation of the pre-existing agreement as one of the options open to a Member State under Article 307(2) EC, the Court expresses its conclusion in the negative: it 'cannot be excluded' in the light of 'difficulties' that may make the adjustment of the agreement 'impossible'. The lack of further criteria has been criticised.[21] However, the elaboration of a detailed set of rules which would dictate the circumstances under which a Member State should denounce a pre-existing agreement would be neither realistic nor useful: the political framework within which states negotiate, carry out their contractual

---

[19] Case C–62/98, n17 above, para 49 and Case C–84/98, n18 above, para 58.
[20] Case C–62/98, n17, above, para 50 and Case C–84/98, n18 above, para 59.
[21] See the annotation on the judgments by C Hillion, (2001) 38 *CMLRev* 1269, 1277 ff.

obligations, and then renegotiate are highly unpredictable and subject to a variety of factors which cannot plausibly be categorised for the purposes of the application of a judicial formula. In acknowledging that renegotiation of a pre-existing agreement may be rendered impossible, in which case denunciation should be considered, the Court accepts, on the one hand, the prime position of renegotiation within the options covered under Article 307(2) EC and, on the other hand, the realities of international relations which may render that option impossible. Furthermore, the judgments of the Court should be viewed within their legal and factual context: in addition to the objective character of the procedure pursuant to which the Court was asked to adjudicate, the action was brought 11 years following the date from which Belgium was required to adjust the agreement in question and five years following the expiry of the period laid down by Regulation 4055/86.

Another point of interest is the tension between the foreign policy interests of the Member State required to adjust its pre-existing agreements and the interest of the Community in having its rules respected by national authorities. The conclusion that, whilst present, such national interest ought to be balanced with the interests of the Community is most significant. The Court implies that the Community legal order may provide the framework within which the Member States may pursue their foreign policy interests. That framework is construed in broad terms: as it cannot possibly dictate the substance of choices that national authorities may make in the foreign policy arena, it merely defines the parameters within which such choices may be made. This approach to the interpretation of Article 307 EC typifies the Court's approach to the legal management of areas in which trade and foreign policy interact. Its central tenet had already been articulated in its interpretation of EC rules imposing sanctions on third countries. In addressing the argument of the British government in *Centro-Com* that the implementation of those rules constituted a foreign policy act which fell within their exclusive competence, the Court had pointed that, whilst Member States did retain their sovereignty in the area of foreign policy, they must exercise it in a manner consistent with Community law.[22] In other words, there is a thread which links the construction of the duty imposed on Member States to reconcile their pre-existing international obligations with Community law with the broader context of the powers of Member States as sovereign subjects of international law. In identifying the limits to the international action of the Member States, the Court's requirement may appear harsh in its implications.[23] However, it also suggests a degree of flexibility: the omnipresent interaction between trade and foreign policy in the conduct of external relations renders the elaboration of a simple formula which could achieve the aims of Article 307 EC impossible. Instead, these aims

---

[22] Case C–124/95 *The Queen, ex parte Centro-Com v HM Treasury and Bank of England* [1997] ECR I–81.

[23] See J Klabbers, 'Moribund on the fourth of July? The Court of Justice on Prior Agreements of the Member States' (2001) 26 *ELRev* 187 where the construction of Art 307(2) EC is viewed as rather narrow.

are to be achieved on the basis of a multi-faceted and inherently flexible system of principles whose application involves a variety of institutional actors. This point was brought home in subsequent case law.

2.2. . . . and Interpretation

In the *Budvar* case, an Austrian court referred questions on the interpretation of the Agreement on intellectual property rights concluded between Austria and the Czechoslovak Socialist Republic in June 1976.[24] That Agreement established a system of protection for certain agricultural and industrial products bearing indications of source, designations of origin and other designations referring to their source. The Czechoslovak designations listed in the Agreement would be reserved exclusively for Czechoslovak products in Austria. Budvar exported and marketed in Austria beer under the name Budweiser Budvar. It brought an action before Austrian courts against Ammersin, a company marketing a beer called American Bud bought from a company in Austria, and relied, *inter alia*, on the Agreement between Austria and Czechoslovakia. In particular, it was argued that the use of the designation American Bud was contrary to the system of protection established under that agreement which reserved the designation Bud exclusively for Czech products.

The first main issue was whether the system of protection set up by that agreement was contrary to EC law. Having established that the existence of a national system protecting simple indications of geographical source was not prohibited under EC secondary legislation on the protection of geographical designation, the Court held that that protection bestowed upon Czechoslovak products was a measure of equivalent effect to a quantitative restriction on imports under Article 28 EC. However, it could be justified under Article 30 EC as necessary for the protection of fair competition if the referring court concluded that, in the Czech Republic, the name Bud was deemed as directly or indirectly referring to the region or place in the territory of the state that it designates. The relevance of Article 307 EC arose in the event that the answer to the above question was negative: was the national court under a duty to apply the system of protection accorded under the pre-existing Agreement, its illegality under Article 28 EC notwithstanding?

In relation to the interpretation of Article 307 EC, the first issue was whether, in the light of the dissolution of Czechoslovakia, the agreement with Austria was applicable at all. The Court engaged in a lengthy analysis of the principles underpinning the phenomenon of state succession in respect of treaties. Having identified the principle of the continuity of treaties as prevailing in the international practice of the law of the treaties, it went on to assess whether both Austria and the Czech Republic actually intended to apply it to the agreement in question. The

---

[24] Case C–216/01 *Budejovicku Budvar v Rudolf Ammersin GmbH* [2003] ECR I–13617.

latter state had expressly accepted the principle of the automatic continuity of treaties. Austria, on the other hand, had indicated in the past that the treaties concluded by a state should be deemed to expire automatically following a complete break-up of that state. However, in the light of a more pragmatic approach adopted by the Austrian authorities in recent years, it fell to the referring court to decide whether both Austria and the Czech Republic actually intended to apply the principle of the continuity of treaties to the agreement in question.

If the answer to that question was affirmative, then the first paragraph of Article 307 EC would apply and the question would be limited to the type of measures the Austrian authorities should take in order to comply with the second paragraph of Article 307 EC by reconciling the system of protection set up under the agreement with Article 28 EC. The Court held as follows:[25]

> [T]he national court must ascertain whether a possible incompatibility between the Treaty and the bilateral convention can be avoided by interpreting the convention, to the extent possible and in compliance with international law, in such a way that it is consistent with Community law.
>
> If it proves impracticable to interpret an agreement concluded prior to a Member State's accession to the European Union in such a way that it is consistent with Community law then, within the framework of Article 307 EC, it is open to that State to take the appropriate steps, while, however, remaining obliged to eliminate any incompatibilities existing between the earlier agreement and the Treaty. If that Member state encounters difficulties which make the adjustment of an agreement impossible, an obligation to denounce that agreement cannot therefore be excluded.

In conclusion, the Court made two observations: on the one hand, the agreement with the Czech Republic did, in fact, provide for the possibility of denunciation by giving notice of at least one year in writing through diplomatic channels; on the other hand, pending the effort of the Austrian authorities to address the incompatibilities of the agreement with Article 28 EC, the former's provisions could continue to apply pursuant to the first paragraph of Article 307 EC in so far as they contain international law obligations which remain binding on Austria.

The Court's judgment in *Budvar* is very useful for our understanding of the proper application of Article 307 EC. It confirms the duty of Member States to consider denunciation of a pre-existing agreement if its adjustment has proved impossible and provided that the agreement in question provides for its denunciation. However, there are two additional elements which further clarify the legal position. The first one is the central role reserved to national courts in the process of addressing conflicts between pre-existing international law duties and Community law. This role is defined in a number of ways: they are expected to assess whether a number of factors relevant to the application of a fundamental Treaty provision are present not only in their territory but also in that of a third country; they are left with the task of determining the position of their national

---

[25] *Ibid*, paras 169–170.

authorities in a matter of public international law, that is state succession; and, most importantly, they are being asked to prevent an incompatibility between a pre-existing international obligation of the Member State and Community law from arising by seeking consistency between the two. Whilst some of these requirements are not surprising in terms of what is expected of a referring court within the context of Article 234 EC, their combination in general and the duty of interpretation in particular place national courts right at the centre of the application of Community law in the area of external relations.

In the broader context of Article 307 EC, the role of national courts had also been highlighted in previous judgments. In the context of preliminary reference proceedings, it is for the referring court to determine whether an agreement concluded by a Member State prior to accession has been effectively annulled by subsequent agreements binding on the same parties, in which case Article 307(1) EC would not apply.[26] Similarly, it is left to the national court to determine the scope and nature of the obligations imposed upon a Member State by a pre-existing agreement.[27] In the context of Community law in general, the interpretative task imposed upon national courts is, of course, hardly a novelty. It is a well-established principle that national courts are to interpret national legislation in the light of a non-directly effective directive.[28] The Court does accept that there is a limit to what national courts can do in that consistent interpretation must be 'possible and in compliance with international law'. Again, this approach had already been adopted in the application of the principle of indirect effect: national courts are required to read the rules of a non-directly effective directive in national legislation 'as far as possible'.[29] On the internal plane, this limit had been deemed to refer 'to the general principles of law which form part of Community law and in particular the principles of legal certainty and non-retroactivity';[30] in the light of the paramount importance of the rights of third countries, it is sensible that the limit to the duty of interpretation imposed upon national courts should be wider, namely 'to the extent possible and in compliance with Community law'. The Court also refers to the possibility of consistent interpretation being 'impracticable'—one wonders what this may mean and whether it should be taken to refer to yet another situation where the duty of interpretation would reach its limit. Be that as it may, the reference to respect of international law is very significant: it would not be acceptable for a national court to engage in so creative an interpretation of an agreement as to undermine the rights of the contracting third country and, ultimately, the objective of the agreement in the name of Community law. In other words, Article 307(2) EC aims at reconciling the international law obligations of the Member States with Community law, not at superseding, even

---

[26] Case C–158/91, n9 above, at paras 20–21.

[27] Case C–13/93 *Office national de l'emploi v Minne* [1994] ECR I–371 at para 18.

[28] Case 14/83 *Von Colson and Kamann v Land Nordrhein-Westfalen* [1984] ECR 1891.

[29] Case C–106/89 *Marleasing SA v La Comercial Internacionale de Alimentacion SA* [1990] ECR I–4135, para 8.

[30] Case 80/86 *Criminal Proceedings against Kolpinghuis Nijmegen BV* [1987] ECR 3969, para 13.

indirectly, international law. Viewed from this angle, the construction of the duty of interpretation imposed upon national courts constitutes a clear link between the first and second paragraphs of Article 307 EC. In rendering national courts involved in the process of achieving the objectives of this EC Treaty provision, the Court follows the ingenious strategy which has marked the introduction of the main principles of Community law leading to the constitutionalisation of the EC Treaty.

The interpretive role of national courts leads us to the second important aspect of the judgment in *Budvar*, namely the paramount importance of international law in the effort to reconcile the pre-existing international obligations of Member States with Community law. What lies at the core of Article 307 EC is respect for the international rules imposing legal obligations on Member States. In its judgment, the Court refers to the options left open to a Member State under Article 307(2) EC. These include interpretation of the existing agreement in a way which would be consistent with Community law, adjustment following renegotiation with the contracting third party and denunciation. These options were mentioned in that order, from the least onerous to the most radical. However, the choice between these options may be neither apparent nor immediate: it may take time for the plausability of a consistent interpretation to be established or accepted, or in the alternative for the negotiations for adjustment to be carried out. There may be exceptional cases where this process may not have a happy conclusion in terms of compliance with Community law: national courts may conclude that to interpret a pre-existing agreement in a manner consistent with Community law would impair its objectives; the agreement in question may not have a denunciation clause or the contracting third party may be unwilling to renegotiate or unable to do so because of internal political conditions. In such a scenario, the ruling in *Budvar* suggests that the principle of Article 307(1) EC should apply and the Member State cannot be accused of violating its EC Treaty obligations.

In other words, international law is accepted as the limit not only to the Community law interpretive duty imposed on national courts but also to the process of seeking to reconcile the pre-existing international duties of Member States with EC law under Article 307(2) EC.[31] In theoretical terms, the significance of this conclusion cannot be overstated in so far as it appears to counterbalance the Court's approach to the exercise of the national foreign affairs power: whilst, in doing so, Member States must act in accordance with Community law, the process of ensuring compliance with the latter must be carried out in accordance with international law. This conclusion further underlines the significance of the role entrusted by the Court to national courts: the way they carried out their task would determine the extent to which alternative methods of ensuring compliance with Community law should be explored and might lead to the conclusion that no such method was in fact appropriate. Entirely consistently with their role in the

---

[31] However, see the concerns expressed in P Manzini, 'The Priority of Pre-Existing Treaties of EC Member States within the Framework of International Law' (2001) 12 *EJIL* 781.

establishment of the single market, national courts are entrusted, in essence, with safeguarding Community law in the area of external relations.

2.3. When is Denunciation Necessary?

Termination of an international agreement is the most extreme action expected of Member States under Article 307(2) EC. Not only must it be carried out in accordance with the procedure laid down in the relevant agreement, but it also targets the totality of the agreement, including provisions compatible with Community law. Therefore, the question of the timing of termination is important, all the more so in the light of the benefits that any delay may bring for the Member State seeking to rely upon Article 307 EC.

This issue was raised before the Court in a recent action brought by the Commission against Austria under Article 226 EC. Its subject-matter was the legality of national legislation on the employment of women in the underground mining industry, in a high-pressure atmosphere and in diving work.[32] For the purpose of this analysis, it is the area of employment in the underground mining industry which is of interest. National rules adopted in 2001 in order to amend legislation originating in 1938 prohibited the employment of women except for a limited number of specified posts; these included management or technical responsibilities without strenuous physical work, social or health services and work in the context of vocational training for the duration of that training or on an occasional basis in an occupation which is not physically strenuous.

The Commission argued that such legislation was contrary to the principle of equal treatment for men and women as enshrined in Articles 2(1) and 3(1) of Directive 76/207.[33] The Austrian government responded by relying upon the exception to the principle of equal treatment laid down in Article 2(3) of Directive 76/207, which refers to the protection of women, particularly as regards pregnancy and maternity. However, that argument was dismissed by the Court, which pointed out that the exception to the principle of sex equality should be interpreted strictly as aiming at protecting the woman's biological condition during and after pregnancy and the special relationship between a woman and her child over the period following pregnancy and childbirth. The Austrian measures were held to go beyond what was necessary in order to meet those objectives, as they excluded women even from work that was not physically strenuous.[34]

It is the second argument put forward by the Austrian government which is of relevance to this analysis. It was argued that the national restriction in question had been adopted in order to implement Convention No 45 of the International Labour Organisations (ILO) ratified by Austria in 1937. Indeed,

---

[32] Case C–203/03 *Commission v Austria*, judgment of the Grand Chamber, 1 Feb 2005, not yet reported.
[33] [1976] OJ L 39/40.
[34] See n32 above, at paras 43–49.

both the prohibition and the exceptions laid down in Austrian legislation mirrored the content of that Convention. The Commission counter-argued that the above Convention ought to have been denounced in accordance with the relevant clause (Article 7(2)). According to this provision, an ILO Member could denounce the Convention within a year after the expiry of each period of ten years following its entry into force. As it had entered into force on 30 May 1937, the Commission argued that Austria ought to have denounced it in the year following 30 May 1997.

In its judgment, the Court accepted that the Austrian rules adopted in order to comply with the Convention did not go beyond its requirements. Having established the incompatibility of the Convention with Directive 76/207, the Court went on to reaffirm the conclusion in Case C–62/98 *Commission v Portugal*, namely that the appropriate steps for the elimination of such incompatibility include denunciation.[35] It concluded that, by maintaining in force the national provisions in question, Austria had not violated the ratio of Article 307(2) EC. This was because on the only occasion following its accession to the Community on which it could have denounced the Convention (the year following 30 May 1997), 'the incompatibility of the prohibition laid down by that Convention with the provisions of Directive 76/207 had not been sufficiently clearly established for that Member State to be bound to denounce the convention'.[36] It was added that the next opportunity for Austria to denounce the Convention would occur in the year following 30 May 2007.

The Austrian government had argued that it could not have known that the rules in question were contrary to the Directive before the Commission issued its first statement on their illegality in September 1998, that is after the expiry of the year during which the Convention could have been denounced legally. That argument was rejected by Advocate General Jacobs as immaterial[37] and was ignored by the Court. The position of the Austrian government is linked to the position that the illegality of the Austrian rules had not been clear and is also vaguely reminiscent of the case law on state liability in damages for a breach of Community law. It is recalled that, in cases where a legislative authority enjoyed wide discretion, the existence of liability for a breach of Community law would depend upon, amongst others, the existence of a sufficiently serious breach; one of the factors which would determine whether that condition occurred would be 'the clarity and precision of the rule breached' and whether 'the position taken by a Community institution may have contributed' towards the violation.[38] In *British Telecommunications*, the adoption of national legislation wrongly implementing Directive 90/351 on procurement procedures in certain utilities sectors was held not to be a sufficiently serious breach of Community law: the provisions of the

---

[35] *Ibid.*
[36] *Ibid*, para 62.
[37] *Ibid*, para 50 of his Opinion.
[38] Joined Cases C–46 and 48/93 *Brasserie du Pêcheur SA v Germany* [1996] ECR I–1029, para 56.

Directive breached were held not to be clear and precise and, *inter alia*, the Commission had not raised the issue when the national rules were adopted.[39] Nonetheless, there can be no connection between the two legal contexts: in relation to state liability, the above conditions were included in a number of factors aiming at assisting national courts in carrying out the complex tasks articulated in *Brasserie du Pêcheur*; in the context of Article 307 EC, the Austrian government had sought to rely upon the non-authoritative approach by the Commission in order to absolve it of its responsibilities under primary law.

In its judgment, the Court appears to suggest a link between the clarity of the state of Community law which triggers the application of Article 307(2) EC and the time when a Member State is bound to denounce an international agreement. Rather than complete certainty, it is 'sufficient clarity' which appears to be the prerequisite for the duty of Member States to apply. However, the conclusion reached in *Commission v Austria* is problematic on two counts. First, both the definition of the principle of equal treatment between men and women and the exception laid down in Articles 2(1) and 2(3) respectively of Directive 76/207 had hardly been unclear in the year following 30 May 1997, that is when Austria had the first opportunity to denounce the Convention legally. For instance, in *Johnston* the Court had already ruled that the exception of Article 2(3) of the Directive should be interpreted strictly, adding that 'it is clear from the express reference to pregnancy and maternity that the Directive is intended to protect a woman's biological condition and the special relationship which exists between a woman and her child'.[40] To that effect, it had held that national legislation preventing women from undertaking general policing duties carrying firearms in Northern Ireland was illegal. That judgment had been delivered in May 1986, that is 11 years prior to the date when Austria had the opportunity to denounce ILO Convention No 45. Indeed, the ruling in *Johnston* was mentioned by the Court in order to substantiate the illegality of the Austrian prohibition.

Secondly, in his Opinion Advocate General Jacobs argued that, because of its failure to denounce the Convention, the Austrian government had lost its right to rely upon Article 307 EC. He referred to the fact that 13 Contracting Parties, including six Member States, had already denounced ILO Convention No 45 and the majority had given as reasons for their denunciation that the Convention was incompatible with the principle of equal treatment for men and women. He also added that the ILO Governing Body had invited the parties to that Convention to contemplate ratifying ILO Convention No 176 on Safety and Health in Mines, applicable equally to men and women, and possibly denouncing Convention No 45.[41] Whilst ignored by the Court, this information further weakens the claim that the inconsistency between the Convention and Directive 76/207 had not been 'sufficiently clearly established'.

---

[39] Case C–392/93 *R v HM Treasury, ex p British Telecommunications plc* [1996] ECR I–1631, para 45.
[40] Case 222/84 *Johnston* [1986] ECR 1651, para 44.
[41] See para 47 of his Opinion.

One way of reading the conclusion reached by the Court is as an effort to strike a balance between the requirement of loyal cooperation which underpins the ratio of Article 307(2) EC and the drastic implications of denunciation of an international agreement. However, as applied to the facts of this case, the Court's line of reasoning tilted the balance in the Member States' favour without proper justification.

3. THE EVOLVING CONTEXT OF THE APPLICATION OF ARTICLE 307 EC

The above section sought to illustrate how Article 307(2) EC has been gradually developed by the Court as the legal foundation of a Community law duty imposed on various national actors in order to ensure compliance with Community law whilst respecting the sanctity of international legal obligations towards non-member states. Striking the balance between those two interests is a delicate exercise. The management of the implications of the judgments in the *Open Skies* litigation illustrates the practical difficulties.[42] The facts of the cases and the judgments of the Court were examined in detail in a previous chapter.[43] For the purpose of this analysis, the Court sidestepped the issue of the applicability of Article 307 EC.[44] There has been considerable difference of opinion as to how the incompatibility between the bilateral air services agreements concluded by Member States and their obligations under Community law is to be remedied. The Commission made it clear quite early on that it deemed the denunciation of the agreements the appropriate remedy.[45] The United States, in a rather combative tone, expressed dissatisfaction with this option. In a statement within three weeks after the judgments had been delivered, the State Department argued that:[46]

> the European Court of Justice's decisions do not *require* the European Union Member Sates to denounce these agreements. The Court also ruled against the Commission's assertion that Member States lacked competence to negotiate *air services* agreements *at all*. Instead, the Court found that our agreements are consistent with EU law, except in three areas. We see no utility in denunciation of our aviation agreements. The United

---

[42] See Case C–467/98 *Commission v Denmark* [2002] ECR I–9519, Case C–468/98 *Commission v Sweden* [2002] ECR I–9575, Case C–469/98 *Commission v Finland* [2002] ECR I–9627, Case C–471/98 *Commission v Belgium* [2002] ECR I–9681, Case C–472/98 *Commission v Luxembourg* [2002] ECR I–9741, Case C–475/98 *Commission v Austria* [2002] ECR I–9797, Case C–476/98 *Commission v Germany* [2002] ECR I–9855.

[43] See Ch 3 above.

[44] See the criticism in CNK Franklin, 'Flexibility vs. Legal Certainty: Article 307 EC and Other Issues in the Aftermath of the Open Skies Cases' (2005) 10 *EFA Rev* 79 which also provides a detailed analysis of further developments.

[45] See COM(2002)649 final at paras 65 and 67.

[46] See House of Lords Select Committee on the European Union, '*Open Skies' or Open Markets? The Effect of the European Court of Justice Judgments on Aviation Relations between the European Union and the United States of America, Session,* 2002–03, 17th Report, at 26–7. See also P Mendes de Leon, 'Before and After the Tenth Anniversary of the Open Skies Agreement Netherlands-US of 1992' (2002) 28 *Air and Space Law* 280 at 300–1.

States is prepared to discuss with the European Union Member States on a bilateral basis how to accommodate the European Court of Justice's specific legal findings. Such discussions can occur without denunciation.

Denunciation was a very unpopular choice with the Member States, too.[47] In practical terms, the determination of whether denunciation was the appropriate response was complicated by the existence of national competence over parts of the Open Skies Agreements and was also tied in with the question of the negotiating mandate which the Commission was seeking. It was this interaction between legal principle and practice which provided an answer: the Commission was granted a complex double negotiating mandate—for an Open Aviation Area Agreement with the United States and a 'horizontal' mandate for amendment of bilateral agreements so that entitlements will be available to any Community controlled airline. The existing agreements have not been denounced and no further infraction proceedings have been brought against the Member States.

This next section will seek to identify other ways in which the evolving international framework may interact with the application of the *ratio* of Article 307 EC.

3.1. Friendship, Navigation and Commerce and Telecommunications Procurement

An example of the multifarious issues that the application of Article 307 EC may raise is provided by the serious dispute between Germany and the Commission about the approach adopted by the former to the Utilities Directive in the early 1990s. Directive 90/531 aimed at bringing the water, energy, transport and telecommunications sectors, until then excluded from the existing secondary legislation, within the scope of public procurement law.[48] Aiming at ensuring free movement, it governed the publication of information about proposed contracts and provided for objective criteria and transparent procedures for their award. What made this set of rules controversial was the inclusion of the so-called rejection and preference clauses: the former allowed national authorities to reject tenders where the proportion of the products originating in third countries would exceed 50 per cent of the total value of the products; the latter provided that, save in certain specified circumstances, in cases where two or more tenders were equivalent on the basis of the award criteria, the national award authorities should prefer the EC bid, that being considered equivalent even if it was up to 3 per cent

---

[47] In relation to the UK, see HL Select Committee Report, n46 above, where, pointing out that the Commission's insistence on formal denunciation seems unnecessarily confrontational, it was stated that 'we saw little value and possibly much harm' in denunciation, and it was recommended that the British government 'resist the Commission's call for denunciation' (para 52).

[48] [1990] OJ L 297/1 consolidated by Dir 93/38 [1993] OJ L 199/84 and followed by Dir 92/13 [1992] OJ L 76/14 which introduced specific remedies in the area.

more expensive. These clauses were to apply only in cases where the third country concerned had not concluded an agreement with the Community granting comparable and effective access for EC undertakings to that country's market.[49]

The German government maintained that those clauses were in conflict with a Friendship, Navigation and Commerce Agreement which it had concluded with the United States in 1954 and, in particular, with its prohibition of discrimination between the two contracting parties in the areas of public procurement.[50] In the light of this interpretation, the German government invoked the Article 307(1) EC proviso and decided in June 1993, that is six months after its entry into force, not to apply the Utilities Directive to US tenders.[51] This development gave rise to a confrontation with the European Commission. In order to appreciate the importance attached to this case by the Commission, two factors need to be highlighted: on the one hand, similar agreements had been concluded between the United States and six other Member States, namely Belgium, Denmark, Ireland, Italy, Greece and the Netherlands; on the other hand, following the adoption of the Utilities Directive, the United States administration had argued that its provisions were contrary to the rules laid down in the GATT. Following two years of negotiations with the Commission, a compromise was reached, albeit confined to the procurement of electrical goods;[52] on EC bids on telecommunications equipment, US sanctions were imposed, to which the Community retaliated.[53] In the light of these internal and external factors, the Commission became alarmed by the German position, all the more so in the light of the ongoing negotiations for the conclusion of the Government Procurement Agreement under the GATT umbrella.

The case of public procurement in the area of telecommunications illustrates with stark clarity both the different, and often conflicting, interests underlying the application of Article 307 EC and, on the other hand, the dynamic process that renegotiation pursuant to Article 307 inevitably entails. Whilst compliance by a Member State with its pre-existing international law obligations is the uncontroversial objective of Article 307, its application in practical terms may serve other functions of a more political nature. For instance, it may offer a Member State a legally acceptable disguise to deviate from rules of Community law adopted despite its opposition—it is noteworthy that the Utilities Directive had been adopted by qualified majority voting.[54] In addition to undermining the effectiveness of

---

[49] For a comment on Dir 90/531, see A Brown, 'The Extension of the Community Public Procurement Rules to Utilities' (1993) 30 *CMLRev* 721.

[50] Under Art 17(2) of the US–Germany Agreement, 'each party shall accord to the nationals, companies and commerce of the other Party fair and equitable treatment, as compared with that accorded to the nationals, companies and commerce of any third country'.

[51] See JM Grimes, 'Conflicts Between EC Law and International Treaty Obligations: A Case Study of the German Telecommunications Dispute' (1994) 35 *Harv Int'l LJ* 535.

[52] See Council Dec 93/323 [1993] OJ L 125/1 and Council Dec 93/324 [1993] OJ L 125/54.

[53] See Council Reg 1461/93 [1993] OJ L 146/1.

[54] In the negotiations leading to the adoption of the Utilities Dir, Germany did not mention its view as to the conflict with its previous Agreement with the US: Grimes, n51 above, 552. See P Eeckhout, *The European Internal Market and International Trade: A Legal Analysis* (Oxford: Clarendon Press, 1994) 318.

Community legislation, undue reliance upon Article 307 EC might have very serious repercussions regarding the international posture of the Community on the economic arena. The application of Community rules to its external relations cannot be examined in isolation; instead, it should be viewed as intrinsically linked to the continuous effort of the Community to present a common stance and negotiate effectively in the context of the ongoing liberalisation of international trade. Viewed from this angle, reliance upon Article 307 EC by a Member State may seriously undermine the negotiating position of the European Community. Again, the example of telecommunications is interesting because the relevance of Article 307 EC arose whilst the Commission was seeking to enhance its negotiating position against, amongst others, the United States in relation to the Government Procurement Agreement.[55] It is recalled that one of the legal bases of the Utilities Directive was Article 133 EC: it was precisely in the context of the common commercial policy that the unitary representation of the Community was deemed so important a function as to justify the exclusive nature of its competence.[56]

Excessive reliance upon Article 307 EC could call into question the extent to which Member States are prepared to accept the normative foundations of the external relations power of the Community. That is not to say that the principle behind Article 307 EC is detrimental to the conduct of EC international relations: quite the contrary, as international relations are carried out on the basis of both Community and national competence, it is vital not only that the main tenets of the international legal order should be complied with, but also that that should be apparent to the trading partners of the Community. However, the intrinsic link between Article 307 EC and the external action of the Community should make the Member States less willing to deviate from Community law and more prepared to adhere by the spirit of Article 307(2) EC. Again this is raised in the case of the Utilities Directive, as the other Member States with similar pre-existing agreements with the United States did not interpret the exclusion and preference clauses as being in conflict with their bilateral obligations. As it happened, the dispute between the Commission and Germany did not give rise to an action before the Court of Justice. Instead, the issue was resolved with the passage of time, as the Utilities Directive ceased to have effect following the adoption of the GATT Government Procurement Agreement.[57]

3.2. Preparing for Accession

The Community institutions have since sought to avoid such legal tensions by addressing potential conflicts before they arise. A noteworthy example is

[55] See M Footer, 'Public Procurement and EC External Relations: A Legal Framework' in N Emiliou and D O'Keeffe (eds), *The European Union and World Trade Law—After the GATT Uruguay Round* (Chichester: Wiley, 1996) 293, 301.

[56] See, for instance, *Opinion 1/75* [1975] ECR 1355 and the analysis in Ch 1.

[57] It was replaced by Dir 98/4 coordinating the procurement procedures of entities operating in the water, energy, transport and telecommunications sectors [1998] OJ L 101/1.

provided by the fascinating process which paved the way for the accession of Central and Eastern European Countries to the European Union. In direct correlation to the scope of this enlargement, the process which led to the accession of the ten new Member States has been extraordinary both in scope and intensity.[58] Within this context, the new Member States had to adjust their international legal commitments in a way which would ensure compliance with the *acquis communautaire*. The Treaty of Accession makes it clear that all the new Member States 'shall withdraw from any trade agreements with third countries, including the Central European Free Trade Agreement'.[59] As the negotiation and conclusion of free trade agreements fall within the exclusive competence of the Community, the retention of such agreements concluded unilaterally by Member States would be clearly contrary to Community law. However, what is most interesting is the process pursuant to which the new Member States gradually adjusted their external policies to those of the Community.[60] The dynamic nature of this process was defined not only by the positions of the Central and Eastern European Countries, but also the development of the Community policies themselves. For instance, Slovenia had requested a ten-year-long transitional period in order to retain the asymmetric trade agreements it had concluded with Croatia, the Former Yugoslav Republic of Macedonia and Bosnia-Herzegovina.[61] In doing so, it put forward a number of economic and political arguments, the latter relating to the disintegration of the former Socialist Federal Republic of Yugoslavia. As it happened, there was no need for such a transitional period as the Community would conclude free trade agreements with those countries. The new Member States would be bound by those agreements, hence the broad scope of Article 6(10) of the Treaty of Accession.

Another interesting feature of the Treaty of Accession is the detailed provision for specific areas of external relations. On the one hand, there is a general cooperation clause according to which 'the new Member States shall take appropriate measures, where necessary, to adjust their position in relation to international organisations, and to those international agreements to which the Community or to which other Member States are also parties, to the rights and obligations arising from their accession to the Union'.[62] As it clearly draws upon Article 307(2) EC, this provision is

---

[58] For an analysis of the pre-accession process, see M Maresceau, 'Pre-accession' in M Cremona (ed), *The Enlargement of the European Union* (Oxford: OUP, 2003) 9. For an analysis of the gradual developments which brought about the approximation of the legislation of the new Member States prior to their accession, see A Ott and K Inglys (eds), *Handbook on European Enlargment—A Commentary on the Enlargement Process* (The Hague: TMC Asser Press, 2002).

[59] Art 6(10). See K Inglis, 'The Union's Fifth Accession Treaty: New Means to Make Enlargement Possible' (2004) 41 *CMLRev* 899, 940–5.

[60] See M Cremona, 'The Impact of Enlargement: External Policy and External Relations' in Cremona, n58 above, 161.

[61] See Republic of Slovenia, *Negotiating Positions of the Republic of Slovenia for Negotiations on Accession to the European Union* (2000) 295 and 297–298.

[62] Art 6(12)(1).

more interesting for its position within the Act of Accession rather than its content:[63] it is the last paragraph in a long Article dealing with external relations and its content is considerably more general than that of the provisions preceding it. This reflects accurately the intention of the Community institutions to deal with pre-existing international obligations of the new Member States in a way which would minimise the risk of legal tensions following accession. Indeed, what precedes Article 6(12) of the Act of Accession is a number of provisions dealing with very specific aspects of external relations. Following a general undertaking that they accede to the mixed agreements concluded or applied provisionally by the present Member States and the Community,[64] there is reference to a number of existing agreements with Belarus, China, Chile, Mercosur and Switzerland to which accession is to be agreed upon by means of the conclusion of additional protocols negotiated by the Commission pursuant to directives by the Council.[65] There is also reference to another category of mixed agreements, for instance with Armenia, Algeria Bulgaria and Ukraine which are to be applied by the Acceding States even pending the conclusion of the additional protocols.[66] Finally, there is reference to the Cotonou Agreement,[67] the European Economic Area Agreement,[68] and a number of areas in which the Community has already concluded bilateral agreements such as textiles[69] and steel.[70] The fisheries agreements previously concluded by the acceding Member States would now be managed by the Community.[71] While understandable in the light of the unprecedented scope of the recent enlargement, the considerable detail of the above provisions becomes all the more striking in the light of the previous Act of Accession concluded on the occasion of the accession by Austria, Sweden and Finland.[72] In addition to a general provision reaffirming the ratio of Article 307 EC, that Act referred only to the rule laid down in the current Art. 6(2)(1), with no reference to agreements provisionally applied, and included the general cooperation rule laid down in the current Art. 6(12)(1).

4. AN INTERESTING APPROACH TO THE APPLICATION OF ARTICLE 307 EC

It was argued above that the structure of Article 6 of the Act of Accession reflects a more active approach to managing the existing international obligations of the new Member States within the context of the EU external relations. Another facet of this dynamic process is highlighted in the case of eight bilateral investment

---

[63] Apart from an apparent glimpse, that is: did it not intend to refer to agreements to which the Community or to which *the Community and* other Member States are also parties?

[64] Art 6(2) of the Treaty of Accession.

[65] See Art 6(2)(2).

[66] Art 6(6).

[67] Art 6(4).

[68] Art 6(5).

[69] Art 6(7).

[70] Art 6(8).

[71] Art 6(9).

[72] [1994] OJ C 241/1.

treaties between the Czech Republic, Estonia, Latvia, Lithuania, Poland, Slovakia, Bulgaria and Romania, on the one hand, and the United States. These agreements had been negotiated after the fall of the Iron Curtain and had entered into force at various dates between 1992 and 2001. A key feature of these agreements is the application of the national treatment principle and the Most-Favoured-Nation principle to undertakings of the contracting parties engaging in direct investment in the other contracting party. A number of their provisions raised serious legal questions as to their compatibility with the *acquis communautaire*. The Commission pointed out that the problem of incompatibility would be more acute in areas such as agriculture and audiovisual services. It was argued that, had the agreements remained unchanged, a number of EC provisions granting preferential treatment to EC operators would have been undermined, hence enabling US investors to benefit from Community subsidies or quotas for the broadcast of European works.[73]

These questions were addressed prior to accession in a multilateral negotiating context involving not only the US Administration and the eight above states but also the European Commission. This resulted in a Memorandum of Understanding (MOU) signed on 22 September 2003 in Brussels. On behalf of the Commission, it was signed by the Director General for Trade. In the MOU, the participants make it clear that their aim is to strike the balance between two main interests: on the one hand, the maintenance and enhancement of a positive framework for US investment in the eight accession and candidate countries; on the other hand, the full compliance and implementation of the *acquis communautaire* in the context of which express reference was made both to Article 307 EC and the Treaty of Accession. To that effect, the ten Participants:

(a) express their intention to address the matters identified [in the MoU] by relying on interpretations and specific amendments to Acceding and Candidate Countries' [Bilateral Investment Treaties] with the US, including specific sectoral exceptions, as well as consultations where appropriate;

(b) intend that making the interpretations and specific amendments outlined in this Understanding will eliminate incompatibilities between obligations of the Acceding and Candidate Countries that arise as a result of membership in the EU and their obligations in their BITs with the US;

and (c) undertake the political commitment to make good faith efforts, as necessary, to seek to avoid or to remedy further incompatibilities.

The MOU refers to a number of areas which the participants deem problematic, an important one being capital movements. The Commission was anxious to ensure respect for the right of the Council to impose restrictions on capital movements and

---

[73] BITs concluded by older Member States (often called Investment Promotion and Protection Agreements) contained a clause ensuring that Community benefits would not be undermined by clauses on Most-Favoured-Nation and national treatment: see, for instance, Art 7(1) of the 1981 Agreement between the UK and Paraguay.

payments originating in or destined for third countries, either under exceptional circumstances involving serious difficulties in the operation of the economic and monetary union[74] or in order to implement a common position or a joint action adopted pursuant to the Common Foreign and Security Policy.[75] The wording of the MOU is non-committal and provides for consultations between the US and the Commission, albeit without prejudice to the latter's powers under the Article 226 EC.

An important area covered by the Memorandum is what the participants call 'sensitive sectors or matters'. In essence, the acceding and candidate countries are allowed to deviate from the non-discrimination principle laid down in the investment agreements in order to meet an EC obligation in areas which include agriculture, audiovisual securities, investment services and other financial services, fisheries, air transport, inland waterways transport and maritime transport. In return, the US Administration ensured that such deviations would not apply to existing US investments in the relevant sector for a considerable period of time.[76] In addition, it was agreed that no exception should be defined in a way which would require divestment, in whole or in part, of an existing investment.

An interesting clause included in the Memorandum is about future developments in EU law. The duty of the acceding states to adjust their pre-existing contractual obligations pursuant to Article 307 EC and the Act of Accession is acknowledged, along with the fact that the provisions of the Memorandum could not possibly envisage the content of future EU law adopted which might raise questions about its compatibility with the content of the investment treaties binding upon the acceding and candidate countries. In order to address this problem, a general provision for consultation is being laid down involving the US Administration and the Commission. This consultation will be carried out by established means, for instance informal contacts between the Commission and US officials, contacts through diplomatic channels, the US–EU Senior Level Coordinating Group; they will be pursued when EU measures affecting foreign investment are proposed and their purpose will be 'to address, consistent with the objective of this Understanding, any incompatibility that would arise from the adoption of any such measure'. The views of the acceding and candidate countries, along with those of Member States with agreements with the USA that may be affected' will be approached by the US Administration and the Commission 'with a good faith effort to be take[n] into account'.

In legal terms, there is no doubt that the Memorandum is not a judicially enforceable set of rules: in its very first paragraph, it is described as a 'political understanding' and the first of its concluding provisions defines it as a 'political arrangement reflecting the participants' intentions with regard to the matters it

---

[74] See Art 57(2) EC.

[75] See Art 60 EC.

[76] That would be either 10 years from the date of the entry into force of the relevant EC or national measure or 20 years from the date of the entry into force of the investment treaty, whichever date was the later.

addresses and . . . not an agreement binding under international law'. This non-binding document nevertheless sets out a framework within which a number of states are to approach, and in certain cases, amend legally binding obligations.

In substantive terms, the informal effect of the agreement is reflected by the content of its provisions. For instance, the distinctly non-committal language used in the Memorandum is noticeable in the issue of the definition of a company or firm under Article 48 EC. Apart from the specific sectors where the acceding and candidate countries can deviate from their bilateral commitments, the Memorandum sets out, in essence, a framework for consultation. This lies at the very core of what the participants view as the inevitable possibility of an eventual conflict between the duty of the acceding and candidate states to comply with EC law and their duty to implement the pre-existing agreement with the USA. This framework of consultation is construed widely: it is to take place between the Commission and the US Administration whenever the accession of new members raises questions concerning the implementation or application by the latter of EU measures that would affect US investments. The objective of the consultation would be the protection of existing investments.

In so far as consultation lies at the very core of the *modus operandi* of the Memorandum, it might appear tempting to dismiss it as of merely rhetorical significance. After all, it is noteworthy that the right of the Commission, in the absence of a mutually satisfactory solution, to have recourse to Article 226 EC against any acceding country deemed to have violated Article 307 EC is acknowledged twice; so is the duty of the acceding countries to adjust their obligations laid down in the investment agreements pursuant to Article 307 EC and the Act of Accession. However, the Memorandum is an interesting document whose main tenor is consistent with other threads of EC external relations and whose implications may be directly relevant to the way in which the Community may manage the coordination of its external posture with that of its Member States. This assessment is based on the following grounds. First, the Memorandum is truly innovative because of its multilateral personal scope as it involves, in effect, three parties, that is the contracting parties to the direct investment agreements and the Commission. Viewed in isolation, their participation is hardly surprising: on the one hand, the acceding and candidate countries and the USA were bound by the agreements in question and, on the other hand, the Commission was responsible for overseeing the whole pre-accession process. However, bringing all these parties together in an effort to set up a common mechanism which would apply to all their agreements was noteworthy, all the more so as it took place prior to the enlargement itself.

It is the role of the Commission which is most interesting. It is recalled that, in *Burgoa*, the Court had established 'a duty on the part of the institutions of the Community not to impede the performance of the obligations of Member States which stem from a prior agreement'.[77] The open-ended nature of that duty notwithstanding, it is clear that it refers to cases where a Member State is called upon to reconcile its international law obligations with its specific Community

---

[77] N7 above, para 9.

law duties. In initiating and participating actively in the process which led to the adoption of the Memorandum of Understanding, the Commission raises this duty to an entirely different level: it adopts a proactive approach in liaising with the third country whose pre-existing bilateral agreements may be affected by EC law and engages in negotiation prior to accession involving even states whose prospect of accession is further apart in time. It intervened in the relationship between acceding and candidate countries and a third country and brought them together under a common umbrella rather than confining them to a set of individual processes regarding the different bilateral agreements. All in all, this was an interesting initiative: far from preparing for yet another round of disputes, the Commission chose to engage the United States in a process which would otherwise be not only fraught with uncertainty but also quite time-consuming.

Whilst the political nature of the Memorandum is not in dispute, its function may be quite relevant to the legal resolution of specific disputes. These are inevitable, as the Memorandum views the reconciliation of the content of the investment agreements with that of Community law as an ongoing process whose parameters cannot be envisaged in advance. However, even for those issues which it fails to resolve, it provides points of reference as to how they ought to be approached. This is relevant not only to the function of the Commission and US officials who are required to liaise in the process of consultation but, also, to the function entrusted to national courts as a matter of Community law, more clearly in *Budvar*. This is the second point which highlights the significance of the Memorandum of Understanding: in setting out the parameters within which certain pre-existing international obligations of the new Member States are to be approached, the Community institutions may attribute concrete meaning to the obligations imposed by the Court upon national institutions. Not only does this illustrate an interesting example of implied synergy between the various Community organs, but it also brings practical benefit to the national authorities.

A final point would be related to the role of Article 307 EC in the management of EC external relations. The scope and intensity of this enlargement can only indicate the prominence that this provision is likely to attain. However, it does not follow that its application would be bound to become the centre of constant legal controversy. This is partly because the case of the Memorandum of Understanding highlights a specific approach to actual and potential conflicts which may become a paradigm for the management of the application of Article 307 EC in an efficient, consensual and timely manner. Most importantly, the application of Article 307 should be placed within the broader context of EC external relations. The Community has exhibited a remarkable momentum in establishing frameworks of cooperation with third countries. In some cases, this effort has played a considerable political, as well as economic, role which should not be overestimated, the case of the Stabilisation and Association Agreements with countries in the West Balkans being an example.[78] The

---

[78] See M Cremona, 'Creating the New Europe: the Stability Pact for South Eastern Europe in the Context of EU–SEE Relations' (1999) 32 *Cambridge Yearbook of European Legal Studies* 463.

intensity of disputes centred around the application of Article 307 EC is in reverse correlation to the scope of and intensity with which the Community is linked to the outside world. The case of the free trade agreements between Slovenia and some of its Balkan neighbours is indicative. This highlights yet again the dynamic nature of the process envisaged under Article 307 EC. This appears to have been grasped by the Community institutions. In the last two years, the Community has appeared eager to pursue its relations with a number of third countries on the basis of a structured approach which would be linked to various strands of its external policy.

5. THE POLITICAL UNDERPINNINGS OF THE APPLICATION OF ARTICLE 307 EC

Another case illustrating the repercussions of Article 307 EC, when addressed within the broader context of EC external relations, is the renegotiation of the Partnership and Cooperation Agreement with Russia. That agreement had been signed in June 1994 as a mixed agreement. In order to ensure the application of its provisions to the new Member States, the Community had been negotiating with the Russian authorities for a considerable period of time only formally to confirm its extension three days prior to the date of accession. A Protocol to the Agreement was signed by all contracting parties forming an integral part of the Agreement[79] and stating that it would apply provisionally with effect from 1 May 2004, that is the date of the new accession.[80]

In the light of the links between the acceding states and Russia, the significance of this development was illustrated by its timing. In fact, it is a parallel development which highlights the economic and political context of the extension of the PCA with Russia. On the date of the signature of the Protocol to the PCA, the European Union and Russia issued a Joint Statement on EU Enlargement and EU-Russian Relations.[81] This document starts off with a reference to the Protocol and, then, highlights a number of issues in relation to which specific arrangements had been agreed upon by the two parties. What follows is a list of areas of economic activity in which the intensity of the wording varies considerably. In a few areas, a positive agreement as to the course of action to be taken is expressed. For instance, in relation to imports of certain steel products, the parties agree to adapt the PCA in a way which would ensure an overall increase of the quota allocated to Russian imports. In the area of anti-dumping duties on Russian imports, transitional special measures were agreed regarding certain specified products,[82] and reviews of others would take place upon 'justified requests by Russian interested parties'. In most areas included in the Joint Statement, it is the intention or wish of the parties that

---

[79] Art 3 of the Protocol.

[80] Art 5(3) of the Protocol.

[81] Brussels, 27 Apr 2004.

[82] The statement refers to specific products exported from Russia such as potassium chloride and grain-oriented electrical sheets.

is stated As regards veterinary measures, for instance, the parties 'confirm their intention to complete the procedures' to introduce new veterinary certificates for EU exports of products of animal origin and to continue negotiations on a veterinary negotiation agreement; they also 'reaffirm [their] commitment to avoid any unnecessary disruption of trade' in animal products. In relation to agricultural products, the parties 'reconfirm their wish to conduct mutual consultations on bilateral tariff quotas'. Following a detailed reference to the arrangements about Kaliningrad, the parties refer to the area of energy in which the Union 'recognises that long term contracts have played and will continue to play an important role in ensuring the stable and reliable supplies of Russian natural gas to the EU market'.

The Joint Statement was clearly instrumental to the agreement on the extension of the PCA to the new Member States. In political terms, this was quite significant. Indeed, so keen was the Russian government to ensure that its concerns would be taken into account that, in certain areas, the Statement merely refers to developments provided in the Act of Accession of the new Member States.[83] Furthermore, and in response to the concern of the Russian government about the treatment of its minorities in the Baltic states, the Joint Statement concludes by 'welcom[ing] EU membership as a firm guarantee for the protection of human rights and the protection of persons belonging to minorities' whereas '[b]oth sides underline their commitment to the protection of human rights and the protection of persons belonging to minorities'.

There is no doubt about the lack of legal effect of the Joint Statement on EU Enlargement and EU–Russian Relations. However, both its timing and content raise the question of its relation to the Protocol to the PCA. In the Statement itself, the parties 'take note' of the Protocol and, 'taking into account the substantial work which has already been done', 'agree to step up [their] efforts to address a number of outstanding issues'. This wording reveals the true dimension of the Statement: rather than clarifying the application of the PCA to the new Member States, it merely sets out the framework within which agreement to the extension of the latter was reached. Viewed from this angle, the adoption of the Joint Statement is relevant to the application of Article 307 EC both directly and indirectly: on the one hand, it enabled the Union to avoid tangible tensions with a most important partner of the new Member States prior to accession; on the other hand, it provided the opportunity to address a whole range of issues of its trade relations with Russia in an era where the Union seeks to consolidate its economic relations with its partners.

6. CONCLUSION

The expansion of the scope of the principles governing Article 307(2) EC as developed by the Court of Justice and the expansion and sophistication of processes

---

[83] For instance, the gradual alignment of Hungarian customs legislation to the Common Customs Tariff lasting for a period of 3 years from accession to Russian exports of non-alloyed aluminium into Hungary.

originating in EC institutions and aiming at forestalling the difficulties of application of that provision have highlighted the multifarious aspects of the interests underpinning Article 307 EC. Viewed as complementary, the above developments have indicated that the application of that provision is necessarily of a dynamic nature, ultimately dependent upon the extent to which a variety of actors may manage to comply with distinct, albeit interacting, Community law duties. Within this context, the nature and interrelationship of the functions imposed upon or assumed by the relevant Community and national institutions becomes clearer: the Commission appears increasingly willing to take initiatives and cooperate with acceding states and their international partners in order to address potential incompatibilities with Community law prior to accession; following accession, the national courts are to interpret pre-existing agreements between Member States and third countries in a manner consistent with Community law, albeit as far as possible and in full compliance with international law; the national executive and legislative authorities are to seek to renegotiate and adjust their agreements in cases where they are deemed to be incompatible with the Community legal order, failing which they should denounce them. It is the individual and cumulative effects of the above functions that define the multi-level and dynamic nature of the evolving construction of Article 307 EC.

Part III

The Practice of EC International Relations

9

Substantive Trade Law – The Case of Anti-dumping

1. INTRODUCTION

THIS BOOK HAS examined the Common Commercial Policy at some length. It has focused on its constitutional foundations and the normative principles introduced by the Court of Justice and developed over the years in its case law. The analysis so far has shown that, far from being sacrosanct doctrines, these principles have developed on a highly differentiated basis and account has been taken of the interactions between the Community institutions and the Member States and the evolving relationship of all of them with the outside world. Against this constitutional and deeply political setting, it would be interesting to see how specific aspects of the Common Commercial Policy (CCP) have been applied in practice. This is the subject-matter of the current chapter. Its aim is not to provide a comprehensive analysis of the substantive content of this policy. Instead, this chapter will provide an overview of the unilateral measures adopted under Article 133 EC and will focus on anti-dumping law, that is the most popular trade instrument currently available. By doing so, it will highlight a number of issues of particular relevance to the broader themes analysed in this book.

2. AN OVERVIEW

The establishment of a customs union between the Member States has internal as well as external effects. In accordance with Article 25 EC, all customs duties on imports and exports and charges having equivalent effect are prohibited. In addition, duties on imports from third countries are imposed on the basis of a Common Customs Tariff decided by the Council by qualified majority voting under Article 26 EC. The relevant Regulation was adopted with effect from 1 July 1968, that is earlier than originally envisaged.[1] The current Regulation contains a

---

[1] Council Reg 950/68 [1968] OJ Spec Ed (I) 275, repealed by Council Reg 2658/87 [1987] OJ L 256/1.

combined nomenclature which the Commission has been delegated to review. The Commission annually adopts a regulation reproducing the complete version of the Combined Nomenclature together with the applicable rates of duty. In addition to the existence of a common nomenclature, the application of the Common Customs Tariff entails the adoption of common rules on the origin of the imported products and the customs arrangements to be applied by the customs authorities.[2]

2.1. Imports and Exports

Following the conclusion of the Uruguay Round, the Community rules on imports were laid down in Regulation 3285/94.[3] After a considerable period of flexible, quota-dominated application of the CCP principles,[4] this regime introduced the principle of free importation into the Community market, albeit subject to safeguard measures provided for under WTO law. In particular, Regulation 3285/94 provides for a Community information, consultation, investigation and surveillance procedure and authorises the EC institutions to impose safeguard measures in cases of products imported in increased quantities or under such conditions as to threaten to cause serious injury to Community producers.[5] Regulation 3285/94 is not of unlimited scope, as special rules apply to imports from non-market economy countries.[6] Traditionally, a specific regime had been provided for certain textile products.[7] However, the Multi-Fibre Agreement on Textiles and Clothing expired on 1 January 2005 and the textiles sector has been fully integrated into the rules laid down in the GATT. As a result, imports from China into United States and the Community have increased considerably. This has given rise to protests by domestic producers urging the authorities to curb those imports.[8] In the Community, in particular, the Commission was caught between these claims from the industry, supported by a number of governments, and the opposition of other Member States which considered any Community intervention unnecessarily protectionist. In June 2005, the Commission reached an agreement with the

---

[2] See Council Reg 2913/92 establishing the Community Customs Code [1994] OJ L 302/1. For a detailed analysis, see T Lyons, *EC Customs Law* (Oxford: OUP, 2001).

[3] Council Reg 3285/94 on the common rules for imports and repealing Regulation 518/94 [1994] OJ L 349/53.

[4] See the analysis in Ch 1 above.

[5] Art 16 *ff* of Reg 3285/94, n3 above.

[6] Reg 519/94 [1994] OJ L 67/89.

[7] Reg 3030/93 on common rules on imports of certain textile products from third countries, [1993] OJ L 275/1; Reg 517/94 [1994] OJ L 67/1 covers imports of textiles from non-market economy countries with no special contractual relationship with the EC.

[8] See J Mayer, 'Not Totally Naked: Textiles and Clothing Trade in a Quota-free Environment' (2005) 39 *JWT* 393.

Chinese authorities whereby imports of ten product categories would be limited until 2008.[9]

In addition, a set of rules governing exports to third countries has been adopted under Article 133 EC. Laid down in Regulation 2603/69,[10] these rules introduce the principle of free exportation and include an exceptional clause concerning public morality, public policy, public security, the protection of the health and life of humans, animals or plants, national cultural treasures and industrial and commercial property. The scope of these rules is not unlimited, as certain categories of products considered to be of a sensitive nature are excluded.[11] In addition, special rules apply to exports of dual-use goods, that is products which may be of both civil and military application.[12] These rules will be examined in a later chapter.

2.2. Trade Policy Instruments

In order to ensure fair conditions of competition in its trade relations with third countries, the Community has adopted a variety of legal instruments. The most commonly used, that is anti-dumping measures, will be discussed separately. A separate legal regime targets subsidised products. First enacted during the transitional period and then amended a number of times, these provisions were given their current form following the completion of the Uruguay Round in order to reflect the content of the Agreement on Subsidies and Countervailing Measures. They are now laid down in Regulation 2026/97.[13] Targeting imports whose subsidised nature is deemed to cause injury to the Community industry, this regime enables the Community to impose duties provided that three conditions are met. First, the subsidy must be specific and consist of any government provision of a financial contribution or any other form of income support which confers a benefit on the exporter. Secondly, the import sales must cause or threaten to cause damage to a substantial part of the Community industry; this includes a loss of market share, reduced prices for producers and resulting pressure on production, sales, profits or productivity. Thirdly, the imposition of the duties must serve the Community interests, a corollary of which is that its costs for the Community should not be disproportionate to the benefits anticipated.[14]

---

[9] See Memorandum of Understanding Between the European Commission and the Ministry of Commerce of the People's Republic of China on the Export of Certain Chinese Textile and Clothing Products to the European Union, agreed on 12 June 2005. For the amendment to the relevant rules, see Commission Reg 1084/2005 amending Annexes II, III and V to Council Reg (EEC) No 3030/93 on common rules for imports of certain textile products from third countries [2005] OJ L 177/19.

[10] Council Reg 2603/69, [1969] OJ L 324/25 amended by Reg 3918/91, [1991] OJ L 372/31.

[11] For instance, oil products: see Reg 1934/82, [1982] OJ L 211/1.

[12] Council Reg 1334/2000 setting up a Community regime for the control of exports of dual-use items and technology [2000] OJ L 159/1.

[13] Council Reg 2026/97 on protection against subsidized imports from countries not members of the European Community [1997] OJ L 288/1.

[14] For a detailed analysis of this regime, see K Adamantopoulos and MJ Pereyra-Friedrichsen, *EU Anti-Subsidy Law and Practice* (Bembridge: Palladian Law Publishing, 2001).

Another important part of the external trade policy of the Community is a set of rules aiming at eliminating trade barriers introduced or maintained by third countries. Laid down in Regulation 3286/94, this regime sets out a procedure which enables the Community industry to lodge a complaint with the Commission regarding trade barriers which third countries are alleged to maintain in order to restrict access to their markets.[15] The function of the Trade Barriers Regulation is distinct from the other trade policy instruments of the Community: rather than defending Community traders from the efforts of third country traders to penetrate the Community market, it aims at assisting Community traders to penetrate third-country markets.[16]

2.3. The 'Everything but Arms' Initiative

An important part of the Community's external trade policy is the Generalised Tariff Preferences scheme. This system ensures that imports from developing countries are not subject to customs duties normally charged, hence facilitating trade with them. Originating in a recommendation by the United Nations Conference on Trade and Development in 1968, the current system is laid down in Council Regulation 980/2005 and is applicable for the period between 1 January 2005 until the end of 2008.[17] The main thrust of this system consists of a combination of preferential arrangements. A general one provides for the complete or partial reduction or suspension of customs duties as laid down in the Common Customs Tariff. There is provision for a special incentive arrangement granted on the basis of the beneficiary's conduct on sustainable development and good governance.

Another special arrangement is related to the 'everything but arms' initiative. Adopted in 2001 by means of a Council Regulation upon a proposal by the Commission,[18] this initiative granted duty-free access to imports of all products from least developed countries and lifted any quantitative restrictions. There are two exceptions to this regime. As suggested by its title, the first consists of arms and munitions which are excluded in their entirety. The second exception refers to the special regime on imports of fresh bananas, rice and sugar and aims at their

---

[15] Council Reg 3286/94 laying down Community procedures in the field of the Common Commercial Policy in order to ensure the exercise of the Community's rights under international trade rules, in particular those established under the auspices of WTO [1994] OJ L 349/71. This instrument was subsequently amended by Council Reg 456/95 [1995] OJ L 41/3. This instrument was originally laid down in the so-called Commercial Policy Instrument adopted in 1984 (Council Reg 2641/84 on the strengthening of the common commercial policy with regard in particular to protection against illicit commercial practices [1984] OJ L 252/1).

[16] For an elaborate analysis of the TBR, see R MacLean and B Volpi, *EU Trade Barrier Regulation – Tackling Unfair Foreign Trade Practices* (Bembridge: Palladian Law Publishing, 2000).

[17] [2005] OJ L 169/1.

[18] Reg 416/2001 [2001] OJ L 60/1.

phased liberalization.[19] At the time of writing, 49 developing countries benefit from this initiative, which is now incorporated into Regulation 980/2005.[20] Whilst the terms of the Community's scheme of generalised preferences are reviewed regularly, the 'everything but arms' provisions are to be maintained for an unlimited period of time.

The success of this initiative is by no means automatic. It depends on a number of factors which, apart from the extension of its scope, are related to the ability of the least developed countries to respond, not least by diversifying their exports.[21] However, it constitutes a significant illustration of the interrelationship between trade and non-trade interests. In addition, it provides a snapshot of the ways in which the Community may adjust its trade policy in order to address non-trade concerns. The analysis in a later chapter will show how this power is linked to other spheres of activity in the EU legal order.

2.4. Anti-dumping Law

Anti-dumping consists of the imposition of duties on imports of products whose price is considered to be lower than that at which they are being sold in the exporting country. There is a healthy debate about the function and objectives of anti-dumping policy. On the one hand, anti-dumping duties have a distinct protective intent which undermines the establishment of a competitive, rule-based international market.[22] Put rather succinctly, 'anti-dumping, as practiced today, is a witches' brew of the worst of policy-making: power politics, bad economics, and shameful public administration'.[23] On the other hand, anti-dumping policy is viewed as a 'legitimate and perfectly normal instrument of trade policy' which aims at ensuring conditions of fair competition on the international market.[24]

An elaborate examination of this debate is beyond the scope of this analysis.[25] Instead, suffice it to point out that the imposition of anti-dumping duties is sanctioned under Article VI GATT 1994 pursuant to which a specific agreement has been concluded. First agreed upon at the Tokyo Round in the form of the Anti-Dumping Code and then clarified at the Uruguay Round, the Agreement on

---

[19] See Commission Reg 1401/2002 laying down detailed rules for the opening and administration of the tariff quotas for rice, originating in the least developed countries [2002] OJ L 203/42 and, for raw sugar cane, Commission Reg 1381/2002 [2002] OJ L 200/14.

[20] [2005] OJ L 169/1.

[21] P Brenton, 'Integrating the Least Developed Countries into the World Trading System: The Current Impact of European Union Preferences Under "Everything But Arms"' (2003) 37 *JWT* 623.

[22] See R Boscheck, 'The Governance of Global Market Relations: The Case of Substituting Antitrust for Antidumping' (2001) 24 *World Competition* 41, especially at 54–62.

[23] JM Finger, 'Reform' in JM Finger (ed), *Antidumping—How It Works and Who Gets Hurt* (Ann Arbor Mich: Michigan University Press, 1993) 57.

[24] See the speech by Sir Leon Brittan, the then Trade Commissioner, at CEEC Anti-dumping Seminar, Brussels 27 Jan 1997.

[25] See the summary in MJ Trebilcock and R Howse, *The Regulation of International Trade* (2nd edn, London: Routledge, 2001) 177–88.

Implementation of Article VI of GATT 1994 sets out the framework within which domestic authorities are to impose anti-dumping measures. Exercised within this context, anti-dumping measures have turned out to be one of the most popular instruments of trade policy on the international scene.

The area of anti-dumping law falls within the Common Commercial Policy of the Community and, hence, is covered by the latter's exclusive competence. The main instrument regulating the application of this policy is Regulation 349/96 (Basic Regulation) adopted under Article 133 EC.[26] This sets out an elaborate procedure carried out under the supervision of the Commission, and provides for the interaction of a number of interested parties. Anti-dumping law and policy is a highly technical and complex area of law whose intricacies and details may be mastered through deep knowledge of legal practice.[27] The following sections will summarise the various elements and stages of the procedure set out in the Basic Regulation and will highlight the ways in which these are approached by the Community judiciary.

3. SUBSTANTIVE ISSUES OF ANTI-DUMPING LAW

Anti-dumping duties are imposed by the Commission on a provisional basis or the Council as a definitive measure. A decision on their imposition is dependent upon three conditions, namely the finding of dumping, the determination of injury to the Community industry and the assessment of the interest of the Community. Within the context of the Basic Regulation, the Commission is in consultation with an Advisory Committee established under Article 15(1) of the Basic Regulation. This consists of representatives of each Member State, with a representative of the Commission as chairman.

3.1. Dumping

In order to determine whether an imported product is 'dumped' in the Community market, a comparison is carried out between the export price and the normal value of the product: the former refers to the price charged in the Community market, whereas the latter refers to the price normally charged in the exporting country.

The rule established under Article 2(1) of the Basic Regulation is that the normal value 'shall normally be based on the prices paid or payable, in the ordinary

---

[26] [1996] OJ L 56/1 last amended by Council Reg 461/2004 [2004] OJ L 77/12.

[27] For a detailed analysis, see van Bael and J-F Bellis, *Anti-Dumping and Other Trade Protection Laws of the EC* (4th edn, The Hague: Kluwer, 2004) at Chs 2–9, W Müller, N Khan and H-A Neumann, *EC Anti-dumping Law—A Commentary on Regulation 384/96* (Chichester: John Wiley and Sons, 1998), and C Stanbrook and P Bentley, *Dumping and Subsidies* (3rd edn, The Hague: Kluwer, 1996), EA Vermulst and P Waer, *EC Anti-dumping Law and Practice* (London: Sweet and Maxwell, 1996).

course of trade, by independent customers in the exporting country'. However, there are cases where the normal value may be disregarded for a number of reasons: sales on the domestic market may be made between companies which are related or which have a compensatory arrangement with each other; imports may come from non-market economy countries; there may be no sales at all in the exporting country or the volume of sales may be insufficient, that is less than 5 per cent of the sales volume of the product to EC. In those cases, the Community authorities assess dumping on the basis of a constructed normal value.

In any case, the determination of the normal value may not take into account sales at a loss, that is at a price below unit production costs including selling, general and administrative costs. These are not considered to occur in the ordinary course of trade if they arise in substantial quantities within an extended period of time and at prices not providing for the recovery of all costs within a reasonable time.

The constructed price is determined under Article 2(3) of the Basic Regulation pursuant to two methods. The first is based on the cost of production in the country of origin, to which the Commission adds a reasonable amount for selling, general and administrative costs and for profits. The second method is based on the export prices to an appropriate third country in the ordinary course of trade, provided that these prices are representative. An interesting illustration of the steps followed by the Commission in order to establish the normal value of a product investigated for dumping in the Community market is set out in Commission Regulation 358/2002 imposing a provisional anti-dumping duty on imports of certain tube and pipe fittings, of iron or steel, originating in the Czech Republic, Malaysia, Russia, the Republic of Korea and Slovakia. In the preamble to the Regulation, the Commission's approach is described as follows:[28]

> As far as the determination of normal value is concerned, the Commission first established, for each exporting producer, whether its total domestic sales of TPFs [ie tube and pipe fittings] were representative in comparison with its total export sales to the Community. In accordance with Article 2(2) of the basic Regulation, domestic sales were considered representative when the total domestic sales volume of each exporting producer was at least 5 % of its total export sales volume to the Community.

> The Commission subsequently identified those types of TPFs, sold domestically by the companies having representative domestic sales, that were identical or directly comparable with the types sold for export to the Community.

> For each type sold by the exporting producers on their domestic markets and found to be directly comparable to the type sold for export to the Community, it was established whether domestic sales were sufficiently representative for the purposes of Article 2(2) of the basic Regulation. Domestic sales of a particular type of TPF were considered sufficiently representative when the total domestic sales volume of that type during the IP

---

[28] [2002] OJ L 56/4, paras 15–21.

represented 5 % or more of the total sales volume of the comparable type of TPF exported to the Community.

An examination was also made as to whether the domestic sales of each type could be regarded as having been made in the ordinary course of trade, by establishing the proportion of profitable sales to independent customers of the type in question. In cases where the sales volume of TPFs, sold at a net sales price equal to or above the calculated cost of production, represented 80 % or more of the total sales volume and where the weighted average price of that type was equal to or above the cost of production, normal value was based on the actual domestic price, calculated as a weighted average of the prices of all domestic sales made during the IP, irrespective of whether these sales were profitable or not. In cases where the weighted average price was below the cost of production or where the volume of profitable sales of TPFs represented less than 80 % but 10 % or more of the total sales volume, normal value was based on the actual domestic price, calculated as a weighted average of profitable sales only.

In cases where the volume of profitable sales of any type of TPF represented less than 10 % of the total sales volume, it was considered that this particular type was sold in insufficient quantities for the domestic price to provide an appropriate basis for the establishment of the normal value.

Wherever domestic prices of a particular type sold by an exporting producer could not be used in order to establish normal value, another method had to be applied. In this regard, the Commission used the prices of the product concerned charged on the domestic market by another producer. In all cases where this was not possible, and in the absence of any other reasonable method, constructed normal value was used.

In all cases where constructed normal value was used and in accordance with Article 2(3) of the basic Regulation, normal value was constructed by adding to the manufacturing costs of the exported types, adjusted where necessary, a reasonable percentage for selling, general and administrative expenses ("SG & A") and a reasonable margin of profit. To this end, the Commission examined whether the SG & A incurred and the profit realised by each of the producing exporters concerned on the domestic market constituted reliable data. Actual domestic SG & A expenses were considered reliable where the domestic sales volume of the company concerned could be regarded as representative. The domestic profit margin was determined on the basis of domestic sales made in the ordinary course of trade.

The choice of the method pursuant to which the normal value is constructed as well as the determination of the criteria on the basis of which this assessment is made is an exercise often fraught with problems. For instance, not infrequently, the Commission has estimated the profit margin on the basis of profitable sales, without taking losses into account and, hence, without averaging profits and losses. As this often led to the inflation of the normal value, the final assessment by the Commission was controversial.

The export price is determined by the Commission under Article 2(8)–(9) of the Basic Regulation. This is the price actually paid or payable for the product when sold for export from the country under investigation to the Community. However, there are cases where no export price may be determined: the imported goods may be exchanged for other goods rather than sold at a price or the export price may be deemed unreliable because of an association or compensatory arrangement between the exporter and the importer. In those cases, the Commission is to determine a constructed export price. This is ascertained on the basis of the price at which the imported products are first resold to an independent buyer. However, if they are not resold, or at least not in the condition in which they were imported, then the constructed export price will be determined 'on any reasonable basis'.[29] In either case, adjustments are to be made for all costs incurred between exportation and resale, including duties and taxes, as well as for profits accruing.

The normal value and the export price of the imported product are to be compared in accordance with Article 2(10) of the Basic Regulation which provides for the comparison to be 'fair'. This refers to a comparison at the same level of trade and regarding sales made as nearly as possible at the same time. In addition, other differences which affect price comparability are to be taken into account. If the comparison may not be carried out on this basis, a number of adjustments will have to be made which may refer to a number of other factors. These include the physical characteristics of the product broadly construed which include its composition; import charges and indirect taxes; discounts, rebates and quantities; level of trade, including differences arising in Original Equipment Manufacturer sales; transport, insurance, handling, loading and ancillary costs; packing; credit; after-sales costs; commission and currency conversions.

The dumping margin is determined in accordance with Article 2(11–12) of the Basic Regulation. The Community institutions may choose one of the following methods: a comparison of a weighted average normal value with a weighted average of prices of all export transactions to the Community; or a comparison of individual normal values and individual export prices to the Community on a transaction-by-transaction basis. A normal value established on a weighted average basis may be compared to prices of all individual export transactions to the Community if there is a pattern of export prices which differs significantly among different purchasers, regions or time periods.

3.2. Injury and Community Interest

The imposition of anti-dumping duties is dependent upon the finding of injury suffered by the Community industry. The definition of the latter is provided in Article 4 of the Basic Regulation. The main principle is that Community industry refers to either all producers of the product under consideration or those whose production is a major proportion of the Community output of the product. This latter definition is explained in the badly drafted provision of Article 5(4) of the

---

[29] Art 8(9) of the Basic Reg.

Basic Regulation: in practice, Community producers who manufacture at least 25 per cent of Community production may be considered as 'Community industry', unless other Community producers accounting for a larger share of such production oppose the complaint which gave rise to the Commission investigation.

There are three deviations from the above principle. First, when Community producers are related to the exporters or importers or are themselves importers of the allegedly dumped product, they may be excluded from the determination of Community industry. Secondly, where the territory of the Community market may be divided into two or more competitive markets, a regional market may be considered to be the Community market.[30] Thirdly, when no separate identification of Community production is possible, that may be defined in terms broader than the characteristics of the imported product under investigation.[31]

The definition of injury is laid down in Article 3 of the Basic Regulation with reference to material injury or threat of material industry or material retardation of the establishment of Community industry. However, no definition of 'material injury' is provided. Instead, it is stated that its determination should be based on 'positive evidence' and should involve examination of both the volume of the dumped imports and their effect on prices in the Community market for like products, as well as the consequent impact of those imports on the Community industry. Whilst vague, this provision highlights the central role of the establishment of a causal link between the dumped products and the material injury.

Article 3(7) of the Basic Regulation refers to 'known factors other than the dumped imports which at the same time are injuring the Community industry'. These should also be examined by the Community institutions which have to ensure that injury caused by them is not attributed to the dumped products. The exporters of products alleged to be dumped in the Community rely upon this provision frequently and seek to point out various deficiencies of the Community industry which prevent it from competing with imported products.

Finally, the determination of the Community interest is carried out in accordance with Article 21 of the Basic Regulation. The Community institutions are to take into account 'all the various interests taken as a whole, including the interests of the domestic industry and users and consumers'. Two issues in particular are given special consideration: on the one hand, the need to eliminate the trade distorting effects of injurious dumping and, on the other hand, the need to restore

---

[30] This was the case regarding imports of ammonium nitrate from Russia: the Community market was divided into at least two distinct markets, one of which was in the UK. The producers in the UK accounted for the whole of UK production, and demand for the product in the UK was not met by supplies from other EC producers; in addition, the allegedly dumped products concentrated on the UK market. Therefore, for the purposes of the investigation, the Community industry was held by the Commission to be the UK industry for ammonium nitrate.

[31] For instance, if badger hair toothbrush are alleged to be causing injury but there are no data on Community production of such products, the Commission would have to assess injury perhaps in relation to all toothbrushes produced in the Community, that is including nylon, travel toothbrushes etc.

effective competition. It is in the light of those considerations that the absence of any reference to the interests and views of the exporters in the Basic Regulation may be understood.

3.3. Non-market Economy Countries

In assessing the conditions necessary for the imposition of anti-dumping duties, there is an assumption that state controlled economies should be treated differently.[32] This is not an assumption confined to the Community's policy: the second interpretative note to Article VI of the GATT 1994 reads as follows:

> It is recognized that, in the case of imports from a country which has a complete or substantially complete monopoly of its trade and where all domestic prices are fixed by the State, special difficulties may exist in determining price comparability for the purposes of paragraph 1, and in such cases importing contracting parties may find it necessary to take into account the possibility that a strict comparison with domestic prices in such a country may not always be appropriate.

To that effect, Article 2(7) of the Basic Regulation provides that the normal value is to be determined on the basis of the price or constructed value in a 'reference country', that is a market economy third country, or the price of imports from such a third country to other countries or, if this is not possible, on any other reasonable basis. An appropriate market economy third country is to be selected in 'a not unreasonable manner'.

The Community has taken the non-market economy status of the importing country into account, a practice illustrated by the special provision for the assessment of the normal value in Article 2(7)(a) of the Basic Regulation. At the time of writing, these countries include Albania, Armenia, Azerbaijan, Belarus, Georgia, North Korea, Kyrgyzstan, Moldova, Mongolia, Tajikistan, Turkmenistan and Uzbekistan. In Regulation 905/98, the Council singled out the rules regarding the constructed normal value for the list of countries considered to be of a non-market economy whilst setting out a specific regime for China and the Russian Federation.[33] In relation to the latter, the rules about normal value laid down in the Basic Regulation may be used by the Commission if it is shown, on the basis of properly substantiated claims by one or more producers subject to the investigation, that market economy conditions prevail for this producer or these producers in respect of the manufacture and sale of the like product concerned. Such a claim would need to be made in writing and contain sufficient evidence that the producer operates under market economy conditions. Regulation 905/98 sets out a number of indications which are worth quoting in full:

---

[32] On the origins and development of the concept, see F Snyder, 'The Origins of the "Nonmarket Economy": Ideas, Pluralism and Power in EC Anti-dumping Law about China' (2001) 7 *ELJ* 369.
[33] [1998] OJ L 128/18.

—decisions of firms regarding prices, costs and inputs, including for instance raw materials, cost of technology and labour, output, sales and investment, are made in response to market signals reflecting supply and demand, and without significant State interference in this regard, and costs of major inputs substantially reflect market values,
—firms have one clear set of basic accounting records which are independently audited in line with international accounting standards and are applied for all purposes,
—the production costs and financial situation of firms are not subject to significant distortions carried over from the former non-market economy system, in particular in relation to depreciation of assets, other write-offs, barter trade and payment via compensation of debts,
—the firms concerned are subject to bankruptcy and property laws which guarantee legal certainty and stability for the operation of firms, and
—exchange rate conversions are carried out at the market rate.

The Commission is to determine whether these criteria are met within three months of the initiation of the investigation. In this process, the specific views of the Advisory Committee must be heard and the Community industry must be given an opportunity to comment.

This special regime has subsequently been extended to Ukraine, Vietnam and Kazakhstan.[34] Furthermore, in 2002 Russia was removed from it and was assimilated, in terms of the determination of normal value, to other market economies. The reason for this was stated in the preamble to the relevant measure: '[i]n view of the very significant progress made by the Russian Federation towards the establishment of market economy conditions, as recognised by the conclusions of the Russia-European Union Summit on 29 May 2002, it is appropriate to allow normal value for Russian exporters and producers to be established in accordance with the provisions of Article 2(1) to (6) of [the Basic Regulation]'.[35] Recently, the British government suggested that China be granted full market economy status too.[36]

4. PROCEDURAL ISSUES OF ANTI-DUMPING LAW

The assessment of whether anti-dumping duties should be imposed is carried out during a tightly regulated investigation period. In accordance with Article 5(1) of the Basic Regulation, the investigation may be initiated by a complaint lodged in writing with the Commission or a Member State by any natural or legal person or any association acting on behalf of a Community industry. In principle, the Commission has the right to initiate anti-dumping investigations on its own motion. However, in practice, this has rarely been the case.

---

[34] Council Reg 2238/2000 of 9 Oct 2000 amending Reg 384/96 on protection against dumped imports from countries not members of the European Community [2000] OJ L 257/2.

[35] Para 5 of the preamble to Council Reg 1972/2002 of 5 Nov 2002 amending Reg 384/96 on the protection against dumped imports from countries not members of the European Community [2002] OJ L 305/1.

[36] See *Financial Times*, 6 July 2005, 12.

The Commission carries out a *prima facie* assessment of the information supplied to it within a period of 45 days. Once the information available has been deemed sufficiently credible to justify the initiation of proceedings, a notice of initiation is published in the Official Journal. Under Article 5(7) of the Basic Regulation, proceedings may not be initiated against countries whose imports represent a market share of below 1 per cent unless such countries collectively account for 3 per cent or more of Community consumption. In principle, anti-dumping investigations last for a year, and in no case for longer than 15 months.

The Commission, in accordance with Article 5(11) of the Basic Regulation, is to inform a number of parties of the initiation of the proceedings. These include the exporters, importers and representative associations of importers or exporters known to it to be concerned, as well as representatives of the exporting country and the complainants. In order to collect information, the Commission produces questionnaires which it disseminates, both on its own initiative and upon request to known importers and exporters and to any other interested party which, then, have at least 30 days to reply. For the purposes of their interaction with the Commission, the interested parties pay particular attention to the notice of initiation as this set out the time limits within which those parties may make themselves known and submit information.

Article 6 of the Basic Regulation provides for a number of procedural rights to be enjoyed by interested parties. These may be summarized as follows. First, the interested parties which have made themselves known to the Commission have the right to be heard. In accordance with Article 6(5) of the Basic Regulation, in a written request submitted within the period defined in the notice of initiation, they must show that they are interested parties, that they are likely to be affected by the outcome of the proceedings and that there are particular reasons why they should be heard.

Secondly, the right to request a meeting is laid down in Article 6(6) for the benefit of importers, exporters, representatives of the government of the exporting country and the complainants. A request for a meeting, which by no means imposes any duty to attend on any other party, must be submitted in writing. Any failure to attend such a meeting is not prejudicial to the case of the relevant party. It should be pointed out that the function of meetings is not superficial as it enables the parties not only further to familiarise themselves with the arguments of the other parties but also to rebut them. However, any oral information given is taken into account by the Commission only if subsequently confirmed in writing.[37]

Thirdly, complainants, importers and association of exporters, users and consumers which have made themselves known to the Commission may, upon a written request, inspect any non-confidential document submitted to the Commission by any party.

---

[37] See T Giannakopoulos, 'The Right to be Orally Heard by the Commission in Antitrust, Merger, Anti-dumping/Anti-subsidies and State Aid Community Procedures' (2001) 24 *World Competition* 541 at 558–561 and 564 *ff*.

Fourthly, Article 20(2) of the Basic Regulation provides for the right of final disclosure. Granted to the complainants, importers, exporters and their representative associations, this denotes the right to be informed of the essential facts and considerations on the basis of which the Commission intends to recommend the imposition of definitive duties or the definitive collection of the amounts secured by way of provisional duties. Again, the exercise of this right depends upon a written request which should be submitted within one month following the publication of the imposition of the provisional duty.

5. JUDICIAL REVIEW IN ANTI-DUMPING LAW

The above overview of the substantive aspects of anti-dumping policy indicated that the assessment of its main elements is subject to a number of factors expressed in a open-ended manner. This raises two interrelated questions, namely the question of the extent to which the Community institutions enjoy discretion in their substantive assessment and the intensity of scrutiny that the Court is prepared to exercise in the review of that assessment.

5.1. Intensity of Review over Substantive and Procedural Issues

The Court of Justice has consistently pointed out that, in carrying out their function by the process laid down in the Basic Regulation, the Community institutions are to make policy choices of a complex economic nature. This entails the conferment of wide discretion. A number of examples illustrate this approach. In relation to the power to determine the constructed normal value, for instance, the wide discretion enjoyed by the Commission has been sanctioned in no uncertain terms. In *Nakajima*, the applicant was a Japanese producer of printers who attacked the precursor to the then Basic Regulation.[38] It argued that its provision regarding the determination of the constructed value in cases where there are no sales in the exporting state was illegal due to lack of essential procedural requirements. In particular, it claimed that the Community institutions were allowed to discriminate against imports by constructing their normal value by reference to undertakings whose structure would not be comparable to that of the importer. For instance, Nakajima argued that it did not have any marketing structure for its products as its entire production output was sold at the 'ex-factory' stage to independent distributors. However, all of the reference undertakings considered by the Commission in order to construct the normal value had a vertically integrated structure designed to ensure distribution of their products within Japan.

---

[38] Case C–69/89 *Nakajima All Precision v Council* [1991] ECR I–2069.

The Court held that '[the text of the then Basic Regulation] left full discretion to the Community authorities by providing for the calculation of SGA (Selling, General and Administrative) expenses and profits on a "reasonable basis"'.[39] This was repeated in relation to the Council Regulation imposing definitive anti-dumping duties on Nakajima: the Court pointed out that it 'has consistently held that [the provision according to which a reasonable amount for SGA expenses had to be included in the constructed normal value] allowed the Community institutions a wide margin of discretion in evaluating that amount'.[40]

The Court then described the objective of the constructed normal value, that is 'to determine the selling price of a product as it would be if that product were sold in its country of origin and consequently, it is the expenses relating to the sales on the domestic markets which must be taken into account'.[41] To that effect, it reached the conclusion that 'normal value of a product must in all cases be constructed as if the product was intended for distribution and sale within the domestic market, regardless of whether or not the producer has, or has access to, a distribution structure'.[42]

A similar approach was also adopted in relation to the determination of the dumping margin. In a cases about ball-bearings, various Japanese companies challenged a Council Regulation imposing definitive anti-dumping duties on imports originating in Japan and Singapore.[43] One of the arguments of the applicant was that the method of calculating the dumping margin adopted by the Commission was arbitrary and unlawful. In particular, it was argued that the transaction-by-transaction method adopted by the Commission to calculate the export price resulted in the export prices below the normal value being left out of account. According to the applicant, that method distorted the calculation of the dumping margin.

The Court rejected this argument and ruled as follows:[44]

[T]he choice between the different methods of calculation . . . requires an appraisal of complex economic situations. The Court must therefore . . . limit its review of such an appraisal to verifying whether the relevant procedural rules have been complied with, whether the facts on which the choice is based have been accurately stated and whether there has been a manifest error of appraisal of a misuse of powers.

---

[39] *Ibid*, para 18.
[40] Para 63.
[41] Para 65.
[42] *Ibid*.
[43] Case 240/84 *NTN Toyo Bearing Company Limited and Others v Council* [1987] ECR 1809.
[44] *Ibid*, para 19. In relation to the choice of a reference country, see Joined Cases 294/86 and 77/87 *Technointorg v Commission and Council* [1988] ECR 6077, at para 29. In addition, see Case 255/84 *Nachi Fujikoshi v Council* [1987] ECR 1861, at para 21, Case C–156/87 *Gestetner Holdings v Council and Commission* [1990] ECR I–781, Case T–155/94 *Climax Paper Converters Ltd v Council* [1996] ECR II–873.

The Court sanctioned the approach taken by the Community institutions. Similarly, in relation to the process of identifying the Community industry, the Court stated in *Nakajima* that:[45]

> it is for the Commission and the Council, in the exercise of their discretion, to determine whether they should exclude from the Community industry producers who are themselves importers of the dumped product. That discretion must be exercised on a case-by-case basis, by reference to all the relevant facts.

The above overview suggests that the discretion enjoyed by the Community institutions in anti-dumping policy is construed by the Court in quite wide terms. In fact, it is very difficult for an applicant to substantiate a violation of EC law on substantive grounds, all the more so in the light of the high threshold raised by the Court's requirements. For instance, misuse of power was held to occur 'only if [the contested decision] appears, on the basis of objective, relevant and consistent indications, to have been adopted in order to achieve purposes other than those for which it was intended'.[46] In the same judgment, the argument of the applicant that anti-dumping duties had been imposed in order to protect mainly the interests of the French industry rather than those of the Community as a whole was dismissed rather summarily: the Court pointed out that a mere reference to the reasons underpinning the imposition of duties set out in contested measure was sufficient and noted that no specific argument had been produced in order to substantiate the claim of misuse of power.

In recent years, there has been a growing concern that review of a more intrusive nature should be considered. In his Opinion in *Gao Yao*, Advocate General Lenz expressed his wish that the Court of First Instance, which at that time was about to assume jurisdiction in anti-dumping cases, exercise a high degree of intensity in its review of such measures. He argued that it appears 'desirable quite generally to investigate very thoroughly the Community institutions' activities in the sphere of anti-dumping law whenever actions are brought'.[47] To a certain extent, the case law of the Court of First Instance has engaged in a close examination of the facts of the cases brought before it.[48] However, the intensity of the review of the Community judiciary appears to be largely confined to the construction of other, non-substantive aspects of anti-dumping legislation.[49] These are examined in the following sections.

---

[45] N38 above, para 80.

[46] Case C–323/88 *Sermes v Directeur des services des douanes de Strasbourg* [1990] ECR I–3027, at para 33.

[47] Case C–75/92 *Gao Yao (Hong Kong) Hua Fa Industrial Co. Ltd v Council* [1994] ECR I–3141, para 95 of his Opinion. See also, for an initial assessment, P Vander Schueren, 'New Anti-dumping Rules and Practice: Wide Discretion held on a Tight Leash?' (1996) 33 *CMLRev* 271.

[48] See, for instance, Case T–161/94 *Sinochem Heilongjiang v Council* [1996] ECR II–695.

[49] See the overview in F Jacobs, 'Judicial Review of Commercial Policy Measures after the Uruguay Round' in N Emiliou and D O'Keeffe (eds), *The European Union and World Trade Law—After the GATT Uruguay Round* (Chichester: John Wiley and Sons, 1996) 329 at 329–37.

5.2. Review of Procedural Issues

The Court has adopted a strict approach to the requirement that the Community institutions comply with the procedural guarantees set out in the Basic Regulation. A clear illustration of this is provided by the judgment in *Al-Jubail*.[50] The applicants challenged a Council Regulation imposing definitive anti-dumping duties on imports of urea originating in Libya and Saudi Arabia. In essence, the applicant's main line of reasoning was centred around the alleged violation of their right to a fair hearing.

One of the specific arguments was focused on the refusal by the Commission to take into account differences in levels of trade and quantities sold in Saudi Arabia and the Community. In particular, the applicant claimed that it had not been informed in advance of the reasons for the Commission's approach. The Court first pointed out that, according to its well-established case law , fundamental rights form an integral part of the general principles of law.[51] Then, it ruled that, when interpreting the rights granted under the Basic Regulation, it is necessary 'to take account in particular of the requirements stemming from the right to a fair hearing, a principle whose fundamental character has been stressed on numerous occasions in the case-law of the Court. Those requirements must be observed not only in the course of proceedings which may result in the imposition of penalties, but also in investigative proceedings prior to the adoption of anti-dumping regulations which, despite their general scope, may directly and individually affect the undertakings concerned and entail adverse consequences for them'.[52]

The Court, then, ruled as follows:[53]

It should be added that, with regard to the right to a fair hearing, any action taken by the Community institutions must be all the more scrupulous in view of the fact that, as they stand at present, the rules in question do not provide all the procedural guarantees for the protection of the individual which may exist in certain national legal systems.

Consequently, in performing their duty to provide information, the Community institutions must act with all due diligence by seeking ... to provide the undertakings concerned, as far as compatible with the obligation not to disclose business secrets, with information relevant to the defence of their interests, choosing, if necessary on their own initiative, the appropriate means of providing such information. In any event, the undertakings concerned should have been placed in a position during the administrative procedure in which they could effectively make known their views on the correctness and relevance of the facts and circumstances alleged and on the evidence presented by the Commission in support of its allegation concerning the existence of dumping and the resultant injury.

---

[50] Case 49/88 *Al-Jubail Fertilizer Company and others v Council* [1991] ECR 3187.
[51] See Case C–260/89 *ERT* [1991] ECR I–2925.
[52] Para 15 with reference to Case 85/87 *Dow Benelux v Commission* [1989] ECR 3137.
[53] Paras 16–17.

Applying these principles to the facts of the case, the Court reached the conclusion that there was nothing in the documents before the Court to show that the Community institutions discharged their duty to place at the applicants' disposal all the information which would have enabled them to defend their interests effectively. The level of intensity applied by the Court in the exercise of its power of review is noteworthy. The Council had relied on an internal mission report after checks in Saudi Arabia and on the minutes of two meetings in Brussels with the representatives of the applicants. However, the information contained in those documents was not subsequently brought to the attention of the applicants. Whilst the Basic Regulation provides for the supply of information orally, the Court pointed out that 'that possibility cannot release the EC authorities from their obligation to ensure that they have evidence to prove that such information was actually communicated'.[54]

Another interesting indication of the scrutiny that the Court is prepared to apply in ensuring compliance with the right to a fair hearing was provided in relation to the applicant's claim that the determination of the injury threshold and the calculation of the allowance for warehousing had been fraught with irregularities. A bone of contention was a letter from the Commission informing the applicant of the rationale and the method chosen to determine the injury threshold. Whilst the Commission claimed to have sent that letter, the applicant insisted that it had not been received. The Court pointed out that the letter had not been sent by registered post and ruled that that 'cannot be regarded as a diligent method of discharging the obligation to provide information laid down in the basic regulation'.[55]

Another case where the right to a fair hearing was raised was *Extramet*.[56] This was an annulment action brought against a Council Regulation imposing anti-dumping duties on the imports of calcium metal originating in China and the Soviet Union. The applicant was the largest importer of calcium metal, essentially from those two countries. These imports constituted the main source of its supplies from which it manufactured granules of pure calcium used primarily in the metallurgical industry. The anti-dumping procedure was brought about after a complaint by the Trade Organization on behalf of Péchiney, that is the only producer of calcium metal in the Community and direct competitor of Extramet.

One of the issues which arose was the determination of injury. Extramet argued that the injury was suferred by Péchiney as a result of its refusal to sell to Extramet. Indeed, that was the reason it had already initiated proceedings before the French authorities. The only statement the Council made about that was in the preamble to the contested Regulation, wherein it merely stated that Péchiney had denied Extramet's allegations. It then pointed out that no final judgment had

---

[54] Para 20.
[55] Para 22.
[56] Case C–358/89 *Extramet Industrie v Council* [1991] ECR I–2501.

been reached by the French authorities and noted that the anti-dumping procedure could be reviewed if a violation of the EC competition rules were found. The
Court ruled that 'none of these statements shows that the Community institutions
actually considered whether Péchiney itself contributed, by its refusal to sell, to
the injury suffered and established that the injury on which they based their conclusions did not derive from the factors mentioned by Extramet. They did not
therefore follow the proper procedure in determining the injury'.[57]

This brief overview illustrates the strict approach to the procedural rights of
interested parties adopted by the Community judiciary. An aspect of this is illustrated by the interpretation of the duty of the institutions to state reasons. As this
is enshrined in Article 253 EC, the Community courts have interpreted this principle strictly. For instance, in relation to a failure by the Council to adopt the
Commission's proposal and impose definitive anti-dumping duties, a statement
that the requisite majority could not be reached is deemed inadequate to satisfy
the obligation to state reasons.[58] All in all, the interpretation of the procedural
provisions of the Basic Regulation may be seen as an attempt to counterbalance
the liberal approach to the discretion enjoyed by the Community institutions.
Another such indication is provided by the interpretation of the EC Treaty
requirements for standing of private applicants.

5.3. A Liberal Approach to Standing

It is recalled that Article 230(2) EC provides for the annulment of Community
measures 'on grounds of lack of competence, infringement of an essential procedural requirement, infringement of this Treaty or of any rule of law relating to its
application, or misuse of powers'. In accordance with the fourth subparagraph of
this provision, 'any natural or legal person may, under the same conditions, institute proceedings against a decision addressed to that person or against a decision
which, although in the form of a regulation or a decision addressed to another
person, is of direct and individual concern to the former'.

In terms of the material scope of the annulment procedure, that is the definition
of the reviewable acts, the approach followed consistently by the Community judiciary is functional in nature: it is the nature of the measure rather than its label
which determines the applicability of Article 230 EC.[59] To that effect, a number of
measures which might be adopted in the process of anti-dumping investigations
are not reviewable. A decision by the Commission to initiate an investigation, for

---

[57] Para 19.

[58] See Case C–76/01P *Comité des industries du coton et des fibres connexes de l'Union européenne (Eurocoton) and Others v Council* [2003] ECR I–10091, at para. 91 and Case T–192/98 *Eurocoton v Council*, judgment of 17 Mar 2005, not yet reported, at paras 34–38.

[59] See, for instance, Case T–84/97 *Bureau européen des unions des consommateurs (BEUC) v Commission* [1998] ECR II–796.

instance, is considered a preparatory act and may not be challenged.[60] The same applies to the decision by the Commission to terminate an investigation without the imposition of anti-dumping duties when the Council opposes such a proposal.[61]

In general, any measure signifying merely the completion of one phase of the investigation is considered to be a preparatory act which is not reviewable under Article 230 EC. Instead, it is the act which signifies the completion of the final phase of the procedure which may be challenged, and it is against that measure that issues pertaining to the preparatory acts may be raised.[62] As the Court put it in another context, 'in the case of acts adopted by a procedure involving several stages, and particularly where they are the culmination of an internal procedure, it is in principle only those measures which definitively determine the position of the Commission or the Council upon the conclusion of that procedure which are open to challenge and not intermediate measures whose purpose is to prepare for the final decision'.[63] However, this is not the case regarding a decision by the Commission to refuse a party access to the file: this is deemed to 'constitute ... not merely a communication but a decision which adversely affects the interests of the [applicant]. The Commission's letter must therefore be regarded as an act adversely affecting the [applicant] which may be the subject of an action under Article [230 EC]'.[64]

Finally, it should be pointed out that, in cases where the Commission proposes the imposition of definitive anti-dumping duties and the Council fails to adopt this proposal, that failure constitutes a reviewable act under Article 230 EC: it is deemed to constitute an implied failure to act which may affect the applicant's interests.[65]

In terms of the personal scope of annulment proceedings, things are more complex. In the area of anti-dumping law, both provisional and definitive duties are imposed by the Commission and the Council respectively by a Regulation. In accordance with Article 249 EC, this measure is of general application, binding in its entirety and directly applicable. However, a strict reading of the requirements for annulment of Community legislation by private applicants would render judicial control over the adoption and content of those measures impossible.[66] Indeed, the wording of the Article 230(4) EC makes it clear that such applicants may not challenge genuine regulations.

---

[60] For instance, see the Order of the CFI in Case T–267/97 *Broome & Wellington v Commission* [1998] ECR II–2191.

[61] Case T–212/95 *Asociación de fabricantes de cemento de España (Oficemen) v Commission* [1997] ECR II–1161 at para 35.

[62] See, for instance, Case C–133/87 *Nashua Corporation and others v Commission and Council* [1990] ECR I–719.

[63] Case C–147/96 *Netherlands v Commission* [2000] ECR I–4723, at para 26.

[64] Case C–170/89 *Bureau Européen des Unions de Consommateurs v Commission* [1991] ECR I–5709, para 11.

[65] Case C–76/01P, n58 above.

[66] See A Arnull, 'Challenging EC Antidumping Regulations: The Problem of Admissibility' (1992) 13 *ECLR* 73 and R Greaves, '*Locus standi* under Article 173 EEC when Seeking Annulment of a Regulation' (1986) 11 *ELRev* 119.

The Community judiciary has gradually accepted that a wide range of private and legal persons may challenge the Commission and Council measures imposing anti-dumping duties. This approach aligns the case law on anti-dumping with that on competition law and state aids.[67] The private applicants granted standing include the exporters of dumped products, as became apparent quite early on in a number of cases about the importation of ball bearings from Japan.[68] Following a complaint by the Federation of European Bearing Manufacturers that Japanese ball-bearings were being dumped in the Community, the Commission adopted a regulation imposing provisional anti-dumping duties. The Council then adopted the contested Regulation on the same date on which the Commission accepted the undertakings of the producers. Four Japanese producers, known as the Big Four, were the main target of the regulation. The Council Regulation imposed a definitive anti-dumping duty on all Japanese ball-bearings, but suspended its application so long as those specific undertakings were observed, imposed on the Commission the duty to be vigilant that the undertakings given by the producers were not violated, and finally ordered the definitive collection of the provisional anti-dumping duties imposed on the products manufactured by the Big Four which were expressly mentioned in the regulation.

In its judgment, the Court made clear at the outset that it accepted that the Big Four and their subsidiaries were sufficiently closely associated. Therefore, in terms of the question whether they were individually and directly concerned by the regulation, there was no need to distinguish between producers and subsidiaries. It then held that their action was admissible because the provision they were contesting was in truth a collective decision relating to named addressees. The Court ruled that that provision concerned only importers who had imported products manufactured by the Big Four and consequently it was of direct and individual concern to them.

In the light of the above, it became clear that in cases where exporters are named in the Regulation challenged under Article 230 EC, their action is admissible. Soon afterwards, it became clear that that liberal reading of *locus standi* requirements was not confined to such cases. In *Allied Corporation*, three American exporters and one independent importer brought annulment proceedings against a Commission regulation imposing provisional anti-dumping duties on imports of chemical fertilizer originating in the United States.[69] The Court, first, pointed out that, according to the Basic Regulation, the imposition of anti-dumping duties is determined on the basis of findings resulting from investigations concerning the production prices of undertakings individually identified. It

---

[67] See P Craig and G de Búrca, *EU Law* (3rd edn, Oxford: OUP, 2003) 506–9.

[68] Case 113/77 *NTN Toyo Bearing v Council* [1979] ECR 1185, Case 118/77 *Import Standard Office v Council* [1979] ECR 1277, Case 119/77 *Nippon Seiko v Council* [1979] ECR 1303, Case 120/77 *Koyo Seiko v Council* [1979] ECR 1337, Case 121/77 *Nachi Fujikoshi v Council* [1979] ECR 1363.

[69] Joined Cases 239/82 and 275/82 *Allied Corporation and others v Commission* [1984] ECR 1005.

[70] *Ibid*, para 12.

then ruled that 'it is . . . clear that measures imposing anti-dumping duties are liable to be of direct and individual concern to those producers and exporters who are liable to establish that they were identified in the measures adopted or concerned by the preliminary investigations'.[70]

In other words, exporters and producers have standing under Article 230(4) EC not only when their identity is mentioned in contested measures, but also when they have participated in the investigations led by the Commission.

Other parties with an interest in the outcome of anti-dumping investigations are those who lodged a complaint with the Commission regarding the products under investigation. The question of their status was raised before the Court in an action brought by Timex, the leading manufacturer of mechanical watches in the Community.[71] The applicant sought to challenge a Council Regulation imposing definitive anti-dumping duties on the importation of mechanical watches originating in the Soviet Union on the ground that the duty imposed was too low.

The Court explained in detail the particular interest of the applicant. The complaint which led to the opening of the investigation procedure owed its origin to complaints originally made by Timex. Indeed, the British Clock and Watch Manufacturers' Association which lodged a complaint on behalf of a number of manufacturers, including Timex, took action because a complaint lodged by the latter itself had already been rejected by the Commission on the ground that it came from only one Community manufacturer. Furthermore, the preambles to both the Commission and the Council Regulations referred to the fact that Timex's views had been heard during the procedure. In addition, a number of other parameters were taken into account: Timex was the leading manufacturer of mechanical watches and watch movements in the Community and the only remaining manufacturer of those products in the United Kingdom; the preambles to the contested measures indicated that the conduct of the investigation procedure was largely determined by Timex's observations and the anti-dumping duty was fixed in the light of the effect of the dumping on Timex. In the light of those considerations, the applicant was granted standing under Article 230(4) EC.

The legal position of importers is more controversial. First, their standing was interpreted in strict terms: in one of the Japanese Ballbearing cases, for instance, standing was granted because, in the course of the anti-dumping investigations, the Commission had deemed them so closely related to the exporter that it had to construct the export price of the product on the basis of their resale price.[72] However, a more liberal approach was adopted subsequently. The judgment in *Extramet* is a case in point.[73] As the facts of the case were outlined above, suffice it to point out that the anti-dumping procedure was brought about following a

---

[71] Case 264/82 *Timex v Council and Commission* [1985] ECR 849.
[72] Case 118/77, n68 above at para 15. See also Joined Cases 277/85 and 300/85 *Canon v Council* [1988] ECR 5731, at para 8.
[73] Case C–358/89 n56 above.

complaint by the trade organisation on behalf of the only producer of calcium metal in the Community and the direct competitor of Extramet.

To the objection of inadmissibility put forward by the Council, Extramet argued that it was individually concerned because it was the largest importer and was also involved in the anti-dumping procedure; in addition, it argued that it could be fully identified in the contested Regulation. The Court examined the preamble to that measure, which states that the 'Community producer' and 'an independent importer' had their views heard during the proceedings. It reached the conclusion that the applicant was individually and directly concerned within the meaning of Article 230(4) EC. The relevant extract is worth-quoting in full: [74]

> In order to determine whether the objection of inadmissibility raised by the Council is well founded, it must be borne in mind that, although in the light of the criteria set out in the second paragraph of Article 230] of the Treaty regulations imposing anti-dumping duties are in fact, as regards their nature and their scope, of a legislative character, inasmuch as they apply to all the traders concerned, taken as a whole, their provisions may none the less be of individual concern to certain traders . . .

> It follows that measures imposing anti-dumping duties may, without losing their character as regulations, be of individual concern in certain circumstances to certain traders who therefore have standing to bring an action for their annulment.

> The Court has acknowledged that this was the case, in general, with regard to producers and exporters who are able to establish that they were identified in the measures adopted by the Commission or the Council or were concerned by the preliminary measures and with regard to importers whose retail prices for the goods in question have been used as a basis for establishing the export prices.

> Such recognition of the right of certain categories of traders to bring an action for the annulment of an anti-dumping regulation cannot, however, prevent other traders from also claiming to be individually concerned by such a regulation by reason of certain attributes which are peculiar to them and which differentiate them from all other persons . . .

> The applicant has established the existence of a set of factors constituting such a situation which is peculiar to the applicant and which differentiates it, as regards the measure in question, from all other traders. The applicant is the largest importer of the product forming the subject-matter of the anti-dumping measure and, at the same time, the end-user of the product. In addition, its business activities depend to a very large extent on those imports and are seriously affected by the contested regulation in view of the limited number of manufacturers of the product concerned and of the difficulties which it encounters in obtaining supplies from the sole Community producer, which, moreover, is its main competitor for the processed product.

The judgment in *Extramet* may appear to provide for a more liberal reading of standing. However, it does raise questions as to the assessment of the quantitative

---

[74] *Ibid*, paras 13–17.

criteria which it appears to recognise, namely in relation to the significance of the importer in the Community market and the damage it would allegedly suffer as a result of the contested measure. In other words, standing was granted on the basis of the very specific facts of the case. In doing so, the Court did not follow the Opinion of Advocate General Jacobs who had argued for an assimilation of the standing criteria for producers, exporters, complainants and importers.[75]

In more general terms, it is important to place the interpretation of the requirements for standing to challenge anti-dumping measures within the broader context of the Court's case law. The construction of *locus standi* has been notoriously strict[76] and given rise to considerable criticism, not least in the Court's own quarters. Indeed, the call by Advocate General Jacobs for a more liberal interpretation of Article 230(4) EC in *Union de Pequeros Agricultores*[77] and the judgment of the Court of First Instance in *Jégo-Quéré*[78] have not been followed up. In this context,[79] it is of considerable significance that measures adopted in the area of anti-dumping policy are subject to review by actions brought by a broader range of parties than those envisaged under the prevailing interpretation of the EC Treaty.[80]

The significance of this approach is illustrated by the indirect interaction between the Community judiciary and the Community institutions to which it has given rise in certain respects. The issue of the rights of associations of users and consumers is a case in point. In a judgment about the interpretation of the precursor to the current Basic Regulation, the Court of Justice ruled that, as practices attributable to consumers or their organizations do not constitute the target of anti-dumping investigations, these could not result in a measure adversely affecting them.[81] The Court concluded that the Commission was under no duty to grant access to the non-confidential documents requested by the applicant. However, it added the following:[82]

> [T]here is nothing in the wording of [the relevant provision] of the basic regulation to prevent the Commission from allowing persons who have a legitimate interest to inspect the non-confidential file.

> It is for the Community legislature to consider whether the basic anti-dumping regulation should grant an association representing the interests of consumers the right to

---

[75] *Ibid*, paras 55–66 of his Opinion.
[76] See the analysis in A Arnull, 'Private Applicants and the Action for Annulment since *Codorniu*', (2001) 38 *CMLRev* 7.
[77] Case C–50/00 P *Union de Pequeros Agricultores v Council* [2002] ECR I–6677.
[78] Case T–177/01 *Jégo-Quéré v Commission* [2002] ECR II–2365.
[79] K Lenaerts and T Korthaut, 'Judicial Review as a Contribution to the Development of European Constitutionalism' in T Tridimas and P Nebbia (eds), *European Union Law for the Twenty-First Century —Rethinking the New Legal Order: Volume I* (Oxford: Hart Publishing, 2004) 17.
[80] This more liberal approach has also been applied in the areas of competition law and state aids.
[81] Case C–170/89 *Bureau Européen des Unions de Consommateurs (BEUC) v Commission* [1991] ECR I–5709.
[82] *Ibid*, paras 29–30.

consult the non-confidential file.

In its current version, the Basic Regulation provides that consumer organisations may obtain access to the non-confidential file.[83] This instance indicates an interesting aspect of the relationship between the Community judiciary and the legislature. That the pronouncements of the former are taken into account by the latter which, in turn, may respond in practical terms is hardly a novelty.[84] What is interesting in the case of anti-dumping is the parallel development between the logic of the Court's approach to the review of anti-dumping measures and the reform of anti-dumping rules by the Community institutions. It was not only the adoption of the Basic Regulation in its current form in 1996 which tightened the legal regime of its precursor and provided for more guarantees for the interested parties involved; it is also the more recent amendment of the Basic Regulation which moves towards this direction. The thrust of Council Regulation 461/2004 is clearly aimed at rendering the proceedings more transparent by setting firm deadlines.[85] To that effect, the Council also appears to take into account the suggestions of the European Parliament for a tighter and more efficient process.[86] All in all, this subtle interaction between the Community judiciary and the legislature and executive puts the more cautious approach of the Court to the substantive aspects of anti-dumping policy in perspective.

A final point which should be emphasised is that an annulment action does not constitute the only way of contesting the legality of anti-dumping measures; proceedings may be brought before national courts, which then refer to the Court of Justice under the preliminary reference procedure. In *Nölle*, for instance, a German importer applied for entry for free circulation of consignments of cleaning and paint brushes from China.[87] When the competent authorities applied a Council Regulation and required that, having paid provisional anti-dumping duties, it then pay definitive anti-dumping duties, the applicant brought proceedings before the national courts. In challenging the national measure, it argued that it implemented a Council measure which was illegal in so far as the choice of reference country was concerned. Having pointed out that the choice of the reference country fell within the scope of its jurisdiction, the Court observed that 'it is

---

[83] Art 6(7). For a rigorous interpretation, see Case T–276/97 *BEUC v Commission* [2000] ECR II–101, at para 76.

[84] See, for instance, the response of the Commission to the articulation of the principle of mutual recognition in Case 120/78 *Rewe v Bundesmonopolverwaltung für Branntwein (Cassis de Dijon)* [1979] ECR 649 in Commission Communication on the consequences of *Cassis de Dijon* [1980] OJ C 256/2.

[85] Council Reg 461/2004 amending Reg 384/96 on protection against dumped imports from countries not members of the European Community and Reg 2026/97 on protection against subsidized imports from countries not members of the European Community [2004] OJ L 77/12.

[86] See, for instance, P5_TA(2002)492 EP Resolution on the Nineteenth annual report from the Commission to the European Parliament on the Community's anti-dumping and anti-subsidy activities [2003] OJ C 300E/120.

[87] Case C–16/90 *Nölle v Hauptzollamt Bremen-Freihafen* [1991] ECR I–5163.

desirable to verify whether the institutions neglected to take account of essential factors for the purpose of establishing the appropriate nature of the country chosen and whether the information contained in the documents in the case were considered with all the care required for the view to be taken that the normal value was determined in an appropriate and not unreasonable manner'.[88] It concluded that the choice of Sri Lanka rather than Taiwan had been insufficiently justified and, therefore, declared the relevant Regulation invalid.

However, it should be recalled that the indirect route of challenging the validity of a Community regulation through national courts is not merely a choice that the interested parties have. As the judgment in *TWD* made clear, if the applicant in the main proceedings clearly had standing to challenge the anti-dumping measure by an action for annulment pursuant to Article 230(4) EC, an action before national courts aiming at having recourse to the Article 234 procedure would be inadmissible.[89]

6. CONCLUSION

It is impossible to convey all the details and complexity of the external trade policies of the Community in a short chapter. This analysis has sought to shed some light on the fundamentals of one of its most important instruments and the variety of issues they raise in terms of the powers of the Community institutions, the rights of private parties and the intensity of judicial control. Central to the interaction of those aspects is the open-ended meaning of a number of concepts upon the assessment of which the Community institutions are to determine whether the imposition of anti-dumping duties is necessary. It should not be forgotten that the inherently controversial role of the Commission in assessing broadly worded concepts in the process of anti-dumping investigations is not carried out in isolation. The definition of the relevant concepts, for instance that of the 'like product', in the WTO context is not necessarily any more helpful.[90]

By way of conclusion, it should be pointed out that the international context within which the Community operates is essential to any proper assessment of its anti-dumping policies. It is noteworthy that the international rules on anti-dumping are now under review as the reform of the Anti-Dumping Agreement is part of the overall development of WTO. The Ministerial Conference in Doha stated that:[91]

---

[88] Para 13.

[89] Case C–188/92 *TWD/Bundesrepublik Deutschland* [1994] ECR I–833. See also Case C–239/99 *Nachi Europe GmbH v Hauptzollamt Krefeld* [2001] ECR I–1197.

[90] See M Bronckers and N McNelis, 'Rethinking the "Like Product" Definition in WTO Antidumping Law' (1999) 33 *JWT* 73.

[91] Para 28 of 4th Ministerial Conference, WT/MIN(01)/DEC 1, adopted on 14 Nov 2001.

In the light of experience and of the increasing application of these instruments by Members, we agree to negotiations aimed at clarifying and improving disciplines under the Agreement[s] on Implementation of Article VI of the GATT 1994 . . . while preserving the basic concepts, principles and effectiveness of these Agreements and their instruments and objectives, and taking into account the need of developing and least-developed participants.

This process will inevitably affect the determination of Community anti-dumping policy and the application of the relevant measures.[92] This is all the more so as the main targets of anti-dumping investigations and duties by the Community, such as China[93] and India, gradually become quite enthusiastic users of this instrument.

---

[92] For an overview of problematic issues, see E Vermulst, 'The 10 Major Problems With the Anti-Dumping Instrument in the European Community' (2005) 39 *JWT* 105. See also G Harpaz, 'The European Community's Anti-Dumping Policy: The Quest for Enhanced Predictability, Rationality, European Solidarity and Legitimacy' (2002–3) 5 *CYELS* 195.

[93] See H Gong, 'Legal Strategies for Challenging the Current EU Anti-dumping Campaign Against Imports from China: A Chinese Perspective' (2002) 27 *Brooklyn Journal of International Law* 575.

10

International Agreements

1. INTRODUCTION

THERE IS A steady proliferation in the number of agreements negotiated and concluded by the European Community,[1] either on its own or along with its Member States, with third countries, groups of countries and international organizations. In the increasingly interdependent international environment, this is not in itself remarkable. However, when assessed against the backdrop of the development of the EU legal order and its constitutional idiosyncrasies, this activity becomes noteworthy. This is partly due to the diversity of the contractual relations of the Community with the rest of the world. Another reason is the sophistication of the development of those relations, the ways in which they interact with each other and the other policies which the Union adopts in its effort to assert its identity on the international scene.

This Chapter will examine this gradual and dynamic process. It will identify broad categories of agreements concluded by the Community, it will define their main function and, then, highlight the linkages established both between themselves and other Union policies. In doing so, it will not examine the Europe Agreements, that is the agreements on the basis of which the recent enlargement was designed. Whilst their significance is more than obvious, their story has been told in detail and well.[2] It will also leave aside the Agreement creating the European Economic Area[3] in which, apart from the EC and its Member States, Iceland, Norway and Liechtenstein participate. The degree of integration prescribed in the Agreement and developed, amongst others, by the European Free Trade Area Court, set it apart from all the other agreements concluded by the Community.[4]

---

[1] For the agreements concluded by the EU under Art 24 TEU, see below at Ch 11.

[2] See M Cremona (ed), *The Enlargement of the European Union* (Oxford: OUP, 2003), C Hillion (ed), *EU Enlargement—A Legal Approach* (Oxford: Hart Publishing, 2004) and A Ott, and K Inglis (eds*), Handbook on European Enlargement—A Commentary on the Enlargement Process* (The Hague: TMC Asser Institute, 2002).

[3] [1994] OJ L 1/3.

[4] For detailed analyses, see T Blanchet, R Piipponen and M Westman-Clement, *The Agreement on the European Economic Area* (Oxford: OUP, 1994), P-C Müller-Graff and E Selvig (eds), *EEA–EU Relations* (Berlin: Berlin-Verlag Spitz, 1999) and S Norberg (ed), *EEA Law—A Commentary on the EEA Agreement* (Berlin: Springer, 1994). On the role of the EFTA Court, see C Baudenbacher, P Tresselt and T örlygsson (eds), The EFTA Court – Ten Years On (Oxford: Hart Publishing, 2005).

2. A WIDE RANGE OF LINKS

The Community has established contractual relations with the rest of the world in a variety of ways. Peers has provided a helpful summary and examined Community practice in terms of legal bases chosen over time.[5] Framework Cooperation Agreements have been concluded pursuant to Articles 133 and 308 EC in order to provide, in addition to trade, for more extensive economic cooperation. Such agreements have been concluded with Latin American countries such as Brazil,[6] Uruguay,[7] Paraguay,[8] Argentina.[9] On the basis of the same EC Treaty provisions, the Community has concluded a Framework Agreement for commercial and economic cooperation with Canada,[10] Trade and Economic Cooperation Agreements with China,[11] Macao,[12] Mongolia[13] and Cooperation Agreements with other Asian countries.[14] Those of the above Agreements concluded after the Maastricht Treaty entered into force, referred to the specific legal basis for development policy agreements introduced thereunder rather than the general enabling clause of Article 308 EC. Furthermore, a Framework Agreement for Trade and Cooperation has been concluded between the Community and the Member States and South Corea[15] and one on Trade, Development and Cooperation with South Africa.[16] Finally, Partnership and Cooperation Agreements have been concluded with the former members of the Soviet Union which will be analysed below.

It becomes, thus, clear that the majority of agreements concluded by the Community are not confined to trade relations. This is also the case, by definition, regarding association agreements. Provision for such agreements is made expressly in the EC Treaty: under Article 310 EC,

> the Community may conclude with one or more States or international organisations agreements establishing an association involving reciprocal rights and obligations, common action and special procedure.

---

[5] S Peers, 'EC Frameworks of Internatioanl Relations: Co-operation, Partnership and Association' in A Dashwood and C Hillion (eds), *The General Law of E.C. External Relations* (London: Sweet and Maxwell, 2000) 160.

[6] [1995] OJ L 262/54.

[7] [1992] OJ L 94/2.

[8] [1992] OJ L 313/72.

[9] This was a Framework Agreement for Trade and Economic Cooperation [1990] OJ L 295/67.

[10] [1976] OJ L 260/2.

[11] [1985] OJ L 250/2.

[12] [1992] OJ L 404/27.

[13] [1993] OJ L 41/46.

[14] These included Cambodia ([1999] OJ L 269/18), Bangladesh ([2001] OJ L 118/48), Vietnam ([1996] OJ L 136/29), Laos ([1997] OJ L 334/15); Cooperation Agreements on partnership and development have been concluded with India ([1994] OJ L 223/24) and Sri Lanka ([1995] OJ L 85/33).

[15] [2001] OJ L 90/46.

[16] [1999] OJ L 311/3.

The significance of this type of agreement is also illustrated by the procedure required for its adoption, namely unanimity in the Council (Article 300(2) subparagraph 1 EC) and the assent of the Parliament (Article 300(3) subparagraph 2 EC). The EC Treaty itself provides no specific criteria as to the definition of association agreements. Accordingly, there is no single form of association established between the Community and third countries.[17] Therefore, a typology of such agreements may only be drawn up on the basis of Community practice.[18] In previous chapters, reference was made to Association Agreements concluded with countries which were to become members of the European Union. Indeed, of the first countries with which agreements were concluded under Article 310 EC, Greece became a Member in 1981 and Turkey has been scheduled to start negotiations for membership on 3 October 2005.[19] The Agreement establishing the European Economic Area is one of the most significant association agreements concluded by the Community and its Member States. Switzerland had signed the agreement but, following a negative vote in a referendum, it did not conclude it. Equally, whilst it had applied for membership, it withdrew its request. Of the wide range of agreements concluded between the Community and Switzerland, seven sectoral agreements agreed upon in 2002 were concluded by the Community under Article 310 EC.[20]

Another important association is the one established with 76 African, Carribean and Pacific countries, now regulated under the Cotonou Agreement: entitled 'Partnership Agreement', it was concluded 'in order to promote and expedite the economic, cultural and social development of the ACP States, with a view to contributing to peace and security and to promoting a stable and democratic political environment'.[21] An association agreement was also concluded recently with Chile and entered into force on 1 March 2005.[22] The association agreements concluded with the Mediterranean countries and the countries in the West Balkans will be examined below.

An interesting aspect of the Union's approach to international relations is its emerging focus on regional forms of cooperation. For instance, along with the Member States, it has concluded an Interregional Framework Cooperation Agreement with Mercosur and its Party Countries, namely Brazil, Argentina,

[17] See M-A Gaudissart, 'Reflexions sur la nature et la portée du concept d'association à la lumière de sa mise en œuvre' in M-FC Tchakaloff (ed.), *Le concept d'association dans les accords passés par la Communauté: essai de clarification* [Brussels: Bruylant, 1999] 3.

[18] See the analysis in *Commentaire Mégret, Vol. 12 Relations Extérieures* (Brussels: Editions de l'Université de Bruxelles, 2005) 293–324.

[19] This date was given by the Brussels European Council in Dec 2004.

[20] Council Dec 2002/309 [2002] OJ L 114/1. The Agreements refer to free movement of persons, trade in agricultural products, public procurement, conformity assessments, air transport, transport by road and rail and Swiss Participation in the 5th Framework Programme for research.

[21] [2000] OJ L 317/3, Art 1. See the analysis in O Babarinder and G Faber, 'From Lomé to Cotonou: Business as Usual?' (2004) 9 *EFA Rev* 27.

[22] [2002] OJ L 352/3.

Uruguay and Paraguay[23] and is currently negotiating a Political and Economic Association Agreement. The Community alone concluded a Framework Agreement on Cooperation with the Andean Community and its Members, namely Bolivia, Colombia, Ecuador, Peru and Venezuela[24] and concluded negotiations on a new Political Dialogue and Cooperation Agreement in October 2003. A Cooperation Agreement has been concluded with the member countries of the South-East Asian Nations, namely Indonesia, Malaysia, the Philippines, Singapore, Thailand, Brunei and Vietnam[25] and one with the countries party to the Charter of the Cooperation Council for the Arab States of the Gulf.[26] Finally, it has concluded a Framework Cooperation Agreement with the group of Central American countries[27] and has completed negotiations on a new Political Dialogue and Cooperation Agreement.

The regional focus of the above contractual relations has been supplemented by the establishment of other structures aimed at broadening the scope of links between the Union and those regional groups. For instance, the Union defined its overall policy on Asia for the first time in 1994,[28] and then, launched the New Asia Strategy. Its aim was to establish a more coherent approach to the Community's relations with East Asia. It is within this framework that the Asia–Europe meetings, that is summits between the respective leaders, have been carried out regularly.[29] Equally, the other frameworks of cooperation mentioned above are also accompanied by additional formalised channels of communication.[30] The emphasis on regional integration is explained not only in economic but also political and security terms. Commissioner Chris Patten, as he then was, points out that:[31]

> [r]egional integration is . . . important for stability and conflict prevention. Closer cooperation can be a catalyst for democracy and improved human rights. Regional integration provides opportunities for countries to become more active and influential partners in, rather than dependant spectators of, global, political, economic and social developments. And it allows countries to work more effectively together to combat global challenges such as narco-trafficking and drugs production.

---

[23] [1999] OJ L 112/66.

[24] [1998] OJ L 127/11.

[25] [1980] OJ L 144/2 as amended in [1985] OJ L 81/2 and [1999] OJ L 117/31.

[26] These include United Arab Emirates, Bahrain, Saudi Arabia, Oman, Qatar and Kuwait: [1989] OJ L 54/3.

[27] Namely, Costa Rica, El Salvador, Guatemala, Honduras, Nicaragua and Panama: [1999] OJ L 63/39.

[28] COM(94) 314 final. *Towards a new Asia Strategy.* The more recent policy paper is COM(2001)369 final *Europe and Asia: A Strategic Framework for Enhanced Partnerships.*

[29] See CM Dent, 'The EU–East Asia Economic Relationship: The Persisting Weak Triadic Link?' (1999) 4 *EFA Rev* 371.

[30] See G Muler-Brandeck-Bocquet, 'Perspectives for a New Regionalism: Relations between the EU and the MERCOSUR' (2001) 5 *EFA Rev* 561.

[31] Speech 04/61 (Canning House, London, 4 Feb 2004).

This emphasis will become more apparent in the evolving approach of the Union to countries located at its borders. These relationships will be examined in the following sections.

3. PARTNERSHIP AND COOPERATION AGREEMENTS

The countries of the ex-Soviet Union, now members of the Commonwealth of Independent States (CIS), concluded a series of agreements with the Community and the Member States in the mid-1990s. These agreements are known as Partnership and Cooperation Agreements (PCAs). The first PCA was concluded with Russia,[32] to be followed by that with Ukraine,[33] the latter entering into force only three months after the former. Following them, the Community concluded a PCA with Moldova[34] and, then, in quick succession with Kazakhstan,[35] Kyrgizstan,[36] Georgia,[37] Uzbekistan,[38] Armenia[39] and Azerbaijan,[40] all of which entered into force on 1 July 1999. Of the other ex-Soviet Republics, PCAs were signed with Belarus in March 1995 and Turkmenistan in May 1998, but neither has yet come into force.[41]

All these agreements are mixed. The relevant decisions concluding them were adopted by the Council as well as the Commission, as the PCAs were concluded not only by the EC but also the European Coal and Steel Community and the European Atomic Energy Community. As for their legal bases, they included a considerable number of EC Treaty provisions.[42]

These agreements with the countries of Eastern Europe and Central Asia were not concluded in a legal vacuum as the Community and its Member States had signed a Trade and Cooperation Agreement with the Soviet Union in 1989.[43] In this context, the new agreements were aimed at replacing that agreement by establishing separate frameworks of bilateral cooperation whilst offering those countries an alternative to accession to the EU.[44]

All PCAs define the objectives of the Partnership in broadly similar terms in their first Article. The one with Moldova, for instance, formulates them as follows:

---

[32] [1997] OJ L 327/3 which entered into force on 1 Dec 1997.
[33] [1998] OJ L 49/3.
[34] [1998] OJ L 181/3 which entered into force on 1 July 1998.
[35] [1999] OJ L 196/3.
[36] [1999] OJ L 196/48.
[37] [1999] OJ L 205/3.
[38] [1999] OJ L 229/3.
[39] [1999] OJ L 239/3.
[40] [1999] OJ L 246/3.
[41] In the case of Belarus because of the authoritarian government of President Lukashenko; in the case of Turkmenistan because it has still not been ratified by all the Parties.
[42] These included Art 44(2), 55, 71, 80(2), 93, 94, 133 and 308 EC.
[43] [1989] OJ L 68/3.
[44] See C Hillion, 'Partnership and Cooperation Agreements between the European Union and the New Independent States of the Ex-Soviet Union' (1998) 3 *EFA Rev* 399.

—to provide an appropriate framework for the political dialogue between the Parties allowing the development of political relations,

—to promote trade and investment and harmonious economic relations between the Parties and so to foster their sustainable economic development,

—to provide a basis for legislative, economic, social, financial, and cultural cooperation,

—to support efforts of the Republic of Moldova to consolidate its democracy and to develop its economy and to complete the transition into a market economy.

Whilst similar to the objectives laid down in the other PCAs, the above formulation is by no means identical to them. For instance, Article 1 of the PCA with Ukraine refers to the development of 'close' political relations, an adjective which is not to be found in any other PCA with the exception of that with Russia which, whilst referring to them as 'close', does not qualify those relations as 'political'. In addition, the cooperation for which the Agreement is to provide a basis is defined as 'mutually advantageous', a qualification absent from all the other PCAs, again with the exception of that with Russia where the requirement for mutuality could not have been overstated: economic, social, financial and cultural cooperation is to be 'founded on the principles of mutual advantage, mutual responsibility and mutual support'.[45]

The above examples provide but one indication of the distinct nature of the PCAs, first, with Russia and, then, with Ukraine. In its Article 1, the former sets out the longest list of objectives to be found in any of the PCAs; in addition to those mentioned above, it includes strengthening political and economic relations, promoting activities of joint interest, providing an appropriate framework for gradual integration between Russia and a wider area of cooperation in Europe and, most importantly, creating the necessary conditions for the future establishment of a free trade area. To a certain extent, Article 1 of the PCA with Russia is indicative of the fact that it was the first agreement to be negotiated with a CIS country and, therefore, its provisions had not yet been streamlined. However, it also illustrates the unique position of Russia in Europe in general and in the then changing geopolitical environment surrounding the Union. The provision for the possibility of establishing a free trade area, for instance (the so-called evolutionary clause), is only included in the PCAs with Russia, Ukraine and Moldova.[46] This distinguishes them from the other PCAs concluded with the Caucasian and Central Asian countries.[47]

Therefore, there is no single definition of partnership within the context of PCAs. Another indication of this is provided by the Agreement with Uzbekistan which is the only one including in its objectives support for the independence and sovereignty of Uzbekistan and assistance in the construction of a civil society in the country based upon the rule of law.

---

[45] Art 1.

[46] Art 3 (PCA with Russia), Art 4 (PCA with Ukraine and Moldova).

[47] For an analysis of the PCAs with the Central Asian countries, see B Berdiyev, 'The EU and Former Soviet Central Asia: An Analysis of the Partnership and Cooperation Agreements' (2003) 22 *YEL* 463.

Integration into the Union structures is not an objective of PCAs. Instead, as rergards their substantive content, they include provisions on political dialogue, trade in goods, provisions affecting business and investment, cross-border supply of services including provisions affecting the establishment and operation of companies, cross-border supply of services, current payments and capital and intellectual property protection, legislative cooperation and economic coopera-tion whose scope ranges from transport and environment to small and medium-sized enterprises and tourism. Again, there is a variation: the agreements with Uzbekistan, Armenia and Azerbaijan, for instance, include, in addition to the Title on Political Dialogue, one on Cooperation on Matters Relating to Democracy and Human Rights.[48] Finally, all PCAs provide for an institutional framework whose bodies, namely a Cooperation Council, a Cooperation Committee and a Parlia-mentary Cooperation Committee, are entrusted with the smooth application of the Agreement. Finally, the Union has adopted two common strategies, one on Russia[49] and one on Ukraine.[50] This additional layer of the relationship between the Union and the newly independent states,[51] along with the emerging approach of the Union to those countries, will be examined below.

4. STABILISATION AND ASSOCIATION AGREEMENTS

The Community has been engaged in the process of concluding a number of asso-ciation agreements under this heading with its neighbours in the West Balkans. At the moment, such agreements have been concluded with Croatia[52] and the Former Yugoslav Republic of Macedonia.[53] Negotiations with Albania have been carried out since January 2003, albeit at a rather slow pace. In relation to Bosnia-Herzegovina, the commencement of negotiations is dependent upon the assess-ment by the Commission that considerable progress has been made in a number of specific areas;[54] once such progress is attested to by the Commission, then the latter may submit a recommendation to the Council that negotiations may com-mence. As to Serbia and Montenegro, the Commission adopted a feasibility study in April 2005 which asserts its readiness to negotiate an Agreement. Once approved by the Council, the Commission submitted a draft negotiating mandate which is currently being discussed at the Council.

---

[48] Art 68 (PCA with Armenia and Uzbekistan) and Art 71 (PCA with Azerbaidjan).

[49] [1999] OJ L 157/1. Its duration was extended by Dec 2003/471/CFSP [2003] OJ L 157/ 68 until 24 June 2004 and has not been further prolonged.

[50] [1999] OJ L 331/1. Its duration was extended by Dec 2003/897/CFSP [2003] OJ L 333/96 until 23 December 2004.

[51] For an analysis of these instruments in the light of recent enlargement, seed M Maresceau, 'EU Enlargement and EU Common Strategies on Russia and Ukraine: An Ambiguous Yet Unavoidable Connection' in Hillion (ed), n2 above, 181.

[52] [2005] OJ L 26/3.

[53] [2004] OJ L 84/13.

[54] COM(2003)692 fin. Report on the preparedness of Bosnia and Herzegovina to negotiate a Stabilisation and Association Agreement with the European Union.

The very term used for the agreements in question highlights the unique geopolitical situation in the Balkans: the war and instability in which the associated states were involved define the stabilising function of the Association. The SAAs cover a range of areas including political dialogue, regional cooperation, free movement of goods, workers, services and capital, the approximation of law and law enforcement, justice and home affairs, cooperation policies and financial cooperation.[55] They provide for the establishment of a free trade area between the Community and FYROM and Croatia within ten and six years respectively after their entry into force.[56] Both agreements include a conditionality clause expressed as follows:[57]

> Respect for the democratic principles and human rights as proclaimed in the Universal Declaration of Human Rights and as defined in the Helsinki Final Act and the Charter of Paris for a New Europe, respect for international law principles and the rule of law as well as the principles of market economy as reflected in the Document of the CSCE Bonn Conference on Economic Cooperation, shall form the basis of the domestic and external policies of the Parties and constitute essential elements of this Agreement.

However, the negotiation and conclusion of stabilisation and association agreements is merely one aspect of the relationship between the EU and the Western Balkans. This relationship is organised on the basis of the stabilisation process which was proposed by the Commission[58] and, then, articulated in the Final Declaration of the Zagreb Summit in November 2000. With the participation of the Heads of State or Government of the Member States and the five countries of the region, along with a representative of Slovenia and other officials, such as the Commission President and the CFSP High Representative,[59] the main aspects of this process were spelled out. On the one hand, EU membership was defined as the objective for the countries of the Western Balkans; on the other hand, these countries would have to meet a number of conditions related to democratic, economic and institutional reforms as already defined three years previously.

The perspective of membership is clearly expressed in both existing Stabilisation and Association Agreements:[60]

> [the contracting parties recall] . . . the European Union's readiness to integrate to the fullest possible extent the [Balkan country in question] into the political and economic mainstream of Europe and its status as a potential candidate for EU membership on the

---

[55] See D Phinnemore, 'Stabilisation and Association Agreements: Europe Agreements for the Western Balkans?' (2003) 8 *EFA Rev* 77.

[56] Such variations are not unusual: in the context of the Europe Agreements, see P Koutrakos, 'Free Movement of Goods' in A Ott and K Inglys (eds), *Handbook on European Enlargement—A Commentary on the Enlargement Process* (The Hague: TMC Asser Institute, 2002) at 369 at 375.

[57] Art 2 of both Agreements.

[58] COM(99)235 final.

[59] See Joint Action 2000/217/CFSP on the holding of a meeting of Heads of State or of Government in Zagreb (Zagreb Summit) [2000] OJ L 290/54.

[60] Last para of the preamble to SAAs with FYROM and Croatia.

basis of the Treaty on European Union and fulfillment of the criteria defined by the European Council in June 1993, subject to successful implementation of this Agreement, notably regarding regional cooperation

Whilst constituting the cornerstone of the stabilisation and association process, the negotiation and implementation of SAAs is not the only component of the process. On the one hand, there are measures adopted by the Community unilaterally aiming at paving the way for the negotiation and conclusion of SAAs. The Lisbon European Council had decided in March 2000 that the negotiation and conclusion of SAAs should be preceded by asymmetrical trade liberalisation. To that effect, the Community has liberalised the imports of most products: they would not be subject to either customs duties or measures of equivalent effect or quantitative restrictions or measures of equivalent effect.[61] Furthermore, there is considerable provision for assistance in the form of CARDS, that is the Community Assistance for Reconstruction, Development and Stabilisation programme. Laid down in a Council Regulation which was adopted in December 2000, this programme brings previous Community programmes within a single framework:[62]

> The existing Community assistance should be expanded and redirected to adjust it to the European Union's political objectives for the region and, particularly, to contribute to the stabilisation and association process and increase the responsibility of recipient countries and entities in relation to that process.

> To that end Community assistance will be focused mainly on building up an institutional, legislative, economic and social framework directed at the values and models subscribed to by the European Union and on promoting a market economy, with due regard for priorities agreed with the partners concerned.

The stabilisation and association process was not launched in a legal and political vacuum. The Union had already sought to structure its approach to the Western Balkans under the form of the so-called Regional Approach: introduced in the aftermath of the civil war and the Dayton Peace Agreement, that programme aimed at consolidating the EU approach to the region by focusing on financial assistance, trade preferences and cooperation agreements between the Community and the Balkan countries.[63] In 1999, the Union launched the Stability

---

[61] Council Reg 2007/2000 introducing exceptional trade measures for countries and territories participating in or linked to the European Union's Stabilisation and Association process [2000] OJ L 240/1 as amended by Council Reg 2563/2000 [2000] OJ L 295/1. Preferential quotas were maintained on imports of wine, baby beef and certain fisheries products. The conclusion of the Interim SAAs with FYROM and Croatia rendered the application of this regime to their imports redundant: see Commission Reg 2487/2001 [2001] OJ L 335/9.

[62] Paras 5–6 of the preamble to Council Reg 2666/2000 [2000] OJ L 306/1; its most recent amendment was by Council Reg 2257/2004 [2004] OJ L 389/1.

[63] See C Pippan, 'The Rocky Road to Europe: The EU's Stabilisation and Association Process for the Western Balkans and the Principle of Conditionality' (2004) 9 *EFA Rev* 219 at 221–9.

Pact for South Eastern Europe.[64] It was within this context that a closer relationship between the Union and the Balkan countries, with the clear objective of broadening its scope beyond trade relations and financial assistance, was developed.[65]

It was against this background that the Feira European Council in June 2000 expressly translated the prospect of closer integration into EU membership. Therefore, the genesis and development of the stabilisation and association process drew upon an evolving body of political and legal initiatives.

The Union's approach to the Western Balkans is characterised by a number of interesting features. The first one is its intense formalisation: it is based on a sophisticated system of various legal instruments and institutional mechanisms established gradually since the Kosovo crisis and covering interlinked areas of activities, all aiming at eventual membership. The negotiation and conclusion of SAAs, whilst a cornerstone of the stabilisation and association process, is also the objective of a formal procedure. A brief overview of the case of Bosnia-Herzegovina will make this point clear. In 2000, the EU adopted a 'Road Map' in which 18 specific steps were identified as essential for the country before the Commission assessed whether Bosnia-Herzegovina was prepared to commence negotiations for an SAA with the Community and its Member States. Three years later, and having concluded that those steps had been substantially completed, the Commission issued a feasibility study where it assessed the country's capacity to meet the obligations of an SAA.[66] This document had two main functions: on the one hand, it pointed out the considerable progress made by Bosnia-Herzegovina in the areas identified in the 2000 Road Map; on the other hand, it identified a number of areas where further progress was required prior to the commencement of negotiations for a SAA. These included compliance with international obligations, in particular by cooperating with the International Criminal Tribunal, more effective governance and public administration, effective human rights provisions and judiciary, tackling organised crime and managing asylum and immigration, customs and taxation reforms, trade and energy policy and others. There were priorities for action in the course of 2004 at the end of which the Commission would ascertain whether sufficient progress had been made and, accordingly, would determine whether it would request a Council authorization to start negotiations for a SAA.

However, another layer was added to the relationship between the EU and the Western Balkans countries. In 2003, the Commission recommended the introduction of European Integration Partnerships:[67]

---

[64] Common Position 1999/345/CFSP [1999] OJ L 133/1.

[65] See M Cremona, 'Creating the New Europe: The Stability Pact for South-Eastern Europe in the Context of EU–SEE Relations' (1999) 2 *CYELS* 463.

[66] COM(2003)692 final. *Report from the Commission to the Council on the preparedness of Bosnia and Herzegovina to negotiate a Stabilisation and Association Agreement with the European Union.*

[67] COM(2003)285 final *The Western Balkans and European Integration.*

Inspired by the pre-accession process, these partnerships would identify priorities for action in supporting efforts to move closer to the European Union. The purpose of these Partnerships would be to identify short and medium-term reforms which the countries need to carry out, to serve as a checklist against which to measure progress, and to provide guidance for assistance under the CARDS programme. They would reflect the particular stage of development of each country and be tailored to its specific needs.

When the Thessaloniki European Council signalled the reorientation of the Union's relationship with the West Balkans in June 2003 and adopted the Thessaloniki agenda for the Western Balkans, it annexed the Commission recommendation to in its Conclusions. The Thessaloniki agenda drew upon the pre-accession experience of the most recent enlargement and, in that context, the Council adopted Regulation 533/2004 where such partnerships are described as follows:[68]

> The European partnerships shall provide a framework covering the priorities resulting from the analysis of Partners' different situations, on which preparations for further integration into the European Union must concentrate in the light of the criteria defined by the European Council, and the progress made in implementing the stabilisation and association process including stabilisation and association agreements, where appropriate, and in particular regional cooperation.

This Regulation also defines the procedure pursuant to which the European partnerships are to materialise: the Council is to define the principles, priorities and conditions of each one of them by qualified majority and pursuant to a proposal by the Commission. The relevant Decisions have already been adopted in respect of all Western Balkan countries.[69]

A second significant feature of the EU approach to the Balkans is the promotion of regional cooperation. This became apparent quite early on. In the Zagreb Declaration, for instance:

> the Heads of State or Government of the five countries concerned undertake to establish between their countries regional cooperation conventions providing for a political dialogue, a regional free trade area and close cooperation in the field of justice and home affairs, in particular for the reinforcement of justice and the independence thereof, for combating organized crime, corruption, money laundering, illegal immigration, trafficking in human beings and all other forms of trafficking. These conventions will be incorporated in the stabilization and association agreements as they are concluded with the European Union. The Heads of State or Government of the five countries concerned

---

[68] [2004] OJ L 86/1, Art 1.
[69] See Council Dec 2004/515/EC [2004] OJ L 221/10 (Bosnia and Herzegovina); Council Dec 2004/520/EC [2004] OJ L 227/21 (Serbia and Montenegro including Kosovo as defined by the United Nations Security Council Resolution 1244); Council Dec 2004/518/EC [2004] OJ L 222/20 (FYROM); Council Dec 2004/519/EC [2004] OJ L 223/20 (Albania); Council Dec 2004/648/EC [2004] OJ L 297/19 (Croatia).

have declared the importance they attach to the training of police officers and magistrates and to the strengthening of border controls.

In practical terms, the conclusion of bilateral trade agreements between the Balkan countries is an important aspect of the stabilisation and association process in general and its regional approach in particular. Under the framework of the Stability Pact and drawing upon a Memorandum of Understanding on Trade Liberalisation and Facilitation signed by these countries, along with Romania, Bulgaria and Moldova, a process of negotiation, conclusion and application of free trade agreements has been set in motion. Evolving in parallel to the stabilisation and association process, this formalised process of regional integration is not of limited scope: it covers energy liberalisation, refugee return, migration, freedom of movement and the fight against organised crime.

The significance of regional cooperation for the relationship between the EU and the Balkan states and the membership perspective of the latter is illustrated by the reference to it in the SAAs. Furthermore, it is repeated in all relevant EU documents. In its first annual report on the stabilisation and association process, the Commission pointed out that 'integration with the EU is only possible if future members can demonstrate that they are willing and able to interact with their neighbours as EU Member States do'.[70] Furthermore, in its 2003 proposals, the Commission referred to regional cooperation as 'an integral part of the preparation for integration into European structures'.[71] This emphasis on the regional element is one of the features of the SAA distinguishing it from the Europe agreements: on the one hand, they further illustrate the very particular context within which they have been conceived and the needs of which the multi-level stabilisation and association process is aimed at addressing; on the other hand, this increases the intensity of obligations imposed upon the West Balkan countries.

The Union's approach to the Western Balkans as summarised in this section is as evolving in its outlook as it is multi-layered in its content: consisting of a variety of legal, economic and political components whose interaction is managed in a highly formalised framework, the stabilisation and association process illustrates an interesting way for the Community to assert its identity on the international scene. The emphasis on the 'stabilisation' component of its evolving relationship with the region highlights the distinct foreign policy function of the Union's approach. It was in that region where, in 1994, the then newly born European Union sought to contribute to the security environment by taking over the administration of the city of Mostar. Having been provided with assistance by the Western European Union pursuant to a most interesting legal document entitled 'Memorandum of Understanding on the European Union Administration of

---

[70] COM(2002)163 final *The Stabilisation and Association Process for South East Europe: First Annual Report.*
[71] N67 above.

Mostar', the Union successfully carried out that task.[72] Whilst not spectacular in terms of its media coverage, that role was nonetheless effective, useful and constituted an original contribution of the EU in the crisis in the Balkans. It is within that context that the structure and implementation of the stabilisation and association process should be examined and their implications assessed: in addition to exporting the *acquis communautaire*,[73] the Union carries out a foreign policy function of considerable significance and sophistication.

5. EURO–MEDITERRANEAN AGREEMENTS

A number of association agreements have been concluded between the Community and the Member States, on the one hand, and a number of Mediterranean countries, on the other hand. These include Egypt,[74] Israel,[75] Jordan,[76] Morocco[77] and Tunisia.[78] The Agreements with Algeria and Lebanon were signed in April and June 2002 respectively but have not yet entered into force.[79] The one with Syria was initialled in October 2004 and is now awaiting ratification. Finally, in terms of the Palestinian Authority, the Community has concluded a Euro–Mediterranean Interim Association Agreement on trade and cooperation with the Palestine Liberation Organisation (PLO) for the benefit of the Palestinian Authority of the West Bank and the Gaza Strip.[80] This Agreement was seen as paving the way for the negotiation of an association agreement.[81] Libya is the only country in the Mediterranean region with which the Union has not got formal relations. It was only following the agreement with the United Kingdom on the Lockerbie bombers and the subsequent decision by Libya to dismantle its weapons of mass destruction programmes that a slow process of gradual engagement appears to have been envisaged.[82] As for Turkey, it was recognised as a candidate country by the Helsinki European Council in December 1999. Following a recommendation by the Commission,[83] the Brussels European Council decided in December 2004 that negotiations with Turkey would start on 3 October 2005.

---

[72] See J Monar, 'Mostar: Three lessons for the European Union' (1997) 2 *EFA Rev* 1.

[73] See A Björkdahl, 'Norm-maker and Norm-taker: Exploring the Normative Influence of the EU in Macedonia' (2005) 10 *EFA Rev* 257.

[74] [2004] OJ L 304/39.

[75] [2000] OJ L 147/3.

[76] [2002] OJ L 129/3.

[77] [2000] OJ L 70/2.

[78] [1998] OJ L 97/2.

[79] The trade and trade-related matters of the Agreement with Lebanon are incorporated in an Interim Agreement which has entered into force: [2002] OJ L 262/2.

[80] [1997] OJ L 187/3.

[81] See Council Dec 97/430 [1997] OJ L 187/1.

[82] See Council Conclusions of 11 Oct 2004.

[83] COM(2004) 656 final.

The Euro–Mediterranean Agreements (EMAs) are association agreements which have replaced a number of Cooperation Agreements concluded between the Community and Mediterranean countries in the 1970s.[84] They are mixed agreements, concluded by both the Community and its Member States,[85] and they cover a wide range of areas. In the trade and economic sphere, they provide for the establishment of a free trade area over a period of varying duration; they also include provisions about political dialogue, intellectual property rights, services, public procurement, competition rules, state aids and monopolies, economic cooperation in various sectors, cooperation relating to social affairs and migration, including re-admission of illegal immigrants and cultural cooperation. In terms of respect for human rights, they include the following clause:[86]

> Relations between the Parties, as well as all the provisions of the Agreement itself, shall be based on respect of democratic principles and fundamental human rights as set out in the universal declaration on human rights, which guides their internal and international policy and constitutes an essential element of this Agreement.

The EMAs constitute the cornerstone of a wider process known as the Euro–Mediterranean Partnership, the origin of which may be found in a meeting of the Ministers of Foreign Affairs of the Euro–Mediterranean countries in Barcelona in November 1995. This launched the Barcelona Process, which is a framework of cooperation between the parties whose main tenets were laid down in the Barcelona Declaration.[87] These included the following three pillars: political and security, economic and financial, and social and cultural. At the very core of the Process is the establishment of a Euro–Mediterranean Free Trade Area by 2010.

Within this context, the EMAs play an important function which is accompanied by a series of parallel initiatives. In the economic sphere, unilateral measures by the Community are quite significant and consist of financial and technical assistance under the MEDA programme. Set out in Council regulations adopted under Article 308 EC,[88] its purpose has been to contribute to initiatives of joint interest in the following three areas: 'the reinforcement of political stability and of democracy, the creation of a Euro-Mediterranean free-trade area, and the development of economic and social cooperation, taking due account of the human and cultural dimension'.[89]

---

[84] See I Macleod, ID Hendry and S Hyett, *The External Relations of the European Communities* (Oxford: Clarendon Press, 1996) 383–4.

[85] This is not the case regarding the Interim Agreement with the Palestinian Authority which has been concluded by the Community alone.

[86] Art 2 of Agreement with Jordan.

[87] See G Edwards and E Philippart, 'The Euro–Mediterranean Partnership: Fragmentation and Reconstruction' (1997) 2 *EFA Rev* 465.

[88] Council Reg 1488/96 on financial and technical measures to accompany (MEDA) the reform of economic and social structures in the framework of the Euro–Mediterranean partnership [1996] OJ L 189/1. This was amended by Council Reg 2698/2000 [2000] OJ L 311/1.

[89] Art 2 of Reg 1488/96. See P Holden, 'The European Community's MEDA Aid Programme: A Strategic Instrument of Civilian Power?' (2003) 8 *EFA Rev* 347.

Central to the functioning of the Euro–Mediterranean Partnership is its regional dimension. For instance, the EMAs refer to it expressly:[90]

> The Parties will encourage operations having a regional impact or associating other countries of the region, with a view to promoting regional cooperation.
>
> Such operations may include:
>
> —trade at intra-regional level,
>
> —environmental issues,
>
> —development of economic infrastructures,
>
> —scientific and technological research,
>
> —cultural matters,
>
> —customs matters.

An interesting feature of the Euro–Mediterranean Partnership, which distinguishes it to a certain extent from the stabilisation and association process, is the degree of multilateral institutionalisation upon which it is based. For instance, the Ministers of Foreign Affairs of all the Euro–Mediterranean countries meet regularly at Euro–Mediterranean conferences; there are other regular sectoral meetings at ministerial level, as well as regular meetings of government experts and representatives of civil society. In addition, there is the Euro–Mediterranean Committee for the Barcelona Process: meeting on a quarterly basis at senior official level, it is chaired by the EU Presidency and acts as an overall steering body for the regional process with the right to initiate activities to be financed pursuant to MEDA and the role of preparing for all the other formal meetings. There are also regional programmes financed by MEDA and covering the three areas mentioned in the Barcelona Declaration, namely the Political and Security Partnership, the Economic and Financial Partnership and the Social, Cultural and Human Partnership.

In addition to the multiplicity of actors and instruments provided for in the context of the Euro–Mediterranean Process at both unilateral and bilateral levels, the Union added another layer to its relations with the region by adopting a Common Strategy in 2000.[91] First introduced at Amsterdam in Article 13 TEU, this instrument is focused on areas where the Member States have important interests in common. Its function is to set out their objectives, duration and the means to be made available by the Union and the Member States. The proper function of common strategies ought to be understood in the light of the constitutional idiosyncrasies of the Union: as its external policies are covered by different competences and are regulated pursuant to different sets of rules, the introduction of common

---

[90] Art 63 EMA with Jordan.
[91] [2000] OJ L 183/5. Its duration was extended by Dec 2004/763/CFSP [2004] OJ L 337/72.

strategies aimed at providing the Union's policies with focus and coherence—or, as a cynical observer might point out, the aim of this instrument was to appear to provide focus and coherence.[92] The Common Strategy on the Mediterranean starts off by setting out 'the vision of the EU for the Mediterranean'. As if the choice of the term 'vision' was not sufficient to raise doubts about the practical role of the instrument, its description provided for in Article 3 is:

> The EU's Mediterranean policy is guided by the principle of partnership, a partnership which should be actively supported by both sides. The EU will work with its Mediterranean partners to: develop good neighbourly relations; improve prosperity; eliminate poverty; promote and protect all human rights and fundamental freedoms, democracy, good governance and the rule of law; promote cultural and religious tolerance, and develop cooperation with civil society, including NGOs. It will do so by supporting the efforts of the Mediterranean partners to attain the goals set out by the Euro-Mediterranean partnership, by using its bilateral relations to pursue these objectives, and by contributing to the creation of a peaceful environment in the Middle East.

This grand statement is followed by an attempt to define the relationship between the Euro–Mediterranean Process and the Common Strategy:

> This Common Strategy builds on the Euro-Mediterranean partnership established by the Barcelona Declaration and its subsequent *acquis*, the Berlin Declaration and the European Union's long-standing policy towards the Mediterranean with its bilateral and regional components.

Then, a list of objectives is laid down, followed by a number of areas of action and initiatives. In substantive terms, the content of the Common Strategy does not add much to the initiatives already undertaken or envisaged within the context of the Euro–Mediterranean Partnership (EMP). In legal terms, it raises a number of questions about the effect of its provisions and its implications for the exercise of Community competence.[93] It is, mainly, in political terms that its adoption should be assessed: it constituted a rhetorical act reaffirming the commitment of the Union to the stabilisation and development of the Mediterranean region. This is also illustrated by the provisions in the Common Strategy seeking to intensify the functioning of the EMP: for instance, the Council is to ensure that each incoming Presidency presents to the Council, in the framework of its general programme, priorities for the implementation of this Common Strategy. In addition, the Council is to review and evaluate the Union's action under this Common Strategy and to report to the European Council on progress towards its objectives not less than annually. But it is mainly its attempt to add momentum to the functioning of the EMP that the Common Strategy signifies.[94]

---

[92] For an analysis of common strategies, see Ch 11 below.
[93] See the analysis in Ch 11 below.
[94] See C Spencer, 'The EU and Common Strategies: The Revealing Case of the Mediterranean' (2001) 6 *EFA Rev* 31.

Furthermore, there is a fine thread which links that instrument and the various initiatives envisaged in the Euro–Mediterranean Partnership, namely the interests of the Member States. On the one hand, their role has been central to the structure and functioning of the EMP[95] and, on the other hand, common strategies are intended to be decided upon by the European Council, that is an intergovernmental body *par excellence*, in areas where the *Member States* have important interests in common.[96] This thread highlights the distinct foreign policy function carried out by the Common Strategy which is explained in Article 5 in the following terms:

> The EU is convinced that the successful conclusion of the Middle East Peace Process on all its tracks, and the resolution of other conflicts in the region, are important prerequisites for peace and stability in the Mediterranean. Given its interests in the region and its close and long-standing ties with its constituent countries, the Union aspires to play its full part in bringing about stability and development in the Middle East. The cooperation that has already been initiated in the framework of the Barcelona Process is a determining factor in laying the foundations for after peace has been achieved. The Union will therefore support the efforts of the parties to implement the peace agreements. In this regard the adoption of the Euro-Mediterranean Charter for Peace and Stability, an objective which predates the adoption of this strategy, should be a deciding factor in the post-conflict process in the Mediterranean.

6. THE EUROPEAN NEIGHBOURHOOD POLICY

The process of enlargement itself has given impetus to the development of a closer relationship between the Union and the countries which lie beyond its borders. This momentum finds its genesis in the so-called 'Wider Europe' initiative. According to the Council, that initiative is 'based on the conviction that the EU's enlargement . . . presents a unique opportunity to strengthen co-operation and interdependence with those countries that will soon find themselves at the Union's frontiers'.[97] Building on this, Commissioner Chris Patten, responsible for external relations, and the high Representative for the Common Foreign and Security Policy, Javier Solana, produced a joint letter on 7 August 2002 entitled 'Wider Europe' in which the EU neighbours were divided into three regional groups, namely the Mediterranean countries, the Western Balkans and the Western Newly Independent States, that is Ukraine, Moldova and Belarus.[98] The

---

[95] See C Flaesch-Mougin, 'Les acteurs des relations euro-méditerranéennes', in *Mélanges en homage à Guy Isaac—50 Ans de droit commnunautaire* (Toulouse: Presses de l'Université des sciences sociales de Toulouse, 2004) 469 at 471–80.

[96] See Art 13(2) TEU (emphasis added).

[97] General Affairs and External Relations Council, Conclusions, 14 Apr 2003.

[98] COM(2003)104 final: *Wider Europe—Neighbourhood: A New Framework for Relations with our Eastern and Southern Neighbours.*

EU relations with these three groups have been carried out on the basis of the structured frameworks described above in this chapter, namely the Barcelona Process, the stabilisation and association process and the Partnership and Cooperation Agreements respectively.

Solana and Patten argued for an opportunity to develop 'a more coherent and durable basis for relations with our immediate neighbours . . . the scope and intensity [of which] will have to be flexible'. In particular, they identified five areas in which concrete measures should be adopted: reinforced political dialogue, economic co-operation and closer trade links, cooperation on Justice and Home Affairs, including border management and migrations issues, financial assistance and integration into EU policies. These ideas were fed into a wider debate which was given the rather cosy, albeit meaningless, name, 'Neighbourhood Policy'. In a communication submitted in March 2003, the Commission sought to articulate this new policy more clearly. It is intended to be based on a wide range of incentives, such as extension of the internal market and regulatory structures, preferential trading relations and market opening, perspectives for lawful migration and movement of persons, intensified cooperation to prevent and combat common security threats, greater EU political involvement in conflict prevention and crisis management, greater efforts to promote human rights, further cultural cooperation and enhanced mutual understanding, integration into transport, energy and telecommunications networks and the European research area, new instruments for investment promotion and protection, support for integration into the global trading system, enhanced assistance and new sources of finance. Admittedly, some of these initiatives appear to be very open-ended—and they are being set out under the title 'a new vision and a new offer'. Whilst there the word 'vision' is disconcertingly vague, there is something attractive in the whole project: the Commission not only refers to the need for a 'differentiated, progressive, and benchmarked approach'[99] but also examines the position of countries such as Libya, thereby broadening the ambit of its policies. Finally, it entertains the idea of launching a new type of contractual framework to be called 'Neighbourhood Agreement'.

The Neighbourhood Policy has been welcomed by the Council[100] and approved by the Thessaloniki European Council.[101] As a result, the Commission produced a further document entitled 'Paving the Way for a new Neighbourhood Instrument'.[102] This is focused on the economic assistance programmes in place and their coordination within the new framework of relationships. The first phase is to last until 2006 and will see the introduction of Neighbourhood Programmes

---

[99] *Ibid*, at 15. It is interesting that the Commission is keen to point out that the aim of its policy is to provide 'a framework for the development of a new relationship which would not, in the medium-term, include a perspective of membership or a role in the Union's institutions'.

[100] General Affairs and External Relations Council, Conclusions, 16 June 2003.

[101] See Conclusions, 12–20 June 2003.

[102] COM(2003)393 final 1 July 2003.

covering the external borders of the enlarged Union aimed at incorporating a number of financial mechanisms such as the Community initiatives concerning trans-European cooperation (INTERREG), the Technical Assistance to the Commonwealth of Independent States Programme (TACIS), the Community Assistance for Reconstruction, Development and Stabilisation Programme (CARDS), the Mediterranean Cooperation Investment Programme (MEDA), and the pre-accession instrument aimed at providing cross-border cooperation (PHARE CBC). The second phase will consist of re-orientating those programmes in a way which would fit in with the broader context of EC external relations. And as if all this activity was not sufficiently dynamic, the Commission recently produced yet another communication under the grand title 'European Neighbourhood Policy—Strategy Paper'.[103] What is interesting about this document is the positive approach adopted towards countries which, for various reasons, have been at the periphery of EC external relations: these include countries in the area of the southern Caucasus, namely Armenia, Azerbaijan and Georgia, in addition to Belarus and Libya.

In its conclusions in June 2004, the Council endorsed the main orientations of the Commission document[104] and stressed one of the main features of the emerging policy, namely its flexibility:

> The Council confirmed that the privileged relationship with neighbours covered by the ENP will be based on joint ownership. It will build on commitments to common values, including democracy, the rule of law, good governance and respect for human rights, and to the principles of market economy, free trade and sustainable development, as well as poverty reduction. Consistent commitments will also be sought on certain essential concerns of the EU's external action including the fight against terrorism, non-proliferation of weapons of mass destruction and efforts towards the peaceful resolution of regional conflicts as well as cooperation in justice and home affairs matters. The level of ambition of the relationship with each neighbour will depend on the degree of the partner's commitment to common values as well as its capacity to implement jointly agreed priorities. The pace of progress of the relationship with each neighbour will acknowledge fully its efforts and concrete achievements in meeting those commitments.

In practical terms, this flexibility is illustrated by the specific ways in which the ENP is to be carried forward, namely through individual action plans agreed jointly between the Union and the partner states. Their minimum duration is set to be three years and they could be renewed by mutual consent. In terms of their content, the action plans, whilst based on common principles, would be differentiated in order to reflect the particular circumstances of the partner country. The starting point for such action plans would be the country reports prepared by the

---

[103] COM(2004)373 final, 12 May 2004.
[104] It also recalls the unwillingness expressed by the Russian government to participate in the policy, content with developing its relations with the EU on a bilateral basis.

Commission. It is noteworthy that a number of such reports have already been produced.[105]

The emerging ENP is designed to draw upon, and yet be distinct from, existing forms of cooperation. In its conclusions in June 2005, the Council pointed out that the ENP 'will bring added value, going beyond existing cooperation, both to partner countries and to the EU'. To that effect, action plans with the Mediterranean countries will be drawn up once the association agreements, provided for in the context of the Euro–Mediterranean Partnership, have entered into force. The interaction between the emerging policy and the existing frameworks of cooperation is illustrated in various ways: for instance, the action plans are to be endorsed by the councils set up under the various association or partnership and cooperation agreements and their implementation monitored by the joint bodies set up thereunder.

The European Neighbourhood Policy is still an emerging policy which seeks to define its function within a rapidly changing neighbourhood. Therefore, it is too early to assess either its effectiveness or its implications for the international identity of the Union. In terms of its general tone and structure, it draws upon the formalisation introduced in EU international relations as illustrated by the stabilisation and association process and the Euro–Mediterranean Partnership. In fact, it adds yet another layer of dense formalisation in an increasingly regional-based conception of international relations.[106] This emphasis on the regional dimension was not only apparent in the genesis of the policy: in its April 2005 Conclusions, the External Relations Council pointed out that, with regard to the south Caucasus countries, 'particular attention will be paid to encouraging regional cooperation and progress in conflict resolution. On this point, the Council welcomes the determination expressed by Armenia, Azerbaijan and Georgia to use the action plans as essential instruments for strengthening regional cooperation'. In placing the regional approach within the broader context of the ENP, the Union highlights the security function of its initiative. It is recalled that one of the goals of the European Security Strategy, endorsed by the European Council in December 2003, is to 'make a particular contribution to stability and good governance in our immediate neighbourhood' and 'promote a ring of well governed countries to the East of the European Union and on the borders of the Mediterranean with whom we can enjoy close and cooperative relations'.[107]

Viewed from this angle, the emergence of the ENP illustrates clearly the evolving nature of EU international relations: drawing upon traditional cooperation

---

[105] See Country Reports on Ukraine (SEC(2004)566), Moldova (SEC(2004)567), Morocco (SEC(2004)569), Tunisia (SEC(2004)570), Jordan (SEC(2004)564), Israel (SEC(2004)568), Palestinian Authority of the West Bank and Gaza Strip (SEC(2004)565) and Egypt (SEC(2005)287/3).

[106] For the regional-based element, see M Cremona, 'The Union as a Global Actor: Roles, Models and Identity' (2004) 41 *CMLRev* 553 at 561–2.

[107] *A Secure Europe in a Better World—The European Security Strategy*, European Council of Thossaloniki, 20 June 2003, 8.

agreements, the Union concluded more advanced forms of contractual relations with its immediate neighbours which were placed within a broader formalised process of wide scope. And within the context of the enlarged Union, an overall framework was further developed, drawing upon the existing frameworks and yet placing them in the context of a broader geopolitical agenda.

However, the addition of this structured overall approach to the already formalised individual policies is bound to raise questions of overlapping functions with legal and practical implications. The Community institutions appear conscious of this: in order to ensure that the ENP brings added value, the Council pointed out that 'it will be essential to maintain the coherence and unity of this policy, in its content, instruments and final goals'.[108] In terms of institutional functions, a considerable degree of interaction is necessary. For instance, for the national reports already drawn up, the Commission worked in close cooperation with the CFSP High Representative. As regards the action plans for the three south Caucasus countries, the Council asked the Commission to contact them and initiate joint discussions in close cooperation, for questions connected with political cooperation and the CFSP, with the Presidency and the High Representative and, where appropriate, with the Special Representative for the South Caucasus for the countries for which he is responsible.[109]

Whilst the specific implications of the ENP for the other structured forms of cooperation are yet to be seen,[110] a note of caution may be worth sounding. The introduction of common strategies by the Amsterdam Treaty and the clarification of their function by the Nice Treaty were also seen as a welcome instrument which could add a significant dimension in the multilayered international relations of the Union. Such expectations have not been met. Admittedly, the ENP appears to be characterised by a degree of institutional sophistication which distinguishes it from other efforts of consolidation of structured cooperation. In addition, the Action Plans, at the core of the emerging Policy, are not envisaged by the Commission to be rhetorical statements; explaining their role in a recent Communication, it pointed out that:[111]

> Individual priorities identified in the Action Plan aim to be both ambitious and realistic, and formulated in a manner as precise and specific as possible so as to allow concrete follow-up and monitoring of the commitments taken by both sides.

---

[108] Conclusions of its June 2004 meeting.

[109] Conclusions of 25 Apr 2005.

[110] In terms of the EMP, see RA Del Sarto and T Schumacher, 'From EMP to ENP: What's at Stake with the European Neighbourhood Policy towards the Southern Mediterranean?' (2005) 10 *EFA Rev* 17 and E Lannon and P van Elsuwege, 'The EU's Emerging Neighbourhood Policy and its Potential Impact on the Euro-Mediterranean Partnership' in PG Xuereb (ed), *Euro–Med Integration and the 'Ring of Friends'* (Msida, European Documentation and Research Centre, University of Malta: 2003) 21.

[111] See COM(2004)795 final, *On the Commission Proposals for Action Plans under the European Neighbourhood Policy* at 3.

7. CONCLUSION

This chapter has offered a snapshot of the gradual development of the Union's relationships with its immediate neighbours. It has focused on the evolution of these relationships into increasingly structured frameworks of cooperation and their development within an evolving system of legal and political links which emerges from the European Neighbourhood Policy. In essence, this analysis has sought to illustrate the renewed momentum and sophistication with which the Union articulates its international role.

In that respect, Marise Cremona has written about the multiplicity of roles assumed by the European Union and defined a number of them: she refers to the notion of a laboratory and model for integration, a market player, a rule genera-tor, a stabiliser and a magnet and neighbour.[112] The development, content and application of the European Neighbourhood Policy suggest that the Union has become increasingly aware of those roles. This consciousness and self-confidence do not appear to be unjustified. Following the referendums in France and the Netherlands, the Balkan leaders were concerned that the fate of the Constitutional Treaty might affect the fate of the integration of the Balkan states into the Union and undermine stability and progress in the region. Serbia's President stated that 'all outstanding issues in our region would be much more difficult to resolve if the EU membership perspective is cancelled'.[113]

The genesis and development of the Union's roles originate in the Community legal order. The analysis in this book has shown how the constitutional idiosyn-crasies of this order have shaped a system of multi-layered and interacting sets of rules and policies within which the Community has defined its external posture. The following chapters will analyse the distinct legal framework within which the Union carries out its foreign and security policy and will examine the ways in which they interact with the Community legal framework.

---

[112] Cremona, n106 above, 553 ff.
[113] See *Financial Times*, 3 June 2005, at 4.

Part IV

EU Political Relations

11

Common Foreign and Security Policy

1. INTRODUCTION

THE ANALYSIS SO far has focused on the constitutional foundations of EC international relations and the various ways in which the Community institutions and the Member States have relied upon them in order to shape the external identity of the Union. The overview of the contractual relations established with third countries and groups of countries has revealed a web of densely regulated and intrinsically intertwined frameworks of cooperation whose focus on their geopolitical and security environment is becoming more pronounced. The implications of these relationships for the Community and the Member States, as well as their international partners, need to be assessed in the light of the Common Foreign and Security Policy of the European Union.

The provisions governing the Common Foreign and Security Policy (CFSP) are laid down in Title V TEU and constitute a set of legal rules whose legal characteristics are distinct from those of the Community legal order. It is this distinct nature and function which the so-called 'pillar' structure of the Union sought to convey when adopted at Maastricht. The fact that the CFSP constitutes one of those pillars, that is one separate legal framework which is nonetheless related to the other 'pillars', is clearly illustrated by the role of the Court of Justice: Article 46 TEU excludes Title V TEU from its jurisdiction. This chapter will examine the distinct normative features of the CFSP framework and will assess them in the light of the development of the Union and its international environment.

2. THE HISTORICAL BACKGROUND

The rules on the Union's Common Foreign and Security Policy were not laid down in a legal and political vacuum. Instead, a considerable body of rules, principles and customs had accumulated since the early days of European integration. Indeed, it was in the area of high politics that the first, albeit doomed, attempt at integration was made: the establishment of the European Defence Community, whilst agreed upon by the original signatories of the European Coal and Steel Community in May 1952, was rejected by the French Parliament in 1954.[1]

---

[1] For a historical account, see E Furdson, *The European Defence Community: A History* (London: Macmillan, 1980).

A detailed analysis of the development of CFSP, from the genesis of its precursor to the evolution of the legal framework at Maastricht and Amsterdam, is beyond the scope of this chapter.[2] Instead, a brief overview will be offered as a necessary prerequisite to a proper understanding of the legal and political context in which the Member States and the Union institutions seek to shape the Union's presence on the international scene.

The failed attempt of establishing a Defence Community was followed by a period of relative stagnation until the beginning of 1970s when the first signs of a collective effort to establish cooperation in the area of high politics became apparent. During this period, which lasted until the adoption of the Single European Act (SEA) in 1986, the Member States of the then European Economic Community sought to develop a culture of cooperation on the basis of three reports presented by their Ministers of Foreign Affairs to the Heads of State and Government. These reports, presented in Luxembourg (October 1970), Copenhagen (July 1973) and London (October 1981),[3] constituted the foundation of the precursor to the CFSP, namely European Political Cooperation (EPC),[4] and sought to set out the objectives and the institutional framework under which the Member States attempted to formulate their stance on the international scene. It is not only for historical reasons that this informal phase of European foreign policy is interesting: when properly examined, it reveals the presence of a number of political and legal factors which are still central to the conduct of CFSP. The three reports formalised to a considerable extent *ad hoc* arrangements, some of which had already been carried out by national officials as a matter of practice: for instance, the Copenhagen Report provided for more frequent meetings of the Council and the Political Committee which had already become standard practice. Therefore, the emerging EPC was incremental in nature, a fact acknowledged by the European Council itself, when it referred to the 'vocation of the Union to deal with aspects of foreign and security policy, in accordance with a sustained evolutionary process and in a unitary manner'.[5]

Another interesting feature of that phase of EPC development was the acknowledgment that security policy had not only political but also economic aspects, and that it was not possible completely to dissociate the former from the latter.[6] Inevitably, this gave rise to the question of how to ensure the creative interaction of those elements without undermining their distinct legal characteristics.

---

[2] See E Denza, *The Intergovernmental Pillars of the European Union* (Oxford: OUP, 2002) Ch 2.

[3] These Reports may be found in *European Political Co-operation (EPC)* (5th ed, Bonn: Press and Information Office of the Federal Government, 1988) at 24 *ff*, 34 *ff* and 61 *ff* respectively.

[4] On EPC in general, see D Allen, R Rummel, and W Wessels, (eds), *European Political Cooperation: Towards a Foreign Policy for Western Europe* (London: Butterwoths, 1982), Holland, M. (ed.), *The Future of European Political Cooperation: Essays on Theory and Practice* (London: Macmillan, 1991), P Ifestos, *European Political Cooperation—Towards a Framework of Supranational Diplomacy?* (Aldershot: Avebery, 1987), S Nuttall, *European Political Cooperation* (Oxford: Clarendon Press, 1992), P de Schoutheete de Tervarent, *La Coopération Politique Européenne* (2nd edn Brussels: Editions Labor, 1986).

[5] Conclusions of the Rome European Council of Dec [1990] *Bull EC* 12–1990 at 7.

[6] This became apparent in the London Report, n3 above..

The Copenhagen Report acknowledged this by pointing out that the development of EPC 'should keep in mind . . . the implications for and the effects of, in the field of international politics, Community policies under construction'.[7]

The Member States were acutely aware of this tension and did their utmost to ensure that the intergovernmental character of EPC would not be undermined by the existence of Community institutions and the exercise of Community policies method. Whilst their sensitivity was understandable in the light of the embryonic development of European foreign policy, it did reach considerable levels of absurdity: it is reported that, in 1973, the Foreign Affairs Ministers, having met in the morning in Copenhagen under the Danish Presidency in order to discuss EPC matters, were prevented from discussing EEC issues in the Danish capital; instead, the French Minister insisted that they all flew to Brussels so that they could discuss these issues as the Council of the European Communities in the afternoon of the same day.[8] Thirty years later, this incident appears amusing. In terms of our understanding of CFSP, it is also instructive in a two-fold manner: on the one hand, it makes it clear that in the area of foreign and security policy semantics matter and national governments are keen to stress to their domestic audience that they remain at the core of decision-making; on the other hand, the formulation of foreign policy pursuant to common rules would not only need to take into account the constitutional particularities underpinning the structure of European integration but would also have to address them in a convincing manner. Therefore, the effectiveness of foreign policy becomes only one of the aims of the relevant legal rules; the regulation and management of decision-making pursuant to common rules turns out to be as much about the internal constitutional balance as about external action. This inward preoccupation, apparent in the conduct of foreign policy at European level, inevitably produced an equally inward preoccupation regarding the choice of legal rules. In other words, procedural and institutional preoccupations became at least as important as matters of substance.

The above characteristics of foreign policy were also apparent in the next stage of the development of EPC which was marked by the attribution of Treaty status to the EPC. The Single European Act laid down a set of rules in its Article 30 which sought to formalise the existing legal arrangements.[9] In doing so, the drafters of the Treaty were keen to stress the inherently limited nature of the commitments undertaken by the Member States. Article 30(1) SEA, for instance, provided that 'the High Contracting Parties shall endeavour to jointly formulate and implement a European foreign policy' and that 'the determination of common policies shall

---

[7] Art 12(b) in n3 above at 34 ff.

[8] E Stein, 'European Political Cooperation (EPC) as a Component of the European Foreign Affairs System' (1983) 43 *ZaöRV* 49 at n14.

[9] See S Nuttall, 'European Political Co-operation and the Single European Act' (1985) 5 *YEL* 203, S Perrakis, 'L'incidence de l'Acte Unique Européen sur la Coopération des Douze en Matière de Politique Etrangère', (1988) XXXIV *AFDI* 807. On the legal effect of those provisions, see C Bosco, 'Commentaire de l'Acte Unique Européen des 17–28 Fevrier 1987' (1987) XXIII *CDE* 355 at 381, J-P Jacqué, 'L'Acte unique européen' (1986) 22 *RTDE* 575 at 611.

constitute a point of reference for the policies of the High Contracting Parties'. Distinctly non-committal, this wording indicates that the subject-matter of EPC as formalised in Title III SEA was the establishment of a culture of cooperation amongst the Member States rather than the definition of a set of specific legal duties. In yet another indication of the significance of semantics in that area of decision-making, Article 30 SEA referred to 'the High Contracting Parties' rather than the 'Member States'. Furthermore, the provisions of the entire Title were expressly excluded from the jurisdiction of the Court of Justice.[10]

It becomes apparent from the above that the then emerging EPC framework, whilst incorporated into the Treaty structure, in fact retained its distinctive character. In its preamble, for instance, the SEA provided that the European Union would be implemented 'on the basis, firstly, of the Communities operating in accordance with their own rules and, secondly, of European Political Co-operation among the Signatory States in the sphere of foreign policy'.[11] Following the establishment of the pillar structure at Maastricht, its consolidation at Amsterdam and Nice and its proposed abolition in the Treaty establishing a Constitution for Europe, this arrangement may appear uncontroversial in terms of its implications for the role of the Member States as fully sovereign subjects of international law. However, the formalisation of EPC in the 1980s was far from uncontroversial as it gave rise to an action against the process of ratification in Ireland before the Supreme Court.[12]

The establishment of the European Union at Maastricht marked the transformation of EPC into a new legal regime which, whilst retaining its distinct legal characteristics, provided for tighter legal duties. The new legal framework was called the Common Foreign and Security Policy and its rules, laid down in Title V TEU, constituted the second pillar of the European Union. At its core was the provision that the Member States 'shall support the Union's external and security policy actively and unreservedly in a spirit of loyalty and mutual solidarity'[13] the wording of which was in stark contrast to the SEA reference to the 'endeavour' of Member States, which had been deemed to be so broad and weak as to be of a declaratory nature.[14]

In addition to their incremental character, the set of rules pursuant to which the Member States and the Community and Union actors have sought to carry out a common foreign policy has been underpinned by a considerable tension: on the one hand, they drew inspiration from the model of foreign policy traditionally carried out by states; on the other hand, they were so keen to rule out any possibility of encroachment upon the dominant role of the Member States as the

---

[10] See Art 31 SEA.

[11] Second recital.

[12] See *Crotty v An Taoiseach and Others* [1987] 2 CMLR 666; for an analysis, see JP McCutcheon, 'The Irish Supreme Court, European Political Co-operation and the Single European Act' (1988) 2 *LIEI* 93, F Murphy, and A Gras, 'L'Affaire *Crotty*: La Cour Suprème d'Irlande Rejette l'Acte Unique Européen' (1988) 24 *CDE* 276, J Temple Lang, 'The Irish Court Case which delayed the Single European Act: *Crotty v. An Taoiseach and Others*' (1987) 24 *CMLRev* 709.

[13] Art J.1(2) TEU.

[14] See J-P Jacqué, 'L'Acte unique européen' (1986) 22 *RTDE* 575 at 611.

ultimate authority of such policy that they were preoccupied with stressing the limits of that policy. In practical terms, this paradox became apparent at various instances: during the war in the former Yugoslavia in the beginning of the 1990s, for instance, the Member States were mainly preoccupied with the issue of state recognition, that is a public international law tool normally relied upon by states. In the process of instrumentalising state recognition, they also introduced a procedural element to it: in December 1991, a Declaration on the Guidelines on the Recognition of New States in Eastern Europe and in the Soviet Union was adopted, in which 'the Community and the Member States' set out conditions pursuant to which new entities would be recognised. These conditions included, amongst others, respect for the Charter of the United Nations, guarantees for the protection of the rights of ethnic and national groups and minorities and respect for the inviolability of borders; entities seeking recognition ought to apply in writing to the Arbitration Committee established by and operated under the auspices of the Community.[15] It is in the light of this experience that the criticism against the Community was often expressed: the failure of the Member States to implement a common position as to how to recognise the new Balkan states and the unilateral recognition of some of them by Germany were seen as indicative of the Community's perceived failure to intervene effectively in the Yugoslav crisis.

The tension between state-inspired common foreign policy and the continuing need for Member States to assert their position as the only effective locus for such policy has entailed the development of the CFSP on the basis of a continuing paradox.[16] This has been succinctly expressed in the EPC context as the achievement by the Member States of 'collective foreign policy harmony together with virtual domestic autonomy'.[17] This paradox has given rise to the oft-quoted phenomenon of 'capabilities–expectations gap'.[18] Quite how this paradox is managed within the current CFSP legal framework, as laid down in Title V TEU last amended at Nice, will be examine in the following sections.

3. THE CURRENT LEGAL FRAMEWORK: OBJECTIVES AND OBLIGATIONS

The objectives of the CFSP are remarkably broad in scope. These are set out in Article 11(1) TEU:

---

[15] For the process of recognition by the Community and its Member States, see DH Bearce, 'Institutional Breakdown and International Cooperation: the European Agreement to Recognize Croatia and Slovenia', (2002) 8 *European Journal of International Relations* 471, R Kherad, 'La Reconnaissance des Etats Issus de la Dissolution de la République Socialiste de Yugoslavie par les Membres de l'Union Européenne' , (1997) 101 *RGDIP* 663 and D McGoldrick, 'Yugoslavia—The Responses of the International Community and of International Law' (1996) 49 *Current Legal Problems* 375.

[16] See P Koutrakos, *Trade, Foreign Policy and Defence in EU Constitutional Law* (Oxford: Hart Publishing 2001) 14–18.

[17] M Holland, 'Three Approaches for Understanding European Political Cooperation: a Case Study of EC South African Policy', (1987) 25 *JCMS* 295 at 303.

[18] C Hill, 'The Capabilities–Expectations Gap, or Conceptualising the European International Role' (1993) 31 *JCMS* 305.

The Union shall define and implement a common foreign and security policy covering all areas of foreign and security policy, the objectives of which shall be:

—to safeguard the common values, fundamental interests, independence and integrity of the Union in conformity with the principles of the United Nations Charter;

—to strengthen the security of the Union in all ways;

—to preserve peace and strengthen international security, in accordance with the principles of the United Nations Charter, as well as the principles of the Helsinki Final Act and the objectives of the Paris Charter, including those on external borders;

—to promote international cooperation;

—to develop and consolidate democracy and the rule of law, and respect for human rights and fundamental freedoms.

The reference to the scope of the CFSP in terms broad enough to cover all areas of foreign and security policy requires a qualification. There is an inherent limit to what the CFSP may cover and, apart from international law, it is defined by the Community legal order. It is the distinct normative characteristics of Title V TEU which make this point central to the conduct of the CFSP and the constitutional order established under the TEU. The significance of the dividing line between the CFSP and those areas where the Member States 'have limited their sovereign powers'[19] will become apparent in the chapter examining the interactions between the first and second pillars. For the purposes of this analysis, suffice it to point out that the Court of Justice, whilst expressly precluded from exercising its jurisdiction over Title V TEU, has held that, 'while it is for Member States to adopt measures of foreign and security policy in the exercise of their national competence, those measures must nevertheless respect the provisions adopted by the Community'.[20]

It is in this context that a number of duties are imposed upon Member States: to 'support the CFSP actively and unreservedly in a spirit of loyalty and mutual solidarity'; to 'work together to enhance and develop their mutual political solidarity; and 'to refrain from any action which is contrary to the interests of the Union or likely to impair its effectiveness as a cohesive force in international relations'.[21] Whilst all these duties are expressed in broad terms, each of them is noteworthy for different reasons. The duty to support the CFSP illustrates clearly the distinct intergovernmental nature of the relevant legal framework, as it is in contrast to the parallel provision of Article 10 EC, according to which 'Member States shall take all the appropriate measures, whether general or particular, to ensure fulfilment of the obligations arising out of this Treaty or resulting from actions taken by the institutions of the Community'. The second duty set out in Article

---

[19] Case 6/64 *Flaminio Costa v ENEL* [1964] ECR 585 at 594.

[20] Case C–124/95 *The Queen, ex parte Centro-Com Srl v HM Treasury and Bank of England* [1997] ECR I–81 at para 27.

[21] Art 11(2) TEU.

11(2) TEU is remarkable for its vagueness even in comparison to other vague CFSP provisions: whilst the existence of mutual political solidarity is a *conditio sine qua non* for the development of an effective foreign policy, to render it the subject-matter of a duty imposed in the context of the CFSP is as meaningless as it is puzzling. After all, the emergence of political solidarity amongst Member States lies firmly beyond the legal sphere of inter-state relations: its development is the progressive and subconscious outcome of the multifarious and often subtle developments based on factors as indeterminate as cultural developments, economic progress, social advancement, education, to a certain extent legal developments and, ultimately, time.

According to Article 11(1) TEU, as amended by the Amsterdam Treaty, one of the objectives of the CFSP is 'to safeguard [amongst others] the integrity of the Union in conformity with the principles of the United Nations Chapter'. This raises the question whether it refers to the territorial integrity of the European Union. In the past, this was answered in the affirmative.[22] In the context of a Union of states where peace and prosperity prevails, this issue might appear of a rather theological nature. However, a number of incidents in the not too distant past have highlighted its significance. In December 1995, Turkey claimed that Greek islets in the Aegean Sea were of disputed sovereignty and invaded one of them, causing a particularly serious deterioration in Greek–Turkish relations which brought to the verge of war a Member State and a state with which the Union has enjoyed contractual relationships from the 1960s and which now is a candidate country. The dispute was resolved through the intervention of the United States, duly acknowledged by the Greek Prime Minister in the Greek Parliament. As for the position of the European Union, Richard Holbrooke, the then Undersecretary of State, pointed out that the EU 'was sleeping through the night'.[23]

This has not been the only incident where the EU appeared embarrassingly unable to rely upon its CFSP framework in order to take a common stance regarding a claim by one of its Member States that its territorial integrity was threatened by a non-Member State. In July 2002, that is approximately six months prior to the entry into force of the Nice Treaty, a similar incident occurred in the Spanish islet Perejil, which Morocco calls Leila, where Morocco took control. This caused an immediate reaction from Spain, giving rise to a military stand-off in the eastern Mediterranean. At that time, the EU did seek to react: following the incident on 11 July, it took the Danish Presidency two days to issue a two-sentence-long statement with no reference whatever to a potential EU reaction, whereas four days later the Political Committee failed to reach agreement as to what statement to produce. In the meantime, the Commission sought to intervene and assert its role: President Prodi held talks over the telephone with the Moroccan Prime Minister[24] and

---

[22] See J Monar, 'The European Union's Foreign Affairs System after the Treaty of Amsterdam: A "Strengthened Capacity for External Action"?' (1997) 2 *EFA Rev* 413 at 415.
[23] *Financial Times*, 1 April 1998, 18.
[24] IP/02/1064.

issued a forceful statement of support for Spain,[25] whilst his spokesman referred to the incident as a threat to EU territory. As this caused dissatisfaction in European capitals,[26] the Commission retreated and offered its services in order to facilitate the restoration of friendly relations between Spain and Morocco. However, in doing so, it caused greater dissatisfaction in Spain, which viewed the Commission's position as an effort to mediate between a Member State claiming to be under attack and a non-Member State. In turn, the Commission was forced to state that in no way would it suggest any mediation.[27] The conflict was resolved, rather predictably, following the intervention by the American Secretary of State Colin Powell.[28]

It is recalled that, in June 2002, the Seville European Council 'acknowledge[d] that the Treaty on European Union does not impose any binding mutual defence commitments'.[29] This statement was made in the context of its response to the National Declaration by Ireland relating to its traditional policy of military neutrality. In any case, the incidents described above illustrate clearly the inherent limitations of the rules laid down in Title V TEU.[30] Indeed, solidarity, both in words and practice, is not to be taken for granted in cases where Member States feel that their sovereignty is under external threat. It might be easy to dismiss the above episodes as irrelevant or even tiresome; after all, both islets in the Aegean Sea and the Eastern Mediterranean were not only tiny but also uninhabitable. However, loyalty and mutual solidarity require that the concerns expressed in one Member State regarding what is perceived to be a threat at the very core of national sovereignty be taken seriously both by the other Member States and the Union institutions. As Advocate General Jacobs pointed out in a different context, 'because of differences of geography and history, each of the Member States has its own specific problems and preoccupations in the field of foreign and security policy. . . . Security is . . . a matter of perception rather than hard fact. What one Member State perceives as an immediate threat to its external security may strike another Member State as relatively harmless'.[31] The Imia and Leila incidents do more than merely reveal the failure of the EU institutions and the Member States to respond in a case where this is required the most; they also indicate that, in addition to the limits to the scope of the CFSP set by the EU legal order, there is an inherent limit set by the absence of genuine solidarity between Member States

---

[25] Statement of 16 July 2002.

[26] See *Financial Times*, 19 July 2002, 7.

[27] Statement of 17 July 2002 (IP/02/1090).

[28] *Financial Times*, 22 July 2002, 8.

[29] Para 4 of the Declaration of the European Council, Annex IV to the Presidency Conclusions.

[30] See the excellent comment in J Monar, 'The CFSP and the Leila/Perejil Island Incident: The Nemesis of Solidarity and Leadership' (2002) 7 *EFA Rev* 251. See also the comment of T Garton-Ash, 'The Price of Parsley', *The Guardian*, 25 July 2002, where he wonders: 'what credibility has Europe as critic and partner if it cannot even resolve such a piffling little dispute on our own front doorstep?' and then concludes 'so much for the great peacemaker and bridgebuilder'.

[31] Case C–120/94 Commission Greece (*re: Former Yugoslav Republic of Macedonia*) [1996] ECR I–1513, at para 54 of his Opinion.

in the area of high politics: as this limit is defined by the enormous diversity of historical, cultural and, hence, political points of reference, this limit may not be addressed automatically by means of legal structures and procedural mechanisms. Instead, its presence will become less pronounced gradually and imperceptibly. In that respect, it is noteworthy that the Treaty Establishing a Constitution for Europe, rather than ensuring the protection of the territorial integrity of the Member States, provides that it shall respect the right of those states to ensure their territorial integrity, viewing this right as part of 'their essential State functions'.[32]

4. THE ROLE OF THE UNION INSTITUTIONS

The role of the European Council is construed in general terms: under Article 13 TEU, it is to 'define the principles of and general guidelines for the common foreign and security policy, including for matters with defence implications'. This description is consistent with its general role under Article 4 TEU, namely to 'provide the Union with the necessary impetus for its development' and to 'define the general political guidelines thereof'.[33] In the light of the distinctly intergovernmental nature of Title V TEU and the highly political nature of its subject-matter, the role of the European Council appears understandable; after all, in the area of foreign affairs, the leverage of the political authority originating in the European Council may facilitate the Union in the assertion of its identity on the international scene.

What is less uncontroversial is its steady development from an impetus-creator into a decision-making actor as marked in the amendment of the TEU at Amsterdam and, then, Nice. An illustration of this more considerable role is provided by the formalisation of its interactions with the EU institutions: for instance, it is to submit to the European Parliament a report after each of its meetings and an annual written report on the progress achieved by the Union.[34] However, it is its participation in the decision-making process that places the European Council at the very centre of the CFSP legal framework: it decides on common strategies, an instrument introduced by the Amsterdam Treaty in order to coordinate the Union's activities in areas where the Member States 'have important interests in common'.[35] The apparent transformation of the European Council into a decision-making institution is significant both in legal and political terms. The European Council has been viewed as a body unsuitable to engage into the decision-making process as laid down in TEU, not least because of the

---

[32] Art I–5(1).

[33] On the role of the European Council, see S Bulmer and W Wessels, *The European Council—Decision-Making in European Politics* (Basingstoke: Macmillan, 1987) and HJ Glaesner, 'The European Council' in D Curtin and T Heukels (eds), *Institutional Dynamics of European Integration Vol II* (Boston, Mass: Martinus Nijhoff, 1994) 101.

[34] Art 3(3) TEU.

[35] Art 13(2) TEU.

informality of its deliberations and the ensuing problems of transparency this raises.[36] In terms of legal principle, this criticism is justified: in the EU constitutional order, the balance of which between supranationalism and intergovernmentalism is carefully reflected by its *sui generis* and multi-faceted institutional structure and the development of which is increasingly underpinned by questions of transparency, to endow the European Council with gradually expanding decision-making powers is tantamount to questioning the way the Union has evolved over the years. The practical implications of this role of the European Council will be assessed later this analysis, in the light of the specific context within which common strategies have been adopted and account being taken of the content of the latter.

It is the Council which is to act on the basis of the guidelines set out by the European Council and adopt the necessary decisions. The Council is also placed at the very core of the CFSP framework in two fundamental respects: in terms of EU policy-making, it is entrusted with the role of 'ensur[ing] the unity, consistency and effectiveness of action by the Union';[37] in terms of the actions by the Member States it is to ensure that the duties imposed upon them under Title V TEU are respected.[38]

The role of the European Commission in the CFSP framework is distinctly inferior to that it has assumed under EC law. It shares with the Council the general responsibility of ensuring the consistency of the Union's external activities as a whole. Other than that, it is confined to being 'fully associated with the work carried out' under Title V (Article 27 TEU). In practical terms, the functions set out in the TEU are secondary: the Commission shares the legislative initiative with the Member States (Article 22(1) TEU); it may be requested by the Council to submit proposals regarding the implementation of a joint action (Article 14(3) TEU); it shall be fully associated with the Presidency in the latter's task of representing the Union (Article 18(4) TEU); it may assist the Presidency in the process of negotiating international agreements in the area of the CFSP (Article 24(1) TEU); it shares with the Member States the right to request that the Presidency convene an extraordinary Council meeting within 48 hours or, in an emergency, within a shorter period (Article 22(2) TEU).

The role of the European Parliament is even less significant. Under Article 21 TEU, the Parliament is to be 'consulted' by the Presidency 'on the main aspects and the basic choices' of CFSP and its views will be 'duly taken into consideration'; in addition, it 'shall be kept regularly informed by the Presidency and the Commission of the development of the Union's foreign and security policy'. Finally, it may submit questions and make recommendations to the Council and hold an annual debate on progress in the CFSP area. The wording of Article 21 TEU is as opaque as it is revealing: all terms chosen by the drafters of the Treaty

---

[36] See A Dashwood, 'Decision-making at the Summit' (2000) 3 *CYELS* 79.
[37] Art 13(2)(3) TEU.
[38] Art 11(2)(3) TEU.

illustrate their intention not only to place the Parliament firmly beyond any position of participating in decision-making but also reducing parliamentary control to merely an exercise in political debate.[39] That this has been the case is attested to by the Parliament itself: in its latest resolution on the annual report from the Council on the main aspects and basic choices of the CFSP, it pointed out that it 'does not consider itself adequately consulted as provided for by Article 21 of the Treaty on European Union through the Council's current practice of simply transmitting a descriptive list of actions for the preceding year rather than consulting Parliament on the main aspects and basic choices for the following year'.[40]

The only way the Parliament has succeeded in interacting with the other EU institutions under Title V is in the area of financing CFSP operations: under the Maastricht Treaty, administrative CFSP expenditure was to be charged to the EC budget, and operating expenditure would be charged to that budget if the Council decided so unanimously, in which case the EC Treaty budgetary procedures would be followed.[41] The different legal implications of administrative and operating expenditure were removed at Amsterdam: under Article 28(2)–(3) TEU, both will be charged to the EC budget except for operating expenditure arising from operations having military or defence implications and cases where the Council, acting unanimously, decides otherwise.

5. CFSP INSTRUMENTS

Article 12 TEU refers to the ways in which the Union is to pursue its objectives in the CFSP arena. These include: the definition of the principles and general guidelines for the common foreign and security policy; decisions on common strategies; adoption of joint actions; adoption of common positions; and strengthening systematic cooperation between Member States in the conduct of foreign policy.

The very enumeration of those means available to the Union is indicative not only of the dynamic nature of the latter's foreign policy but also of an acknowledgment of its incomplete state. This is illustrated by the last indent of Article 12 TEU: to refer to the systematic cooperation of the Member States in that context is to indicate that, ultimately, the foreign policy envisaged under Title V TEU depends upon the continuous interaction between sovereign subjects of international law. In particular, this provision also appears to suggest that, in terms of its formulation and substantive content, the effectiveness of this policy relies upon a

---

[39] See RA Wessel, 'Good Governance and EU Foreign, Security and Defence Policy' in DM Curtin and RA Wessel (eds), *Good Governance and the European Union: Reflections on Concepts, Institutions and Substance* (Antwerp: Intersentia, 2005) 215 at 219–23.

[40] A6–0062/2005 final at A.

[41] Art J.11(2) of the Maastricht Treaty: see J Monar, 'The Finances of the Union's Intergovernmental Pillars: Tortuous Experiments with the Community Budget' (1997) 35 *JCMS* 57 and 'The Financial Dimension of the CFSP' in M Holland (ed), *Common Foreign and Security Policy—The Record and Reforms* (London: Pinter, 1997) 34. On the financing of military operations in particular, see D Scannell, 'Financing ESDP Military Operations' (2004) 9 *EFA Rev* 529.

culture of cooperation between the Member States whose development can only be subject to such indeterminate factors as political rapport between leaders, international circumstances, economic realities and time. This is illustrated by the history of Article 12 TEU itself: the reference to *strengthening* systematic cooperation between Member States, introduced at Amsterdam and maintained at Nice, replaced the Maastricht formulation of the *establishment* of such cooperation.[42]

The principles and general guidelines for the CFSP, to be defined by the European Council pursuant to Article 13(1) TEU, do not constitute, strictly speaking, a CFSP instrument: even if Article 13 TEU made no reference to it, it would follow from the general function of the European Council that their articulation was essential to the framing of the CFSP. Indeed, Article 4 TEU provides that 'the European Council shall provide the Union with the necessary impetus for its development and shall define the general political guidelines thereof'. After all, due to its intergovernmental nature, the second pillar would provide the natural domain for the Heads of State or Government of the Member States to act. In any case, Conclusions of the European Council are mentioned in joint actions adopted by the Council.

5.1. Common Strategies

Common strategies were introduced by the Amsterdam Treaty, and their function was clarified at Nice. Focused on areas where the Member States have important interests in common, they are to 'set out their objectives, duration and the means to be made available by the Union and the Member States'.[43] The Council is entrusted with the power both to recommend common strategies to the European Council and to implement them. Within the institutional machinery available under Title V TEU, common strategies carry out a very particular function which is distinct from that of the other instruments referred to in Article 12 TEU. This is illustrated by the very wording of Article 13(2) TEU, which provides for adoption in areas where the *Member States* rather than the Union have important interests in common, whilst their implementation is a matter for the Union on the basis of measures adopted by both the Union and the Member States. As regards implementing measures, there is no limit to the actions to be undertaken by the Council as, under Article 13(3)(2) TEU, these include 'in particular' joint actions and common positions.

The European Council has adopted three common strategies pursuant to Article 13 TEU, namely on Russia,[44] Ukraine[45] and the Mediterranean region.[46] A

---

[42] Art J.1(3).

[43] Art 13(2) TEU.

[44] [1999] OJ L 157/1. Its duration was extended by Dec 2003/471/CFSP [2003] OJ L 157/68 until June 2004.

[45] [1999] OJ L 331/1. Its duration was extended by Dec 2003/897/CFSP [2003] OJ L 333/96 until 23 December 2004.

[46] [2000] OJ L 183/5. Its duration was extended until 21 Jan 2005 by Dec 2004/763/CFSP [2004] OJ L 337/72.

Common Strategy on the Western Balkans was commissioned by the Vienna European Council in December 1998[47] and was then referred to by the Cologne European Council.[48] The significance of all three areas for the Union had already been illustrated by a number of legal and political acts adopted by the Union institutions. In relation to Russia, for instance, the EC and the Member States had concluded a Partnership and Cooperation Agreement,[49] the Council had responded to a communication by the Commission[50] and set out various aspects of multifaceted engagement in November 1995. In the case of Ukraine, a Partnership and Cooperation Agreement was negotiated and concluded following the definition of the objectives and priorities of the Union's approach soon after the entry into force of the Maastricht Treaty.[51] As for the Mediterranean region, the EU had already expressed its interest by drawing up an ambitious framework of trade and political relations in the form of the Euro–Mediterranean Partnership which was launched at the 1995 Barcelona Conference and covered the conclusion of bilateral association agreements.

Whilst, at the time of writing, not all three Common Strategies are in force, their content and overall role are worthy of further examination. In terms of their structure, the common strategies have certain characteristics in common. In their initial part, the European Council sets out the 'vision' of the EU for its partnership with either the third country or the Mediterranean region as a whole; in addition to grandiose statements, the First Part of the Common Strategies also serves to highlight the overarching objective of the policies and initiatives set out therein: the one on Ukraine, for instance, '*acknowledges* Ukraine's European aspirations and *welcomes* Ukraine's pro-European choice' whilst referring to 'further rapprochement with the EU'.[52] The next part of the Common Strategies set out their objectives, which are as vague as they are uncontroversial: they include consolidation of democracy, the rule of law and public institutions, economic reforms, cooperation on security and stability and common challenges on the European continent. In the case of the Common Strategy on the Mediterranean, the objectives are focused on the Barcelona Declaration and the achievement of peace in the Middle East. Furthermore, the instruments and means to be invoked are laid down and areas of action and specific initiatives are outlined.

In terms of their substance, all three Common Strategies adopted so far share the same degree of vagueness and platitudes: that on Russia, for instance, 'welcomes Russia's return to its rightful place in the European family' and refers to 'the common heritage of European civilisation'.[53] Placed in a section the title of which includes the term 'vision', this language does not appear surprising. However, the

---

[47] 11–12 Dec 1998: see para 74 of the Presidency Conclusions.
[48] 3–4 June 1999: see para 69 of the Presidency Conclusions.
[49] [1997] OJ L 327/3.
[50] COM(95)223 final, *The European Union and Russia: The Future Relationship*.
[51] See Council Dec 98/149 [1998] OJ L 49/1 and Common Position 94/779 [1994] OJ L 313/1 respectively.
[52] N45 above, at 2 (emphasis added).
[53] N44 above, at 1.

terms in which the substantive provisions of the Common Strategies are couched vary considerably from the specific and policy-oriented[54] to the general and non-committal.[55]

The personal scope of the actions set out in the Common Strategies is defined in all-encompassing terms: these instruments refer to action to be undertaken at three levels, namely by the EU, the EC and the Member States; accordingly, the involvement of the Council, the Commission and national authorities is provided for. The Common Strategy on Russia, for instance, provided as follows:[56]

> The European Union will work to achieve the objectives of this Common Strategy by making appropriate use of all relevant instruments and means available to the Union, the Community and to the Member States.

In the light of the above, the implementation of common strategies gives rise to multiple competences and involves a variety of institutional and policy actors. This phenomenon raises important questions. First, in substantive terms, how are the various actors to coordinate and the coherence of the ensuing actions to be ensured? It is noteworthy that all three Common Strategies adopted so far deal with the question of coherence in a two-fold manner. On the one hand, they include a general provision according to which their implementation will be carried out in accordance with the applicable procedures of the Treaties, hence enabling them to provide as follows:[57]

> The European Council calls on the Council and the Commission in accordance with the responsibilities defined in Articles 3 and 13 of the Treaty on European Union to ensure the unity, consistency and effectiveness of the Union's actions in implementing this Common Strategy.

On the other hand, they include a section on 'coordination' which, invariably, is to be ensured at various levels: between the Member States, both independently and in regional and international organisations; between the Member States and the Commission; between the Council, the Commission and third countries, regional and international organisations; between the EU and the then candidate countries.[58] Even on the basis of the far from widespread practice pursuant to Article 13 TEU, there is an interesting shift of emphasis: the latest Common Strategy goes further by providing as follows:[59]

---

[54] The Common Strategy on the Mediterranean, for instance, refers to the progressive harmonisation of rules of origin in terms of South-South trade: n46 above, at para 16.

[55] *Ibid*, at para 13 where, in terms of political and security aspects, the EU commits itself 'to identify common ground on security issues aiming at establishing a common area of peace and stability'.

[56] N44 above, at 3.

[57] See that on Russia, n44 above, at 3. Also, para 38 of that on Ukraine, n45 above, and para 26 of that on the Mediterranean region, n46 above.

[58] See Common Strategy on Russia, n44 above, at 3; on Ukraine, n45 above, at paras 42–45; on the Mediterranean, n46 above, at paras 29–32.

[59] N46 above, at para 26.

The effectiveness of this Common Strategy will be optimised by ensuring the greatest possible coherence between the various instruments and areas of activities of the Union and those of the Member States. The Union will ensure complementarity between its Mediterranean policy and other policies.

Secondly, in terms of constitutional order, how is the dividing line to be drawn between competences which arise in distinct legal frameworks and powers which involve distinct legal actors? All three Common Strategies stress the distinct nature of the relevant competences and appear keen to ensure that their limits are respected. The one on the Mediterranean, for instance, provides as follows:[60]

This Common Strategy will be implemented by the EU institutions and bodies, each acting within the powers attributed to them by the Treaties, and in accordance with the applicable procedures under those Treaties.

Thirdly, a specific issue which emerges from the above is the legal implications of common strategies within the EU constitutional structure: can they constitute the basis of a legal duty imposed upon the EU institutions? In the CFSP context, it has been argued that Article 13 EC entails the imposition of an unconditional legal duty on the Council to act in the areas covered by a common strategy.[61] In the context of the EU order in general, the question of the nature of the duty imposed under a common strategy may be of profound significance in the light of the distinct legal characteristics of Title V TEU, and hence the instruments adopted thereunder, the exclusion of the jurisdiction of the Court of Justice[62] and the comprehensive character of the policies covered by common strategies. In this respect, the substantive content of common strategies is noteworthy; the first one, that on Russia, provided as follows:

The European Council calls on the Council, the Commission and Member States:

— to review, according to their competencies and capacities, existing actions, programmes, instruments and policies to ensure their consistency with this Strategy; and, where there are inconsistencies, to make the necessary adjustments at the earliest review date,

— to make full and appropriate use of existing instruments and means, in particular the PCA, as well as all relevant EU and Member States' instruments and Member States' programmes, and to develop and maintain to this end an indicative inventory of the resources of the Union, the Community and Member States through which this Common Strategy will be implemented.

Not only are the relevant provisions open-ended in terms of the activities that the EU institutions are expected to undertake, but they also illustrate acute awareness of the variety of competences underpinning the range of those activities. In

---

[60] N46 above, at para 24.
[61] RA Wessel, *The European Union's Foreign and Security Policy—A Legal Institutional Perspective* (The Hague: Kluwer Law International, 1999) 184.
[62] See Art 46 TEU.

that respect, Denza has pointed out that, whilst of a legal character, these instruments 'have more of the flavour of political obligations than of legal texts'.[63] Be that as it may, the issue was considered sufficiently important to justify the insertion of a European Council Declaration annexed to all three Common Strategies adopted so far. This reads as follows:[64]

> The Council acts by qualified majority when adopting joint actions, common positions or any other decisions within the scope of Title V of the Treaty on European Union (common foreign and security policy), on the basis of the Common Strategy.
>
> Acts adopted outside the scope of Title V of the Treaty on European Union shall continue to be adopted according to the appropriate decision-making procedures provided by the relevant provisions of the Treaties, including the Treaty establishing the European Community and Title VI of the Treaty on European Union.

Finally, the host of legal questions related to the application of Article 13 TEU raises further questions, not only in terms of the institutional functioning of the EU, but also in terms of the substantive consistency of the external policies of the Union. It had been argued, for instance, that the Common Strategies on Russia and Ukraine had the potential of undermining the effectiveness of the policies originally provided for in the Partnership and Cooperation Agreements with those countries.[65] The role of common strategies emerging from the above analysis appears to be more important in terms of policy projection than substance. It is interesting, for instance, that, in the case of the Mediterranean region, the British Secretary of State for Foreign and Commonwealth Affairs stated in the House of Commons EU Select Committee that 'the Barcelona process should take clear precedence over the CMS as a means of advancing European interests in the region and building partnerships. It is the instrument to which our Mediterranean partners respond best.'[66] This secondary function of common strategies is also borne out by the more recent Commission initiative on Russia: whilst stating that 'the current structure of cooperation and in particular the PCA is neither outdated nor exhausted',[67] it is very clear from the document as a whole that that conclusion applies to the PCA rather than the Common Strategy: the latter is mentioned only twice, once descriptively and once in terms of its eventual abolition.[68] It is noteworthy that, in its conclusions, the Commission document

---

[63] N2 above, at 134. To that effect, she notes that the European Council is to 'decide on' them rather than actually adopt them.

[64] The Declaration attached to the Common Strategy on the Mediterranean Region also contains references to the EU contribution to the Middle East process.

[65] See C Hillion, 'Institutional Aspects of the Partnership between the European Union and the Newly Independent States of the Former Soviet Union: Case Studies of Russia and Ukraine' (2000) 37 *CMLRev* 1211.

[66] House of Commons EU Select Committee, 9th Report, 2000–2001: *The Common Mediterranean Strategy*, para 64.

[67] COM(2004)106 final, *Communication from the Commission to the Council and the European Parliament on relations with Russia.*

[68] *Ibid*, at 7.

recommends to the Council that the EU 'engage with Russia . . . moving away from grand political declarations and establishing an issues-based strategy and agenda':[69] to observers of a cynical and suspicious disposition, this might appear to refer to the Common Strategy on Russia

The picture of common strategies which emerges from the above analysis is one of an instrument which, whilst it appears capable of providing a policy thread which would link various legal initiatives together, is problematic in terms of its constitutional, institutional and substantive implications. However, their legal interest notwithstanding, the above questions have not given rise to serious problems in practice. This is partly because of reasons mentioned above: within the multi-level policy approach adopted by the EU, common strategies have become largely irrelevant. The fact that this fate of theirs is hardly lamented is due to their original conception: rather than functioning as an effective policy instrument, common strategies were introduced in order to appear to provide coherence and consistency in the Union's external action. Adopted in areas where the vital interests of the Union had given rise to policy responses of considerable scope, diversity and depth, they purported to enable the Union to provide the thread which would link those responses, their distinct legal qualities notwithstanding. Viewed from this angle, the introduction of common strategies should be understood within the constitutional and political climate prevailing at the time of the adoption of the Amsterdam Treaty: at a time when the existence of the pillar structure had come under attack,[70] the introduction of common strategies seeks to assuage concerns over the potential undermining implications of the functioning of the second pillar alongside the Community legal framework. Therefore, common strategies emerge as an instrument indicative of the decisively introverted nature of the CFSP rules: rather than addressing the specific policy needs of the Union and enhancing the substantive effectiveness of its approach, they aim at addressing the constitutional particularities of EU integration and dealing with the internal consistency of their policy outcomes. In other words, rather than the country or region with which they deal, common strategies appear to target mainly an internal audience.

5.2. Joint Actions and Common Positions

Joint actions and common positions constitute the very first CFSP instruments which became available to the EU under the Maastricht Treaty. The Amsterdam Treaty clarified the distinction between them: under Article 14(1) TEU:

> Joint actions shall address specific situations where operational action by the Union is deemed to be required. They shall lay down their objectives, scope, the means to be

---

[69] *Ibid*, at 6.

[70] The Parliament, for instance, had argued for the incorporation of the CFSP framework within the EC. See the overview in Denza, n2 above, 123 *ff.*

made available to the Union, if necessary their duration, and the conditions for their implementation.

whereas under Article 15:

Common positions shall define the approach of the Union to a particular matter of geographical or thematic nature. Member States shall ensure that their national policies conform to the common positions.

Whilst referring to the institution adopting joint actions, the provisions of Article 14 TEU do not make reference to the institution proposing their adoption. The Commission, which enjoys the exclusive legislative initiative in the Community legal order, is now given the right, under Article 14(4) TEU, to put forward proposals 'to ensure the implementation of a joint action'. This provision, added by the Amsterdam Treaty and left unchanged by the Nice Treaty, appears to enhance the Commission's position in the CFSP; it is recalled that, in general, the Commission shares the right of initiative with the Member States under Article 22(1) TEU.[71] However, the provision for this additional role merely expresses what should follow from the general responsibility of the Commission as defined in Article 3(2) TEU, that is to ensure the consistency of the Union's external activities as a whole in the context of its external relations, security, economic and development policies: the central role of the Commission in the initiation of a number of those areas and the operational character of joint actions render the right of initiative both necessary and rather self-evident.

In the absence of a specific provision, it is assumed that the Presidency is the main policy initiator regarding the adoption of joint actions, as well as the other CFSP instrument, that is common positions.[72] The central role of the Presidency is acknowledged by the 1996 IGC which annexed a Declaration on the establishment of a policy planning and early warning unit to the Amsterdam Treaty.[73] Set to operate in the context of the Council Secretariat General and under the responsibility of the CFSP High Representative, this body is to put forward, amongst others, policy options for CFSP action to be considered by the Council; these options are to be presented to the Council under the responsibility of the Presidency irrespective of whether the Unit would articulate them at the request of the Council or the Presidency or on its own initiative.

As joint actions have an operational character, Article 14(2)–(7) TEU deals with a number of eventualities which might require reassessment of the EU action, namely substantial change in circumstances, imperative need failing a Council decision and major difficulties in the implementation process. In all these cases, the Council emerges as the central institution the role of which is not only to

---

[71] This has been the position since the establishment of the second pillar (see Art J(8)(3) TEU as agreed at Maastricht).

[72] See also A Dashwood, 'External Relations Provisions of the Amsterdam Treaty' (1998) 35 *CMLRev* 1019, 1033 and Denza, n2 above, at 145.

[73] Declaration No 6.

respond to the circumstances by adjusting the joint action but also to provide the forum for the management of the existing actions.

Assessed against the remaining provisions of Title V TEU referring to the position of the Member States, the binding effect of joint actions is expressed in Article 14(3) TEU in the strongest terms. It is recalled that, in terms of the effect of Title V TEU in general, Article 11(2) TEU refers to a duty of active and unreserved support in a spirit of loyalty and mutual solidarity whilst requiring that the Member States 'refrain from any action which is contrary to the interests of the Union or likely to impair its effectiveness as a cohesive force in international relations'. The distinctly stronger wording of Article 14(3) TEU is justified in the light of the operational function of joint actions which is, hence, envisaged to require that Member States undertake specific measures in order to give effect to the Union's position. In certain cases, the core of the initiative described in a joint action may be undertaken by a specific Member State or group of states: under Joint Action 2004/796/CFSP, for instance, the Union set up a scheme aiming to support a project for the implementation of physical protection measures at the Bochvar Institute in Moscow of the Russian Federal Agency for Atomic Energy; whilst Article 2 of that measure provides, quite predictably, that the Presidency, assisted by the High Representative for the CFSP, will be responsible for the implementation of the Joint Action, Article 3 provides that Germany will be responsible for its technical implementation in the framework of its bilateral programme in that area.[74]

Joint actions have covered a wide range of activities[75] the most significant of which include the following. First, in the area of the European Security and Defence Policy, it has been pursuant to joint actions that the Union has undertaken its most important operations in terms of both the military and civilian aspects of that policy.[76] Secondly, the European Defence Agency, whose role was referred to by the 2003 Brussels European Council,[77] was established pursuant to a Joint Action.[78] Thirdly, after the European Council had adopted the Common Strategy on Russia, the Council adopted a joint action setting up a Cooperation Programme for non-proliferation and disarmament in Russia[79] following the expiry of which a number of other initiatives have been undertaken in that area pursuant to Article 14(1) TEU.[80] Fourthly, the Union's special representatives in

---

[74] See Joint Action 2004/796/CFSP [2004] OJ L 349/57.

[75] See the typology in Wessel, n61 above, at 162–169.

[76] See Ch 13 below in Section 4.

[77] See Presidency Conclusions of 1 Oct 2003 at para 65.

[78] See Joint Action 2004/551/CFSP [2004] OJ L 245/17. The EU Satellite Centre (Joint Action 2001/555/CFSP [2001] OJ L 200/5) and the EU Institute for Security Studies (Joint Action 2001/554/CFSP [2001] OJ L 200/1) were also established under joint actions.

[79] Joint Action 1999/878/CFSP [1999] OJ L 331/11.

[80] See, for instance, the establishment of a unit of experts the function of which is to support the Russian authorities in the process of non-proliferation and disarmament pursuant to Joint Action 2003/472 on the continuation of the European Union cooperation programme for non-proliferation and disarmament in the Russian Federation [2003] OJ L 157/69.

areas of major strategic significance for the Union have been appointed pursuant to joint actions.[81] Finally, the fight against the proliferation of weapons of mass destruction has been carried out mainly on the basis of joint actions.[82]

Common positions, on the other hand, lack the operational character of joint actions. Whilst this may make them appear rather similar in nature to the statements and declarations which are frequently used by the Presidency in order to express the Union's position on specific issues, in fact common positions constitute a concrete legal act which is viewed as such by the drafters of the Treaty: whilst, under the Maastricht Treaty, the Council was to 'define' a common position,[83] the Amsterdam amendment dedicates an entire Article to this instrument and makes it clear that it is to be 'adopted' by the Council.

The legal position of Member States in terms of the application of common positions is set out in Article 15 TEU in terms which differ from that laid down in Article 14(3) TEU regarding joint actions: whilst the latter required that Member States be committed in their positions and activities, the former merely requires that their policies 'conform to the common positions'. In terms of their legal effect, the difference in the TEU wording should not be taken to entail a legal duty of a different nature: whilst clearly excluded from the jurisdiction of the Court of Justice, common positions impose a legal duty upon Member States. Instead, the difference in wording reflects the more declaratory content of the instrument provided for in Article 15 TEU; it is for this reason that compliance with the latter may take less concrete form when compared to the more specific implications raised by joint actions. Whilst not challenging their legally binding effect, the fact that common positions lack the operational character of joint actions might appear to question their significance. Prior to the adoption of the Amsterdam Treaty, Koskenniemi had pointed out that they tended not to set up 'definite behavioural guidelines' and, instead, 'either repeat duties set up elsewhere or coordinate positions in open-ended terms liberating the Presidency to participate in the great game of diplomacy with maximal freedom and leaves the rest free of substantial involvement'.[84]

Whilst this is the case in relation to a number of common positions, it would be a mistake to dismiss this instrument as irrelevant. One reason for this is the fact

---

[81] See, for instance, Joint Action 2003/873 extending and amending the mandate of the Special Representative of the European Union for the Middle East Process [2003] OJ L 326/46. Under Art 18(5) TEU, special representatives may be appointed by the Council in order to deal with particular policy issues; they are appointed by qualified majority in accordance with Art 23(2) TEU. The Council has, so far, appointed Special Representatives in FYROM, South Caucasus, Afghanistan, Bosnia-Herzegovina, African Great Lakes Region, Moldova, Sudan, Central Asia and two more in order to oversee the Stability Pact for South Eastern Europe and contribute to the Middle East peace process.

[82] See, for instance, Joint Action 2004/495 on support of IAEA activities under Nuclear Strategy Programme and in the framework of the implementation of the EU Strategy against Proliferation of Weapons of Mass Destruction [2004] OJ L 182/46.

[83] Art J(2)(2).

[84] M Koskenniemi, 'International Law Aspects of the Common Foreign and Security Policy' in M Koskenniemi (ed), *International Law Aspects of the European Union* (The Hague: Kluwer Law International, 1998) 27 at 32–33.

that the substantive distinctions between joint actions and common positions are not always apparent. The imposition of economic sanctions against third countries is a case in point. Since the establishment of the European Union, the imposition of economic sanctions by means of a Council Regulation under Article 301 EC has always been preceded by the adoption of a CFSP measure in which the Council expresses its will for economic sanctions to be imposed as a means of foreign policy.[85] Whilst, in practice, it has always been a common position which expressed the will of the Council to have recourse to a Community measure imposing sanctions, it is interesting that the EC Treaty should provide for either. In addition, arms embargoes in particular are imposed pursuant to common positions.[86] Finally, another example of the occasionally blurred line between joint actions and common positions is their adoption by the Council interchangeably: for instance, Joint Action 96/195/CFSP on participation by the EU in the Korean Peninsular Energy Development Organisation (KEDO),[87] along with Common Position 97/484/CFSP,[88] were replaced by a single Common Position.[89]

Going further than merely expressing support or disapproval, a common position may indicate the direction in which the Union institutions may act: Common Position 2000/420/CFSP concerning EU support for the Organisation of African Unity peace process between Ethiopia and Eritrea, for instance, notes that the Commission 'may direct its action towards achieving the objectives of this Common Position, where appropriate, by relevant Community measures';[90] in doing so, the common position in question highlights the synergy between Community and Union policies which is essential not only for the effectiveness but also the coherence of the CFSP.

Measures adopted under Article 15 TEU may provide the overall framework for most important EU policies as well as laying down more specific duties imposed not only upon Member States but also the Community institutions: this is illustrated by the common positions adopted in order to combat terrorism.[91]

Following the above analysis of the functions of joint actions and common positions, it is worth examining a case where neither was deemed suitable in order to enable the Union to articulate its approach. This is the regulation of exports of arms pursuant to the adoption by the Council of a Code of Conduct in June 1998. Neither that nor a subsequent measure laying down a list of military equipment

---

[85] On sanctions imposed by the Union and the legal problems they raise, see the analysis in Ch 12 below.

[86] See, for instance, Common Position 2004/31/CFSP concerning the imposition of an embargo on arms, munitions and military equipment on Sudan [2004] OJ L 6/55 amended by Common Position 2004/510/CFSP [2004] OJ L 209/28.

[87] [1996] OJ L 63/1.

[88] [1997] OJ L 213/1.

[89] Common Position 2001/869/CFSP [2001] OJ L 325/1.

[90] [2000] OJ L 161/1, Art 3.

[91] See Common Position 2001/930/CFSP [2001] OJ L 344/90 on the criminalisation of the use of funds, financial assets and economic resources for terrorist activities; also Common Position [2001] OJ L 344/93 on providing for the freezing of funds and assets of persons, groups and entities involved in terrorist activities, the latter defined in the body of the measure.

over which that conduct applies[92] was adopted on the basis of Title V TEU. The adoption of this measure beyond the formal set of instruments provided for under Title V TEU is as indefensible as it is unwise:[93] not only does it question the seriousness of the oft-proclaimed commitment of the Union to manage the arms trade in a sensible and responsible manner, but it also undermines the effect that the formal legal machinery available to the CFSP may carry. This is all the more so in the light of the significance of this policy, as illustrated by the central role of the intended amendment of the Code of Conduct in the issue of lifting the arms embargo on China and the ensuing dispute with the USA. The failure of the Council to have recourse to the formal instruments available to it under Title V TEU is all the more extraordinary when viewed against the manner in which the Council has chosen to act in order to ensure compliance with parts of the Code of Conduct: a Common Position has been adopted concerning the control of arms brokering 'in order to avoid circumvention of UN, EU or OSCE embargoes on arms exports, as well as of the Criteria set out in the European Union Code of Conduct on Arms Exports'.[94]

6. DECISION-MAKING PROCEDURES

Consistently with the intergovernmental character of the CFSP framework, the rule in decision-making is unanimous agreement in the Council (Article 23(1) TEU). However, this is not a rule of universal application: there is a range of exceptions applied to different circumstances.

First, the Treaty provides for three express derogations where qualified majority voting applies: in the adoption of any decision, including joint actions and common positions, on the basis of a common strategy; in the adoption of any decision, including the conclusion of an international agreement,[95] implementing a joint action or a common position; in the appointment of a special representative. It should be pointed out that these exceptions do not apply to decisions having military or defence implications (Article 23(2)(3) TEU).

Secondly, there is a provision for constructive abstention: under Article 23(1) TEU, abstentions by members of the Council in person or represented shall not prevent the adoption of decisions by the Council for which unanimity is required. In abstaining, the representatives of the Member States may also make a formal declaration which, whilst accepting the binding effect of the relevant decision upon the Union, will absolve their Member States from their duty to apply them. However, there is a limit to the extent to which constructive abstention may be

---

[92] Council Declaration of 13 June 2000 [2000] OJ C 191/1 and was updated on 17 Nov 2003 [2003] OJ C 314/1.

[93] See the criticism in Koutrakos, n16 above, at 204–7.

[94] Art 1(1) of Common Position 2003/468/CFSP on the control of arms brokering [2003] OJ L 156/79.

[95] Art 24(3) TEU.

relied upon: the Council may not adopt a decision for which unanimity is required if its members qualifying their abstention represent more than one third of the votes (Article 23(1)(2) TEU).

It is not only the possibility of constructive abstention upon which the TEU sets a limit—it is also the extent to which the express procedural derogations may be relied upon by the Council which is limited. Article 23(2)(2) TEU provides for an 'emergency break': the Council is prevented from acting by qualified majority in cases where one of its members declares that, 'for important and stated reasons of national policy, it intends to oppose the adoption of [such] decision'. In that case, the Council may refer the matter, by qualified majority voting, to the European Council which is, then, to act under unanimity. The effect of this provision is to prevent the Council from acting under this exceptional procedure whilst enabling it to rely upon it in order to ask the European Council to act unanimously.

The above overview illustrates the limited scope of the deviations from the rule of unanimity: the first category of exceptions appears to be based on the principle that majority voting is suitable for measures of an operational character, as these aim at implementing the political will of the EU institutions which the latter have already expressed unanimously; as for constructive abstention, it is a reasonable formula which aims at addressing a very specific situation, namely to prevent 'the lone dissenter' from bringing the Union to a halt. In other words, the rule of unanimity is still central to the conduct of the CFSP. This has attracted criticism: it has been argued that unanimous voting, the expression of intergovernmentalism *par excellence*, prevents the Union from realising its full potential on the international scene.[96] This procedural provision appears to be viewed as the main obstacle to the conduct of an efficient and influential foreign policy, a matter which attracted considerable attention following the failure of the European Union to agree on a single view as to how to deal with the regime of Saddam Hussein in the light of the expressed wish of the United States to intervene militarily. As this issue will be analysed further in this chapter, at this juncture suffice it to point out the following: the effectiveness of a common, that is not a single, foreign policy depends upon the successful interaction of a number of multifarious interdependent factors of which legal rules are but one. This is all the more so in the context of a Union of sovereign states which are still engaged in an extraordinary process to define the ever elusive line between autonomy and convergence.[97] The assertion of the Union's identity on the international scene pursuant to a common foreign policy requires more than a set of rules which may appear convenient at the time. That there is a reality beyond that set of rules is clear in the way that the Member States deal with their international affairs: for instance, Turkish armed fighter-jets fly over

---

[96] See the article by former Commissioner Pascal Lamy entitled 'Europe's Policymakers Live in the Real World' in *Financial Times,* 28 Oct 2002, at 27.

[97] On the inherent limitations of the CFSP framework, see P Koutrakos, 'Constitutional Idiosyncracies and Political Realities: the Emerging Security and Defence Policy of the European Union' (2003) 10 *Columbia Journal of European Law* 69.

the northern and central Aegean Sea every day, much to the protestations of the Greek government, which argues that, in doing so, they violate Greek airspace. The Turkish government counter-argues that its conduct is entirely consistent with international law. As a result, Greek combat aircraft are sent to intercept them and there are almost daily reports of engagements between them. In the event of an accident, the limits of the solidarity proclaimed in the area of the CFSP and the legal rules of Title V TEU are bound to be tested—and the experience of the Imia and Perejil/Leila incidents is not encouraging. This is a constant reminder of the complex reality which the rules laid down in Title V TEU seek to reflect.

7. INTERNATIONAL AGREEMENTS CONCLUDED UNDER TITLE V TEU

The Treaty of Amsterdam provided for the negotiation and conclusion of international agreements in the area of the CFSP. It is recalled that such capacity had been central to the international posture of the European Community: expressly provided in certain areas in the original Treaty of Rome, the treaty-making power of the Community had also been consolidated considerably by the Court of Justice in its implied competence case law. In *AETR*, the judgment which introduced such competence in the area of external relations, the starting point for the line of reasoning which led to the so-called *AETR* doctrine was the existence of legal personality under EC law.[98]

It was against this background that the question of the legal means, or the absence thereof, enabling the Union to relate to the outside world in the conduct of its foreign policy arose. The clearest indication concerned the Union's position in the Yugoslav conflict. In July 1994, that is shortly after the Maastricht Treaty entered into force, the European Union was about to take over the administration of the city of Mostar. The legal framework pursuant to which this operation was to be carried out was set out in a legal document entitled 'Memorandum of Understanding on the European Union Administration of Mostar'. In that document, the Western European Union was requested to assist the Union administrator to restore public order and security in that city in former Yugoslavia. The administration of Mostar was an example of a non-traditional foreign policy act which proved to be quite successful: whilst less spectacular in principle, quite effective in practice.[99] For the purposes of this analysis, suffice it to focus on the legal dimension of the incident: in the absence of express legal personality, the memorandum, signed on behalf of the Member States by the Presidency,[100] was signed between, on the one hand, 'the Member States of the European Union

---

[98] Case 22/70 *Commission v Council* [1971] ECR 263.

[99] See J Monar, 'Mostar: Three lessons for the European Union' (1997) 2 *EFA Rev* 1.

[100] For the relevant basis, see Dec 93/603/CFSP concerning the joint action decided by the Council on the basis of Art J.3 TEU on support for the convoying of humanitarian aid in Bosnia and Herzegovina [1993] OJ L 286/1, adapted by Dec 94/308/CFSP [1994] OJ L 134/1 and supplemented by Dec 94/510/CFSP [1994] OJ L 205/3.

acting within the framework of the Union in full association with the European Commission' and, on the other hand, 'the Member States of the Western European Union'.

This procedural formula was relied upon in order to disguise the fact that, whilst in its foreign policy the EU was capable of engaging in policy-making, there was no provision for treaty-making.[101] Therefore, what proved to be a genuinely original contribution of the EU in the crisis in the Balkans became possible only by means of an *ad hoc* legal method. This raised the more general question whether the Union should be endowed with legal personality. Both the Irish and Dutch Presidencies suggested that the Intergovernmental Conference which would adopt the Amsterdam Treaty confer legal personality on the EU.[102] However, neither at Amsterdam nor at Nice were such proposals endorsed. In a compromise of the type not infrequently reached at IGC level, the TEU amendments provided for treaty-making capacity on the basis of a provision which raised as many questions as it answered.

The relevant provisions of Article 24 TEU, as amended at Nice, read as follows:

1. When it is necessary to conclude an agreement with one or more States or international organisations in implementation of this title, the Council may authorise the Presidency, assisted by the Commission as appropriate, to open negotiations to that effect. Such agreements shall be concluded by the Council on a recommendation from the Presidency.

2. The Council shall act unanimously when the agreement covers an issue for which unanimity is required for the adoption of internal decisions.

3. When the agreement is envisaged in order to implement a joint action or common position, the Council shall act by a qualified majority in accordance with Article 23(2).

4. The provisions of this Article shall also apply to matters falling under Title VI. When the agreement covers an issue for which a qualified majority is required for the adoption of internal decisions or measures, the Council shall act by a qualified majority in accordance with Article 34(3).

5. No agreement shall be binding on a Member State whose representative in the Council states that it has to comply with the requirements of its own constitutional procedure; the other members of the Council may agree that the agreement shall nevertheless apply provisionally.

6. Agreements concluded under the conditions set out by this Article shall be binding on the institutions of the Union.

In procedural terms, Article 24 TEU departs quite significantly from the pattern underpinning the negotiation and conclusion of agreements in the EC sphere:

---

[101] M Cremona, 'The European Union as an International Actor: The Issues of Flexibility and Linkage' (1998) 3 *EFA Rev* 67 at 67–8.

[102] See A Dashwood, 'External Relations Provisions of the Amsterdam Treaty' in D O'Keeffe, and P Twomey, (eds), *Legal Issues of the Amsterdam Treaty* (Oxford: Hart Publishing, 1999) 201 at 218–21.

instead of the Commission, it is the Presidency which negotiates them, the former only 'assisting as appropriate'. In terms of voting, Article 24(3) TEU treats agreements concluded pursuant to Title V TEU similarly to any other formal CFSP act deemed necessary in order to implement another act unanimously adopted.

As a matter of practice, a number of agreements have been concluded under Article 24 TEU. These may be categorised as follows. First, agreements concerning the objectives and status of EU crisis management missions concluded with the third countries hosting the operation, such as those with the Federal Republic of Yugoslavia,[103] the Former Yugoslav Republic of Macedonia,[104] Albania,[105] Bosnia-Herzegovina[106] and Georgia.[107] Secondly, agreements concerning the participation and status of the personnel or forces of third countries in EU crisis management operations.[108] Thirdly, agreements on the exchange of classified information, such as with NATO, FYROM and Romania.[109] Fourthly, agreements with third countries or international organizations on permanent arrangements for the participation of third countries in the EU crisis management operations.[110] Fifthly, other agreements, such as those concluded under both the second and the third pillars, with the United States on extradition and on mutual legal assistance.[111]

The question whether, pursuant to Article 24 TEU, the EU enjoys international legal personality has attracted considerable academic attention.[112] There is no doubt

---

[103] [2002] OJ L 125/2.

[104] [2001] OJ L 241/2, [2003] OJ L 82/46 and [2004] OJ L 16/66.

[105] [2003] OJ L 93/50.

[106] [2002] OJ L 293/2.

[107] [2004] OJ L 389/42.

[108] These included agreements with Poland [2003] OJ L 064/38, Russia [2003] OJ L 197/38, Cyprus [2003] OJ L 239/2, Iceland [2003] OJ L 239/5, Czech Republic [2003] OJ L 239/8, Lithuania [2003] OJ L 239/11, Switzerland [2003] OJ L 239/14, Latvia]2003] OJ L 239/17, Hungary [2003] OJ L 239/20, Romania [2003] OJ L 239/23, Estonia [2003] OJ L 239/26, Slovenia [2003] OJ L 239/29, Norway [2003] OJ L 239/32, Turkey [2003] OJ L 239/35, Ukraine [2003] OJ L 239/38, Bulgaria [2003] OJ L 239/41 and Slovak Republic [2003] OJ L 239/44. In relation to EU POL Proxima in FYROM, see the agreements with Switzerland [2004] OJ L 354/78, Ukraine [2004] OJ L 354/82, Norway [2004] OJ L 354/86 and Turkey [2004] OJ L 354/90. In relation to EU forces in FYROM, see agreements with Poland [2003] OJ L 285/44, Latvia [2003] OJ L 313/79, Slovak Republic [2003] OJ L 012/54, Romania [2004] OJ L 120/62, Estonia [2003] OJ L 216/61, Czech Republic [2003] OJ L 229/39, Turkey [2003] OJ L 234/23. For the participation of Cyprus in Congo, see [2003] OJ L 253/23. On participation in Bosnia-Herzegovina, see the agreements with Morocco [2005] OJ L 34/47, Albania [2005] OJ L 65/35 and New Zealand [2005] OJ L 127/28.

[109] [2003] OJ L 80/36 (with NATO), [2005] OJ L 94/38 (with FYROM) and [2005] OJ L 118/48 (with Romania).

[110] Agreements have been concluded with Bulgaria [2005] OJ L 46/50, Iceland [2005] OJ L 67/2, Norway [2005] OJ L 67/8 and Romania [2005] OJ L 67/14.

[111] [2003] OJ L 181/27 and [2003] OJ L 181/34 respectively. For an analysis, see V Mitsilegas, 'The New EU–USA Cooperation on Extradition, Mutual Legal Assistance and the Exchange of Police Data' (2003) 8 *EFA Rev* 515.

[112] Wessel had argued early on that the EU already enjoyed legal personality: RA Wessel, *The European Union's Foreign and Security Policy—A Legal Institutional Perspective* (The Hague: Kluwer 1999) Ch 7. See also E Bribosa, and A Weyembergh, 'La personalité juridique de l'Union européenne' in M Dony, (ed), *L'Union européenne et le Monde après Amsterdam* (Brussels: Editions de l'Université de Bruxelles, 1999) 37, JW de Zwaan, 'The Legal Personality of the European Communities and the European Union' (1999) 30 *Netherlands Yearbook of International Law* 75, N Neuwahl, 'A Partner with a Troubled Personaltiy: EU Treaty-Making in Matters of CFSP and JHA After Amsterdam' (1998) 2 *EFA Rev* 177.

that the implications of Article 24 TEU are not entirely without ambiguity. On the one hand, it has been suggested that it enables Member States to instrumentalise EU procedures and render EU institutions their agent in order to act on the international scene.[113] This position is based not only on the lack of legal means to hold the EU as such internationally responsible but also on Article 24(5) TEU, according to which 'no agreement shall be binding on a Member State whose representative in the Council states that it has to comply with the requirements of its own constitutional procedure'. On the other hand, it has been argued that reliance upon that procedure so far has made it clear that it is the EU which has entered into contractual relations with third parties, hence suggesting its implied legal personality.[114]

Indeed, the wording of the decisions adopted pursuant to Article 24 TEU could not be any clearer. A case in point is the Council Decision 2003/222/CFSP on the conclusion of the Agreement between EU and FUROM on the status of the European Union-led Forces in the Former Yugoslav Republic of Macedonia (FYROM), Article 2 of which authorises the President of the Council 'to designate the person empowered to sign the Agreement in order to bind the European Union'. Be that as it may, the procedure laid down therein has enhanced the ability of the EU to act on the international scene.[115] It has also rendered the question of express legal personality less controversial: Article 6 of the Treaty Establishing a Constitution for Europe states that 'the Union shall have legal personality'. Whilst the fate of this Treaty is uncertain, the agreement at IGC level to introduce this clause is significant.

8. RULES CHALLENGED: THE WAR IN IRAQ

The detailed study of the legal rules underpinning the conduct of the CFSP enables a proper understanding of the functioning of the Union legal order, the dynamics of European integration and the mechanisms of decision-making. However, high politics are not confined by legal frameworks. When the Iraqi crisis occurred and the international community sought to decide how to deal with the regime of Saddam Hussein, the relevance of the legal regime laid down in Title V TEU was questioned. As the Member States appeared seriously divided, a host of questions was raised: was it the rule of unanimity which prevented the Union from asserting its identity on the international scene? Had the procedural framework been different, would the outcome have also been different? Has the CFSP failed completely?

---

[113] See Denza, n2 above, at 174–7.

[114] See A Dashwood, 'Issues of Decision-making in the European Union after Nice' in A Arnull, and D Wincott, (eds), *Accountability and Legitimacy in the European Union* (Oxford: OUP, 2002) 13 at 17–21 and S Marquardt, 'The Conclusion of International Agreements under Article 24 of the Treaty on European Union' in V Kronenberger (ed), *The European Union and the International Legal Order: Discord or Harmony?* (The Hague: TMC Asser Press, 2001) 333.

[115] See Editorial Comment, 'The European Union—A New International Actor' (2001) 38 *CMLRev* 825.

On 27 January 2003, the General Affairs and External Relations Council expressed its 'deep concern' about the situation in Iraq, 'urge[d] the Iraqi authorities to engage in full and active cooperation' with the United Nations inspectors and 'reaffirm[ed] the role of the UNS[ecurity] C[ouncil] in the implementation of UNSCR 1441', concluding that '[t]he responsibility of the UNSC in maintaining international peace and security must be respected'.[116] On 30 January 2003, the leaders of five Member States of the European Union (Great Britain, Spain, Italy, Portugal and Denmark) and three then candidate states (the Czech Republic, Poland and Hungary) issued a statement on 'the real bond between the United States and Europe' which was viewed as 'a guarantee of our freedom' and stated that 'Resolution 1441 is Saddam Hussein's last chance to disarm using peaceful means'. On the same day, the European Parliament declared its opposition to any kind of preventive war or unilateral military action, and insisted that the EU speak with one voice on the basis of a common position.[117] Finally, at an extraordinary meeting in Brussels on 17 January 2003, the European Council 'recognis[ed] that the primary responsibility for dealing with Iraqi disarmament lies with the Security Council'.[118]

The then President of the Commission, Romano Prodi, 'regret[ed] that it has not been possible to agree on a common European Union position' and stated that '[w]e must all work together to reduce potential long-term damage to . . . our efforts to build a Common Foreign and Security Policy for the Union'.[119] In a statement on 20 March 2003, that is the date the war began, President Prodi stated that '[w]hatever the outcome of the war, there can be no denying this is a bad time for the Common Foreign and Security Policy, for the European Union as a whole' and pointed out the following:[120]

> These difficult circumstances also show it is time to draw the lessons from this crisis. Europe can make an effective contribution to peace in the world only if its nations pull together within the European Union. We all agree that we owe our wealth and prosperity to the Union. It is not in our interest to continue relying on others when it comes to defending our values militarily.

There can be no doubt that the war in Iraq seriously tested not only the procedural provisions of the TEU but also the culture of cooperation fostered by the development of the CFSP rules and that of their precursor. The failure, for instance, of the Member States holding a permanent seat at the UN Security Council to carry out systematic and meaningful discussions of the Iraqi crisis in

---

[116] Conclusions, 5396/03 at 14.
[117] *Agence Europe*, 31/Jan/03 at 4.
[118] Conclusions, POLGEN 7, 6466/03 at 1.
[119] Statement of 20/Mar/03.
[120] IP/03/419.

the Council was highly regrettable.[121] However, to argue that the Iraqi crisis signified the failure of the CFSP is not only overly dramatic but also indicative of a very selective reading of the CFSP framework. It should not be forgotten that that crisis challenged all the structures of international cooperation which had dominated the post-World War II arena: not only were the United Nations marginalised and NATO seriously split, but also very considerable opposition was expressed within most individual states; it is recalled, for instance, that there were serious demonstrations in Continental Europe and considerable parliamentary disquiet in Great Britain, whilst Turkey, a traditional ally of the United States, refused to cooperate as required by the American administration.

In other words, the Iraqi conflict was so profound in its implications that it challenged the entire system of international cooperation. To expect the Union to succeed where the United Nations and the Western powers, both individually and collectively, failed is as unrealistic as it would be to disregard the CFSP idiosyncrasies. The rules laid down in Title V TEU and the *acquis politique* formed after years of practice and experience had by no means produced a framework strictly confined to legal principles and procedures. On the contrary, in the process of asserting its identity on the international scene, the Union has tolerated considerable deviations from the model of 'togetherness' advocated in the TEU as ad hoc coalitions of varying membership, albeit mainly representing the big Member States, have been frequent. For instance, in the past, there were biannual meetings between the Prime Ministers of the UK, France, Spain, Italy and Germany with the Turkish Prime Minister which, to a considerable extent, set the tone of the relationship between the EU and Turkey; more recently, the so-called EU-3, that is France, the United Kingdom and Germany, have been very active in seeking not to alienate Iran from the international community whilst ensuring a system of control of its nuclear facilities.[122]

Active beyond the institutional framework set out in Title V TEU, such groupings are identified with the pathological aspects of the CFSP, and yet, they may be associated with an initiative viewed as distinctly European. The case of EU-3 is a case in point, in so far as neither the EU institutions nor other Member States have expressed reservations on the autonomous efforts of these three Member States to define an approach to Iran which would be both alternative to that advocated by

---

[121] The then Director for External Relations at the Council Secretariat later wrote that 'there was intermittent superficial discussion and the occasional minimalist declaration to show that the EU was at least aware that there was an Iraqi problem. But . . . the UK and France made sure that the subject was reserved for handling only in New York at the UN. The other Member States connived at their own irrelevance (and impotence) partly out of respect for the primacy of UN over EU obligations for Britain and France, but more particularly because they knew that any attempt to forge a common EU position on Iraq would be more damaging than helpful to a still fragile CFSP which was making real progress in other areas, notably the Balkans and even the Middle East': Sir Brian Crowe, 'A Common Foreign policy After Iraq?' in M. Holland (ed), *Common Foreign and Security Policy—The First Ten Years* (2nd edn, London: Continuum, 2004) 28 at 30.

[122] See, for instance, *Financial Times*, 27 May, See also E Denza, 'Non-proliferation of Nuclear Weapons: The European Union and Iran' (2005) 10 *European Foreign Affairs Review* 289.

the United States and indicative of the evolving 'European' role on the international scene. That is not say that such initiatives are uncontroversial: whilst the European Union debated the issue of its participation in operations in Afghanistan, the British Prime Minister, the French President, along with his Prime Minister, and the German Chancellor organised a meeting just prior to the European Council summit in Ghent on 19 October 2001. The dissatisfaction expressed by other Member States was met with an invitation by the British Prime Minister to his above interlocutors to a meeting in London on 4 November 2001. This caused such consternation that a number of other leaders were also invited either because they represented a big Member State (the Spanish and Italian Prime Ministers), or because they formally represented the Union (the Belgian Prime Minister whose country held the Presidency) or were closely associated with the CFSP (the High Representative). That meeting became notorious in its symbolism of the limits of the rules laid down in Title V TEU.[123] Therefore, as heterogeneity has been a constant feature of the evolving CFSP, in a crisis of the magnitude of the Iraqi one it should be less surprising.

This raises the question of decision-making procedures and their role in the effective conduct of foreign policy. There appears to be a widely shared assumption that the rule of unanimity which prevails under Title V TEU is both unjustified and unduly restrictive of the ability of the Union to meet its objectives as set out in Article 11 TEU. This view of unanimity has not changed in the light of the Treaty Establishing a Constitution for Europe: it has been argued, for instance, that that Treaty 'continues to provide ... far too many "sensitive" issues to be decided upon by unanimity and accordingly does not allow the Union to adequately face the challenges of our times and to be taken seriously, in particular by the USA, its foremost partner'.[124] However, to argue that it is the requirement for unanimity which prevents the Union from taking its well-deserved place at the centre of the international arena is to ignore not only the prevailing political realities but also the history, development and idiosyncrasies of the CFSP. It is for issues such as those outlined in this chapter that there are 'sensitive areas' in Title V TEU: the question of territorial integrity of the Member States, the extent to which CFSP initiatives are inspired by and draw upon national practices, the heterogeneity of representation, all in all the peculiarities and tensions inherent in a polity seeking to define a common rather than a single policy determine both the strengths and the limitations of the CFSP. Therefore, what the Iraqi crisis revealed is that there is an inherent limit to the potential of legal rules in the case of the *sui generis* policies of the Union: to argue that the Union would have adopted a different approach had there been a requirement for majority voting is to ignore, not only the ability of the states to rely upon ingenious arrangements when the core of their sovereignty is impinged upon in the area of high politics, but also the capacity of the Union framework to accommodate and absorb such deviations. In

---

[123] See Written Questions H–900/1 [2001] OJ C 318E/148 and E–3214/01 [2002] OJ C 160E/74.
[124] D von Kyaw, 'The EU after the Agreement on a Constitutional Treaty' (2004) 9 *EFA Rev* 455 at 456.

any case, even in policy terms, majority voting is far from a panacea for the cohesiveness of the Union and the effectiveness of its foreign policy: as Denza puts it succinctly, 'in foreign relations, the power to shoot from the hip is not always an advantage'.[125]

9. CONCLUSION

In the context of international law, Hilary Charlesworth has argued against focusing unduly on crises.[126] Transposing this to the EU context, it is argued that the cries of lament for the failure of the Common Foreign and Security Policy in the Iraqi crisis were not only unduly alarmist but also based on wrong assumptions about the CFSP itself. Rather than the failure of the Union to define a common approach to that crisis, it is the momentum which that failure appears to have generated that is noteworthy. This momentum is apparent at two levels. In terms of practice, the area of security and defence policy has proved to be the centre of considerable activities.[127] In rhetorical terms, the focus of the now moribund Treaty Establishing a Constitution for Europe on international relations has been presented, albeit not altogether convincingly, as the opportunity for the Union to assume a role commensurate with its economic stature. The following chapters will examine this momentum and its various manifestations.

---

[125] N2 above, at 121.
[126] H Charlesworth, 'International Law: A Discipline of Crisis' (2002) 65 *MLR* 377.
[127] See A Menon, 'From Crisis to Catharsis: ESDP after Iraq' (2004) 80 *International Affairs* 631.

12

Foreign Policy and External Trade

1. INTRODUCTION

THE ANALYSIS SO far has shown that the European Union carries out its foreign and security policy on the basis of legal rules the nature of which is distinct from that of the Community legal order. The decision-making role of the European Council, the prevailing function of the Council, the secondary role of the Commission, the express exclusion of Title V TEU from the jurisdiction of the Court of Justice, the prevailing requirement for unanimous voting, all have shaped a set of rules aiming at attaching the development of the Common Foreign and Security Policy (CFSP) to that of European integration without compromising in any way, or even appearing to do so, the ability of the Member States to act as fully sovereign subjects of international law. The distinct nature of the CFSP rules becomes all the clearer when examined against the factors which have shaped the external economic policies of the Community: the gradual articulation of the existence of the Community's implied external competence, the definition of the implications of exclusivity, the longstanding debate about the scope of the Common Commercial Policy, all developed on the basis of the *acquis communautaire* as articulated by the Court of Justice.

However, the conduct of international political relations may not be isolated from that of international economic relations. From a historical perspective, the development of the CFSP itself illustrates this point clearly: the combined economic strength following the development of European integration and the leverage which it enabled the EC to exercise in the international arena gave rise to expectations that the Community would assume a concomitant international political role. Widely shared by the European political elites as well as third countries, this expectation gave rise to the gradual evolution of the incremental and *sui generis* foreign policy of the Union and the development of its legal framework. From a policy-making point of view, trade has always been a most important component of foreign affairs. This has always been the case and is quite apparent in the context of the post-Cold War international geopolitical environment and characterised by two phenomena: on the one hand, the proliferation of organisations pursuing formalised regional cooperation such as the North American Free Trade Association (NAFTA), the Southern Common Market (MERCOSUR), the Andean Community and the Association of Southeast Asian Nations (ASEAN); on the other hand, the increasingly formalised development of the international economic order within the framework of the World Trade Organisation (WTO).

Whilst trade has become central to the international economic arena, the specific ways in which it interacts with foreign and security policy raise a host of legal questions within the constitutionally idiosyncratic order of the European Union. This chapter will examine how such questions have been raised in relation to three areas in which trade measures with foreign policy implications have been most prominent, namely exports of dual-use goods, economic sanctions against third countries and exports of armaments.

2. A QUESTION OF BOUNDARIES

To observe that the legally distinct sets of rules on the EC and the CFSP, as laid down in the EC Treaty and Title V TEU respectively, are bound to give rise to legal conflicts is to point out the obvious. The Treaty on European Union itself acknowledges this in Article 47:

> Subject to the provisions amending the Treaty establishing the European Economic Community with a view to establishing the European Community, the Treaty establishing the European Coal and Steel Community and the Treaty establishing the European Atomic Energy Community, and to these final provisions, nothing in this Treaty shall affect the Treaties establishing the European Communities or the subsequent Treaties and Acts modifying or supplementing them.

It is not merely the structure of the institutional machinery of the Union which may give rise to problems: that the institutions of the Union are to act in different areas serving different objectives pursuant to different rules is not in itself either unprecedented[1] or automatically destabilising. After all, the provision for 'a single institutional framework' in Articled 3 TEU is one of the normative links between the distinct legal pillars of the European Union. It is their material scope which sheds a different light on both the institutional structure of the Union and the diverse legal characteristics of its pillars. It is recalled that the CFSP covers 'all areas of foreign and security policy'.[2] And yet, this apparently all-encompassing scope is inherently limited in accordance with the origins and development of the *acquis communautaire* as supervised and articulated by the Court of Justice. It is this inherent limitation and the various ways in which it may be undermined to which Article 47 TEU refers.

The most apparent tensions raised by the coexistence of the legally distinct sets of rules laid down in the first and second pillars are related to the choice of the

---

[1] See, for instance, Joined Cases C–181/91 and C–248/91 *Parliament v Council and Commission (Bangladesh)* [1993] ECR I–3685 and Case C–316/91 *Parliament v Council* [1994] ECR I–625 where the Court sanctioned the practice whereby Member States relied upon the EC institutional machinery and procedures in the exercise of their shared competence within the framework of EC external relations.

[2] Art 11(1) TEU.

appropriate legal framework: should a trade measure with foreign policy implications be regulated under EC law or pursuant to measures adopted under Title V? In the light of their distinct normative characteristics and, not least, the express exclusion of the latter from the jurisdiction of the Court of Justice, the choice of legal framework appears to be of immense significance. The Court of Justice has ruled on this issue directly in an Article 230 EC action against a Council measure adopted under the third pillar. In the *Airport Transit Visa* case, the Commission challenged the adoption of a Joint Action adopted under the then provision of Article K.3 TEU on airport transit arrangements.[3] The measure in question aimed at introducing common rules on issuing visas for transit through the international areas of the airports of the Member States. The Commission argued that its adoption was illegal as it ought to have been adopted pursuant to the rule laid down in Article 100c EC (pre-Amsterdam); according to that provision, it was for the Council to adopt rules on the third countries whose nationals ought to be in possession of a visa when crossing the external borders of the Member States and, from January 1996, it should have done so by qualified majority.

The first issue which was raised was the very existence of the jurisdiction of the Court. The British government, which supported the Council before the Court, argued that the annulment of acts adopted beyond the Community legal order was excluded from the jurisdiction of the Court pursuant to Article 46 TEU. Therefore, it claimed, the action brought by the Commission should be declared inadmissible. The Court rejected that argument. In doing so, it relied upon Article 47 TEU which made it clear that the TEU rules providing for the adoption of EU measures should not affect the provisions of the EC Treaty. The Court, then, opined that Article 46 TEU also makes it clear that the EC Treaty provisions on the powers of the Court of Justice and the exercise of those powers applied to Article 47 TEU. It then concluded as follows:[4]

> It is therefore the task of the Court to ensure that acts which, according to the Council, fall within the scope of [then] Article K.3(2) of the Treaty of the European Union do not encroach upon the powers conferred by the EC Treaty on the Community.
>
> It follows that the Court has jurisdiction to review the content of the [Joint Action] in the light of Article 100c of the EC Treaty in order to ascertain whether the Act affects the powers of the Community under that provision and to annul the [Joint Action] if it appears that it should have been based on Article 100c of the EC Treaty.

The Court went on to dismiss the annulment action. It concluded that measures on an airport visa for third country nationals who, flying from a third country to another third country, need to remain in the international area of an airport within the territory of Member States were correctly based on the third

---

[3] Case C–170/96 *Commission v Council* [1998] ECR I–2763; the measure challenged was Joint Action 96/197 [1996] OJ L 63/8.

[4] *Ibid*, paras 16–17.

pillar.[5] However, as is often the case in the history of European integration, the party winning the battle does not necessarily win the war. The action brought by the Commission enabled the Court to declare in quite uncompromising terms that, whilst the second and third pillars are excluded from its jurisdiction, it is for the Court to determine where the dividing line between the distinct sets of rules upon which the EU is based lies. Viewed within the context of the specific dispute, the line of reasoning underpinning the judgment in *Airport Transit Visa* is entirely consistent with past case law. It is a well-established principle that the form of a measure by no means determines its legal implications: it is for this reason, for instance, that, in terms of EC secondary legislation, an act beyond the formal classification envisaged in the EC Treaty may be challenged before the Court.[6]

In other words, the Court, at various junctures, has favoured a functional approach in order to determine the circumstances under which it would supervise the application of Community law. However, articulated in the context of the constitutional foundations of the EU legal order, this approach sheds considerable light not only on the role of the Court of Justice but also on how the Union may work in practice. It suggests that the requirements that the Union act on the basis of a single institutional framework and that the integrity of the Community legal order be not undermined by decision-making under TEU provisions do not constitute statements of merely rhetorical significance: they are legal provisions the application of which is for the Court of Justice to ensure. Viewed from this angle, the definition of its jurisdiction in functional terms sheds light for the first time on the linkages between the pillars. It also raises the following question: if it is for the Court of Justice to protect the legal integrity of the Community legal order by relying upon the Article 47 TEU proviso, is it not possible for the coexistence and, furthermore, interaction between the EC and the CFSP rules to be ensured? Rather than two distinct frameworks destined to coexist in a legally awkward manner because of a political compromise, could the different provisions upon which the Union is based not operate as a dynamic system of interrelated rules?

Any answer to the above questions is dependent upon a number of other related factors such as the approach to the relationship between EC and CFSP rules by the EU legislature as well as the relevant case law of the Court of Justice. In terms of the choice of the appropriate legal framework, a similar conclusion has been reached by the Court of First Instance.[7] Two annulment actions brought by Yugoslav citizens against CFSP common positions placing them on a list of persons not admitted to the territories of the Member States have been removed from

---

[5] For a comment on the substance of the judgment, see A Oliveira, annotation on Case C–170/96 (1999) 36 *CMLRev* 149.

[6] See Case 22/70 *Commission v Council (ETR)* [1971] ECR 263 at para 42. In a similar vein, the formal designation of a national authority is relevant to its status in terms of the application and enforcement of a directive: see Case C–188/89 *Foster* [1990] ECR I–3313 at para 18.

[7] See Case T–338/02 *Segi, Araitz Zubimendi Izaga and Aritza Galarraga v Council*, Order of 7 June 2004, not yet reported.

the Court's register.[8] There is one annulment action brought by the Commission under Article 230 EC against a Council decision implementing a Joint Action in relation to the Moratorium on Small Arms and Light Weapons.[9] This is a most interesting case, as it raises the question of the relationship between substantive policies adopted within the CFSP framework and commitments undertaken in the context of the Cotonou agreement.

3. EXPORTS OF DUAL-USE GOODS

Dual-use goods are products which may be of both civil and military application. As such, the regulation of their export appears to be a matter of trade as well as foreign and security policy. An overview of their legal regime is interesting, not only in terms of the legal questions that it raises about the relationship between EC and CFSP rules, but also in terms of the ingenuity to which the Union institutions and the Member States have had recourse in order to address politically sensitive issues by what they deem to be legally convenient formulas.

The legal regulation of exports of dual-use goods touches upon the longstanding debate about the scope of the Common Commercial Policy. Export measures are expressly referred to in the non-exhaustive list of activities of Article 133 EC and common rules on exports were adopted as early as of 1969.[10] The exclusive competence of the Community over the CCP, as introduced by the Court in early 1970s and articulated and refined in later jurisprudence, would appear to preclude any role for individual Member States in determining the legal regime of exports of dual-use goods. However, the very notion of 'dual-use' attached to those products illustrated their special nature: military products have long been presumed to lie either in a twilight zone between Community law and national law or beyond the sphere of Community law altogether.[11] In any case, exports of such products were seen to be so intrinsically linked to the conduct of foreign policy as to be subsumed by the legal rules governing the latter; and as the latter fell within national sovereignty, the right of Member States to restrict exports of dual-use goods was argued to be entirely within their sovereignty too.

In a way, the conflicting claims as to which approach should govern the legal rules on exports of dual-use goods provided the starkest illustration yet of the instrumental-objective debate regarding the scope of CCP. This debate, first put forward before the Court in a comprehensive manner by the Commission and the Council in *Opinion 1/78*,[12] shaped the debate about the proper construction of

---

[8] See Case T–349/99 *Miskovic v Council* [2000] OJ C 79/35 challenging Council Dec 1999/612/CFSP and Case T–350/99 *Karic v Council* [2000] OJ C 79/36 challenging Council Dec 1999/62/CFSP, both removed ([2001] OJ C 161/50 and 51 respectively).

[9] Case C–91/05 *Commission v Council* [2005] OJ C 115/10.

[10] Council Reg 2603/69 [1969] OJ L 324/25, subsequently amended by Reg 3918/91 [1991] OJ L 372/31.

[11] Whether this view is justified in legal terms is a different question altogether: see P Koutrakos, *Trade, Foreign Policy and Defence in EU Constitutional Law* (Oxford: Hart Publishing, 2002) Ch 8.

[12] *Opinion 1/78* [1979] ECR 2871.

Article 133 EC and defined the various arguments about the applicability of that provision to services and intellectual property rights.[13] In the area of dual-use goods, the nature of such products and the practical and political implications of their regulation rendered the conflict between the instrumental and objective approaches all the more controversial: if the former approach was endorsed, the trade nature of the measures in question would render them within the scope of the CCP and the Member States would be able to adopt unilateral measures only pursuant to a specific Community law authorisation;[14] if the latter approach was adopted, the foreign policy objective of the exports of dual-use goods would render their regulation beyond the scope of the CCP and firmly within that of national sovereignty.

3.1. A First Indication of the Court's Approach

Before the Union institutions had agreed on how to regulate exports of dual-use goods, the Court of Justice had the opportunity to rule on the compatibility of national restrictions on such exports in *Richardt*.[15] In that preliminary reference from Luxembourg courts, criminal proceedings were brought against a company established in France which had drawn up a contract with the then Soviet central purchasing agency. Richardt had agreed to sell a unit for the production of bubble memory circuits consisting of a number of machines. Once the relevant export formalities had been complied with, it transpired that the flight from Paris which had been booked in order to transport the goods to Moscow has been cancelled. The goods were, then, transported to Luxembourg by road and then loaded on to another flight to Moscow. However, customs checks in Luxembourg revealed that one of the machines fell within a category of goods which Luxembourg legislation subjected to a special transit licensing procedure due to its potentially strategic nature. As the machine in question had not been accompanied by such licence, the national authorities initiated proceedings against Richardt for violation of the national transit legislation.

The question which arose was whether the special licensing requirement imposed under Luxembourg legislation on the transit of products deemed to be of a strategic nature was contrary to Community law on transit. The relevant secondary measure, that is the so-called Export Regulation, required that the transit permit granted in one Member State be recognised as valid by the competent authorities in the other Member States.[16] Two views were put before the Court: on the one hand, four Member States and, rather surprisingly, the Commission argued that a Member State should be free to require that strategic products be

---

[13] See *Opinion 1/94 (WTO Agreements)* [1994] ECR I–5267.

[14] Case 41/76 *Suzanne Criel, née Donckerwolcke and Henri Schou v Procureur de la République au Tribunal de Grande Instance, Lille and Director General of Customs* [1976] ECR 1921.

[15] Case C–367/89 *Criminal Proceedings against Aim Richard and Les Accessoires Scientifiques SNC* [1991] ECR I–4621.

[16] Council Reg 222/77 on Community transit [1977] OJ L 38/1.

subject to a special authorising licence in addition to the general one provided under Regulation 222/77; on the other hand, Richard argued that such an additional requirement would be contrary to Community law as the nature of the products in transit should be irrelevant.

The Court started off by pointing out that, whilst the Community rules on transit applied in principle to all products, Article 10 of Regulation 222/77 did not preclude Member States from imposing restrictive measures in so far as such measures were compatible with the EC Treaty. What was crucial, therefore, was whether the national requirement for special authorisation was consistent with primary law on free movement of goods, and in particular Article 30 EC which enables Member States to deviate from free movement in order to protect certain clearly defined interests. The Court pointed out that, whilst the interests laid down in the latter provision enable the Member States to deviate from the rules on free movement of goods, they do not reserve the protection of those interests to their exclusive jurisdiction. Instead, Article 30 EC constitutes an exception to the rule of free movement, and as such it should be interpreted strictly so as to ensure that the national measures under review are such as to serve the interests laid down therein and 'they do not restrict intra-Community trade more than is absolutely necessary'.[17]

The Court, then, examined whether the Luxembourg measures were justifiable in order to protect public security as laid down in Article 30 EC. It held that the notion of public security referred to both the internal and external security of the Member States. As there was no doubt that the importation, exportation and transit of products capable of being used for strategic purposes might affect the public security of a state, the national measures were justifiable. The question whether they were actually justified depended on their compliance with the principle of proportionality. This was central to the reference before the Court, because it had been argued that the penalty prescribed under national law, namely confiscation and the initiation of criminal proceedings, was disproportionate to the aim that the deviation from Community law had purported to serve. The Court concluded that compliance with the principle of proportionality was a matter for the referring court which ought to apply it by:[18]

> taking account of all the elements of each case, such as the nature of the goods capable of endangering the security of the State, the circumstances in which the breach was committed and whether or not the trader seeking to effect the transit and holding documents for that purpose issued by another Member State was acting in good faith.

The judgment in *Richardt* provided an early indication of the Court's approach to national measures on dual-use goods as within the system of EC law.[19]

---

[17] Para 20. See also Case 72/83 *Campus Oil Ltd v Minister for Industry and Energy* [1984] ECR 2727, paras 32–37.

[18] Para 25.

[19] For a comment, see I Govare and P Eeckhout, 'On Dual Use Goods and Dualist Case Law: the *Aimé Richardt* Judgment and Export Controls' (1992) 29 *CMLRev* 941.

In particular, two points may be identified in the judgment which would define not only subsequent case law but also the subsequent approach taken by the Union institutions. The first was about the status of such measures: the right of the Member States to define and protect their security did not render the Community legal framework redundant; on the contrary, it was within that framework that national authorities would be expected to act. The second point was about the limits that that framework placed upon the right of the Member States to protect their security by means of export restrictions: the broad construction of the notion of security and the central role of the referring court defined a liberal approach which appeared to take into account the concerns of the Member State.

Whether the main tenets of the judgment in *Richardt* were but another facet of the combination of legal principle and political realism that the Court had been known to demonstrate in its EC external relations case law would remain to be seen. At this juncture, suffice it to focus on the role of the national court. Central to the preliminary reference procedure is the principle that it is for the referring court to apply the interpretation of EC law given by the Court of Justice to the facts of the case referred.[20] The application of the principle of proportionality and the assessment of whether a national deviation from EC law complies with that principle is one of the tasks traditionally bestowed upon national courts.[21] However, not only do the parameters within which national courts are expected to act differ, but also the assistance they get from the Court of Justice may vary. In the context of the law on free movement of goods, for instance, there have been cases where the Court of Justice provides no guidance at all as to how the principle of proportionality is to be applied,[22] and in other cases it outlines the factors which the referring court is to take into account;[23] in some other cases it applies the test itself, either because of the apparent difficulty experienced by national courts in reaching a uniform conclusion on the matter[24] or on its own motion.[25] However, in the area of the interface between trade and foreign policy, the involvement of national courts is significant in a more fundamental way due to the subject-matter of the disputes.

[20] See the analysis of the procedure laid down in Art 234 EC in P Craig and G de Búrca, *EU Law* (3rd eds, Oxford: OUP, 2003) ch 11.

[21] On the principle of proportionality in general, see E Ellis (ed.), *The Principle of Proportionality in the Laws of Europe* (Oxford: Hart Publishing, 1999) and N Emiliou, *The Principle of Proportionality in European Law* (The Hague: Kluwer, 1996).

[22] See, for instance, Case C–405/98 *Konsumentombudsmannen (KO) v Gourmet International Products AB (GIP)* [2001] ECR I–1795; in that case, Jacobs AG had applied the proportionality test himself and had found the Swedish advertising restriction disproportionate. For criticism of the Court's approach, see A Biondi, 'Advertising Alcohol and the Free Movement Principle: the *Gourmet* Decision' (2001) 26 *ELRev* 616.

[23] See, for instance, the onerous task for the national court outlined in Case 368/95 *Vereinigte Familiapress Zeitungsverlags- und Vertriebs GmbH v Heinrich Bauer Verlag* [1997] ECR I–3689.

[24] See Case C–312/89 *Union départementale des syndicats CGT de l Aisne v SIDEF Conforama Societe Arts et Meubles and Société Jima* [1991] ECR 1–997 at para. 12 and Case C–169/91 *Council of the City of Stoke-on-Trent and Norwich City Council v B & Q plc.* [1992] ECR 1–6635 at para. 16.

[25] See, for instance, Case C–112/00 *Schmidberger* [2003] ECR I–5659. On the role of national courts in the area of free movement of goods, see M Jarvis, *The Application of EC Law by National Courts* (Oxford: OUP, 1998).

3.2. Seeking to Square the Circle

Following the judgment in *Richart*, it became apparent that any attempt to regulate exports of dual-use goods could not ignore the Community legal framework in general and the CCP in particular. The establishment of a separate set of rules at Maastricht aiming at the conduct of a common foreign policy offered the Member States and the Union institutions a third way: instead of addressing the question of the appropriate legal framework by making a choice between Community competence and national sovereignty, the Union actors decided to involve both. Therefore, common rules on exports of dual-use goods were adopted, whereby certain issues were governed by Community law and certain others by CFSP rules: Council Regulation 3381/94 laid down the rules pursuant to which such exports were to be regulated[26] and Council Decision 94/942/CFSP set out the list of products to which the common rules would apply and would determine the application of those rules. [27]

The term 'dual-use' might appear to apply to a vast range of products covering a desk used by an army commander or the pairs of boots worn by soldiers. Such an interpretation would render it of potentially unlimited scope; however, due to the special nature of such products, the legal regime applicable to exports of dual-use goods is exceptional in legal terms and, as such, should be interpreted strictly. Accordingly, such a broad interpretation of the notion should be rejected. Indeed, the common rules on exports of dual-use goods, whilst themselves controversial in legal terms, have clearly confined their scope to products enumerated in an exhaustive manner. This is illustrated by the first measure detailing the list of products deemed to be of dual use within the meaning of EU common rules: whilst divided into categories broadly phrased,[28] these preducts were defined by Decision 94/942/CFSP in very specific terms. The same applied to the subsequent amendments to the list.

A detailed examination of the substantive content of Regulation 3381/94 and Decision 94/942/CFSP is of historic significance only, as the system laid down therein has now been abolished.[29] However, our understanding of the logic as well as the main structure of the system they established is central to our understanding of the evolving relationship between trade and foreign policy in the system of EU interna-

---

[26] [1994] OJ L 367/1.

[27] [1994] OJ L 367/8. This was amended a number of times by the following Council measures: Dec 95/127/CFSP [1995] OJ L 90/2; Dec 95/128/CFSP [1995] OJ L 90/3; Dec 96/423/CFSP [1996] OJ L 176/1; Dec 96/613/CFSP [1996] OJ L 278/1, Dec 97/100/CFSP [1997] OJ L 34/1; Dec 97/419/CFSP [1997] OJ L 178/1, Dec 97/633/CFSP [1997] OJ L 266/1; Dec 98/106/CFSP [1998] OJ L 32/1; Dec 98/232/CFSP [1998] OJ L 92/1; Dec 99/54/CFSP [1999] OJ L 18/1; Dec 2000/243/CFSP [2000] OJ L 82/1.

[28] These included: nuclear materials; facilities and equipment; materials, chemicals microorganisms and toxins; materials processing; electronics; computers; telecommunications and information security, sensors and lasers; navigation and avionics; marine; propulsion systems, space vehicles and related equipment.

[29] See the analysis in P Koutrakos, 'Exports of Dual-Use Goods under the Law of the European Union' (1998) 23 *ELRev* 235.

tional relations. The adoption of common rules on exports of dual-use goods was deemed necessary in order to address the security concerns of Member States as to the ultimate destination of exports of dual-use goods without compromising the establishment of the internal market and the free movement of goods which this entailed. Therefore, the common rules established under those measures were aimed at replacing the national controls which had existed until then with an effective system of export control on a common basis which would also improve the international competitiveness of the European industry.

The thrust of the system lies upon two interrelated principles: on the one hand, exports of the products specified in the list annexed to Council Decision 94/942/CFSP were subject to authorisation to be granted by the competent authorities of the Member state of exportation; on the other hand, once granted by the competent authorities of that State pursuant to the provisions of Regulation 3381/94, an export authorisation was deemed valid throughout the Community.

The criteria on the basis of which national authorities were to grant export licences were listed in an Annex to Decision 94/942/CFSP. These consisted of the following: the commitments that the Member States had undertaken under international agreements on non-proliferation and the control of sensitive goods; their obligations under sanctions imposed by the UN Security Council or agreed in other international *fora*; considerations of national foreign and security policy, including, where relevant, those covered by the criteria the Member States had agreed at the Luxembourg and Lisbon European Council in 1991 and 1992 respectively; considerations about intended end-use and the risk of diversion.

The *raison d'être* of the establishment of the system of common rules pursuant to two separate measures was set out in Regulation 3381/94 itself: 'decisions concerning the content of these lists are of strategic nature and consequently fall within the competence of the Member States'.[30] In establishing a system of rules based on two distinct and yet interconnected measures, the Union institutions and the Member States sought to square the circle: on the one hand, the integrity of the CCP appeared to be preserved as the legal mechanism pursuant to which export authorisations were to be granted was set out in an Article 133 EC instrument; on the other hand, the ability of the Member States to define their security interests appeared to be intact.

However, this system was deeply flawed.[31] The criteria on the basis of which national authorities were to assess requests for export authorisations constituted the very core of the mechanism laid down in Regulation 3381/94: to exclude them from its scope was tantamount to depriving the mechanism of its *modus operandi* and seriously impairing its effectiveness. In addition to the political symbolism that such exclusion might have carried, its objective was to prevent any judicial

---

[30] Fourth preambular para.
[31] See the criticism in Koutrakos, n11 above, at 101–6.

control over the action of national authorities; not only would the Court of Justice have been expected to have no jurisdiction over the interpretation and application of the criteria pursuant to which export authorisations were to be granted, but also national courts would have to declare inadmissible actions brought by private applicants. This legal formula was clearly based on a formalistic conception of the pillars: it was assumed that the adoption of a measure beyond the Community legal order would in itself entail the legal consequences of that measure. Following the judgment in the *Airport Transit Visa* case, there is no doubt that such conception is incorrect. This formalistic construction of regulations which suggested that a trade measure could be strictly separate from its foreign policy component was rejected by the Court in its subsequent case law.

3.3. The Approach of the Court of Justice

In *Werner*[32] and *Leifer*,[33] two judgments delivered on the same day, the Court dealt directly with the relationship between the CCP and the right of Member States to protect their public security. Both cases were references from German courts enquiring about the legality of the Law on Foreign Trade, and in particular its requirement that exports of certain products be subject to an export licence. This requirement had been imposed in order to guarantee the security of Germany, prevent disturbance to the peaceful co-existence of nations and prevent the external relations of Germany from being seriously disrupted. In *Werner*, the plaintiff was an exporter who had agreed to supply a number of industrial products to Libya. His application for an export licence in 1991 had been rejected on the ground that the supply of those goods would seriously jeopardise public security as defined in the above Law. In *Leifer*, criminal proceedings had been initiated against an exporter for having delivered certain products, including chemical ones, to Iraq over a period of four years without having applied for the necessary export licences.

In both cases, the Community rules in question were laid down in secondary legislation adopted within the framework of the Common Commercial Policy. Council Regulation 3918/92 on common rules on exports (Export Regulation)[34] prohibited the imposition of quantitative restrictions, hence introducing the principle of free exportation subject to the exceptions specifically provided therein. Such an exception is laid down in Article 11 of the Export Regulation: Member States were allowed to impose quantitative restrictions on exports in order to protect a number of specific non-trade interests, namely public morality, public policy, public security, the health and life of humans, animals or plants, national

---

[32] Case C–70/94 *Fritz Werner Industrie-Ausruestüngen GmbH v Germany* [1995] ECR I–3189.
[33] Case C–83/94 *Criminal Proceedings against Peter Leifer and Others* [1995] ECR I–3231.
[34] [1991] OJ L 372/31 amending Council Reg 2603/69 [1969] OJ Spec Ed (II) 590.

treasures possessing artistic, historic or archaeological value, industrial and commercial property.

The first issue raised before the Court was whether the framework within which the EC export rules had been adopted was broad enough to cover export measures with foreign policy implications. Drawing upon the *dicta* of its case law in the 1970s about the non-restrictive interpretation of the scope of CCP,[35] the Court pointed out that a national measure whose effect was to prevent or restrict the export of certain products did not fall beyond the scope of the CCP on the ground that its objectives were related to foreign and security policy:

> The specific subject-matter of commercial policy, which concerns trade with non-member countries and, according to Article [133] is based on the concept of a common policy, requires that a Member State should not be able to restrict its scope by freely deciding, in the light of its own foreign policy or security requirements, whether a measure is covered by Article [133].[36]

Having approached the German requirement for export licensing as within the scope of the CCP, the Court pointed out that the Export Regulation and the principle of free exportation applied to the facts of the two cases. This also entailed the application of the other central principle of the CCP, that is the exclusive nature of Community competence: according to its oft-repeated formulation, national measures of commercial policy are legal only if adopted pursuant to a specific Community law authorisation.[37] The Court accepted that the exceptional clause laid down in Article 11 of the Export Regulation amounted to such an authorisation and went on to assess whether the German rule was justifiable.

Whilst national security fell undoubtedly within the scope of public security as laid down in Article 11 of the Export Regulation, the position of the prevention of a serious disturbance to foreign relations or protection of the peaceful coexistence of nations was less clear. The Court drew upon the wide construction of public security in *Richardt* and opined that the foreign policy considerations underpinning the objectives of the German measure should fall within the scope of public security: not only was it difficult to distinguish the former from security policy considerations but also the interdependent international environment had made it less possible to assess the security of a state separately from that of the international community. Having concluded that the German measure deviating from the Export Regulation was justifiable, the Court left it to the referring court to decide whether it was in fact justified, that is both necessary and proportionate in order to protect its stated objective.

However, the Court relied once more upon its earlier judgment in *Richardt* and made it clear that the exportation of goods capable of being used for military purposes to a country at war with another country might affect the public security of

---

[35] See *Opinion 1/78 (re: Agreement on Natural Rubber)* [1979] ECR 2871, para 45.
[36] *Werner*, n32 above, para 11.
[37] See Case 41/76 *Donckerwolcke* [1976] ECR 1921, para 32 and Case 174/84 *Bulk Oil* [1986] ECR 559, para 31.

a Member State.[38] In *Leifer,* the Court went further to examine whether the principle of proportionality was met by the legal conditions under which the German measure was applied. In particular, it dealt with the question whether it was consistent with EC law for the national measure to impose on applicants for an export licence the burden of proving that dual-use goods were, in fact, for civil use; it also examined whether it was problematic, from the point of view of EC law, that the competent national authorities could refuse a licence if the products in question were objectively suitable for military use. Whilst it left it for the referring court to assess the compatibility of those provisions with the principle of proportionality, the Court referred to the general nature of the role of national authorities:[39]

> depending on the circumstances, the competent national authorities have a certain degree of discretion when adopting measures which they consider to be necessary in order to guarantee public security in a Member State . . . When the export of dual-use goods involves a threat to the public security of a Member State, those measures may include a requirement that an applicant for an export licence show that the goods are for civil use and also, having regard to specific circumstances such as *inter alia* the political situation in the country of destination, that a licence be reused if those goods are objectively suitable for military use.

It was also for the national court to determine whether the initiation of criminal proceedings constituted a sanction proportionate to the public security objective that the national measure purported to serve: the only guidance provided by the Court was to repeat the parameters already stated in *Richardt* within which the national court ought to carry out its assessment, namely to take into account all the elements of each case, such as the nature of the goods capable of endangering the security of the state, the circumstances in which the breach was committed and whether the exporter had acted in good faith.

Both judgments in *Werner* and *Leifer* made it clear that the foreign policy implications of a trade measure could not render it beyond the scope of the Community legal order.[40] This conclusion is significant in two respects. In terms of Article 133 EC, it sheds further light on the longstanding debate about its scope: indeed, the early statement of the Court that a broad construction of the CCP was necessary for a worthwhile external trade policy[41] is particularly apt in the case of trade policy measures with foreign implications. To allow Member States to determine the types of measures which would fall beyond the scope of Article 133 EC in the light of their specific political dimension would be tantamount to introducing an inherently indeterminate criterion capable of eroding the coherence of the external trade policies of the Community and undermining the jurisdiction of the Court of Justice. This is all the more so in the light of the

---

[38] Para 28 of *Werner,* n 32 above and 29 of *Leifer,* n33 above.
[39] N33 above, para 35.
[40] For a comment on the judgments, see N Emiliou, annotation in (1997) 22 *ELRev* 68.
[41] See *Opinion 1/78 (re: International Agreement on Natural Rubber)* [1979] ECR 2781.

intrinsically intertwined nature of trade and foreign policy: as Advocate General Jacobs was to point out in a subsequent case, '[m]any measures of commercial policy may have a more general foreign policy or security dimension. When for example the Community concludes a trade agreement with Russia, it is obvious that the agreement cannot be dissociated from the broader political context of the relations between the European Union, and its Member States and Russia'.[42]

In terms of the regulation of trade measures with foreign policy implications, the judgments in *Werner* and *Leifer* suggested that the Community legal order was capable of accommodating national concerns: not only was the right of the Member States to define their security acknowledged but also their discretion to assess how best to protect it was guaranteed. On the one hand, the limits to the exercise of that discretion, as set out in the context of the principle of proportionality, would be ensured by the national courts; on the other hand, the broad construction of the notion of public security illustrated a pragmatic approach. All in all, the interpretation put forward by the Court of Justice indicated that, far from constituting two strictly separate spheres of activity, trade and foreign policy were in fact interlinked. The implication of this conclusion for the formalistic approach underpinning the common rules on exports of dual-use goods was clear: the inter-pillar formula set out in Regulation 3381/94 and Decision 94/942/CFSP was not only flawed in legal terms but also redundant in practical terms. This conclusion became abundantly clear in the subsequent case law of the Court of Justice on economic sanctions.

4. SANCTIONS AGAINST THIRD COUNTRIES

Economic sanctions against third countries is another example of the interaction between trade and foreign policy whose regulation has raised legal questions similar to those examined above. In terms of their effectiveness, there has been a longstanding debate in international relations and political science literature.[43] Within that context, quantitative criteria have been developed on the basis of which specific regimes may be assessed.[44] For the purpose of their legal analysis, suffice it to point out that sanctions constitute an instrument of foreign policy

---

[42] Case C–124/95 *The Queen, ex parte Centro-Com Srl v HM Treasury and Bank of England* [1997] ECR I–81, para 41 of his Opinion.

[43] See, for instance, D Baldwin, *Economic Statecraft* (Princeton, NJ: Princeton University Press, 1985), PAG van Bergeijk, *Economic Diplomacy, Trade and Commercial Policy—Positive and Negative Sanctions in a New World Order* (Aldershot: Edward Elgar, 1995), MP Doxey, *International Sanctions in Contemporary Perspective* (Basingstoke: Macmillan 1996), DW Drezner, *The Sanctions Paradox: Economic Statecraft and International Relations* (Cambridge: Cambridge University Press, 1999).

[44] See GC Hufbaer, JS Scott and KA Elliot, *Economic Sanctions Reconsidered* (2nd edn Washington, DC: Institute for International Economics, 1992). For a critique of existing literature, see DW Drezner, 'The Hidden Hand of Economic Coercion' (2003) 57 *International Organization* 643. See also N Marinov, 'Do Sanctions Help Democracy? The US and EU's Record 1997–2004' (2004) Stanford Institute for International Studies, Center for Democracy, Development and the Rule of Law Working Power No 28).

the popularity of which with both states and international organisations has not waned.[45]

In the context of European integration, the regulation of sanctions against third countries may be examined in the framework of three distinct phases.[46] The first one was in the late 1960s and 1970s when the Member States were required to implement United Nations Security Council Resolutions by imposing sanctions on Rhodesia. They did so by adopting national measures, their rationale being that the foreign policy nature of sanctions rendered them beyond the Community legal framework. This argument, now known as the 'Rhodesia doctrine', justified any deviation from Community law that such unilateral measures had entailed on the basis of Article 297 EC. One of the most obscure provisions of the EC Treaty, this badly drafted rule enables Member States to deviate from the entire body of Community law provided that certain truly extraordinary circumstances occur.[47] However, the implementation of those sanctions by means of disparate national measures proved to be fraught with problems, especially regarding the lack of uniformity in terms of the content of the national regimes and the time of their imposition.[48]

It was for that reason that another solution, capable of guaranteeing a degree of uniformity and, hence, effectiveness of sanctions, was soon found within the framework of the Common Commercial Policy. Indeed, Article 133 EC, with its express reference to measures of export policy, had always been the most obvious legal basis within the Community system. However, their political dimension, along with the ongoing debate about the scope of the CCP between the Commission, the Council and the Member States had rendered reliance upon Article 133 EC controversial. Therefore, a legal formula was devised whereby economic sanctions were imposed by means of a Council Regulation adopted under Article 133 EC only following the adoption of a decision by the Member States within the framework of European Political Cooperation: the latter expressed the political will of the Member States to rely upon the Community legal framework in order to impose sanctions upon specific third states, whereas the former actually laid down the rules governing those sanctions. This combination of Community and non-Community measures was first relied upon following

---

[45] For a comprehensive legal analysis of unilateral and multilateral sanctions, see L Picchio Forlati and LA Sicilianos (eds), *Les sanctions économiques en droit international* (Leiden/Boston, Mass: Martinus Nijhoff, 2004).

[46] See Koutrakos, n11 above, 58–66.

[47] Art 297 EC reads as follows: 'Member States shall consult each other with a view to taking together the steps needed to prevent the functioning of the common market being affected by measures which a Member State may be called upon to take in the event of serious internal disturbances affecting the maintenance of law and order, in the event of war, serious international tension constituting a threat of war, or in order to carry out obligations it has accepted for the purpose of maintaining peace and international security'. For an analysis, see P Koutrakos, 'Is Article 297 EC a "Reserve of Sovereignty"?' (2000) 37 *CMLRev* 1339.

[48] See PJ Kuyper, 'Sanctions against Rhodesia, the EEC and the Implementation of General International Legal Rules' (1975) 12 *CMLRev* 231 and P Willaert, 'Les sanctions économiques contre la Rhodésie (1965–1979) (1985) 18 *RBDI* 216.

the declaration of martial law in Poland in December 1981 and underpinned the imposition of sanctions on third countries until the establishment of the European Union at Maastricht.[49] It is noteworthy that the political genesis of the sanctions imposed under Article 133 EC was described in a non-uniform manner: for instance, in the above case of sanctions against the Soviet Union, the relevant Council Regulation only referred to the 'Community interests',[50] whereas the one against Argentina, imposed during the Falklands war, referred specifically to discussions between the Member States under Article 297 EC and within the EPC context.[51]

From a legal point of view, the compromise illustrated by the dual system of an Article 133 EC act and a non-Community measure is significant: it indicated that the EPC, a framework of political cooperation launched in a non-formalised manner and developed incrementally over the years until its incorporation into the EC Treaty, had matured sufficiently to be treated by the Member States as their most important forum for consultation in the area of foreign policy. On the other hand, it was precisely this political genesis of Article 133 EC measures which rendered sanctions a somewhat distinct area within the CCP. It was not only the wording of the relevant instruments which made this clear by referring to the agreement between the Community and the Member States to rely upon EC law in order to ensure the uniform implementation of sanctions;[52] it was also their scope which was articulated as if the longstanding debate about the scope of Article 133 EC had been irrelevant: for instance, sanction regimes imposed under Article 133 EC covered services and transport.[53] That is not to say that the Member States intended the CCP to be construed widely in any way: quite apart from the saga of reform of Article 133 EC from Amsterdam to Nice, as the Court pointed out in *Opinion 1/94*, the practice of Community institutions could not deviate from the principles underpinning the Community's express competence.[54] Instead, their non-Community political genesis and practical implications defined them as a distinct area within the scope of the CCP.

The above was confirmed by the Treaty on European Union at Maastricht: the establishment of the Union on three distinct legal frameworks, the so-called 'pillars', changed the way in which sanctions were imposed and gave them their current form by introducing a specific legal basis. This is Article 301 EC which reads as follows:

---

[49] See PJ Kuyper, 'Trade Sanctions, Security and Human Rights and Commercial Policy' in M Maresceau (ed), *The European Community's Commercial Policy after 1992: The Legal Dimension* (Dordrecht: Martinus Nijhoff, 1993) 395 and P Sturma, 'La participation de la Communauté européenne à des "sanctions" internationales' [1993] *RMC* 250.

[50] Sixth recital of preamble to Reg 596/82 [1982] OJ L 72/15.

[51] See Council Reg 877/82 [1982] OJ L 102/1. For that sanctions regime, see J Verhoeven, 'Sanctions internationales et Communautés européennes—A propos de l'affaie des iles Falklands (Malvinas)' [1984] *CDE* 259.

[52] See, for instance, Council Reg 2340/90 preventing trade by the Community as regards Iraq and Kuwait [1990] OJ L 213/1.

[53] *Ibid*, and 3155/90 [1990] OJ L 304/1.

[54] N13 above.

Where it is provided, in a common position or in a joint action adopted according to the provisions of the Treaty on European Union relating to the common foreign and security policy, for an action by the Community to interrupt or to reduce, in part or completely, economic relations with one or more third countries, the Council shall take the necessary urgent measures. The Council shall act by a qualified majority on a proposal from the Commission.

A similar rule is provided for financial sanctions in Article 60 EC.[55] The provision for an inter-pillar approach to sanctions, that is their imposition by means of a CFSP measure followed by a Council Regulation, formalised the principle pursuant to which sanctions had been imposed since the early 1980s. However, in doing so, the TEU also acknowledged that sanctions were, indeed, a distinct area within the sphere of EC external relations: despite the procedural similarities between Articles 301 and 133 EC (the provision for a Council Regulation, qualified majority voting), the removal of sanctions from the purview of the latter clearly illustrated the idiosyncratic way in which the CCP had applied to them *de lege lata*. In a similar vein, it also illustrated the maturity of the foreign policy rules of the Union, so much so that they were formally construed as an essential requirement for the application of Article 301 EC.

It is not only the formalisation of the inter-pillar approach introduced at Maastricht which illustrates the distinct nature of economic sanctions within the constellation of trade instruments available to the Union; the wording of Article 301 EC also delineates the scope of the sanctions regimes imposed thereunder in terms quite distinct from the debate surrounding the interpretation of Article 133 EC. The reference to 'economic sanctions' indicates that the scope of the measures envisaged under that provision is broader than that of the CCP; not only does this constitute the formal acknowledgment of pre-existing practice, but it is also further illustrated by the measures actually adopted pursuant to Article 301 EC which cover trade, financial and transport services construed quite widely.[56] In a limited number of areas, sanctions have been imposed pursuant to Article 308 as well as Articles 60 and 301 EC.[57]

---

[55] Art 60(1) EC reads as follows: 'If, in the cases envisaged in Article 301, action by the Community is deemed necessary, the Council may, in accordance with the procedure provided for in Article 301, take the necessary urgent measures on the movement of capital and on payments as regards the third countries concerned'.

[56] See Koutrakos, n11 above, at 68–72. For the relationship between Art 301 EC and other EC Treaty provisions, see *ibid*, at 79 *ff*.

[57] See Council Reg 2580/2001 on specific restrictive measures directed against certain persons and entities with a view to combating terrorism [2001] OJ L 344/70; Council Reg 881/2002 imposing certain specific restrictive measures directed against certain persons and entities associated with Usama bin Laden, the Al-Qaida network and the Taliban [2002] OJ L 139/9; Council Reg 1763/2004 imposing certain restrictive measures in support of effective implementation of the mandate of the International Criminal Tribunal for the former Yugoslavia [2004] OJ L 315/14; Council Reg 560/2005 imposing certain specific restrictive measures directed against certain persons and entities in view of the situation in Côte d'Ivoire [2005] OJ L 95/1. See Case T-306/01 *Ahmed AH Yusuf and Al Barakaat International Foundation v Council* and Case T-315/01 *Kadi v Council and Commission*, judgments delivered on 21 September 2005, not yet reported.

The inter-pillar formula laid down in Article 301 EC may appear similar to that underpinning the common rules on exports of dual-use goods as set out originally in Regulation 3381/94 and Decision 94/942/CFSP. In fact, it is distinct from the latter in an important respect: rather than excluding the *modus operandi* of the sanctions regime, the inter-pillar formula provides for the legal expression of the political choice involved in the adoption of such rules. This choice needs to be made and expressed not *ipso facto* and *a priori*, but individually and every time that the political and legal circumstances call for it.

Sanctions imposed by the Community under Article 301 EC may cover a variety of areas. In terms of trade sanctions, they may restrict or prohibit imports from and exports to the target state, the material scope of the products in question varying from very specific to quite broad; in addition, trade sanctions may also be indirect, that is apply to aircraft carrying cargo to or from that state and prevent them from taking off from, landing in or overflying the territory of the Community. In relation to financial sanctions imposed pursuant to Articles 60 and 301 EC, the relevant Regulations may prohibit investments, the transfer of certain or any financial assets or freeze the assets of the target state. In relation to transport sanctions, the Union may prohibit flights between the target state and the Member States.

In practical terms, it has been a common position adopted by the Council which expresses the will of the Union to have recourse to Community law in order to impose sanctions on third countries. An examination of the various regimes adopted under this formula reveals a number of characteristics which they share.[58] The common position carries out a two-fold function: on the one hand, it refers to the legal and political context which rendered the imposition of sanctions necessary; on the other hand, it refers to the thrust of the regime to be adopted by the Council under Article 301 EC. For instance, in relation to sanctions imposed on Côte d'Ivoire, the relevant Common Position referred in its preamble extensively to the UN Security Council Resolutions requiring that its Members impose sanctions and to the initiatives of the Economic Community of West African States and the African Union, albeit in the latter case very briefly.[59]

An important aspect of the sanctions regimes imposed by the EU is the scope for independent action left to the Member States: indeed, the competent national authorities are allowed to authorise activities which fall within the scope of the various deviations provided for in the relevant Council Regulations provided that certain conditions are met. In addition, it is for the Member States to determine the penalties for any violation of the Community rules on sanctions. Furthermore, there is a cooperation procedure established under the Article 301 EC measures which provides for exchange of information between the Member States and the Commission.

---

[58] See Koutrakos, n11 above, 72–76.
[59] Common Position 2004/852/CFSP [2004] OJ L 368/50 following which the Council adopted Reg 174/2005 [2005] OJ L 29/5 amended by Reg 560/2005 [2005] OJ L 95/1.

The imposition of economic and financial sanctions on the basis of the coexistence of Community and non-Community legal measures raises important legal questions: how does their distinct normative nature affect the implementation of sanctions? Is the intergovernmental nature of the CFSP measure mentioned in Article 301 EC likely to undermine the Community law characteristics of the Council Regulation adopted thereunder? Does the political genesis of the latter measure subsume it under a set of rules which is expressly excluded from the jurisdiction of the Court of Justice? Even if the coexistence of such measures did not undermine the existence of the Court's jurisdiction, would it affect the intensity of its exercise?

5. THE APPROACH OF THE COURT OF JUSTICE TO ECONOMIC SANCTIONS

In a number of cases about the interpretation and application of sanctions based on the pre-Maastricht formula, that is the combination of an Article 133 EC Regulation with an EPC decision, the Court elaborated on the legal regulation of trade measures with foreign policy implications.

5.1. Asserting Jurisdiction

The first such judgment was in *Bosphorus*,[60] a reference from the Irish Supreme Court. In that case, a Turkish air charterer and travel organiser had leased for a period of four years two aircraft owned by the Yugoslav national airline. Under the lease agreement, the latter retained ownership of the aircraft for the period of the lease, whereas Bosphorus had complete control of their day-to-day management. The problem was that the lease agreement had been concluded in April 1992, that is after sanctions had been imposed on the Federal Republic of Yugoslavia pursuant to Community secondary legislation implementing the relevant United Nations Security Council Resolutions. In particular, Article 18 of Regulation 990/93 provided that all vessels in which a majority or controlling interest was held by a person or undertaking in or operating from Serbia and Montenegro should be impounded by the authorities of the Member States.[61]

In essence, two issues were raised before the Court of Justice: the first dealt with the application of the above provision of the Regulation against an undertaking which, whilst leasing the vessels in question, was neither their owner nor established or operating in Serbia and Montenegro; the second issue was whether such an interpretation of Regulation 990/93 would run counter to fundamental rights and the principle of proportionality.

---

[60] Case C–84/95 *Bosphorus Hava Yollari Turizm ve Ticaret AS v Minister for Transport, Energy and Communications and others* [1996] ECR I–3953.
[61] Council Reg 990/93 concerning trade between EEC and FRY (Serbia and Montenegro) [1993] OJ L 102/14.

The Court answered the first question in the affirmative: the wording of Article 8 of Regulation 990/93 made no distinction between ownership of an aircraft and its day-to-day operation and control; in addition, to render the latter the decisive criterion for the application of the sanctions imposed under that Regulation 'would jeopardize the effectiveness of the strengthening of the sanctions, which consist in impounding all means of transport of [Serbia and Montenegro] and its nationals ... in order further to increase the pressure on that republic'.[62]

For the purposes of this analysis, it is the methodology followed by the Court of Justice which is of interest. It was pointed out that Regulation 990/93 had been adopted by the Council pursuant to Article 133 EC following the adoption of a non-Community measure: indeed, in a decision of the Community and its Member States meeting within the framework of European Political Cooperation, it had been decided that the imposition of sanctions provided for in UN Security Council Resolutions should be carried out pursuant to EC rules. There is reference to that decision in the preamble to Regulation 990/93 and, in its interpretation of the latter, the Court expressly took into account the text and aim of the Resolutions which the non-Community decision and, hence, Regulation 990/93 itself, purported to implement.

As to whether a broad construction of the prohibition laid down in Regulation 990/93 was contrary to fundamental human rights and to the principle of proportionality, the Court replied in the negative. It pointed out that the specific rights invoked by the plaintiff in the main proceedings, namely the right to peaceful enjoyment of property and the freedom to pursue a commercial activity, were not absolute: instead, they were subject to restrictions justified by objectives of general interest pursued by the Community.[63] It was, then, pointed out that the imposition of any sanctions impinges upon the rights of persons who are not responsible for the situation which had led to their adoption. It then added that the importance of the aims pursued by such regimes was such as to justify negative consequences 'even of a substantial nature' for some operators.[64] To that effect, the Court made detailed reference to the objectives of the sanctions regime as expressed in the preamble to Regulation 990/93 and reached the following conclusion:[65]

> as compared with an objective of general interest so fundamental for the international community, which consists of putting an end to the state of war in the region and to the massive violations of human rights and humanitarian international law in the Republic of Bosnia-Herzegovina, the impounding of the aircraft in question, which is owned by an undertaking based in or operating from the Federal Republic of Yugoslavia, cannot be regarded as inappropriate or disproportionate.

[62] Para 18.
[63] See para 21 of the judgment with reference to Case 44/79 *Hauer v Land Rheinland-Pfalz* [1979] ECR 3727, Case 5/88 *Wachauf v Bundesamt für Ernährung und Forstwirtschaft* [1989] ECR 2609 and Case C–280/93 *Germany v Council* [1994] ECR I–4973.
[64] Para 23.
[65] Para 26.

In terms of legal reasoning, the method followed by the Court appears somewhat curious in so far as the wording of the requirement in the UN Council Resolution that aircraft be impounded was identical to that in Article 8 of Regulation 990/93. And yet, the Court chose to rely upon the former in order to substantiate the broad definition of the terms of the Sanctions Regulation. It is in terms of judicial principle that this route may be understood. In interpreting an international instrument[66] which a non-Community measure undertakes to implement by means of Community legislation, the Court makes it clear that the interaction between different measures adopted pursuant to different sets of rules by no means undermine its intention to exercise fully its jurisdiction. Viewed from this angle, the approach of the Court constitutes a statement aimed at affirming its jurisdiction within the multi-level legal context within which sanctions are implemented by the Member States following a UN Resolution. It is noteworthy that the substantive conclusion of the exercise of its jurisdiction was to sanction as broad a scope of the embargo as the wording of the Sanctions Regulation and the UN Security Council Resolution could possibly carry. In other words, the exercise of the Court's jurisdiction also conveyed the message that the *effet utile* of the sanctions regimes would be ensured.

It was against this background that the judgment in *Bosphorus* illustrated a strict approach to the human rights defence upon which the plaintiff sought to rely in the main proceedings. The Court did not engage in a detailed assessment of the specific restriction entailed by the application of the sanctions rules—instead, it gave precedence to the objectives pursued by the Regulation in a rather automatic manner, assuming that the application of any sanctions regime would entail restrictions on the legal position of trade operators. In relation to the criticism which this approach has attracted,[67] two points may be made. First, the sweeping scope of this part of the judgment appears to suggest that the Court would be unwilling to be drawn into a detailed substantive analysis of the specific ways in which the legal position of traders would be affected by EU sanctions and the extent to which the latter would meet the requirement of proportionality. However, should this be correct, it would also be qualified in so far as it would apply only to rights invoked before the Court which were not absolute in nature.[68] Put in another way, the *effet utile* interpretation of rules on exports is directly related to the intensity of judicial control over the repercussions of such rules for the legal position of individual traders. Secondly, in a way, the position assumed by the Court in *Bosphorus* is not dissimilar to that of national courts as envisaged in the judgments in *Werner* and *Leifer*: instead of assessing the right of Member States to deviate from Community law in order to protect their public security, it

---

[66] See the comments in N Burrows, 'Caught in the Cross-Fire' (1997) 22 *ELRev* 170.

[67] See I Canor, '"Can Two Walk Together, Except They be Agreed?" The Relationship Between International Law and European Law: The Incorporation of United Nations Sanctions Against Yugoslavia Into European Community Law Through the Perspective of the European Court of Justice' (1998) 35 *CMLRev* 137.

[68] See, similarly, the analysis in Case 112/00 *Schmidberger*, n25 above.

examines the right of Member States to rely upon Community law in order to pursue collectively a foreign policy objective. Whilst it was in the context of the former that the Court recognised the exercise of wide discretion, it is also in the context of the latter that, rather than questioning, it actually supported the quest of the Member States to achieve as effective an application of the relevant rules as possible.[69]

5.2. Discouraging Deviations

In *Centro-Com*,[70] the Full Court dealt with the extent to which a Member State could legally deviate from Community rules laying down sanctions against third countries. In this reference from the English High Court, the plaintiff was a company exporting pharmaceutical products from Italy to Montenegro. The relevant Community measure, namely Regulation 1432/92,[71] prohibited the export of all commodities and products originating in or coming from the Community. However, in implementing the rules laid down in UN Security Council Resolution 757 (1992), it also provided for an exception regarding those commodities and products intended for strictly medical purposes; such exports would be deemed legal once notified to the Sanctions Committee set up under UN Security Council Resolution 724 (1991) and also granted an export authorisation by the competent national authorities. Having complied with both requirements, Centro-Com exported from Italy a number of consignments of pharmaceutical products and blood-testing equipment to two wholesalers in Montenegro whose bank account held by the National Bank of Yugoslavia with Barclays Bank would be debited. The latter was subject to authorisation by the Bank of England and, as a matter of course, was granted for exports authorised by the Sanctions Committee and the national authorities of the exporting state, irrespective of whether that State was the United Kingdom or another Member State. Indeed, of the total number of consignments meeting those requirements, a considerable number were paid for following authorisation by the Bank of England. However, the Treasury changed its policy of automatic authorisation following reports of abuse of the above authorisation procedure. Instead, it decided to authorise payment from bank accounts held in Britain only for exempt products exported from United Kingdom and authorised by the British competent authorities.

---

[69] Bosphorus then challenged the implementation of the sanctions regime by the Irish government before national courts. In a unanimous judgment, the Grand Chamber of the European Court of Human Rights ruled that there was no manifest deficiency in the protection of the applicant's ECHR rights by the Court of Justice in Case C–84/95 *Bosphorus*: see *Bosphorus Hava Yollari v Ireland*, App No 45036/98, judgment of 30 June 2005.

[70] Case C–124/95 *The Queen, ex parte Centro-Com Srl v HM Treasury and Bank of England* [1997] ECR I–81.

[71] Council Reg 1432/92 prohibiting trade between the EEC and the Republics of Serbia and Montenegro [1992] OJ L 151/4.

The reference to the Court of Justice was about the compatibility of the British deviation from the rules of the Sanctions Regulation with Article 133 EC in general and the sanctions rules adopted thereunder in particular. In its judgment, the Full Court addressed directly the relationship between Community competence over trade and national sovereignty in the area of foreign policy. The starting point for its analysis was to acknowledge the latter: indeed, the Court pointed out that it was precisely in the exercise of their sovereignty in that area that sanctions against Serbia and Montenegro had been adopted, as Regulation 1432/92 had been adopted following a decision of the Member States within the framework of European Political Cooperation to impose sanctions upon those Balkan states. However, the power of the Member States should be exercised in accordance with Community law; having repeated the *Werner dictum* that the export measures adopted by Member States may not be viewed as beyond the scope of the CCP because of their foreign policy objective, the Court concluded as follows:[72]

> while it is for Member States to adopt measures of foreign and security policy in the exercise of their national competence, those measures must nevertheless respect the provisions adopted by the Community in the field of the common commercial policy provided for by Article 133 of the Treaty.

Having asserted the applicability of CCP rules to the reference before it and, consequently, the existence of its own jurisdiction over the interpretation and application of the relevant measures, the Court went on to assess the validity of the British measure. It pointed out that, as the export prohibition constituted an exception to the rules laid down in the Export Regulation, the latter would still apply to those exports which were not prohibited under the former. It is recalled that the Export Regulation introduced the principle of free exportation and only allowed Member States to impose restrictions in order to protect some exhaustively defined interests such as public security.

Drawing upon the broad construction of public security first in *Richardt* and then in *Werner* and *Leifer*, the Court had no difficulty in concluding that:[73]

> a measure intended to apply sanctions imposed by a resolution of the United Nations Security in order to achieve a peaceful solution to the situation in Bosnia-Herzegovina, which forms a threat to international peace and security, ... falls within the exception provided for in Article 11 of the Export Regulation.

However, whilst the British restriction was justifiable, it was held not to be justified as Community rules were already in existence in order to ensure that the interest which the national restriction purported to protect had already been protected at Community level. In other words, the effective application of sanctions, that is the interest purported to be served by the British restriction, could be

---

[72] Para 27.
[73] Para 45.

ensured by the authorisation procedures applied by other Member States and, in particular, the competent authorities of the state of exportation. The Court opined that the Member States should place trust in each other in relation to checks made by the authorities of the exporting state and pointed out that there was nothing regarding the authorisation granted by the Italian authorities to suggest that the system provided under the Sanctions Regulation had not functioned properly.[74]

The line of reasoning followed by the Court in *Centro-Com* leaves no doubt as to its implications: the political genesis of a Community trade measure beyond the Community legal framework would in no way impinge on the effectiveness of the latter. As a matter of fact, the references in the judgment to the political choice made by the Member States to have recourse to EC law suggest that the opposite is the case: its integrity is all the more reinforced as recourse to EC law is the outcome of the political will of the Member States to deal with an international issue of particular seriousness. As if the message had not already been brought home, the Court concluded that part of its judgment as follows:[75]

> even where measures such as those in issue in the main proceedings have been adopted in the exercise of national competence in matters of foreign and security policy, they must respect the Community rules adopted under the common commercial policy.

The conclusion that, in the exercise of their sovereignty, Member States may not undermine Community law is not unique in the area of the interface between trade and foreign policy. It has been the starting point for the Court's case law in other areas of activity which, whilst diverse in scope, are closely related to the core of what states deem to be their sovereign functions, such as direct taxation,[76] criminal legislation[77] and, more recently and quite controversially, health care.[78] In defining the Community legal order as a limit in compliance with which Member States may exercise their powers, the Court also asserts its jurisdiction. In terms of the general approach of the Court, it is interesting that the judgment in *Centro-Com* was devoid of the flexibility that the Court had demonstrated in an earlier case in the context of the internal market where public security was at issue. In *Campus Oil*, it is recalled that the Irish government was allowed to retain

---

[74] The Court also dismissed the argument of the British government that the contested restriction was necessary under Art 307 EC: see para 60 of the judgment and the analysis in Ch 8 above.

[75] Para 30.

[76] See, for instance, Case C–80/94 *Wielockx* [1995] ECR I–2493 at para 16, Case C–107/94 *Asscher* [1996] ECR I–3089, at para 36, Case C–311/97 *Royal Bank of Scotland* [1999] ECR I–2651 at para 17, Joined Cases C–397/98 and C–410/98 *Metallgesellschaft and Others* [2001] ECR I–1727, at para 37 and Case C–324/00 *Lankhorst-Hohorst GmbH v Finanzamt Steinfurt* [2002] ECR I–11779, at para 26 and Case C–319/02 *Manninen* [2004] ECR I–7477 para 19.

[77] See Cases 299/86 *Drexl* [1988] ECR 1213, at para 17.

[78] See Cases C–158/96 *Raymond Kohll v Union des caisses de maladie* [1998] ECR I–1931 at para 19 and C–120/95 *Nicolas Decker v Caisse de maladie des employs privs* [1998] ECR I–1831, at para 23, Case C–157/99 *B.S.M. Geraets-Smits and H.T.M. Peerbooms v Stichting Ziekenfonds VGZ and Stichting CZ Groep Zorgverzekeringen* [2001] ECR I–5473 at para 46.

a procurement provision discriminating overtly in favour of the national oil refinery in order to be able to maintain sufficient resources at all times despite the fact that this interest was purported to have already been served under secondary Community legislation.[79] The sympathetic approach to the definition of the specific security requirements to the detriment of the existing Community legislation is in contrast to the robust approach to the arguments put forward by the British government in *Centro-Com*.

In that respect, two points are worth making. First, by deviating from the Sanctions Regulation, rather than protecting national security, the British authorities acted in complete disregard for the existing legal framework. It is this aspect which was examined by the Court which, having established that the British deviation from the Export Regulation, whilst justifiable, was not justified, went on to engage in a discussion of proportionality: it pointed out that, as the British measure amounted to a requirement that all goods exempt from the sanctions rules be exported only from its own territory, it constituted a disproportionate restriction on the principle of exportation. Instead, had there been concerns about the effectiveness of the sanctions due to specific aspects of the application of the authorisation procedure by the Italian authorities, the British authorities should have relied upon the collaboration procedures between national administrative authorities established under secondary Community legislation.[80] All in all, the arguments put forward before the Court seeking to justify the national deviation had precisely the same objective as the strict interpretation adopted by the Court, namely the effective application of the Community rules on sanctions. It was the question of the choice of the appropriate legal means which was approached differently by the Court. Secondly, whilst the intensity of judicial control in *Centro-Com* was considerable, the overall tone of that judgment was not dissimilar to that in *Bosphorus* in so far as the *effet utile* of the Community rules setting out sanctions was ensured, in both cases, by strict compliance with the letter of the relevant legislation.

5.3. Highlighting the Role of National Courts

Whilst in *Bosphorus* and *Centro-Com* the Court asserted the existence of its jurisdiction, demonstrated the intensity of its control and ensured the *effet utile* of Community rules on sanctions, in the subsequent judgment in *Ebony Maritime* it also highlighted the significance of national courts in the application of those rules.[81] This reference from the Italian highest administrative court (*Consiglio di*

---

[79] Case 72/83 *Campus Oil v Minister for Industry and Energy* [1984] ECR 2727.

[80] Reference was made to Council Reg 1468/81 on mutual assistance between the administrative authorities of the Member States and the cooperation between the latter and the Commission to ensure the correct application of the law on customs or agricultural matters [1981] OJ L 144/1.

[81] Case C–177/95 *Ebony Maritime SA and Loten Navigation Co. Ltd v Prefetto della Provincia di Brindisi and others* [1997] ECR I–1111. For a comment, see N Burrows, 'Reinforcing International Law' (1998) 23 *ELRev* 79 and C Vedder and H-P, Folz, annotation on *Centro-Com* and *Ebony Maritime* (1998) 35 *CMLRev* 209.

Stato) was, again, about the interpretation and application of Regulation 990/93 on trade between the Community and the Federal Republic of Yugoslavia.[82] This time the focus was on the prohibition on maritime trade: Article 1 of the Regulation prohibited the entry into the territorial sea of the Federal Republic of Yugoslavia by all commercial traffic, whereas Article 9 required that all vessels, aircraft and cargoes suspected of having violated, or being in violation of, the above prohibition be detained by the competent authorities of the Member States pending investigations. It was the application of these provisions which gave rise to the dispute before the Italian courts. A tanker owned by one of the plaintiffs in the main proceedings had been carrying a cargo of petroleum products belonging to the other plaintiff. It left the Italian port of Brindisi to set sail for the Croatian port of Rijeka. During its journey, the vessel started taking on water and its master sent out distress signals indicating that he had to change course towards the nearest coastline of Montenegro, his declared intention being to run the vessel aground. However, a helicopter from the NATO/Western European Union (WEU) forces landed on the vessel's deck before the latter had even entered Yugoslav territorial waters. A Dutch military squad took control of the vessel, which was then towed back into Brindisi where it was handed over to the Italian authorities.

The case referred to the Court originated in the action brought by the two plaintiffs against the decision of the Italian authorities to impound their vessel and confiscate their cargo. What made their case controversial was the fact that their vessel had been in international waters flying the flag of a non-Member State and belonging, along with its cargo, to non-Community companies. Being asked to assess the applicability of Regulation 990/93 in that context, the Court adopted a broad and *effet utile*–oriented approach to the prohibition contained therein: in terms of its material scope, it opined that neither the wording of the Regulation nor the wording and purpose of the relevant UN Security Council Resolution made any distinction, hence indicating that the vessel's flag and owner were irrelevant. The same conclusion applied to the territorial scope of the prohibition which was construed broadly enough to cover international waters: not only actual but also attempted entries into Yugoslav territorial waters were covered by the prohibition on all commercial traffic for 'any other interpretation would risk rendering the prohibition ineffective'.[83] Finally, a domestic provision prescribing confiscation of the cargo in case of infringement of the prohibition is not ruled out by Regulation 990/93.

A final point was made in relation to the remedies imposed by Italian legislation. The plaintiffs in the main proceedings had argued that these amounted to a system of strict liability and were contrary to the principle of proportionality. However, the Court responded that, in the absence of a Community provision, it was for the Member States to choose the penalties they deem necessary for a violation of Community law. In doing so, they should ensure that the substantive and

---

[82] N61 above.
[83] Para 25.

procedural conditions under which infringements of Community law are penalised are analogous to those applicable for national law of a similar nature and significance. In addition, the Member States should ensure that the penalties they choose are effective, proportionate and dissuasive. It was for the national court to ascertain whether national law met those conditions.

In interpreting the terms of the Sanctions Regulation as widely as possible in *Ebony Maritime*, the Court renders its *effet utile* approach a theme underpinning its case law on sanctions. What is noteworthy in its judgment, though, is its construction of the principle of proportionality. The significance of this principle in terms of the interface between foreign policy and external trade was highlighted above in the context of exports of dual-use goods. It is recalled, for instance, that in *Richardt* compliance with the national deviation from the EC transit rules was left for the national court to determine, albeit within the parameters set out in the judgment. In *Ebony Maritime*, it was also left for the referring court to ascertain whether the penalties for the violation of the EU sanctions were proportionate. However, not only did the Court point out that a system of strict liability penalising breach of a regulation had already been held to be consistent with Community law, but it also repeated the parameters within which the assessment of the principle of proportionality ought to be carried out by the referring court: it referred to the objective of Regulation 990/93, that is to bring to an end the state of war in the Balkans and the massive violations of human rights and humanitarian international law in Bosnia-Herzegovina and stressed that, as such, that was of fundamental general interest for the international community.[84] Finding its place in the concluding paragraph of the judgment, following the acknowledgment of the role of the referring court, this statement, short of absolving national courts of that role, is as close to a substantive assessment of the issue of proportionality as the Court could make. This becomes another thread in the case law on the interactions between foreign policy and trade: by indicating clearly how the test of proportionality should be applied by national courts, the Court of Justice renders it a judicial tool in striking the balance between the effective application of Community law and the gradual development of a symbiotic relationship with national administrations. This instrumentalisation of the principle of proportionality enables the Court of Justice to define a normative space where national concerns about foreign policy and national security would be received sumpathetically, albeit not unreservedly.

6. MANAGING THE RELATIONSHIP BETWEEN FOREIGN POLICY AND TRADE

The thread which brings the various judgments on the interface between foreign policy and trade together is the rejection of formalism: an understanding of foreign

---

[84] Para 38 with reference to Case C–84/95 *Bosphorus*, n60 above, at para 26.

policy and trade as strictly separate areas of activity is treated as unrealistic; a construction of distinct sets of rules aimed at regulating these areas separately is viewed as unworkable; a line of reasoning excluding the Court of Justice *ipso facto* from the exercise of its jurisdiction in areas where the Community legal order is involved or affected is flatly rejected as contrary to the linkages between the EC framework and the CFSP rules laid down in the TEU itself. Instead, the Court defines its jurisdiction in functional terms whilst making it clear that the intensity of control exercised both by Community judges and national judges would not undermine the substantive choices of foreign policy as expressed by the Member States in the exercise of their powers as sovereign subjects of international law. The emergence of this functional approach has had implications for both exports of dual-use goods and economic sanctions: as the main questions of their legal regulation have now been answered in a legally sensible and politically realistic manner, the emphasis has turned to the management of the interface between trade and foreign policy.

6.1. A New regime on Exports of Dual-use Goods

The functional construction of the interaction between trade and foreign policy suggested that the legal system based on Regulation 3381/94 and Decision 94/942/CFSP was both redundant in practical terms and flawed in legal terms. As this became apparent to the Union institutions and the Member States, it was repealed and replaced by a set of rules adopted solely pursuant to Article 133 EC. It is noteworthy that the Council measure repealing Decision 94/941/CFSP refers expressly to the case law of the Court.[85] The new set of rules is set out in Regulation 1334/2000.[86] In terms of legal principle, it incorporated all the elements of the regime which had previously been deemed to be of a strategic nature and, thus, beyond the scope of the Community legal order. Therefore, the material scope of the common rules on exports of dual-use goods is defined in a list of products annexed to the Regulation itself. This list covers ten categories of products which include the following: nuclear materials, facilities and equipment; materials, chemicals, 'microorganisms' and 'toxins'; material processing; electronics; computers; telecommunications and 'information security'; sensors and lasers; navigation and avionics; marine; propulsion systems, space vehicles and related equipment. Each of these broadly defined categories includes a number of products divided into further subcategories covering equipment, test and inspection equipment, materials, software and technologies.

The various types of authorisation provided for in Regulation 1334/2000 are applicable to the above items. However, Member States are to impose an authorisation requirement for products not included in the lists annexed to the

---

[85] See preamble to Council Dec 2000/402/CFSP [2000] OJ L 159/218.

[86] [2000] OJ L 159/1 amended by Council Reg 149/2003 [2003] OJ L 30/1 and Council Reg 1504/2004 [2004] OJ L 281/1. In addition, the control of technical assistance related to certain military end-uses was regulated under Joint Action 2000/401/CFSP [2000] OJ L 159/216.

Regulation provided that certain conditions regarding the purchasing country or the country of destination are met. This should not be read as opening up the scope of the notion of dual-use goods to any products which might be used in any way by the military; this would entail too broad an interpretation of the material scope of the exceptional rules laid down in Regulation 1334/2000. Indeed, the Regulation itself defines the outer limit of the products which, whilst not covered by the list annexed to it, might nonetheless be subject to an authorisation requirement by the Member State; Article 4(2), for instance, refers to products which are or may be intended, in their entirety or in part, for a military end-use.[87]

As to the criteria pursuant to which national authorities are to decide whether to grant an export authorisation or not, Article 8 of Regulation 1334/2000 provides a list which appears indicative in nature; the Member States are to take into account 'all relevant considerations including:

(a)   the obligations and commitments they have each accepted as a member of the relevant international non-proliferation regimes and export control arrangements, or by ratification of relevant international treaties;

(b)   their obligations under sanctions imposed by a common position or a joint action adopted by the Council or by a decision of the OSCE or by a binding resolution of the Security Council of the United Nations;

(c)   considerations of national foreign and security policy, including those covered by the European Union Code of Conduct on arms exports;

(d)   considerations about intended end-use and the risk of diversion'.

In substantive terms, Regulation 1334/2000 streamlined the common rules on exports of dual-use goods. The current system provides for a Community general export authorisation which covers exports of those products exhaustively defined in a list annexed to it to a limited number of countries, namely the USA, Canada, Japan, Australia, New Zealand, Switzerland and Norway. In addition, three other types of authorisation are provided: an individual authorisation which applies to one exporter and covers a transaction to one end-user; a global authorisation which may be granted to a specific exporter and applies to a specified type or category of dual-use goods and is valid for exports to one more specified countries; finally, a national general export authorisation which may exist in individual Member States.

At the core of the system established under Regulation 1334/2000 is the principle of mutual recognition, which had underpinned the content of the previous inter-pillar regime. In rendering this fundamental principle of the establishment of the internal market the foundation of the common rules on exports of dual-use

---

[87] Military end-use is defined as covering incorporation into military items listed in the military list of Member States, use of production, test or analytical equipment and components therefore, for the development, production or maintenance of military items listed in the abovementioned list and use of any unfinished products in a plant for the production of military items listed in the abovementioned list (Art 4(2)(a)–(c)).

goods, the Council amplified its application in two ways. On the one hand, there is considerable scope for Member States to determine whether their security should be protected by restricting exports of dual-use products. This is ensured in a number of ways. For instance, Member States are allowed to adopt or maintain national legislation imposing an authorisation requirement on the export of dual-use goods items not covered by the list annexed to the Regulation. This would be the case provided that the exporter had grounds for suspecting that those items were or might be intended, in their entirety or in part, for use in connection with the development, production, handling, operation, maintenance, storage, detection, identification or dissemination of chemical, biological or nuclear weapons or other nuclear explosive devices or the development, production, maintenance or storage of missiles capable of delivering such weapons.[88] Moreover, Member States may prohibit or impose an authorisation requirement on the export of goods not listed in the Annex for reasons of public security or human rights considerations, provided that such measures are notified to the Commission which then publishes them.[89] Furthermore, the substantive and procedural duties imposed upon the Member State do not prejudice their right to take unilateral measures under the exceptional clause laid down in the Export Regulation.[90] In addition, in cases where a Member State concludes that an export of dual-use goods to be authorised by the authorities of another Member State might prejudice its essential security interests, it may request the latter not to grant an export authorisation or, accordingly, to annul, suspend, modify or revoke it. In these cases, the Regulation imposes a duty of immediate consultation upon the authorities of the exporting Member State:[91] this is of a non-binding nature and is to be terminated within ten working days. Finally, export authorisation is also required for the export of products which, whilst not listed in the list annexed to Regulation 1334/2000, are or may be intended for use in connection with weapons of mass destruction or missiles for delivery of such weapons or in connection with military products for countries subject to an arms embargo imposed by the Union or other international *fora*.[92] Finally, it is for the Member States to lay down the penalties to be imposed for any violation of the common rules.[93]

The considerable role with which national administrations are endowed illustrates in a concrete manner that the establishment of common rules solely within the framework of the CCP by no means entails the marginalisation of the Member States in the application of Community law. The acknowledgement of their role *de lege lata* may be viewed as the substantive equivalent of the wide

---

[88] Art 4(5) and (1) of Reg 1334/2000, n 86 above.
[89] Art 5; as for a list of national measures published by the Commission, see the Information Note in [2003] OJ C 273/2.
[90] Art 4(8) of Reg 1334/2000, n 86 above.
[91] Art 7(2).
[92] See Art 4(1) and (2); in addition, the exporter ought to have been informed that the products in question might be used for a military end-use.
[93] Art 19.

discretion which Member States are deemed to enjoy in terms of the protection of their security pursuant to the judgments in *Werner* and *Leifer*.

The second central feature of the common rules is the formalisation of the continuous interaction between the competent authorities of the Member State of exportation and the Commission and the authorities of the other Member States. For instance, in cases where the authorities of the exporting state refuse to grant an export authorisation or annul, suspend, modify or revoke one already granted, they are under a duty to inform both the competent authorities of the other Member States and the Commission and exchange the relevant information with them.[94] In cases where a Member State is about to authorise the export of products for which authorisation has been denied by another Member State within the previous three years, the authorities of the former are bound to consult the authorities of the latter; if, this consultation notwithstanding, the authorities of the exporting state decided to grant the relevant export authorisation, they would be under a duty to inform both the other Member States and the Commission and provide them with all the relevant information to explain the decision.[95] A further illustration of the proceduralisation of the system introduced by Regulation 1334/2000 is provided by the establishment of a Coordinating Group: chaired by a Commission official and comprising one representative from each Member State, the Group is responsible for examining any question raised by the application of the Regulation and providing guidance to Member States.[96]

This overview of the new regime on exports of dual-use goods raises the following two points. First, the development of the system of administrative cooperation provided for under the previous inter-pillar regime had been one of the principal areas in which the Commission had recommended considerably tighter mechanisms in its proposals for the reform of the common rules on exports of dual-use goods.[97] In addition to the principle of mutual recognition, the proceduralisation introduced by Regulation 1334/2000 and the ensuing establishment of formal channels of communication between national administrations and the Commission are further illustrations of the effect that internal market principles may have on the formulation of external policies. Indeed, the duty of notification and the establishment of consultation procedures between national administration and the Member States has been a central feature of the new approach to technical harmonisation.[98] It is interesting that the regulation of such a controversial area should provide the terrain where the main principles underpinning the

---

[94] Art 9(2) of Reg 1334/2000, n 86 above.
[95] Art 9(3) of *ibid.*
[96] Art 18.
[97] See COM(1998)258 final At 10 *ff.*
[98] An example is provided by Council Dir 83/189 [1983] OJ L 109/8 amended various times, most significantly by Dir 98/48 [1998] OJ L 217/18; for a detailed analysis of its content, see S Weatherill, 'Compulsory Notification of Draft Technical Regulations: the Contribution of Directive 83/189 to the Management of the Internal Market' (1996) 16 *YEL* 129. See also P Koutrakos, 'The Elusive Quest for Uniformity in EC External Relations' (2002) 4 *CYELS* 243.

establishment and management of the internal market and those aiming at addressing the security concerns of the Member States interact within the framework of the CCP. Secondly, whilst the discretion enjoyed by national authorities is at the core of Regulation 1334/2000, the new approach set out in that instrument is not without important legal implications for the management of the overall competence of the Community. In that respect, Eeckhout points out that the establishment of the new regime raises the prospect of the exercise of Community competence in future international negotiations in this area within the formula of mixity.[99]

6.2. Managing Sanctions

Whilst in the case of exports of dual-use goods the Court's case law clearly suggested, and the Community legislature accepted, that the CCP provided the appropriate framework, the regulation of sanctions pursuant to both EC and CFSP measures is provided for as a matter of primary law. In its approach in the *Centro-Com* line of judgments, the Court illustrated its willingness to exercise its jurisdiction fully as a matter of Community law and, therefore, ensure the effectiveness of the sanction regimes. However, it did not and could not pronounce on the complications that the legal formula laid down in Article 301 EC might entail as a matter of course. Such problems, as illustrated by the implementation of sanctions under the inter-pillar approach, vary in nature: there may be a considerable delay between the adoption of the common position declaring the will of the Member States to impose sanctions and the Council Regulation actually laying down the sanctions regime; the wording of the Common Position is often vague and, as such, pending the adoption of the Article 301 EC measure, it renders the content of the obligations imposed upon the Member States uncertain; as a result, the uniformity of implementation of sanctions and the effectiveness of the ensuing regime are undermined.[100]

In December 2003, the Council approved a set of guidelines on implementation and evaluation of sanctions in the framework of CFSP.[101] These guidelines, drawn up by the Working Party of Foreign Relations Counsellors, further discussed by the Political Committee and then submitted to the Permanent Representatives Committee (COREPER), constitute the first effort by the Union to enhance the effectiveness of its sanctions regimes in a comprehensive manner. Rather than containing political statements and oft-repeated platitudes about the role of sanctions in promoting the Union values on the world stage, the Guidelines explore specific ways which would regularise various aspects of the regulation of sanction regimes and contribute to the enhancement of their effectiveness.

---

[99] P Eeckhout, *External Relations of the European Union—Legal and Constitutional Foundations* (Oxford: OUP, 2004) 463.
[100] See the overview in Koutrakos, n11 above, at 86–90.
[101] Council conclusions 15535/03 (PESC 356) of 8 Dec 2003.

The Guidelines seek to cover 'the entire process from imposition of restrictive measures, through effective monitoring of their application, to developing a more consistent approach for reporting and assessing the effectiveness of the restrictive measures'.[102] They set out the main principles underpinning issues such as targeted measures, that is measures affecting a clearly defined category of persons and entities, exemptions, expiration or review of sanctions, implementation of UN Security Council Resolutions and jurisdiction. Throughout the Guidelines, the approach adopted is practical and its focus sharp. A standard wording is suggested for various issues such as different types of sanctions measures and products, exception clauses or sanctions to be taken in cases of infringement; the issue of the time difference between the adoption of the Common Position and that of the Council Regulation is raised.

This practical focus is noteworthy. The Guidelines deal with the reference to Community measures in the CFSP instrument expressing the will of the Member States to have recourse to Community law in order to impose sanctions. As a matter of practice, the latter mentions that 'action by the Community is needed to implement certain measures'; the Guidelines suggest that 'where precision is needed to ensure that all measures are implemented in time, the CFSP instrument should indicate expressly how each measure or part of measure will be implemented'.[103] Whilst this arrangement might enhance the smoother elaboration of the sanction regimes by the Community institutions, it would also raise questions about the institutional implications of the inter-pillar position: would the Commission, which is the sole initiator of legislation in the Community legal order, be under a legal duty to conform to a mandate set out in a non-Community measure? Should such questions arise, would it be for the Court of Justice to resolve them, hence preserving the institutional balance which is central to the functioning of the Community system? The answer to such questions depends inevitably upon the degree of detail in which the relevant provisions of the Common Position would be expressed in the light of the Guidelines. Be that as it may, in legal terms the Commission has the right to determine the content of its proposal as it deems fit; in practical terms, in the light of the significance of the subject-matter and the fact that time would be of essence, it is unlikely that the reference to the Community action in the Common Position would give rise to substantive debates which would require judicial resolution.

A central feature of the Guidelines, and one that makes their approval by the Council all the more interesting, is their focus on the management of sanctions rather than the overall process leading to their adoption. To that effect, they make it very clear that the political process leading to the decision to impose or repeal sanctions is not addressed at all.[104] Instead, the process of monitoring and evaluating sanctions is quite prominent. Having pointed out that the existing mechanisms

---

[102] PESC 757, FIN 568, at para 2.

[103] *Ibid*, at para 35.

[104] See n102 above, at para 2.

for overseeing implementation and enforcement by Member States has often been unsatisfactory, the Council approved the establishment of a 'Sanctions Formation' of the Foreign Relations Counsellors Working Group. Its main function being to exchange experience and develop best practice in the implementation and application of sanctions, this Council body has its mandate defined in terms of specific, practical aspects of sanctions management: these include collecting all information available on alleged circumventions of EU sanctions and other international sanctions regimes, exchanging information and experience, including with third states and international organisations, on the implementation of international sanctions regimes, assisting in evaluating the results and difficulties in the implementation of sanctions and examining all relevant technical issues relating to the implementation of EU sanctions. In addition, provision for regular reporting on the implementation of sanctions is to be made both in the CFSP and EC measures setting out sanctions regimes.

Focusing on the management of EU sanctions and seeking to address specific issues with practical, standardised solutions, the Guidelines further develop the regulatory approach underpinning the new regime on exports of dual-use goods. They set aside the normative issues raised by the coexistence of the EC and non-EC measures at the core of the adoption of EU sanctions. In the light of the functional jurisdiction of the Court of Justice, as defined clearly in the *Airport Transit Visa* case and articulated in *Centro-Com* and the other judgments on sanctions, this move is sensible. This emerging emphasis on management rather than regulation is not unique to economic sanctions in particular and the interface between foreign policy and trade in general; it is also consistent with the underlying tone of the case law of the Court of Justice on the delineation of competence in the sphere of EC external relations.

7. THE CASE OF EXPORTS OF ARMAMENTS

Whilst economic sanctions and restrictions on exports of dual-use goods have been regulated pursuant to a variety of legal arrangements in order to ensure the harmonious coexistence of national sovereignty and Community competence, the regulation of exports of arms in general and arms embargoes in particular has been less controversial. The reason for this is the assumption that armaments fall entirely within the sphere of national sovereignty.[105] The need to ensure that exports of armaments would be contained has been shared in the international community for a long time. A number of initiatives have been undertaken in order to produce common criteria on the basis of which arms exports will be controlled. Following the end of the Cold War, the most prominent initiative has been the Wassenaar Arrangement on Export Controls for Conventional Arms and

---

[105] See the analysis in Ch 13 below.

Dual-Use Goods and Technologies. With its diverse membership,[106] this organisation, which began to operate in September 1996 and is based in Vienna, acknowledges the complete discretion of its members to authorise exports of arms and related goods. What it does require is that the participating states exchange information and exercise their discretion in accordance with a number of agreed procedures and criteria.[107]

After years of lobbying by non-governmental organisations and negotiations between national administrations, in June 1998 the Council adopted a document entitled 'EU Code of Conduct on Arms Exports'. Its aim is to express the 'determination' of the Member States 'to set high common standards which should be regarded as the minimum for the management of, and restraint in, conventional arms transfers by all EU Member States, and to strengthen the exchange of relevant information with a view to achieving greater transparency'.[108] It seeks to do so by establishing channels of communication between the authorities of the Member States competent to authorise exports of arms. In addition, the Code sets out eight criteria which the above authorities are to take into account. These may be summarised as follows:

—respect for the international commitments of the Member States;
—respect for human rights in the country of final destination;
—a proper assessment of the internal situation of the country of destination regarding the existence of tensions or armed conflicts;
—the preservation of regional peace, security and stability;
—the security of the Member States and of the territories whose external relations are the responsibility of a Member State, as well as the security of friendly and allied countries;
—the behaviour of the buyer country with regard to the international community, in particular as regards its attitude to terrorism, the nature of its alliances and respect for international law;
—the existence of a risk that the equipment would be diverted within the buyer country or re-exported under undesirable conditions;
—the compatibility of the exportation under review with the technical and economic capacity of the country of destination, taking into account the desirability that states should achieve their legitimate needs of security and defence with the least diversion for armaments of human and economic resources.

[106] This comprises Argentina, Australia, Austria, Belgium, Bulgaria, Canada, Czech Republic, Denmark, Finland, France, Germany, Greece, Hungary, Ireland, Italy, Japan, Luxembourg, Netherlands, New Zealand, Norway, Poland, Portugal, Republic of Korea, Romania, Russian Federation, Slovakia, Slovenia, Spain, Sweden, Switzerland, Turkey, Ukraine, the UK and the USA.
[107] These were amended more recently in July 2004. For a review of the interaction of this system with EU rules in the light of the recent enlargement, see S Jones, 'EU Enlargement: Implications for EU and Multilateral Export Controls' [2003] *The Nonproliferation Review* 80.
[108] For an analysis of the Code, see Koutrakos, n11 above, at 202–7.

It is an indication of the acute political sensitivity of the subject-matter that, when adopted in 1998, the Code of Conduct did not include a list of products to which its provisions would apply. The parallel with Council Regulation 3381/94 setting out the original regime on exports of dual-use goods is obvious: whilst the latter was so controversial that its material scope was excluded from its ambit, in the case of the Code of Conduct there was no definition of its material scope. It was in June 2000 that the Council agreed on the list of arms and related products to the export of which the above criteria would apply.[109] A review of the implementation of the Code, along with the identification of possible improvements, is carried out annually.[110]

The Code of Conduct was intended to outline certain broad parameters within which the Member States would purport to act *in tandem*. Its adoption beyond the formal instruments laid down in Title V illustrates not only their highly sensitive content but also the reluctance of the Member States to commit themselves even to the lowest common denominator. Indeed, the implementation of the Code, and hence its effectiveness, is entirely a matter for the discretion of the Member States.[111]

In terms of the imposition of arms embargoes, the interaction between the CFSP and EC measures formalised under Article 301 EC has proved irrelevant: such measures are adopted solely on the basis of a common position adopted under Article 15 TEU.[112] These measures are implemented by means of national legislation. Like economic sanctions, they often provide for certain exemptions: for instance, Common Position 2002/829/CFSP on the supply of certain equipment into Congo[113] did not apply to supplies temporarily exported for the personal use only of United Nations personnel, supplies of non-lethal military equipment intended solely for humanitarian or protective use temporarily exported for the personal use only of representatives of the media and humanitarian and development workers and associated personnel, as well as equipment to be used for the clearance and destruction of anti-personnel landmines. As the Community legal framework is excluded, the effectiveness of the arms embargoes relies entirely upon intergovernmental channels of coordination and cooperation often established on an *ad hoc* basis. Such channels become all the more significant in the light of the exemptions provided for in the relevant Common Positions: the broader the scope for national action independently of a tightly regulated and enforced set of rules, the broader the scope for deviating from and, potentially, undermining the embargo. In this respect, it is recalled that the effectiveness of the economic sanctions

---

[109] [2000] OJ C 191/1 amended twice so far: [2000] OJ C 314/1 and [2005] OJ C 127/1.

[110] The most recent one was the Sixth Report: [2004] OJ C 316/1.

[111] See, for instance, the Council's Reply to Written Questions E–1801/04 and P-1883/04, as well as the Commission's Answer to Written Question E–1884/03, not yet published.

[112] See, for instance, Common Position 2004/31/CFSP concerning the imposition of an embargo on arms, munitions and military equipment on Sudan [2004] OJ L 6/55 amended by Council Common Position 2004/510/CFSP [2005] OJ L 209/28.

[113] [2002] OJ L 285/1.

against Serbia and Montenegro, an issue in *Centro-Com*, was supervised by the Court itself. This mechanism is absent from the system of implementation of arms embargoes.

Therefore, the effectiveness of arms embargoes relies upon the willingness of the Member States to comply with certain rules adopted beyond the formal CFSP machinery. For instance, Common Position 2004/137/CFSP, imposing, amongst others, arms restrictions on Liberia, requires that, in applying the relevant exemptions and deciding whether to grant an export authorisation on an *ad hoc* basis, national authorities 'take full account' of the criteria set out in the EU Code of Conduct on arms exports.[114] It is precisely the interaction between the rules laying down an arms embargo and the Code of Conduct which highlights the pathology of both. Following the violent suppression of demonstrations in Tienanmen Square in Beijing in June 1989, the European Council issued a declaration in which 'it strongly condemns the brutal repression taking place in China' and asked the Member States to halt all programmes of military cooperation and impose an embargo on trade in arms with China. As the years went by, a number of Member States, with France and the United Kingdom quite active amongst them, formed the view that the embargo should be lifted. To the various reservations to this proposal expressed by the United States the response by European officials was that the lifting of the embargo would be accompanied by a considerable tightening of the rules laid down in the Code of Conduct. In the light of the increasingly hostile reaction by the United States, this proposal was temporarily shelved.[115] For the purposes of this analysis, the terms in which the various actors expressed their positions were noteworthy: the proponents of the embargo seriously doubted that any meaningful control of arms exports could be maintained on the basis of the Code of Conduct; in a similar vein, the advocates of lifting the embargo focused mainly on the symbolic significance of this gesture, rather than its substantive effect.[116] All in all, neither the Code nor the embargo regime was deemed sufficiently tight to pursue effectively their stated objectives.

8. CONCLUSION

The analysis of the interactions between trade and foreign policy in this chapter has shown that a formalistic distinction between those two areas of activities is impossible to maintain, in practical terms, and defend, in legal terms. The approach of the Court of Justice, as elaborated gradually in its case law and accepted by the Union institutions and the Member States, has clearly highlighted a normative sphere in which trade may be regulated and foreign policy carried

---

[114] Art 1(3), of [2004] OJ L 40/35.
[115] See *Financial Times*, 15 Apr 2005, 8.
[116] See the interview by the French Defence Minister in *International Herald Tribune*, 9 Mar 2005, in which she suggested that the retention of the embargo would in fact facilitate the development of defence industries in China.

out with neither the Community competence being undermined nor national sovereign threatened. In addition to this general conclusion, there is a thread which links the construction of the relationship between trade and foreign policy by the Court with other areas of EU international relations law. Two points in particular are noteworthy. The first is about the genesis and development of the Common Commercial Policy. Previous chapters have highlighted the flexible application of the notion of exclusivity during the process of the consolidation of the CCP. This flexibility had been apparent both in the Court's case law and the regulatory measures of the Community institutions. It was also shown that, with the establishment of the internal market, the Court was less willing to sanction deviations from the principles of the CCP. Its approach to the exports of dual-use goods and sanctions, as elaborated in this Chapter, indicates that, rather than being abandoned altogether, exclusivity has merely taken a different form. The consolidation of the broad scope of Article 133 EC is accompanied by the acknowledgment of the wide discretion enjoyed by national authorities. In other words, the judgments analysed in this chapter follow the tone which the Court set in its judgments in the 1980s whilst adapting to the new challenges facing the conduct of the CCP.

The second point follows from the above and is about the role of national courts. Previous chapters identified a number of areas in which national courts become increasingly prominent, such as the interpretation of international agreements concluded by the Member States prior to their accession to the European Union or the determination of various important aspects of mixed agreements. The approach of the Court of Justice to the interactions between trade and foreign policy confirms this position. By assessing whether national deviations from Article 133 EC are necessary and proportionate in the exercise of the discretion granted to Member States, national courts become central to the application of the Common Commercial Policy in an area of increasing significance for the EU international action.

13

European Security and Defence Policy

1. INTRODUCTION

T HE ADVANCED STAGE of European integration and the preparation for, and completion of, the recent enlargement have raised questions about the identity of the European Union. Its international role was at the centre of the these developments. In the Laeken Declaration on the Future of the European Union, the European Council wondered, '[d]oes Europe not, now that it is finally unified, have a leading role to play in a new world order, that of a power able both to play a stabilising role worldwide and to point the way ahead for many countries and peoples?' By addressing this question, the Member States and the Union institutions turned their attention to the European Security and Defence Policy. The significance attached to it had been illustrated clearly by the first Declaration adopted by the Nice Intergovernmental Conference and annexed to the Final Act of the Treaty of Nice: it stated that the Union's objective was for that policy 'to become operational quickly', for which the entry into force of the Treaty of Nice was expressly ruled out as a precondition; instead, the Union institutions were asked to act on the basis of the TEU provisions as amended at Amsterdam. It is the evolution of the European Security and Defence Policy (ESDP), its implementation and the various factors which shape its development that will be analysed in this chapter.

2. RULES AND STRUCTURES

In setting out the objectives of the European Union, Article 2 TEU referred to the assertion of its identity on the international scene 'in particular through the implementation of a common foreign and security policy including the progressive framing of a common defence policy, which might lead to a common defence'. The wording of this provision, retained in the Amsterdam Treaty, is slightly changed when compared to its original form at Maastricht: Article B of that Treaty had referred to the 'eventual' framing of a common defence policy which might 'in time' lead to a common defence. The removal of those terms at Amsterdam signified the wish of the drafters of the Treaty to remove defence policy from the sphere of political aspiration and bring it closer to the development of the Common Foreign and Security Policy (CFSP). In addition to this textual indication, the more central role of defence policy is also supported by its inclusion in the scope of general principles and guidelines drawn up by the European Council under Article 13(1) TEU.

The main principles of the legal framework of the security and defence policy are set out in Article 17 TEU. The wording and structure of its provisions make it clear that, in addition to setting out the main parameters of the development of the Union's defence policy, Article 17 TEU also aims at underlining the limits of that policy. In its very first paragraph, it states the following:[1]

> The policy of the Union in accordance with this Article shall not prejudice the specific character of the security and defence policy of certain Member States and shall respect the obligations of certain Member States, which see their common defence realised in the North Atlantic Treaty Organisation (NATO), under the North Atlantic Treaty and be compatible with the common security and defence policy established within that framework.

As if the point has not been brought home, Article 17(3) TEU states the following:

> Decisions having defence implications dealt with under this Article shall be taken without prejudice to the policies and obligations referred to in paragraph 1, second subparagraph.

It is not only the need to stress the same point twice in the course of a single Treaty Article that is noteworthy: in addition to the reference to the status of neutral Member States,[2] the statement in Article 17(1) TEU that certain Member States 'see their common defence realized in NATO' was added at Amsterdam and maintained at Nice. This suggests that the qualification expressed in Article 17(3) TEU was not considered sufficiently clear an indication as to the role of NATO at the core of the defence of a number of Member States.[3] The overall emphasis leaves no doubt as to the message that the drafters of Article 17 TEU sought to convey: whilst a distinct possibility, the development of a common defence policy is not envisaged as undermining the fundamental policy choice made by certain Member States. In a similar vein, Article 6(3) TEU makes it clear that the Union shall respect the national identities of the Member States.

The scope of the Union's security and defence policy, as laid down in Article 17 TEU, covers humanitarian and rescue tasks, peacekeeping tasks and tasks of combat forces in crisis management, including peacemaking. This list duplicates the

---

[1] 2nd subpara.

[2] On the neutrality of Ireland in particular, see R Doherty, *Ireland, Neutrality and European Security Integration* (Aldershot: Ashgate, 2002); on the neutrality of Austria, Finland, Sweden and Denmark too, see E Denza, *The Intergovernmental Pillars of the European Union* (Oxford: OUP, 2002) 347–350.

[3] On the role of the enlarged NATO, along with that of the EU, in European security, see F Schimmelfennig, *The EU, NATO and the Integration of Europe—Rules and Rhetoric* (Cambridge: Cambridge University Press, 2003).

activities defined by the Western European Union Council of Ministers in June 1992 in the now famous Petersberg Declaration. The wording of Article 17(2) TEU, introduced at Amsterdam and maintained at Nice, indicates that the list of the so-called 'Petersberg tasks' is indicative rather than exhaustive.

The function of the development of defence policy pursuant to Article 17 TEU is not exclusive: closer cooperation between two or more Member States in the Western European Union (WEU) or NATO framework is allowed as long as 'such cooperation does not run counter to or impede that provided for in this title' (Article 17(4) TEU). This provision not only translates into legal language a fact of political reality but it also follows from the previous provisions of Article 17 TEU: having acknowledged quite emphatically that the core of national defence within NATO is not affected by the development of the EU defence policy, it makes perfect sense for the right of the relevant Member States to engage in close cooperation to be affirmed. As a matter of fact, the relevant clause is slightly broader in scope: the right to develop close cooperation is not confined to those Member States which see their defence realised in NATO, but is extended to all Member States. Furthermore, such cooperation is accepted not only within NATO but also within the WEU. On the other hand, there is a limit to such cooperation, that is not to run counter to or impede cooperation provided for in Title V TEU, compliance with which is assumed to be ensured by the Council. However, this limit is not as clearly defined as it may appear: rather than 'policy' or 'decisions' or 'activities', Article 17(4) TEU refers to cooperation under Title V TEU which should not be undermined. This choice of an inherently indeterminate notion referring to an incremental process brings the relevant clause to the realm of political declaration rather than legal obligation.

One final point that needs to be made is about the role of the WEU. The Nice amendment of Article 17 TEU removed all but one reference to it; it is recalled that, under the Amsterdam Treaty, the elaboration and implementation of EU decisions and actions with defence implications would be entrusted to the WEU. The only remaining reference to the latter is in Article 17(4) TEU where the WEU along with NATO provides the framework within which individual Member States may develop close cooperation.[4]

It was not only in terms of the Union's commitment that the Treaty of Nice laid more emphasis on the development of the ESDP; it also adjusted the CFSP infrastructure to reflect this new focus. To that end, not only did it require that the Political Committee develop into a Political and Security Committee,[5] but it also broadened the scope of its tasks considerably: in addition to monitoring the international

---

[4] See RA Wessel, 'The EU as a Black Widow: Devouring the WEU to Give Birth to a European Security and Defence Policy' in V Kronenberger (ed), *The European Union and the International Legal Order: Discord or Harmony?* (The Hague: TMC Asser Press 2001) 405.

[5] Established under a Council Dec [2001] OJ L 27/1. An Interim Political and Security Committee had been established under Council Dec 2000/143/CFSP [2000] OJ L 49/1.

situation in the areas covered by the CFSP, contributing to the definitions of policies by delivering opinions to the Council and monitoring the implementation of agreed policies, Article 25(2) TEU provides as follows:

> Within the scope of this Title, this Committee shall exercise, under the responsibility of the Council, political control and strategic direction of crisis management operations.

The remaining provisions of Article 25 TEU spell out the practical implications of this: the Political and Security Committee (PSC) may be authorised by the Council to take the relevant decisions concerning the political control and strategic direction of specific crisis management operations. In legal terms, this role of the PSC raises questions of competence, jurisdiction and institutional propriety: are the many functions of this newly established body which is to act pursuant to a Council authorisation excluded by the jurisdiction of the Court not a threat to the legal integrity of the Community framework and the institutions and bodies acting within it? Article 25 requires that the authorisation by the Council and the functions of the PSC will be without prejudice to Article 47 TEU, that is to say they may not affect the Community legal order.

In addition to the Political and Security Committee, the Helsinki European Council provided for the establishment of the Military Committee and the Military Staff. The overall function of all three bodies is to exercise 'the necessary political control and strategic direction' regarding the Petersberg tasks carried out by the Union. The Political and Security Committee consists of national senior representatives, normally at ambassadorial level, based in Brussels. It interacts with the Military Committee to which it forwards guidelines. The latter[6] is composed of the Chiefs of Defence, normally represented by their military delegates, and its task is give military advice and make recommendations to the Political and Security Committee. In addition, it provides military direction to the Military Staff,[7] that is the body with military expertise entrusted with performing early warning, situation assessment and strategic planning for Petersberg tasks including the identification of European national and multinational forces.

In practical terms, the exercise of political control and strategic direction of the various ESDP operations by the Political and Security Committee entails a range of tasks such as the appointment of the Head of Mission,[8] pursuant to a

---

[6] Established by Council Dec 2001/79/CFSP [2001] OJ L 27/4. Its chairman was appointed first under Council Dec 2001/309/CFSP [2001] OJ L 109/1 and then Council Dec 2003/401/EC [2003] OJ L 139/34.

[7] Established by Council Dec 2001/80/CFSP [2001] OJ L 27/7 as amended by Council Dec 2005/395/CFSP [2005] OJ L 132/17.

[8] See PSC Dec EUPOL Kinshasa/1/2004 [2004] OJ L 396/61, PSC Dec Proxima/2/2004 [2004] OJ L 367/29, PSC Dec THEMIS/1/2004 [2004] OJ L 239/35, PSC Dec EUJUST LEX/1/2005 [2005] OJ L 72/29, PSC Dec BiH/2/2004 [2004] OJ L 324/22, PSC Dec BiH/4/2004 [2004] OJ L 357/38.

request by the Council,[9] the provision of strategic direction to the Operation Commander and the exercise of political control over him/her and the operation in the implementation of the operation's mandate, the establishment of a Committee of Contributors[10] and the acceptance of non-acceding third states' contributions.[11]

3. THE DEVELOPMENT OF THE ESDP FRAMEWORK

In the last seven years, that is since the meeting between the British Prime Minister, Tony Blair, and French President, Jacques Chirac, at St Malo, the security and defence policy of the European Union has been at the very centre of Union activities. The Laeken Declaration, for instance, which was adopted by the European Council in December 2001 and set the Union on to the long road leading to the adoption of the Treaty Establishing a Constitution for Europe, referred to the expectation that European citizens were assumed to share regarding greater European involvement in that area.

It is an interesting feature of the development of the ESDP framework that, whilst drawing upon a broadly worded TEU provision, its main parameters have emerged on as incremental a basis as the CFSP itself prior to its incorporation in the Treaty. Indeed, not only is the genesis of its momentum located in the rather unlikely alliance of two Member States, but also its foundation is to be found in the guidelines set out in successive European Council meetings and the Presidency reports adopted thereunder. The meeting between Prime Minister Blair and President Chirac took place in December 1998 in St Malo, where the two leaders expressed their wish that a stronger European presence in the area of security and defence policy be forged.[12] The momentum that this incident was to bring was illustrated by the reference to the British–French initiative by President Chirac as the 'Franco-British motor',[13] a statement all the more striking in the light of the traditional relationship between France and Germany at the very core

---

[9] In the case of the EU Police Mission in the Former Yugoslav Republic of Macedonia (FYROM), for instance, see Art 9(7) of Joint Action 2004/789/CFSP [2004] OJ L 348/40 amended by Joint Action 2005/142 [2005] OJ L 48/45.

[10] See PSC Dec EUPM/1/2005 [2005] OJ L 72/23 regarding the Police Mission in Bosnia-Herzegovina and PSC Dec Proxima/3/2005 [2005] OJ L 72/25, PSC Dec BiH/3/2004 [2004] OJ L 325/64 amended by PSC Dec BiH/5/2004 [2004] OJ L 357/39, PSC Dec DRC 2/2003 [2003] OJ L 184/13, PSC Dec FYROM/1/2003 [2003] OJ L 62/1.

[11] See PSC Dec Proxima/1/2004 [2004] OJ L 60/54; PSC Dec BiH/1/2004 [2004] OJ L 324/2; PSC Dec DRC 1/2003 [2003] OJ L 170/19 as amended by PSC Dec DRC 3/2003 [2003] OJ L 206/32; PSC Dec FYROM/2/2003 [2003] OJ L 170/15 as amended by PSC Dec FYROM/3/2003 [2003] OJ L 170/17 and PSC Dec FYROM/4/2003 [2003] OJ L 170/18.

[12] See *Agence Europe*, 7–8 Dec 1998, at 4. See the analysis in J Howorth, 'Britain, NATO and CESDP: Fixed Strategy, Changing Tactics' (2000) 3 *EFA Rev* 1.

[13] *Financial Times*, 26 Dec 1999, at 1.

of Union integration. Within six months, the stakes had been raised and the initiative was undertaken at EU level. In June 1999, the Cologne European Council signalled the first step of an ongoing process which has not yet been completed: a Declaration on Strengthening the Common European Policy on Security and Defence annexed to the Presidency Conclusions started with the following grand statement:[14]

> We, the members of the European Council, are resolved that the European Union shall play its full role on the international stage. To that end, we intend to give the European Union the necessary means and capabilities to assume its responsibilities regarding a common European policy on security and defence.

The main focus of the emerging momentum was on the ability of the Council to take decisions on the full range of the Petersberg tasks. To that end, the European Council declared that:

> the Union must have the capacity for autonomous action, backed up by credible military forces, the means to decide to use them, and a readiness to do so, in order to respond to international crises without prejudice to actions by NATO. The EU will thereby increase its ability to contribute to international peace and security in accordance with the principles of the UN Charter.

It was in this context that the European Council endorsed a Presidency report on strengthening of the common European policy on security and defence which described, in rather general terms, options as to the guiding principles of the ESDP, the decision-making procedures, implementation and the modalities of participation and cooperation.

The specific objective of the emerging policy became clearer at the Helsinki European Council which stated that the Union should be able:[15]

> to agree to deploy rapidly and then sustain forces capable of the full range of Petersberg tasks as set out in the Amsterdam Treaty, including the most demanding, in operations of up to corps level (up to 15 brigades or 50,000–60,000 persons). These forces should be militarily self-sustaining with the necessary command, control and intelligence capabilities, logistics, other combat support services and additionally, as appropriate air and naval elements. Member States should be able to deploy in full at this level within 60 days, and within this to provide smaller rapid response elements available and deployable at very high readiness. They must be able to sustain such a deployment for at least one year. This will require an additional pool of deployable units (and supporting elements) at lower readiness to provide replacements for the initial forces.

---

[14] Para 1, Annex 3 to Presidency Conclusions.
[15] Progress Report by the Finnish Presidency on Strengthening the Common European Policy on Security and Defence, submitted to the Helsinki European Council in Dec 1999 and annexed to the Presidency Conclusions.

These became known as the 'Helsinki Headline Goals' for the achievement of which the deadline was set for 2003.

In defining the framework within which the Union was intended to develop its security and defence policy, the European Council set in motion a process the pace of which was developed steadily and as a matter of course on the basis of work carried out by the Presidency, as presented in reports endorsed by the European Council, and the definition by the latter of further goals: the Lisbon European Council required that further work be carried out in the area of civil crisis management;[16] the Feira European Council endorsed a Presidency report which provided a comprehensive and detailed account of overall EU capabilities, both in the military and civil spheres;[17] in November 2000, the Member States participated in a Capabilities Commitment Conference in Brussels in which they set out their specific voluntary commitments to the Union and in which they identified a number of capability shortfalls; whilst declaring the ESDP operational, the Laeken European Council in December 2001 launched the European Capabilities Action Plan in the framework of which the above shortfalls would be addressed;[18] in May 2003, a second Capabilities Conference took place in Brussels in which the Defence Ministers declared that the Union had operational capability across the whole range of the Petersberg tasks, albeit one which was 'limited and constrained by recognized shortfalls'.[19] To that effect, the Headline Goal 2010, adopted by the General Affairs and External Relations Council in May 2004 and endorsed by the European Council in June 2004, set new goals in order to provide the EU with the necessary capabilities. These goals are quite specific: for instance, they include the availability of an aircraft carrier with its associated air wing and escort by 2008 and the implementation by 2005 of EU strategic lift joint coordination, with a view to achieving by 2010 the necessary capacity and full efficiency in strategic lift in support of anticipated operations in air, land and sea.

The picture emerging from the above summary is that of an intense process aiming at shaping the ESDP whilst addressing the practical elements necessary for its implementation. A number of features of this evolving process are noteworthy. First, there is an unmistaken emphasis on what the ESDP is not to be, namely the foundation of a European army responsible for the defence of the Member States. By repeating this negative definition, the EU underlines the existing role of NATO and seeks to assuage any concerns shared by the more Atlanticist of its Members as well as the United States. To that effect, the Helsinki European Council stressed that 'NATO remains the foundation of the collective defence of its members, and

---

[16] 23–24 Mar 2000, paras 42–45 of the Presidency Conclusions.

[17] Feira European Council, 19–20 June 2000, Presidency Conclusions, Annex 1: Presidency Report on the Strengthening the Common European Security and Defence Policy.

[18] European Council, Presidency Conclusions 14–15 Dec 2001, Annex II: Declaration on the Operational Capability of the Common European Security and Defence Policy.

[19] Council, 19–20 May 2003, Declaration on EU Military Capabilities.

will continue to have an important role in crisis management'.[20] Secondly, all related developments are accompanied by the official assurance that any ESDP initiative, rather than entailing the application of supranational methods, would be based upon the existence and maintenance of national sovereignty. The Helsinki European Council, for instance, pointed out that 'the commitment of national assets by Member States to such operations will be based on their sovereign decision'.[21] Thirdly, due to the idiosyncracies of the EU constitutional structure, the relationship between the EC and CFSP frameworks has not been overlooked. The European Council at Helsinki declared that 'taken within the single institutional framework, decisions will respect European Community competences and ensure inter-pillar coherence in conformity with Article 3 of the EU Treaty'.[22] Finally, a sense of dissatisfaction with grand rhetoric seems to transpire from these activities: for instance, the realisation that the practical aspects of security related to the Union capabilities had not been satisfactorily addressed led not only to the re-evaluation of the relevant targets but also questioned the significance of the declaration of the rapid reaction force at Laeken as operational. In that respect, the qualitative focus of the Headline Goal 2010 is noteworthy.[23]

A defining moment in the development of the ESDP has been the *European Security Strategy*. Under the grand subtitle, *A Secure Europe in a Better World*, this document, presented by the EU High Representative, Javier Solana, and approved by the European Council in December 2003, has been a 'key framework for policy formulation'.[24] It purports to become the first formalised effort to spell out what the strategic priorities of the EU are.[25] One of its interesting points is its strategic outlook: having pointed out in the Introduction that in the post-Cold War era 'no single country is able to tackle today's complex problems on its own', with an express reference to the dominant position of the United States as a military actor, it goes on to declare the following: 'Europe should be ready to share in the responsibility for global security and in building a better world'. These are grand words. The European Security Strategy seeks to meet this objective by, first, identifying the main strategic objectives of the European Union in the rapidly changing international environment and, then, ascertaining the policy implications for the European Union. The key threats identified are, rather predictably, terrorism, the

---

[20] N15 above.

[21] *Ibid.*

[22] *Ibid.*

[23] See S Biscop, 'Able and Willing? Assessing the EU's Capacity for Military Action' (2004) 9 *EFA Rev* 509 at 516 ff.

[24] Brussels European Council, July 2004, Presidency Conclusions, para 50.

[25] The elaboration of such a doctrine is considered essential by international relations theorists: 'In the absence of a functioning transnational security concept west European powers, both big and small, react too late, with too little, to crises that seem increasingly beyond the scope and range of either their diplomatic or military capabilities, built as they are upon false strategic assumptions': J Lindley-French, 'In the Shadow of Locarno? Why European Defence is Falling' (2002) 78 *International Affairs* 789 at 809.

proliferation of weapons of mass destruction, regional conflicts, state failure and organised crime.

In the light of these threats and in order to defend its security, the Union has three strategic objectives: to address threats as early as possible and with recourse to a variety of instruments including, but by no means confined to, military means; to build security in its neighbourhood not only by the Union's enlargement but also by 'promoting a ring of well governed countries to the East of the European Union and on the borders of the Mediterranean with whom we can enjoy close and cooperative relations';[26] to contribute to the establishment of an international order based on effective multilateralism with emphasis on the WTO and the international financial institutions, the transatlantic relationship and regional organisations.

In order to meet its strategic objectives, the European Security Strategy advocates the need for the Union to be more active, more coherent and more capable. Reference is made to the need 'to develop a strategic culture that fosters early, rapid, and when necessary, robust intervention'.[27] This entails the development of the Union's capabilities, not only in military terms, but also as regards civilian and diplomatic resources. Finally, there is reference to the need for coherence between EC and EU instruments as well as national and international initiatives.

In keeping with the broad terms of its content, the European Security Strategy concludes in the following terms:[28]

> This is a world of new dangers but also of new opportunities. The European Union has the potential to make a major contribution, both in dealing with the threats and in helping to realise the opportunities. An active and capable European Union would make an impact on a global scale. In doing so, it would contribute to an effective multilateral system leading to a fairer, safer and more united world.

The implications of the European Security Strategy for the substantive content of ESDP are difficult to discern: its vague character along with its failure to define actual targets and prioritise its policy objectives appears to question its actual significance. In other words, it comes across as an 'inspirational sketch'.[29] And yet, its adoption constitutes a rhetorical act which is noteworthy for at least two reasons. First, it illustrates the growing self-confidence of the Union as an international actor. It is interesting, for instance, that it should have taken its name after the United States National Security Strategy.[30] Whilst it by no means follows that this self-confidence is borne out by its content, the European Security Strategy

---

[26] *European Security Strategy*, European Council of Thessaloniki, 20 June 2003, at 8.

[27] *Ibid*, at 11.

[28] *Ibid*, at 14.

[29] The reference in S Duke, 'The European Security Strategy in a Comparative Framework: Does it make for Secure Alliances in a Better World?' (2004) 9 *EFA Rev* 459 at 460.

[30] See A Toje, 'The 2003 European Union Security Strategy: A Critical Appraisal' (2005) 10 *EFA Rev* 117 at 120 ff who provides a parallel analysis of the two documents.

illustrates the emerging focus of the Union on raising the visibility of its international stature. In other words, this document has more to do with the identity that the Union seeks to project on to the international scene and less with the definition of its policies. What is interesting about this process is the extent to which the EU institutions refer to the responsibility of the Union rather than its ambition: the Security Strategy claims that 'Europe should be ready to share in the responsibility for global security and in building a better world',[31] a statement repeated in subsequent documents.[32]

The second interesting feature of the European Security Policy is its emphasis on 'an international order based on effective multilateralism'. It is pointed out that 'the United Nations Security Council has the primary responsibility for the maintenance of international peace and security. Strengthening the United Nations, equipping it to fulfil its responsibilities and to act effectively is a European priority'.[33] This emphasis is not merely a statement included in a strategic document: the Union's commitment to multilateralism is expressed in various ways and at various levels. A previous chapter offered an overview of the focus of the Union's international policies on regionalism, as illustrated by its increasing links with regional organisations such as, the Southern Common Market (MERCOSUR) and the structured frameworks of cooperation with the Mediterranean countries, the West Balkans and the South Caucasus. The emerging emphasis on multilateralism is also apparent in the recent efforts by the Commission to develop the Union's relationship with the United Nations.[34] In addition, a number of Member States proposed the establishment of 'battle groups' aiming, amongst others, at offering the United Nations rapid reaction capability. Submitted by the British, French and German governments in February 2004, this initiative suggested that the Union be able to deploy nine such groups, each consisting of 1,500 troops; these would be ready for launch in ten days from command, and be in the theatre of operations in 15 days. The EU Defence Ministers endorsed this initiative and, in November 2004, agreed to establish 13 such groups which would be operational by 2007. Furthermore, at its meeting in December 2003 when it adopted the European Security Strategy, the European Council identified four areas for initial work, namely effective multilateralism with the UN at its core, the fight against terrorism, a strategy towards the region of the Middle East and a comprehensive policy towards Bosnia-Herzegovina. It is noteworthy that the latter two touch upon areas which had already been viewed by the Union as part of its structured relationship with the West Balkans and the Euro–Mediterranean respectively: both those frameworks have a clear focus on regional cooperation.[35]

---

[31] N26 above, at 1.
[32] See, for instance, the Headline Goal 2010 approved by the General Affairs and External Relations Council on 17 Mar 2004 and endorsed by the European Council of 17 and 18 June 2004.
[33] N26 above at 9.
[34] COM(2003)526 final, *The European Union and the United Nations: The choice of multilateralism*.
[35] The Union's focus on those priority areas is continuing: see Presidency Conclusions of Brussels European Council of 17–18 June 2004.

4. THE ESDP RECORD—AN OVERVIEW

In the context of a legal analysis of the ESDP, an overview of the initiatives undertaken by the European Union is useful: the range of the relevant activities, their development, their legal infrastructure, the involvement of the various institutional actors, all contribute to our understanding of how legal rules apply to this area of activity which lies at the very core of high politics.[36]

Apart from its military aspects, the civilian aspects of crisis management have been an interesting case of foreign policy intervention in so far as it enables the Union to develop a policy area of its own, hence differentiating the model of its activity from that traditionally pursued by sovereign states. In other words, it attributes a more distinct character to the CFSP, all the more so in the light of its reliance upon the combined and coherent employment of a range of EU/EC instruments, involving a host of actors, institutions and procedures. In June 2000, the Feira European Council adopted a report produced by the Portuguese Presidency on Strengthening the Common European Security and Defence Policy. This Report refers in detail to civilian aspects of crisis management and highlights the potentially distinctive nature of its approach:

> Particular attention could be paid to those areas where the international community so far has demonstrated weaknesses. It would provide 'added value' as it would improve the Union's capacity to react as well as the Union's capability to meet the requests of the other lead organisations: they would be able to count—on a more systematic basis — on a sizeable quantitative and qualitative contribution which could represent the nucleus of some of their missions. This would, in turn, increase the Union's visibility.[37]

A number of priority areas are singled out, namely police, strengthening the rule of law, strengthening civilian administration and civil protection. These, in addition to military operations, have been at the centre of the ESDP initiatives undertaken so far.

4.1. Police Missions

The Union has carried out three police mission operations: in Bosnia and Herzegovina under the name EUPM,[38] in the Former Yugoslav Republic of Macedonia under the name EUPOL PROXIMA[39] and in Kinshasa, Democratic

---

[36] For an elaborate analysis of ESDP operations within the context of conflict prevention, see V Kronenberger and J Wouters (eds), *The European Union and Conflict Prevention—Policy and Legal Aspects* (The Hague: TMC Asser Press, 2004).

[37] Feira European Council, 18–20 June 2000, Presidency Conclusions, Annex I, Appendix 3, Part A.

[38] Council Joint Action 2002/210/CFSP [2002] OJ L 70/1, amended by Joint Actions 2003/141/CFSP [2003] OJ L 53/63 and 2003/188/CFSP [2003] OJ L 73/9.

[39] Joint Action 2003/681/CFSP [2003] OJ L 249/66, amended by Joint Action 2004/789/CFSP [2004] OJ L 348/40.

Republic of Congo, under the name EUPOL Kinshasa.[40] The first one was the very first operation undertaken in the ESDP framework. Taking over from the United Nations International Police Force, its main objectives, along with provisions on its management and structure, were originally determined by the Council in February 2002[41] and then incorporated in the Joint Action adopted the following month. Based in Serajevo, the mission is focused on establishing sustainable policing arrangements under the authorities of the host state in accordance with best European and international practice by the end of 2005. Most of its personnel consists of seconded police officers and the remainder includes international civilians and national staff from Bosnia and Herzegovina.

The mission in FYROM is of a broader scope in so far as it defines its objective within the context of a 'broader rule of law perspective' which expressly covers institution building programmes as well as police activities, both being 'mutually supportive and reinforcing'.[42] Finally, the mission in Kinshasa is quite narrow in its scope: to 'monitor, mentor and advise the setting up and the initial running of the Integrated Police Unit in order to ensure that [the latter] acts following the training received in the Academy Centre and according to international best practice in this field'.[43]

What is interesting in relation to all three police missions launched so far in the context of the ESDP is the fact that the Union institutions are noticeably keen to emphasise the position of their initiative as an intrinsic part of a multi-level international approach to this troubled area. There are two aspects to this. In terms of the relationship between the Union and the rest of the world, all the documents related to EUPM, that is Council Conclusions,[44] the Joint Action itself and the Presidency Declaration on the launch of the mission,[45] refer to the 'seamless' transition from UN control, the support expressed by the United Nations Security Council and the Union's undertaking to coordinate with the UN and consult international organisations, in particular NATO and OSCE; most importantly, the participation of non-Member States is not only welcomed but actively sought as an important component of the mission.[46] Furthermore, the CFSP High Representative informs the UN Security Council of the progress of the operation by regularly submitting a report.[47] In a similar vein, the initiative undertaken in FYROM was within a very specific international framework, namely the Ochrid Framework Agreement: signed by representatives of the main FYROM and Albanian

[40] Joint Action 2004/847/CFSP [2004] OJ L 367/30.
[41] See General Affairs Council Conclusions, Brussels, 18/19 Feb 2002 at 16 ff.
[42] See first para of preamble to and Art 3 of Joint Action 2003/681/CFSP, n 39 above.
[43] Art 3 of Joint Action 2004/847/CFSP, n40 above.
[44] See for instance General Affairs Council Conclusions, Brussels, 10 Dec 2002, Doc 15182/02.
[45] Brussels, 31 Dec 2002 P202/02.
[46] See, for instance, Art 8 of Joint Action 2002/210/CFSP, n38 above, and Art 9 of Joint Action 2003/681/CFSP, n39 above.
[47] The last report covered the second half of 2004: see S/2005/66 of 11 Feb 2005.

ethnic parties in August 2001, the Agreement aimed at securing the future of FYROM's democracy and facilitating the development of closer and more integrated relations between the country and the Euro-Atlantic community. To that effect, it expressly asked the EU along with the OSCE and USA to participate in police training.[48] Finally, the mission in Kinshasa is closely related to the Global and All-inclusive Accord on the transition of the Democratic Republic of Congo signed in December 2002: not only was the establishment of the integrated police unit provided for in that agreement, but also the United Nations Security Council had encouraged all donors to support its establishment and functioning.[49] Furthermore, there has been a gradually developing formalised process of cooperation between the UN and EU in the area of crisis management.[50]

In terms of their position within the overall Union approach, the Balkan missions are viewed as an intrinsic component of the Union's overall approach to the Balkans. In particular, it is stated that the operation is intended to contribute to the achievements of the stabilisation and association process and, to that effect, reference is made to the support to be provided by the Community's assistance programme in this context under the CARDS Regulation.[51] It is for this reason that an entire Article in the Joint Action establishing either of the missions is dedicated to Community action: in those provisions, the Council 'notes the intention of the Commission to direct its action towards achieving the objectives of this Joint Action, where appropriate, by relevant Community measures' whereas it is also pointed out that the Council 'also notes that coordination arrangements in Brussels and Sarajevo are required'.[52] The identical wording of those provisions is noteworthy in so far as it seeks to point out the comprehensive nature of the Union approach whilst avoiding the pitfall of appearing to impose a direct legal duty on EC institutions.[53]

The case of the mission in Kinshasa is equally interesting in terms of the interactions it entails between Community and Union instruments. Rather than taking an initiative in a legal and political vacuum, the Council established the police mission in the light of the following policies: on the one hand, in response to the establishment of the integrated police union in Kinshasa and following the UN Security Council Resolution urging support and training for it, the Commission had adopted a financing decision within the context of the European Development

---

[48] Art 5(2) and (3): see http://www.usip.org/library/pa/macedonia/pa_mac_08132001.html.

[49] See UN SC Resolution 1493 (2003).

[50] See, for instance, the Declaration by the European Council on EU–UN co-operation in Military Crisis Management Operations—Elements of Implementation of the EU-UN Joint Declaration, 17–18 June 2004.

[51] Reg 2666/00 [2000] OJ L 306/1.

[52] Art 10(1) and (2) of Joint Action 2002/210, n38 above, and Art 11(1) and (2) of Joint Action 2003/681/CFSP, n39 above.

[53] On the substantive content of the operations, see M Merlingen and R Ostrauskaite, 'ESDP Police Missions: Meaning, Context and Operational Challenges' (2005) 10 *EFA Rev* 215.

Fund for a project on technical assistance, rehabilitation of the training centre, the provision of certain equipment and adequate training; on the other hand, the Council had adopted a CFSP action in the context of which the Union and its Member States contributed financially or in kind to provide the Democratic Republic of Congo with clearly specified law enforcement equipment, arms and ammunitions.[54]

4.2. Military Missions

There were two such operations, now concluded, namely the military operations on Congo (DRC/ARTEMIS)[55] and FYROM (CONCORDIA),[56] both conducted on the basis of UN Security Council resolutions. Currently, the only military operation undertaken within the ESDP framework is in Bosnia and Herzegovina under the name ALTHEA.[57] Its function, to provide deterrence and contribute to a safe and secure environment in that state, is to be carried out within a legal context already predetermined multilaterally at an international level: it is continued compliance with the General Framework Agreement for Peace, that is the Paris Agreement of 1995 between Bosnia and Herzegovina, Croatia and Federal Republic of Yugoslavia, that the EU mission is to ensure, in particular regarding the military aspects of peace settlements and boundaries issues defined in that agreement. In doing so, the EU took over from NATO whose Stabilisation Force had carried out that function since the entry into force of the above agreement. In assuming this role, the European Union was not only welcomed by the United Nations Security Council but authorised to become the legal successor the NATO-led Stabilisation Force.[58]

Once again, the position of Operation ALTHEA as part of the EU's wide-ranging approach is underlined in all the relevant documents: as High Representative Solana put it at the launch of the operation, 'EUFOR will mesh with the EU's substantial engagement in so many areas: a formidable economic commitment, a Police mission deployed, a solid political relationship'.[59] However, it is precisely this multiplicity of roles which renders the issue of coherence both crucial and complex as it applies to at least three levels of activities: first, within the ESDP framework in relation to the EU police mission which had already been operating

---

[54] Joint Action 2004/494/CFSP [2004] OJ L 182/41.

[55] Joint Action 2003/423/CFSP [2003] OJ L 143/50 following UN Security Council Resolution 1484 of 30 May 2003. The operation was launched pursuant to Council Dec 2003/432/CFSP [2003] OJ L 147/42.

[56] Joint Action 2003/92/CFSP [2003] OJ L 34/26. The operation was launched pursuant to Council Dec 2003/202/CFSP [2003] OJ L 76/43, extended by Council Dec 2003/563/CFSP [2003] OJ L 190/20.

[57] Launched under Council Dec 2004/803/CFSP [2004] OJ L 353/21, following Joint Action 2004/570/CFSP [2004] OJ L 252/10.

[58] Resolution 1575/2004 of 22 Nov 2004.

[59] His speech was delivered in Sarajevo on 2 Dec 2004: SO337/04.

in Bosnia and Herzegovina; secondly, within the EU framework in relation to the activities undertaken by the Community in the context of the stabilisation and association process; thirdly, within the international context in relation to NATO with whose assets and capabilities the EU operation is carried out.

The terms in which the EU draws upon NATO assets and capabilities were agreed upon in advance after long and tortuous negotiations concluded in March 2003 at the NATO Washington Summit and are commonly known by the name 'Berlin Plus'. As for the coherence between the EU activities in Bosnia and Herzegovina, it is not only the range of roles assumed within distinct but overlapping legal frameworks which may become problematic; it is also the multiplicity of actors whose involvement appears to serve different purposes and whose coexistence may appear to become difficult to manage. In addition to the main EU institutional actors and the bodies established within the CFPS framework, an EU Special Representative in Bosnia and Herzegovina was also appointed by the Council.[60] Rather than further overcrowding the scene, this new functionary is entrusted with the task of the overall coordination of the EU presence in the country. Suggesting that the EU institutions appreciate the challenge involved, Joint Action 2004/570/CFSP dedicates an Article on the issue of coherence of EU response; Article 7 reads as follows:

1   The operation shall be part of a closely coordinated EU presence in BiH. The Council shall ensure the maximum coherence and effectiveness for the EU effort in BiH. Without prejudice to Community competence, the EUSR [that is the EU Special Representative] shall promote overall EU political coordination in BiH. The EUSR shall chair a coordination group composed of all EU actors present in the field, including the EU Force Commander, with a view to coordinating the implementation aspects of the EU's action.
2   The EU Force Commander shall, without prejudice to the chain of command, take EUSR local political advice into account, especially with regard to matters for which the EUSR has a particular or stated role, and shall, within his/her mandate, endeavour to take into account any request from the EUSR.
3   The EU Force Commander shall liaise, as appropriate with the EUPM.

The above provisions seek to address the issue of coherence of EU action in all its ramifications. In terms of the legal tension regarding the Community participation and the ever-controversial issue of its legal 'subordination' to an intergovernmental framework, the reference to respect for Community competence in Article 7(1) of the Joint Action should also be read along with what appears to have become a provision *sine qua non* for ESDP operations: the Council 'notes' the intention of the Commission to direct, where appropriate, its actions towards achieving the objectives set out in the CFSP instrument establishing the mission.[61]

---

[60]   Joint Action 2004/569/CFSP [2004] OJ L 252/7.
[61]   Art 15 of Joint Action 2004/570/CFSP, n57 above.

That is not to say that the effort to address the legal issues in question in a comprehensive manner is necessarily convincing or practical: for instance, what precisely does the political nature of the coordination carried out by the Special Representative entail? And how is it to be exercised 'without prejudice to Community competence'? Be that as it may, and despite the fact that this sounds like a truism, all these arrangements can only be tested in practice. This is all the more so in the light of the nature of the operation and the seriousness of the political situation in the area: as time is of the essence and the stakes are very high, the EU actors in the area are likely to turn out to be rather unwilling to test the legal limits of the above arrangements.

4.3. Rule of Law Missions

The Union has already undertaken two initiatives in the area of the rule of law, one in Georgia and one in Iraq. The mission in Georgia, called EUJUST THEMIS, was actually launched in July 2004.[62] Comprising experts seconded by Member States and located in the Commission delegation in Tbilisi, the main aims of the mission are to provide urgent guidance for the new criminal justice reform strategy, support the overall coordinating role of the relevant Georgian authorities in the field of judicial reform and anti-corruption and support planning for new legislation such as a Criminal Procedure Code. In practical terms, a number of experts are located within the relevant Georgian authorities such as the Ministry of Justice, the General Prosecutor's Office and the courts.

The genesis of this mission is indicative both of the legal framework within which ESDP operations may develop and the variety of sets of rules which such operations are bound to involve. In particular, a Partnership and Cooperation Agreement with Georgia had been concluded by the EC and the Member States and entered into force in July 1999; in addition, the main framework for technical assistance to countries in Eastern European and Central Asia, that is TACIS, had been set out by means of Community law as early as 1991.[63] Not only is there assistance provided to Georgia under this framework, but the objective of strengthening the rule of law and supporting the establishment of a credible and efficient criminal justice system also featured prominently in the Country Strategy Paper adopted by the Commission in 2003.[64]

In other words, there had been a considerable body of economic support and legal infrastructure already provided for pursuant to Community instruments upon which the Union was able to draw in order to plan, structure and carry out

---

[62] Established under Joint Action 2004/523/CFSP [2004] OJ L 228/21.

[63] The current framework covering the period 2000–2006 is set out in Council Reg 99/2000[2000] OJ L 12/1.

[64] Country Strategy Paper 2003–2006, TACIS National Indicative Programme 2004–2006, Georgia, adopted by the Commission on 23 Sept 2003, at 21–22.

its ESDP operation. This is illustrated by the very content of the CFSP instrument which set up the Rule of Law Mission: on the one hand, Joint Action 2004/523/CFSP refers in its preamble to the aim of the Union to support the transition process in Georgia through the full range of EU instruments, referring expressly to the PCA and its implementation by EC programmes; on the other hand, an entire Article is dedicated to Community action. This provision is rather carefully worded: it seeks to point out the comprehensive nature of the Union approach whilst not appearing to impose a direct legal duty on EC institutions: in Article 11(1) of the Joint Action, the Council 'notes the intention of the Commission to direct its action towards achieving the objectives of this Joint Action, where appropriate, by relevant Community instruments', whereas in Article 11(2) the Council 'also notes that coordination arrangements are required in Tbilisi as well as in Brussels'.

The distinct nature of the second Rule of Law Mission launched by the Union is illustrated by its very name, that is the EU *Integrated* Rule of Law Mission *for* Iraq. Formally launched under the name EUJUST LEX in March 2005,[65] this operation covers police, rule of law and civilian administration matters, that is three out of the four priority areas defined by the Feira European Council.

The explosive situation in Iraq and the difficult political context within which the Union has sought to define its approach are illustrated in the somewhat cautious wording of the Joint Action: in its preamble, it points out that 'the success of the mission will depend on an effective strategic and technical partnership with the Iraqis throughout the operation'. Indeed, the genesis of this operation was very different from that in Georgia: the possibility of an integrated mission following the first post-war elections was stated in the Presidency Conclusions of the Brussels European Council of November 2004, following which the Council adopted a Joint Action setting up an expert team in order to explore the possibility of launching such a mission.[66] It was in this context that the Council launched the integrated mission. In terms of its functions, the Mission aims to train a total of approximately 770 judges, investigating magistrates and senior police and penitentiary officers, both in senior management and criminal investigation.

Once again, the sensitive political underpinnings of the mission and the effort of the Union to find its own distinct voice in international affairs are expressed:[67]

EUJUST LEX shall be secure, independent and distinct but shall be complementary and bring added value to ongoing international efforts, in particular of the United Nations, as well as develop synergies with ongoing Community and Member States' efforts . . .

The above provision constitutes a more forceful formulation of a statement included in the preamble to Joint Action 2004/909/CFSP; the latter also included

---

[65] Joint Action 2005/190/CFSP [2005] OJ L 62/37.
[66] Joint Action 2004/909/CFSP [2004] OJ L 381/84.
[67] Joint Action 2005/190/CFSP, n65 above, Art 2(5).

a reference to the security concerns in Iraq which was again developed into the following forcefully worded statement in the preamble to Joint Action 2005/190/CFSP:

> EUJUST LEX will implement its mandate in the context of a situation posing a threat to law and order, the security and safety of individuals, and to the stability of Iraq and which could harm the objectives of the Common Foreign and Security Policy as set out in Article 11 of the Treaty.

In the light of the above, it becomes less surprising that this training is envisaged not to take place in Iraq except pursuant to an amendment of the Joint Action and provided that the security conditions in Iraq so permit.[68]

4.4. Other Missions

In addition to its police mission in Kinshasa regarding the integrated police unit, the European Union has launched another mission in the Democratic Republic of the Congo. Under the name EUSEC DR Congo, its function is to provide advice and assistance for security sector reform by providing practical support for the integration of the Congolese army. [69] In carrying out this operation, the Union gives concrete form to the 'long-term conflict prevention and peace-building initiatives' in Africa which it had undertaken to adopt as a matter of principle.[70]

5. THE ECONOMIC ASPECTS OF SECURITY

The Treaty of Nice maintained a provision originally introduced at Amsterdam about cooperation in the area of armaments which reads as follows:[71]

> The progressive framing of a common defence policy will be supported, as Member States consider appropriate, by cooperation between them in the field of armaments.

Its opaque wording notwithstanding, this provision illustrates a developing awareness of the link between the emerging defence identity of the Union and the state of its defence industries. The approach of the Union institutions and the Member States to what may be called 'the economic aspects of security' has been, at best, ambivalent and fragmented. Defence industries in general have faced serious challenges in adjusting to the post-Cold War era. However, the European ones

---

[68] *Ibid*, Art 2(3)(2).
[69] Council Joint Action 2005/355/CFSP [2005] OJ L 112/20.
[70] See preamble to Council Common Position 2005/304/CFSP concerning conflict prevention, management and resolution in Africa [2005] OJ L 97/57, which repealed Common Position 2004/85/CFSP [2004] OJ L 21/25.
[71] Art 17(1)(3)TEU.

in particular suffer from considerable and chronic structural difficulties, including fragmentation, excess production capability, reduced budgetary resources and failure to engage in increasingly costly research.[72] The financial problems of national defence industries have become more serious in the light of intensified international competition.[73] Whilst there has been considerable momentum in other defence markets, particularly in the United States, to address fragmentation with consolidation, in the European Union any such discussion has been markedly difficult and slow.

In addition to the political reasons related to the reluctance of the Member States to engage in the consolidation of strategic industries, there are also legal reasons for this stagnation. Defence industries have been widely held to be entirely beyond the scope of the Community legal framework.[74] This view has been based upon a broad reading of Article 296(1)(b) EC: this 'wholly exceptional' provision[75] enables Member States to deviate from the entire body of Community law in order to protect the essential interests of their security by taking measures relating to the production of or trade in arms, munitions and war material.[76] In the light of this view, the Member States have been very reluctant to engage in any formalised effort of coordinating the management of their defence industries; instead, the existing attempts to consolidate have been market-led, fragmented in nature and limited in scope.[77]

It has been the European Commission, that is one of the least powerful institutions in the CFSP sphere, which has been the main advocate of a different approach. In two documents published in the late 1990s, it articulated a comprehensive approach to the restructuring and consolidation of the defence industries of the Member States. The first one, entitled *The Challenges facing the European Defence-Related Industry. A Contribution for Action at European Level*,[78] outlined the economic problems facing the fragmented European defence industries and the challenges they would have to face in a globalised economic environment. In the second document, entitled *Implementing European Union Strategy on Defence*

---

[72] See the overview in P Cornish, *The Arms Trade and in Europe* (London: Pinter, 1995) and, more recently, K Hartley, 'Defence Industries' in P Johnson (ed), *Industries in Europe: Competition, Trends and Policy Issues* (2nd edn, Cheltenham: Edward Elgar, 2003)

[73] See K Hartley, 'The Future of European Defence Policy: An Economic Perspective' (2003) 14 *Defence and Peace Economics* 107.

[74] See, for instance, the Commission Answer to Written Questions E–1568/04 and E–1569/04 not yet published in 05.

[75] See Case 222/84 *Marguerite Johnson v Chief Constable of the Royal Ulster Constabulary* [1986] ECR 1651 at para 27 and the Opinion of Jacobs AG in Case C–120/94 *Commission v Greece (FYROM)* [1996] ECR I–1513 at para 46.

[76] For a different reading of that provision, see P Koutrakos, *Trade, Foreign Policy and Defence in EU Constitutional Law* (Oxford: Hart Publishing, 2001) at 182–197. See also M Trybus, 'The EC Treaty as an Instrument of Defence Integration: Judicial Scrutiny of Defence and Security Exceptions' (2002) 39 *CMLRev* 1347.

[77] For a positive assessment of the relevant developments, see T Guay and R Callum, 'The Transformation and Future Prospects of Europe's Defence Industry' (2002) 78 *International Affairs* 757.

[78] COM(96)10 final, adopted on 24 Jan 1996.

Related Industries,[79] the Commission put forward a detailed strategy as to the legal measures required for the consolidation and restructuring of national defence industries. This was comprehensive in scope and covered areas such as public procurement, defence and technological development, standardisation and technical harmonisation, competition policy, structural funds, export policies and import duties on military equipment.

The Commission's initiative was noteworthy for a number of reasons.[80] First, it constituted the first serious attempt by an EU actor to define a common approach to what had been perceived to be the unmanageable sum of disparate national units. Secondly, the policies suggested by the Commission were based on a wide range of legal measures whose legal foundation varied: they included EC instruments, CFSP measures and even measures beyond the EU framework the adoption of which would require close coordination between EU and other international organisations. Thirdly, whilst the Community legal framework was suggested to be relied upon to a considerable extent, the Commission proposals left no doubt as to how acutely aware they were of the ways in which defence industries were intrinsically linked to the exercise of national sovereignty. In the context of public procurement, for instance, products defined as highly sensitive equipment which fall within the scope of Article 296(1)(b) EC would be exempted from the EC measures suggested therein; in addition, the proposals emphasised this specific character of the industries and accepted the need to provide for confidentiality of information as well as to maintain guaranteed sources of supply.

The approach advocated by the Commission was comprehensive in scope, coherent in substance and imaginative in its legal thinking. However, it did not succeed in dealing effectively with the reluctance of the Member States to engage in the restructuring of their defence industries. The Finnish Presidency Report of December 1999 made no suggestions about their consolidation, the Military Capabilities Commitment Declaration adopted by the General Affairs Council and Defence Ministers in December 2000 mentioned them in very general terms and the Presidency Conclusions of the Seville European Council in June 2002 included a mere reference to the 'prospects for cooperation on armaments'.[81] Five years after its original proposals, the Commission responded to a request by the European Parliament and revisited these issues. In a document adopted in March 2003, it reiterated the need for a coherent cross-pillar approach to the legal regulation of defence industries with special emphasis on standardisation, intra-Community transfers, competition, procurement, exports of dual-use goods and research.[82]

---

[79] COM(97)583 final, adopted on 12 Nov 1997.

[80] For analysis of these issues, see Koutrakos, n76 above, 207–220.

[81] Para 12.

[82] COM(2003)113 final, *European Defence—Industrial and Market Issues. Towards an EU Defence Equipment Policy* (adopted on 11 Mar 2003).

The failure of the Member States to address the problems of their defence industries and respond to the Commission's initiative has not enhanced the ability of the Union to develop a security and defence identity with some teeth.[83] The traditional view is that reduced defence budgets are largely responsible for the current state of the national defence industries: during the recent Iraqi war, the then US Ambassador to NATO, and now State Department Under Secretary, stated that 'Europe needs to reflect on the low level of defence spending, which has left most European militaries in a state of disrepair'.[84] However, the problems facing the defence industries of the Member States are also structural and due to duplication and fragmentation, as well as lack of strategic thinking in terms of interoperability, structures and programmes. In other words, it is the absence of substantive cooperation which has been at the core of the ability of the Union to develop its defence policy in meaningful ways.

It has been only recently that a number of developments have suggested the distinct possibility of a different approach. Prominent amongst them is the renewed focus on armaments cooperation illustrated in the Treaty Establishing a Constitution for Europe. The content of this Treaty will be examined in detail in the next chapter. However, its provisions on armaments cooperation are worth examining in the context of this analysis as they have already added momentum to cooperation in the area of defence capabilities. The proposed Treaty refers to the position of the Member States in tighter legal language: on the one hand, they 'shall make civilian and military capabilities available to the Union for the implementation of the common security and defence policy, to contribute to the objectives defined by the Council' (Article I–41(3)); to that effect, they 'shall undertake progressively to improve their military capabilities' (Article I–41(3)(2)). In practical terms, the Treaty Establishing a Constitution for Europe provides for the establishment of an agency under the name European Defence Agency (EDA) which is specialised in the area of defence capabilities development, research, acquisition and armaments. (Article I–41(3)(2)). The function of the Agency is set out in that provision in rather general terms: to identify operational requirements; to promote measures to satisfy those requirements; to contribute to identifying and, where appropriate, implementing any measure needed to strengthen the industrial and technological base of the defence sector; to participate in defining a European capabilities and armaments policy; to assist the Council in evaluating the improvement of military capabilities. The function of the Agency is envisaged as limited and circumscribed—the terms mentioned above ('identify', 'promote', 'participate' and 'assist') leave no doubt about this.

---

[83] See P Koutrakos, 'Inter-pillar Approaches to the European Security and Defence Policy—The Economic Aspects of Security' in Kronenberger, n4 above, 435.

[84] See interview with Nicholas Burns in *Financial Times*, 3 Mar 2005 at 4.

The EDA membership will be open to all Member States wishing to be part of it.[85] As far as its position in the Union institutional structure is concerned, the EDA is to operate under the authority of the Council and in liaison with the Commission where necessary. The precise tasks entrusted to the EDA are set out in Article III–311(1) as follows:

(a)   contribute to identifying the Member States' military capability objectives and evaluating observance of the capability commitments given by the Member States

(b)   promote harmonisation of operational needs and adoption of effective, compatible procurement methods

(c)   propose multilateral projects to fulfil the objectives in terms of military capabilities, ensure coordination of the programmes implemented by the Member States and management of specific cooperation programmes

(d)   support defence technology research, and coordinate and plan joint research activities and the study of technical solutions meeting future operational needs

(e)   contribute to identifying and, if necessary, implementing any useful measure for strengthening the industrial and technological base of the defence sector and for improving the effectiveness of military expenditure

At its meeting in Thessaloniki in June 2003, the European Council decided that the Council create an intergovernmental agency in the field of defence capabilities in the course of 2004. It is noteworthy that that was the same meeting at which the draft Treaty Establishing a Constitution for Europe, as elaborated by the European Convention, was presented to the European Council. Having responded to the European Council,[86] the Council adopted a Joint Action on the establishment of the European Defence Agency in July 2004.[87] The objective of the Agency is 'to support the Council and the Member States in their effort to improve the EU's defence capabilities in the field of crisis management and to sustain the ESDP as it stands now and develops in the future';[88] in doing so, it is to act without prejudice to either the competences of the EC[89] or those of the Member States in defence matters.[90] The Agency is given four functions, namely defence capabilities development, armaments cooperation, the European defence, technological and industrial base and defence equipment market and, finally, research and development. All in all, the Agency is entrusted with promoting coherence in place of fragmentation in the area of the defence industries. The main decision-making body of the Agency is the Steering Committee where all Member States, with the exception of Denmark, are represented.

---

[85] Art III–311(2) which also provides that the statute, seat and operational rules of EAD will be defined in a European decision adopted by the Council by qualified majority voting.

[86] See Council Dec 2003/834/EC creating a team to prepare for the establishment of the agency in the field of defence capabilities development, research, acquisition and armaments [2003] OJ L 318/19.

[87] 2004/551/CFSP [2004] OJ L 245/17.

[88] *Ibid*, Art 2(1).

[89] *Ibid*, Art 1(2).

[90] *Ibid*, Art 2(2).

An interesting feature of the new Agency is its reluctance to engage in grand rhetoric about the defence identity of the Union and its apparent determination to focus on tangible aspects of the management of defence industries. Its Chief Executive, Nick Witney, for instance, stated in an interview that 'the EDA's success will actually be determined by whether 24 defence ministers spend—at least at the margin—their individual budgets in a way which is a bit different from now'.[91] This attractively modest objective is borne out by the emphasis of the Agency's work on interoperability issues and potential for collaboration in a number of concrete projects which either have raised problems for European troops when deployed in the past or are already in progress in the context of *ad hoc* national collaborative programmes.

Another indication of a renewed interest in the economic aspects of security originates, again, in the European Commission. In response to the European Security Strategy, it has focused on 'the combined and relatively untapped strengths of the "security" industry and the research community in order to effectively and innovatively address existing and future security challenges'.[92] In doing so, it drew upon its previous proposals and has produced a document about the need to focus on research and development in the area of security.[93] This document endorses the conclusions of a report delivered by a group of Personalities in the field of security research convened by the Commission itself. The main objective of the Commission's proposal is the development of a coherent security research programme at EU level which would be 'capability-driven, targeted at the development of interoperable systems, products and services useful for the protection of European citizens, territory and critical infrastructures as well as for peacekeeping activities' whilst also directly linked to 'the good functioning of such key European services as transport and energy supply'.[94] To that effect, it proposes action in four different areas: consultation and cooperation with users, industry and research organisations under the umbrella of a European Security Research Advisory Board; the establishment of a European Security Research Programme implemented as a specific programme with its own set of procedures, rules for participation, contracts and funding arrangements; cooperation with other institutional actors established under the CFSP and ESDP framework and in particular the European Defence Agency; the establishment of a structure which would ensure the flexible and effective management of the European Security Research Programme.

The Commission's initiative on security research is as apposite as it is astute: not only has the principal influence of technology on the conduct of warfare been

[91] See his interview of 15 Apr 2005 at www.euractiv.com.
[92] COM(2004)72 final, *Towards a programme to advance European security through Research and Technology.*
[93] COM(2004)590 final, *Security Research: The Next Step.*
[94] *Ibid*, at 4.

highlighted in Afghanistan and Iraq,[95] but also research and development has been at the very centre of the Lisbon Agenda. According to this initiative agreed by the European Council in March 2000, the EU would become 'the most competitive and dynamic knowledge-driven economy by 2010'. This reform process had become largely moribund until a new Commission led by José Manuel Barroso took over in November 2004 and placed its reform at the centre of its policies. In addition, there is renewed interest in research and technology development in the light of the activities of the newly established European Defence Agency, which has also focused on this area.

Following up on its earlier initiatives, the Commission also issued a Green Paper on Defence Procurement.[96] Two elements of this document are noteworhty for the puproses of this analysis. First, the Commission raises the issue of the need for clarity in terms of the rules governing defence procumerent, including the possibility of an interpretative communication on Article 296 EC. Whilst it has taken more than 45 years for such a suggestion to be made, the Commission's proposal is significant; it entails that that Treaty provision cease to be shrouded in an interpretative vacuum and that defence industries be removed from the twilight zone between national sovereignty and Community law in which they have been left since the establishment of the Community. The fact that it is merely the possibility of such a position which has been raised, and only for discusssion, does not make this gesture any less significant. It indicates that the momentum in the development of the security and defence policy of the Union will inevitably have legal implications for a number of issues related to the defence industries which have been thought to be an area too sensitive to handle. That the Commission responded to this challenge should be applauded. The second feature of the Green Paper on Defence Procurement is its suggestion that a Community directive be adopted coordinating the award of contracts on goods, services and work. This measure would be based on a strict reading of Article 296 EC pursuant to the case law of the Court and would recognise the need for flexibility which would suit the specific features of the relevant contracts.

6. CONCLUSION

The European Security and Defence Policy has been fertile ground for grand statements ever since the Franco-British initiative of St Malo put it back on the agenda of Union development. However, the rhetoric about the role of the Union as a 'superpower', almost mesaianic in its promises, has been accompanied by the gradual realisation that a number of economic and practical factors, whilst

---

[95] See the special report on worldwide security in *Financial Times*, 9 May 2005, in particular at 2C.
[96] COM(2004)608 final.

ignored for a long time, were essential prerequisites for the effective development of ESDP. The establishment of the European Defence Agency and the renewed focus of the Commission on the economic aspects of security, along with the new Headline Goal 2010, illustrate this gradual shift. The European experience of the Iraqi crisis, rather perversely, has concentrated the minds of the Member States on the practical realities of security. Even within the context of the European Security Strategy, the areas which the Union has deemed of priority are those where structured frameworks of cooperation, already evolving, had been established involving both the Community and its Member States, namely the Mediterranean and the West Balkans. The ESDP operations undertaken so far are also underpinned by a cautious, yet effective, approach.

May these developments indicate that, amidst various calls for a grand design for Europe, the fundamentals of its security and defence identity are finally addressed? It is too early to tell. In relation to the EDA, the EU High Representative for CFSP described its prospects as follows: '[t]he EDA is the best hope to ensure that defence budgets are spent to better effect. It is ideally positioned to identify the intersection of economic and operational imperatives. It provides both a forum and a catalyst for member states to look at common problems and develop shared solutions. But its success will crucially depend on political will'.[97] Whilst almost a truism, it is political will which will determine the fate of the above early signs of a more focused approach to security. This will is shaped by a number of factors, both external, such as the transatlantic relationship,[98] and internal. The process leading to the adoption of the Treaty Establishing a Constitution for Europe, for instance, added considerable dynamism to the development of ESDP, as illustrated by the establishment of the EDA itself. As to whether the uncertain fate of that Treaty would undermine this process, this will be examined in the next chapter.

---

[97] Article entitled 'Europe should pool its defence resources', *Financial Times*, 24 May 2005, 15.

[98] See I Peters, 'ESDP as a Transatlantic Issue: Problems of Mutual Ambiguity' (2004) 6 *International Studies Review* 381.

Part V

A New Framework?

14

A New Framework for EU International Relations?

1. INTRODUCTION

O N 20 OCTOBER 2004, the Heads of State or Government of the enlarged European Union signed the Treaty Establishing a Constitution for Europe in Rome.[1] This was the outcome of the Intergovernmental Conference launched on 4 October 2003 which followed an extraordinary process of deliberation outlined in the European Council Laeken Declaration of December 2001.[2] In launching the Convention on the Future of Europe, it entrusted it 'to consider the key issues arising for the Union's future development and try to identify the various possible responses'. This Convention produced a draft Treaty Establishing a Constitution for Europe which its Chairman, the former President of the French Republic, Valéry Giscard d'Estaing, presented to the European Council at its Thessaloniki summit in June 2003.

For its entry into force, the Constitutional Treaty requires ratification by all the Member States. However, a declaration annexed to the Treaty provides that 'if, two years after the signature of the Treaty establishing a Constitution for Europe, four fifths of the Member States have ratified it and one or more Member States have encountered difficulties in proceeding with ratification, the matter will be referred to the European Council'. At the moment of writing, and following the negative votes in the French and the Netherlands referendums, the fate of the Constitutional Treaty is uncertain. At its meeting of 18 June 2005, the European Council adopted a declaration on the ratification of the Treaty which called for 'a period of reflection' which:

> will be used to enable a broad debate to take place in each of our countries, involving citizens, civil society, social partners, national parliaments and political parties. This debate, designed to generate interest, which is already under way in many Member States, must be intensified and broadened. The European institutions will also have to make their contribution, with the Commission playing a special role in this regard.

---

[1] [2004] OJ C/310/1.
[2] See C Closa, 'The Convention Method and the Transformation of EU Constitutional Politics' in EO Eriksen, JE Fossum and AJ Manendez (eds), *Developing a Constitution for Europe* (London: Routledge, 2004) 183.

According to this Declaration, it will be in the first half of 2006 that a decision as to how to proceed will be taken. However, its uncertain fate notwithstanding, the Constitutional Treaty is directly relevant to this book, as the international relations of the European Union were at the core of the work carried out in the Intergovernmental Conference. This is apparent in the Declaration of Rome, adopted at the European Council summit in October 2003. Launching the 2004 Intergovermental Conference (IGC), the Heads of State or Government of the Member States and the candidates for membership of the European Union and the Presidents of the European Parliament and Commission:

—reaffirm that the process of European integration is our continent's essential calling as the instrument for a more efficacious international role for the Union in supporting peace, democracy, prosperity and solidarity in all member States;

—highlight the fact that the imminent enlargement constitutes a historical moment which renders the Union richer in terms of identity and culture and extends the possibility of promoting shared values and of conferring weight and authority to Europe's role in world;

—confirm the importance of the commitment to endow the European Union with a constitutional text based on the equality of its States, people and citizens that assures the efficacy, consistency and efficiency of Europe's role in the world and take up the Convention's Draft Treaty as a good basis for starting in the Intergovernmental Conference;

—stress that the adoption of a Constitutional Treaty represents a vital step in the process aimed at making Europe more cohesive, more transparent and democratic, more efficient and closer to its citizens, inspired by the will to promote universal values above all through cooperation with international multilateral organisations and confirming a strong and balanced transatlantic relationship;

The focus on the international role of the European Union could not have been described in starker terms. Similarly, the agreement on the content of the Constitutional Treaty and its signature was seen as offering a unique opportunity to the Union to assert its identity on the international scene. The then President of the Commission, Romano Prodi, stated that 'today, Europe is reaffirming the unique nature of its political organization in order to respond to the challenges of globalisation, and to promote its values and play its rightful role on the international scene'.[3] The High Representative for the CFSP, Javier Solana, went even further: he wrote that 'neither Europe nor the world could afford the self-inflicted would of a rejection of the constitution'.[4]

Another reason for examining the Constitutional Treaty and its possible implications for the Union's international relations is the momentum that the long

---

[3] Speech delivered in Rome at the ceremony on the signing of the Constitutional Treaty (29/Oct/2004) (at the time of writing, available at http://www.europa.eu.int/constitution/speeches_en.htm).

[4] Article entitled 'The Case for Europe', *International Herald Tribune*, 28 May 2005.

process of its preparation has created. A previous chapter referred to recent developments in relation to the European Security and Defence Policy, including the area of armaments. The analysis of the Constitutional Treaty will confirm this emerging emphasis on this sphere of activities. In the chapters dealing with the foundations, regulation and management of EC international relations, reference was made to the relevant provisions of the Constitutional Treaty. The remainder of this analysis will focus on its implications for the overall conduct of EU international relations, with particular emphasis on the areas of foreign, security and defence policy.

2. REORGANISATION: VALUES, PRINCIPLES AND OBJECTIVES

The Constitutional Treaty is divided into four parts. Part I sets out the general framework within which the Union is to function. It includes the following: the definition and objectives of the Union, general provisions on fundamental rights and Union citizenship, the Union competences and the ways in which they are to be exercised, institutions and bodies, provisions for membership. Part II includes the Charter of Fundamental Human Rights which, therefore, is given primary law status. Part III sets out the various policies of the Union and the ways in which they are to be carried out by the EU institutions. Finally, Part IV includes the general and final provisions of the Constitutional Treaty.

The principal innovation introduced by the Constitutional Treaty appears to be the abolition of the pillar structure and the incorporation of the CFSP, along with Title VI TEU on Police and Judicial Cooperation in Criminal Matters, within the unitary structure of the European Union.

The CFSP provisions are laid down in Parts I and III of the Treaty and are preceded by the Union's objectives which are set out in Article I–3. The fourth paragraph of this provision refers specifically to the international posture of the Union. It reads as follows:

> In its relations with the wider world, the Union shall uphold and promote its values and interests. It shall contribute to peace, security, the sustainable development of the Earth, solidarity and mutual respect among peoples, free and fair trade, eradication of poverty and the protection of human rights, in particular the rights of the child, as well as to the strict observance and the development of international law, including respect for the principles of the United Nations Charter.

These objectives are expressly linked to the Union's values. It is recalled that safeguarding the 'common values' of the Union is already one of the CFSP objectives under Article 1(1) TEU. However, under the Constitutional Treaty, these values are defined for the first time in primary law. Article I–2 reads as follows:

> The Union is founded on the values of respect for human dignity, freedom, democracy, equality, the rule of law and respect for human rights, including the rights of persons belonging to minorities. These values are common to the Member States in a society in

which pluralism, non-discrimination, tolerance, justice, solidarity and equality between women and men prevail.

In addition to these values and objectives of the Union, the very first provision of Title V, that is the specific Title of Part III of the Constitutional Treaty governing the Union's external action, elaborates on the latter's principles and objectives. Article III–292(1) reads as follows:

> The Union's action on the international scene shall be guided by the principles which have inspired its own creation, development and enlargement, and which it seeks to advance in the wider world: democracy, the rule of law, the universality and indivisibility of human rights and fundamental freedoms, respect for human dignity, the principles of equality and solidarity, and respect for the principles of the United Nations Charter and international law.

What is significant about this list of uncontroversial principles is its application to the entirety of the Union's international relations, namely the CFSP, the Common Security and Defence Policy, the CCP, cooperation with third countries and humanitarian aid, economic, financial and technical cooperation with third countries, humanitarian aid, economic sanctions, the negotiation and conclusion of international agreements and the EU relations with international organisations and third countries.

Another illustration of the Treaty's attempt to provide coherence in EU international relations is the provision of Article I–292(1)(2) which reads as follows:

> The Union shall seek to develop relations and build partnerships with third countries, and international, regional or global organisations which share the principles referred to in the first subparagraph. It shall promote multilateral solutions to common problems, in particular in the framework of the United Nations.

Previous chapters of this book identified the commitment to multilateralism as a thread linking together the development of structured relations between the Union and the rest of the world and the emerging EU security identity. The express acknowledgment of this thread by the Constitutional Treaty is one of the positive aspects of its suggested reorganisation of the EU international relations.

The objectives of the EU international action are set out in Article III–292(2) as follows:

> The Union shall define and pursue common policies and actions, and shall work for a high degree of cooperation in all fields of international relations, in order to:
>
> (a) safeguard its values, fundamental interests, security, independence and integrity;
>
> (b) consolidate and support democracy, the rule of law, human rights and the principles of international law;
>
> (c) preserve peace, prevent conflicts and strengthen international security, in accordance with the purposes and principles of the United Nations Charter, with the principles of

the Helsinki Final Act and with the aims of the Charter of Paris, including those relating to external borders;

(d) foster the sustainable economic, social and environmental development of developing countries, with the primary aim of eradicating poverty;

(e) encourage the integration of all countries into the world economy, including through the progressive abolition of restrictions on international trade;

(f) help develop international measures to preserve and improve the quality of the environment and the sustainable management of global natural resources, in order to ensure sustainable development;

(g) assist populations, countries and regions confronting natural or man-made disasters;

(h) promote an international system based on stronger multilateral cooperation and good global governance.

The provision of an express set of principles and objectives overarching the entire range of the Union's relations with the rest of the world is an important innovation of the Constitutional Treaty. The definition of overall principles and objectives reflecting the Union's values, whilst unclear both in themselves and their interactions, adds clarity to the requirement of coherence in EU international actions.[5] In addition, it renders the process of defining the EU international posture more distinctive. In terms of its position within the system set out in the Treaty, this innovation reflects the emerging focus on the international identity of the European Union.

3. THE POSITION OF THE CFSP WITHIN THE CONSTITUTIONAL TREATY

Provisions on the Common Foreign and Security Policy are included in both Parts I and III of the Constitutional Treaty. The former describes the Union competence in Article I–16 and then includes a set of provisions in Article I–40 which is accompanied by a set of provisions on Security and Defence Policy in Article I–41; the latter Part deals with the detailed aspects of these frameworks.

As far as the CFSP in particular is concerned, its competence within the unitary structure of the Union is described in Article I–16. It reads as follows:

> The Union's competence in matters of foreign and security policy shall cover all areas of foreign policy and all questions relating to the Union's security, including the progressive framing of a common defence policy that might lead to a common defence.

Article I–16(2) sets out the general duty imposed upon the Member States in the CFSP area as follows:

[5] On how the EU values are reflected by the principles and objectives of the Union's external action, see M Cremona, 'Values in the EU Constitution: the External Dimension' in S Millns and M Aziz (eds), *Values in the Constitution of Europe* (Aldershot, Ashgate, 2005) (forthcoming).

Member States shall actively and unreservedly support the Union's common foreign and security policy in a spirit of loyalty and mutual solidarity and shall comply with the Union's action in this area. They shall refrain from action contrary to the Union's interests or likely to impair its effectiveness.

In its very first paragraph, Article I–40 defines the conduct of the Union's foreign and security policy as based on three factors, namely the development of mutual political solidarity among Member States, the identification of questions of general interest and the achievement of an ever-increasing degree of convergence of Member States' actions. This formulation constitutes a pragmatic depiction of the state and likely evolution of the Union's common foreign policy. It suggests that the mutual political solidarity is a *conditio sine qua non* for the effectiveness of the CFSP and that the convergence of national actions is the gradual outcome of a dynamic process. This is further acknowledged in Article I–40(5) where the commitment of the Member States to this process of convergence is described with greater clarity:

Member States shall consult one another within the European Council and the Council on any foreign and security policy issue which is of general interest in order to determine a common approach. Before undertaking any action on the international scene or any commitment which could affect the Union's interests, each Member State shall consult the others within the European Council or the Council. Member States shall ensure, through the convergence of their actions, that the Union is able to assert its interests and values on the international scene. Member States shall show mutual solidarity.

The remaining provisions of Article I–40 deal with the principal parameters of the CFSP institutional structure: a general duty of consultation within the European Council and the Council, as well as a duty of 'mutual solidarity', is laid down in Article I–40(5); European decisions become the main CFSP instrument the adoption of which will be unanimous in principle and pursuant to an initiative from a Member State or a proposal from the Union Minister for Foreign Affairs or on a proposal from the Minister with the Commission's support (Article I–40(6)); the Council may act by qualified majority subject to the unanimous authorisation by the European Council expressed in a European decision (Article I–40(7)).

3.1. Institutions

The Constitutional Treaty gives the European Council formal institutional status.[6] Whilst not exercising legislative functions,[7] its decision-making role, along with its central position in the CFSP sphere, is reaffirmed. As for the European Parliament, its role is again confined to regular consultation on the main aspects

---

[6] See Art I–19(1).
[7] Art I–21(1).

and basic choices of the CFSP and to being informed of its evolution.[8] The only improvement in its position is confined to the debate on progress in implementing the CFSP which, instead of being held annually, would now be held twice a year and would also include the common security and defence policy.

The CFSP provisions are, again expressly excluded from the jurisdiction of the Court of Justice. According to Article III–376:

> The Court of Justice of the European Union shall not have jurisdiction with respect to Articles I–40 and I–41 and the provisions of Chapter II of Title V concerning the common foreign and security policy and Article III–293 insofar as it concerns the common foreign and security policy.

> However, the Court shall have jurisdiction to monitor compliance with Article III-308 and to rule on proceedings, brought in accordance with the conditions laid down in Article III-365(4), reviewing the legality of European decisions providing for restrictive measures against natural or legal persons adopted by the Council on the basis of Chapter II of Title V.

One of the main innovations of the Constitutional Treaty is the establishment of the post of Union Minister for Foreign Affairs (EUMFA) whose responsibility will be to ensure, along with the Council, that the principles guiding the Member States in their conduct in the areas covered by the CFSP are complied with (Article III–294(2)). In addition, he/she is responsible for ensuring the consistency of the Union's overall external action (Article I–28(4)).

The Minister will participate in decision-making: in addition to a national initiative, it would be following a proposal by him/her, which may, but not is required to be, supported by the Commission, that the European Council and the Council will act (Article I–40(6)). The main characteristic of this post is its twin institutional hats: the Minister will chair the Foreign Affairs Council under Articles I–28(3) and III–296(1) whilst being one of the Vice-Presidents of the Commission under Article I–28(4). How is this going to work? The Constitutional Treaty seeks to distinguish between the activities which will fall within the Minister's responsibilities as a member of the Commission and those in the CFSP area. In terms of the former, Article I–28(4) states that the Minister will be bound by Commission procedures for the 'responsibilities incumbent on [the Commission] in external relations and for coordinating other aspects of the Union's external action'. There is a caveat attached to this provision and which applies 'only … for exercising these responsibilities': the Minister will be bound by Commission procedures 'to the extent that this is consistent with paragraphs 2 and 3 [that is his/her CFSP functions]'.

The functions that the Minister for Foreign Affairs is envisaged to assume go beyond those currently carried out by the High Representative for the CFSP under Article 26 TEU. They are considerable and multifarious: the Minister will be responsible for the implementation of the European decisions adopted by the

---

[8] See Art I–40(8) which mainly repeats the provision of Art 21(1) TEU.

European Council and the Council (Article III–296(1)); he/she shall represent the Union in CFSP areas and shall present the Union's position in international organisations and at international conferences (Article III–296(2)); as a coordinator, he/she is responsible for the organisation of the coordination of national actions in international organisations and at international conferences (Article III–305); as the representative of the Union, he/she will present the Union's position to the UN Security Council in cases where such position has been defined by the Union prior the UNSC meeting and following a request from those Member States which sit on the Security Council, one which they 'shall' put forward (Article III–305(2)(3); he/she may request the Political and Security Committee to deliver opinions to the Council (Article III–307(1)); he/she will be responsible for ensuring that the European Parliament is consulted and informed on the main aspects, basic choices and development of the CFSP and that its views are duly taken into consideration (Article III–304(1) and I–40(8)). Finally, the Commission delegations to third countries, which are to become Union delegations, will be placed under the authority of the Minister (Article III–328(2)).

A most important aspect of the role of the Minister is the assistance to be provided by a European External Action Service. This service will consist of officials from both the Council and the Commission as well as staff seconded from national diplomatic services of the Member States (Article III–296(3)). In relation to the establishment of that service, a Declaration attached to the Constitutional Treaty provides as follows:

> To assist the future Union Minister for Foreign Affairs, introduced in Article I-27 of the Constitution, to perform his or her duties, the Convention agrees on the need for the Council of Ministers and the Commission to agree, without prejudice to the rights of the European Parliament, to establish under the Minister's authority one joint service (European External Action Service) composed of officials from relevant departments of the General Secretariat of the Council of Ministers and of the Commission and staff seconded from national diplomatic services.

> The staff of the Union's delegations, as defined in Article III–230, shall be provided from this joint service.

> The Convention is of the view that the necessary arrangements for the establishment of the joint service should be made within the first year after entry into force of the Treaty establishing a Constitution for Europe.

In his/her coordinating role, the Minister for Foreign Affairs is expected to interact with various actors, namely the Ministers of Foreign Affairs of the Member States within the Council in cases where a common approach has been defined by the European Council o the Council in the meaning of Article I–40(5).

The provision of the post of the Minister for Foreign Affairs is one of the distinctive amendments of the CFSP institutional structure aimed at enhancing the unity of the Union's international representation, ensuring the coherence of its policies and raising the visibility of its distinct international identity. The idea of streamlining the process of the international representation of the Union in the CFSP areas is sensible, not least because the fragmentation mirrored by the currently rotating Presidency is without doubt unsatisfactory.[9] The functions of the Minister, as described above, are considerable, which is the main reason why the introduction of this post is seen as one of the main achievements of the Constitutional Treaty.

However, once again, the integration of structures does not necessarily do away with institutional complexity. The double-hatting attached to the new Minister is deeply problematic.[10] In practical terms, the choice of rendering the Minister both the Vice-President of the Commission and the chairperson of the Council was due to the inability of the Member States to decide between the conflicting proposals put forward at the Convention. However, it raises serious questions, not only of institutional loyalty, but also substantive efficiency across the range of areas falling within the Minister's responsibilities. In relation to international agreements, for instance, it is for the Minister rather than the Commission to recommend that the Council authorise the opening of negotiations, provided that the subject-matter of the agreement in question relates exclusively or principally to the common foreign and security policy.[11] However, it is precisely questions of delineation of responsibilities and, therefore, competence which have given rise to considerable disputes before the Court of Justice in the area of international treaty-making. Far from bringing clarity into the current state of affairs, the new provisions appear to replace existing legal tensions with new ones.

Another source of potential conflicts is related to the function of the Minister regarding the international representation of the Union, that is one of the reasons for the introduction of the new post. Far from being the only institutional actor whom the US State Department Secretary will have to call when he/she wants to speak to Europe, the Minister will coexist with the President of the European Council. Article I–22(2) provides that the latter 'shall, at his or her level and in that capacity, ensure the external representation of the Union on issues concerning its common foreign and security policy, without prejudice to the powers of the Union Minister for Foreign Affairs'. Its last qualification notwithstanding, this new provision indicates that the international representation of the Union will still be the responsibility of more than one actor the delineation of whose functions will have to be determined on an *ad hoc* basis, account being taken of the

---

[9] See B Crowe, *Foreign Minister of Europe* (London: The Foreign Policy Centre, 2005) where a positive overall assessment of the new post, albeit with a call for the new authority to be used cautiously. Also, see S Duke, 'The Convention, the Draft Constitution and External Relations: Effects and Implications for the EU and its International Role', EIPA Working Paper 2003/W/2, at 14–20.

[10] J Wouters, 'The Union's Minister for Foreign Affairs: Europe's Single Voice or Trojan Horse?' in JW de Zwaan, JH Jans and FA Nelissen (eds), *The European Union—An Ongoing Process of Integration: Liber Amicorum Alfred E. Kellermann* (The Hague: TMC Asser Press, 2004) 77.

[11] Art III–325(3).

subject matter of the issue in question.[12] In other words, whether the requirement that the Union 'speak with one voice' is met once again depends upon the substance of the Union's approach rather than the identity of the actor(s) expressing it. All in all, the tensions created by the existing system between the High Representative, on the one hand, and the Commissioner for External Relations[13] and the Presidency, on the other hand, are merely covered by a veneer of integration of functions. In fact, the tensions are maintained and the only variable which appears to change is the structure of the institutional setting against which they will arise.

3.2. Instruments

In defining the means by which the CFSP is to be carried out, the Constitutional Treaty refers to general guidelines, European decisions and systematic cooperation between Member States. As regards the articulation of the Union's approach, Article III–295(1)(1) refers to the 'strategic lines of the Union's policy' which the European Council may be called upon to define following its convention at an extraordinary meeting by its President, should international developments so require.

As for the formal legal armoury available to the CFSP, the existing CFSP instruments, namely common strategies, common positions and joint actions, are replaced by European decisions. These are defined in Article I–33 as 'non-legislative act[s], binding in [their] entirety' unless they specify their addresses, in which case they are binding only upon them. Such measures will state the reasons on which they are based. They are to refer to any proposals or opinions required by the Constitution (Article I–37(2)) and will be published in the Official Journal (Article I–38(2)).

Whilst joint actions and common positions are removed from the CFSP framework, their function is to be carried out by European decisions, a fact to which the wording of Article III–294(3) alludes: they shall define *actions* to be undertaken by the Union and *positions* to be taken by the Union. However, there is no reference to the function of common strategies; instead, their reincarnation in the post-Nice constitutional landscape by means of European decisions is not confined to the CFSP area and, instead, applies to the Union's external action in all its forms. Under Article III–293(1)(2), the European Council may adopt

---

[12] It has been argued that the tensions likely to arise between the Minister for Foreign Affairs and the President of the European Council would not be dissimilar to those raised in France between the President and the Prime Minister pursuant to the provisions on foreign policy under the French Constitution: see D Thym, 'Reforming Europe's Common Foreign and Security Policy' (2004) 10 *EFA Rev* 5 at 22.

[13] See F Cameron and D Spence, 'The Commission-Council Tandem in the Foreign Policy Arena' in DG Dimitrakopoulos (ed), *The Changing European Commission* (Manchester: Manchester University Press, 2004) 121.

European decisions on the strategic interests and objectives of the Union following a recommendation by the Council; such decisions may concern the Union's relations with a specific country or region or may be thematic in approach. Whilst common strategies have hardly been either the most effective or substantial CFSP instruments, the European decisions on the strategic interests and objectives of the Union do not appear to add any clarity to the legal machinery of the Union. What their provision in the Constitutional Treaty does is to confirm the very specific function of common strategies which was internal to the constitutional structure of the Union rather than external in terms of pursuing substantive effectiveness. That instrument sought to prove that the legally distinct nature of the pillars would not undermine the coherence of the external action of the Union, a point made redundant in formal terms in the light of the abolition of the pillar structure. However, the formalisation of the right of the European Council to adopt such European decisions in all the areas covered by the Union's external action is significant in legal terms in so far as it consolidates and further expands the decision-making function of the European Council in the Union' structure.[14]

In assuming the function of joint actions, European decisions will be adopted by the Council 'where the international situation requires operational action by the Union', whereas the remainder of Article III–297 generally reproduces the existing provisions of Article 14 TEU. There is one aspect in which the Constitutional Treaty differs from Article 14 TEU, in relation to a change in circumstances having a substantial effect on issues covered by a European decision, Article III–297(1)(2) provides that the Council '*shall* review the principles and objectives of that decision and adopt the necessary decisions'. In addition to removing the reference to the validity of the decision in the absence of a Council intervention, the new wording appears to necessitate it in such circumstances. The implications of this amended wording should not be overstated: it is doubtful whether the Council would become subject to a legal duty to adopt a decision should the circumstances change in the way envisaged in the provision in question. In assuming the function of common positions, European decisions are defined by Article III–298 in terms identical to those of Article 15 TEU.

It becomes clear from the above that, whilst the Constitutional Treaty appears to simplify the institutional machinery of the CFSP by providing for the single instrument of a European decision, in fact it merely transposes the existing instruments in a new setting. As the wording of Title V, Chapter II, Part III indicates, there is provision for a number of European decisions: those adopted by the European Council on the strategic interests and objectives of the Union; those adopted by the Council defining a Union action; those adopted by the Council defining a Union position; and those adopted by the Council implementing another European decision defining a Union action or position.

---

[14] For criticism of the emerging role of the European Council, see A Dashwood, 'Decision-making at the Summit' (2000) 3 *CYELS* 79.

3.3. Decision-making

The Constitutional Treaty maintains unanimity as the rule in decision-making within the CFSP framework. Whilst the wording of Article III–300(1)(2) makes it clear that the existing rule of Article 23(1)(1) TEU on abstentions is maintained, the reference to the second indent of the latter provision is removed. Whilst this omission is regrettable, it can only be inferred that the existing rule of abstention by members present either in person or represented would still apply. Of the existing exceptions to the rule of unanimity, the Constitutional Treaty maintains them by reformulating them as follows. First, in European decisions adopted by the Council in order to implement a European decision adopted by the European Council, the latter related to the Union's strategic interests and objectives. Secondly, in cases of European decisions adopted by the Council in order to implement a previous European decision also adopted by the Council, the latter defines a Union action or position. Thirdly, in cases of European decisions concerning the appointment of a special representative. In addition, two further exceptions are introduced: the first one applies to European decisions adopted by the Council on a proposal presented by the Minister for Foreign Affairs following a specific request to him/her from the European Council;[15] the second exception leaves it open to the European Council to authorise the Council by means of a European decision adopted unanimously to act by a qualified majority in cases not mentioned in Article III–300(2). This latter provision constitutes a variation of a procedure introduced at Maastricht and then removed by the Amsterdam Treaty: according to the then Article J.3(2), the Council, in adopting unanimously a joint action, could define areas in which subsequent measures could be adopted by qualified majority. This provision had never been invoked by the Council.

Article III–300(2) also maintains the 'emergency break' to voting by qualified majority currently applicable pursuant to Article 23(2) TEU. However, this is amended in two ways. On the one hand, a Member State may block the adoption of a European decision by qualified majority when invoking 'vital', rather than 'important', and 'stated' reasons of national policy. This new wording appears to illustrate more clearly the highly exceptional nature of this provision. On the other hand, should this occur, there is another procedural stage prior to the possible referral of the matter by the Council to the European Council: the Minister for Foreign Affairs is asked to search for a solution acceptable to the objecting Member State by engaging in close consultation with it. Whilst highlighting the important role that the Minister is envisaged to play under the new arrangements, this amendment sits uncomfortably with the tighter wording of the new formulation of the 'emergency break': the negotiation process entailed by his/her involvement renders the requirement for qualified majority voting redundant, hence undermining the actual significance of this derogation from the unanimity rule.

---

[15] Art III–300(2)(b). The request by the European Council may have been made either on its own initiative or following a proposal by the Minister for Foreign Affairs.

Finally, the Constitutional Treaty maintains the ability of the Union to respond speedily and efficiently to the often unpredictable pace of the development of international relation by convening an extraordinary meeting of the Council. Article III–299(2) confers upon the Minister of Foreign Affairs the right, either of his/her own motion or at the request of a Member State, to convene such a meeting in cases requiring a rapid decision within 48 hours or, in an emergency, within a shorter period.

3.4. Depillarisation

The so-called 'depillarisation' of the Union[16] is one of the main innovations of the Constitutional Treaty which is purported to simplify the Union's constitutional structure, integrate its disparate legal frameworks and facilitate the coherence of its policies. However, a close analysis of the Treaty's provisions reveals a somewhat different picture.

The much-maligned pillar structure, introduced by the Treaty on European Union at Maastricht and maintained in its two subsequent amendments at Amsterdam and Nice, sought to translate in legal terms a self-evident fact: whilst Member States were determined to broaden the scope of their cooperation in areas deemed to be closer to the functions traditionally performed by states, and whilst they thought it sensible to rely upon institutions and processes of the Community legal order, they wished to do so at a different pace, pursuant to a different mode of integration and in order to achieve qualitatively different objectives. It was this fundamental differentiation that the establishment of distinct, albeit interrelated, sets of rules sought to convey. Put in another way, the pillar structure sought to leave no doubt as to the distinct nature and implications of the activities falling within the scope of foreign, security and defence policy.

It was the complexities to which the management of the pillars gave rise that the depillarisation of the Union under the Constitutional Treaty sought to address. In its report to the President of the European Council, the Presidency of the Convention argued that the merger and reorganisation of the existing Treaties responded to the requirements of clarity and simplification.[17] However, whether the normative integration of the CFSP framework follows its organisational integration into a single structure is a separate issue. This requires an examination of the specific ways in which the competence of the Union in that area is construed within the scheme of the Constitutional Treaty. It was pointed out above that that competence was laid down in Article I–16. The position of this provision within the structure of the Treaty is noteworthy: it follows the listing of areas of exclusive competence (Article I–13), those of shared competence (Article I–14) and the separate provision on the coordination of economic and employment policies

---

[16] See Editorial Comments, 'The CFSP under the EU Constitutional Treaty—Issues of Depillarization' (2005) 42 *CMLRev* 325.
[17] See CONV 851/03 at para 7.

(Article I–15) and precedes the listing of the areas of supporting, coordinating or complementary action (Article I–17). This constitutes the first indication that the CFSP, whilst integrated within the unitary structure established by the Constitutional Treaty, is, in fact, distinguished by the other areas of activities over which the Union is to act. This is also illustrated by the provision of Article I–12, which lists briefly the different categories of the Union competence and refers to the CFSP separately too in paragraph (4).

The fact that the areas covered by the CFSP are mentioned in the same group of provisions dealing with other areas of EU competence might appear to create the illusion of integration. As the drafters of the TEU sought to convey the construction of the CFSP as an area of distinct normative features, so the drafters of the Constitutional Treaty sought to convey the construction of the CFSP as an area integrated within the unitary structure of the Union; put in another way, in the former case, the message that was sought to be conveyed was that the pillar structure was legally significant just as the message, in the latter case, is that the abolition of that structure is legally significant. In reality, the construction of Articles I–12 and I–16 signifies only the appearance of change: in legal terms, the CFSP is dealt with as an area of competence distinct from all the other types of EU competence.

This indicates that, whilst integrated in a single structure, in fact the content of the existing second pillar maintains its distinct normative features. In institutional terms, this is illustrated by the express elevation of the European Council to the position of the main decision-making institution alongside the Council.[18] In procedural terms, the legally distinct characteristics of the CFPS are acknowledged by the provision of Article III–308, that is the last provision of Section 1, Chapter II, Part III of the Constitutional Treaty, which reads as follows:

> The implementation of the common foreign and security policy shall not affect the application of the procedures and the extent of the powers of the institutions laid down by the Constitution for the exercise of the Union competences referred to in Articles I–13 to I–15 and I–17.

> Similarly, the implementation of the policies listed in those Articles shall not affect the application of the procedures and the extent of the powers of the institutions laid down by the Constitution for the exercise of the Union competences under this Chapter.

This provision transposes the ratio of Article 47 TEU into the new unified constitutional setting. This, along with the points made above, indicates that the integration of the CFSP rules into the apparently unified legal structure set out by the Constitutional Treat has been achieved principally in organisational rather than normative or substantive terms. Another issue raising questions of organisational and normative integration is the legal personality of the Union. The Constitutional

---

[18] See Art I–40(3) and (6). For what appears to be an increasingly wide range of activities falling within its scope, see Arts III–295 and, particularly, III–293.

Treaty provides for express legal personality in Article I–(7). It should be noted that the considerable exercise of the treaty-making power currently provided for in Article 24 TEU[19] has already rendered this issue a matter of somewhat theological debate. Whilst the new Treaty suggests a welcome clarification, it does not clarify the implications of the exercise of the Union's competence to negotiate and conclude international agreements in the area of the CFSP for the powers of the Member States to act on the external plane in that area. The provision on exclusivity laid down in Article I–13(2) not only fails to convey the subtleties of this principle as developed over the years by the Court, but appears to apply to CFSP agreements, too.[20] However, a number of factors might appear to militate against this view: the Union's competence in the CFSP is not strictly speaking shared,[21] the distinct normative characteristics of the CFSP are maintained and Article I–13(2), for all its failings, clearly seeks to codify the Court's case law on the development of the Community's external competence.

All in all, one of the characteristics of the Constitutional Treaty appears to be the discrepancy between the general rhetoric about Union competence and the differentiated ways in which such competence is construed. It is recalled, for instance, that, according to Article I–1(1), the Union is to exercise the competences conferred by the Member States 'on a Community basis'. This provision is as remarkable for its extraordinary vagueness as it is for its apparent disregard for the subtleties of the development of the Community legal order and the distinct terms in which the CFSP is articulated within the new Constitutional structure.

3.5. Primacy

The other principal feature of the new Treaty is the express provision for the primacy of EU law in its Article 1–6, which reads as follows:

> The Constitution and law adopted by the institutions of the Union in exercising competences conferred on it shall have primacy over the law of the Member States.

In dealing with one of the foundation principles of the Community legal order, one deeply entrenched in our vocabulary since the very early days of the Community, this provision incorporates it for the first time in primary law. However, this raises questions about its effects on CFSP provisions and measures adopted thereunder. The principle of primacy does not merely connote higher legal status; such an interpretation would ignore the subtleties developed in a very

---

[19] See Ch 11 above.

[20] Art I–13(2) reads as follows: 'The Union shall also have exclusive competence for the conclusion of an international agreement when its conclusion is provided for in a legislative act of the Union or is necessary to enable the Union to exercise its internal competence, or insofar as its conclusion may affect common rules or alter their scope'. See the analysis in Ch 3 above.

[21] See M Cremona, 'The Draft Constitutional Treaty: External Relations and External Action' (2003) 40 *CMLRev* 1347 at 1352.

long and complex line of case law which links the supremacy of primary and secondary Community law to the ability of national courts to apply it in national legal orders, either directly or indirectly, and, in any case, under the supervision of the European Court of Justice. Would this principle apply to CFSP rules? The Constitutional Treaty appears to suggest an affirmative answer despite the fact that the Court of Justice is expressly excluded from the CFSP sphere and, hence, will be unable further to develop the principle and supervise its application in the new constitutional setting. It is not only the self-evident sensitivity of the subject-matter of the CFSP rules, but also the content of the obligations they impose, that questions this assumption. For instance, Article I–40(5) requires that, prior to undertaking any action on the international scene or any commitment which could affect the Union's interests, each Member State consult the others within the European Council or the Council. Dashwood raises the 'hypothetical' example of a Member State joining with a third country in a military action overseas without first consulting its European partners formally, and wonders whether it could be argued before a national court that such action was illegal.[22] The wording of the Constitutional Treaty does not appear to rule out such an eventuality. And yet, both the exclusion of the jurisdiction of the Court and the Treaty's construction of the Union competence over the CFSP in quite distinct terms militate against the application of such principle.[23]

In that respect, two clarifications need to be made. First, to rely upon the exclusion of the Court's jurisdiction in order to argue against the application of the principle of primacy in the CFSP area is not to confuse the effect of a legal rule and its enforcement. However, primacy has been developed since the early 1970s on the basis of the constant interaction between the Community judiciary and national courts, not least because its application is related to the issue of validity of Community law, the absence of which only the Court of Justice may pronounce.[24] Secondly, it might appear to follow from the above that primacy of CFSP rules might have different legal implications in so far as it would be for the national courts to determine quite what status they would confer upon them within their own national legal orders.[25] However, such an effect would not amount to the application of the principle of primacy as we know it, not least because it clearly dissociates it from the objective of uniformity of law which has underpinned both its inception and development. Instead, it would constitute a call to national courts to endow CFSP rules with higher status, whatever that might mean. Should that be the case, the applicability of Article I–6 in the CFSP area would not only become a statement of rhetorical significance and very little

---

[22] A Dashwood, 'The Relationship between the Member States and the European Union/European Community' (2004) 41 *CMLRev* 355 at 380.

[23] See Editorial Comments, n16 above, at 327.

[24] See Case 314/85 *Foto-Frost v Hauptzollamt Lübeck-Ost* [1987] ECR 4199.

[25] K Lenaerts and D Gerard, 'The Structure of the Union according to the Constitution for Europe: the Emperor is Getting Dressed' (2004) 29 *ELRev* 289 at 307.

practical purpose, but it would also render the effectiveness of the CFSP a matter of continuous uncertainty.

The picture emerging from the above overview of the position of the CFSP within an apparently unified EU structure as set out in the Constitutional Treaty is not one of integration. It does not indicate normative integration because the Member States quite clearly did not wish to abandon their right to conduct their foreign relations as fully sovereign subjects of international law; it does not indicate substantive integration either, because procedural integration may not in itself entail integration of actions. Instead, the new constitutional arrangement is based on the nominal integration of structures which appears to have created an illusion of integration. Is this a case of the pillars being abolished in all but name? In fact, rather than merely contradicting the objective of clarity which this constitutional exercise had purported to serve, the proposed arrangements are more seriously problematic. As Denza points out, 'to introduce into the Treaties uncertainties over primacy in the conduct of foreign affairs, over the nature of Union competence to establish and conduct foreign policy and over whether the Member States retain any power of independent action in foreign affairs would call into question the separate nation status of the Member States' and concludes as follows: 'the changes are not necessary in order to create an effective common foreign policy and they would radically alter the balance of power between the Union and its Member States'.[26]

4. COMMON SECURITY AND DEFENCE POLICY

The examination of the European Security and Defence Policy in a previous Chapter suggested that that area has recently attracted considerable attention both by Union institutions and the Member States. The Constitutional Treaty illustrates this renewed interest, not least by renaming it the Common Security and Defence Policy (CSDP). This constitutes a change from 'European Security and Defence Policy', the title with which it has become known pursuant to various European Council Conclusions and other documents and initiatives. The substance of the amendments also attests to this renewed emphasis. As the provisions related to armaments cooperation were examined in a previous chapter, this section will focus on the position of the CSDP within the suggested new order and the detailed provisions governing its function.

The provisions on the CSDP are grouped together in a manner which distinguishes them from those on the CFSP. Therefore, in Part I, the main tenets of this policy are laid down in Article I-41, entitled 'Specific provisions relating to the common security and defence policy', immediately following the 'Specific provisions relating to the common foreign and security policy' in Article I-40. The

---

[26] E Denza, 'Lines in the Sand: Between Common Foreign Policy and Single Foreign Policy' in T Tridimas and P Nebbia (eds), *European Union Law for the Twenty-First Century—Rethinking the New Legal Order* (Oxford: Hart Publishing, 2004) Vol. 1, 259 at 272.

same organisational logic underpins Title III, where Section 2 is dedicated to the CSDP. These semantic changes are indicative of a renewed focus on the role of its security and defence in the context of the conduct of the Union's international relations. Article I–41(1) states that the CSDP 'shall be an integral part of the common foreign and security policy'.

4.1. Principles, Tasks and Procedures

In terms of the ESDP objectives as within the CFPS framework, the Treaty Establishing the Constitution for Europe retains the Nice formulation: the competence of the Union will cover 'the progressive framing of a common defence policy that might lead to a common defence' (Article I–16(1)). However, the specific provisions relating to that policy go considerably further: Article I–41(2) states that the progressive framing of a common defence policy '*will* lead to common defence, when the European Council, acting unanimously, so decides'. Apart from illustrating the sensitivity of the underlying issues, this textual discrepancy is of questionable significance in legal terms: even in the absence of the firm commitment in Article I–41(2), it is for the European Council to decide the establishment of a common Union defence, in which case it 'shall recommend to the Member States the adoption of such a decision in accordance with their respective constitutional requirements'.[27]

The function of the CSDP is given clarity by the Constitutional Treaty. It 'shall provide the Union with an operational capacity drawing on civil and military assets' to be used 'on missions outside the Union for peace-keeping, conflict prevention and strengthening international security in accordance with the principles of the United Nations Charter' (Article I–41(1)). This list, bringing together objectives currently set out in Article 11(1) TEU, seeks to provide broad categories of security activities, and is further defined in Article III–309(1) so as to include the following: joint disarmament operations, humanitarian and rescue tasks, military advice and assistance tasks, conflict prevention and peacekeeping tasks, tasks of combat forces in crisis management including peace-keeping and post-conflict stabilisation. This non-exhaustive listing of activities covers all those currently laid down in Article 17(2) TEU and goes even further in terms of specificity; for instance, it is the first time that conflict prevention is expressly mentioned in primary law.

There is another aspect of the formulation laid down in Article I–41(2) which is noteworthy. A Protocol with a sole article provides that 'the Union shall draw up, together with the Western European Union, arrangements for enhanced cooperation between them'. According to its preamble, this was drawn up by the High Contracting Parties 'bearing mind the need to implement fully the provisions of

---

[27] Art I–41(2). See F Naert, 'European Security and Defence in the EU Constitutional Treaty' (2005) 10 *Journal of Conflict and Security Law* 187 at 192 which links the wording of this provision to the future role of the neutral States, should a common defence be established.

Article I–41(2) of the Constitution'. The scope for such cooperation is not clarified further.

The Minister for Foreign Affairs has an important role in the area of security
and defence as he/she is entrusted with ensuring coordination of the civilian and
military aspects of CSDP tasks, albeit under the authority of the Council and in
close and constant contact with the Political and Security Committee.[28] As for
decision-making, the rule of unanimity is imposed upon the Council, which is to
adopt European Decisions pursuant to a proposal from the Minister for Foreign
Affairs or an initiative from a Member State.[29]

4.2. Flexibility

One of the central features of the Constitutional Treaty is the acknowledgment
that defence and security tasks may be carried out by groups rather than the totality of the Member States within a framework laid down by Union law. This may
take one of three forms. First, a group of Member States may assume the role of
implementing a CDSP task. In doing so, the Member States involved will 'protect
the Union's values and serve its interests'.[30] Article III–310 makes this conditional
upon two main factors: on the one hand, the relevant Member States should be
both willing to undertake and have the necessary capability for the task in question; on the other hand, they will carry out this function within the framework of
the European decisions adopted by the Council. In addition, a number of procedural duties are imposed upon the Member States in question: they are to keep the
Council regularly informed of progress either on their own initiative or at the
request of another Member State; they are to inform the Council immediately in
cases where the completion of the required task would entail 'major consequences
or require amendment of the objective scope and conditions determined for the
task in the [relevant] European decisions'.[31]

The provision of such a role for Member States is significant in so far as it introduces a degree of flexibility in the conduct of defence policy:[32] the Union would
be enabled to assert its identity on the international scene without necessarily having first to develop a fully-fledged operational structure. In the same vein, an element of inevitability is also present: to enable the willing and the able Member
States to assume, in a legal and formalised manner, security and defence functions
which they could otherwise assume beyond the CSDP framework is gradually to
render the development of that framework less controversial.

It would not be unique to the Union legal order for states to assume functions
of the Union: it is recalled that in the Community legal order, Member States may

---

[28] Art III–309(2).

[29] Art I–41(4).

[30] Art I–41(5).

[31] In this case, the necessary European decisions would be adopted by the Council.

[32] J Howorth, 'The European Draft Constitutional Treaty and the Future of the European Defence
Initiative: A Question of Flexibility' (2004) 9 *EFA Rev* 483.

be required to act as the Community's legal agents and exercise the latter's competence, for instance by participating in international agreements which provide only for the accession of states.[33] The obvious differences regarding the legal implications of such cases aside, the provision of Article III–310 is noteworthy for the considerable margin of discretion it enables the participating Member States to exercise: it is for them to agree on the management of the CDSP task entrusted to them under the relevant European Decision, albeit in association with the Union Minister. In addition to the presumed informality, in procedural terms, of its exercise, their discretion becomes all the more apparent in the light of the weak nature of the procedural duties imposed upon them by Article III–310(2): it is noteworthy, for instance, that the participating Member States should merely 'inform' the Council of their progress rather than consult with it.

The second way in which groups of Member States may act separately from the remaining states is through the mechanism of permanent structured cooperation. There are two criteria which the participating Member States should meet: they should have military capabilities which themselves fulfil higher criteria and they should have more binding commitments to one another in the CSDP area. As to its material scope, Article I–41(6) make it applicable to 'the most demanding missions'.

In terms of decision-making, permanent structured cooperation is to be established by means of a European decision following the notification of the participating states' intention to the Council and the Minister for Foreign Affairs. Following consultation with the Minister, the Council is to act by a qualified majority defined in terms drawn upon the general rule introduced under Article I–25: at least 55 per cent of the participating Member States comprising at least 65 per cent of their population.[34] The same procedure applies to the participation of any other states at a later stage as well as the suspension of the participation of states no longer fulfilling the relevant criteria or no longer able to meet the relevant commitments. In both cases, the required European decision is to be adopted only by Council members representing the participating Member States. The formalisation of the participation of Member States in the permanent structured cooperation notwithstanding, the wording of Article III–312 suggests that it is for them, rather than the Union institutions, to decide on participation. For instance, in cases where a state decides to join this mechanism at a later stage, the European decision adopted by the Council is to 'confirm' its participation.[35] Similarly, in cases where a state wishes to withdraw, the Council 'shall take note that the Member State in question has ceased to participate', albeit not in a European decision.[36]

---

[33] See *Opinion 2/91* (re: *Convention No 170 ILO on safety in the use of chemicals at work*) [1993] ECR I–1061, para 5.

[34] A blocking minority is defined as the minimum number of participating states representing more than 35% of the population of those states, plus one more member (Art III–312(3) (4)).

[35] Art III–312(3) subpara 2.

[36] Art III–312(5).

In contrast to the decision-making procedure provided for the establishment and membership of the permanent structured cooperation, the voting rule for the European decisions and recommendations of the Council within that mechanism is unanimity,[37] whereas there is no reference to any contribution by the Minister of Foreign Affairs.

The mechanism of permanent structured cooperation is set out in Article III–312. To the criteria mentioned in Article I–41(6), this provision adds another one related to the commitments on military capabilities that the participating Member States should make in compliance with Protocol 23 annexed to the Treaty. The provisions of that Protocol are noteworthy. Its rather long preamble seeks to assuage fears that the enhanced military capacity of the Union might undermine NATO. To that effect, and having repeated the qualifications already mentioned in the Constitutional Treaty about the fundamental defence policy choices of the Member States, it is stated that 'a more assertive Union role in security and defence matters will contribute to the vitality of a renewed Atlantic Alliance'. As for the main provisions of the Protocol, two sets of commitments are laid down. The first deals with the general objectives of the mechanism of permanent structured cooperation which, under Article 1 of the Declaration, include the following:

(a) proceed more intensively to develop its defence capacities through the development of its national contributions and participation, where appropriate, in multinational forces, in the main European equipment programmes, and in the activity of the . . . (European Defence Agency), and

(b) have the capacity to supply by 2007 at the latest, either at national level or as a component of multinational force groups, targeted combat units for the missions planned, structured at a tactical level as a battle group, with support elements including transport and logistics, capable of carrying out the tasks referred to in Article III–309, within a period of 5 to 30 days, in particular in response to requests from the United Nations Organisation, and which can be sustained for an initial period of 30 days and be extended up to at least 120 days.

The second set of commitments that Member States need to undertake in order to be able to participate in the mechanism of permanent structured cooperation are of a more specific nature. They are worth-quoting in full:[38]

(a) cooperate, as from the entry into force of the [Constitutional Treaty], with a view to achieving approved objectives concerning the level of investment expenditure on defence equipment, and regularly review those objectives, in the light of the security environment and of the Union's international responsibilities;

---

[37] Art III–312(6) which also provides that unanimity is to be constituted by the votes of the representatives of the participating Member States only.

[38] Art 2 of the Declaration.

(b)   bring their defence apparatus into line with each other as far as possible, particularly by harmonising the identification of their military needs, by pooling and, where appropriate, specialising their defence means and capabilities, and by encouraging cooperation in the fields of training and logistics;

(c)   take concrete measures to enhance the availability, interoperability, flexibility and deployability of their forces, in particular by identifying common objectives regarding the commitment of forces, including possibly reviewing their national decision-making procedures;

(d)   work together to ensure that they take the necessary measures to make good, including through multinational approaches, and without prejudice to undertakings in this regard within the North Atlantic Organisation, the shortfalls perceived in the framework of the 'Capability Development Mechanism';

(e)   take part, where appropriate, in the development of major joint or European equipment programmes in the framework of the European Defence Agency.

The above commitments are expressed in such terms that their effectiveness relies entirely upon the discretion of the participating Member States. However, qualified though their fulfilment is envisaged to be, it is significant that they should be set out in the Protocol: their clear focus on military capabilities and the relative detail in which this is expressed is yet another indication of the Union's increasingly prominent focus on the economic and technical aspects of defence policy. As such, the requirements laid down in the Protocol establish a link between the participating Member States and the Council, on the one hand, and the European Defence Agency, on the other: the latter shall contribute to the regular assessment of participating states' contributions regarding their capabilities and shall report at least once a year. These reports 'may serve as a basis' for Council recommendations and European decisions adopted pursuant to Article III–312.[39]

Finally, the Constitutional Treaty introduces a solidarity clause in the CSDP. This is distinct from the general solidarity clause laid down in Article I–43 which refers to cases where a Member State is the object of a terrorist attack or the victim of a natural or man-made disaster.[40] In the area of the CSDP in particular, Article I–41(7) provides as follows:

If a Member State is the victim of armed aggression on its territory, the other Member States shall have towards it an obligation of aid and assistance by all the means in their

---

[39] Art 3 of the Protocol on Permanent Structured Cooperation established by Art I–41(6) and Art III–312 the Constitution.

[40] Art I–43(1) reads as follows: '1.   The Union and its Member States shall act jointly in a spirit of solidarity if a Member State is the object of a terrorist attack or the victim of a natural or man-made disaster. The Union shall mobilise all the instruments at its disposal, including the military resources made available by the Member States, to: (a) prevent the terrorist threat in the territory of the Member States; protect democratic institutions and the civilian population from any terrorist attack; assist a Member State in its territory, at the request of its political authorities, in the event of a terrorist attack; (b) assist a Member State in its territory, at the request of its political authorities, in the event of a natural or man-made disaster.' Art III–329 provides for the implementation of this clause.

power, in accordance with Article 51 of the United Nations Charter. This shall not prejudice the specific character of the security and defence policy of certain Member States.

Commitments and cooperation in this area shall be consistent with commitments under the North Atlantic Treaty Organisation, which, for those States which are members of it, remains the foundation of their collective defence and the forum for its implementation.

This is one of the general CSDP provisions which is not elaborated upon any further in Part III. The scope of the duty of Member States 'to aid and assist by all the means in their power' is very broad[41] and appears to cover military assistance against the aggressor. Whilst stronger than the existing clause of Article 17 TEU,[42] this formulation is problematic. What is the scope of 'aid and assistance by all the means in [the Member States'] power'? However, how would a broad interpretation be reconciled with the neutrality of certain of the Member States without undermining the cohesiveness and effectiveness of the action it envisages?[43] And if the scope of this clause were to be interpreted broadly, would the criterion pursuant to which Member States are to express their assistance be defined from an objective point of view? In other words, does this provision impose a legal duty, one that is to have primacy over national law pursuant to Article I–6, to utilise their military capabilities in order to assist another Member State under attack? The nature of the duty is such as to render its interpretation subject to inherently indeterminate criteria: for instance, in a case where a Member State argues that, whilst enjoying considerable military capabilities, it is not within its power to deploy them for reasons related to their readiness, it is impossible to envisage any meaningful discussion in the Council as to the validity of this claim. This is all the more so considering that, should the extreme circumstances envisaged under Article I–41(7) arise, time would be of the essence and the pace of events would be such as to confine any negotiations between the Member States and third states to the political sphere. Another question raised by the formulation of Article I–41(7) has to do with the very definition of the event the occurrence of which is purported to trigger the application of the solidarity clause: what would happen in a case where the Member States under the duty to assist had doubts about the existence and nature of the armed aggression claimed by the state under attack? In the case of Imia, for instance, between Greece and Turkey or that of the Leila islet, between Spain and Morocco, it became clear very soon that the claim of the two Member States that their territorial sovereignty had been under attack was

---

[41] Art 51 UN Charter reads as follows: '[n]othing in the present Charter shall impair the inherent right of individual or collective self-defence if an armed attack occurs against a Member of the United Nations, until the Security Council has taken measures necessary to maintain international peace and security. Measures taken by Members in the exercise of this right of self-defence shall be immediately reported to the Security Council and shall not in any way affect the authority and responsibility of the Security Council under the present Charter to take at any time such action as it deems necessary in order to maintain or restore international peace and security'.

[42] See J Howorth, 'The European Draft Constitutional Treaty and the Future of the European Defence Initiative' (2004) 9 *EFA Rev* 483 at 493–4.

[43] See the analysis in Naert, n27 above, at 193 *ff*.

not taken seriously by the other Member States. Would things turn out to be different just because there was a provision, albeit broadly worded, in the Constitutional Treaty?

The above does not mean to suggest that the inclusion of the solidarity clause of the type set out in Article I–41(7) is completely irrelevant: no meaningful foreign and security policy, let alone common defence policy, would ignore the issue of the territorial integrity of the Member States. To that effect, the solidarity clause is indicative of not only the sharper focus of the Constitutional Treaty on defence policy but also the momentum that the security and defence policy of the Union appears to have gathered.   However, the very subject matter of this clause inevitably highlights the inherent limitations of its applications: the extreme circumstances to which it refers and the nature of the duty which it entails render the expression of solidarity by Member States, or the absence thereof, beyond the limits of the legal sphere and place it firmly within the sphere of high politics. To that effect, it is noteworthy that no reference should be made to any role for the Union institutions.

5. CONCLUSION

In the Laeken Declaration on the Future of European Union in December 2001, the European Council referred to 'Europe's new role in a globalised world'. It raised the question 'what is Europe's role' and, then, asked rhetorically: '[d]oes Europe not, now that is finally unified, have a leading role to play in a new world order, that of a power able both to play a stabilising role worldwide and to point the way ahead for many countries and peoples?'

The provisions of the Constitutional Treaty examined in this chapter were not intended to answer this question. Instead, they aimed at providing the legal framework which would facilitate the assumption of this role by the Union institutions. In doing so, they addressed the issue of the effectiveness and coherence of EU international relations in the context of the task of simplification as laid down in the Laeken Declaration. Setting out the agenda for the work of the Convention for the Future of Europe, it stated that 'the image of a democratic and globally engaged Europe admirably matches citizens' wishes'. It went on to state that citizens 'want to see Europe more involved in foreign affairs, security and defence, in other words, greater and better coordinated action to deal with trouble spots in and around Europe and in the rest of the world'.

The legal framework within which the European Union has carried out its international relations from Maastricht to Amsterdam and, then, Nice is indeed complex. For instance, the legal possibility of the conclusion of an international agreement by the European Community, the European Union and the Member States, that is 27 parties, is unlikely to set the hearts of Europeans with enthusiasm for the European project. And yet, the complexity of the Union structures illustrates the constitutional idiosyncrasies of the EU legal order. The abandonment of the existing structures in organisational terms neither removes the underlying reasons for their existence in the first place nor guarantees the coherence and effectiveness of EU action. For instance, as the analysis in this chapter suggested, the pillars would be present in all but name, as was the current CFSP instruments. Furthermore, the existing questions about the coherence between Community and Union actions and the respective functions of the institutions have been replaced by a whole different set of questions. This conclusion also applies to the definition of the Union's external competences in Part I of the Constitutional Treaty: the analysis in an earlier chapter showed that the attempt to transpose the complex case law of the Court of Justice into Article I–13 failed to convey the subtleties of the existing state of law.

This brings us back to 'Europe's new role' as set out in the Laeken Declaration. That document went on to point out the following:

> Now that the Cold War is over and we are living in a globalised, yet also highly fragmented world, Europe needs to shoulder its responsibilities in the governance of globalisation. The role it has to play is that of a power resolutely doing battle against all violence, all terror and all fanaticism, but which also does not turn a blind eye to the world's heartrending injustices. In short, a power wanting to change the course of world affairs in such a way as to benefit not just the rich countries but also the poorest. A power seeking to set globalisation within a moral framework, in other words to anchor it in solidarity and sustainable development.

These are grand words and their implementation requires more than the removal of the appearance of complexity from the Treaty structures. It should not be forgotten that the existing rules have proved sufficiently flexible to enable the Union to assume various significant roles in its international relations. This book has focused on the content, potential and limitations of those rules. Within the Community legal order, for instance, it has shown how, through principle and pragmatism, the Community institutions and the Member States have managed their coexistence under the creative supervision of the Court of Justice. In the area of the Common Foreign and Security Policy, whilst highlighting the inherent limits of the relevant legal rules, the above analysis pointed out their potential within the actively interacting pillars. As for the European Security and Defence Policy, the clarity and effectiveness of its emerging identity have been shown to depend more on concrete steps about its capabilities and considerably less on grand security concepts.

The analysis so far has highlighted the dynamic and multi-layered nature of EU international relations law. This has been one of the main themes of this book. It is recalled that this started off with a reference to the comment made by Anthony Aust about the complexity of EU external relations rules. The analysis in the previous chapters hardly refuted that claim. However, the emphasis on the complexity of the rules should not underestimate the overall contribution of the other components of the system of EU external relations. This book has sought to highlight the rules, principles, procedures, actors and practices pertaining to the relationships of the Union with the outside world and, mainly, focus on the various threads which bring them together. It is pursuant to the interaction between these factors that one should assess the extent to which the Union carries out its international relations in an efficient and legally sensible manner. As this interaction is both constant and evolving, its legal implications raise various questions. This book has sought to illustrate how the complexity of legal rules and the state of uncertainty prevailing in certain areas have not prevented the system of EU international relations from developing in a dynamic manner and dealing with theoretical problems both flexibly and pragmatically. For instance, whilst there is considerable debate about the issue of the international legal personality of the Union, there has been a steadily growing number of agreements concluded under Article 24 TEU; whilst the legal framework on defence has been far from detailed, there has been growing emphasis on the development of the security and defence policy of the Union and some promising signs regarding its economic aspects. Similar conclusions were reached in the context of EC external relations regarding the flexible construction of exclusivity by the Court of Justice and the development of various mechanisms ensuring the management of mixity. In addition to the various mechanisms emerging as a matter of practice, the multilayered nature of EC international relations law also relies upon the interaction of various legal developments, such as the wide jurisdiction of the Court of Justice, the differentiated construction of direct effect, the articulation of alternative ways of applying international rules, the emerging role of national courts. All in all, the dynamic and multi-layered legal system governing EU international relations is considerably more subtle in its continuous development and implications than any conception of the Union as originating in Mars or Venus may possibly convey.

Bibliography

ABEYRATNE, R, 'The Decision of the European Court of Justice on Open Skies and Competition Cases' (2003) 26 *World Competition* 335.

ADAMANTOPOULOS, K and PEREYRA-FRIEDRICHSEN, MJ, *EU Anti-Subsidy Law and Practice* (Bembridge, Palladian Law Publishing, 2001).

ALLEN, D, RUMMEL, R and WESSELS, W (eds), *European Political Cooperation: Towards a Foreign Policy for Western Europe* (London, Butterworth Scientific, 1982).

ANDERSON, DWK and DEMETRIOU, M, *References to the European Court* (2nd edn, London, Sweet & Maxwell, 2002).

ANTONIADIS, A, 'The Participation of the European Community in the World Trade Organisation: An External Look at European Union Constitution-Building' in T TRIDIMAS and P NEBBIA (eds), *European Law for the Twenty-First Century: Rethinking the New Legal Order* (Oxford, Hart Publishing, 2004) i, 321.

APPELLA, A, 'Constitutional Aspects of Opinion 1/94 of the ECJ Concerning the WTO Agreement' (1996) 45 *International and Comparative Law Quarterly* 440.

ARNULL, A, 'The Use and Abuse of Article 177 EEC' (1989) 52 *Modern Law Review* 622.

——, 'Challenging EC Antidumping Regulations: The Problem of Admissibility' (1992) 13 *European Competition Law Review* 73.

——, 'Left to Its Own Devices? Opinion 2/94 and the Protection of Fundamental Rights in the European Union' in A Dashwood and C Hillion (eds), *The General Law of EC External Relations* (London, Sweet & Maxwell, 2000) 61.

——, 'Private Applicants and the Action for Annulment since *Codorniu*' (2001) 38 *Common Market Law Review* 7.

——, et al, *Wyatt and Dashwood's European Union Law* (4th edn, London, Sweet & Maxwell, 2000).

AUST, A, *Modern Treaty Law and Practice* (Cambridge, Cambridge University Press, 2000).

BABARINDER, O and FABER, G, 'From Lomé to Cotonou: Business as Usual?' (2004) 9 *European Foreign Affairs Review* 27.

BAIL, C, DECAESTECKER, J-P and JOERGENSEN, M, 'European Union' in C BAIL, R FALKNER and H MARQUARD (eds), *The Cartagena Protocol on Biosafety: Reconciling Trade in Biotechnology with Environment and Development?* (London, Royal Institute of International Affairs, 2002) 166.

BALDWIN, DA, *Economic Statecraft* (Princeton, NJ, Princeton University Press, 1985).

BARENTS, R, 'The European Communities and the Commodity Organisations' (1984) 10 *Legal Issues of European Integration* 77.

BARTELS, L, *Human Rights Conditionality in the EU's International Agreements* (Oxford, Oxford University Press, 2005).

BEARCE, DH, 'Institutional Breakdown and International Cooperation: The European Agreement to Recognize Croatia and Slovenia' (2002) 8 *European Journal of International Relations* 471.

BENVENISTI, E, 'Judicial Misgivings Regarding the Application of International Law: An Analysis of Attitudes of National Courts' (1993) 4 *European Journal of International Law* 159.

BERDIYEV, B, 'The EU and Former Soviet Central Asia: An Analysis of the Partnership and Cooperation Agreements' (2003) 22 *Yearbook of European Law* 463.

BERKEY, JO, 'The European Court of Justice and Direct Effect for the GATT: A Question Worth Revisiting' (1998) 9 *European Journal of International Law* 626.

BETLEM, G, 'The Doctrine of Consistent Interpretation-Managing Legal Uncertainty' (2002) 22 *Oxford Journal of Legal Studies* 397.

BIEBER, R, 'Democratic Control of International Relations of the European Union' in E Cannizzaro (ed), *The European Union as an Actor in International Relations* (The Hague, Kluwer Law International, 2002) 105.

BIONDI, A, 'Advertising Alcohol and the Free Movement Principle: The *Gourmet* Decision' (2001) 26 *European Law Review* 616.

BISCOP, S, 'Able and Willing? Assessing the EU's Capacity for Military Action' (2004) 9 *European Foreign Affairs Review* 509.

BJOERKLUND, M, 'Responsibility in the EC for Mixed Agreements - Should Non-Member Parties Care?' (2001) 70 *Nordic Journal of International Law* 373.

BJÖRKDAHL, A, 'Norm-Maker and Norm-Taker: Exploring the Normative Influence of the EU in Macedonia' (2005) 10 *European Foreign Affairs Review* 257.

BLANCHET, T, PIIPPONEN R and WESTMAN-CLÉMENT M, *The Agreement on the European Economic Area (EEA): A Guide to the Free Movement of Goods and Competition Rules* (Oxford, Clarendon Press, 1994).

BLIN, O, 'L'article 113 CE après Amsterdam' [1998] *Revue du marché commun et de l'Union européenne* 420.

BONO, RG, 'The International Powers of the European Parliament, the Democratic Deficit, and the Treaty of Maastricht' (1992) 12 *Yearbook of European Law* 85.

BOSCHECK, R, 'The Governance of Global Market Relations: The Case of Substituting Antitrust for Antidumping' (2001) 24 *World Competition* 41.

BOSCO, G, 'Commentaire de l'Acte Unique Européen des 17–28 fevrier 1987' (1987) 23 *Cahiers de Droit Européen* 355.

BOURGEOIS, JHJ, 'Effects of International Agreements in European Community Law: Are the Dice Cast?' (1984) 82 *Michigan Law Review* 1250.

——, 'The Common Commercial Policy: Scope and Nature of the Powers' in ELM VÖLKER (ed), *Protectionism and the European Community: Import Relief Measures Taken by the European Economic Community and the Member States, and the Legal Remedies Available to Private Parties* (2nd edn, Deventer, Kluwer Law, 1987) 1.

——, 'The EC in the WTO and Advisory Opinion 1/94: An Echternach Procession' (1995) 32 *Common Market Law Review* 763.

——, 'The European Court of Justice and the WTO: Problems and Challenges' in JHH WEILER (ed), *The EU, the WTO and the NAFTA: Towards a Common Law of International Trade* (Oxford, Oxford University Press, 2000) 71.

——, 'The EC's Trade Policy Powers after Nice: Painting Oneself in a Corner?' in VANDERSANDEN G (ed), *Mélanges en hommage à Jean-Victor Louis* (Brussels, Editions de l'Université de Bruxelles, 2003) i, 29.

BRENTON, P, 'Integrating the Least Developed Countries into the World Trading System: The Current Impact of European Union Preferences under "Everything But Arms"' (2003) 37 *Journal of World Trade* 623.

BRIBOSA, E and WEYEMBERGH, A, 'La personalité juridique de l'Union européenne' in M DONY (ed), *L'Union européenne et le monde après Amsterdam* (Brussels, Editions de l'Université de Bruxelles, 1999) 37.

BRONCKERS, M and McNELIS, N, 'Rethinking the "Like Product" Definition in WTO Antidumping Law' (1999) 33 *Journal of World Trade* 73.

BRONCKERS, MCEJ, 'A Legal Analysis of Protectionist Measures Affecting Japanese Imports into the European Community' in ELM VÖLKER(ed), *Protectionism and the European Community: Import Relief Measures Taken by the European Economic Community and the Member States, and the Legal Remedies Available to Private Parties* (2nd edn, Deventer, Kluwer Law, 1987) 57.

BRONKHORST, HJ, 'The Valid Legislative Act as a Cause of Liability of the Communities' in T HEUKELS and A McDONNELL (eds), *The Action for Damages in Community Law* (The Hague, Kluwer Law International, 1997) 153.

BROWN, A, 'The Extension of the Community Public Procurement Rules to Utilities' (1993) 30 *Common Market Law Review* 721.

BROWNLIE, I, 'International Law at the Fiftieth Anniversary of the United Nations: General Course on Public International Law' (1995) 255 *Recueil des Cours* 9.

——, *Principles of Public International Law* (6th edn, Oxford, Oxford University Press, 2003).

BULMER, S and WESSELS, W, *The European Council: Decision-Making in European Politics* (Basingstoke, Macmillan, 1987).

BURROWS, N, 'Caught in the Cross-Fire' (1997) 22 *European Law Review* 170.

——, 'Reinforcing International Law' (1998) 23 *European Law Review* 79.

CAMERON, F and SPENCE, D, 'The Commission–Council Tandem in the Foreign Policy Arena' in DG DIMITRAKOPOULOS (ed), *The Changing European Commission* (Manchester, Manchester University Press, 2004) 121.

CANNIZZARO, E, 'The Scope of the EU Foreign Policy Power: Is the EC Competent to Conclude Agreements with Third States Including Human Rights

Clauses?' in E CANNIZZARO (ed), *The European Union as an Actor in International Relations* (The Hague, Kluwer Law International, 2002) 296.

CANOR, I, '"Can Two Walk Together, except They Be Agreed?" the Relationship between International Law and European Law: The Incorporation of United Nations Sanctions against Yugoslavia into European Community Law through the Perspective of the European Court of Justice' (1998) 35 *Common Market Law Review* 137.

CATHAIN, CN, 'The European Community and the Member States in the Dispute Settlement Understanding of the WTO: United or Divided?' (1999) 5 *European Law Journal* 461.

CAZALA, J, 'La contestation de la compétence exclusive de la Cour de justice des communautés européennes' (2004) 40 *Revue trimestrielle de droit européen* 505.

CHALMERS, D, 'Legal Base and the External Relations of the European Community' in N EMILIOU and D O'KEEFFE (eds), *The European Union and the World Trade Law: After the GATT Uruguay Round* (Chichester, Wiley, 1996) 46.

CHARLESWORTH, H, 'International Law: A Discipline of Crisis' (2002) 65 *Modern Law Review* 377.

CHAYTOR, B, GERSTER, R and HERZOG, T, 'The Convention on Biological Diversity —Exploring the Creation of a Mediation Mechanism' (2002) 5 *Journal of World Intellectual Property* 157.

CHEYNE, I, 'Haegeman, Demirel and Their Progeny' in A DASHWOOD and C HILLION (eds), *The General Law of EC External Relations* (London, Sweet & Maxwell, 2000) 20.

——, 'International Instruments as a Source of Community Law' in A DASHWOOD and C HILLION (eds), *The General Law of EC External Relations* (London, Sweet & Maxwell, 2000) 254.

CHRISTIANOS, V, 'Compétence consultative de la Cour de justice des communautés européennes à la lumière du Traité sur l'Union européenne' (1994) 374 *Revue du Marché Commun et de l'Union Européenne* 37.

CHURCHILL, R and SCOTT, J, 'The Mox Plant Litigation: The First Half-Life' (2005) 53 *International and Comparative Law Quarterly* 643.

CORNISH, P, *The Arms Trade and Europe* (London, Pinter, 1995).

CRAIG, P and DE BÚRCA, G, *EU Law: Text, Cases, and Materials* (3rd edn, Oxford, Oxford University Press, 2002).

CREMONA, M, 'The Completion of the Internal Market and the Incomplete Commercial Policy of the European Community' (1990) 15 *European Law Review* 283.

——, 'Case C-360/93, European Parliament v. Council of the European Union' (1997) 34 *Common Market Law Review* 389.

——, 'The European Union as an International Actor: The Issues of Flexibility and Linkage' (1998) 3 *European Foreign Affairs Review* 67.

——, 'Creating the New Europe: The Stability Pact for South Eastern Europe in the Context of EU-See Relations' (1999) 2 *Cambridge Yearbook of European Legal Studies* 463.

——, 'The EU and the External Dimension of Human Rights Policy' in SV KONSTADINIDIS (ed), *A People's Europe: Tuning a Concept into Content* (Aldershot, Ashgate, 1999) 155.

——, 'External Relations and External Competence: The Emergence of an Integrated Policy' in P CRAIG and G DE BÚRCA (eds), *The Evolution of EU Law* (Oxford, Oxford University Press, 1999) 137.

——, 'EC External Commercial Policy after Amsterdam: Authority and Interpretation within Interconnected Legal Orders' in JHH WEILER (ed), *The EU, the WTO and the NAFTA: Towards a Common Law of International Trade* (Oxford, Oxford University Press, 2000) 27.

——, 'A Policy of Bits and Pieces? The Common Commercial Policy after Nice' (2001) 4 *Cambridge Yearbook of European Legal Studies* 61.

——, 'The External Dimension of the Single Market: Building (on) the Foundations' in C BARNARD and J SCOTT (eds), *The Law of the Single European Market: Unpacking the Premises* (Oxford, Hart Publishing, 2002) 352.

——, 'The Draft Constitutional Treaty: External Relations and External Action' (2003) 40 *Common Market Law Review* 1347.

——, 'The Impact of Enlargement: External Policy and External Relations' in M Cremona (ed), *The Enlargement of the European Union* (Oxford, Oxford University Press, 2003) 161.

——, 'The Union as a Global Actor: Roles, Models and Identity' (2004) 41 *Common Market Law Review* 553.

——, 'Values in the EU Constitution: The External Dimension' in M Aziz and S Millns (eds), *Values in the Constitution of Europe* (Aldershot, Ashgate, 2005) (forthcoming).

——, (ed), *The Enlargement of the European Union* (Oxford, Oxford University Press, 2003).

CROSBY, S, 'The Single Market and the Rule of Law' (1991) 16 *European Law Review* 451.

CROWE, B, 'A Common Foreign Policy after Iraq?' in M Holland (ed), *Common Foreign and Security Policy: The First Ten Years* (2nd edn, London, Continuum, 2004) 28.

——, *Foreign Minister of Europe* (London, The Foreign Policy Centre, 2005).

DAILLIER, P and PELLET, A, *Droit International Public* (7th edn, Paris, LGDJ, 2002).

DASHWOOD, A, 'Why Continue to Have Mixed Agreements at All?' in JHJ BOURGEOIS, J-L DEWOST and M-A GAIFFE (eds), *La Communauté Européenne et les Accords Mixtes: Quelles Perspectives?* (Brussels, Presses interuniversitaires européennes, 1997) 93.

——, 'External Relations Provisions of the Amsterdam Treaty' (1998) 35 *Common Market Law Review* 1019.

——, 'Implied External Competence of the EC' in M KOSKENNIEMI (ed), *International Law Aspects of the European Union* (The Hague, Kluwer Law International, 1998) 113.

——, 'External Relations Provisions of the Amsterdam Treaty' in D O'KEEFFE and PM TWOMEY (eds), *Legal Issues of the Amsterdam Treaty* (Oxford, Hart Publishing, 1999) 201.

——, 'The Attribution of External Relations Competence' in A DASHWOOD and C HILLION (eds), *The General Law of EC External Relations* (London, Sweet & Maxwell, 2000) 115.

——, 'Decision-Making at the Summit' (2000) 3 *Cambridge Yearbook of European Legal Studies* 79.

——, 'Preliminary Rulings on the Interpretation of Mixed Agreements' in D O'KEEFFE and A BAVASSO (eds), *Liber Amicorum in Honour of Lord Slynn of Hadley: Judicial Review in European Union Law* (The Hague, Kluwer Law International, 2000) 167.

——, 'Issues of Decision-Making in the European Union after Nice' in A ARNULL and D WINCOTT (eds), *Accountability and Legitimacy in the European Union* (Oxford, Oxford University Press, 2002) 13.

——, 'Opinion 2/00, Cartagena Protocol on Biosafety' (2002) 39 *Common Market Law Review* 353.

——, 'The Relationship between the Member States and the European Community/European Union' (2004) 41 *Common Market Law Review* 355.

——, and HELISKOSKI J, 'The Classic Authorities Revisited' in A DASHWOOD and C HILLION (eds), *The General Law of EC External Relations* (London, Sweet & Maxwell, 2000) 3.

DE LA ROCHÈRE, JD, 'L'ère des Compétences Partagées' [1995] *Revue du Marché Commun et de l'Union Européenne* 461.

DE LEON, PM, 'Before and after the Tenth Anniversary of the Open Skies Agreement Netherlands–US of 1992' (2002) 27 *Air and Space Law* 280.

DE SCHOUTHEETE, P, *La Coopération Politique Européenne* (2nd edn, Paris, Editions Labor, 1986).

DE VEL, G, 'L'Union Européenne et les activités du Conseil de l'Europe' in D DORMOY (ed), *L'union Européenne et les Organisations Internationales* (Brussels, Bruylant, 1997) 105.

DE WITTE, B, 'Old-Fashioned Flexibility: International Agreements between Member States of the European Union' in G DE BÚRCA and J SCOTT (eds), *Constitutional Change in the EU: From Uniformity to Flexibility?* (Oxford, Hart Publishing, 2000) 31.

DEL SARTO, RA and SCHUMACHER T, 'From EMP to ENP: What's at Stake with the European Neighbourhood Policy Towards the Southern Mediterranean?' (2005) 10 *European Foreign Affairs Review* 17.

DEMPSEY, PS, *European Aviation Law* (The Hague, Kluwer Law International, 2004).

DENT, CM, 'The EU-East Asia Economic Relationship: The Persisting Weak Triadic Link?' (1999) 4 *European Foreign Affairs Review* 371.

DENZA, E, 'The Community as a Member of International Organisations' in N EMILIOU and D O'KEEFFE (eds), *The European Union and the World Trade Law: After the GATT Uruguay Round* (Chichester, Wiley, 1996) 3.

——, *The Intergovernmental Pillars of the European Union* (Oxford, Oxford University Press, 2002).

——, 'The Relationship between International and National Law' in MD EVANS (ed), *International Law* (Oxford, Oxford University Press, 2003) 415.

——, 'Lines in the Sand: Between Common Foreign Policy and Single Foreign Policy' in T TRIDIMAS and P NEBBIA (eds), *European Law for the Twenty-First Century: Rethinking the New Legal Order* (Oxford, Hart Publishing, 2004) i, 259.

——, 'Non-Proliferation of Nuclear Weapons: The European Union and Iran' (2005) 10 *European Foreign Affairs Review* 289.

DILLON, S, *International Trade and Economic Law and the European Union* (Oxford, Hart Publishing, 2002).

DOHERTY, R, *Ireland, Neutrality and European Security Integration* (Aldershot, Ashgate, 2002).

DOLMANS, MJFM, *Problems of Mixed Agreements: Division of Powers within the EEC and the Rights of Third States* (The Hague, Asser Instituut, 1985).

DOUGAN, M, 'The "Disguised" Vertical Direct Effect of Directives?' (2000) 59 *Cambridge Law Journal* 586.

——, 'Case C–390/99, Canal Satélite Digital, Case C–159/00, Sapod Audic v. Eco-Emballages' (2003) 40 *Common Market Law Review* 193.

DOXEY, MP, *International Sanctions in Contemporary Perspective* (2nd edn, Basingstoke, Macmillan, 1996).

DREZNER, DW, *The Sanctions Paradox: Economic Statecraft and International Relations* (Cambridge, Cambridge University Press, 1999).

——, 'The Hidden Hand of Economic Coercion' (2003) 57 *International Organisation* 643.

DUKE, S, 'The Convention, the Draft Constitution and External Relations: Effects and Implications for the EU and Its International Role' (2003) *EIPA Working Paper 2003/W/2*.

——, 'The European Security Strategy in a Comparative Framework: Does It Make for Secure Alliances in a Better World?' (2004) 9 *European Foreign Affairs Review* 459.

Editor, 'The Aftermath of *Opinion 1/94* or How to Ensure Unity of Representation for Joint Competence' (1995) 32 *Common Market Law Review* 385.

——, 'The European Union—a New International Actor' (2001) 38 *Common Market Law Review* 825.

——, 'The CFSP under the EU Constitutional Treaty—Issues of Depillarization' (2005) 42 *Common Market Law Review* 325.

EDWARDS, G and PHILIPPART, E, 'The Euro—Mediterranean Partnership: Fragmentation and Reconstruction' (1997) 2 *European Foreign Affairs Review* 465.

EECKHOUT, P, *The European Internal Market and International Trade: A Legal Analysis* (Oxford, Clarendon Press, 1994).

——, 'The Domestic Legal Status of the WTO Agreements: Interconnecting Legal Systems', (1997) 34 *Common Market Law Review* 11.

——, *External Relations of the European Union: Legal and Constitutional Foundations* (Oxford, Oxford University Press, 2004).

EHLERMANN, C-D, 'Six Years on the Bench of the "World Trade Court". Some Personal Experiences as Member of the Appellate Body of the World Trade Organisation' (2002) 36 *Journal of World Trade* 637.

ELLIS, E (ed), *The Principle of Proportionality in the Laws of Europe* (Oxford, Hart Publishing, 1999).

ELSIG, M, *The EU's Common Commercial Policy: Institutions, Interests and Ideas* (Aldershot, Ashgate, 2002).

EMILIOU, N, 'The Death of Exclusive Competence?' (1996) 21 *European Law Review* 294.

——, *The Principle of Proportionality in European Law: A Comparative Study* (The Hague, Kluwer Law International, 1996).

——, annotation on *Werner* and *Leifer* (1997) 22 *European Law Review* 68.

ERIKSEN, EO, FOSSUM, JE and MENÉNDEZ AJ, *Developing a Constitution for Europe* (London, Routledge, 2004).

FERNÁNDEZ-MARTÍN, JM and O'LEARY, S, 'Judicial Exceptions to the Free Provision of Services' (1995) 1 *European Law Journal* 303.

FINGER, M, 'Reform' in JM FINGER and NT ARTIS (eds), *Antidumping: How It Works and Who Gets Hurt* (Ann Arbor, Mich, University of Michigan Press, 1993) 57.

FLAESCH-MOUGIN, C, 'Le Traité de Maastricht et les compétences externes de la Communauté européenne: à la recherche d'une politique externe de l'Union' (1993) 29 *Cahiers de Droit Européen* 351.

——, 'Les acteurs des relations euro-méditerranéennes' in M BLANQUET (ed), *Mélanges en hommage à Guy Isaac: cinquante ans de droit communautaire* (Toulouse, Presses de l'université des sciences sociales de Toulouse, 2003) 469.

FLORY, T and MARTIN, F-P, 'Remarques à propos des avis 1/94 et 2/92 de la Cour de justice des Communautés européennes au regard de la notion de Politique Commerciale Commune' [1996] *Cahiers de Droit Européen* 376.

FOOTER, M, 'Public Procurement and EC External Relations: A Legal Framework' in N EMILIOU and D O'KEEFFE (eds), *The European Union and the World Trade Law: After the GATT Uruguay Round* (Chichester, Wiley, 1996) 293.

FORLATI, L and SICILIANOS, L-A (eds), *Les sanctions économiques en droit international* (Leiden, Martinus Nijhoff, 2004).

FRANKLIN, CNK, 'Flexibility vs. Legal Certainty: Article 307 EC and Other Issues in the Aftermath of the Open Skies Case' (2005) 10 *European Foreign Affairs Review* 79.

FRID, R, *The Relations between the EC and International Organisations: Legal Theory and Practice* (The Hague, Kluwer Law International, 1995).

FROWEIN, JA, 'The Competences of the European Community in the Field of External Relations' in J SCHWARZE (ed), *The External Relations of the European Community, in Particular EC-US Relations* (Baden-Baden, Nomos, 1989) 29.

FURSDON, E, *The European Defence Community: A History* (London, Macmillan, 1980).

GAGLIARDI, AF, 'The Right of Individuals to Invoke the Provisions of Mixed Agreements before the National Courts: A New Message from Luxembourg?' (1999) 24 *European Law Review* 276.

GATTINARA, G, 'La compétence consultative de la Cour de justice après les avis 1/00 et 2/00' [2003] *Revue du Droit de l'Union européenne* 687.

GAUDISSART, M-A, 'Reflexions sur la nature et la portée du concept d'association à la lumière de sa mise en oeuvre' in M-FC TCHAKALOFF (ed), *Le concept d'association dans les accords passés par la Communauté: essai de clarification* (Brussels, Bruylant, 1999) 3.

GAZA, G, 'Trends in Judicial Activism and Judicial Self-Restraint Relating to Community Agreements' in E CANNIZZARO (ed), *The European Union as an Actor in International Relations* (The Hague, Kluwer Law International, 2002) 118.

GIANNAKOPOULOS, T, 'The Right to Be Orally Heard by the Commission in Antitrust, Merger, Anti-Dumping/Anti-Subsidies and State Aid Community Procedures' (2001) 24 *World Competition* 541.

GILSDORF, P, 'Portée et délimitation des compétences communautaires en matière de Politique Commerciale' [1989] *Revue du Marché Commun* 195.

GLAESNER, HJ, 'The European Council' in D CURTIN, T HEUKELS and HG SCHERMERS (eds), *Institutional Dynamics of European Integration* (Boston, Mass Martinus Nijhoff, 1994) ii, 101.

GONG, H, 'Legal Strategies for Challenging the Current EU Anti-Dumping Campaign against Imports from China: A Chinese Perspective' (2002) 27 *Brooklyn Journal of International Law* 575.

GOVAERE, I, CAPIAU, J and VERMEERSCH, A, 'In-between Seats: The Participation of the European Union in International Organisations' (2004) 9 *European Foreign Affairs Review* 155.

——, and EECKHOUT P, 'On Dual Use Goods and Dualist Case Law: The *Aimé Richardt* Judgment and on Export Controls' (1992) 29 *Common Market Law Review* 941.

Government of the Federal Republic of Germany, *European Political Co-Operation (EPC)* (5th edn, Bonn, Press and Information Office of the Federal Government, 1988).

GRARD, L, 'La Cour de justice des Communautés européennes et la dimension externe du marché unique des transports aériens—a propos des huit arrêts du 5 novembre 2002 dans l'affaire dite "Open Skies"' [2002] *Cahiers de Droit Européen* 695.

——, 'L'Union européenne et le droit international de l'aviation civile' (2004) 49 *Annuaire Français de Droit International* 492.

GREAVES, R, '*Locus Standi* under Article 173 EEC when Seeking Annulment of a Regulation' (1986) 11 *European Law Review* 119.

——, 'The Community's External Competence: Air Transport Services' (2003) 52 *International and Comparative Law Quarterly* 499.

GRILLER, S, 'Judicial Enforceability of WTO Law in the European Union— Annotation to Case C-149/96 Portugal v Council' (2000) 3 *Journal of International Economic Law* 441.

GRIMES, JM, 'Conflicts between EC Law and International Treaty Obligations: A Case Study of the German Telecommunications Dispute' (1994) 35 *Harvard International Law Journal* 535.

GROUX, J, 'Mixed Negotiations' in D O'Keeffe and HG Schermers (eds), *Mixed Agreements* (Deventer, Kluwer Law, 1983) 87.

GUAY, T and CALLUM, R, 'The Transformation and Future Prospects of Europe's Defence Industry' (2002) 78 *International Affairs* 757.

HALFORD, AJ, 'Public Procurement and Community External Relations' (1996) 21 *European Law Review* 478.

HANSON, BT, 'What Happened to Fortress Europe? External Trade Policy Liberalization in the European Union' (1998) 52 *International Organisation* 55.

HARDY, M, '*Opinion 1/76* of the Court of Justice: The Rhine Case and the Treaty-Making Powers of the Community' (1977) 14 *Common Market Law Review* 561.

HARPAZ, G, 'The European Community's Anti-Dumping Policy: The Quest for Enhanced Predictability, Rationality, European Solidarity and Legitimacy' (2003) 5 *Cambridge Yearbook of European Legal Studies* 195.

HARTLEY, K, 'Defence Industries' in PS JOHNSON (ed), *Industries in Europe: Competition, Trends, and Policy Issues* (2nd edn, Cheltenham, Edward Elgar Publishing, 2003).

HARTLEY, TC, *Constitutional Problems of the European Union* (Oxford, Hart Publishing, 1999).

HAUSER, H and ROITINGER, A, 'Renegotiation in Transatlantic Trade Disputes' in EU PETERSMANN and MA POLLACK (eds), *Transatlantic Trade Disputes: The EU, the US, and the WTO* (Oxford, Oxford University Press, 2003) 487.

HEDEMANN-ROBINSON, M, 'An Overview of Recent Legal Developments at Community Level in Relation to Third Country Nationals Resident within the European Union, with Particular Reference to the Case Law of the European Court of Justice' (2001) 38 *Common Market Law Review* 525.

HEFFERNAN, L and MCAULIFFE, C, 'External Relations in the Air Transport Sector: The Court of Justice and the Open Skies Agreements' (2003) 28 *European Law Review* 601.

HELISKOSKI, J, 'The "Duty of Cooperation" between the European Community and Its Member States within the World Trade Organisation' (1996) 7 *Finnish Yearbook of International Law* 59.

——, 'Should There Be a New Article on External Relations?' in M KOSKENNIEMI (ed), *International Law Aspects of the European Union* (The Hague, Kluwer Law International, 1998) 273.

——, 'Joint Competence of the European Community and Its Member States and the Dispute Settlement Practice of the World Trade Organisation' (1999) 2 *Cambridge Yearbook of European Legal Studies* 61.

——, 'Internal Struggle for International Presence: The Exercise of Voting Rights within the Fao' in A DASHWOOD and C HILLION (eds), *The General Law of EC External Relations* (London, Sweet & Maxwell, 2000) 79.

——, 'The Jurisdiction of the European Court of Justice to Give Preliminary Rulings on the Interpretation of Mixed Agreements' (2000) 69 *Nordic Journal of International Law* 395.

——, *Mixed Agreements as a Technique for Organizing the International Relations of the European Community and Its Member States* (The Hague, Kluwer Law International, 2001).

——, 'The Nice Reform of Article 133 EC on the Common Commercial Policy' (2002) 1 *Journal of International Commercial Law* 1.

HERRMANN, C, 'Common Commercial Policy after Nice: Sisyphus Would Have Done a Better Job' (2002) 39 *Common Market Law Review* 7.

——, 'Monetary Sovereignty over the Euro and External Relations of the Euro Area: Competences, Procedures and Practice' (2002) 7 *European Foreign Affairs Review* 1.

HILF, M, 'The ECJ's *Opinion 1/94* on the WTO—No Surprise, but Wise?' (1995) 6 *European Journal of International Law* 245.

HILL, C, 'The Capabilities–Expectations Gap, or Conceptualising Europe's International Role' (1993) 31 *Journal of Common Market Studies* 305.

HILLION, C, 'Partnership and Cooperation Agreements between the European Union and the New Independent States of the Ex-Soviet Union' (1998) 3 *European Foreign Affairs Review* 399.

——, 'Institutional Aspects of the Partnership between the European Union and the Newly Independent States of the Former Soviet Union: Case Studies of Russia and Ukraine' (2000) 37 *Common Market Law Review* 1211.

——, 'Case C–62/98 Commission of the European Communities v. Portugal, and Case C–84/98 Commission of the European Communities v. Portugal' (2001) 38 *Common Market Law Review* 1269.

——, 'Tobacco Advertising: If You Must, You May' (2001) 60 *Cambridge Law Journal* 486.

——, (ed), *EU Enlargement: A Legal Approach* (Oxford, Hart Publishing, 2004).

HOLDEN, P, 'The European Community's MEDA Aid Programme: A Strategic Instrument of Civilian Power?' (2003) 8 *European Foreign Affairs Review* 347.

HOLDGAARD, R, 'The European Community's Implied External Competence after the Open Skies Cases' (2003) 8 *European Foreign Affairs Review* 365.

HOLLAND, M, 'Three Approaches for Understanding European Political Cooperation: A Case Study of EC South African Policy' (1987) 25 *Journal of Common Market Studies* 295.

——, *The Future of European Political Cooperation: Essays on Theory and Practice* (London, Macmillan, 1991).

HOUBÉ-MASSE, M-L, *La CEE et les crédits à l'exportation: l'intégration en question* (Rennes, Apogée, 1992).

HOWORTH, J, 'Britain, NATO and CESDP: Fixed Strategy, Changing Tactics' (2000) 5 *European Foreign Affairs Review* 377.

——, 'The European Draft Constitutional Treaty and the Future of the European Defence Initiative: A Question of Flexibility' (2004) 9 *European Foreign Affairs Review* 483.

HOWSE, R and NICOLAIDIS, K, 'Legitimacy and Global Governance: Why Constitutionalizing the WTO is a Step Too Far' in RB PORTER *et al* (eds), *Efficiency, Equity, and Legitimacy: The Multilateral Trading System at the Millennium* (Washington, DC, Brookings Institution Press, 2001) 227.

HUDEC, RE, 'The New WTO Dispute Settlement Procedure: An Overview of the First Three Years' (1999) 8 *Minnesota Journal of Global Trade* 1.

HUFBAUER, GC, SCHOTT, JJ and ELLIOTT, KA, *Economic Sanctions Reconsidered* (2nd edn, Washington, DC, Institute for International Economics, 1990).

IFESTOS, P, *European Political Cooperation: Towards a Framework of Supranational Diplomacy?* (Aldershot, Avebury, 1987).

INGLIS, KM, 'The Union's Fifth Accession Treaty: New Means to Make Enlargement Possible' (2004) 41 *Common Market Law Review* 937.

JACKSON, J, 'International Law Status of WTO Dispute Settlement Reports: Obligation to Comply or Option to buy Out?' (2004) 98 *American Journal of International Law* 109.

JACOBS, F, 'Judicial Review of Commercial Policy Measures after the Uruguay Round' in N EMILIOU and D O'KEEFFE (eds), *The European Union and the World Trade Law: After the GATT Uruguay Round* (Chichester, Wiley, 1996) 329.

JACQUÉ, J-P, 'L'Acte unique européen' (1986) 22 *Revue Trimestrielle de Droit Européen* 575.

JARVIS, MA, *The Application of EC Law by National Courts: The Free Movement of Goods* (Oxford, Oxford University Press, 1998).

JOHNSON, M, *European Community Trade Policy and the Article 113 Committee* (London, Royal Institute of International Affairs, 1998).

JONES, S, 'EU Enlargement: Implications for EU and Multilateral Export Controls' (2003) 10 *The Nonproliferation Review* 80.

KADDOUS, C, 'L'arrêt France c. Commission de 1994 et le contrôle de la "légalité" des accords externes en vertu de l'art. 173 CE: la difficile réconciliation de l'orthodoxie communautaire avec l'orthodoxie internationale' (1996) 32 *Cahiers de Droit Européen* 613.

——, *Le droit des relations extérieures dans la jurisprudence de la Cour de justice des Communautés européennes* (Basel/Brussels, Helbing & Lichtenhahn/Bruylant, 1998).

KHERAD, R, 'La reconnaissance des états issus de la dissolution de la République Socialiste Fédérative de Yougoslavie par les membres de l'Union européenne' (1997) 101 *Revue Générale de Droit International Public* 663.

KLABBERS, J, 'Moribund on the Fourth of July? The Court of Justice on Prior Agreements of Member States' (2001) 26 *European Law Review* 187.

——, 'The *Bustani* Case before the ILOAT: Constitutionalism in Disguise?' (2004) 53 *International and Comparative Law Quarterly* 455.

KOOPMANS, T, 'The Role of Law in the Next Stage of European Integration' (1986) 35 *International and Comparative Law Quarterly* 925.

KOSKENNIEMI, M, 'International Law Aspects of the Common Foreign and Security Policy' in M KOSKENNIEMI (ed), *International Law Aspects of the European Union* (The Hague, Kluwer Law International, 1998) 27.

KOUTRAKOS, P, 'Exports of Dual-Use Goods under the Law of the European Union' (1998) 23 *European Law Review* 235.

——, 'Is Article 297 EC a "Reserve of Sovereignty"?' (2000) 37 *Common Market Law Review* 1339.

——, 'Inter-Pillar Approaches to the European Security and Defence Policy—the Economic Aspects of Security' in V KRONENBERGER (ed), *The European Union and the International Legal Order: Discord or Harmony?* (The Hague, TMC Asser Press, 2001) 435.

——, 'On Groceries, Alcohol and Olive Oil: More on Free Movement of Goods after Keck' (2001) 26 *European Law Review* 391.

——, *Trade, Foreign Policy, and Defence in EU Constitutional Law: The Legal Regulation of Sanctions, Exports of Dual-Use Goods and Armaments* (Oxford, Hart Publishing, 2001).

——, 'The Elusive Quest for Uniformity in EC External Relations' (2002) 4 *Cambridge Yearbook of European Legal Studies* 243.

——, 'Free Movement of Goods' in A OTT and K INGLIS (eds), *Handbook on European Enlargement: A Commentary on the Enlargement Process* (The Hague, TMC Asser Press, 2002) 369.

——, 'The Interpretation of Mixed Agreements under the Preliminary Reference Procedure' (2002) 7 *European Foreign Affairs Review* 25.

——, 'Constitutional Idiosyncrasies and Political Realities: The Emerging Security and Defence Policy of the European Union' (2003) 10 *Columbia Journal of European Law* 69.

——, '"I Need to Hear You Say It": Revisiting the Scope of the EC Common Commercial Policy' (2003) 22 *Yearbook of European Law* 407.

——, annotation on 'Case C–29/99, Commission v. Council (Re: Nuclear Safety Convention)' (2004) 41 *Common Market Law Review* 191.

KRAJEWSKI, M, 'External Trade Law and the Constitution Treaty: Towards a Federal and More Democratic Common Commercial Policy?' (2005) 42 *Common Market Law Review* 91.

KRENZLER, HG and PITSCHAS, C, 'Progress or Stagnation? The Common Commercial Policy after Nice' (2001) 6 *European Foreign Affairs Review* 291.

KRITIKOS, M, 'Mixity and Ad Hoc Arrangements in EU Negotiating Strategies for the Biosafety Protocol' in F SNYDER (ed), *International Food Security and Global Legal Pluralism* (Brussels, Bruylant, 2004) 153.

KRONENBERGER, V and WOUTERS, J (eds), *The European Union and Conflict Prevention: Policy and Legal Aspects* (The Hague, TMC Asser Press, 2004).

KUIJPER, PJ, 'Sanctions against Rhodesia, the EEC and the Implementation of General International Legal Rules' (1975) 12 *Common Market Law Review* 231.

——, 'Trade Sanctions, Security and Human Rights and Commercial Policy' in M MARESCEAU (ed), *The European Community's Commercial Policy after 1992: The Legal Dimension* (Dordrecht, Martinus Nijhoff, 1993) 395.

——, 'The Conclusion and Implementation of the Uruguay Round Results by the European Community' (1995) 6 *European Journal of International Law* 222.

——, 'From Dyestuffs to Kosovo Wine: From Avoidance to Acceptance by the European Community Courts of Customary International Law as Limit to Community Action' in IF DEKKER and HHG POST (eds), *On the Foundations and Sources of International Law* (The Hague, TMC Asser, 2003)

——, 'The Evolution of the Third Pillar from Maastricht to the European Constitution: Institutional Aspects' (2004) 41 *Common Market Law Review* 609.

——, and PAASIVIRTA, E, 'Further Exploring International Responsibility: The European Community and the ILC's Project on Responsibility of International Organisations' (2004) 1 *International Organisations Law Review* 111.

KUILWIJK, KJ, *The European Court of Justice and the GATT Dilemma: Public Interest Versus Individual Rights?* (Beuningen, Centre for Critical Legal Studies, 1996).

KUMM, M, 'The International Rule of Law and the Limits of the International Model' (2004) 44 *Virginia Journal of International Law* 19.

LANNON, E and ELSUWEGE, PV, 'The EU's Emerging Neighbourhood Policy and Its Potential Impact on the Euro-Mediterranean Partnership' in PG XUEREB (ed), *Euro-Med Integration and the 'Ring of Friends'* (Msida, European Documentation and Research Centre, University of Malta, 2003) 21.

LAVRANOS, N, 'European Court of Justice, 5 November 2002, Cases C–466/98 – C–469/98, C–471/98 – C–472/98, C–475/98 – C–476/98, Commission v. UK, Dk, S, Fin, B, L, Aus, G' (2003) 30 *Legal Issues of European Integration* 81.

——, *Decisions of International Organisations in the European and Domestic Legal Orders of Selected EU Member States* (Groningen, Europa Law Publishing, 2004).

LEE, P and KENNEDY, B, 'The Potential Direct Effect of GATT 1994 in European Community Law' (1996) 30 *Journal of World Trade* 67.

LENAERTS, K and GERARD, D, 'The Structure of the Union According to the Constitution for Europe: The Emperor Is Getting Dressed' (2004) 29 *European Law Review* 289.

——, and KORTHAUT, T, 'Judicial Review as a Contribution to the Development of European Constitutionalism' in T TRIDIMAS and P NEBBIA (eds), *European Law for the Twenty-First Century: Rethinking the New Legal Order* (Oxford, Hart Publishing, 2004) i, 17.

——, and SMIJTER, ED, 'The United Nations and the European Union: Living Apart Together' in K WELLENS (ed), *International Law: Theory and Practice: Essays in Honour of Eric Suy* (The Hague, Martinus Nijhoff, 1998) 493.

LINDLEY-FRENCH, J, 'In the Shadow of Locarno? Why European Defence Is Failing' (2002) 78 *International Affairs* 789.

LOUIS, J-V, VANDERSANDEN, G and WAELBROECK, D, *Commentaire J. Mégret Vol 10* (2nd edn, Brussels, Editions de l'Université de Bruxelles, 1993).

——, and DONY, M, *Commentaire J. Mégret Vol 12, Relations Extérieures* (Brussels, Editions de l'Université de Bruxelles, 2005).

LOWENFELD, AF, *International Economic Law* (Oxford, Oxford University Press, 2002).

LYONS, TJ, *EC Customs Law* (Oxford, Oxford University Press, 2001).

MACLEAN, RM and VOLPI, B, *EU Trade Barrier Regulation: Tackling Unfair Foreign Trade Practices* (Bembridge, Palladian Law Publishing, 2000).

MACLEOD, I, HENDRY, ID and HYETT, S, *The External Relations of the European Communities: A Manual of Law and Practice* (Oxford, Oxford University Press, 1996).

MADELIN, R, 'Trade Policy—Opening World Markets for Business' in M DARMER and L KUYPER (eds), *Industry and the European Union: Analysing Policies for Business* (Cheltenham, Edward Elgar, 2000) 155.

MADURO, MP, *We the Court: The European Court of Justice and the European Economic Constitution: A Critical Reading of Article 30 of the EC Treaty* (Oxford, Hart Publishing, 1998).

MAIZELS, A, *Commodities in Crisis: The Commodity Crisis of the 1980s and the Political Economy of International Commodity Policies* (Oxford, Clarendon Press, 1992).

MANZINI, P, 'The Priority of Pre-Existing Treaties of EC Member States within the Framework of International Law' (2001) 12 *European Journal of International Law* 781.

MARESCEAU, M, 'Pre-Accession' in M CREMONA (ed), *The Enlargement of the European Union* (Oxford, Oxford University Press, 2003) 9.

——, 'EU Enlargement and EU Common Strategies on Russia and Ukraine: An Ambiguous yet Unavoidable Connection' in HILLION C (ed), *EU Enlargement: A Legal Approach* (Oxford, Hart Publishing, 2004) 181.

MARINOV, N, 'Do Sanctions Help Democracy? The US and EU's Record 1997–2004' (2004) Stanford Institute for International Studies, Center for Democracy, Development and the Rule of Law Working Paper No 28.

MARQUARDT, S, 'The Conclusion of International Agreements under Article 24 of the Treaty on European Union' in V KRONENBERGER (ed), *The European Union and the International Legal Order: Discord or Harmony?* (The Hague, TMC Asser Press, 2001) 333.

MARTENCZUK, B, 'Decisions of Bodies Established by International Agreements and the Community Legal Order' in V KRONENBERGER (ed), *The European Union and the International Legal Order: Discord or Harmony?* (The Hague, TMC Asser Press, 2001) 141.

MASON, M, 'Elements of Consensus: Europe's Response to the Japanese Automotive Challenge' (1994) 32 *Journal of Common Market Studies* 433.

MATSUSHITA, M, SCHOENBAUM, T and MAVROIDIS, PC *The World Trade Organisation: Law and Practice* (Oxford, Oxford University Press, 2003).

MAUNU, A, 'The Implied External Competence of the European Community after the ECJ *Opinion 1/94*—Towards Coherence or Diversity?' (1995) 2 *Legal Issues of European Integration* 115.

MAVROIDIS, PC, 'Remedies in the WTO Legal System: Between a Rock and a Hard Place' (2000) 11 *European Journal of International Law* 763.

MAYER, J, 'Not Totally Naked: Textiles and Clothing Trade in a Quota-Free Environment' (2005) 39 *Journal of World Trade* 393.

McCUTCHEON, JP, 'The Irish Supreme Court, European Political Co-Operation and the Single European Act' (1988) 2 *Legal Issues of European Integration* 93.

McGOLDRICK, D, 'Yugoslavia—the Responses of the International Community and of International Law' (1996) 49 *Current Legal Problems* 375.

——, *The International Relations Law of the European Union* (London, Longman, 1997).

MENON, A, 'From Crisis to Catharsis: ESDP after Iraq' (2004) 80 *International Affairs* 631.

MERLINGEN, M and OSTRAUSKAITE, R, 'ESDP Police Missions: Meaning, Context and Operational Challenges' (2005) 10 *European Foreign Affairs Review* 215.

MICHALOPOULOS, C, *Developing Countries in the WTO* (Basingstoke, Palgrave, 2001).

MITSILEGAS, V, 'The New EU–USA Cooperation on Extradition, Mutual Legal Assistance and the Exchange of Police Data' (2003) 8 *European Foreign Affairs Review* 515.

MONAR, J, 'The Finances of the Union's Intergovernmental Pillars: Tortuous Experiments with the Community Budget' (1997) 35 *Journal of Common Market Studies* 57.

——, 'The Financial Dimension of the CFSP' in M Holland (ed), *Common Foreign and Security Policy: The Record and Reforms* (London, Pinter, 1997) 34.

——, 'Mostar: Three Lessons for the European Union' (1997) 2 *European Foreign Affairs Review* 1.

——, 'The CFSP and the Leila/Perejil Island Incident: The Nemesis of Solidarity and Leadership' (2002) 7 *European Foreign Affairs Review* 251.

MULER-BRANDECK-BOCQUET, G, 'Perspectives for a New Regionalism: Relations between the EU and the Mercosur' (2001) 5 *European Foreign Affairs Review* 561.

MÜLLER-GRAFF, P-C and SELVIG, E (eds), *EEA–EU Relations* (Berlin, Arno Spitz, 1999).

MÜLLER, W, KHAN, N and NEUMANN H-A, *EC Anti-Dumping Trade Law, a Commentary on Regulation 384/96* (Chichester, Wiley, 1998).

MURPHY, F and GRAS, A, 'L'affaire Crotty: la Cour Supreme d'Irlande rejette l'Acte unique européen' (1988) 24 *Cahiers de Droit Européen* 276.

NAERT, F, 'European Security and Defence in the EU Constitutional Treaty' (2005) 10 *Journal of Conflict and Security Law* 187.

NEUWAHL, N, 'Freedom of Movement for Workers under the EEC Treaty Association Agreement' (1988) 13 *European Law Review* 360.

——, 'Individuals and the GATT: Direct Effect and Indirect Effects of the General Agreement on Tariffs and Trade in Community Law' in N EMILIOU and D O'KEEFFE (eds), *The European Union and the World Trade Law: After the GATT Uruguay Round* (Chichester, Wiley, 1996) 313.

——, 'Shared Powers or Combined Incompetence? More on Mixity' (1996) 33 *Common Market Law Review* 667.

——, 'A Partner with a Troubled Personality: EU Treaty-Making in Matters of CFSP and JHA after Amsterdam' (1998) 3 *European Foreign Affairs Review* 177.

NIEMANN, A, 'Between Communicative Action and Strategic Action: The Article 113 Committee and the Negotiations on the WTO Basic Telecommunications Services Agreement' (2004) 11 *Journal of European Public Policy* 379.

NOLTE, G, 'Case 12/86, Meryem Demirel v. Stadt Schwäbisch Gmünd' (1988) 25 *Common Market Law Review* 403.

NORBERG, S (ed), *EEA Law: The European Economic Area: A Commentary on the EEA Agreement* (Stockholm: CE Fritzes AB (Kluwer), 1993).

NUTTALL, S, 'European Political Co-Operation and the Single European Act' (1985) 5 *Yearbook of European Law* 203.

——, *European Political Co-operation* (Oxford, Oxford University Press, 1992).

O'KEEFFE, D, 'Exclusive, Concurrent and Shared Competence' in A DASHWOOD and C HILLION (eds), *The General Law of EC External Relations* (London, Sweet & Maxwell, 2000) 179.

——, and SCHERMERS HG (eds), *Mixed Agreements* (Deventer, Kluwer Law, 1983).

OLIVEIRA, Á, 'Case C–170/96, Commission of the European Communities v. Council of the European Union' (1999) 36 *Common Market Law Review* 149.

OTT, A and INGLIS, K (eds), *Handbook on European Enlargement: A Commentary on the Enlargement Process* (The Hague, TMC Asser Press, 2002).

OUCHTERLONY, T, 'The European Communities and the Council of Europe' (1984) 1 *Legal Issues of European Integration* 59.

PEERS, S, 'Case C–268/94, Portugal v. Council' (1998) 35 *Common Market Law Review* 539.

——, 'EC Frameworks of International Relations: Co-operation, Partnership and Association' in A DASHWOOD and C HILLION (eds), *The General Law of EC External Relations* (London, Sweet & Maxwell, 2000) 160.

——, 'Fragmentation or Evasion in the Community's Development Policy? The Impact of Portugal v Council' in A DASHWOOD and C HILLION (eds), *The General Law of EC External Relations* (London, Sweet & Maxwell, 2000) 100.

——, 'Fundamental Right or Political Whim? WTO Law and the European Court of Justice' in G DE BÚRCA and J SCOTT (eds), *Constitutional Change in the EU: From Uniformity to Flexibility?* (Oxford, Hart Publishing, 2000) 111.

PERRAKIS, S, 'L'incidence de l'Acte unique européen sur la coopération des douze en matière de politique étrangère' (1988) XXXIV *Annuaire Francais de Droit International* 807.

PESCATORE, P, 'Les relations extérieures des Communautés européennes: contribution à la doctrine de la personnalité des organisations internationales' (1961) 103/II *Recueil des cours* 1.

——, 'External Relations in the Case-Law of the Court of Justice of the European Communities' (1975) 12 *Common Market Law Review* 615.

——, 'The Doctrine of "Direct Effect": An Infant Disease of Community Law?' (1983) 8 *European Law Review* 155.

——, 'Opinion 1/94 on Conclusion of the WTO Agreement: Is There an Escape from a Programmed Disaster?' (1999) 36 *Common Market Law Review* 387.

PETERS, I, 'ESDP as a Transatlantic Issue: Problems of Mutual Ambiguity' (2004) 6 *International Studies Review* 381.

PETERSMANN, E-U, 'The EEC as a GATT Member—Legal Conflicts between GATT Law and European Community Law' in M HILF, FG JACOBS and EU PETERSMANN (eds), *The European Community and GATT* (Deventer, Kluwer, 1986) 23.

——, 'National Constitutions and International Economic Law' in M HILF and EU PETERSMANN (eds), *National Constitutions and International Economic Law* (Deventer, Kluwer, 1993) 3.

——, 'The Dispute Settlement System of the World Trade Organisation and the Evolution of the GATT Dispute Settlement System since 1948' (1994) 31 *Common Market Law Review* 1157.

——, 'The GATT Dispute Settlement System as an Instrument of the Foreign Trade Policy of the EC' in N EMILIOU and D O'KEEFFE (eds), *The European Union and the World Trade Law: After the GATT Uruguay Round* (Chichester, Wiley, 1996) 253.

——, 'European and International Constitutional Law: Time for Promoting "Cosmopolitan Democracy" in the WTO' in G DE BÚRCA and J SCOTT (eds), *The EU and the WTO: Legal and Constitutional Issues* (Oxford, Hart Publishing, 2001) 81.

——, 'From State Sovereignty to the "Sovereignty of Citizens" in the International Relations Law of the EU?" in N WALKER (ed), *Sovereignty in Transition* (Oxford, Hart Publishing, 2003) 145.

PHILLIPS, PWB and KERR, WA, 'The WTO versus the Biosafety Protocol for Trade in Genetically Modified Organisms' (2000) 34 *Journal of World Trade* 63.

PHINNEMORE, D, 'Stabilisation and Association Agreements: Europe Agreements for the Western Balkans?' (2003) 8 *European Foreign Affairs Review* 77.

PIPPAN, C, 'The Rocky Road to Europe: The EU's Stabilisation and Association Process for the Western Balkans and the Principle of Conditionality' (2004) 9 *European Foreign Affairs Review* 219.

PLENDER, R, 'The European Court's Pre-emptive Jurisdiction: Opinions under Article 300(6) EC' in D O'KEEFFE and A BAVASSO (eds), *Liber Amicorum in Honour of Lord Slynn of Hadley: Judicial Review in European Union Law* Vol. 1 (The Hague, Kluwer Law International, 2000) 203.

PRECHAL, S, *Directives in EC Law* (2nd edn, Oxford, Oxford University Press, 2005).

RASMUSSEN, H, 'The European Court's Acte Claire Strategy in CILFIT' (1984) 9 *European Law Review* 242.

REICHMAN, JH, 'Securing Compliance with the Trips Agreement after *US v India*' (1998) 1 *Journal of International Economic Law* 585.

RIDEAU, J, 'Les accords internationaux dans la jurisprudence de la Cour de justice des Communautés européennes: réflexions sur les relations entre les ordres juridiques international, communautaire et national' (1990) 94 *Revue Générale de Droit International Public* 289.

RIVERA-TORRES, O, 'The Biosafety Protocol and the WTO' (2003) 26 *Boston College International and Comparative Law Review* 263.

ROESSLER, F, 'The Institutional Balance between the Judicial and the Political Organs of the WTO' in R QUICK, JH JACKSON and MCEJ BRONCKERS (eds), *New Directions in International Economic Law: Essays in Honour of John H. Jackson* (The Hague, Kluwer Law International, 2000) 325.

ROSAS, A, 'Mixed Union—Mixed Agreements' in M KOSKENNIEMI (ed), *International Law Aspects of the European Union* (The Hague, Kluwer Law International, 1998) 125.

——, 'Case C–149/96, Portugal v. Council ' (2000) 37 *Common Market Law Review* 797.

——, 'The European Union and Mixed Agreements' in A DASHWOOD and C HILLION (eds), *The General Law of EC External Relations* (London, Sweet & Maxwell, 2000) 201.

SACK, J, 'The European Community's Membership of International Organisations' (1995) 32 *Common Market Law Review* 1227.

SCANNELL, D, 'Financing ESDP Military Operations' (2004) 9 *European Foreign Affairs Review* 529.

SCHIMMELFENNIG, F, *The EU, NATO and the Integration of Europe: Rules and Rhetoric* (Cambridge, Cambridge University Press, 2003).

SCHMITTER, C, 'Article 228a' in V CONSTANTINESCO, R KOVAR and D SIMON (eds), *Traité sur l'Union européenne (signé à Maastricht le 7 février 1992): commentaire article par article* (Paris, Economica, 1995) 763.

SCHOISSWOHL, I, 'The ECJ's Atlanta Judgment: Establishing a Principle of Non-Liability?' in F BREUSS, S GRILLER and E VRANES (eds), *The Banana Dispute: An Economic and Legal Analysis* (Vienna, Springer, 2003) 309.

SCHUEREN, PV, 'New Anti-Dumping Rules and Practice: Wide Discretion Held on a Tight Leash?' (1996) 33 *Common Market Law Review* 271.

SCHÜTZE, R, 'Parallel External Powers in the European Community: From "Cubist" Perspectives Towards "Naturalist" Constitutional Principles?' (2004) 23 *Yearbook of European Law* 225.

SELMAYR, M and ZILIOLI, C, 'The External Relations of the Euro Area: Legal Aspects' (1999) 36 *Common Market Law Review* 273.

SHANY, V, 'The First Mox Plant Award: The Need to Harmonize Competing Environmental Regimes and Dispute Settlement Procedures' (2004) 17 *Leiden Journal of International Law* 815.

SIMMONDS, KR, 'The Community's Participation in the U.N. Law of the Sea Convention' in D O'KEEFFE and HG SCHERMERS (eds), *Mixed Agreements* (Deventer, Kluwer Law, 1983) 179.

——, 'The European Community and the New Law of the Sea' (1989) 218 *Recueil des Cours* 9.

SLAUGHTER, A-M, STONE SWEET, A and WEILER, J, *The European Court and National Courts: Doctrine and Jurisprudence: Legal Change in Its Social Context* (Oxford, Hart Publishing, 1998).

SLOT, PJ and DUTHEIL DE LA ROCHÉRE, J, 'Case C–466/98, Commission v. United Kingdom; C–467/98, Commission v. Denmark; C–468/98, Commission v. Sweden; C–469/98, Commission v. Finland; C–471, Commission v. Belgium; C–472/98, Commission v. Luxemburg; C–475/98, Commission v. Austria;' (2003) 40 *Common Market Law Review* 697.

SNYDER, F, 'The Origins of the "Nonmarket Economy": Ideas, Pluralism and Power in EC Anti-Dumping Law About China' (2001) 7 *European Law Journal* 369.

SPENCER, C, 'The EU and Common Strategies: The Revealing Case of the Mediterranean' (2001) 6 *European Foreign Affairs Review* 31.

STANBROOK, C, BENTLEY, P and CUNNARE, J, *Dumping and Subsidies: The Law and Procedures Governing the Imposition of Anti-Dumping and Countervailing Duties in the European Community* (3rd edn, The Hague, Kluwer Law International, 1996).

STEIN, E, 'European Political Cooperation (EPC) as a Component of the European Foreign Affairs System' (1983) 43 *Zeitschrift für ausländisches öffentliches Recht und Völkerrecht* 49.

——, 'External Relations of the European Community: Structure and Process' (1990) 1 *Collected Courses of the Academy of European Law* 115.

STOLL, P-T and STEINMANN, A, 'WTO Dispute Settlement: The Implementation Stage' (1999) 3 *Max Planck Yearbook of United Nations Law* 407.

STURMA, P, 'La participation de la Communauté européenne de sanctions internationales' [1993] *Revue du Marché Commun* 250.

SWAAK, CRA, *European Community Law and the Automobile Industry* (The Hague, Kluwer Law International, 1999).

TEMPLE LANG, J, 'The Irish Court Case Which Delayed the Single European Act: *Crotty v. An Taoiseach and Others*' (1987) 24 *Common Market Law Review* 709.

THIEME, D, 'European Community External Relations in the Field of the Environment' (2001) 10 *European Environmental Law Review* 252.

THYM, D, 'Reforming Europe's Common Foreign and Security Policy' (2004) 10 *European Foreign Affairs Review* 5.

TIMMERMANS, CWA 'Common Commercial Policy (Article 113 EEC) and International Trade in Services' in F CAPOTORTI *et al* (eds), *Du droit international au droit de l'intégration: liber amicorum Pierre Pescatore* (Baden-Baden, Nomos, 1987) 675.

——, 'The EU and Public International Law' (1999) 4 *European Foreign Affairs Review* 181.

——, 'Organising Joint Participation of EC and Member States' in A DASHWOOD and C HILLION (eds), *The General Law of EC External Relations* (London, Sweet & Maxwell, 2000) 239.

——, 'The Constitutionalization of the European Union' (2002) 21 *Yearbook of European Law* 1.

——, 'Community Commercial Policy on Textiles: A Legal Imbroglio' in ELM VÖLKER (ed), *Protectionism and the European Community: Import Relief Measures Taken by the European Economic Community and the Member States, and the Legal Remedies Available to Private Parties*, (2nd edn, Deventer, Kluwer Law, 1987) 159.

TOJE, A, 'The 2003 European Union Security Strategy: A Critical Appraisal' (2005) 10 *European Foreign Affairs Review* 117.

TOMUSCHAT, C, 'The International Responsibility of the European Union' in CANNIZZARO E (ed), *The European Union as an Actor in International Relations* (The Hague, Kluwer Law International, 2002) 177.

TREBILCOCK, MJ and HOWSE, R, *The Regulation of International Trade* (2nd edn, London, Routledge, 2001).

TREVES, T, 'The European Community and the Law of the Sea Convention: New Developments' in E CANNIZZARO (ed), *The European Union as an Actor in International Relations* (The Hague, Kluwer Law International, 2002) 279.

TRIDIMAS, G and TRIDIMAS, T, 'The European Court of Justice and the Annulment of the Tobacco Advertisement Directive: Friend of National Sovereignty or Foe of Public Health?' (2002) 14 *European Journal of Law and Economics* 171.

——, 'The WTO and OECD Opinions' in A DASHWOOD and C HILLION (eds), *The General Law of EC External Relations* (London, Sweet & Maxwell, 2000) 48.

——, 'Black, White and Shades of Grey: Horizontality of Directives Revisited' (2002) 21 *Yearbook of European Law* 327.

——, 'Knocking on Heaven's Door: Fragmentation, Efficiency and Defiance in the Preliminary Reference Procedure' (2003) 40 *Common Market Law Review* 9.

——, and EECKHOUT, P, 'The External Competence of the Community and the Case-Law of the Court of Justice: Principle versus Pragmatism' (1995) 14 *Yearbook of European Law* 143.

TRYBUS, M, 'The EC Treaty as an Instrument of European Defence Integration: Judicial Scrutiny of Defence and Security Exceptions' (2002) 39 *Common Market Law Review* 1347.

VAN BAEL, I and BELLIS, J-F, *Anti-dumping and Other Trade Protection Laws of the EC* (4th edn, The Hague, Kluwer Law International, 2004).

VAN BERGEIJK, PAG, *Economic Diplomacy, Trade and Commercial Policy: Positive and Negative Sanctions in a New World Order* (Aldershot, Edward Elgar, 1994).

VAN DARTEL, RJPM, 'The EEC's Commercial Policy Concerning Textiles' in ELM VÖLKER (ed), *Protectionism and the European Community: Import Relief Measures Taken by the European Economic Community and the Member States, and the Legal Remedies Available to Private Parties* (2nd edn, Deventer, Kluwer Law, 1987) 121.

VAN DEN BROEK, N, 'Legal Persuasion, Political Realism and Legitimacy: The European Court's Recent Treatment of the Effects of WTO Agreements in the EC Legal Order' (2001) 4 *Journal of International Economic Law* 411.

VEDDER, C and FOLZ, H-P, annotation on Case C–124/95, *the Queen v HM Treasury and the Bank of Engalnd ex parte Centro-Com Sr* and Case C–177/95, *Ebony Maritime SA, Loten Navigation Co Ltd v Prefetto della Provincia di Brindisi and Others* (1998) 35 *Common Market Law Review* 209.

VERHOEVEN, J, 'Sanctions internationales et Communautés européennes—à propos de l'affaire des Iles Falklands (Malvinas)' [1984] *Cahiers de Droit Européen* 259.

VERMULST, E, 'The 10 Major Problems with the Anti-Dumping Instrument in the European Community' (2005) 39 *Journal of World Trade* 105.

——, and WAER, P, *EC Anti-Dumping Law and Practice* (London, Sweet & Maxwell, 1996).

VERWEY, DR, *The European Community, the European Union and the International Law of Treaties: A Comparative Legal Analysis of the Community and Union's External Treaty-Making Practice* (The Hague, TMC Asser Press, 2004).

VOGELENZANG, P, 'Two Aspects of Article 115 EEC Treaty: Its Use to Buttress Community-Set Subquotas, and the Commission's Monitoring System' (1981) 18 *Common Market Law Review* 169.

VÖLKER, ELM, 'Case 174/84, Bulk Oil (Zug) A.G. v. Sun International Limited and Sun Oil Trading' (1987) 24 *Common Market Law Review* 99.

——, and STEENBERGEN, J, *Leading Cases and Materials on the External Relations Law of the EC: With Emphasis on the Common Commercial Policy* (Deventer, Kluwer Law, 1985).

VON BOGDANDY, A, 'Case C–53/96, Hermès International v. FHT Marketing Choice BV' (1999) 36 *Common Market Law Review* 663.

VON BOGDANDY, A, 'Legal Effects of World Trade Organisation Decisions within European Union Law: A Contribution to the Theory of the Legal Acts of International Organisations and the Action for Damages under Article 288(2) EC' (2005) 39 *Journal of World Trade* 45.

VON KYAW, D, 'The EU after the Agreement on a Constitutional Treaty' (2004) 9 *European Foreign Affairs Review* 455.

VRANES, E, 'From *Bananas I* to the 2001 Bananas Settlement: A Factual and Procedural Analysis of the WTO Proceedings' in F BREUSS, S GRILLER and E VRANES (eds), *The Banana Dispute: An Economic and Legal Analysis* (Vienna, Springer, 2003) 1.

WALKER, N, 'The EU and the WTO: Constitutionalism in a New Key' in G DE BÚRCA and J SCOTT (eds), *The EU and the WTO: Legal and Constitutional Issues* (Oxford, Hart Publishing, 2001) 31.

WASSENBERGH, H, 'A Mandate to the European Commission to Negotiate Air Agreements with Non-EU States: International Law versus EU Law' (2003) 28 *Air and Space Law* 139.

WEATHERILL, S, 'Compulsory Notification of Draft Technical Regulations: The Contribution of Directive 83/189 to the Management of the Internal Market' (1996) 16 *Yearbook of European Law* 129.

——, 'Breach of Directives and Breach of Contract' (2001) 26 *European Law Review* 177.

——, and BEAUMONT, PR, *EU Law* (3rd edn, London, Penguin, 1999).

WEILER, JHH, 'The Community System: The Dual Character of Supranationalism' (1981) 1 *Yearbook of European Law* 257.

——, 'The External Legal Relations of Non-Unitary Actors: Mixity and the Federal Principle' in D O'KEEFFE and HG SCHERMERS (eds), *Mixed Agreements* (Deventer, Kluwer Law, 1983) 35.

——, 'Thou Shalt Not Oppress a Stranger: On the Judicial Protection of the Human Rights of Non-EC Nationals - a Critique' (1992) 3 *European Journal of International Law* 65.

——, *The Constitution of Europe: "Do the New Clothes Have an Emperor?" and Other Essays on European Integration* (Cambridge, Cambridge University Press, 1999).

——, 'The Rule of Lawyers and the Ethos of Diplomats: Reflections on WTO Dispute Settlement' in RB Porter *et al* (eds), *Efficiency, Equity, and Legitimacy: The Multilateral Trading System at the Millennium* (Washington, DC, Brookings Institution Press, 2001) 334.

——, and FRIES, SC, 'A Human Rights Policy for the European Community and Union: The Question of Competences' in P ALSTON (ed), *The EU and Human Rights* (Oxford, Oxford University Press, 1999) 147.

WELLENSTEIN, E, 'Participation of the Community in International Commodity Agreements' in SJ BATES (ed), *In Memoriam J.D.B. Mitchell* (London, Sweet & Maxwell, 1983) 65.

WESSEL, RA, *The European Union's Foreign and Security Policy: A Legal Institutional Perspective* (The Hague, Kluwer Law International, 1999).

——, 'The EU as a Black Widow: Devouring the WEU to Give Birth to a European Security and Defence Policy' in V KRONENBERGER (ed), *The European Union and the International Legal Order: Discord or Harmony?* (The Hague, TMC Asser Press, 2001) 141.

——, 'Good Governance and EU Foreign, Security and Defence Policy' in DM CURTIN and RA WESSEL (eds), *Good Governance and the European Union: Reflections on Concepts, Institutions and Substance* (Antwerp, Intersentia, 2005) 215.

WILLAERT, P, 'Les sanctions économiques contre la Rhodésie (1965–1979)' (1985) 18 *Revue Belge de Droit International* 216.

WOLL, C, *Transatlantic Relations as a Catalyst to European Integration—the Activism of the European Commission in the Case of International Aviation* (Washington, DC, American Institute for Contemporary German Studies, The Johns Hopkins University, 2003).

WOUTERS, J, 'The Union's Minister for Foreign Affairs: Europe's Single Voice or Trojan Horse?' in ZWAAN JW *et al* (eds), *The European Union: An Ongoing Process of Integration: Liber Amicorum Alfred E. Kellerman* (The Hague, TMC Asser Press, 2004) 77.

——, and VAN EECKHOTTE, D, 'Giving Effect to Customary International Law through European Community Law' in JM PRINSSEN and AAM SCHRAUWEN (eds), *Direct Effect: Rethinking a Classic of EC Legal Doctrine* (Groningen, Europa Law Publishing, 2002) 183.

ZONNEKEYN, G, 'The Status of WTO Law in the Community Legal Order: Some Comments in the Light of the Portuguese Textiles Case' (2000) 25 *European Law Review* 293.

——, 'EC Liability for Nonimplementation of Adopted WTO Panels and Appellate Body Reports—the Example of the "Innocent Exporters" in the Banana Case' in V KRONENBERGER (ed), *The European Union and the International Legal Order: Discord or Harmony?* (The Hague, TMC Asser Press, 2001) 251.

——, 'EC Liability for the Non-Implementation of WTO Dispute Settlement Decisions' (2003) 6 *Journal of International Economic Law* 761.

——, 'The ECJ's *Petrotub* Judgment: Towards a Revival of the "Nakajima Doctrine"?' (2003) 30 *Legal Issues of European Integration* 249.

ZWAAN, JW, 'The Legal Personality of the European Communities and the European Union' (1999) 30 *Netherlands Yearbook of International Law* 75.

Index